ROCOCO: THE CONTINUING CURVE, 1730–2008

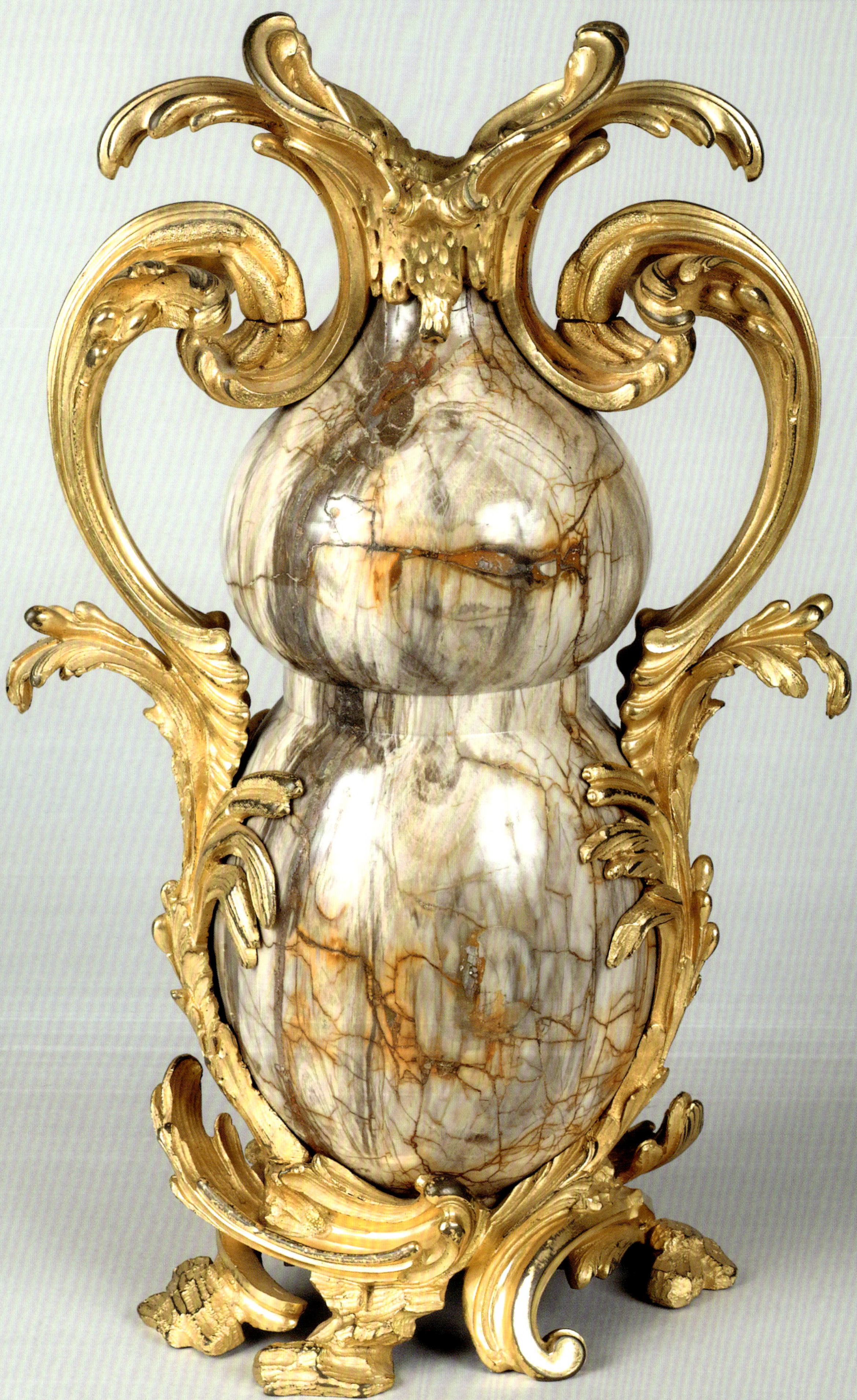

ROCOCO

THE CONTINUING CURVE, 1730–2008

Sarah D. Coffin
Gail S. Davidson
Ellen Lupton
Penelope Hunter-Stiebel

Smithsonian
Cooper-Hewitt, National Design Museum

New York

Rococo: The Continuing Curve

Contents

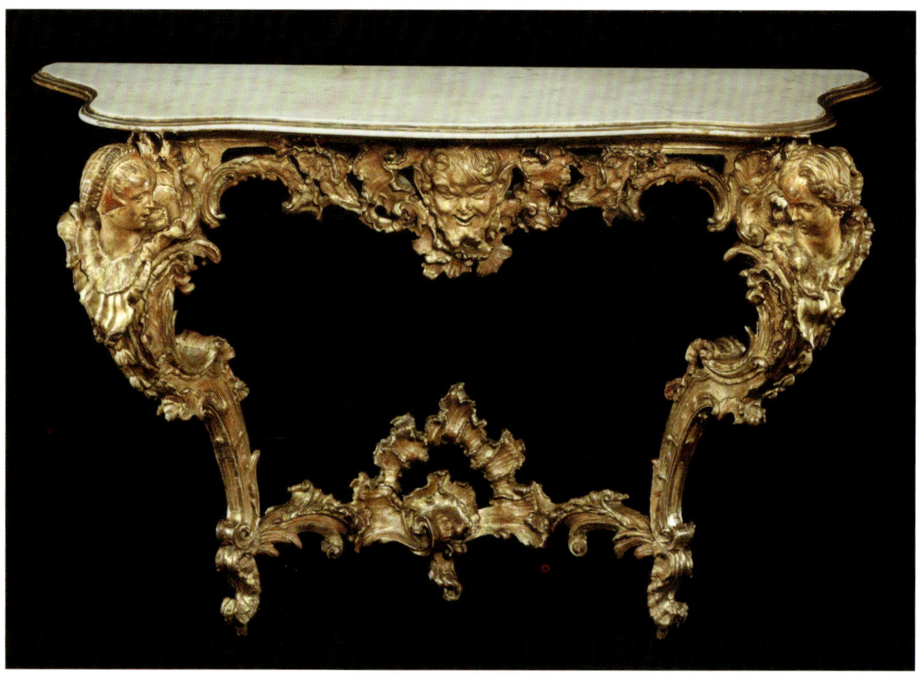

Console table. Germany, ca. 1745. Gilt wood, marble. Courtesy of Carlton Hobbs LLC

Foreword

Paul Warwick Thompson, Director
Cooper-Hewitt, National Design Museum, Smithsonian Institution

Museum exhibitions on rococo have, to date, focused on national expressions of the movement or the predilections of a particular patron. *Rococo: The Continuing Curve, 1730–2008*, however, surveys the rococo impulse across centuries and continents—from Paris and provincial France to the Netherlands, Britain, Germany, down into Italy and the Iberian Peninsula, and across the Atlantic to the western hemisphere. With each border crossing, one can discern new stylistic impulses and different social and political persuasions that temper a curlicue or embellish a surface. And through the centuries, the courtly patrons of the eighteenth century give way to the mercantile classes of the industrialized world, academic style succumbs to the natural flow of Art Nouveau, and so on, until we arrive at the present day, in Europe or California, where an extravagance of form is discerned in the work of such seemingly unlikely candidates as Frank Gehry, Ron Arad, and Cindy Sherman.

I wish to thank the four curators of this exhibition—Sarah D. Coffin, Gail S. Davidson, and Ellen Lupton of Cooper-Hewitt; and guest curator Penelope Hunter-Steibel—who have enlarged, with tremendous verve and audacious imagination, a traditionally narrow aperture on rococo and broadened our vista, helping us to understand how and why rococo style has mutated and created a terrain far removed from the boudoir of Madame de Pompadour or the studio of François Boucher. Their fundamental thesis is close to my vision of design: Movements and innovations can only be deeply understood when placed within a historic continuum. It is only with closer scrutiny that one recognizes the correspondences and motivations among designers and clients of different eras.

I also wish to thank the essayists in this catalogue, all of them prominent scholars who have contributed much to the study of rococo's place in decorative-arts history; Nurit Einik, Jackie Killian, and Cindy Trope for their invaluable help in organizing the book and exhibition; Chul R. Kim, Head of Publications; Jocelyn Groom, Head of Exhibitions; Jill Bloomer and Annie Chambers for their work on the more than 380 images in this catalogue; and, of course, Cooper-Hewitt's Curatorial Director Cara McCarty, who has guided the team throughout. With deep appreciation, I would like to acknowledge the many institutions and individuals who have been extraordinarily forthcoming in their willingness to lend to this landmark exhibition, as well as those whose generosity has helped to make this exhibition possible, including The Grand Marnier Foundation, Kay Allaire, the Consulate-General of The Netherlands, and an anonymous donor. This beautiful publication is supported in part by The Andrew W. Mellon Foundation, with additional funding from Furthermore: a program of the J. M. Kaplan Fund. And finally, much gratitude and congratulations to exhibition designers Leven Betts Studio and exhibition graphics and catalogue designers Tsang Seymour Design, who have fully immersed themselves in the spirit of rococo and delivered a superb installation and book design.

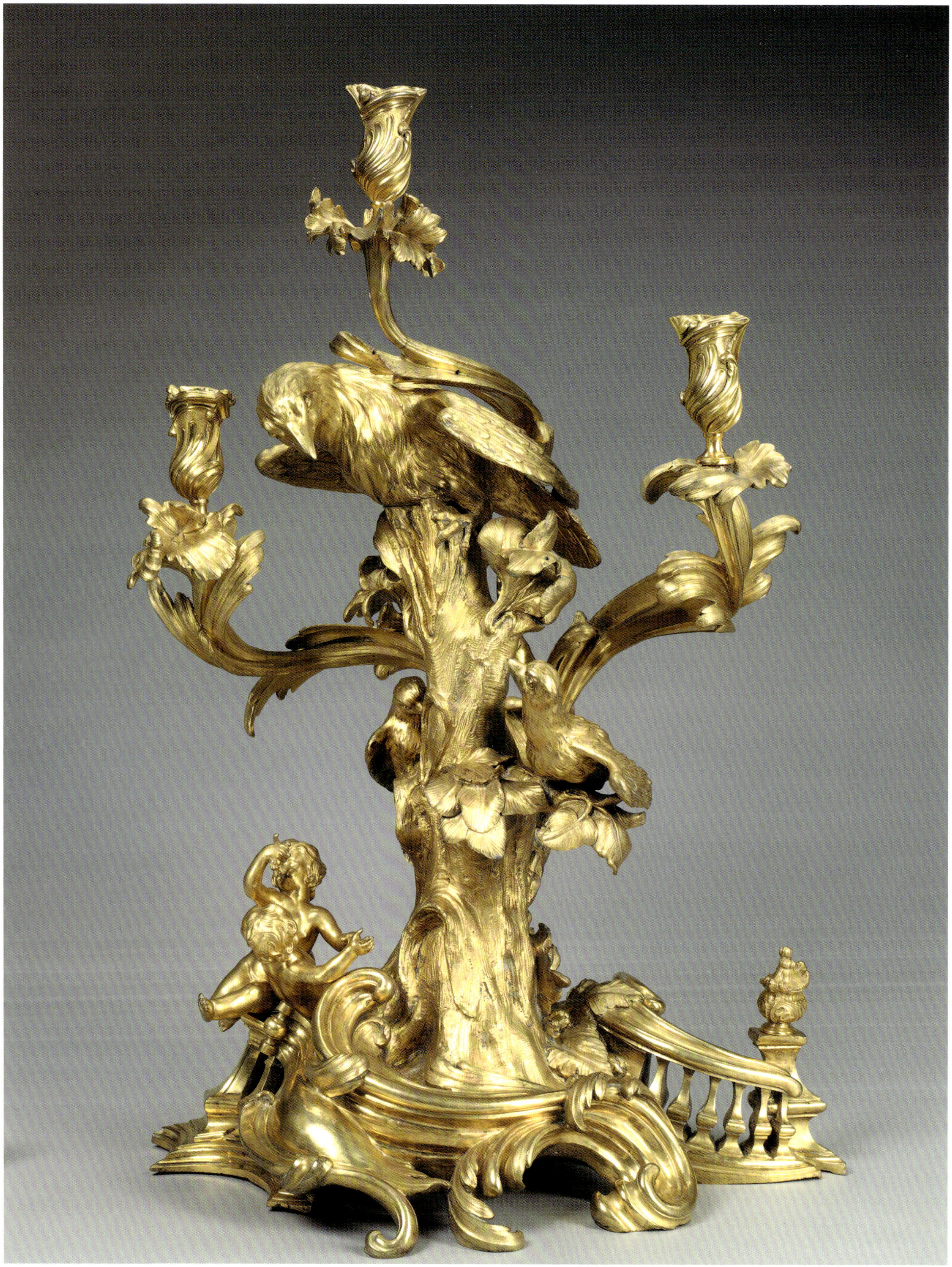

FIG. 2 Candelabrum. Jean-Joseph de Saint-Germain (French, 1720–1791). France, ca. 1750. Gilt bronze. The Cleveland Museum of Art, John L. Severance Fund, 1946.81

The Continuing Curve

Penelope Hunter-Stiebel

The fashioning of implements is a benchmark in the evolution of man. It began as pure function: how will this object make life easier? But soon after came the desire to make objects that were pleasing. As society advanced, this yin-yang tension found expression in a creative contrast of styles. The yang—aggressive, male creativity associated with daylight, wind, and air—can be seen from the architectural orders of classical Greece through latter-day modernism. The yin—passive, resilient, female creativity associated with darkness, earth, and water—has an equally long history that reached its apex in the eighteenth-century style we call rococo. This fundamentally human desire to appeal to the senses with softened forms is traced in the works of art presented on these pages and in the exhibition they document.

STYLE

This sensuous impulse looks to nature for models that feature the sinuous S-curve. It celebrates tactile as well as visual values. On a deeper level, it represents the rejection of mere intellect in favor of a broader appeal to the senses, the rebellion against regimented order, the embrace of the bizarre and the subconscious, the assertion of individuality through innovation. The term rococo invokes the period from around 1730 to 1765 when this impulse was dominant. In only one other period, from 1880 to 1910, did its periodic eruptions gather the magnitude of an international movement, as what is now generally termed Art Nouveau. Whenever it has exceeded the force of an undercurrent, it has aroused passionate critical censure, as if the snaking line insinuating itself into furnishings and decoration posed a threat to society.

Sinuous, organic, sensuous—that is the mantra of this project. To lay bare this tendency, the most extreme examples have been selected. They are often exceptional works in a designer's oeuvre that encompasses more traditional creations. The works are presented individually, not in the pairs or sets that made their eccentricity more palatable to a public accustomed to repetition and symmetry. Paintings and sculpture are largely absent; the applied arts made to give private pleasure and soften the rigors of daily life offer the clearest evidence of the movement. Historically, the importance of subject matter in the so-called "fine arts" makes stylistic nuance less obvious. The outstanding exception is the depiction of the female nude (figs. 1), where the idealized form, whether painted, sculpted, cast, or drawn, embodies the values of sensuous curves. It is hardly surprising that female nudes appeared in eighteenth-century rococo decorations and became a leitmotif in Art Nouveau.

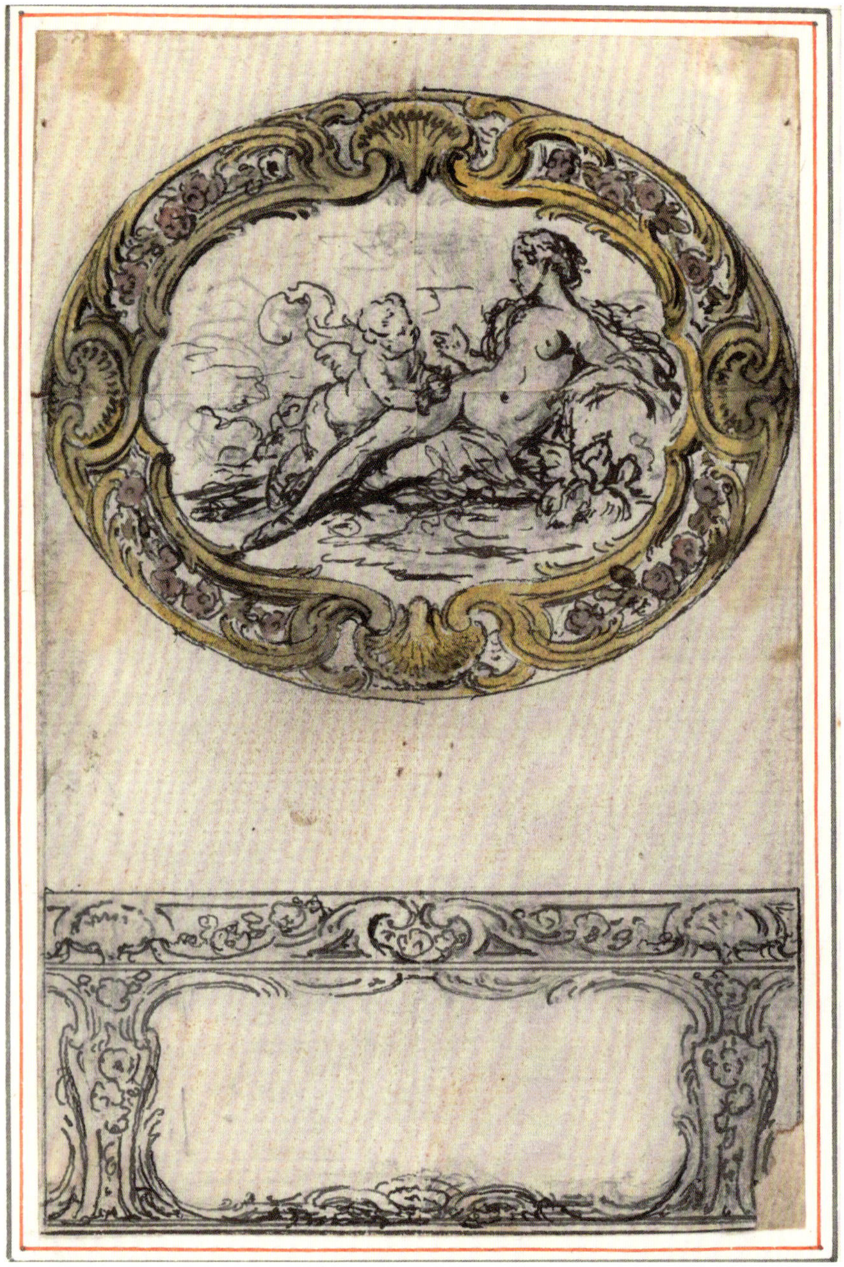

FIG. 1 *Design for an Oval Gold Box.* Hubert-François Gravelot (French, 1699–1773). England, ca. 1745. Pen and black ink over graphite. The Metropolitan Museum of Art, 44.54.42

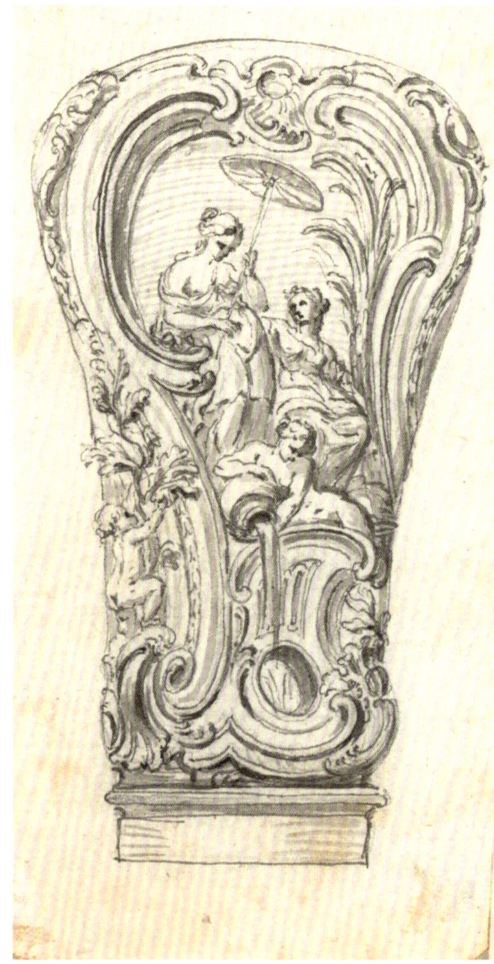

FIG. 3 *Ornament Design.* Juste-Aurèle Meissonnier (French 1675–1750). France, ca. 1740. Pen and brown ink, brush and gray wash over graphite underdrawing. The Metropolitan Musuem of Art, Rogers Fund, 1986, 1986.1032.1

CIRCUMSTANCE

The rococo impulse rose to prominence in societies that were stable, prosperous, and open enough to encourage this clearly nonessential production. The circumstance was ideal in France during the reign of Louis XV (r. 1715–74) (fig. 2): The country was the most powerful in Europe. It had known decades of internal peace and steadily growing prosperity. The arts were supported as part of the nation-state structure established by Louis XIV. Furthering France's international prestige and providing exports for a favorable balance of trade required continuing innovation. To this end, the royal policy of attracting talent from abroad overrode the protectionism of the guild system.

The time was ripe for a genius, and one arrived in the person of Juste-Aurèle Meissonnier (1695–1750) (fig. 3). Born into a southern French family and trained as a silversmith in Turin, Italy, Meissonnier came to Paris to work under royal protection and went on to court appointment as designer to the king's cabinet. Although the pan-European Baroque style employed curves and leaf motifs, it was always contained within a framework of order intended for the public appreciation of grandeur. In an ambitious drive to distance himself from the competition, Meissonnier led France from the decorously ornamented dissipation of Baroque splendor to the surging nature-based invention that exploded into the uncharted territory of asymmetry. Publishing his most aggressive designs in prints, he spread his fame and made his novel design vocabulary the lingua franca of Europe. Eagerly adopted and adapted in countries and principalities habituated to French leadership, rococo style took on the character of an epidemic: design prints and model books spread it swiftly

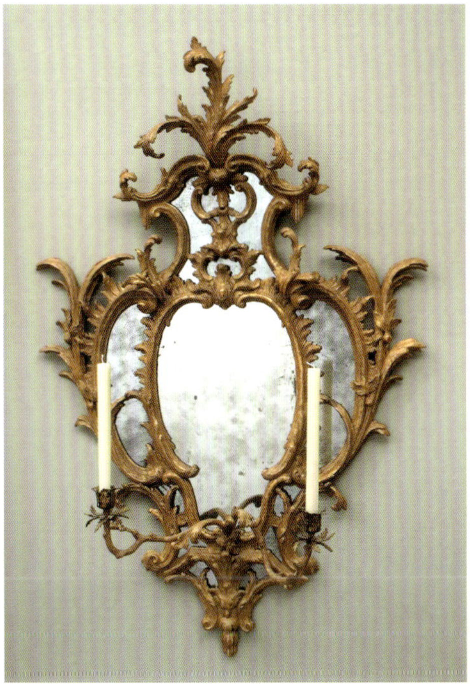

FIG. 4 Mirror. England, ca. 1755. Gilt wood. Colecciòn Patricia Phelps de Cisneros, Caracas, 2000.14

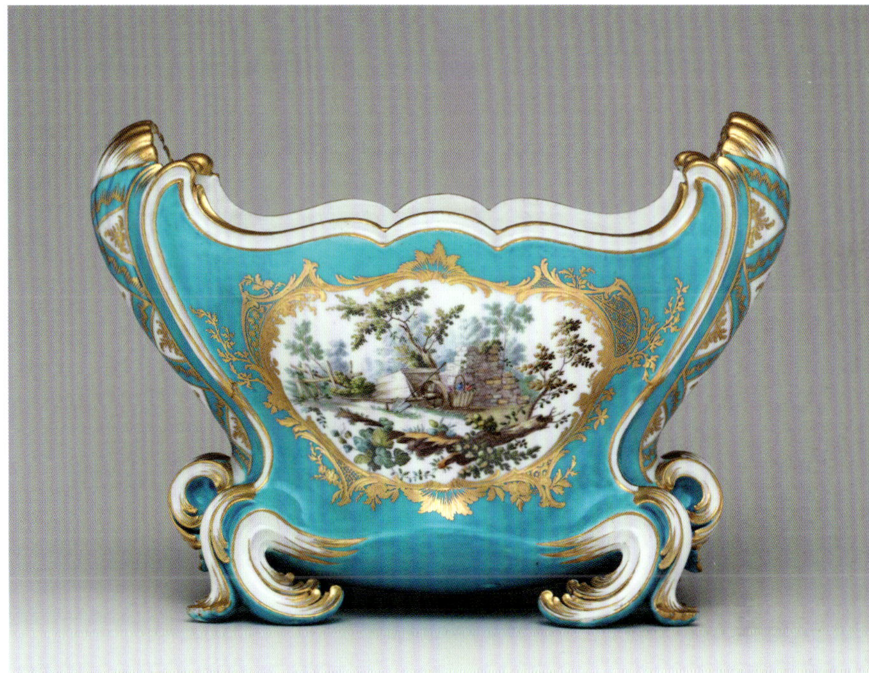

FIG. 5 Cuvette Mahon (flower vase). Sèvres Porcelain Manufactory. Sèvres, France, ca. 1757–60. Soft paste porcelain, gilding. The Metropolitan Museum of Art, The Lesley and Emma Sheafer Collection, Bequest of Emma A. Sheafer, 1974.356.528

throughout the Western world. Designers and craftsmen who mastered and improvised in the idiom were much in demand, and the research in this volume reveals the extent to which their travels contributed to the initial triumph of the style and its periodic resurgence (fig. 4).

PATRONAGE

The enthusiasm of individual patrons launched the style. Louis XV endorsed the rococo movement, which abetted his predilection for an intimate private life. His official mistress, Madame de Pompadour, fostered it, particularly in the new field of porcelain (fig. 5). There were also outstanding patrons outside France, with Meissonnier receiving commissions from the King of Portugal to the nobility of Poland. Louis XV's father-in-law, the former Polish King Stanislas, transformed Nancy, the capital of his principality of Lorraine, by taking the style public. He lavishly applied rococo ironwork ornament to the urban spaces he created (fig. 6). The rulers in Munich and Berlin, enamored of the French style, hired French-trained architects to make over their courts. François Cuvilliés (1695–1768), Johann August Nahl (1710–1773), and their followers gratified their patrons' ambitions by turning up the volume of the French statement, amplifying the scale and ornamental themes in a distinctively Germanic manner.

FIG. 6 Triangular console element. Attributed to the workshop of Jean Lamour (French, 1698–1771). Nancy, France, ca. 1755. Gilded iron, forged. Musée Lorrain, Nancy, D.07.05.14.336

SILVER

Precious metals led this luxury trend, and gold boxes and silver tureens and candelabra projected the wealth and daring taste of their owners.

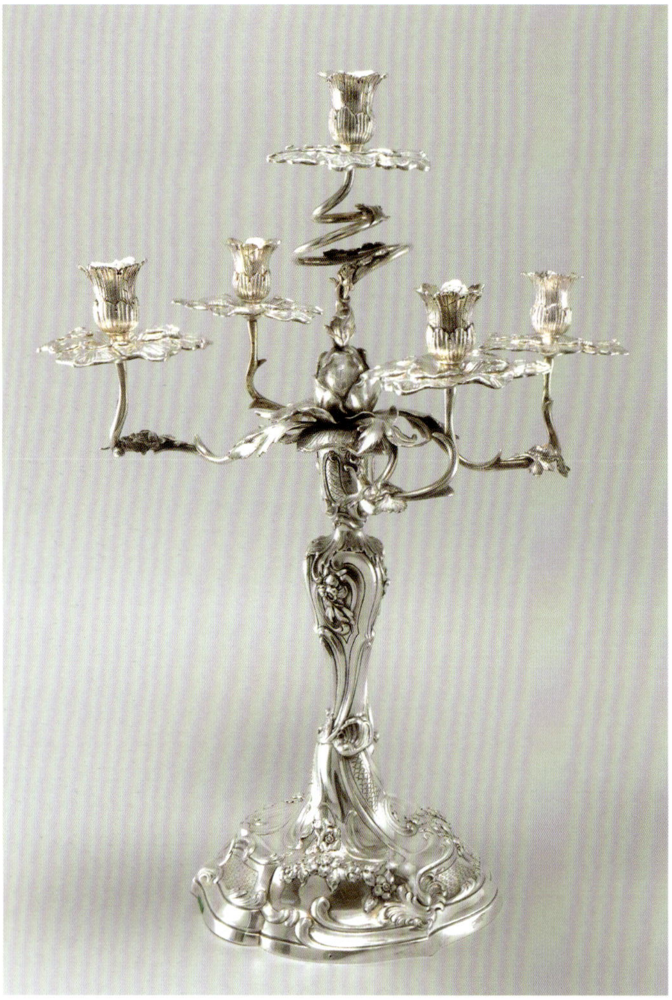

FIG. 7 Five-light candelabrum. Hermann Neupert II (German, 1727–1807) (arms); Gebruder Friedlander (base). Berlin, Germany, ca. 1764 (arms), late 19th century (base). Silver. Private collection

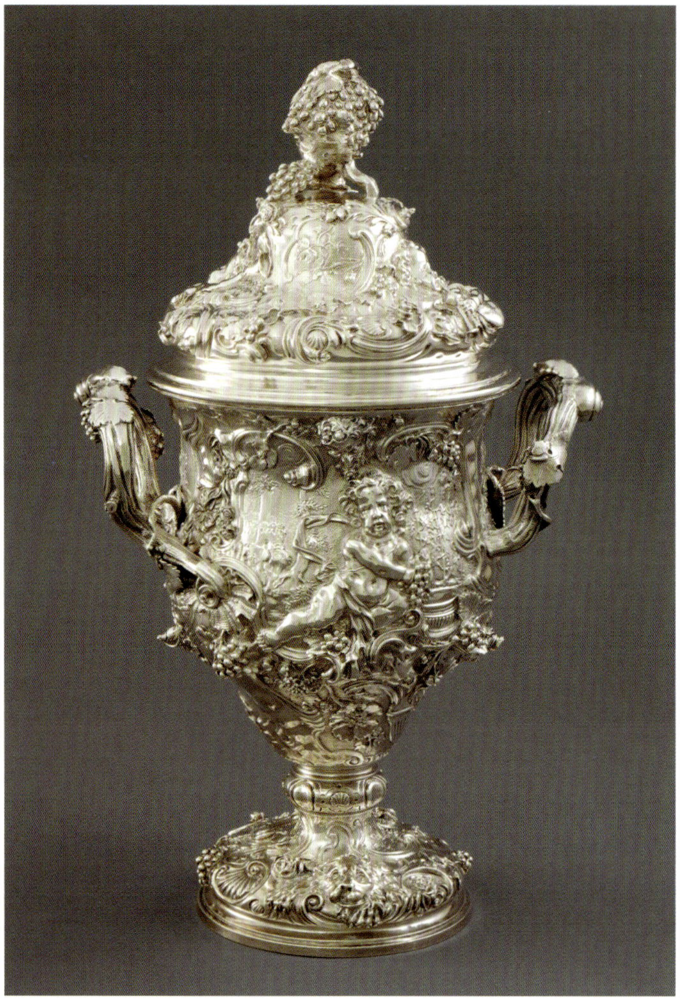

FIG. 8 Two-handled cup and cover. Paul de Lamerie (English, 1688–1751). London, England, 1742–43. Silver. The Sterling and Francine Clark Institute, 413

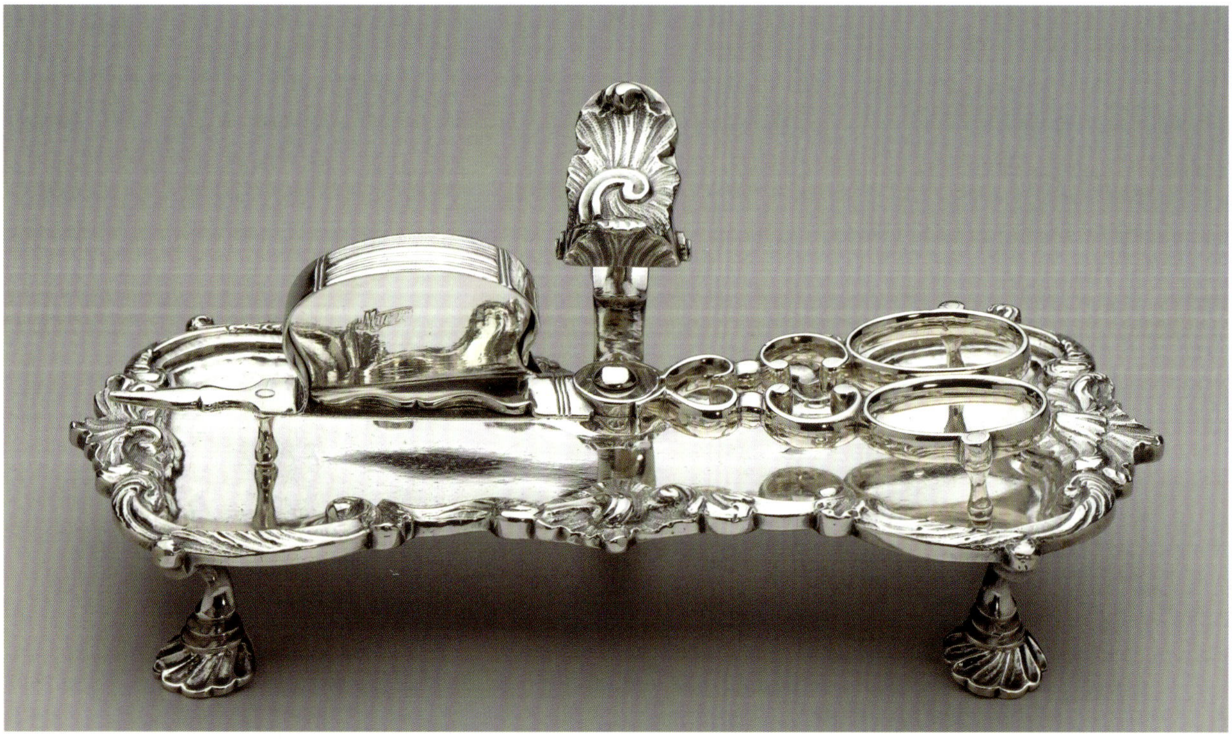

FIG. 9 Snuffers and stand. Myer Myers (American, 1723–1795). New York, NY, ca. 1755–70. Silver. Yale University Art Gallery. Mabel Brady Garvan Collection, 1936.147a-b

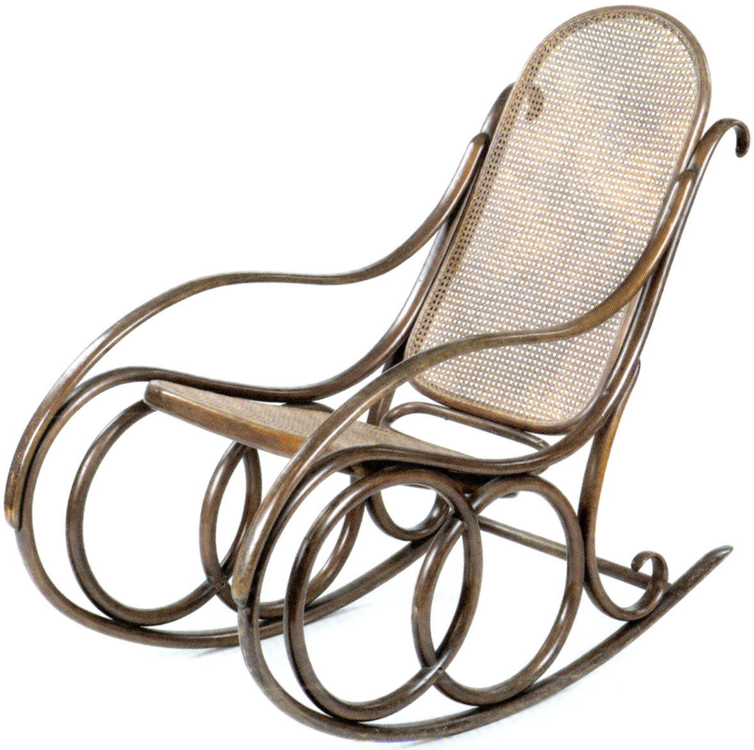

FIG. 10 Rocking chair "No. 4." Thonet Brothers. Austria, ca. 1860. Bent beech wood, caning. Cooper-Hewitt, National Design Museum, Smithsonian Institution, Museum purchase through gift of American Institute of Interior Designers, 1969-103-2

Aesthetically, the gleam and flow attainable in silver and gold made them ideal media for rococo-style objects. Moreover, the techniques of silversmithing, particularly chasing, required a level of sculptural virtuosity essential to mastering the style.

The most prominent precursors of rococo were the Dutch silversmiths Adam van Vianen (1568–1627) and his brother Paulus van Vianen (ca. 1570–1613). They devised a novel amorphous and flowing ornament, dubbed "auricular," and took it from border applications to the fashioning of entire objects. The auricular style enjoyed brief popularity in the Netherlands before it was subsumed by more regular floral ornament. It was not until the 1740s that Dutch silver became part of the international current of rococo, in variations developed according to local taste, from the extravagance of wealthy Amsterdam merchants to the lyric elegance of courtiers of The Hague.

In Germany, the established silver industry in Augsburg quickly adapted to the new style (fig. 7). When the Hanoverian dynasty assumed the English throne, the flow of talent from Germany to England increased, and silversmiths working in London, Paul de Lamerie (1688–1751) foremost among them, applied the decorative idiom to tablewares in myriad variations (fig. 8). Examples made in the American colonies joined with English wares to become the delight of silver collectors for centuries to come (fig. 9). In the nineteenth and early twentieth centuries, silver showpieces made the most extravagant spectacular statements of the rococo revival styles.

REVIVAL VERSUS INVENTION

Following the decline of Napoleon, nostalgia for the *ancien régime* of pre-Revolutionary Europe supported a spate of historic revivals. Louis XV rococo ornament was often conflated with Louis XIV Baroque and Louis XVI Neoclassicism. The Victorian predilection for coziness, however, could be interpreted as a bourgeois expression of the Louis XV celebration of intimacy. True invention surfaced in the mid-nineteenth-century proliferation of ornament through the new technology of bentwood. In New York City, German immigrant John Henry Belter (1804–1863) (See Busch, fig. 5) patented a lamination process that produced lavish curves and ornament ideally suited to the Victorian parlor. At the same time, Michel Thonet (1796–1871) formed a company with his sons in Vienna for the manufacture of experimental bentwood furniture (fig. 10). He turned his sights toward mass production as his bentwood technique allowed for sinuous, linear structures that were as inexpensive and sturdy as they were aesthetically pleasing.

ART NOUVEAU

Confused historical design and shoddy industrial execution were rejected in explosions of creativity toward the close the nineteenth century. The first of these movements occurred in Nancy, the eastern French center of eighteenth-century rococo. Emile Gallé (1846–1904) (fig. 11) inspired a regional renaissance, using the Louis XV style as a springboard to inventions based on the observation of nature (fig. 12). René Lalique elevated

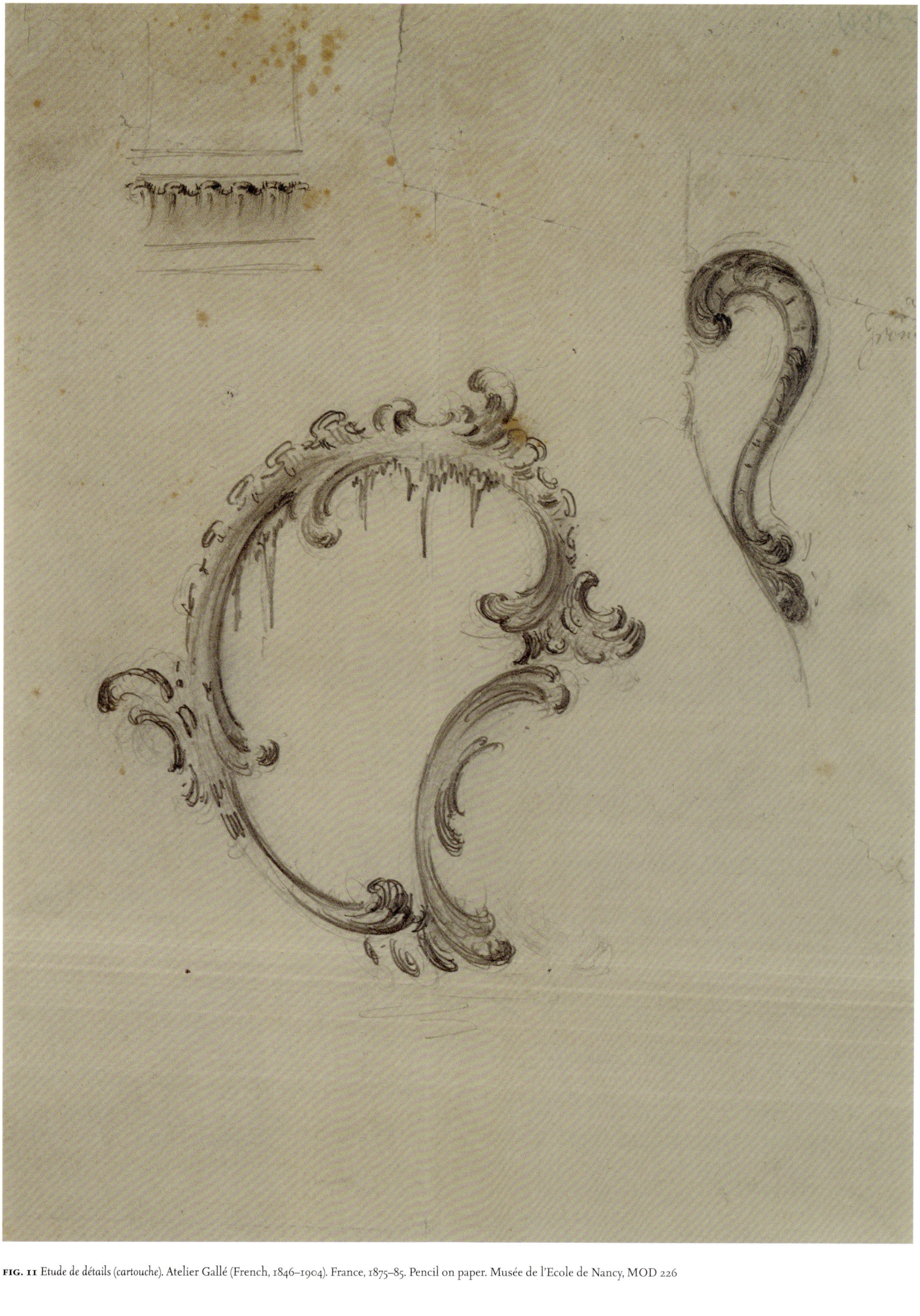

FIG. 11 *Etude de détails (cartouche)*. Atelier Gallé (French, 1846–1904). France, 1875–85. Pencil on paper. Musée de l'Ecole de Nancy, MOD 226

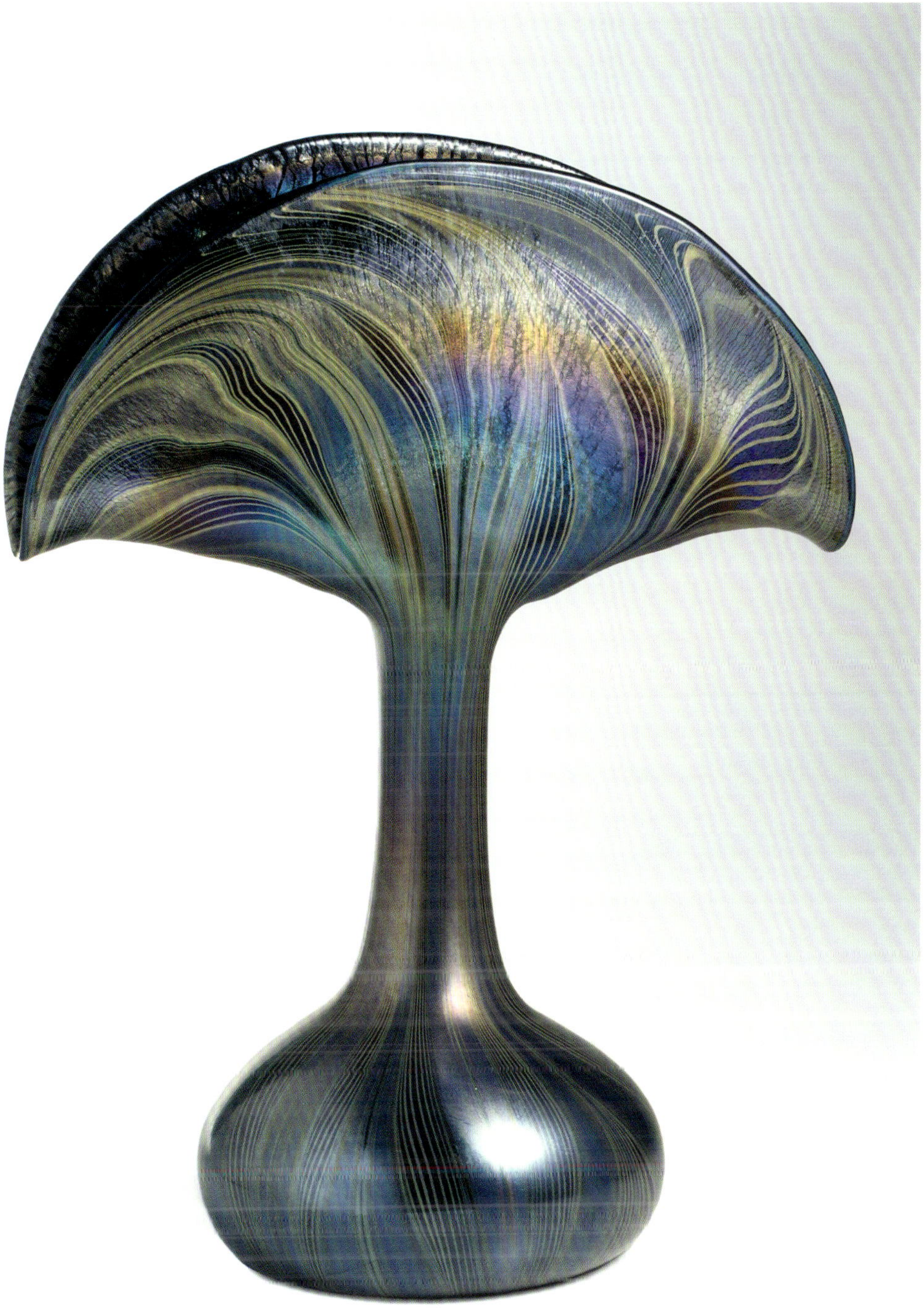

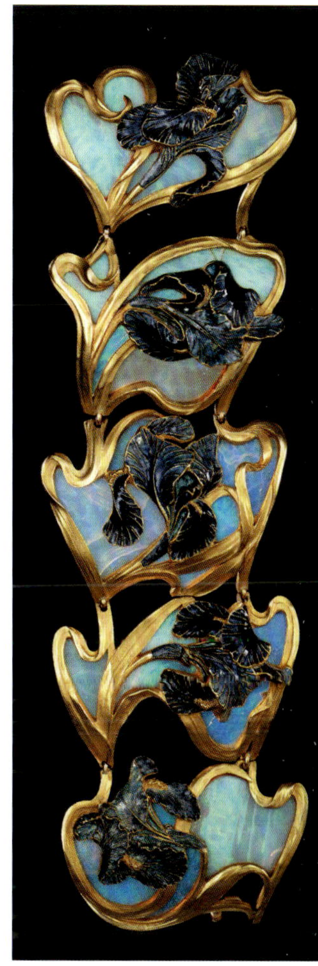

FIG. 14 "Iris" bracelet. René Lalique (French, 1860–1945). France, ca. 1897. Gold, enamel, opals. Private collection, New York

FIG. 13 "Peacock" vase. Louis Comfort Tiffany (American, 1848–1933). Produced by Tiffany Studios. New York, NY, designed ca. 1900, produced 1900–28. Glass. Cooper-Hewitt, National Design Museum, Smithsonian Institution, Gift of Stanley Siegel, from the Stanley Siegel Collection, 1975-32-11

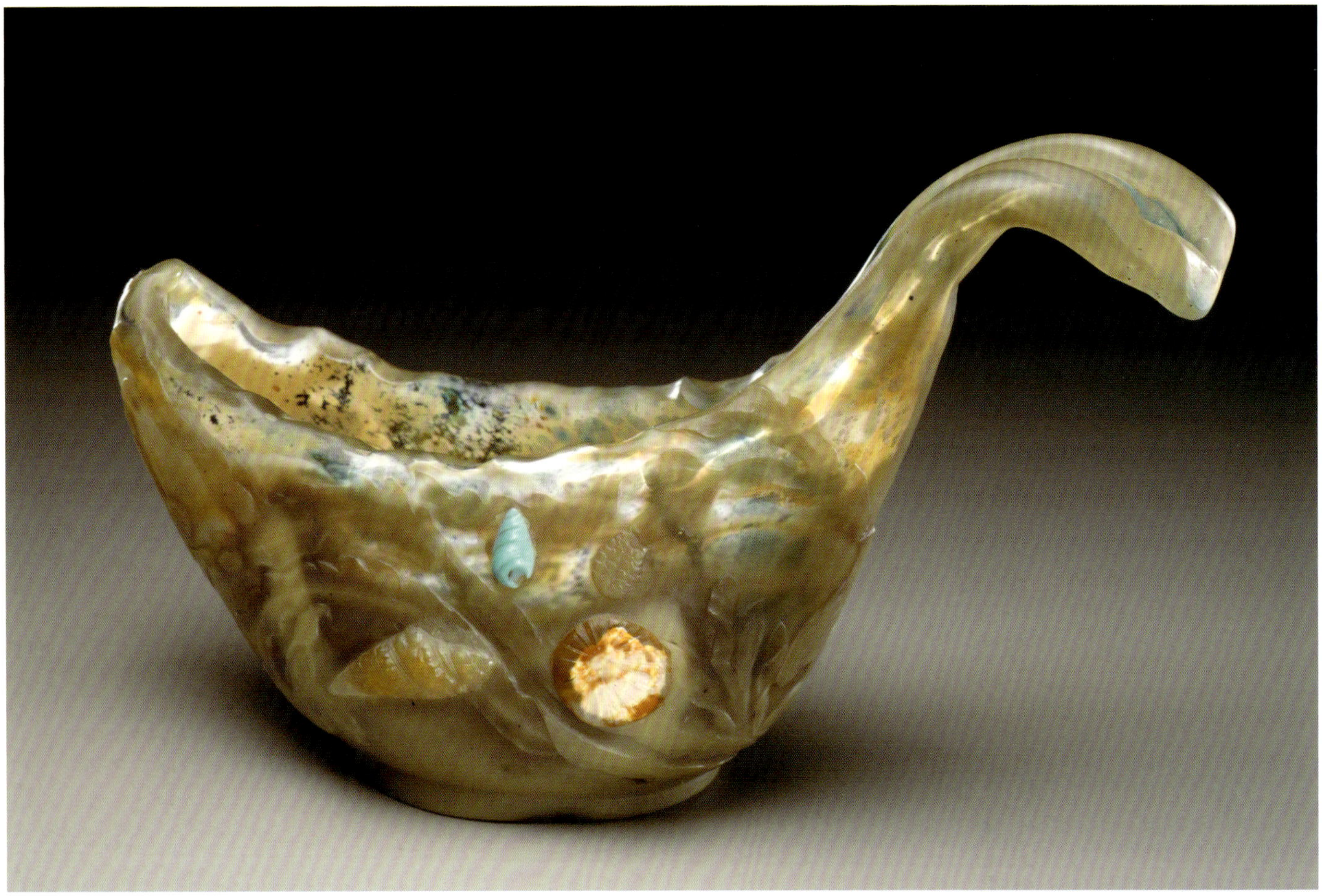

FIG. 12 Ladle. Emile Gallé (French, 1846–1904). France, ca. 1900. Marquetry, acid-etched, engraved, internally decorated blown glass. Virginia Museum of Fine Arts, Richmond; The Sydney and Frances Lewi Art Nouveau Fund, 75.6

jewelry to a new level of artistry with sculptural forms that prioritized design in a flowing, Symbolist-inspired idioom over traditional stone-setting. The dealer Siegfried Bing (1838–1905) showcased various manifestations of the resurgence of the rococo impulse. The name Bing gave his gallery, Art Nouveau, came to designate the movement that ranged from the whiplash designs of the Belgian Victor Horta (1861–1947) to the organic complexities of Parisian Hector Guimard (1867–1942) and the sensuous glass of the American Louis Comfort Tiffany (1848–1933) (fig. 13).

YESTERDAY AND TOMORROW

Though widespread and vigorous at the turn of the last century, sensuous creativity was trumped by the intellectual asceticism of modernism during the 1920s. Still, there was a perceptible softening in aspects of modernist design in the 1930s and 1950s. Molded plastic offered the potential of supple strength to postwar designers, and Verner Panton used it to achieve lyricism in his colorful, utilitarian stacking side chair (see Lupton, fig. 5). Although institutions, corporations, and banks continue to adopt classic modernist furnishings to brand themselves as forward-looking, the postwar consumer age has allowed for individual indulgence in alternative modes. The Studio Craft movement burgeoned in the United States in the 1970s (fig. 15), celebrating a return to handcraftsmanship and organic form and spawning outstanding masters of various media, from Albert Paley in metal (see Lupton, fig. 29) and Wendell Castle in wood (see Lupton, fig. 19) to Dale Chihuly in glass (see Lupton, figs. 14, 15). Today's hottest designers employ technology to achieve innovative creations that often correspond to rococo sensibility.

The evidence of three centuries suggests that the rococo spirit is alive and well. Whatever may be touted as tomorrow's trend, somebody, somewhere, will be creating something sinuous, organic, and sensuous.

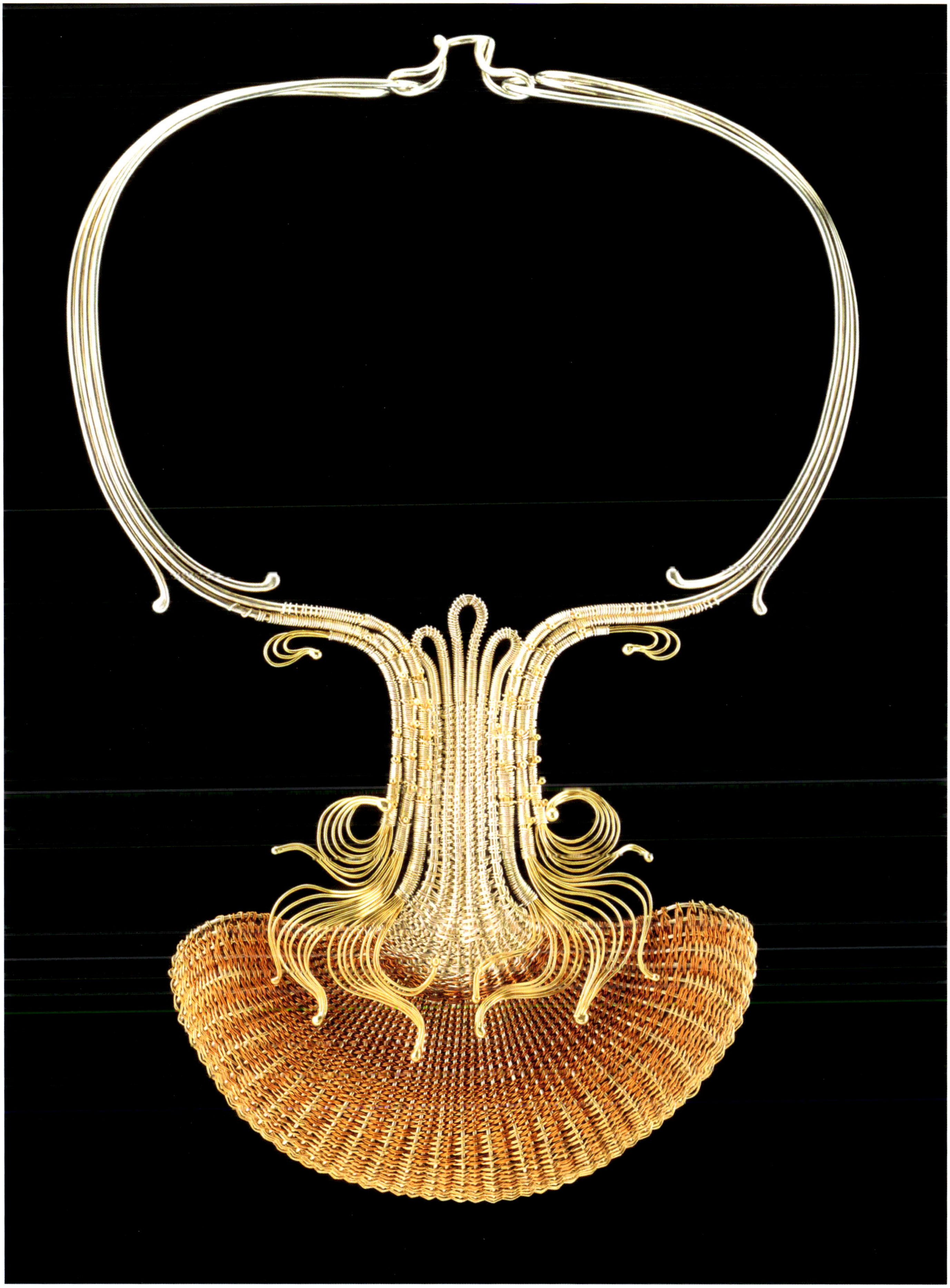

FIG. 15 Choker #38. Mary Lee Hu (American, b. 1943). United States, 1978. Silver, gold, copper. Smithsonian American Art Museum, Gift of the James Renwick Alliance, 1985.22

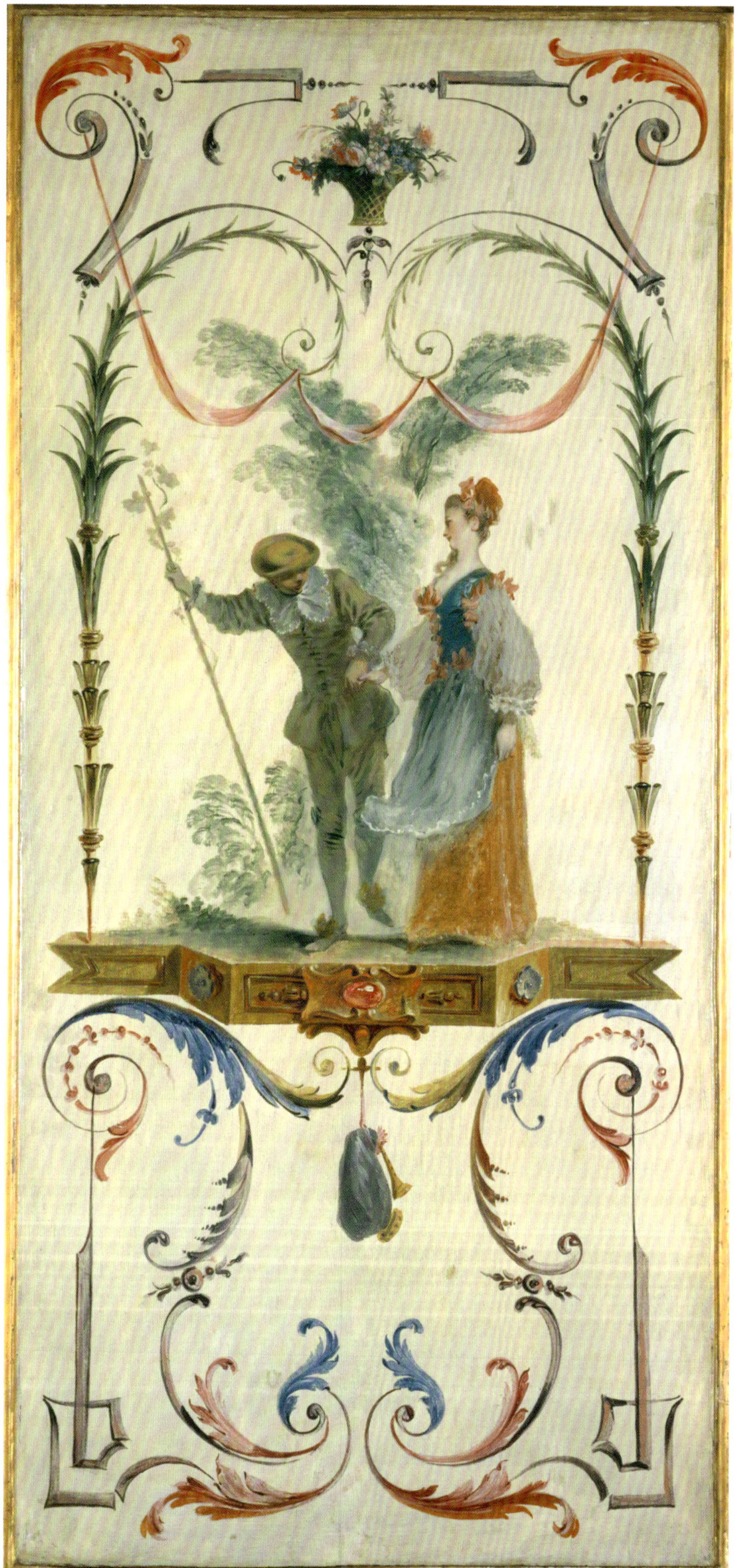

FIG. 1 *The Coaxer: Arabesque.* Jean-Antoine Watteau (French, 1684–1721). France, 1709. Oil on panel. Private collection, Paris, France

Rococo Redux

FROM THE STYLE MODERNE OF THE EIGHTEENTH CENTURY TO ART NOUVEAU

Melissa Lee Hyde

The word rococo is often synonymous with old-fashioned. There is a certain irony in this, since the style associated with it was the first self-consciously modern one in the history of art. For better or worse, rococo has also long been identified with the feminine, a characterization that has come back into vogue (and *Vogue*) thanks to Vivienne Westwood, Madonna, and Sofia Coppola—the Express clothing store on Madison Avenue even has a Jean-Honoré Fragonard-inspired mural. In these current reincarnations, rococo is more vehemently "feminine" than ever, making it the most recent chapter in a continuing history of a style that goes back to the eighteenth century—a history that involves revolutions, culture wars, and gender politics.

Rococo was the predominant artistic style in Europe for much of the eighteenth century. Yet, in the eighteenth century, there was no "rococo" art—the word itself was not invented until after the French Revolution and not commonly used until the 1830s. The exuberant, playful, elegant style of decoration and design that we now call rococo was known in its own time as *le style rocaille*, *le style moderne*, or *le goût nouveau*. Born out of an early eighteenth-century French mode of interior decoration and ornament marked by asymmetry, sinuous lines, and motifs both fanciful and naturalistic, rococo enjoyed numerous revivals and reincarnations in the nineteenth century.

The word rococo, with its rhyming syllables and echoing cadences, seems to connote frivolity and excess. These certainly numbered among its original meanings. The expression first arose in the wake of the French Revolution as studio slang used by painters to scorn art (or anything else) they deemed outmoded, mannered, or which otherwise smacked of the era of Louis XV and his longtime favorite, the Marquise de Pompadour. On these points specialists generally agree, although the exact origins and etymology of rococo have long been a subject of debate.[1] Used variously to denominate a period or an artistic style, or as a pejorative expression, its origins are as uncertain as its meanings.

Etymologically, rococo probably derived from a combination of the first two syllables of the French words *rocaille* (a form of colorful and irregular rockwork used to embellish grottoes and fountains) and *coquillage* (shell motifs that accompanied the rocaille).[2] It is also possible that the expression combined rocaille with the Italian adjective *barocco*, meaning misshapen, malformed, and convoluted (as in a "baroque" pearl). Barocco was a word nineteenth-century writers used to denigrate works of seventeenth-century artists like Giovanni Lorenzo Bernini, who was sometimes identified, erroneously, as the "father" of rococo.[3]

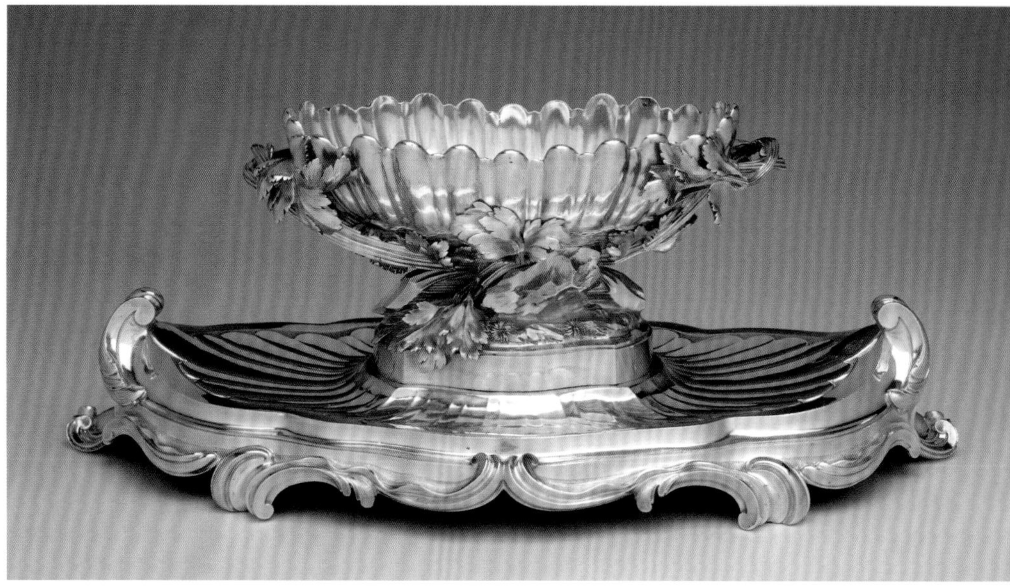

FIG. 3 Sauceboat and Stand. François-Thomas Germain (French, 1726–1791). Paris, France, 1756–59. Silver. Museum of Fine Arts, Boston; Elizabeth Parke Firestone and Harvey S. Firestone Jr. Collection, 1993.515.2a-b

In French, rocaille was, and is, a synonym for rococo, though it has never shared the broader meanings of rococo, which applies to many other forms of visual and material culture, from dress fashions to paintings to church façades.[4] The rocaille form was first adapted to ornament and decoration by designers like Pierre Lepautre in the 1680s, then years later by Jean-Antoine Watteau in his decorative paintings (fig. 1). In works like *Pilgrimage to the Isle of Cythera* (1717), he adopted rocaille arabesque forms in more pictorial terms. Le style rocaille reached its fullest flowering in the designs of Juste-Aurèle Meissonnier and Thomas Germain (1673–1748), both master silversmiths (figs. 2, 3). A frame Meissonnier designed in 1730 for a Jean-Baptiste Oudry painting appears to be the first instance of the rocaille as new form of ornament rather than decorative rockwork.[5] (fig. 4) In it, Meissonnier incorporated the arabesques, scrollwork, leaves, and shell motifs of an asymmetrical rocaille cartouche (see Fuhring, fig. 18) into the design of the frame, making it a lively, undulating form that dissolved rather than defined boundaries.

Etienne-Jean Delécluze, a student and biographer of the neoclassical painter Jacques-Louis David, wrote in 1855 that the expressions Pompadour and rococo were first used by David's students in 1796–97 to refer to "the taste that was in fashion during the reign of Louis XV."[6] In the 1820s and 1830s, French authors from Stendhal to Honoré de Balzac deployed the term with a variety of meanings.[7] It did not appear in the official lexicon of the French language, the *Dictionnaire de l'Académie Française*, until 1842, in which it was defined somewhat vaguely as a style of ornament and design associated with Louis XV.[8] As David's students had done almost fifty years earlier, the *Dictionnaire* definition linked rococo with Pompadour.

By 1836, rococo entered the English language. In her perceptive account of the "new-born" word, Frances Trollope noted in *Paris and the Parisians in 1835* that it was "applied by the young and innovating to everything which bears the stamp of the taste, principles or feelings of the past."[9] Trollope also observed that the meaning of rococo depended upon the speaker's political vantage point. For "the innovating" to be rococo might be a question of adhering to ancien-régime fashion or to its royalist politics. For republicans—the political radicals of the 1830s—to be rococo was to be subservient to all forms of authority. Subsequently, rococo art was seen to symbolize the cultural and political authority of successive French nineteenth-century regimes; in particular, the Second Empire's interest in pre-Revolutionary art was part of official efforts to establish legitimacy through identification with a period when royalty was as yet unchallenged.[10] Later in the century, as capitalism and middle-class democracy triumphed decisively in politics and the economy, the affluent and well born championed rococo art as a way of contesting what they deemed an oppressive and stern bourgeois morality and political authority.[11]

In Trollope's usage, rococo was not an art-historical term. Until the end of the nineteenth century, it was not widely used as such, except in Germany. It remained a general label for the Louis XV style or for anything old-fashioned. By the 1840s, Jacob Burckhardt began to use it as a generic art-historical term for any decadent phase of a period style (e.g., he described a "rococo" phase in Romanesque, Gothic, and Hellenistic art). Soon thereafter, other German art historians began to use rococo as a formal classification of the general period and style of Louis XV, and undertook the first critical analyses of the style. These scholars were concerned largely with theorizing the style in relation to baroque architecture in Germany and Italy.

Since Fiske Kimball's groundbreaking 1943 book *The Creation of the Rococo*, many scholars—especially in France—have continued to use rococo in the narrow sense, to name a style of decoration and ornament developed by a small number of French designers, ornamentalists, and architects during the first half of the eighteenth century.[12] However, the word is still used to designate the broad historical period from the regency to the reign of Louis XVI (r. 1774–1792), known as the "Rococo Age," or to refer to a pan-European style "capable of suffusing all spheres of art."[13] Some scholars have argued that it was the first "modern" style; others have denied that it qualifies as a style at all. Lately, it has become possible to speak of rococo as a cultural mode of being, thought, and representation rather than exclusively as a formal idiom. As Mary Sheriff recently noted,

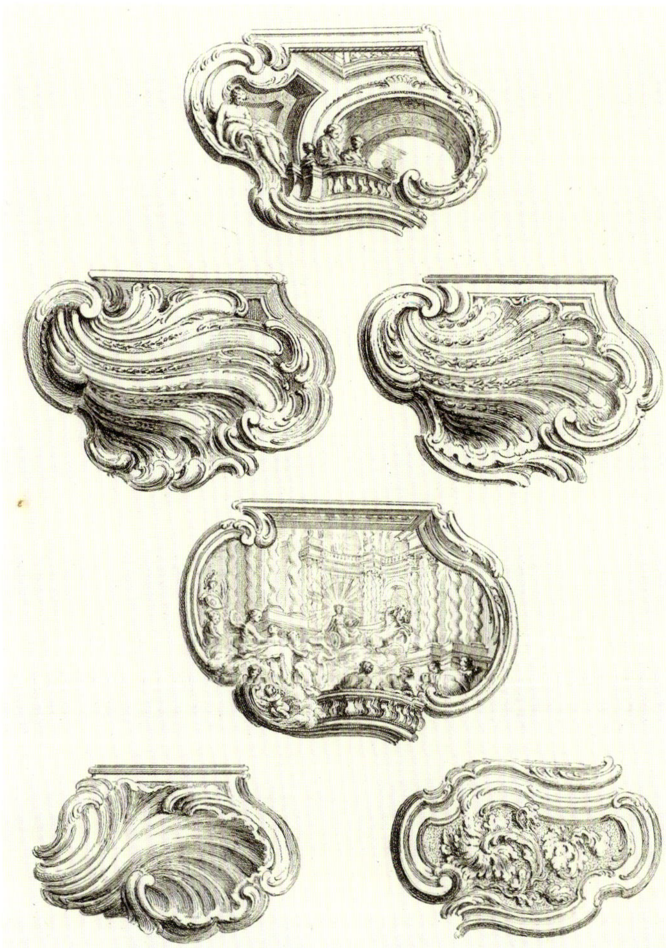

FIG. 2 *Differents desseins de Tabatieres* (Various Designs for Tobacco Boxes), plate 50 in *Oeuvre de Juste-Aurèle Meissonnier*. Juste-Aurèle Meissonnier (French, 1695–1750). Etched by Gabriel Huquier (French, 1695–1772). Paris, France, 1748. Etching on off-white laid paper. Cooper-Hewitt, National Design Museum, Smithsonian Institution, Purchased for the Museum by the Advisory Council, 1921-6-212-19-a

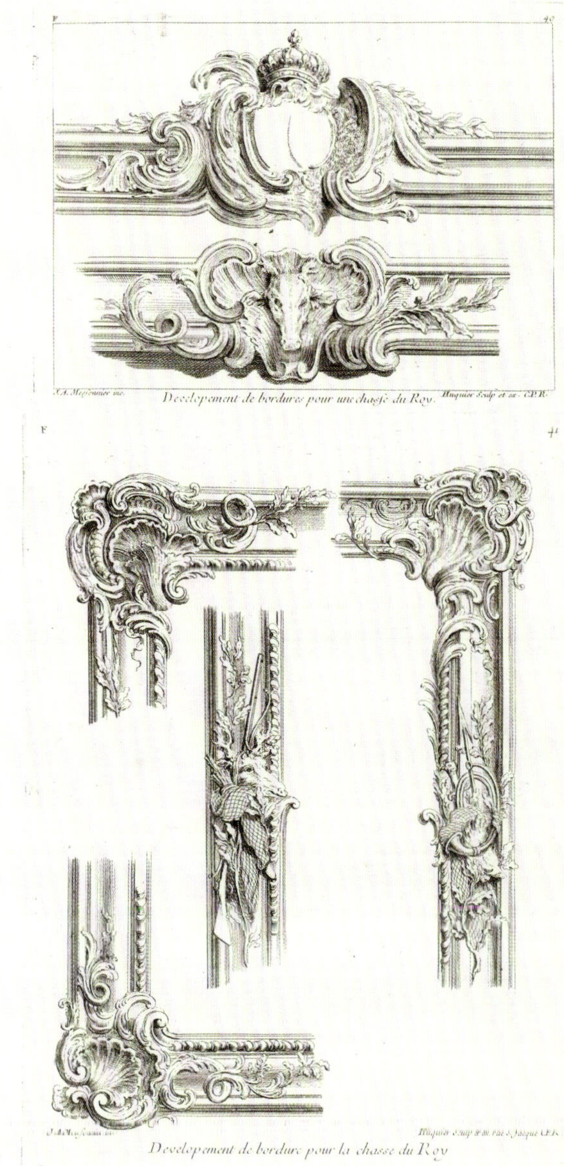

FIG. 4 *Développement de bordures pour une chasse du Roy* (Frame for the King's Hunt), plates 40–41 in *Oeuvre de Juste-Aurèle Meissonnier*. Juste-Aurèle Meissonnier (French, 1695–1750). Etched by Gabriel Huquier (French, 1695–1772). France, 1748. Etching and engraving on white laid paper. Cooper-Hewitt, National Design Museum, Smithsonian Institution, Purchased for the Museum by the Advisory Council, 1921-6-212-14-a,b

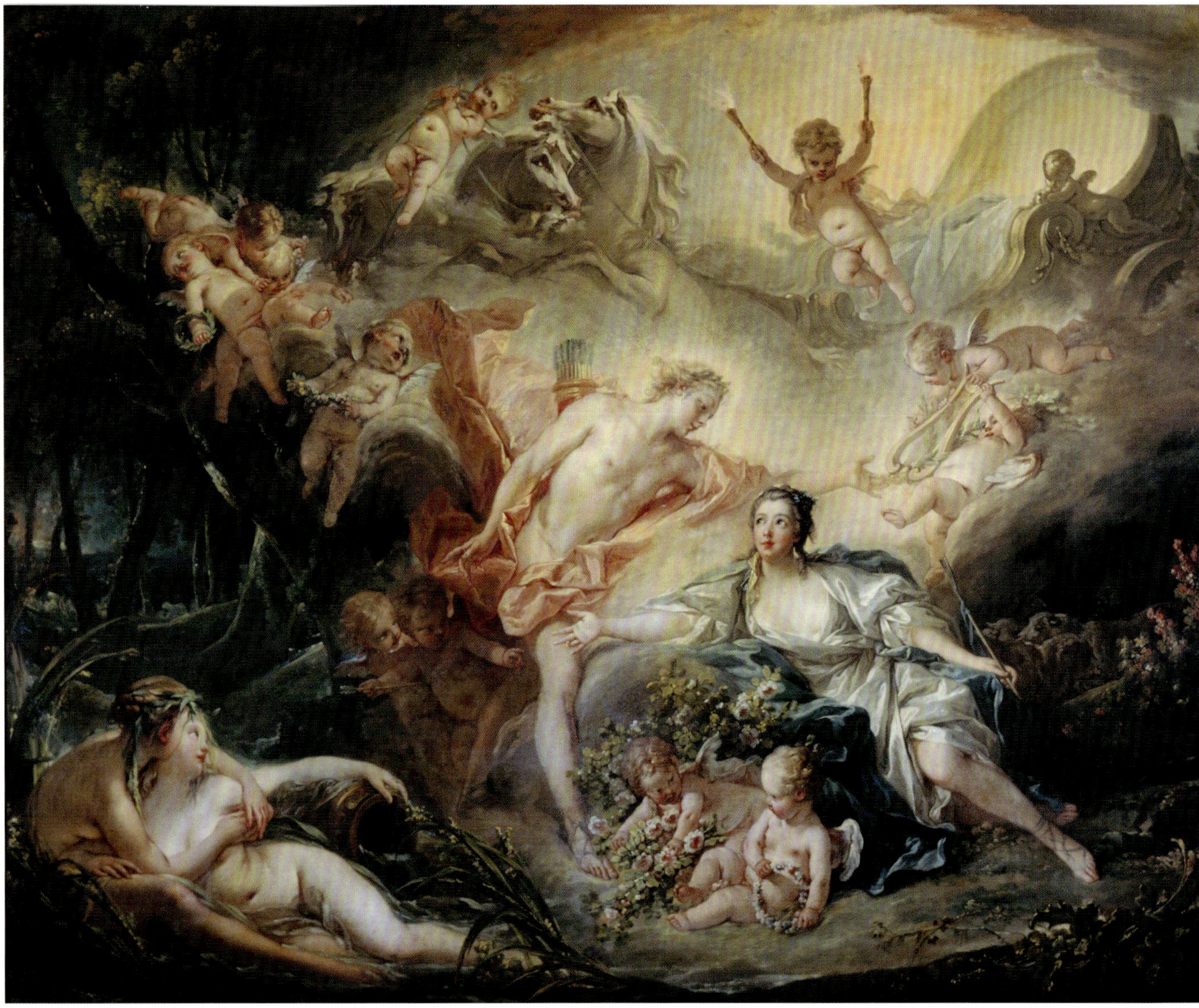

FIG. 5 *Apollo Revealing His Divinity to Issé*. François Boucher (French, 1703–1770). France, 1750. Brush and oil on panel. Musée des Beaux-Arts, Tours, France

"It is as unstable and provocative as the art it describes." She also pointed out that, in the eighteenth century, there was no expressly defined theory of rococo; rather, "the style's adversaries first articulated its characteristics negatively and retrospectively, and those who appreciate the rococo have wrestled with their definition ever since."[14]

By any definition, Meissonnier's work is rococo. However, there is another artist closely connected to him, François Boucher (1703–1770), whose work blurs the distinctions between its broader and narrower definitions. Boucher is best known as an emblematic figure of rococo painting, but he was also intimately involved with the development and diffusion of rocaille ornament. As others have noted, in Boucher's art (and that of Jean-Antoine Watteau before him), the boundary between painting and the decorative arts is porous.[15] As is the case in rocaille designs, paintings like *Apollo Revealing His Divinity to Issé* (fig. 5) feature no rectilinear forms and eschew perspectival space, and there is an apparently improvisational, even haphazard, quality to the lush arrangement of objects. Even though *Apollo* has a rectangular format, the figures are keyed to a compositional form that recalls a rocaille cartouche, and they bear little relation to the rectangular frame.[16] More usual in Boucher's oeuvre are paintings like *Summer* (ca. 1750), in which the figures seem subordinate to the frame's animated curves, which encroach on and meld with the pictorial space.

Elements of rococo's ornamental vocabulary—flowers and other vegetation, rocks, vases, masks, shells, mythical marine creatures, pearls—also appear very often in the picturesque abundance of beautiful objects in Boucher's painting.[17] Paintings such as *A Lady Fastening Her Garter* (*La Toilette*) feature acutely observed décors, furniture, decorative objects, and fashions that epitomize rococo, and their characteristically rococo painterly qualities—the play with surface and depth, the nimble brushwork, lightness, delicacy, and flirtatious sensuality.[18]

Apollo Revealing His Divinity to Issé and *Summer* are two of the many works that Boucher produced for Madame de Pompadour. In 1860, the Goncourt brothers, whose celebratory, if sometimes fabulous, writings on eighteenth-century art have had a lasting impact on art-historical analysis of the period, declared Pompadour "the godmother and queen of the rococo."[19] The Goncourts' general belief in the eighteenth century as the "century of Woman" led them to overstate Pompadour's role in the development of rococo.[20] Nevertheless, she was instrumental in making

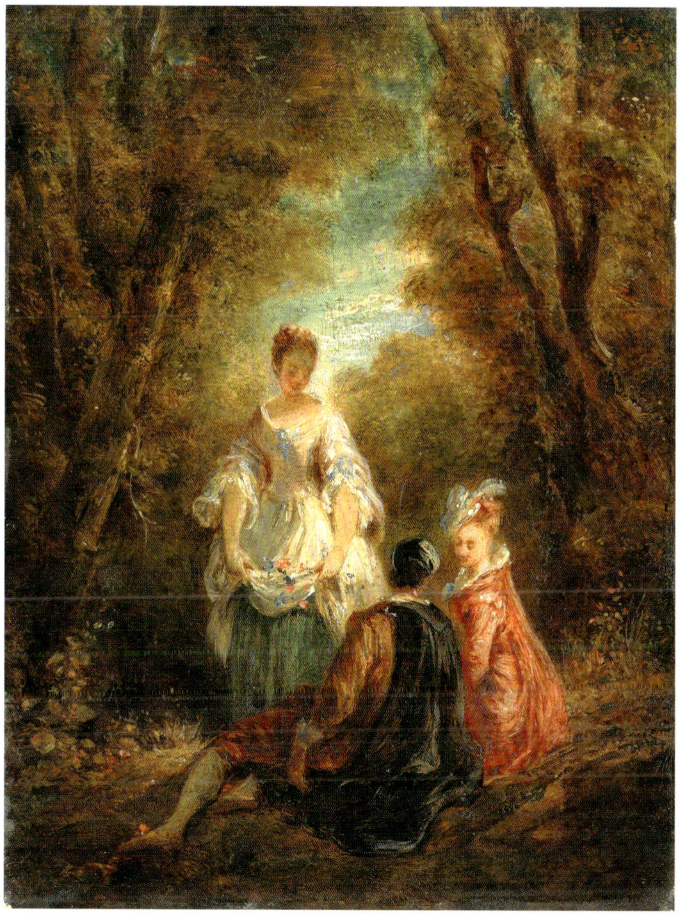

FIG. 6 *Conversation in a Park*. Jules-Robert Auguste (French, 1789–1850). France, first half of 19th century. Musée du Louvre, Paris, France

it the most fashionable style of her day. Her association with rococo art fueled the notion that it was a feminine style, despite its having been a fully developed stylistic idiom long before her time and the fact that it was a style elaborated by male artists, mainly for male patrons—and not only in France. Frederick the Great, King of Prussia (r. 1740–86), was one of the most avid collectors of Watteau's paintings and the patron of important rococo architectural projects such as Sanssouci. Moreover, the popularity of Boucher's art in his own time, indicated by the demand for prints after his work and by his success as a designer of theatrical décors, also casts doubt on whether rococo art was a purely aristocratic style, despite assertions by the Goncourts and others that it was.

Enlightenment critics of elite society claimed that women's involvement in culture and politics, symbolized by Pompadour, her interest in art, and her role at court, was leading to the effeminization of France. Though far from the truth, these critics also claimed that rococo art was made almost exclusively for women of the court and salon society (*le monde*)—more than once Boucher's art was referred to as "fan painting."[21] The Goncourts reaffirmed the notion that rococo was aristocratic and feminine, but their celebration of the reign of woman was meant to ascribe positive values to the terms of eighteenth-century critiques of the style.

Due to its associations with the hated ancien régime, rococo fell from favor during the Revolution and the reign of Napoleon that followed.[22] Rococo enjoyed its first real revival during the years of the Bourbon Restoration (1814–30). Emigrés returning to the elegant Faubourg St. Germain attempted to regain something of their previous status by collecting eighteenth-century art, furnishing their *hôtels* with period decorations (both Louis XV and Louis XVI), and patronizing new artists who imitated rococo or simply captured some of its flavor (fig. 6).[23] Newer members of the aristocracy and ambitious, wealthy members of the bourgeoisie also adopted rococo as a symbol of legitimacy and cultural distinction. (Until the Goncourts, proponents of rococo did not regard it as an inherently feminine style, but as one signifying elite refinement and privilege.)

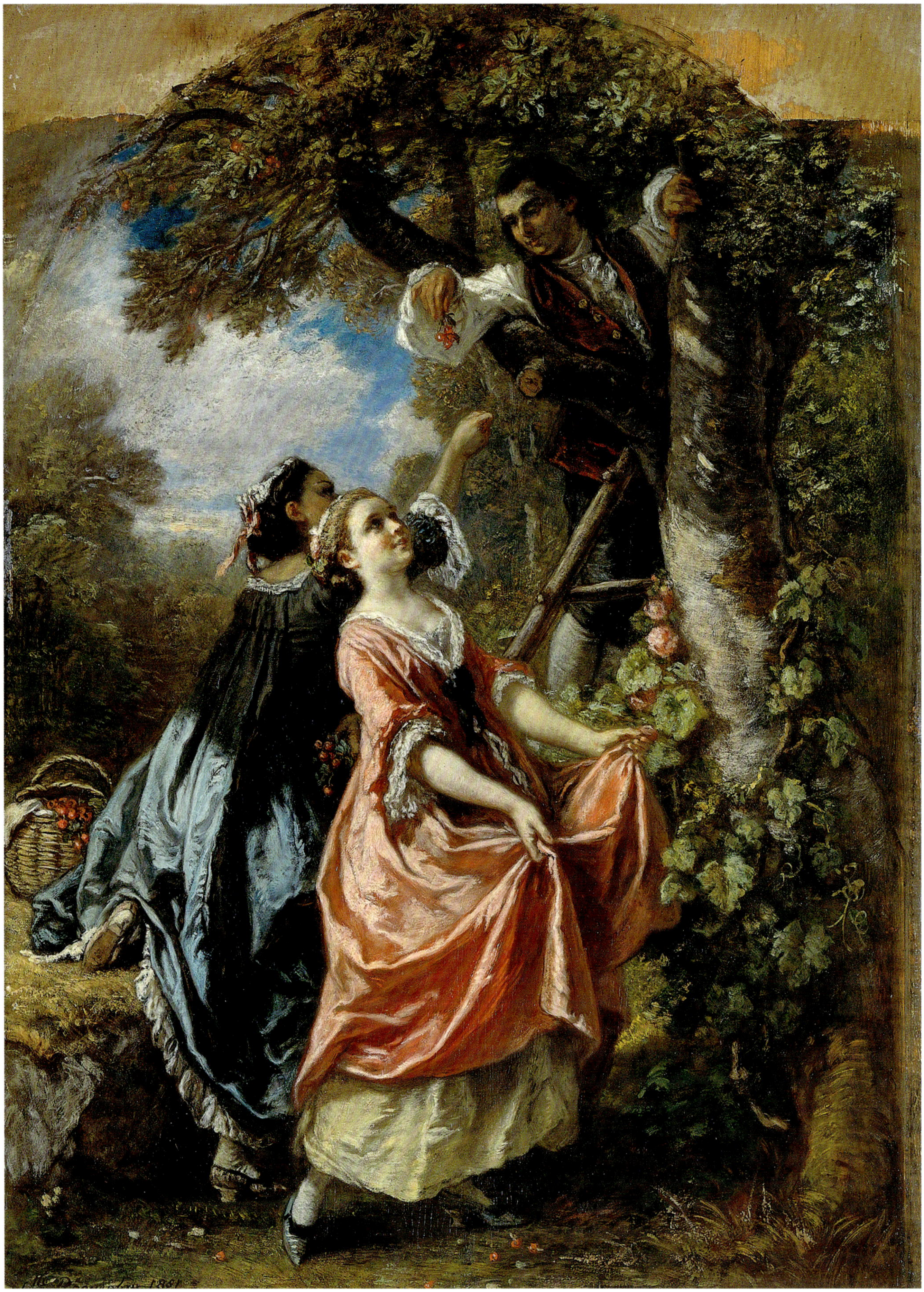

FIG. 7 *Rousseau and Mademoiselle Galley Gathering Cherries*. Camille Roqueplan (French, 1800–1855). France, 1851. Brush and oil on panel. The Wallace Collection, London, England

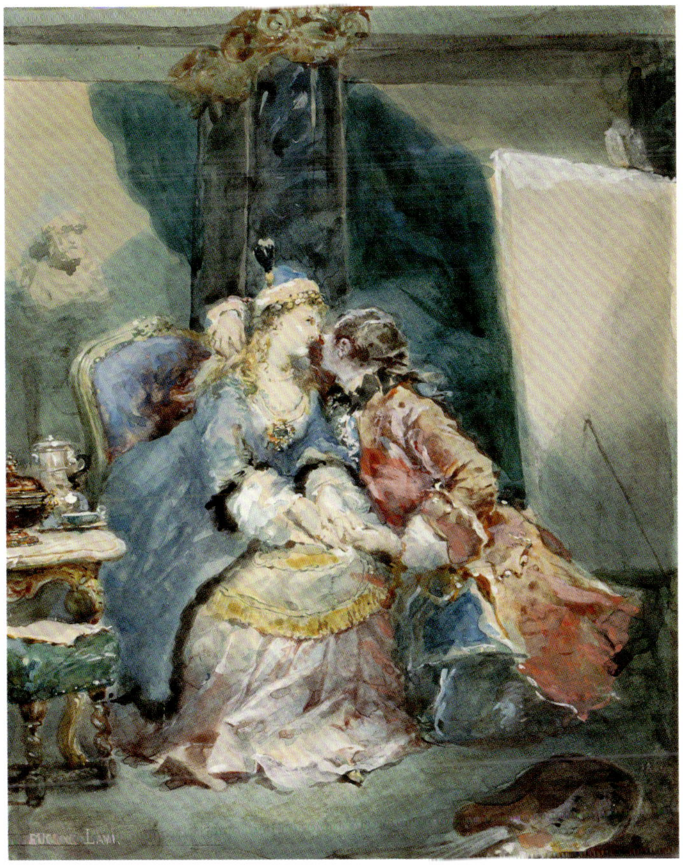

FIG. 8 *A Couple Embracing in an Artist's Studio.* Eugène Lami (French, 1800–1890). France, 1881. Brush and watercolor, white gouache over black chalk on paper. The J. Paul Getty Museum, Los Angeles, California, Gift of Dr. and Mrs. Richard A. Simms in honor of John Walsh on the occasion of his retirement as Director, 2000.49

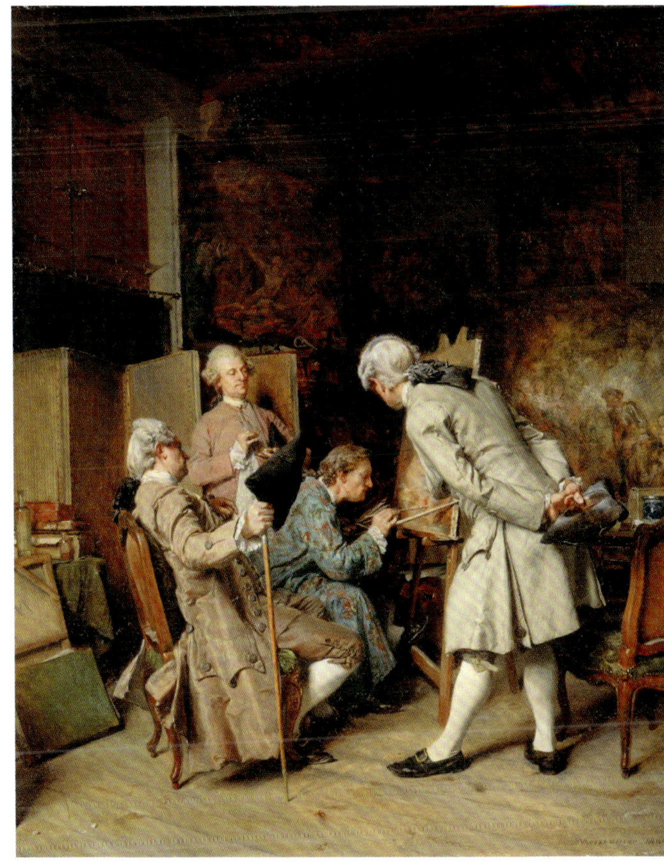

FIG. 9 *The Painting Lovers (in the Taste of the 18th Century).* Ernest Meissonier (French, 1815–1891). France, 1860. Brush and oil on panel. Musée d'Orsay, Paris, France

As Frances Trollope wrote, to embrace rococo after the Bourbon Restoration was to return to the pictorial and social ideals of the ancien régime, and was, in that sense, a political gesture. It also suggested the belief that art was for and about the aristocracy's amorous moods and pleasures.

It was not only the wealthy elite who developed a taste for rococo. In the 1820s and 1830s, young romantics discovered in the likes of Watteau, Nicolas Lancret, and Fragonard a colorist aesthetic wholly in tune with their own Bohemian l'art pour l'art credo.[24] Some, like Camille Roqueplan (1800–1855) (fig. 7), made important contributions to the early rococo revival in France through their eighteenth century-inspired works and their copies after eighteenth-century artists. An enormous number of late nineteenth-century artists, from Eugène Lami (1800–90) (fig. 8) to Edouard Manet, Pierre-Auguste Renoir, and Berthe Morisot, would also be inspired by rococo art. Throughout the nineteenth century, rococo art was increasingly sought after by collectors, many of whom were artists, but none more obsessively than the Goncourts.

The brothers came of age during the July Monarchy (1830–48) and the Second Republic (1848–52), when rococo art, décor, and fashions were a mark of the social and cultural elite. After 1840, the eighteenth century took on a broader cultural significance as the single most important source for the design of fashions and decorative arts. However, it was during the Second Empire (1852–70) that the interest in and imitation of eighteenth-century visual and material culture became a phenomenon.[25] In painting, this fascination with the eighteenth century is apparent in the spectacular success enjoyed by Ernest Meissonier (1815–1891), who, in the early 1830s, began to exhibit small genre paintings of eighteenth-century subjects, rendered with a crisp documentary realism that captivated Salon audiences (fig. 9). His success spawned legions of imitators who continued to work through the end of the century.[26]

The taste for the eighteenth century was much encouraged by the ever-increasing bourgeois audiences "for whom it presented an optimistic outlook on life appropriate to the new Parisian 'nobility' of the late Second Empire," as Caroline Igra recently argued. However, the popularity of images of eighteenth-century life and of rococo-inspired art involved more than a shift in patronage and taste: "Reviving this earlier regime was a means of flattering themselves and emphasizing their own imperialist claims, in the hope of achieving the awe and respect of the populace supposedly enjoyed by the former regime."[27]

This suggests why the wife of Napoleon III, Empress Eugénie, did so much to promote a taste for the eighteenth century.[28] To furnish her various residences, she procured eighteenth-century paintings and furniture from state collections (fig. 10). Eugénie commissioned painters like Giraud, Chaplin, and Monticelli to decorate her suites in the royal residences with allegories and mythologies in the manner of Boucher. She commissioned furniture in a style dubbed by one scholar "the Second Rococo."[29] In 1867, she sponsored an exhibition of Marie-Antoinette's possessions at the Petit Trianon.[30] Before that, in 1854, Franz-Xavier

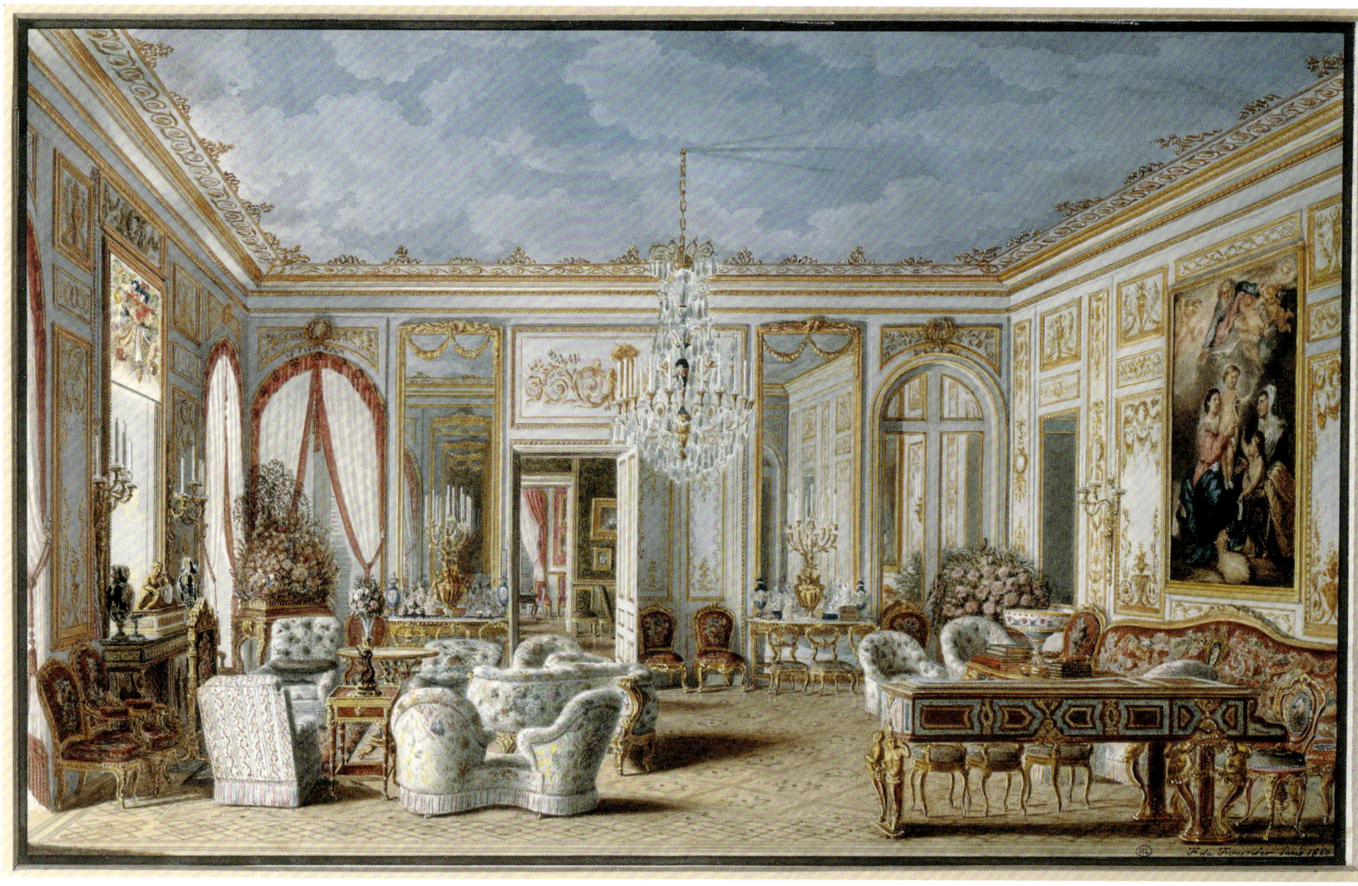

FIG. 10 *The Empress' Salon at St. Cloud, Second Empire.* Jean-Baptiste Fortuné de Fournier (French, 1798–1864). France, 1860. Brush and watercolor on paper. Château, Compiegne, France

Winterhalter painted her portrait *en Marie-Antoinette*, which began a vogue for women's portraits in eighteenth-century costume.[31] This high-profile woman's taste for and promotion of eighteenth-century rococo art surely added to its feminine associations.

Nineteenth-century conceptions of the "feminine" aesthetic of rococo art, its charming "triviality," and its particular appeal to women are summed up in Pascal-Adolphe-Jean Dagnan-Bouveret's 1889 painting *The Watercolorist in the Louvre* (fig. 11). Here Watteau's *Pilgrimage to Cythera* is presented as the kind of art appropriate for pretty dilettantes who paint fans. In Dagnan-Bouveret's painting, the woman's presence seems to function as a kind of alibi for Dagnan-Bouveret's own engagement with Watteau. Both the copy of the masterful rendition of *Pilgrimage* and the fan painter herself allowed Dagnan-Bouveret to paint in a "feminine" mode, without compromising his own masculinity as an artist.[32]

For their part, the Goncourts were not satisfied with works merely inspired by the eighteenth century; they sought to recover the real thing. They began writing a series of scholarly books on eighteenth-century art in 1859, but their engagement with the art and culture of the period went far beyond any conventional literary or historical endeavor. Believing it to be the golden past, they worked to recreate and inhabit it, both in their writings about the period and more materially in their authentically rococo home in the Parisian suburb of Auteuil, which housed their magnificent collection of furniture, objets d'art, and drawings by Boucher, Fragonard, St. Aubin, and others.

The Goncourt brothers' knowledge and appreciation of rococo style, reflected in the decoration of their home and their writings, had a direct impact on the formation of the Art Nouveau style late in the century.[33] The "feminine" rococo that was so meticulously recreated by the Goncourts unified the elements of interior space into undulating and asymmetrical forms derived from the flowing tendrils of vines, flowers, and other plant life, the scroll and serpentine fan shapes of rocaille grottoes, and shells.[34] Many of its features—not least of all its emphasis on sinuous lines—would be continued in the whiplash curves of Art Nouveau (see Hunter-Stiebel, *Art Nouveau*), another totalizing artistic style intimately associated with the "eternal feminine."

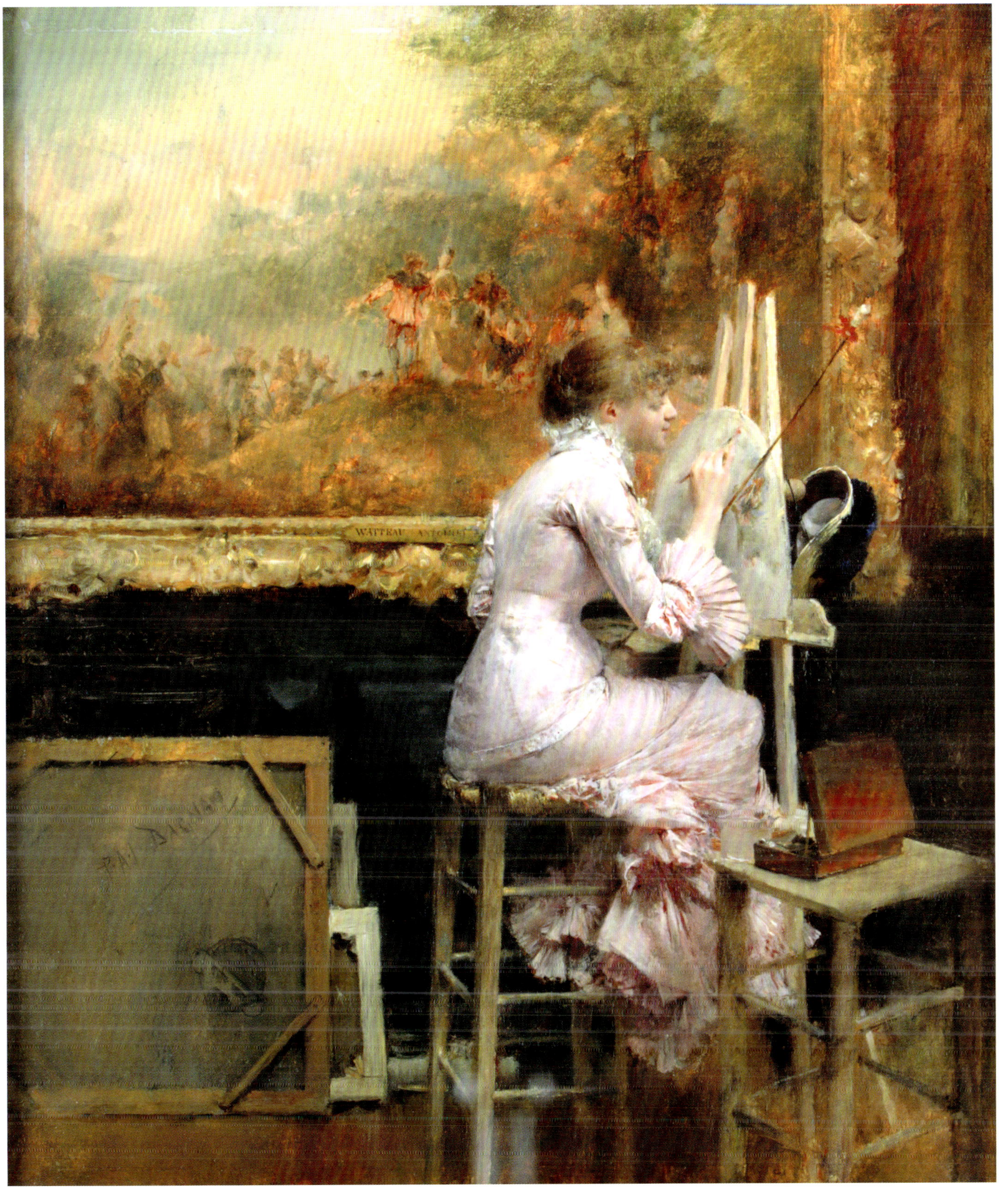

FIG. 11 *The Watercolorist in the Louvre*. Pascal-Adolphe-Jean Dagnan-Bouveret (French, 1852–1929). France, ca. 1889. Brush and oil on panel. State Hermitage Museum, Saint Petersburg, Russia, GE9787

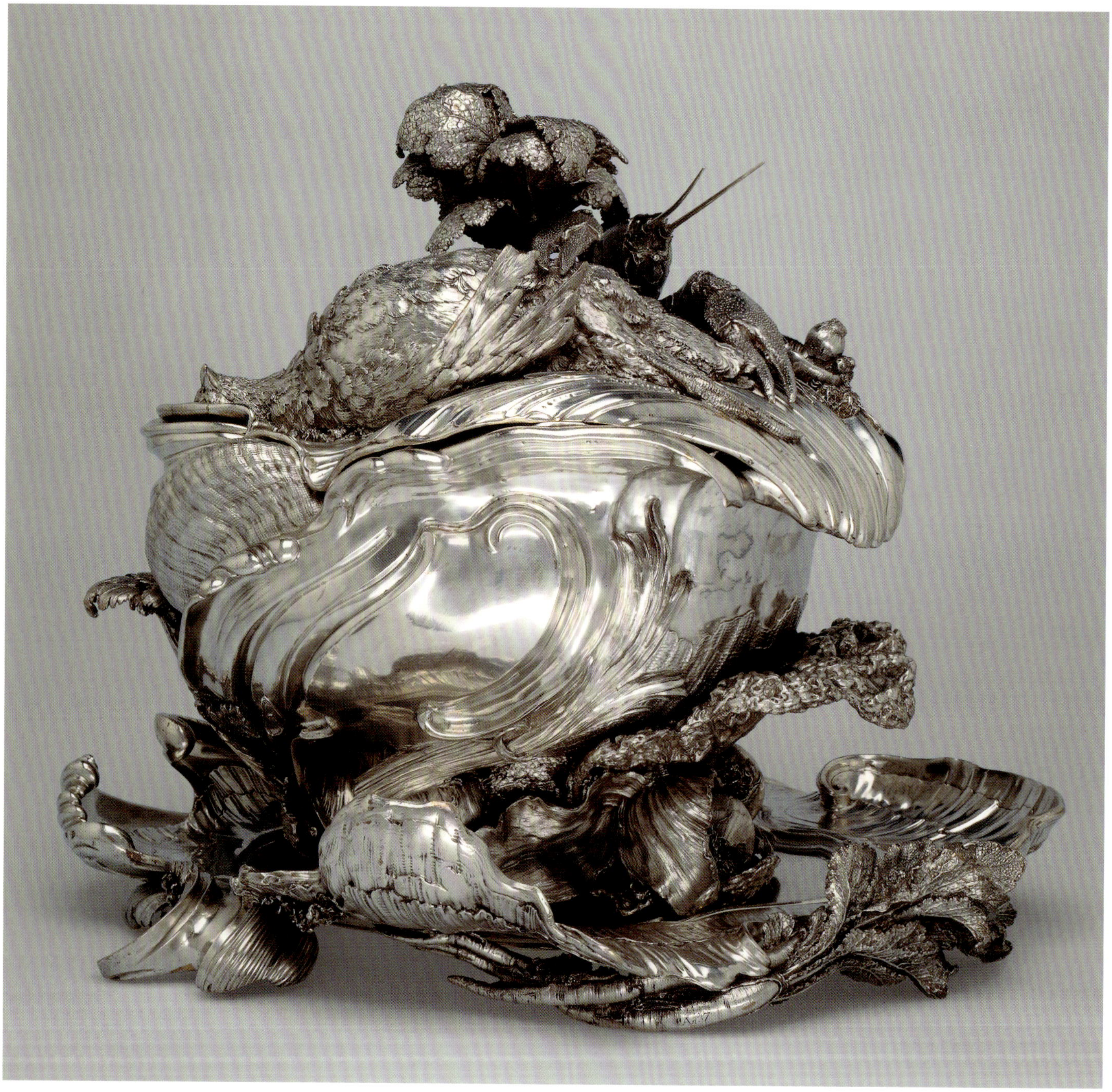

FIG. 15 Covered tureen and platter. Juste-Aurèle Meissonnier (French, 1695–1750). Executed by Henry-Guillaume Adnet (French, 1683–1745) and Pierre-François Bonnestrenne (French, 1682–after 1740). Paris, France, 1735–40. Silver. Cleveland Museum of Art, Leonard C. Hanna Jr. Fund, 1977.182.a–c

Juste-Aurèle Meissonnier and His Patrons

Peter Fuhring

When Fiske Kimball published his book *The Creation of the Rococo* in 1943, it was immediately recognized as a groundbreaking study of lesser-known issues of the early eighteenth-century arts of decoration that proved to be major. In his review of the book, Anthony Blunt boldly stated that "the exaggerated importance usually attached to the position of Juste-Aurèle Meissonnier in French Art is corrected, and the author rightly emphasizes that his main success was abroad."[1] Blunt further stressed how little the early phase of rococo style was affected by foreign influences. But, at the same time, he considered Italy's influence on the generation of Gilles-Marie Oppenord and Vassé more important than Kimball allowed, and urged further study on the Italian influence on Oppenord. Georges Wildenstein formulated a more tempered opinion of Kimball's book, stating that foreign influences were always welcomed by France, but that French artists synthesized them in ways that expressed the national characteristics of France's own artistic genius.[2] Both critics focused in different ways on a phase in art history when issues of nationality and style were not only intertwined, but seen as the touchstones by which art was judged. Today, a different understanding of art history has made it possible to inventory the achievements of an artist or designer before judging them, if at all. What matters more now is to understand to what extent an artist responded to the expectations of his patron or to the laws of the luxury market. In the eighteenth century, a much more open society already existed than is generally understood. Ideas and artists traveled, and people were open to the sometimes daring and innovative proposals of designers. Only rarely did these propositions go beyond the unwritten rules of decorum, but innovation was recognized, and the resulting accomplishments were held in high esteem. The loss of so many works makes it difficult to even partially reconstruct the rich creation in all fields of the arts of decoration of the first half of the eighteenth century. It is important to remember here that Kimball's and Blunt's knowledge of Meissonnier's work was only fragmentary, and almost exclusively based on the prints made after his designs. They also failed to acknowledge that the published works offered a selection made by the artist and shed no light on the purpose of the publication. The lack of visual documentation depicting the many works of his contemporaries also led to an unbalanced appreciation of Meissonnier and his time.

The negative connotations of rococo proved to have a long life. However insignificant the origin of the term rocaille (the small stones and shells used to embellish grottoes and fountains) may seem, it is significant that it had a precise meaning.

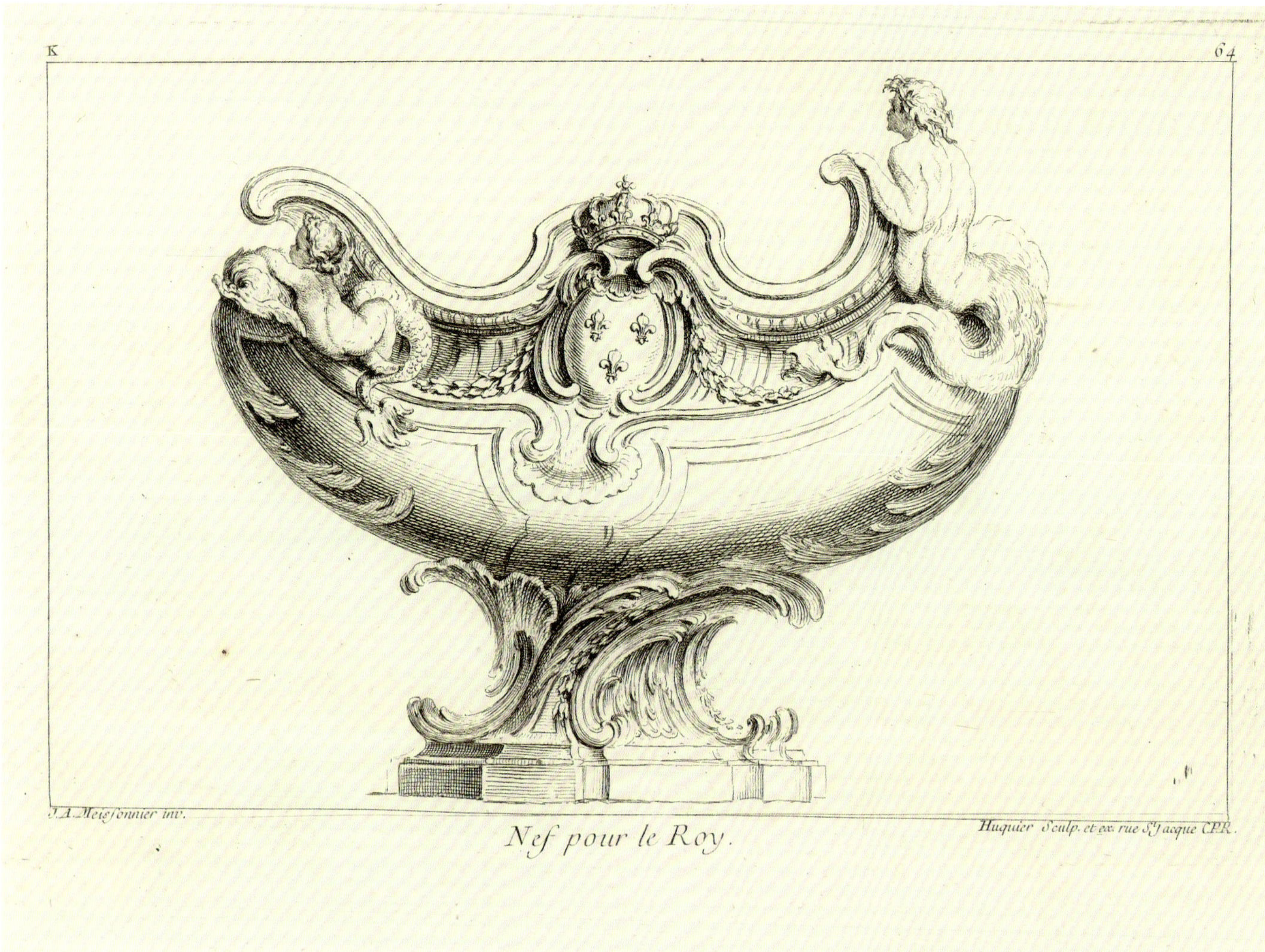

FIG. 1 *Nef pour le Roy (Design for a Standing Ship)*, plate 64 in *Oeuvre de Juste-Aurèle Meissonnier*. Juste-Aurèle Meissonnier (French, 1695–1750). Etched by Gabriel Huquier (French, 1695–1772). Paris, France, 1748 (designed 1728–29). Etching on off-white laid paper. Cooper-Hewitt, National Design Museum, Smithsonian Institution, Purchased for the Museum by the Advisory Council, 1921-6-212-25-b

Indeed, the introduction of elements from nature into interior decoration in the early eighteenth century was a break with the grand style of the preceding period. At the same time, experimenting with rocaille led to its transformation to a new ornament in the regency and early reign of Louis XV, which contributed so much to characterize the new style. This said, ornament is but one element of design, and, like the work of a designer or artist, it is judged by more than one criterion. The perfect understanding of ornament by an artist like Meissonnier, together with his profound interest in sculpture, made it possible for him to develop a "free" approach to traditional objects and transcend craft-based boundaries. His new solutions, different from anyone else's, astonished his contemporaries.[3] Not surprisingly, several designs by Meissonnier were immediately copied and interpreted in France and abroad.

It is extremely difficult to reconstruct the balance between issues of prestige, innovation and tradition, design and craftmanship, feasability and price that determined discussions in the luxury market, where patrons commissioned works from artists rather than bought finished products in a shop. Did a patron address himself to Meissonnier because a relative had done so, the artist had worked for the crown, he liked earlier work by the artist, or was favorably impressed by the drawing presented to him? What made the patron aware of the artist in the first place? How was an artist's reputation made, promoted, sustained, or broken? We do know that contemporaries of Meissonnier were well aware of his excellence as a craftsman and of his capacity to propose novel and surprising designs. There is the opinion of abbé Jean-Bernard Le Blanc, guest at the Duke of Kingston's London house in 1737–38, who thought that the most capable goldsmiths in London were nothing but craftsmen, but a Thomas Germain or a Meissonnier was entirely different—they were designers, sculptors, great men in their genre.[4] Pierre-Jean Mariette formulated a similar idea about the exceptional gifts of Meissonnier as a goldsmith, which he considered his true profession, and who would have had, if any, only one competitor, Thomas Germain.[5] Mariette regretted that the artist indulged in architecture, and he considered Meissonnier's taste alone insufficient for success. On the other hand, Jacques-François Blondel lauded Meissonnier's study of architecture as having enriched his art.[6] When one considers these remarks, it becomes clear that major arbiters of taste, all contemporaries and acquaintances of Meissonnier, had a high opinion of him as an artist. When a trained craftsman, in this case a silversmith, is given credit as an artist, this implies much more than mere excellence of execution: it confers praise on his designs as

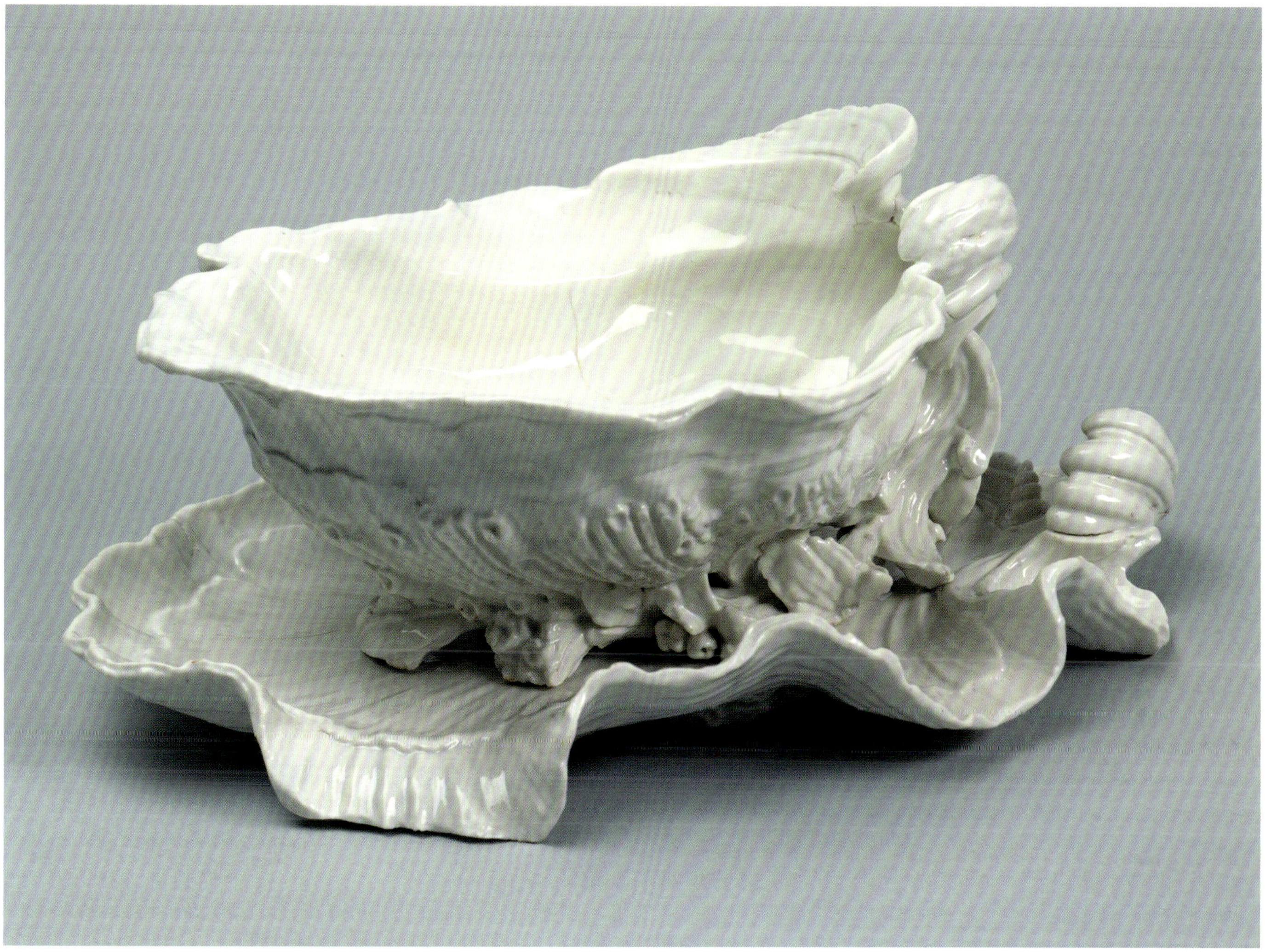

FIG. 2 "Shell-Form" bowl and platter. Juste-Aurèle Meissonnier (French, 1695–1750). Manufactured by Chantilly Porcelain Factory. Chantilly, France, ca. 1730–35. Soft-paste porcelain. The David and Alfred Smart Museum of Art, The University of Chicago; Gift of Mrs. Helen Regenstein, 1976.10a-b

well. The notion of design is crucial in this context and offers part of the explanation for Meissonnier's success among his various patrons from France, Portugal, England, and Poland.

His support among the highest social circles and the French court offer important information about the beginning of Meissonnier's career. In French society of the eighteenth century, many artists were welcomed from abroad, continuing the policy of the preceding period. Under Louis XIV, numerous foreign craftsmen were employed at the Manufacture des Gobelins to work on the embellishment of the royal palaces. After the reopening of the Gobelins at the beginning of the eighteenth century, tapestry weaving was recommenced, and workshops were used by some silver- and goldsmiths such as Meissonnier, but the once centralized control of artistic matters was not reestablished by the state. It is unclear whether his occupation of a workshop at the Gobelins was connected to his first commission in France, soon after he had arrived in 1714. Meissonnier engraved a medal for the famous "Medal History of King Louis XIV" series commemorating the naval battle of Malaga in 1704. The work fell under the supervision of the marquis de la Vrillière, but the director of the Royal Mint, the royal goldsmith Nicolas Delaunay (ca. 1650–1727), watched over the day-to-day practice. The drawing was supplied by Antoine Coypel, the official designer of the mint, thus allowing Meissonnier to show only his workmanship.

Meissonnier was trained in Turin by his father, the goldsmith Etienne (Stefano) Meissonnier (1660–1746), which made it impossible for him to enter the corporation of Parisian silver- and goldsmiths or to open shop and work for the public. However, Meissonnier was granted permission by royal decree in 1724 to enter the corporation and to call himself a royal goldsmith.[7] An official document records his working for the crown at the Gobelins, but the royal archives remain silent about this work, and not a single design from this period was selected by Meissonnier for his published *Oeuvre*. Immediately after his official enrollment, Meissonnier received two significant commissions, one from Orléans for the reliquary of Saint-Aignan (1725–30) and the other from the French court for five gold sword hilts as marriage presents from Louis XV and Maria Lesczynska to Polish gentlemen from the household of the queen's father, King Stanislas (1725). In both cases, Meissonnier was responsible for both design and execution, and, when the reliquary was finished, it was exhibited in his workshop in Paris. The opening lines of the *Mercure de France* dedicated to the event revealed the festive mood: "We are attentive to celebrate the progress of the arts in France and cannot refrain from saying something about an important goldsmith work, recently made by M. Meissonnier, and which a large number of curious persons came to see to their great satisfaction."[8]

Meissonnier also made several new pieces for the state-dinner service ordered for the young Louis XV. In his role as *grand maître de la maison du roi*, Louis-Henri, Prince of Condé, Duke of Bourbon (1692–1740), supervised the refurbishing of the royal silver and gold services that had been greatly diminished by Louis XIV's melting campaigns. The first minister had already commissioned from Meissonnier in 1723, for his private use, a silver wine cooler known today by a print and numerous nineteenth-century copies in silver and bronze. The minister's mother, Louise-Françoise, Duchess of Bourbon (1673–1743), also favored the artist's career, but no tangible evidence exists among the documents related to her estate. Nothing was executed from Meissonnier's designs for the gold service, but two prints preserve his designs for a small tureen and a ship. Louis XV's desire to break with tradition may have stimulated the search for novel ideas, and Meissonnier's design for the king's ship (fig. 1) illustrates this to perfection in its masterful, dynamic rendering of a ship floating on sea waves. The idea was certainly welcomed, but precedence, not style, determined the final choice of one of the three royal goldsmiths appointed by the crown in 1723 to succeed Nicolas Delaunay.

The Duke of Bourbon created a porcelain manufactory around 1724 at Chantilly, where he was in exile. He invited Meissonnier to conceive models in the new style based on rocaille ornament. Among the models is a tureen known from an experimental version.[9] (fig. 2) There is also a possibly later finished version, along with salt shakers[10] and a pair of girandoles with branches in porcelain embellished in gold,[11] all dating from the years 1730 to 1735. These pieces were clearly in opposition to the general imitations of Japanese porcelain for which the factory is mainly known.[12] The new material provided a challenge for Meissonnier, but the few surviving pieces associated with his designs suggest his possible dissatisfaction with the limitations imposed by soft porcelain, in contrast to the precision and excellence that he could achieve only by working in silver or gilt bronze.

The multiplication of prestigious commissions enhanced Meissonnier's reputation, and, not surprisingly, he was chosen to succeed Jean-Baptiste Berain as designer to the king's cabinet in 1726. Louis II de Rochechouart, Duke of Mortemart (1681–1746), Pair de France and *premier gentilhomme de la Chambre du Roi*, favored Meissonnier's nomination. They must have known each other, as the Duke had commissioned from the artist two years earlier a "Cadran à vent" (barometer) in 1724.[13] (fig. 3)

Another patron of Meissonnier was Jean-Frédéric Phélipeaux (1701–1781), Count of Maurepas and Pontchartrain and secretary of state, who was church warden of the Saint-Sulpice church council from 1720 and first church warden from January 1730. He likely suggested to the priest Jean-Baptiste Languet de Gergy (1675–1750) that he ask Meissonnier to supply some ideas for the main façade of Saint-Sulpice, one of the most important churches in Paris. Other church patrons included the Duke of Bourbon, the Cardinal of Polignac and the Duke of Orléans, patron of Gilles-Marie Oppenord (1672–1742), architect of the church since 1718. The proposition by Meissonnier came at an opportune moment: Oppenord found himself in a difficult position due to the construction of a lantern over the cupola in 1726 which proved to be too heavy. Meissonnier's design for the façade, the last part of the church to be constructed, is well known from a drawing and a corresponding large print included in the artist's *Oeuvre*.[14]

Apparently, the initiative was premature, and, in 1730–32, a competition was organized to find a definitive solution for the façade. Together with several other architects, Meissonnier sent in a proposal, but his design, radically changed to a French vocabulary in comparison to the strong Borrominian influence present in his first design, was discarded, and Giovanni Niccolo Servandoni (1695–1766) was declared the winner. Maurepas favored the project of the highly acclaimed stage-set designer Servandoni, as can be gleaned from a later eighteenth-century source, but he continued to support Meissonnier in other ways.

Maurepas, who had become secretary to the Saint-Esprit Order in 1725, could well have invited the artist to propose his vision for the new palace and church of the most important royal order, Saint-Esprit. Despite the forced accommodation of this order in the small and rather old-fashioned church of the cloister of the Augustine order, Meissonnier submitted a spectacular proposition dating from the years 1727–31.[15] It was Louis XV's express wish that plans be drawn to improve the house of the Saint-Esprit order, and some of Meissonnier's patrons shared the desire to enrich the center of Paris with important buildings topped by cupolas. Their initiatives could be seen both as an emulation of Rome and a wish to shift the center of power from Versailles to Paris. The fact that Meissonnier's proposal did not win the Saint-Sulpice competition did not deter Maurepas from commissioning private items from Meissonnier, such as a silver inkstand made in 1731 whose astoundingly complex shape is only known today from a print.[16]

During this period, Meissonnier continued his research of novel forms based on the traditional rocaille, allowing asymmetrical and shell-shaped finishings to play a dominant role. His designs for snuffboxes were considered exemplary, and Meissonnier supplied models for them to other goldsmiths and jewelers such as Daniel Govaers. The gold and lapis lazuli box from 1728–29 bearing the arms of Marie-Anne de

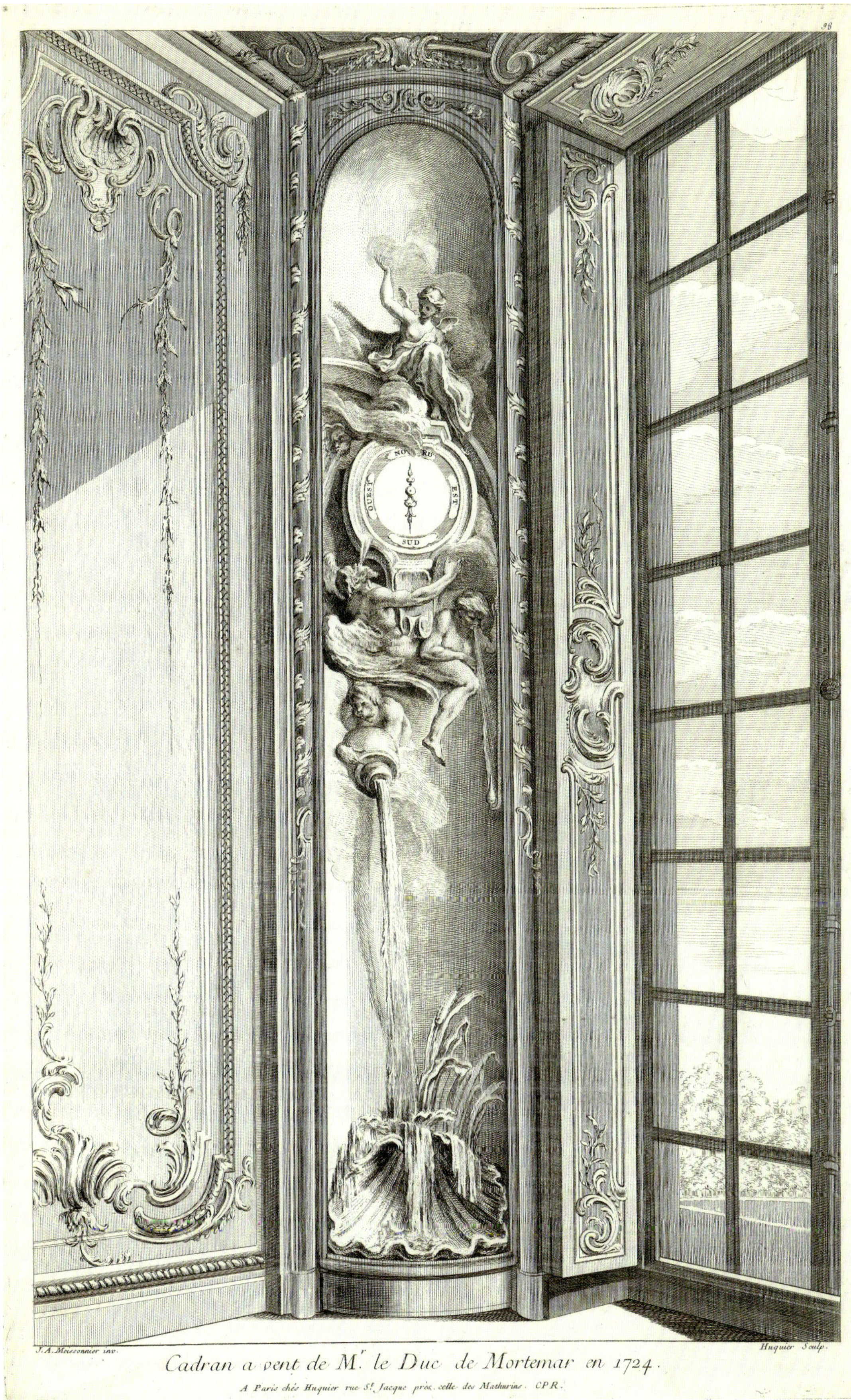

FIG. 3 Cadran à vent de M. le Duc de Mortemar [sic] en 1724 (Design for a Barometer for the Duc of Mortemart in 1724), plate 98 in Oeuvre de Juste-Aurèle Meissonnier. Juste-Aurèle Meissonnier (French, 1695–1750). Etched by Gabriel Huquier (French, 1695–1772). Paris, France, 1748 (designed 1724). Etching on white laid paper. Cooper-Hewitt, National Design Museum, Smithsonian Institution, Purchased for the Museum by the Advisory Council, 1921-6-212-56

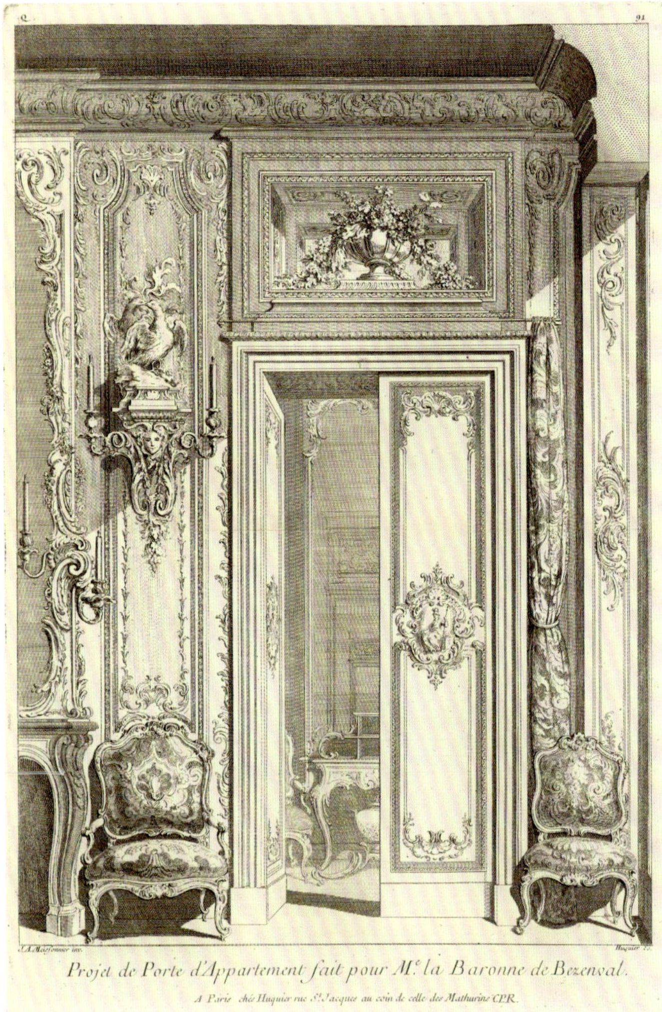

FIG. 4 Projet de Porte d'Appartement fait pour Mme la Baronne de Bezenval (Design for the Doorway in the Apartment of the Baronness of Bezenval), plate 91 in Oeuvre de Juste-Aurèle Meissonnier. Juste-Aurèle Meissonnier (French, 1695–1750). Etched by Gabriel Huquier (French, 1695–1772). Paris, France, 1748 (designed 1730–34). Etching on white laid paper. Cooper-Hewitt, National Design Museum, Smithsonian Institution, Purchased for the Museum by the Advisory Council, 1921-6-212-49

Neubourg, widow of Charles II of Spain, who had retired to Bayonne, bears his maker's mark. It is one of the first boxes executed in a complex cut-out shape, which demanded great skill in its execution. The circumstances of its commission are still unknown, but it was most likely made as a present. Designs for snuffboxes served as the starting point for a series of small, horizontal panels of ornament, among the first prints issued under the artist's direction in the spring of 1734.[17] In the announcement of the publication in the *Mercure de France*, they were described as "fountains, cascades, ruins, rockswork, and shells, morsels of architecture with bizarre and picturesque effects, intriguing, extraordinary forms, parts of which often do not relate to any others, yet do not make the ensemble less rich and agreeable. There are also some kinds of platforms with figures of humans and animals, grouped with intelligence, whose borders are extremely ingenious and varied."[18] Their success was immediate, copied by craftsmen and admired by collectors all over Europe.

As a royal goldsmith and designer to the king's cabinet for festival décors, Meissonnier had direct access to the court's inner circles. This privileged position undoubtedly played a role in the decision of Luis da Cunha, Portuguese ambassador in Paris, to invite Meissonnier to be the official adviser in matters of art to the king of Portugal. Apart from Meissonnier's status as an "official" artist, da Cunha's personal preferences in art were nourished by the works of the great Bernini and Pietro da Cortona. His choice for the work and approach of Meissonnier found a firm advocate in Robert-Alexandre d'Hermand (1660–1739), who lived at the Louvre and was in charge of the education of Louis XV. Gilles-Marie Oppenord, architect of the Orléans family, was suggested by Pierre Crozat for the post, but could not compete with Meissonnier. The latter's knowledge of the court's ceremonial protocol and the latest tastes guaranteed the best possible advice to the Portugese king, who imitated the style of the French crown.[19] For instance, Meissonnier advised him on the iconographic program of the tapestries designed for the new throne of Portugal, and supplied around 1728 designs for the fauteuil, executed by unidentified silversmiths in gilt solid silver.[20] The artist made also several designs for the interior decoration of a series of apartments in the royal palace, all of which were executed from 1731 to 1734.[21]

In the second half of the 1720s, everything seemed possible for Meissonnier, but his deep wish to become an architect somewhat overshadowed his natural gifts as a silversmith. The merchant and shipowner Léon Brethous (1693–1751) from Bayonne first offered Meissonnier the opportunity to see one of his architectural projects realized.[22] Due to restricted space, Brethous needed the authorization of the city of Bayonne to use some public grounds to build his new residence, on the bank of the Nive river, at the entrance of the city. According to documents from July 1729, Brethous submitted a plan that was examined by "des architectes les plus habilles, et par des personnes les plus experimentées de Paris." Brethous obtained access to high court circles and was favorably received as *Ecuyer gentilhomme de la Grande Vénerie de France*.[23] The concept of the building, with its rounded corners and, consequently, rooms with four round corners, was a novelty at the time. Archival documents make it possible to determine that, contrary to the opinion formulated by F. Kimball in 1942,[24] the character of the interior decoration (not executed) was in fact innovative for its time, and was contemporary to or slightly

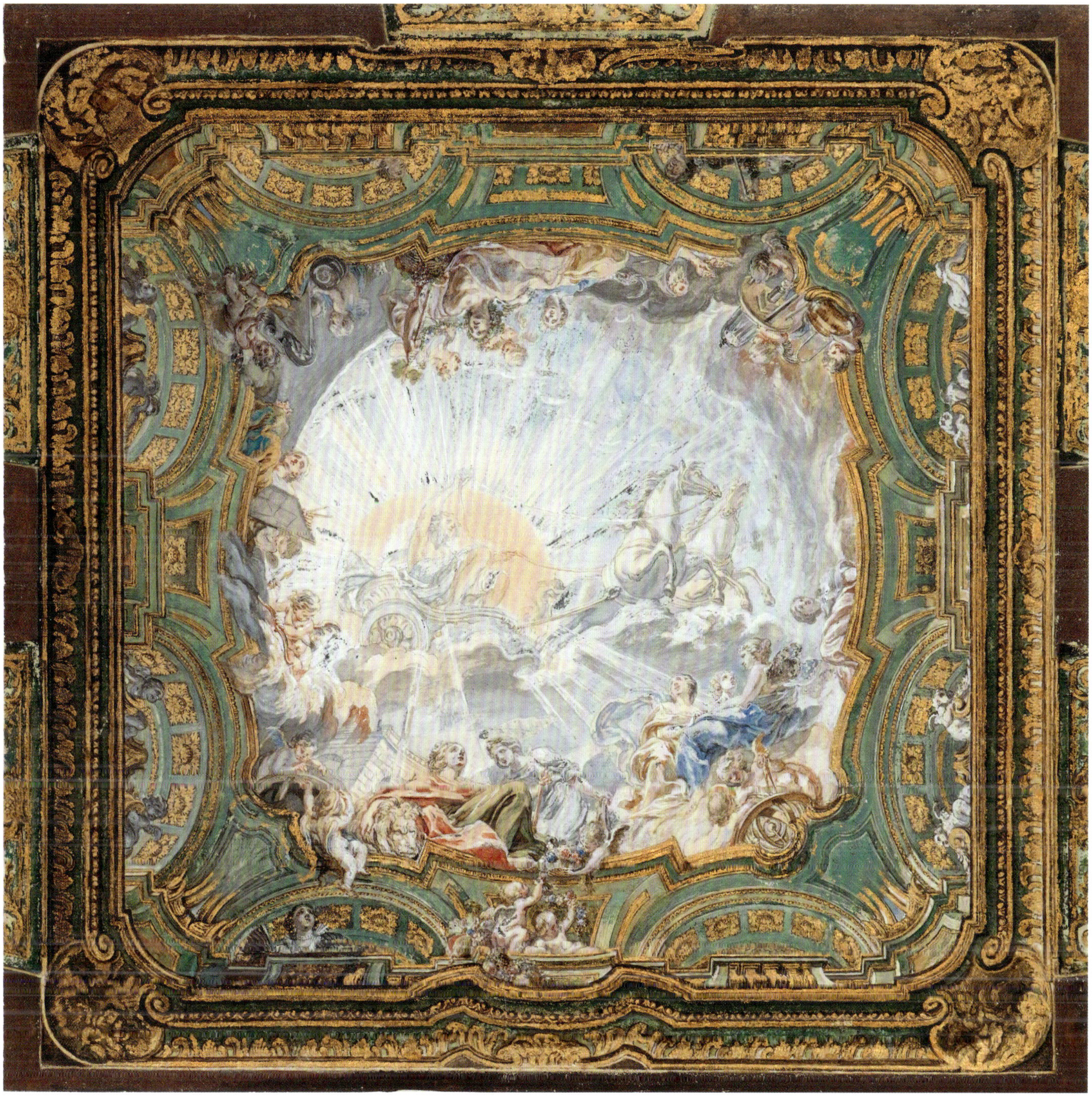

FIG. 5 "Chariot of Apollo," Ceiling Design for Count Bielinski's Cabinet, Warsaw, Poland. Juste-Aurèle Meissonnier (French, 1695–1750). Paris, France, 1734. Pen and gray ink, brush and watercolor, gouache, gold paint over black chalk on white laid paper. Cooper-Hewitt, National Design Museum, Smithsonian Institution, Purchased for the Museum by the Advisory Council, 1911-28-214

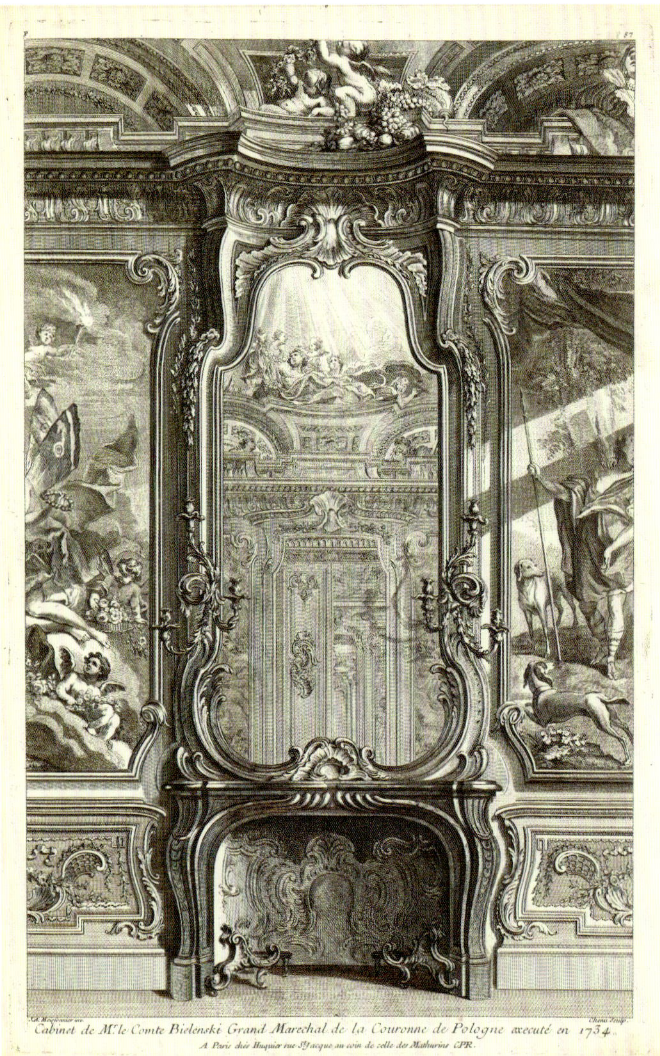

FIG. 6 Cabinet de Mr. le Comte Bielenski [sic], Grand Maréchal de la Couronne de Pologne (The Cabinet of Count bielinski, Grand Marshall of Poland), plate 87 in *Oeuvre de Juste-Aurèle Meissonnier*. Juste-Aurèle Meissonnier (French, 1695–1750). Etched and engraved by Pierre Chenu (French, 1718–after 1767). Paris, France, 1742–48 (designed 1734). Etching and engraving on white laid paper. Cooper-Hewitt, National Design Museum, Smithsonian Institution, Purchased for the Museum by the Advisory Council, 1921-6-212-45

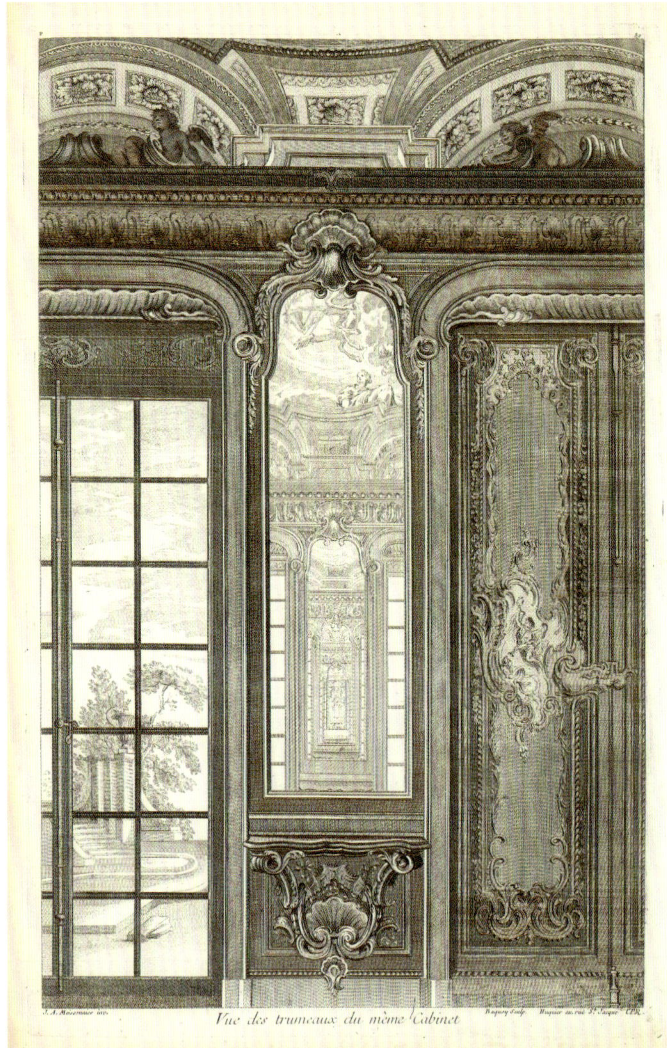

FIG. 7 Vue des trumeaux du même Cabinet (View of Same [Count Bielinski's] Cabinet), plate 89 in *Oeuvre de Juste-Aurèle Meissonnier*. Juste-Aurèle Meissonnier (French, 1695–1750). Etched and engraved by Pierre Chenu (French, 1718–after 1767) Paris, France, 1742–48 (designed 1734). Etching and engraving on white laid paper. Cooper-Hewitt, National Design Museum, Smithsonian Institution. Purchased for the Museum by the Advisory Council, 1921-6-212-47

predated similar schemes by Nicolas Pineau (1684–1754). Several changes in the details of the façade, like the simplified design of the entrance portal, seem to indicate that Meissonnier was not present at the building site. As with his designs for gold objects, he was content to leave the execution of his plans to others.

Like his father, the young Louis-Paul de Rochechouart, Prince of Tonnay-Charente and Duke of Mortemart (1710–1731), was familiar with Meissonnier and, as first gentleman of the bedchamber, he accepted the execution of the artist's design for the fireworks display realized on December 5, 1729, in the forecourt of Versailles castle to celebrate the birth of Louis XV's son. Only a select few saw the incredibly complex decoration, executed in several layers of trompe-l'oeil painted set pieces, which served as the background for the fireworks. The rich iconography of the decoration staged the story of the arrival of representatives from the four continents to congratulate France on the birth of the dauphin, supervised by the gods of Olympus. The subject proved to be too complicated for most in the audience, who preferred to be amused rather than edified on the mythological background of the royal house once favored under Louis XIV. Despite the lengthy descriptions published in the newspapers, critics like the Count of Caylus noted that the backdrop was not sufficiently linked to the fireworks and disparaged the absence of transparent paintings. The ensuing disappointment must have formed the basis for the court's decision not to publish a print commemorating the event. Infuriated, Meissonnier decided to do so himself, and the subject appears on the list he supplied to the crown in order to obtain a general privilege for the publication of his works in November 1733. Paradoxically, Meissonnier commissionned Laureolli to etch the plate but did not succeed in publishing the print of his first and only executed festival decoration. It finally appeared under the auspices of his second publisher and friend Gabriel Huquier between 1757 and 1761, long after

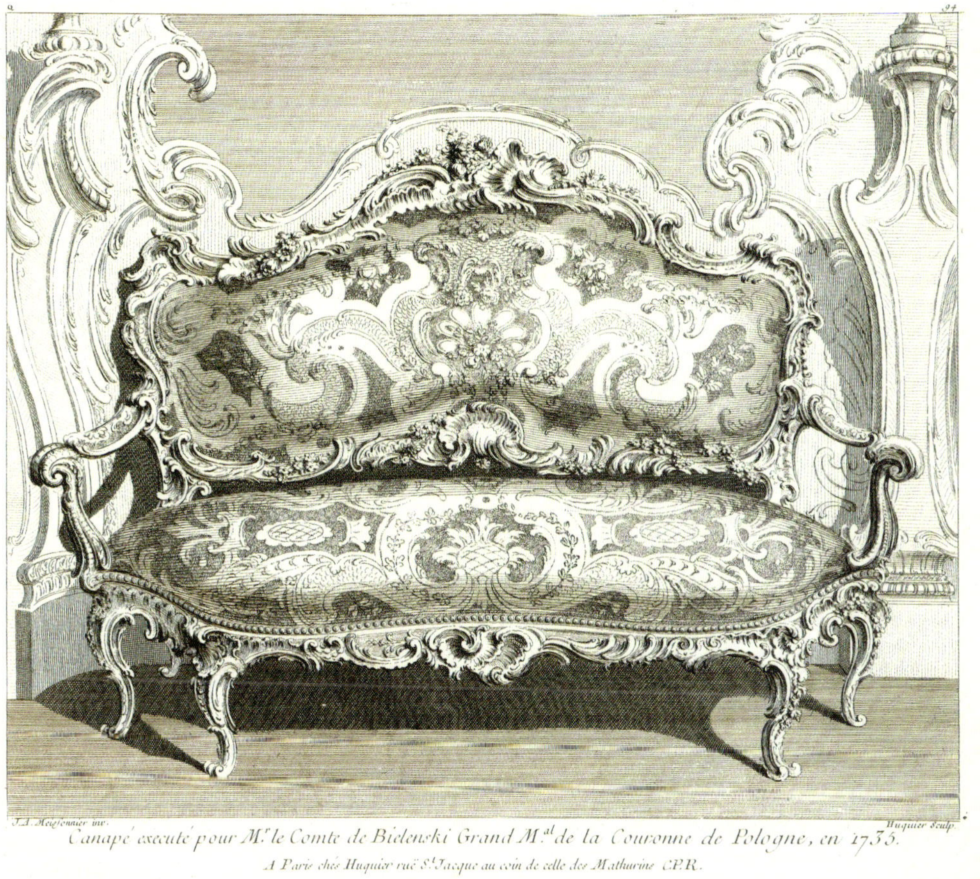

FIG. 8 Canapé exécuté pour Mr. le Comte de Bielenski [sic], Grand Marechal de la Couronne de Pologne, en 1735 (Small Sofa for Count Bielenski, Grand Marshall of Poland, 1735), plate 94 in Oeuvre de Juste-Aurèle Meissonnier. Juste-Aurèle Meissonnier (French, 1695–1750). Etched by Gabriel Huquier (French, 1695–1772). Paris, France, 1748 (designed 1735). Etching on white laid paper. Cooper-Hewitt, National Design Museum, Smithsonian Institution, Purchased for the Museum by the Advisory Council, 1921-6-212-52

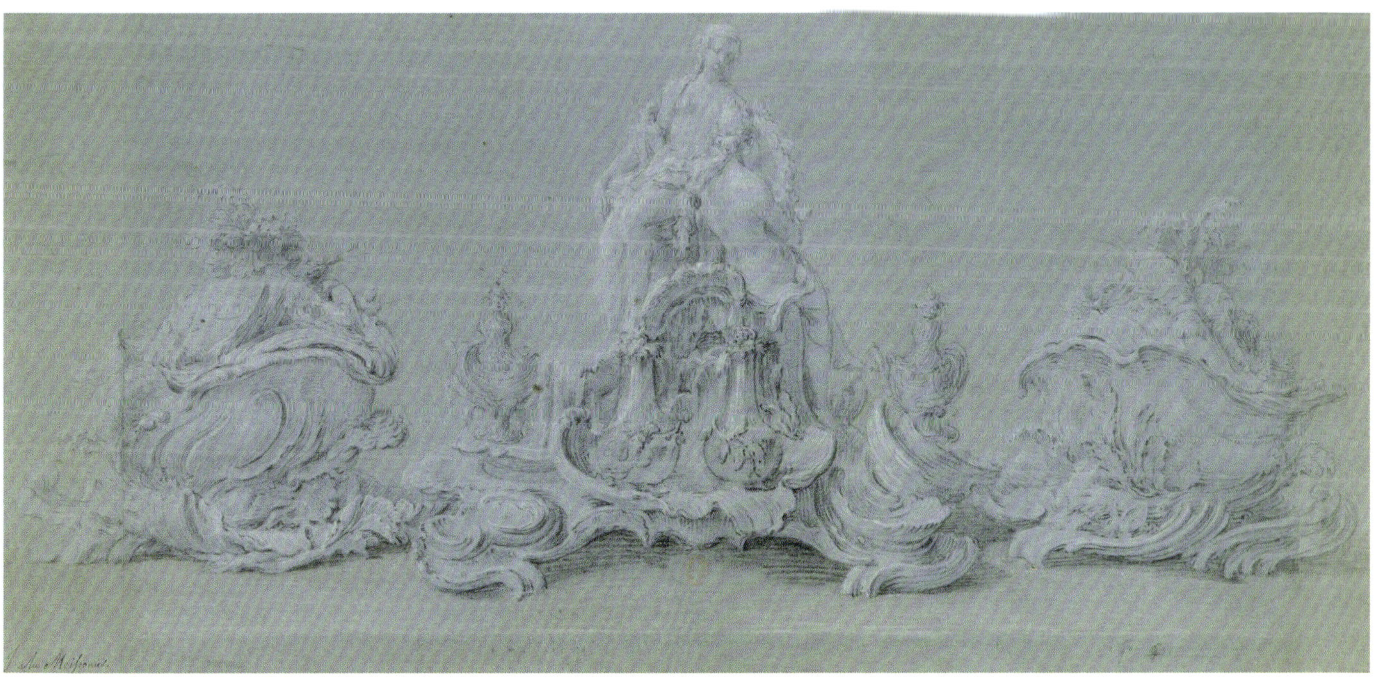

FIG. 9 First Design for a Centerpiece and Two Tureens for the Duke of Kingston. Juste-Aurèle Meissonnier (French, 1695–1750). Black chalk, brush and white gouache on blue laid paper. Paris, France, 1733–34. Bibliothèque Nationale de France, Cabinet des Estampes et Photographie, inv. B. 11 rés., fol. 4

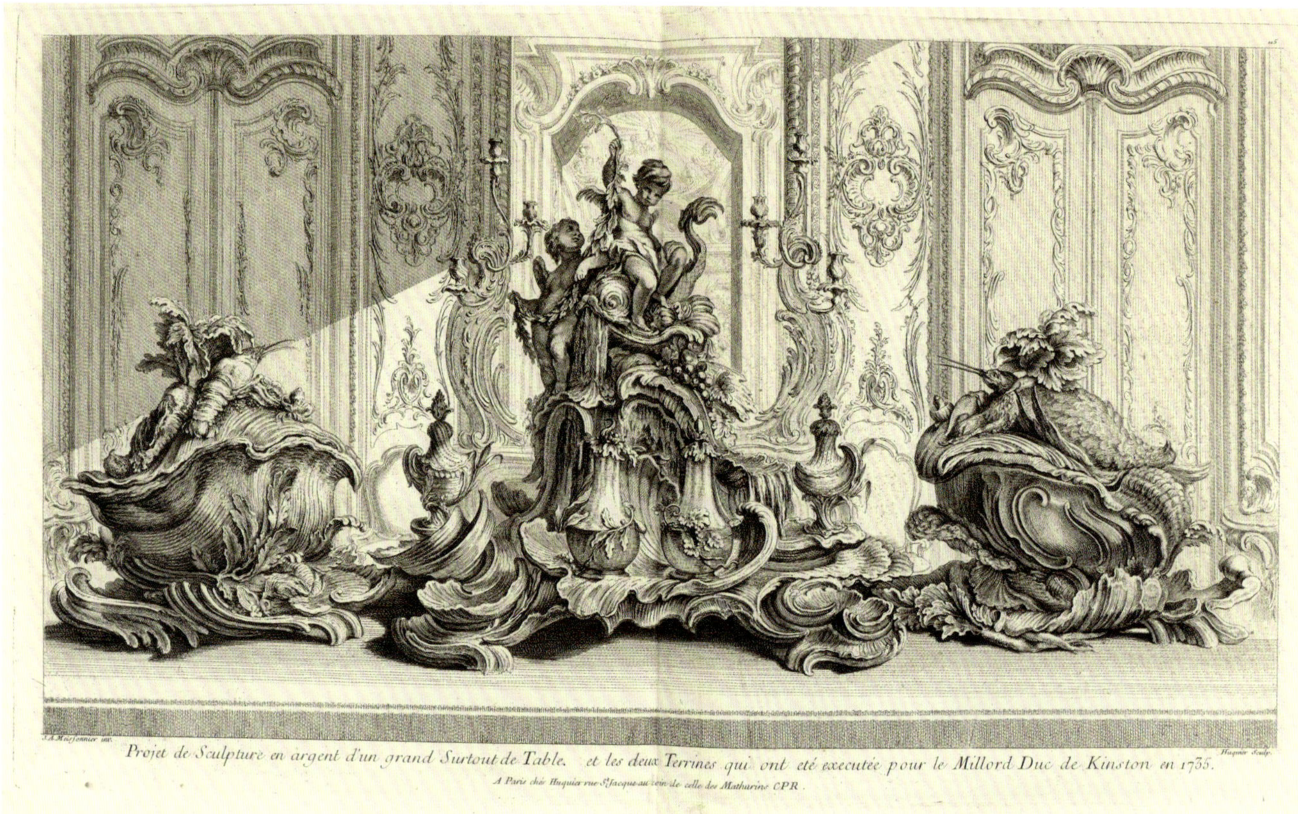

FIG. 10 Projet de Sculpture en argent d'un grand Surtout de Table et les deux Terrines qui ont été Executée pour Millord Duc de Kingston in 1735 (Design for a Centerpiece and Two Tureens Executed for the Duke of Kingston in 1735), plate 115 in Oeuvre de Juste-Aurèle Meissonnier. Juste-Aurèle Meissonnier (French, 1695–1750). Etched by Gabriel Huquier (French, 1695–1772). Etching on white laid paper. Paris, France, 1748. Cooper-Hewitt, National Design Museum, Smithsonian Institution, Purchased for the Museum by the Advisory Council, 1921-6-212-72

the event had taken place.[25] The experience left Meissonnier badly positioned for future commissions in festival decorations. Spanish ambassadors decommissioned from Meissonnier a second fireworks display to be put up on the Seine river opposite the Tuileries, replacing him with the painter and stage designer Servandoni, who later won the Saint-Sulpice competition mentioned earlier. A similar situation arose over the fireworks display designed for the 1739 marriage of Elisabeth, daughter of Louis XV, with the Spanish prince Dom Fernando.[26] In spite of this setback, Meissonnier held the position of designer to the king's cabinet till the end of his life, and, in defense of the employment of other designers for court festivities, he called himself in the late 1740s the *premier dessinateur de la chambre et du cabinet du Roy*.

Meissonnier's apparent desire to compete with fellow craftsmen and designers in all fields also led him to the field of interior decoration. Countess Catherine Bielinska (1684–1761), sister of Count François Bielinski (1684–1766), commissioned him to decorate her apartment in 1730–34. This project is known solely by one print in his *Oeuvre*, entitled "Projet de Porte d'Appartement fait pour Me. la Baronne de Bezenval."[27] (fig. 4) As with other titles in the book, the description of the work should be taken literally, and it confirms the project was executed. The specific mention of the project status of the decoration probably indicates that there were some alterations, but lack of documentation about this commission makes it impossible to know what happened.[28] In 1718, Countess Bielinska had married Jean Victor de Besenval (1671–1736), who was, from 1713 to 1721, the French royal envoyé extraordinaire in Poland.

In 1734, Countess Bielinska probably suggested to her brother that he order from Meissonnier the decoration of a cabinet for his hotel at 29-33 Krolewska Street in Warsaw. The Polish War of Succession (1733–35) may well have created a delay in the execution of the room in Paris, but, when it was finally finished in 1735, it was mounted in the king's presence at the Tuileries Palace from September 1735 to July 1736 before transported to Warsaw.[29] This may well have been the first exhibition of decorative arts in Western Europe. Three newspaper articles published in Holland and France are essential in grasping the complexity of the decoration, which is also known by one drawing of the ceiling (fig. 5) and four large engravings.[30] (figs. 6, 7) The curious public came to admire the room, described as "très-magnifique, & d'un goût nouveau,"[31] and, according to eyewitness reports, the combination of painting, sculpture, and architecture was achieved with discernment and taste, presenting a most flattering view of the progress of the arts in France.[32] The same appreciation applied to the sofa designed by Meissonnier for Bielinski in 1735.[33] (fig. 8) Its extreme cut-out shape and the delicacy of the wooden frame's asymmetric carved ornaments are consistent with the contemporary works of Avisse, Sené, and Tilliard.[34]

In the years of the Besenval and Bielinski commissions, Meissonnier returned to silversmith work. The temptation must have been great to demonstrate his superiority to his fellow silversmiths, and the occasion was offered by the young Evelyn Pierrepont, Duke of Kingston (1712–1773), only son of William, Earl of Kingston (d. 1713). In 1726, he set off on a grand tour of the continent of Europe. He traveled through France,

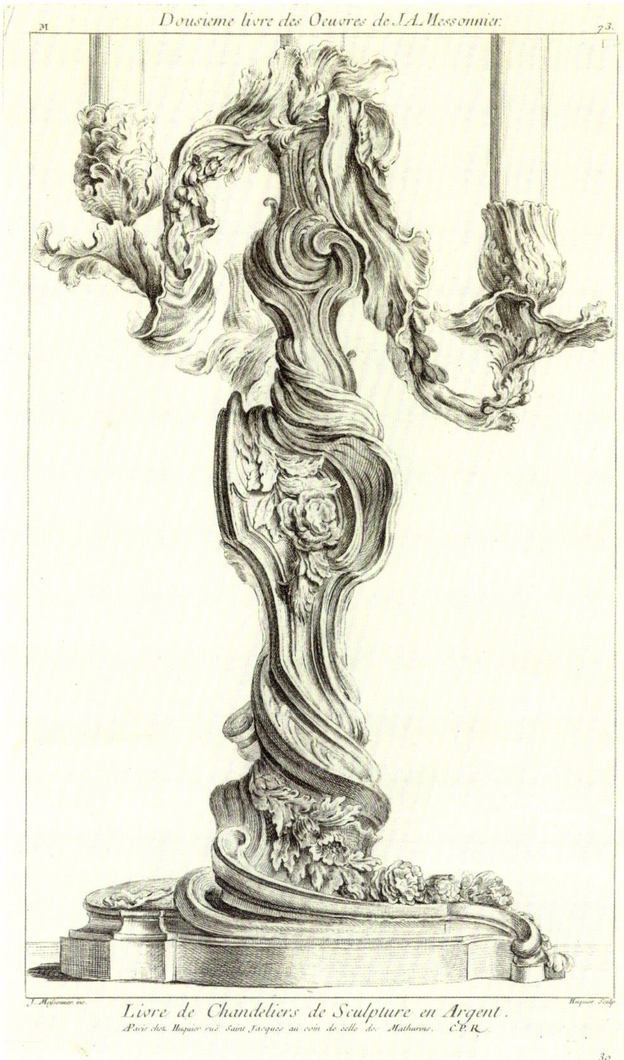

FIG. 11 *Livre de Chandeliers de Sculpture en Argent* (Book of Candelabrum in Silver [Design for the Candelabra for the Duke of Kingston]), plate 73 in *Oeuvre de Juste-Aurèle Meissonnier*. Juste-Aurèle Meissonnier (French, 1695–1750). Etched by Gabriel Huquier (French, 1695–1772). Etching on white laid paper. Paris, France, 1748 (designed 1734). Cooper-Hewitt, National Design Museum, Smithsonian Institution, Purchased for the Museum by the Advisory Council, 1921-6-212-31-a

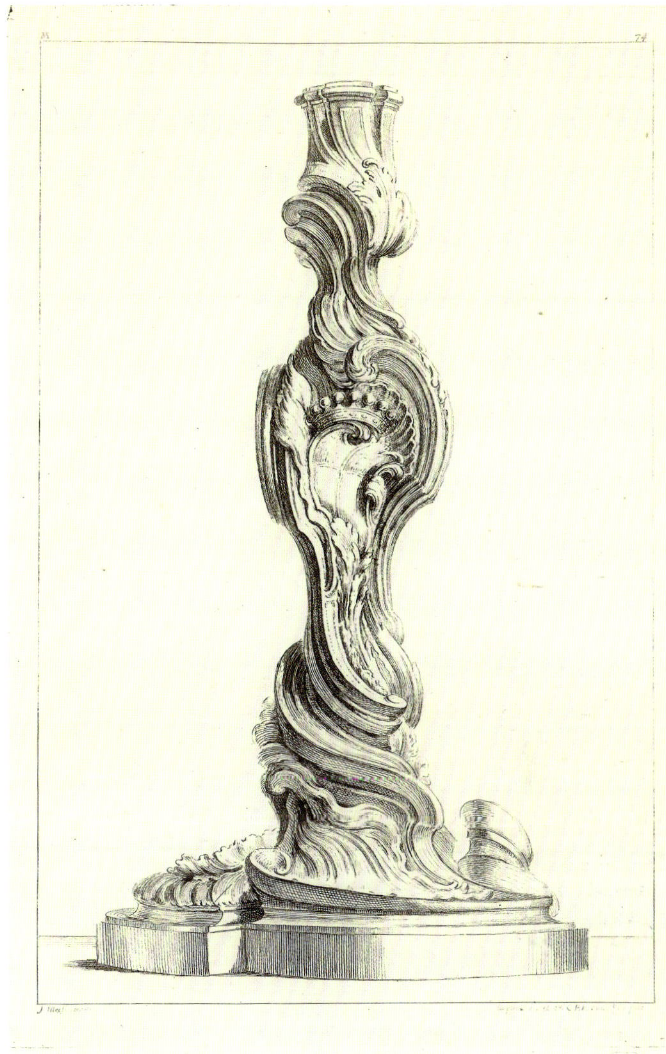

FIG. 12 *Design for a Candlestick*, plate 74 in *Oeuvre de Juste-Aurèle Meissonnier*. Juste-Aurèle Meissonnier (French, 1695–1750). Etched by Gabriel Huquier (French, 1695–1772). Etching on off-white laid paper. Paris, France, 1748 (designed 1734). Cooper-Hewitt, National Design Museum, Smithsonian Institution, Purchased for the Museum by the Advisory Council, 1921-6-212-32-a

went to Rome, then spent some time in Paris in the spring of 1732 in the company of his governor, Nathan Hickham, and his preceptor, Peter Patel, son of the goldsmith Pierre Patel. In July 1733, Kingston obtained full control of his estate and prepared to return to Paris. He intended to purchase French silver, and the authorization of the French state in October 1733 for him to bring from London to Paris 300 marcs of silver offers definitive proof of his intention to commission a considerable number of new works. French law obliged clients of French silversmiths to supply silver for more important commissions, and this was customarily done by melting old family silver. The document further proves that Kingston's decision predates the duke's visit to Chantilly in July 1734 and December 1735. The supposed role of the Duke of Bourbon, who was well acquainted with Meissonnier, to introduce Kingston to the artist is cast in doubt. Kingston's familiarity with the new style and his keen wish to play his part in the court circles of London as first gentleman of the bedchamber to George III offer a plausible explanation for his choice of the "illustrious" Meissonnier to renew the family silver. Whether "his Grace's aversion to all Forms," as Kingston's preceptor Hickham related in his correspondence of June 1732, would have enhanced his master's interest in innovative designs is difficult to establish. On the other hand, the presence of two young girls as crowning elements in the first design for a centerpiece pay hommage to Kingston's well-known amorous relationships in Paris.[35] (fig. 9) Kingston, once described by Walpole as a man of the "greatest beauty," had the daring and the financial resources to place an important order with one of France's top silversmiths. Producing the pieces took much longer than expected, and not all the pieces he commissioned were made.

Today, one candlestick and two tureens, but not the accompanying centerpiece, exist. For all three pieces, Meissonnier supplied the designs and models (figs. 10–12), supervised the work done by fellow silversmiths, and finished the chasing himself. The silversmith Claude Duvivier (1688–1744) executed two candlesticks in 1734–35, and they were

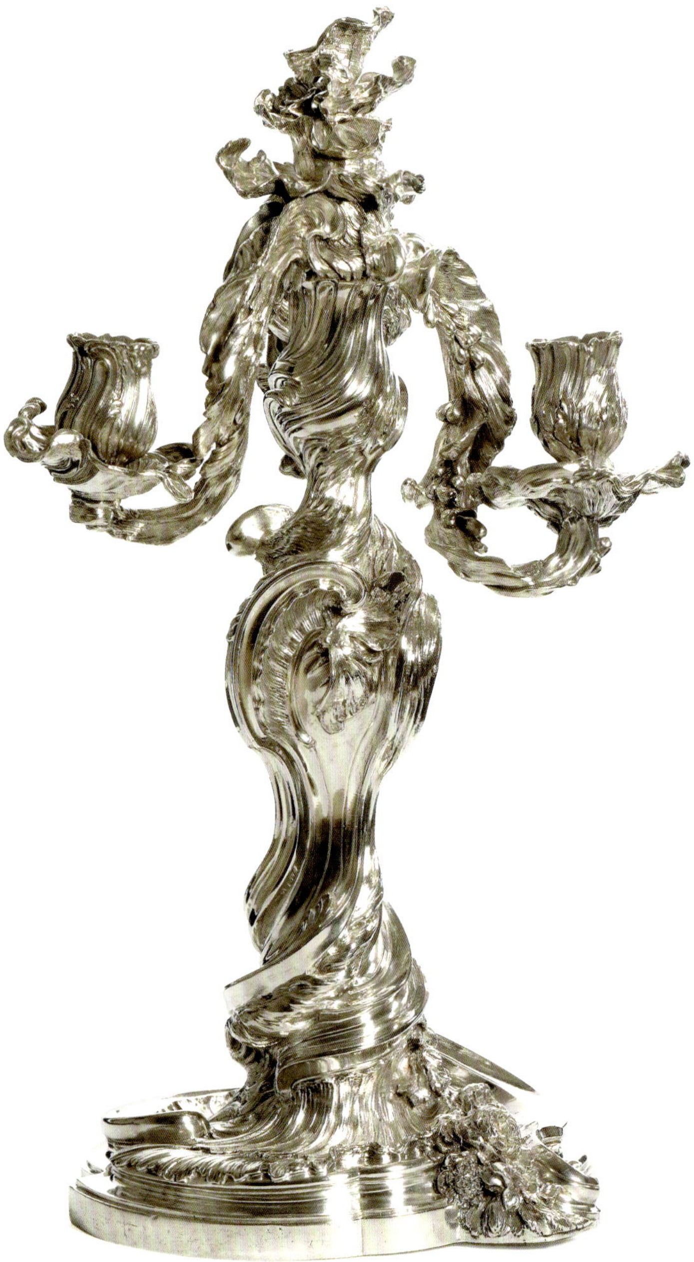

FIG. 13 Candlestick for the Duke of Kingston. Juste-Aurèle Meissonnier (French, 1695–1750). Made by Claude Duvivier (French, 1688–1747) and Juste-Aurèle Meissonnier. Paris, France, 1734–35. Silver. Musée des Arts Décoratifs, Paris; Gift of David and Flora David-Weill, 1937, Inv. 32632

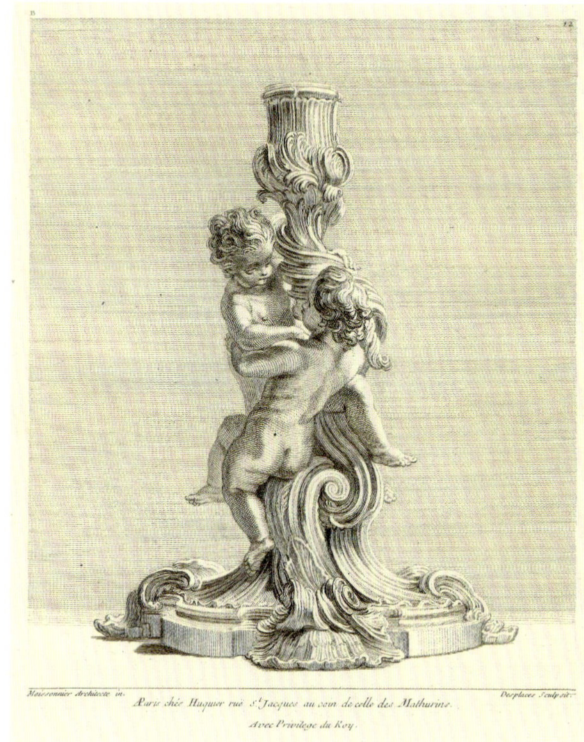

FIG. 14 Design for a Candlestick, plate 12 in Oeuvre de Juste-Aurèle Meissonnier. Juste-Aurèle Meissonnier (French, 1695–1750). Etched by Philippe-Louis Compagnon-Desplaces (French, 1682–1739). Etching on off-white laid paper. Paris, France, 1748 (designed 1728, first published 1734). Cooper-Hewitt, National Design Museum, Smithsonian Institution, Purchased for the Museum by the Advisory Council, 1921-6-212-8-b

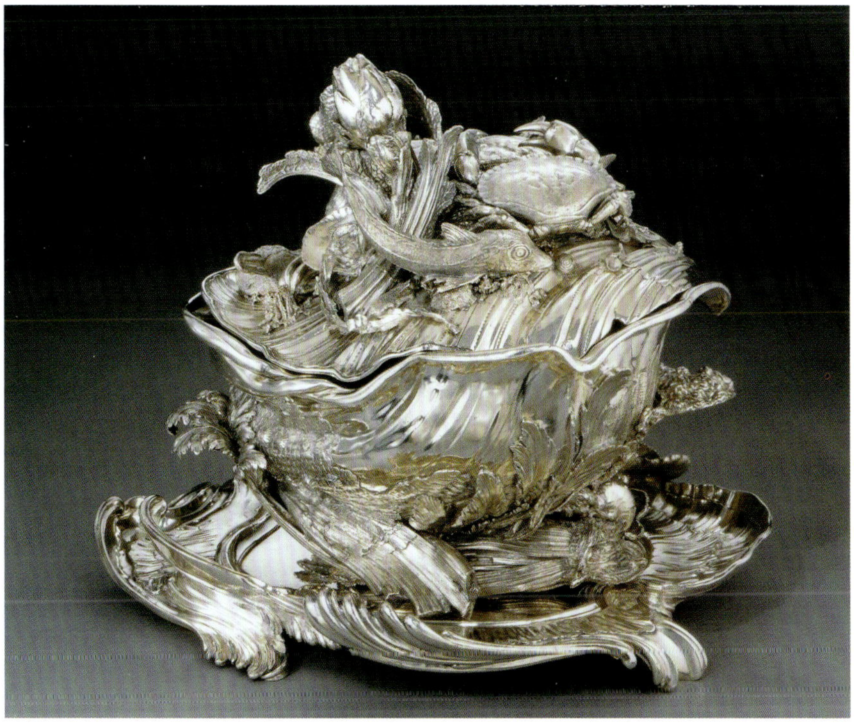

FIG. 16 Tureen for the Duke of Kingston. Juste-Aurèle Meissonnier (French, 1695–1750). Executed by Henry-Guillaume Adnet (French, 1683–1745) and Pierre-François Bonnestrenne (French, 1682–after 1740). Paris, France, 1734–40. Silver. Private collection

registered in Kingston's inventory in March 1737.[36] The model, an evolved version of a candlestick design from 1728 (figs. 13, 14), is characterized by a fluid upward spiral from the base to the stem and branches, in which the elements of the candlestick are not individually defined. The success of this model was instant—probably even before three prints of it were published by Gabriel Huquier showing each of the three sides, and numerous versions of it were executed in porcelain and gilt bronze.[37] The tureens, or *pots à oglie*, were executed in 1734–37 by the silversmiths Henry-Guillaume Adnet (1683–1745) and François Bonnestrenne (1682–after 1740) (figs. 15, 16). According to an article in the *Gazette d'Utrecht*, the chasing of the tureens was in good progress in March 1738,[38] but Meissonnier needed more time to finish them, as they did not enter Kingston's inventory until November 1740.[39] Meissonnier's decision to involve other silversmiths to execute his designs is not surprising in light of the earlier cases mentioned. Consequently, none of the three works bears his maker's mark, but his authorship is clearly stated on the bodies and covers of the tureens by his engraved name, MEIS=ER or MEISSONIER, and on the platters with his engraved signature, -FAIT-PAR-I-A-MEISSONIER-ARCHITECTTE-. Indeed, all three works demonstrate Meissonnier's unsurpassed excellence in bringing alive the complex shapes of the candlestick and tureens. In October 1741, Carl Gustave Tessin mentioned in a letter to the architect Carl Hårleman, a staunch admirer of Meissonnier, the high price that the Duke of Kingston paid for the tureens. The price of 32,000 livres may have seemed high to the Swedish representative, but not higher than that charged for similar works by the royal goldsmiths Besnier or Germain. The Kingston tureens, with their astounding movement and dynamic unity, are a delight to the eye, and offer the best illustration of what rococo is about. The asymmetric forms are inspired by shells and rocaille; and the inclusion of vegetables, fishes, and game testify to the renewed interest in nature, whose elements were introduced in interior decoration and turned into art.

In 1748, the minister Maurepas would encounter Meissonnier one last time. He was asked by the city of Paris to supervise the competition for the design of a town square to accommodate an equestrian statue of Louis XV. The participation of Meissonnier was part of his endeavor to enter the Royal Academy of Architecture, for which he was considered a fitting member in official reports as early as 1737. Meissonnier supplied several designs and a three-dimensional model for this prestigious competition. He also designed a new town hall of the city of Paris (1748–50). Magnificently situated on the top end of the Ile de la Cité, opposite the equestrian statue of Henry IV, the building was crowned by a splendid dome, offering an appealing answer to the request for embellishment of the city center.[40] This design should be seen in conjunction with Meissonnier's project for the Order of Saint-Esprit, the remodeling of the Hôtel de Conti, and the addition of domes on the corner pavilions of the colonnade of the Louvre. One small print, part of the illustrations of Meissonnier's treatise on universal architecture, records his daring proposition for the city center.[41] None of them was ever executed. Meissonnier's design for the remodeling of the choir of the Saint-Germain l'Auxerrois church, opposite the Louvre, was almost built. According to a report in the *Mercure de France*, the church fathers preferred Meissonnier's project, presented by his friend Gabriel Huquier, after his sudden death in 1750. The uniqueness of Meissonnier's proposals can be gleaned from a rare set of prints, which reveals a remarkable combination of Gothic design principles and mature rocaille ornamentation (fig. 17). However, the church wardens felt forced to work with a living artist, and they chose the

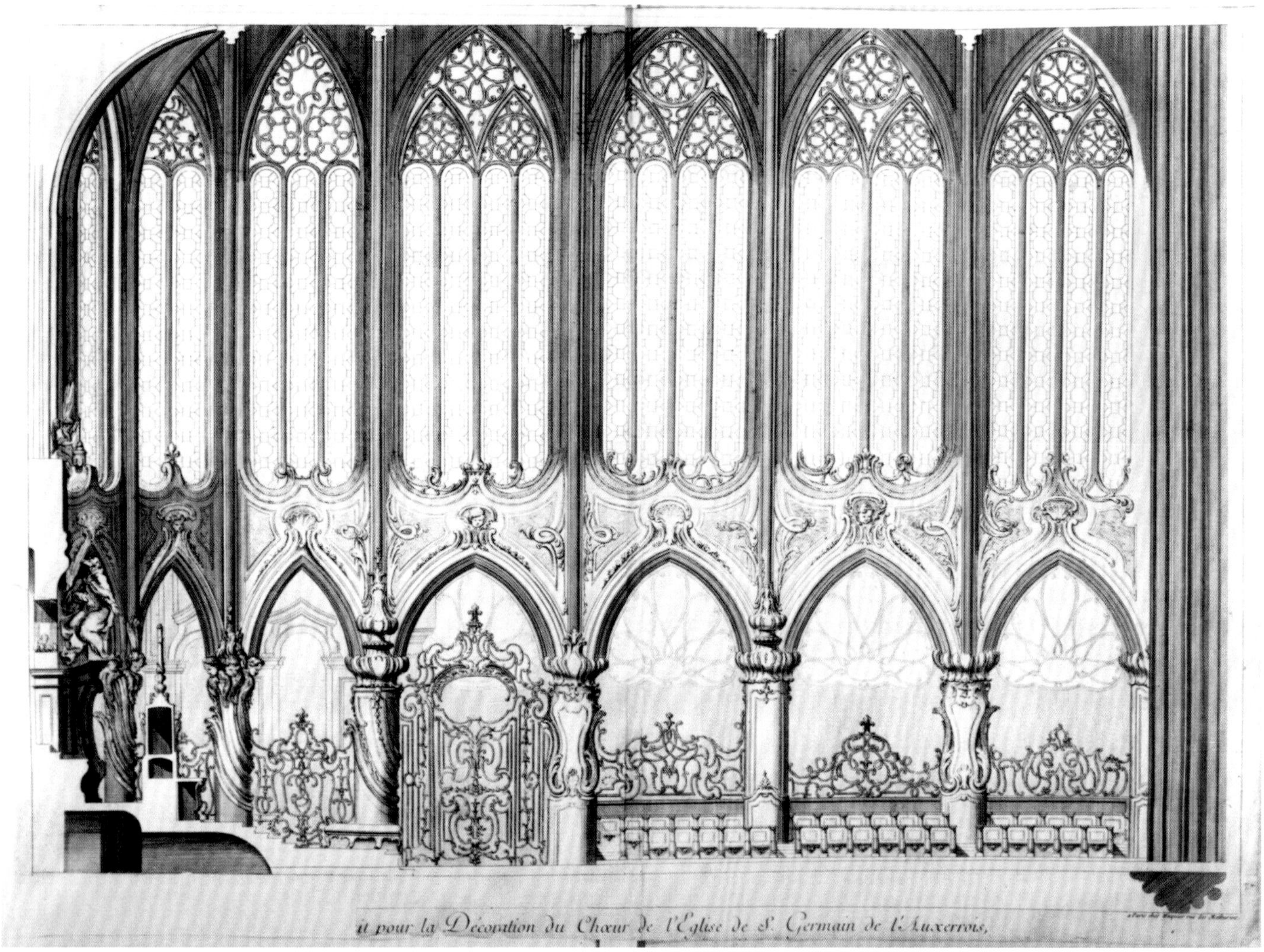

FIG. 17 Projet fait pour la Décoration du Choeur de l'Eglise de S. Germain de l'Auxerrois (Design for the Choir of Saint Germain l'Auxerrois). Juste-Aurèle Meissonnier (French, 1695–1750). Etched by Gabriel Huquier (French, 1695–1772). Paris, France, 1757–61 (designed 1745–50). Etching on off-white laid paper. Bibliothèque de l'Institut national d'histoire de l'art, collections Jacques Doucet, Fol Est 473

little-known Claude Baccarit (d. 1785), who worked with his brother-in-law, the sculptor Louis-Claude Vassé (1716–1772). In doing so, the church accepted a much less innovative proposal, whose decorations were largely destroyed in the nineteenth century.

The publication of a selection of Meissonnier's designs further confirmed, enlarged, and kept vivid the memory of his works. Gabriel Huquier had taken over from the widow of François Chéreau the initiative of publishing Meissonnier's designs in spring 1734. From the initial publication of separate sets and one large plate, Huquier changed the presentation in Meissonnier's *Oeuvre*, for which the artist chose the works himself.[42] For this folio-size presentation, Meissonnier designed an allegorical title plate, added his portrait, and organized in sets and numbered all of the prints. This initiative can be dated to about 1738; and the fact that a copy of Meissonnier's *Oeuvre* appeared in a posthumous inventory of Thomas Germain in August 1748 provides evidence that it was completed before then.

The enumeration of Meissonnier's activities—"painter, sculptor, architect, etc.," to which he added his role as a designer of the king's room and cabinet—on the title plate of his *Oeuvre* clearly indicates his wish to escape the position of the goldsmith by not including his original profession after his name (fig. 18). At the same time, the presence in the title plate of the goldsmith's tools in the hands of Minerva attest to his former training. Today, we would simply call Meissonnier an artist or a designer. On January 7, 1747, Meissonnier returned his maker's mark to the Parisian corporation of goldsmiths. This action can be explained by his wish to become an architect and member of the Royal Academy of Architecture, but this would have been possible only if he had cut his association with the world of crafts and commerce. It is in this light that his treatise on universal architecture should be seen, but the text remained unpublished, and its illustrations only saw the light of day about ten years after he died.

The 1748 publication date of Meissonnier's *Oeuvre* explains why the rendering of the design of his last Polish commission, from Princess Czartoryska, did not exactly correspond to the finished design, since a change in ideas could not be incorporated in print. From the correspondence of Prince Auguste-Alexandre Czartoryski (1696–1782) in Poland, we learn that, in 1732, Besenval advised the prince to commission from the sculptor Jacques Caffieri (1678–1755) a project for the wainscoting

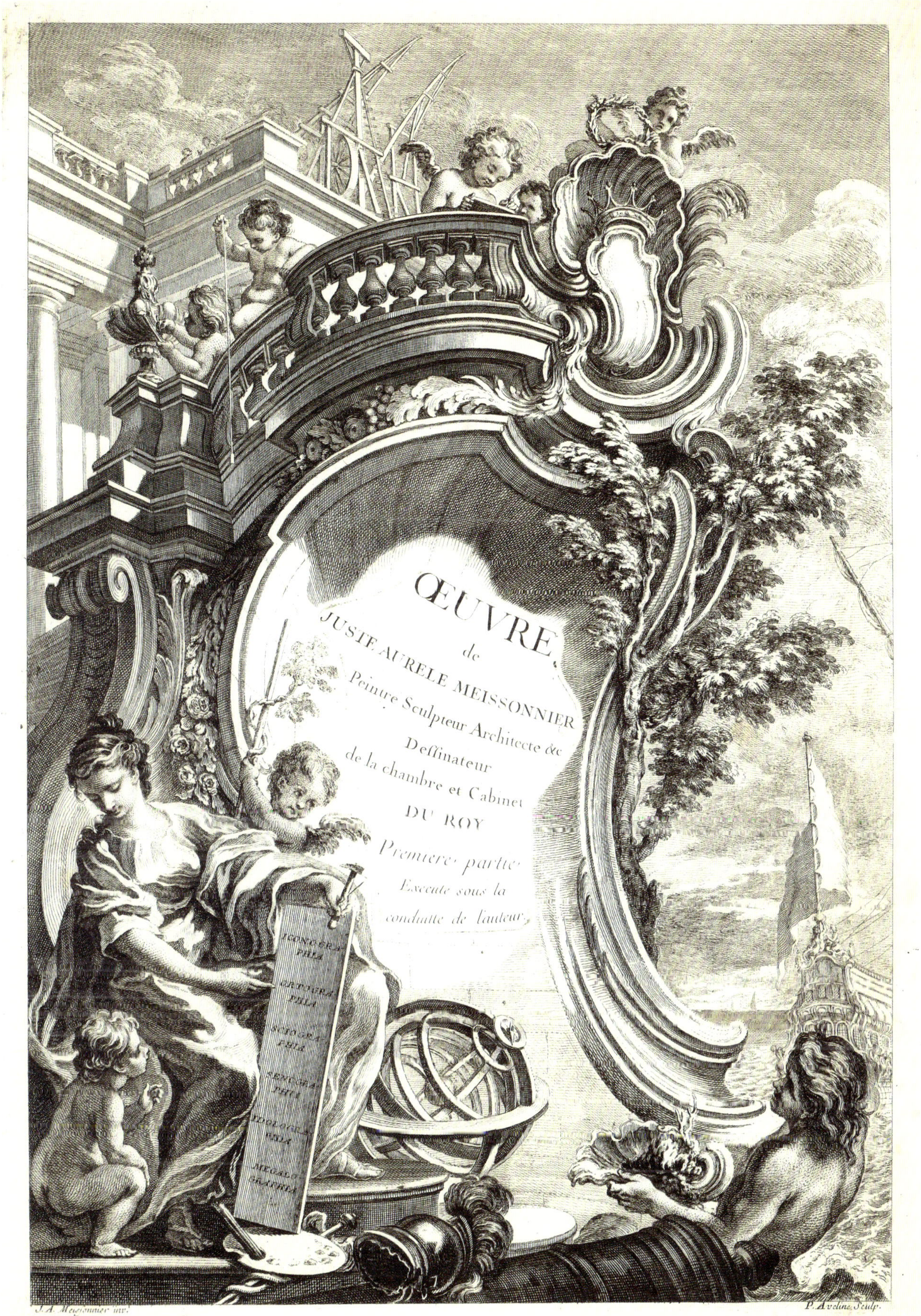

FIG. 18 Title page, Oeuvre de Juste-Aurèle Meissonnier. Juste-Aurèle Meissonnier (French, 1695–1750). Etched by Gabriel Huquier (French, 1695–1772). Paris, France, 1748. Etching on off-white laid paper. Cooper-Hewitt, National Design Museum, Smithsonian Institution, Purchased for the Museum by the Advisory Council, 1921-6-212-1

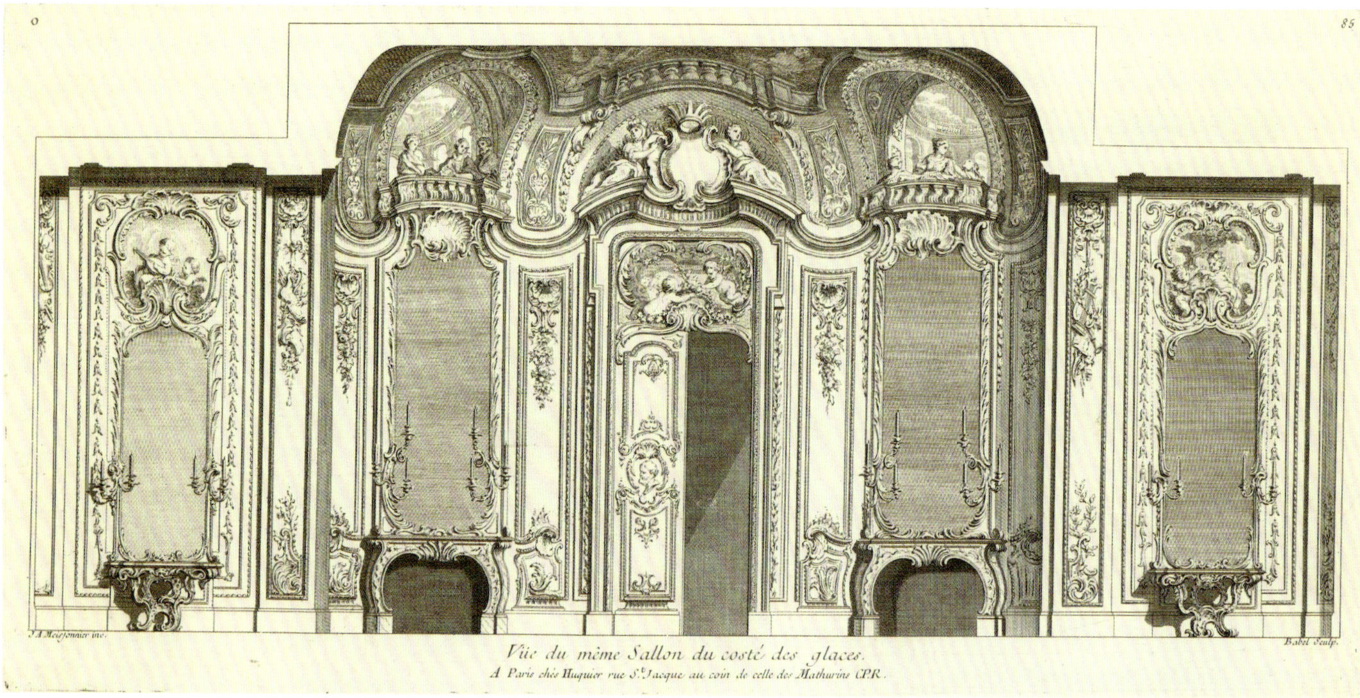

FIG. 19 Vue de même (Czartoryski) Sallon du costé des glaces (Design for the Salon Czartoryski), plate 85 in Oeuvre de Juste-Aurèle Meissonnier. Juste-Aurèle Meissonnier (French, 1695–1750). Etched by Pierre-Edmé Babel (French, 1720–1775). Paris, France, 1748. Etching on off-white laid paper. Cooper-Hewitt, National Design Museum, Smithsonian Institution, Purchased for the Museum by the Advisory Council, 1921-6-212-43

of an unidentified room.[43] The reluctance of French artists to work for foreign clients is legendary, particularly when they needed to supervise work abroad. The Polish War of Succession possibly brought to a halt the commissioning of works from French artists. Once the prince reconciled with August III of Poland, his influence grew steadily, and Czartoryski's interest in involving French artists for the renovation of his residence was renewed. In February 1748, Meissonnier signed a contract with Czartoryski's wife, Marie Sophie Denhoff (née Sieniawska), Princess Czartoryska, to deliver the wainscoting and ceiling of a large room in October 1749 (fig. 19). The death of Meissonnier in August 1750 left the salon unfinished. The salon no longer exists, but the record drawings of the palace executed around 1760 by Jean-Sigismond Deybel the Younger prove the installation of the room, which was probably sent to Poland by Meissonnier's widow shortly before September 1753. When the room was dismantled around 1840, several elements of the wainscoting were used to built a laquered black wardrobe, but, when it was discovered that it had been made out of the remains of the mythical salon, the wardrobe was dismantled and the carvings restored to their original state.[44] (fig. 20) The strong, striking carved ornaments adhere to a vocabulary that still appeals to us today. Meissonnier's personal touch is visible in its deep plasticity, in the strong upward movement of its lines, and in its details.

Meissonnier's patrons clearly were aware of his exceptional gifts. Through their commissions for his silver, interior decorations, and other works, they demonstrated their acceptance of the new style he employed and his startling results, yet this was never openly expressed. These were times when reputation or the advice of friends was the deciding factor in the choice of a designer. We can only hypothesize that his patrons desired objects and decorative schemes in the latest fashion, befitting their status, and guaranteeing the admiration of their family, friends, and visitors. Meissonnier's Italian heritage—his father, grandfather, and great-grandfather were all goldsmiths in Aix-en-Provence—likely led him to create designs that were different from what the French were accustomed to. At the same time, his understanding of French aesthetics brought him broad support among court circles and beyond. His ability to at once renew classic design and execute his designs at the highest level of artistry is what made Meissonnier exceptional.

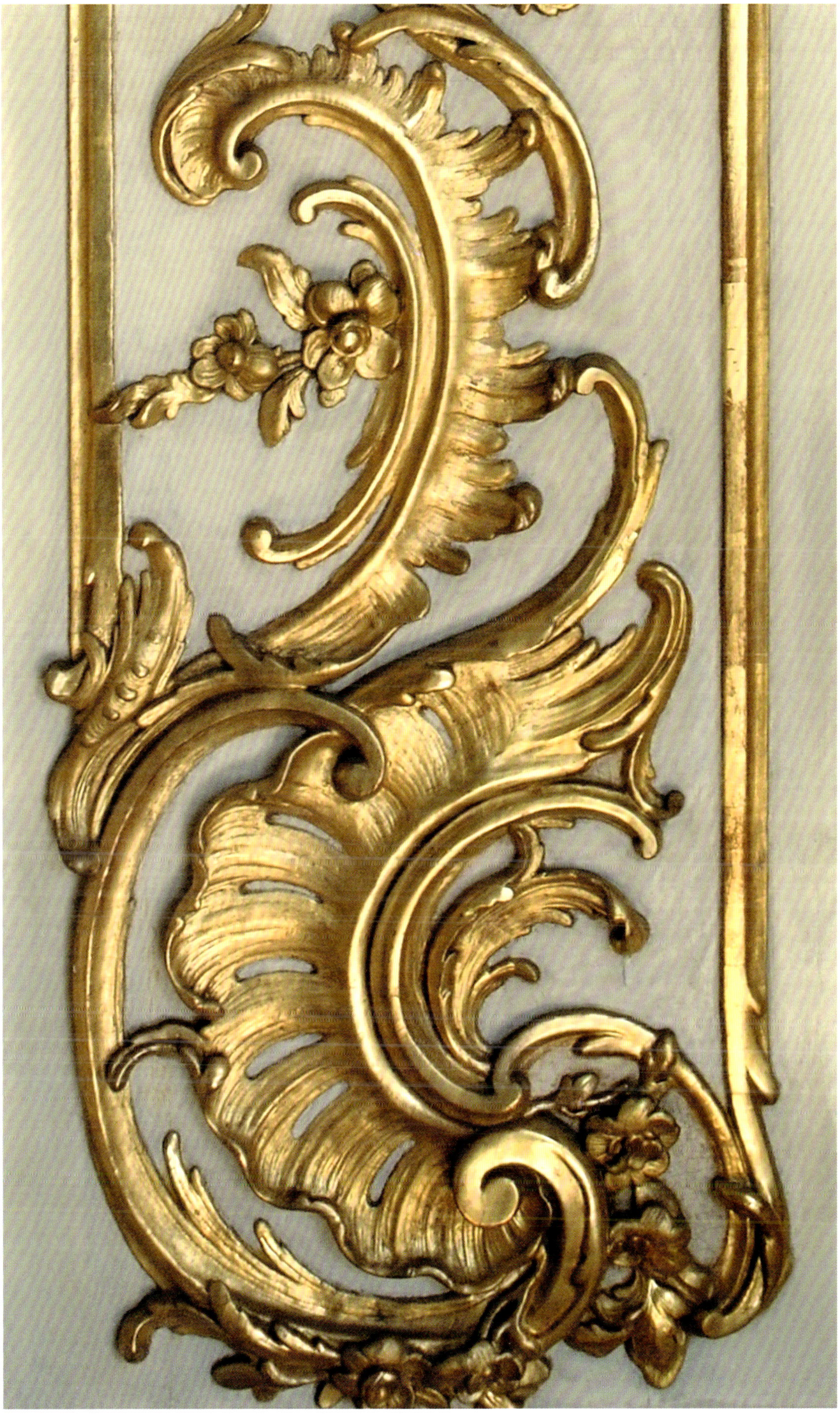

FIG. 26 Detail of Wainscoting of the Czartoryski Salon. After a design by Juste-Aurèle Meissonnier (French, 1695–1750). Paris, France, 1748–53 (restoration 1966). Wood, gilding, oil paint. Przypkowskis Museum, Jedrzejow, Poland

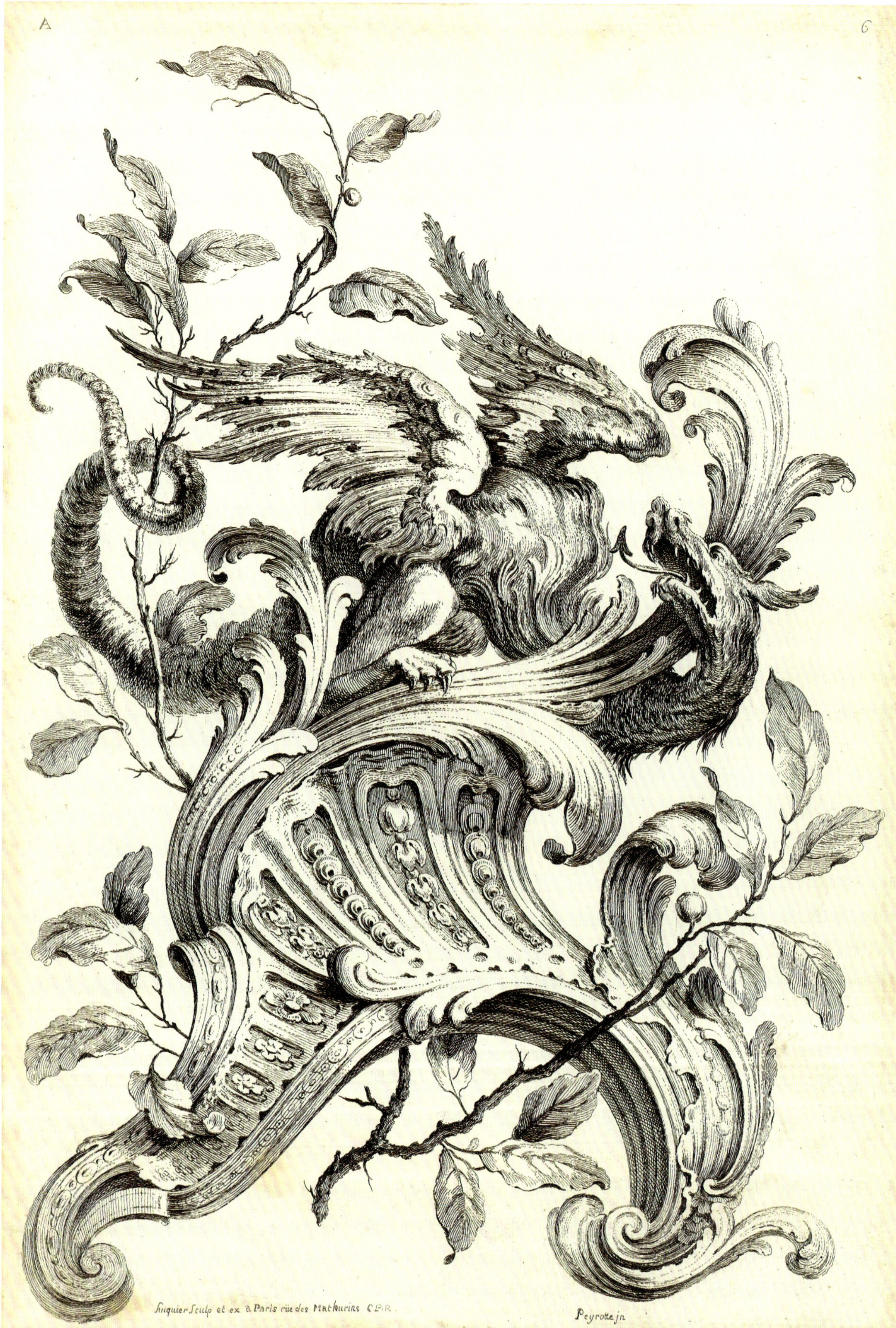

FIG. 1 Winged Griffin *on a Rocaille Bracket*, plate 6 in *Première Partie divers Ornements*. Alexis Peyrotte (French, 1699–1769). Etched by Gabriel Huquier (French, 1695–1772). Paris, France, ca. 1745. Etching on white laid paper. Cooper-Hewitt, National Design Museum, Smithsonian Institution, Purchased for the Museum by the Advisory Council, 1921-6-213-6

Ornament of Bizarre Imagination

ROCOCO PRINTS AND DRAWINGS FROM COOPER-HEWITT'S LÉON DECLOUX COLLECTION

Gail S. Davidson

Looking back on *le goût nouveau* (rococo) in domestic interiors from the last quarter of the eighteenth century, committed classicist and architect Jacques-François Blondel quipped, "[designers] abandoned regular forms; they were busy confounding design in all kinds of ways, under the pretext of creating something new, of lightening and enlivening domestic interiors. The Lajoües, the Pineaus, the Meissoniers, and their imitators, so to speak, produced a kind of irrational architecture. They only used extraordinary contours in decoration, only a confused mixture of attributes placed indiscriminately, allied with ornament of bizarre imagination, where one finds a ridiculous jumble of irregular cartouches of rockwork, dragons, reeds, palms, and all sorts of imaginary plants that have created such a stir in the world of interior decoration... The large quantity of prints which have circulated among the public, in addition to the numerous extant apartments with this bad decoration, publicize the extravagance of these frivolous compositions."[1]

In stark contrast, what Blondel found bizarre, excessive, and frivolous, rococo decorators found enchanting, original, and just plain fun. Nevertheless, as Blondel asserted, prints flooding the markets as well as design drawings, fabricated objects, and interior decoration helped make rococo style the "fad du jour" in Paris from about 1730 to 1750.[2] Because prints were published generally in unbound booklets or *cahiers* of four, six, eight, or more sheets (later bound to a collector's wishes), they, or pirated editions of them, could be easily rolled and transported by craftsmen. Their portability helped spread rococo design within France and on to Germany, England, Italy, Spain, the Netherlands, and as far as the United States.

It was advantageous for designers like Juste Aurèle Meissonnier, Jacques de Lajoüe (1686–1761), and Nicolas Pineau (1684–1754) to create designs for engravings and etchings. If they were able to obtain the king's patent (*brevet*), publishing their designs with the phrase *avec le privilège du roi* prevented other designers or publishers from passing off copies of the prints as their own without being fined and the counterfeit prints confiscated.[3] By making or hiring printmakers to reproduce his designs, an artist could advertise his creative expertise and secure commissions from clients, who could leaf through different tureen concepts, for example, to select a model or variation for fabrication. Prints also helped diffuse the ideas of a designer beyond the borders of France and secure commissions from royal and noble clients in other countries. Etchings and engravings were also a way of documenting executed design projects for the artist's or client's records. Artists' prints were also used for teaching purposes, to show shop members or design students how an object would look from the top and from head-on.

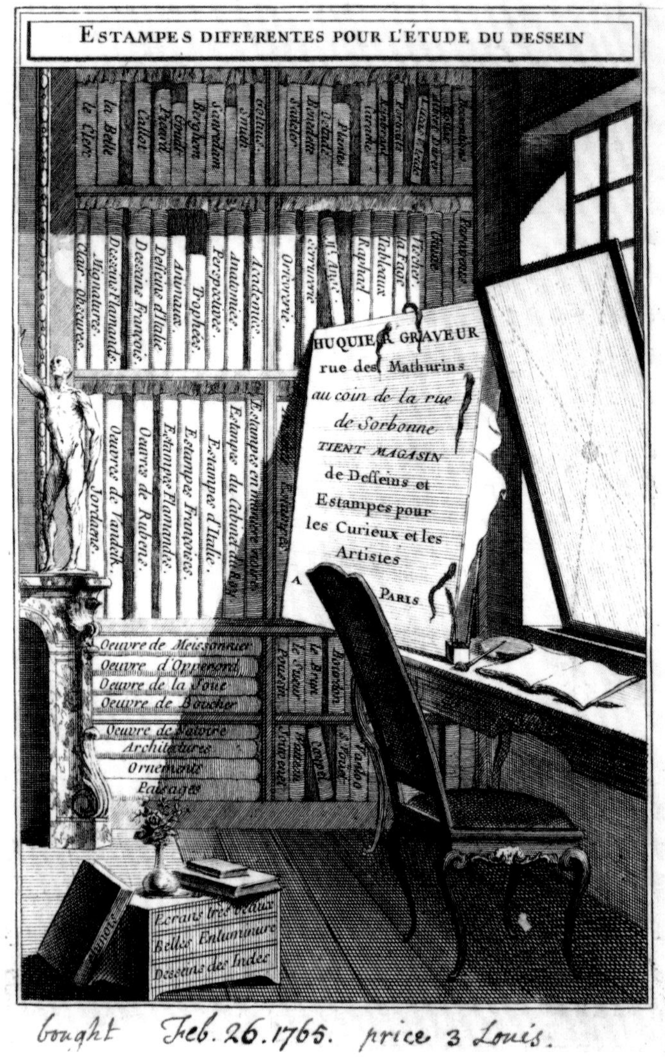

FIG. 2 Business card. Gabriel Huquier (French, 1695–1772). Paris, France, ca. 1749. Etching on white laid paper. Private collection

Moreover, they served as demonstrations of a designer's creative ingenuity or fantasy; often the objects depicted were too fanciful to have functioned in the real world (fig. 1). Finally, prints were used to give instructions to a fabricator, influence taste, and support French hegemony in the decorative arts.

Printed designs for decorative arts, called ornament prints, covered every aspect of the interior and exterior decoration of buildings as well as transportation vehicles.[4] Ornament prints included designs for furniture, lighting, wall paneling, metalwork, textiles, jewelry, glasswork, screens, fans, carriages, fountains and gardens, ironwork, festival decorations, and architecture. They also covered ornamental motifs used to embellish objects such as cartouches, chinoiseries, fruits, and plants as well as vegetal designs and geometric motifs. They were frequently published in allegorical suites such as the months or seasons of the year, the times of the day, the senses, and the elements, which were reproduced in marquetry or on painted furniture, wall decoration, ceramics, etc.[5]

If a designer wanted to produce prints after his designs, he could apply for a royal patent in his own name, as the textile designer Jean-Antoine Fraisse did in 1734,[6] and Meissonnier in 1733, for the printing of the *Livres d'ornements*. This group of about forty to fifty prints was published by the Veuve [Widow] Chéreau, who took over a well-established publishing business upon the death of her husband, the engraver François Chéreau (1680–1729).[7] But usually the engraver or publisher applied for the patent. The Chéreau family, through its two branches, was an important publisher and dealer of ornament prints in Paris.[8] They published the works of rococo designers Pierre-Edmé Babel and Pierre-Quentin Chedel and the neoclassical designers Jean-François Forty, Richard de Lalonde, and Henri Salembier. Other publishers of decorative-arts prints included Etienne Charpentier (ca. 1707–after April 1792), Nicolas III de Larmessin (1684–1755), Robert-Menge Pariset (1680/90–before 1775), and Nicolas-Jean-Baptiste de Poilly (1707–1780). If publishing families intermarried, copperplates, which had commercial value because of the prints made from them, became the dowry that a woman brought to the marriage. They were also passed down as inheritance.

In the world of eighteenth-century French ornament prints, Gabriel Huquier (1695–1772) was the most innovative and crucial figure. He was a prolific printmaker, designer of ornament, collector, dealer, and major print publisher, whose editions aided in establishing the careers

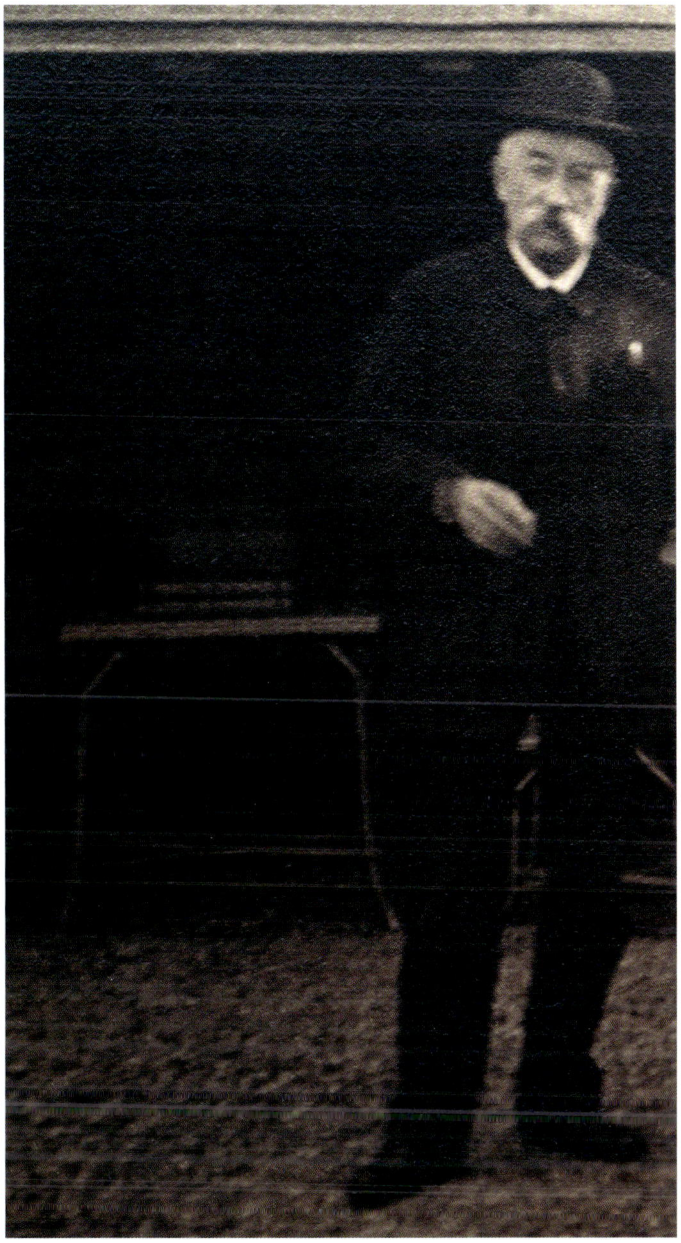

FIG. 3 Jean-Léon Decloux, ca. 1911. Cooper-Hewitt, National Design Museum Property Files

and influence of individual rococo designers and, in a more general way, in disseminating rococo style throughout Europe. During the 1730s, he published small series of his own etchings after François Boucher drawings, including the *Recueil de fontaines* (Album of Fountain Designs) (1736), *Livre de cartouches* (Series of Cartouches), and *Scenes de la vie chinoise* (Scenes of Chinese Life); and Jacques de Lajoüe's *Recueil nouveau de differens Cartouches…Second Livre de Cartouches..Troisieme Livre de Cartouches…*(First, Second, and Third Albums of Cartouches) (before 1738). His entrepreneurial breakthrough came around 1740, when he conceived the idea of working with living designers on the publication of large-format *oeuvre* catalogues containing a selection of an artist's designs, introduced by a title page and the designer's portrait. These catalogues undoubtedly helped propel the careers of these individuals, turning them into design celebrities within and outside France.

Huquier proudly advertised his unique venture on his business card of about 1749 (fig. 2), which depicted on a shelf the *Oeuvres* of Meissonnier, Gilles-Marie Oppenord, Lajoüe, Boucher, and Charles-Joseph Natoire.[9] Unfortunately, he only completed the first two of these projects. He started with the Oppenord publication, but put it aside in the early 1740s to pick up the Meissonnier *Oeuvre* (probably due to Oppenord's death in 1742 and the growing market for images of Meissonnier's new rocaille ornament), which he completed by 1748. This volume of 115 plates, executed in consultation with the artist and etched for the most part by Huquier after Meissonnier's drawings, was his masterpiece. An example of this impressive publication, in Cooper-Hewitt, National Design Museum's collection, was acquired by the Museum's former incarnation, the Cooper Union Museum for the Arts of Decoration, among an exceptional group of 410 ornament-print albums and around 500 drawings from the collection of Jean Léon Decloux of Paris and Sèvres, France (fig 3)

The history behind the Decloux acquisition, never explored in detail until now, is pertinent to the following discussion. When the Cooper Union Museum was founded in 1897 by Sarah, Eleanor, and Amy Hewitt, granddaughters of industrialist Peter Cooper, the sisters were determined to acquire examples of rococo and neoclassical objects, as they believed these styles represented the greatest achievements in design history. It was a propitious time for collecting, especially in the area of prints and drawings. Many collectors, who had acquired ornament prints and drawings in the nineteenth century as professional architects, as amateurs for their libraries, or because of increased interest in historical revivals, were divesting themselves of large holdings. In France, the architect André-Denis Bérard (d. 1873), producer of two important catalogues of the prints of Jean-François Cuvilliés, father and son, among other designers, collected more than 3,000 ornament prints plus rare and important ornament drawings. They were put on the market after the death of his son in 1890 (February 16-25, 1891). With the passing of architect Hippolyte Destailleur (1822–1893), owner of the greatest collection of ornament drawings and prints in France, his "second collection" of drawings, prints, and books was auctioned at the Hôtel Drouot on May 19–23, 1896. After selling a collection of ornament prints and drawings to Russia, Alfred Beurdeley (1847–1919) sold another group of French and English eighteenth-century ornament drawings in Paris in 1905 (Galerie Petit, March 13–15) and eighteenth-century ornament prints in 1913 (March 8); and a

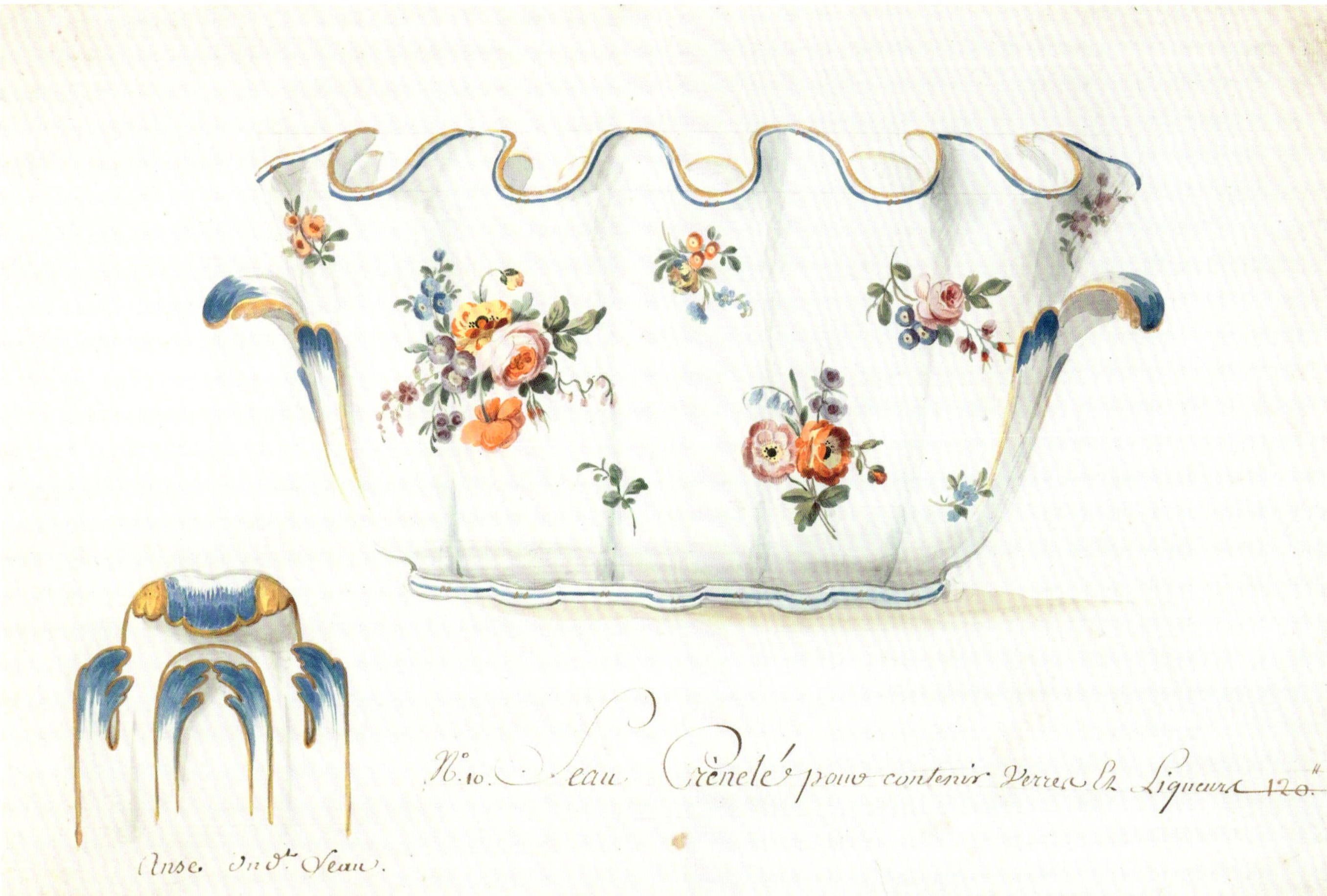

FIG. 4 *Design for a Verrière* (Monteith) *with Detail of Handle, for Sèvres Porcelain Manufactory, Paris.* Attributed to Jacques-François Micaud (French, ca.1732–1811). Sèvres, France, ca. 1765–75. Pen and brown ink, brush and watercolor on off-white laid paper. Cooper-Hewitt, National Design Museum, Smithsonian Institution, Museum purchase through gift of various donors and from Eleanor G. Hewitt Fund, 1938-88-8316

third group of ornament drawings and prints in Paris on May 28, 29, and 31, 1920. Finally, the extensive holdings of ornament-print series belonging to Edmond Foulc (d. 1916) came on the Paris market at the Hôtel des Commissaires-Priseurs on June 3–6, 1914. This superb collection of 479 ornament folios and architectural books featured 187 albums/books of eighteenth-century ornament prints, including works after Babel, Boucher, Cuvilliés, Lajoüe, Meissonnier, and Jean-Baptiste Pillement. Léon Decloux acquired objects from many of these collections. In Italy, Giovanni Piancastelli (1845–1926), drawing master, curator, and director of the Borghese collection in Rome, disposed of 15,000 drawings between 1901 and 1907 when he retired to Bologna.[10]

The Hewitt sisters' first major drawings purchase came in 1901 when they acquired, sight unseen, about 3,800 Piancastelli drawings of eighteenth- and nineteenth century ornament and architecture. They purchased an additional 8,663 drawings from the same collection in 1938, formerly acquired by Mr. and Mrs. Edward D. Brandegee of Cambridge, Massachusetts.[11]

The Piancastelli holdings were mainly Italian, but there were some major deposits of French rococo drawings in the 1938 group. A series of ten drawings for a Sèvres porcelain dinner service included a *Design for a Verrière* (Monteith) (fig. 4), in which the rippling, curved rim, supporting the glass stems, carries the eye in an undulating rhythm around the body of the vessel. Another Piancastelli drawing by Johann Michael Hoppenhaupt II (1709–1778-86), architect and designer for the Prussian court, shows a design for a light, open carriage known as a cabriolet (fig. 5), whose wooden seat frame, carved with sculptural shell-like pierced ornament, sprouts a fanciful open parasol.

By 1911, the sisters convinced the Museum's Advisory Council to purchase a collection of French rococo and neoclassical drawings for decorative arts and architecture from Decloux's collection.[12] A former painting contractor who specialized in ornamental gilded paneling, Decloux devoted himself to acquiring and auctioning off several collections of objects. As early as 1891, he sold an encyclopedic collection of French, German, and Italian enamels, ceramics, metalwork, furniture, and textiles.[13] The sale's proceeds enabled him to gather a new collection of old master and decorative-arts drawings, including works attributed to Jean-Antoine Watteau, Boucher, and Jean-Honoré Fragonard, which were sold in 1898.[14] Seven years later, he met the Hewitts at a luncheon given by the former Marcellite Thorn Garner of New York, the second wife of Henri-Charles-Joseph Letonnelier, marquis de Breteuil, who had hired the Decloux family firm to decorate the interior walls in the newly constructed Hôtel de Breteuil on avenue Foch. The sisters were in Paris for one of their annual study and buying trips to Europe on behalf of their newly established museum.[15] Within the year, Decloux secured an ongoing relationship with the Hewitts, functioning as their Paris agent for the purchase of ornament books and objects for the Museum's

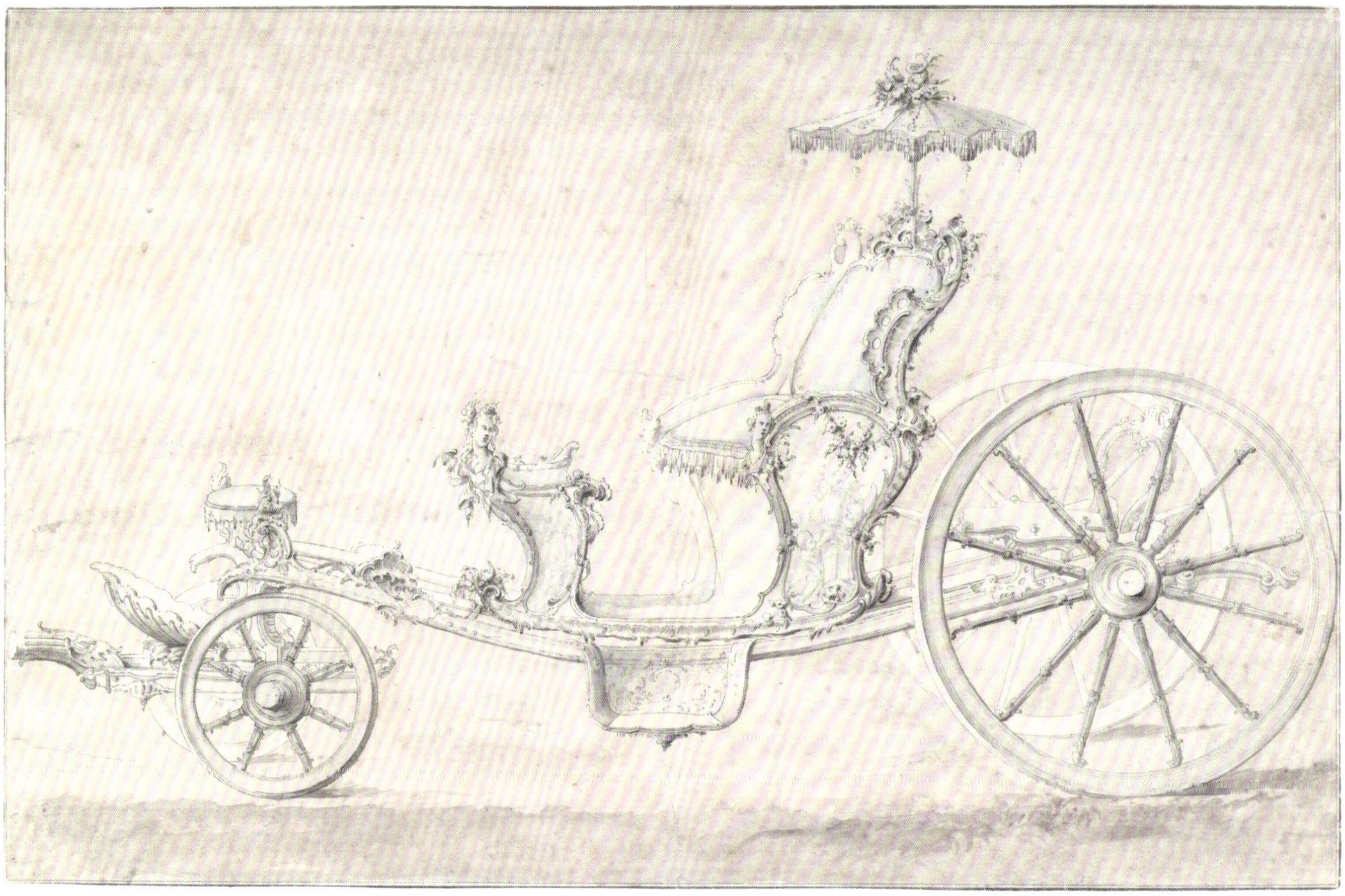

FIG. 5 *Design for a Cabriolet*. Johann Michael Hoppenhaupt II (German, 1709–1778-86). Berlin, Germany, before 1750. Pen and black ink, brush and watercolor over black chalk on white laid paper. Cooper-Hewitt, National Design Museum, Smithsonian Institution, Museum purchase through gift from Eleanor G. Hewitt Fund and various donors, 1938-88-3188

collection.[16] He also courted as a client their friend Mrs. George T. Bliss, and purchased objects for her as well as for Charles W. Gould, a member of the Museum Advisory Council.[17] Extant letters from Decloux to Eleanor Hewitt between 1906 and 1911 document in detail the evolution of these early transactions.[18]

As early as February 1907, Decloux purchased albums of late eighteenth-century prints after designs by Forty, Lalonde, Salembier, and François Boucher fils, which he sent on approval to the sisters for possible acquisition. A year later, he purchased a 250-page album of Jean-François Cuvilliés the Elder prints in an old binding, which he restored and added a handwritten title page. He encouraged the Hewitts to buy this album as well as two Oppenord print albums that were coming up for sale, with the often repeated line "L'on ne reverra sans doute jamais" ["This opportunity will never come again"]. Decloux also pressed them to acquire many examples of carved and painted wood from the Renaissance through the eighteenth century, together with copper, iron, and pewter objects. By August 1908, he received 32, 220 francs for objects sent, not including the freight charges and payment for ten ornament-print albums.

Drawings presented more of a problem, wrote Decloux, due to their rarity. In an October 21, 1908, letter, he mentioned a gouache drawing by Meissonnier that a dealer was trying to secure for him, which may well be Cooper-Hewitt's splendid gouache ceiling design from the Decloux collection, *Chariot of Apollo*, for the cabinet of Count Bielinski in Poland (see Fuhring, fig. 5). (Other than a published description in the *Mercure de France* of July 1736 of this cabinet giving the color of the marble, written when it was on view in the Tuileries Palace prior to its shipment to Warsaw, this drawing provides the only secure documentation of the coloring in this room.) In January 1910, Decloux mentioned fifty drawings previously in the Destailleur collection, acquired from the Destailleur sale by a Rothschild family member, which were being sold by a dealer friend. Included in this group were later eighteenth-century drawings attributed to Gilles-Paul Cauvet, Jean-Charles Delafosse, Jean-Louis Prieur, and Richard de Lalonde, along with drawings by Oppenord, Boucher, and Watteau. Decloux boasted that the prestigious Destailleur acquisition had increased his collection to 300 sheets.

By October 1910, Decloux alerted Eleanor Hewitt that he was downsizing his real-estate and art holdings, and had decided to offer the Museum his entire decorative-arts drawings and decorative paintings collections, numbering 350 objects, to avoid inheritance taxes at his death. To encourage the sale, Decloux sent a catalogue and photographs he had taken of each object, which were displayed at a special meeting of the Museum Advisory Council in March 1911. After dutifully bargaining down the asking price from 300,000 to 280,000 francs, to be paid over four years, the Council agreed to fund the acquisition from donations by its members. An announcement of the pending acquisition, totaling $56,000 (equivalent to $1,225,798.05 as of 2006), appeared in the

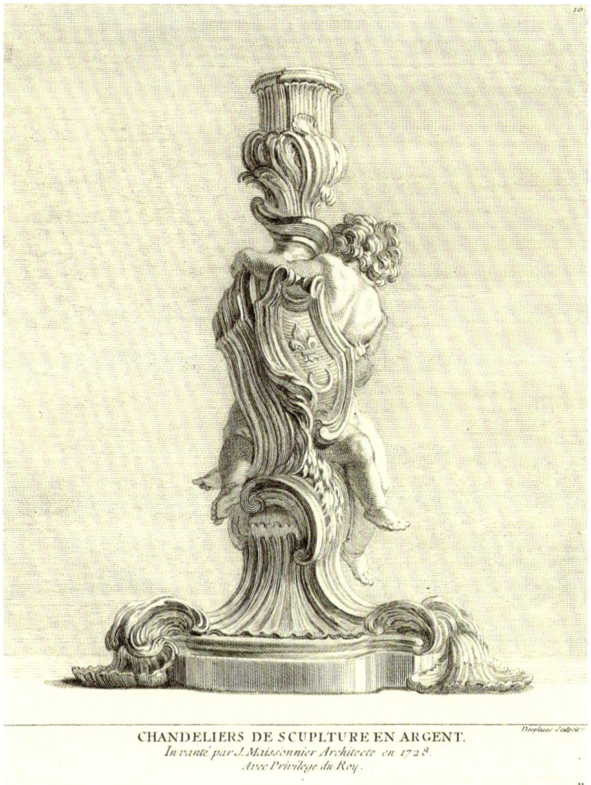

FIG. 6 *Chandeliers de Sculpture en Argent* (*Design for a Candlestick*), plate 10 in *Oeuvre de Juste-Aurèle Meissonnier*. Juste-Aurèle Meissonnier (French, 1695–1750). Etched by Philippe-Louis Compagnon-Desplaces (French, 1682–1739). Paris, France, 1748 (designed 1728, first published 1734). Etching on white laid paper. Cooper-Hewitt, National Design Museum, Smithsonian Institution, Purchased for the Museum by the Advisory Council, 1921-6-212-6-b

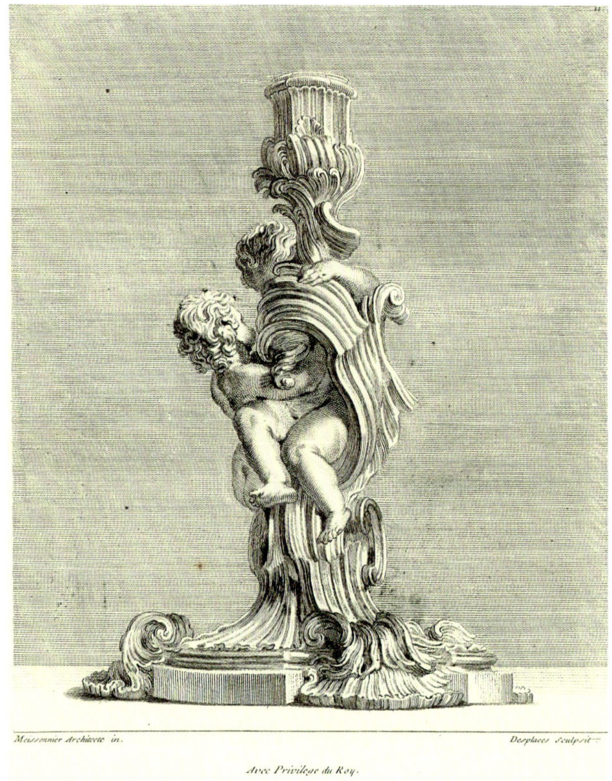

FIG. 7 *Design for a Candlestick*, plate 11 in *Oeuvre de Juste-Aurèle Meissonnier*. Juste-Aurèle Meissonnier (French, 1695–1750). Etched by Philippe-Louis Compagnon-Desplaces (French, 1682–1739). Paris, France, 1748 (designed 1728; first published 1734). Etching on white laid paper. Cooper-Hewitt, National Design Museum, Smithsonian Institution, Purchased for the Museum by the Advisory Council, 1921-6-212-7-b

Museum's 1911 Annual Report. In the next year's report, discussion of the Decloux collection continued, which lauded the "broad-minded wisdom" of the Council; the educational value of the drawings, "an untold mine of wealth for suggestions of decorative ideas"; and the prestige the Decloux collection would bring to the Museum and its educational mission. With the goals of promoting its new educational resource for design students and increasing the institution's profile in the New York cultural community, the Museum exhibited the collection with a special opening for art professionals, which was covered by the *New York Times* (November 9, 1911, p. 10).

The Hewitt sisters and Cooper Union Museum profited once again from Decloux's hard times during World War I. After auctioning off a third collection of paintings, drawings, miniatures, and objets d'art in 1920,[19] Decloux offered the Hewitts another portion of his collection, comprising 413 albums of ornament prints and related preparatory drawings. The $27,118.64 purchase (equivalent to $305,425.58 as of 2006), once again funded by Council members, contained many albums of prints by or after the greatest rococo designers including Meissonnier, in addition to neoclassical ornamentalists.

As most modern scholars would attest, Meissonnier was the creative genius of French rococo.[20] Even his greatest eighteenth-century critics recognized his originality—which was exactly what they condemned in his work. As his obituary writer Pierre-Jean Mariette charged in the *Mercure de France*, he was born with a fertile imagination, but his search for novelty caused him to break all the rules, and he "gave birth with his pen & pencil compositions without order or measure which perverted and spoiled so many minds." The orders to which Mariette alluded were the architectural orders inherited from antiquity, and the rules were the rules of "good taste"; or, to put it succinctly, the "goût nouveau" equaled the "goût mauvais."[21]

If his detractors found Meissonnier's ingenuity mutinous, his peers in the design community, whether metalworkers, porcelain modelers, or two-dimensional designers, were overcome with the master's originality, and turned to the *Oeuvre* as a wellspring of design ideas for candlesticks, tobacco boxes, sword hilts, watch cases, wall paneling, and furniture (including consoles, chairs, and settees), though it is not known how many of these designs were ever fabricated. Through the print medium, his designs carried the newest rococo style to Germany, England, the Netherlands, and elsewhere. His model, *Design for a Candlestick* (1728) (figs. 6, 7; also see Fuhring, fig. 14), from the group of prints published by the Widow Chéreau in 1734 and reprinted by Huquier in the *Oeuvre*, was reproduced with some alterations in proportions in a porcelain candlestick modeled by J. F. Eberlein (1696–1749) as part of the celebrated 1739 Meissen "Swan" service for Count Heinrich von Brühl (fig. 8). Along the route from France to Germany, however, the spiraling, energetic movement in Meissonnier's design, which the master demonstrated by showing three different views of the object, became more static and restrained, and the plastic character of the original was similarly lost in translation, in the German porcelain.[22]

A Meissonnier tureen design, with a cover composed of a crayfish

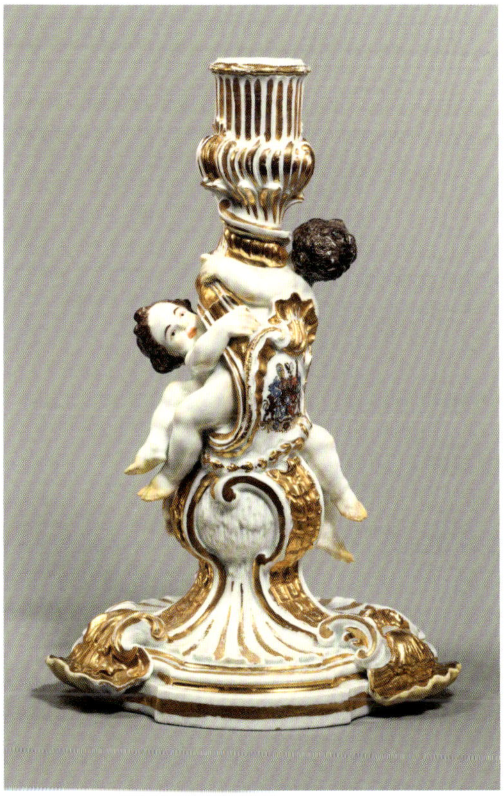

FIG. 8 Candlestick from the "Swan" Service, for Count Heinrich von Brühl. After a design by Juste-Aurèle Meissonnier (French, 1695–1750). Modeled by Johann Friedrich Eberlein (German, 1695–1749). Manufactured by Meissen Porcelain Manufactory. Meissen, Germany, 1737–41. Hard-paste porcelain. The Metropolitan Museum of Art, Gift of R. Thornton Wilson, in memory of Ellsworth Wilson, 1950.50.211.234

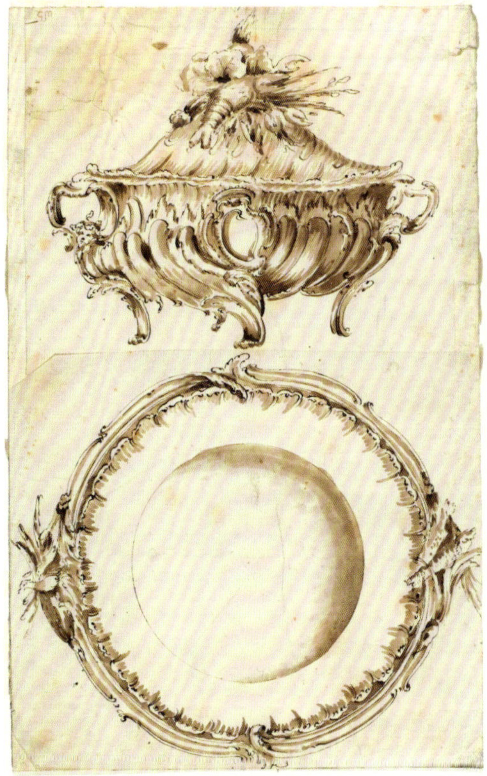

FIG. 10 *Design for a Tureen and Platter*. France, ca. 1748. Graphite, pen and brown ink, brush and sepia wash on two joined sheets of paper. Cooper-Hewitt, National Design Museum, Smithsonian Institution, Purchased for the Museum by the Advisory Council, 1911-28-160-a, b

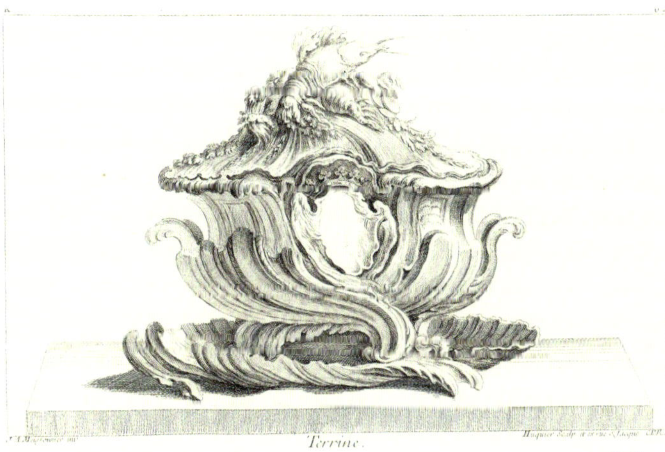

FIG. 9 *Design for a Tureen*, plate 62 in *Oeuvre de Juste Aurèle Meissonnier*. Juste-Aurèle Meissonnier (French, 1695–1750). Etched by Gabriel Huquier (French, 1695–1772). Paris, France, 1748 (first published 1734). Etching on white laid paper. Cooper-Hewitt, National Design Museum, Smithsonian Institution, Purchased for the Museum by the Advisory Council, 1921-6-212-24-b

and vegetables, a body formed from cabbage leaves swirling outward from a central, undecorated coat of arms, and handles created by the body's outermost leaves, is illustrated in the *Oeuvre*, plate 62 (fig. 9). It presumably inspired a *Design for Tureen* by an unknown French artist in Cooper-Hewitt's collection (fig. 10). This tureen's body of up-curving leaves surrounding a crowned cartouche, with a cover of crayfish and vegetables, is a poor cousin of Meissonnier's exuberant design. Its handles spring more traditionally from the edge of the bowl and, while they might function better, are much less innovative than those of the original. The platter has nothing at all to do with Meissonnier.

The same Meissonnier tureen design appears to have been a source for a *pot à oille* depicted in the lower half of a drawing in the Bibliothèque Nationale (fig. 11). This sheet has been attributed to Jacques III Roëttiers due to the similarity of the upper design to a Roëttiers pot à oille in Pierre Germain's *Éléments d'orfèvrerie* (1748).[13] (fig. 12) It may well be that the double sheet depicts designs by Roëttiers but was drawn by Jacques-Jean Pasquier (1718–1785), who etched the plates in Germain's book with a delicacy equal to the fine brushwork in the Bibliothèque Nationale sheet. Regardless of the authorship of the latter drawing, these feathery designs that almost fly off the page are concept sketches created to secure a commission, while Meissonnier's robust and muscular tureen design was clearly intended as instruction for professional modelers on how to replicate his design in three dimensions. Meissonnier collaborated with his printmaker Gabriel Huquier to employ a system of long, thin curvilinear strokes together with crosshatchings of varying densities to both define

FIG. 11 *Designs for a Tureen and a Pot à Oille*. Attributed to Pierre Germain (French, 1716–1783) or Jacques III Roëttiers (French, 1707–1784). Paris, France, ca. 1748. Brush and black and brown ink, wash over slight traces of black chalk on off-white laid paper. La Bibliothèque Nationale de France, Cabinet des Estampes et Photographie. Le 39, Fol. 28

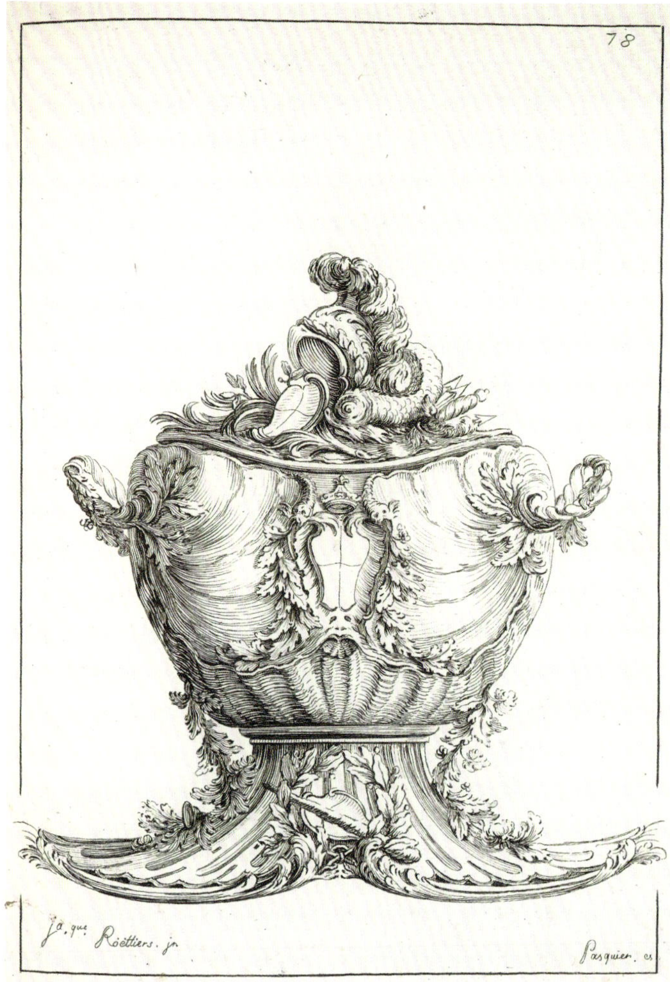

FIG. 12 *Design for a Pot à Oille*, plate 78 in Pierre Germain, *Elements d'Orfevrerie*, second part (Paris, 1748). Jacques III Roëttiers (French, 1707–1784). Etched by Jacques Jean Pasquier (French, 1718–1775). Paris, France, 1748. Etching on white laid paper. Cooper-Hewitt, National Design Museum, Smithsonian Institution, Purchased for the Museum by the Advisory Council, 1921-6-313-78

the plastic character of the leaves and perhaps indicate where the surface would receive a high polish and where the chiseling was to be left matte.

The second in Blondel's triumvirate responsible for the degenerate goût nouveau was Jacques de Lajoüe. Unlike Meissonnier, Lajoüe, joined the Académie royale de Peinture et Sculpture in 1721, and enjoyed great success as a painter of marine views, landscapes, and gardens with terraces, fountains, and hunting scenes, which served as framed easel paintings or decorative canvases for insertion in paneling.[24] Yet his talent for rococo style is best seen not in his paintings, but in his designs for cartouches, carriages, fountains, theater sets, chinoiseries, fans, textiles, and screens, most of which are known from print portfolios published between 1730 and 1740. These included *Recueil nouveau de differens Cartouches* (Paris, 1734), with second and third books; *Livre de cartouches de Guerre* (1735); *Livre de buffets* (Paris, 1735); *Livre Nouveau de Douze Morceaux de Fantaisie* (Paris, 1736); and *Premier Livre de divers morceaux d'architecture, paysage et perspective* (Paris, ca. 1740), with second, third, and fourth parts. Undated portfolios include *Livre de vases*; *Nouveaux tableaux d'ornements et rocailles*, with a second book; and *Livre de divers esquices et grifonemens*. Most of these print series were etched and published by Huquier, who planned on publishing a Lajoüe *Oeuvre* catalogue.

With the change in taste around 1750, Lajoüe's career went into decline—which may be the reason Huquier never produced the publication—but he remained influential all over Europe as a decorative designer by virtue of the almost 200 prints after his designs which he and/or Huquier cleverly organized to appeal to market demand. Cooper-Hewitt's Decloux collection includes an album of rocaille cartouches from the first, second, and third sets. These designs for framing elements, which could be themed for different publishing needs, are individually innovative, humorous, satirical, and clever. A preparatory drawing in Cooper-Hewitt's collection, *Design for an Escutcheon in the Form of a Sailboat* (fig. 13), for a plate etched by Julien in the *Recueil nouveau de differens Cartouches*, ranks among the most whimsical of these ornaments.[25] Its shell-shaped sailing ship, ornamented with bizarre beasts, was especially useful for printed maps, where the title could be inserted on the sail. Other sea-themed escutcheons were similarly employed by cartographers.[26] Lajoüe's cartouche designs enjoyed great popularity all of Europe, and were published (in reverse) in Germany by the Augsburg publisher Johann Georg Merz as well as in England.[27] Drawings (mostly signed) for different cartouches exist today in the collections of the École des Beaux-Arts, the Hermitage, and formerly in the Houthakker collection;

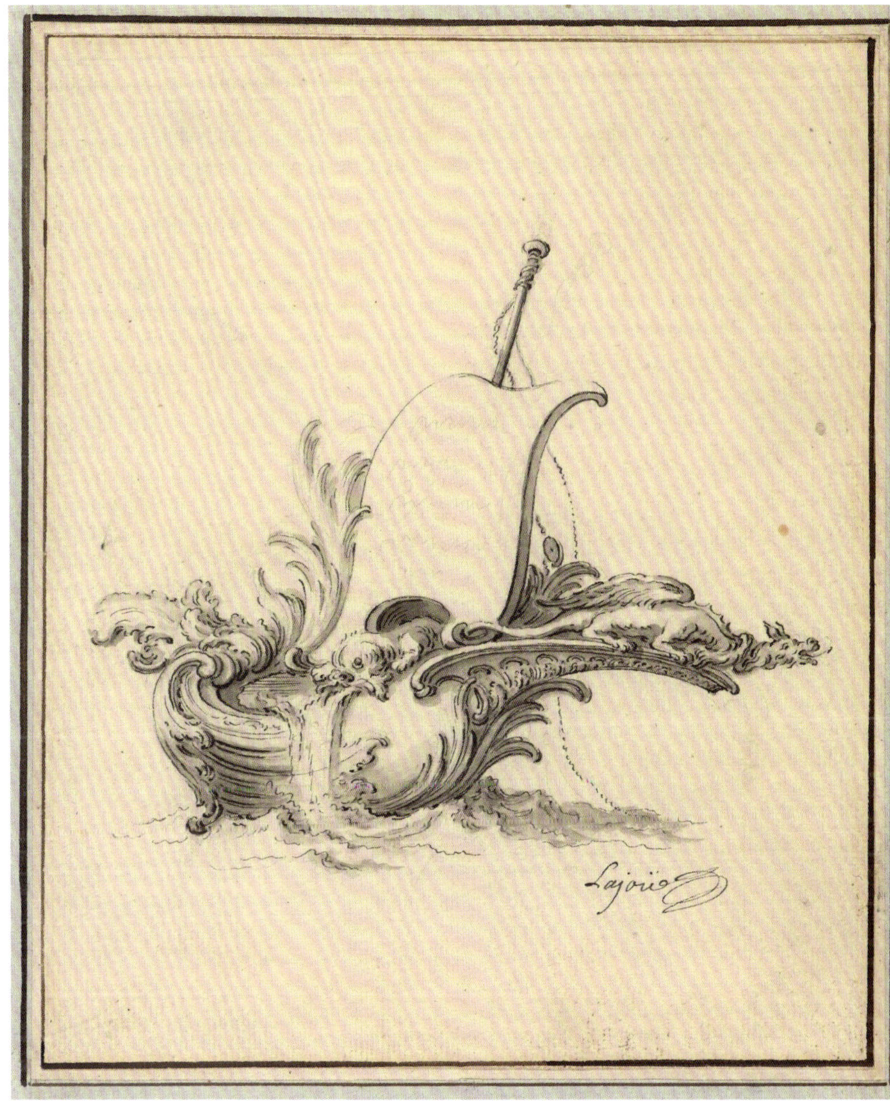

FIG. 13 *Design for an Escutcheon in Form of Sailboat, for Recueil Noveau de differens Cartouches.* Jacques de Lajoüe (French, 1687–1761). Paris, France, 1734. Pen and brush and black ink, wash, graphite on cream laid paper. Cooper-Hewitt, National Design Museum, Smithsonian Institution, Gift of Eleanor and Sarah Hewitt, 1914-21-29

all are characterized by Lajoüe's facile, easily recognizable brush- and brown-wash manner of draftsmanship (often colored with watercolor).

A second album of designs after Lajoüe in Cooper-Hewitt's Decloux collection comprises prints from several series, including nine plates from the *Second Livre de tableaux d'ornemens et rocailles*. For these designs, Lajoüe dipped into his painting vocabulary of fantastic architecture, staircases, gardens, and fountains, and adapted these motifs for smaller scale use as designs for box covers and other ornament. The idea for this effort seems to have been inspired by Meissonnier's early designs for ornament published in 1734 (figs. 14, 15). Without taking any motif directly from Meissonnier, Lajoüe adopted the *de sotto in su* perspective (often with more than one vanishing point): figures standing or seated on architectural fragments, fountains spilling water off the edges of the design, and encroaching rocaille scrolls that challenge the landscape for top billing in the composition. To this mix, the designer added his ubiquitous trellised garden pavilions, which also served as standard dressing for his theater sets (fig. 16). Several of his prints were divided down the middle to offer a design choice, giving these images an especially raucous appearance. You can almost imagine Lajoüe chuckling, "This will really knock their socks off!" No wonder Blondel commented that Lajoüe

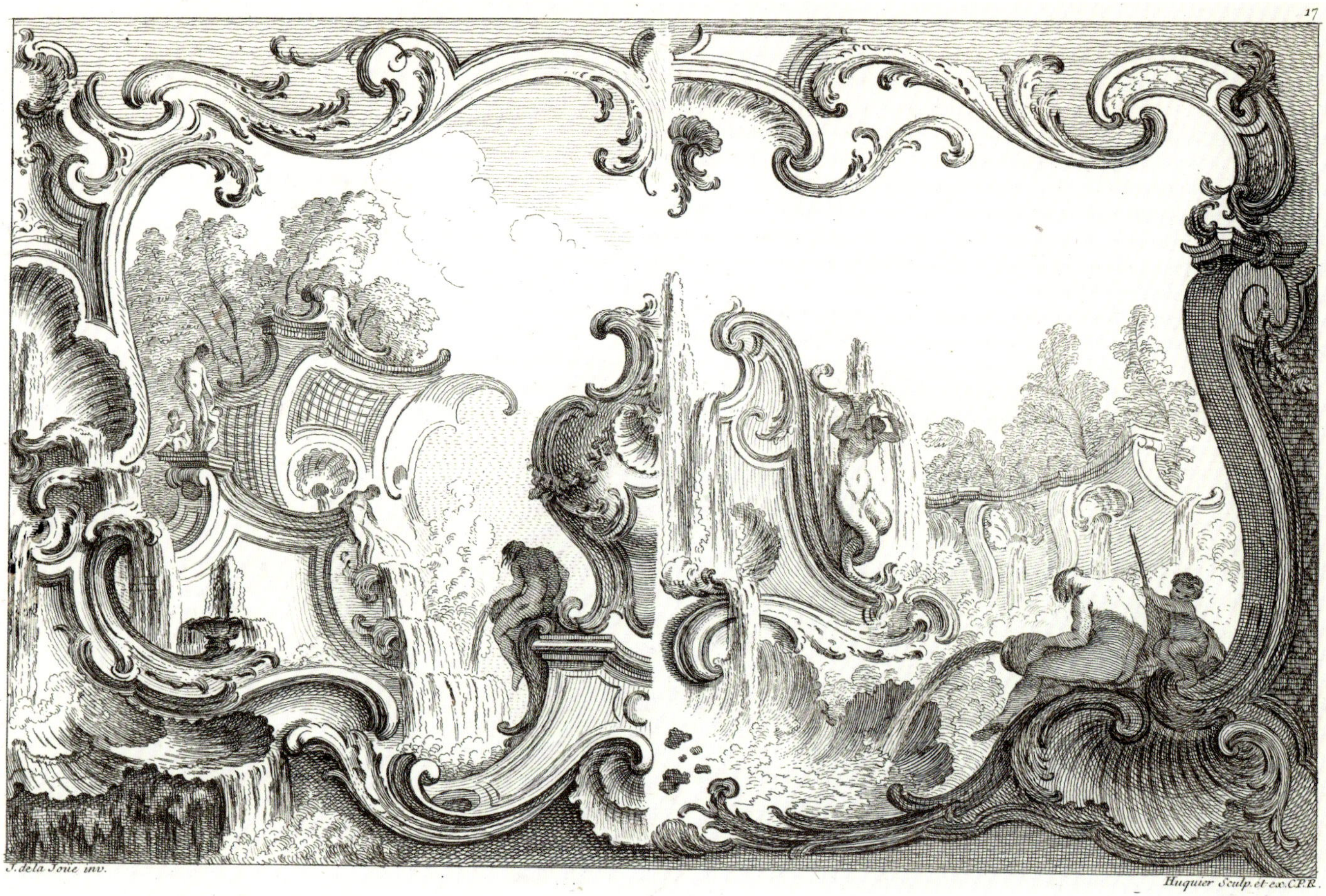

FIG. 14 Design for Ornament, plate 17 in *Second Livre de tableaux d'ornemens et rocailles*. Jacques de Lajoüe (French, 1687–1761). Etched by Gabriel Huquier (French, 1695–1772). Paris, France, ca. 1734. Etching on white laid paper. Cooper-Hewitt, National Design Museum, Smithsonian Institution, Gift of Eleanor and Sarah Hewitt, 1921-6-327-8

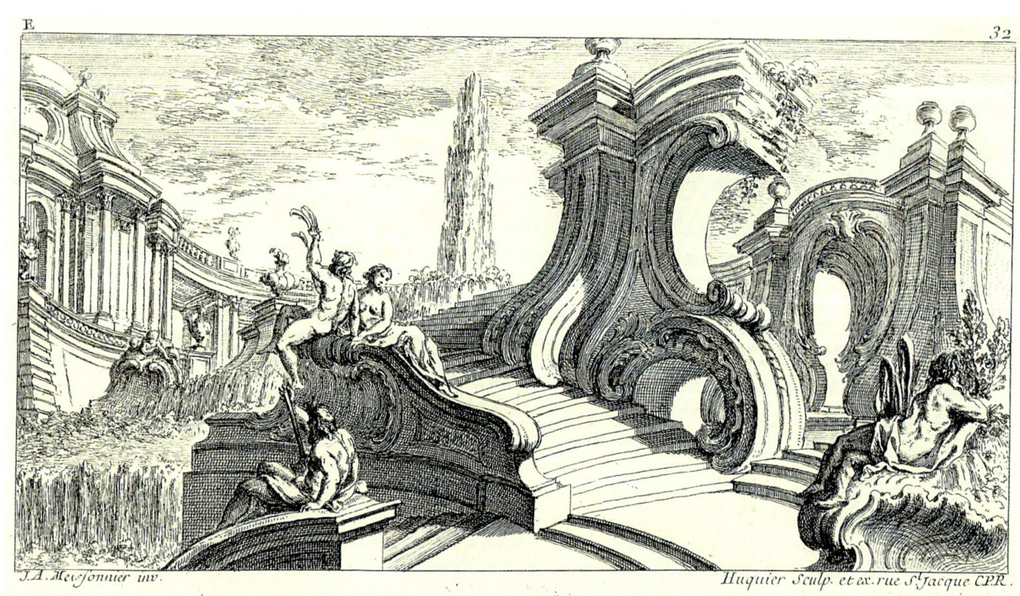

FIG. 15 Design for Ornament, plate 32 in *Oeuvre de Juste-Aurèle Meissonnier*. Juste-Aurèle Meissonnier (French, 1695–1750). Etched by Gabriel Huquier (French, 1695–1772). Paris, France, 1748 (first published 1734). Etching on white laid paper. Cooper-Hewitt, National Design Museum, Smithsonian Institution, Purchased for the Museum by the Advisory Council, 1921-6-212-33-b

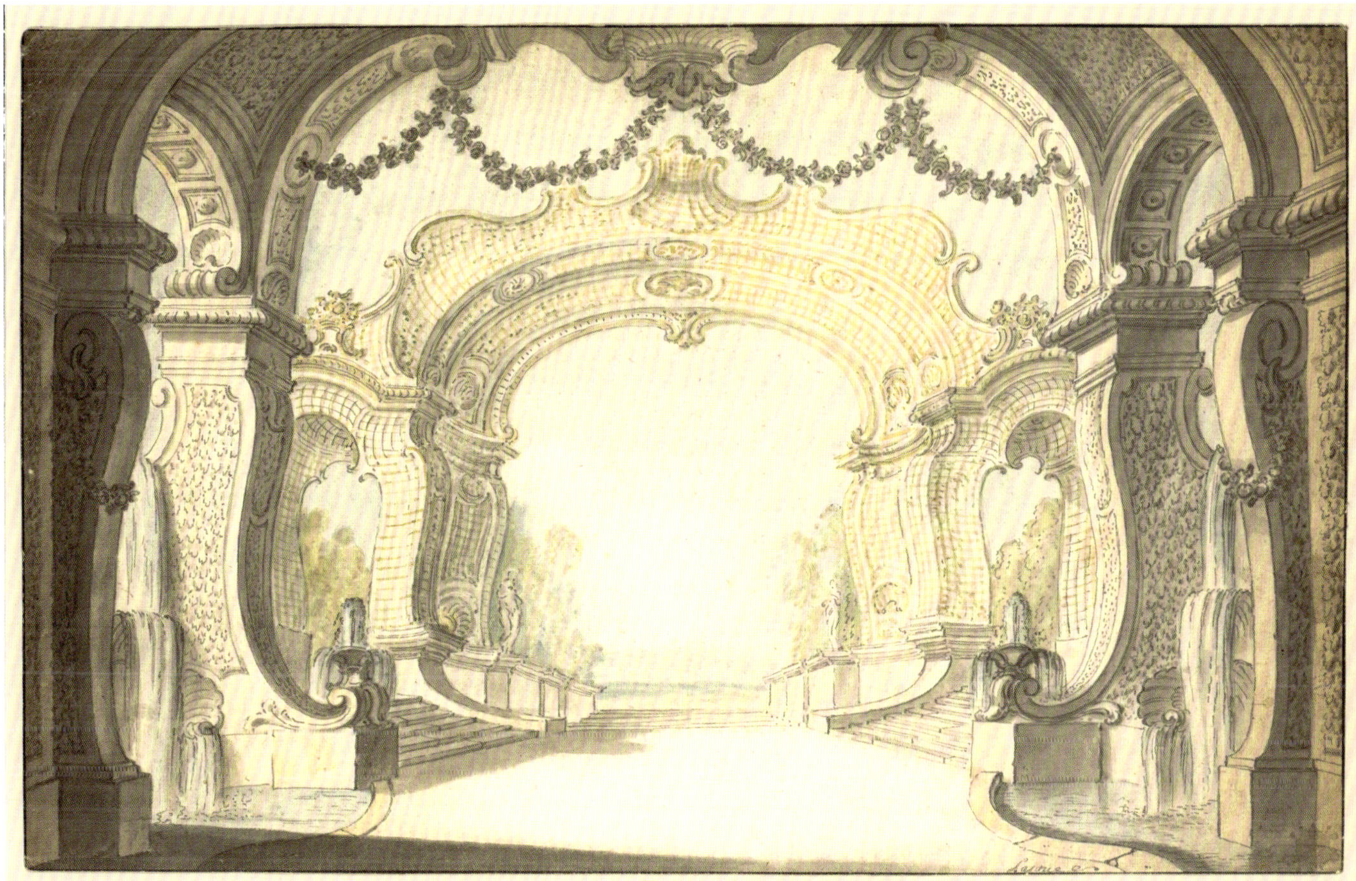

FIG. 16 *Design for a Stage Set.* Jacques de Lajoüe (French, 1687–1761). Paris, France, ca. 1735. Pen and gray ink, brush and watercolor, black chalk, graphite on cream laid paper, framing lines in pen and black ink. The Metropolitan Museum of Art, Harris Brisbane Dick Fund, 1935, 35.76.1

"contributed even more than Pinault et Meissonnier…to the bad taste in ornaments and in bizarre compositions."[28]

As an artist essentially working in two dimensions, Lajoüe (or his publisher Huquier) saw a profit in adapting the designer's decorative motifs to consumer items such as fans, fire screens, and folding screens, all essential fixtures of eighteenth-century domestic life.[29] François Boucher and Watteau before him also created designs for screen panels. Boucher's *Nouveaux Morceaux pour des paravants* comprised five designs: the *Triumph of Pomona*, engraved by Charles-Nicolas Cochin fils; and four other plates including the iconic *Rocaille* (fig. 17), masterfully etched by Claude Duflos the Younger, who brilliantly captured the texture and rich chiaroscuro of Boucher's black chalk drawings. Lajoüe's *Design for a Panel of a Folding Screen*, blocks out a single screen panel divided in three registers, each framed with rocaille ornament (fig. 18). The designer used the same tripartite organization for a six-panel painted screen on paper (fig. 19), the front side of which depicts the three elements of water (fountains) below; earth (a port scene and parks) in the middle; air (sky filled with flying birds) in the uppermost section[30]; and, on the rear, central cartouches surrounded on three sides by garlands.[31] The similarity of the symmetrical shellwork fountains in the lower registers of these panels to a small painting in the Musée des Arts Décoratifs (fig. 20) of a naiad and putto in a shell-shaped wall fountain (referencing fertility) raises the possibility that the little painting was cut out from a similar screen.[32]

According to Marianne Roland Michel, the six-panel screen most likely belonged to Huquier,[33] which provokes a comment on the relationship of designers to their publishers. Could Huquier have commissioned

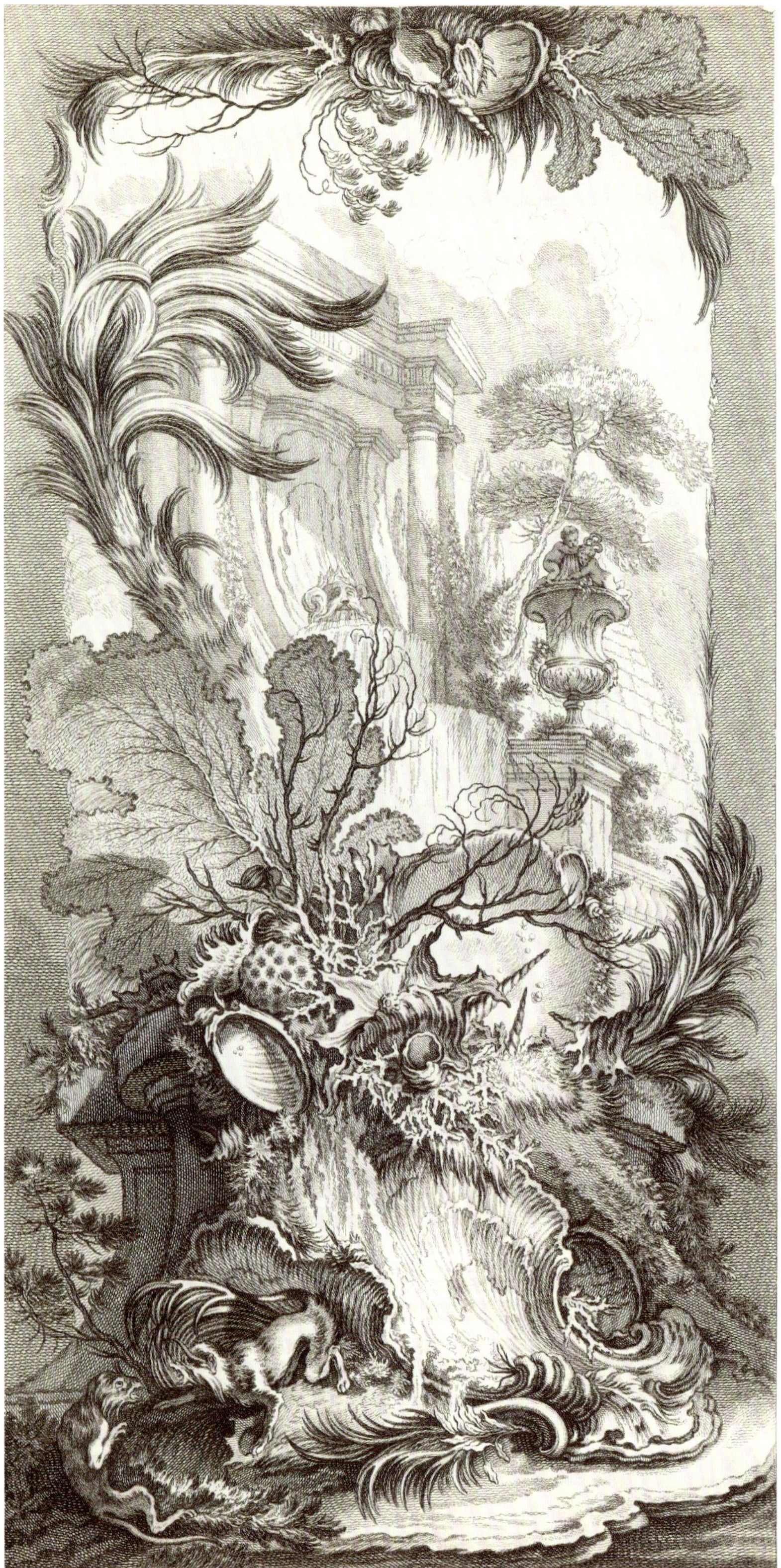

FIG. 17 *Rocaille (Rococo Design), in Nouveaux Morceaux pour des paravents.* François Boucher (French, 1703–1770). Etched and engraved by Claude-Augustin Duflos (French, 1700–1786). Paris, France, ca. 1737. Etching with engraving on white paper. Cooper-Hewitt, National Design Museum, Smithsonian Institution, Gift of Eleanor and Sarah Hewitt, 1931-94-11

FIG. 18 *Design for Panel of a Folding Screen.* Jacques de Lajoüe (French, 1687–1761). Paris, France, ca. 1735. Pen and gray ink, wash, over traces of black chalk, graphite, framing lines in pen and black ink, lined. The Metropolitan Museum of Art, Purchase, Harris Brisbane Dick Fund and Joseph Pulitzer Bequest, 1971, 71.513.3

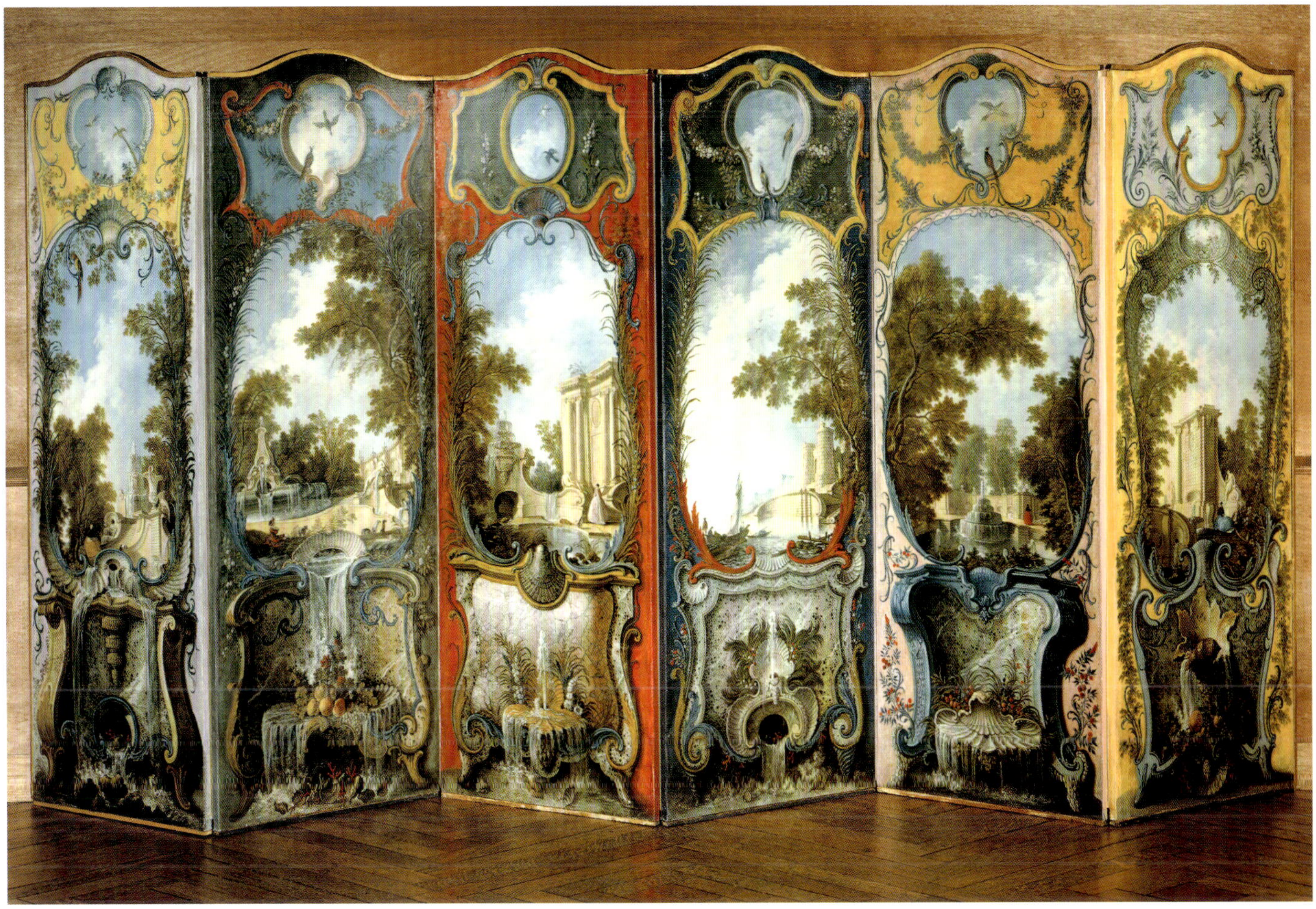

FIG. 19 Screen with Six Leaves. Jacques de Lajoüe (French, 1687–1761). Paris, France, ca. 1740. Brush and oil paint over black chalk on paper, mounted. Musée du Petit Palais, Collection Dutuit PDUT00874

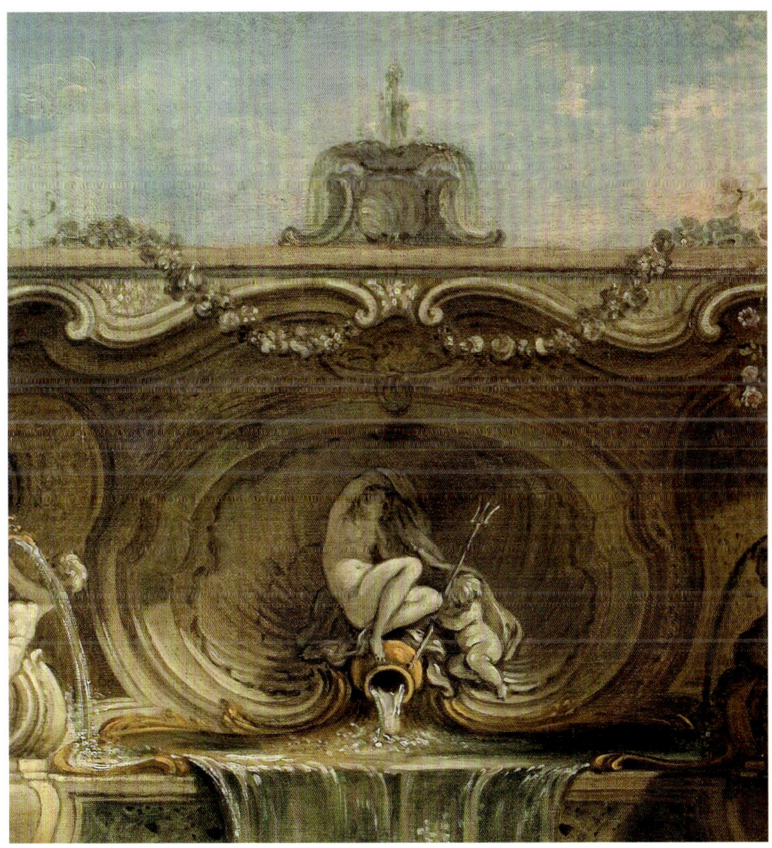

FIG. 20 Amphitrite and Cupid. Jacques de Lajoüe (French, 1687–1761). Paris, France, ca. 1740. Brush and oil on canvas. Musée des Arts Décoratifs, Paris; Maciet gift 1904, Inv. 11304

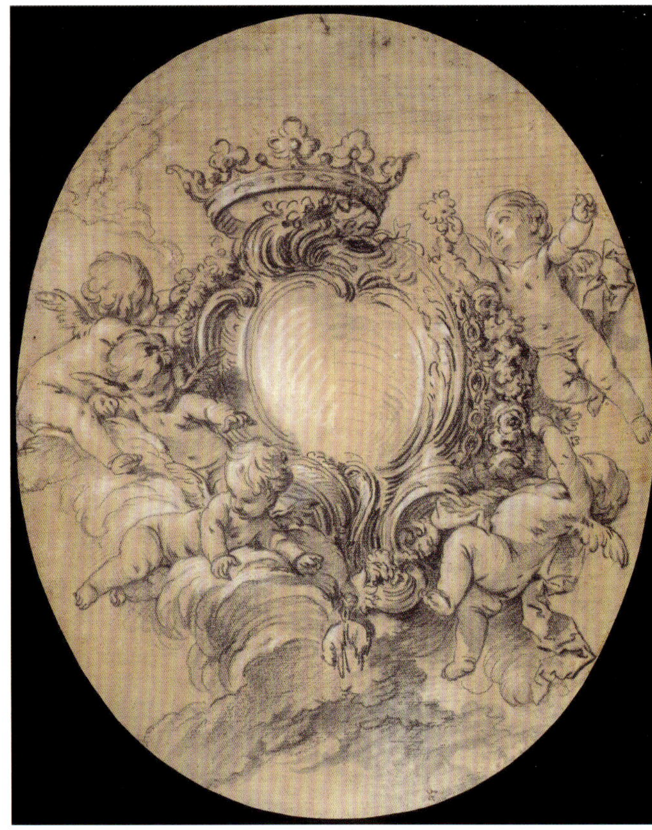

FIG. 21 *Crowned Rocaille Escutcheon with Putti.* François Boucher (French, 1703–1770). Paris, France, 1734–48. Black chalk heightened with white on light brown antique laid paper. The Horvitz Collection, Boston

the screen for his shop and apartment to show clients how works on paper were easily adapted for inexpensive fire or folding screens, rather than the more upscale versions decorated with tapestries or textiles? The screen also highlights how Lajoüe and other painter/designers were able to capitalize on their existing oeuvre by reusing their painted compositions to embellish decorative-arts objects. As another example, Boucher incorporated the playful putti that inhabit his pictures in a design for an armorial escutcheon (fig. 21) to be used most likely as a decoration for a royal carriage.[34]

While Lajoüe has been called the "meilleur représentant d'un genre particulier: la peinture rocaille,"[35] there were many other designers who contributed to the fad for rocaille ornament. Alexis Peyrotte (1699–1769) was an exceptionally creative designer of textiles, ornament, and furniture whose career has only recently emerged from relative obscurity.[36] However, in his own day, one of the future critics of rococo, Charles-Nicolas Cochin, held Peyrotte in higher esteem than the highly touted textile designer Jean Pillement.[37] Born in the small Vaucluse village of Mazan, Peyrotte began his design career in Lyon (ca. 1740–45), working with the printmaker Jean-Charles François and the publisher Robert Pariset, creating large-scale compositions with figures in fantasy landscapes to use as fire screens,[38] as well as other decorative ornament, for what is termed in French *découpure*—ornament that was cut-out, hand-colored, and pasted onto furniture, fire screens, or folding screens.[39]

In 1745, Peyrotte moved to Paris, where he gained the favor of Gaspard-Moïse-Augustan de Fontanieu (1694–1767), *intendant du garde-meuble de la couronne*, who was charged with commissioning furniture and furnishings for the many royal households.[40] Peyrotte gained, probably through Fontanieu, a commission in 1747 to paint wall decorations in the apartments of the dauphin and dauphine in Versailles.[41] Two years later, he was appointed *peintre du roi et dessinateur du garde-meuble de la couronne*, and in that capacity he created floral and chinoiserie textile patterns, which he painted directly on silk, or for embroideries and woven silks. These decorative fabrics were incorporated as curtains, bed hangings, and upholstery at Versailles, Fontainebleau, Choisy-le-Roi, and Bellevue.

One of Peyrotte's textiles used to decorate Louis XV's bedroom at Versailles, a green silk brocaded with silver-gilt thread in a cornucopia pattern,[42] may have been somewhat like a design, attributed to Peyrotte, of a cornucopia of fruit resting precariously on a shell supported by a dolphin that is currently on the New York market (fig. 22). This drawing appears to be by the same hand as Peyrotte's resplendent pastel drawing of a squash vine sprouting from a tipsy rocaille vase.[43] (fig. 23) On the other hand, these designs may have been intended for hand-painted patterns on silk.

Additional examples of Peyrotte's floral and chinoiserie textile designs, gorgeously colored in gouache, count among the sixty-two drawings from the *Recueil de dessins pour meubles et pour ornaments* submitted to Fontainieu as suggestions or incentives for royal commissions.[44] An example showing one half of a textile design (a common technique in drawings for symmetrical patterns, which merely had to be repeated in reverse to create the full design) includes sprigs of pink roses overlaid with lush yellow rocaille tracery, which may have been made out of taffeta

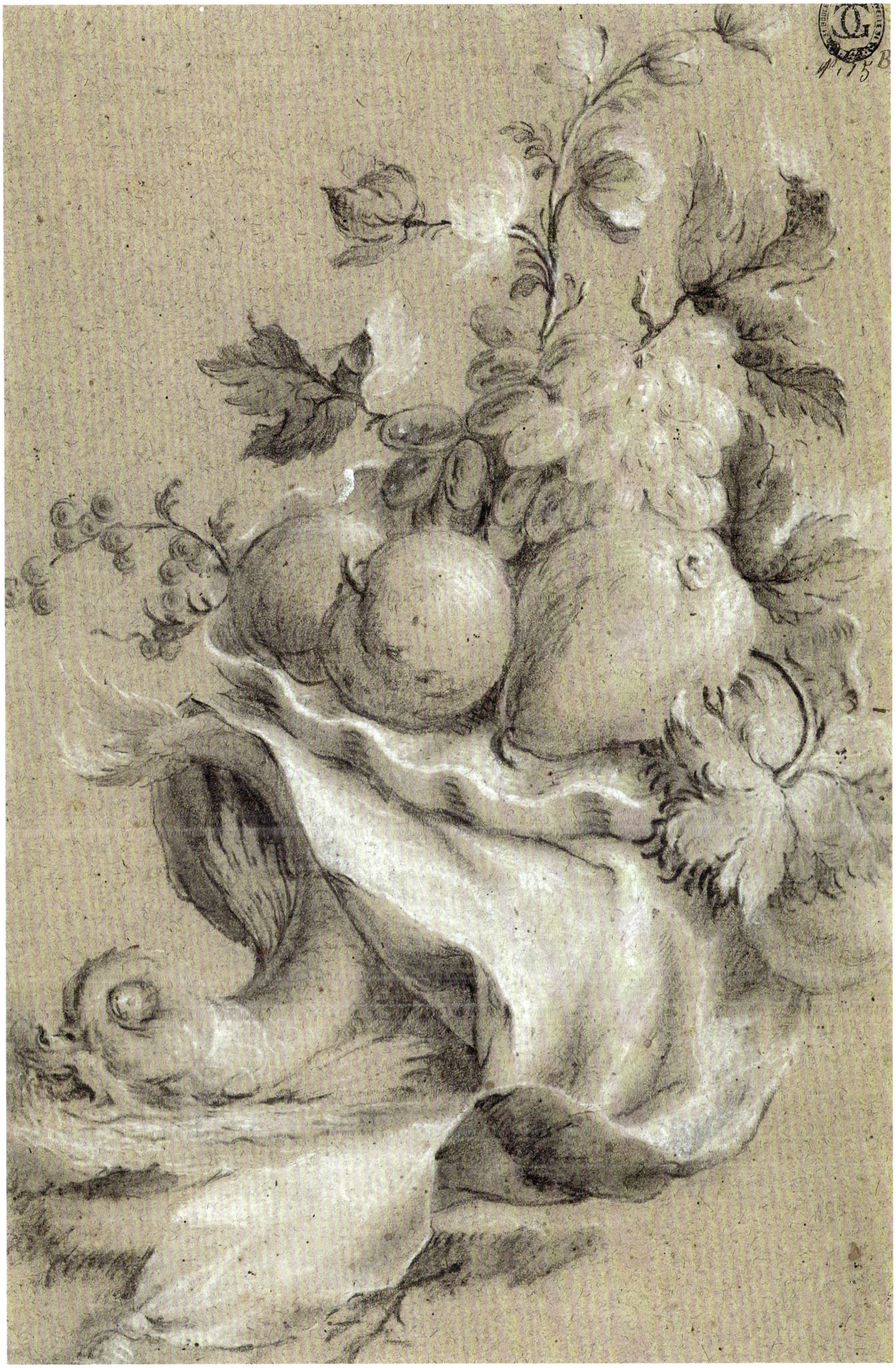

FIG. 22 *Cornucopia of Fruit with Shell and Dolphin.* Attributed to Alexis Peyrotte (French, 1699–1769). Paris, France, ca. 1749. Charcoal and white chalk on buff laid paper. Courtesy of L'Antiquaire and the Connoisseur, Inc.

and applied on top of the flowered silk design.[45] (fig. 24) The meandering bands of shell-inspired ornament, which intermittently sprout flourishes resembling bird feathers, are close cousins to Peyrotte's rocaille decoration in the print series *Seconde Partie divers Ornements* (fig. 25). These elegant and exuberant designs rank among Peyrotte's most flamboyant and impressive creations. With their size, texture, and visual weight, they could easily be imagined in the medium of gold-plated bronze. Indeed, the design of a winged griffon with forked tongue perched on top of a curling rocaille base recalls a pair of andirons, one with a wild boar and the other a lion, created by Jacques Caffiéri.[46] (see fig. 1 Hunter-Stiebel, p. 84, fig. 17)

As a designer of so much talent and creativity, Peyrotte deserves his revived reputation. (Even the Web site of his hometown, at the base of Mount Ventoux in Provence, boasts of this designer, along with the Marquis de Sade, as one of its great native sons.) The politically savvy Peyrotte, hoping to secure interior-design commissions, dedicated the *Divers ornemens* to the architect Michel Tannevot (ca. 1685–1762), a prominent designer of Parisian hotels who favored interiors in the nascent rococo style. This is the same Tanevot whom Blondel castigated, along with Jean-Baptiste Leroux (ca. 1677–1746) and an architect named Legrand, as men who "scarcely knew how to draw plans and had to rely on the decorations of Pineau, Meissonnier, Lajoüe, and their followers" to hide their lack of architectural know-how.[47] Blondel included in the band of followers François-Thomas Mondon (ca. 1709–1755), whose eccentric rocaille designs included chinoiserie and other exotic references, such as those in his *Quatrieme Livre de formes ornées de rocailles;* Jean-François Cuvilliés the Elder (1695–1768); and his son François Cuvilliés the Younger (1731–1777).

While Blondel tarred Jean-François Cuvilliés with the same brush as other French rococo designers, this prolific French-trained ornamentalist worked in Germany, exporting French rocaille decoration to the area along the French border controlled by Maximillian II Emanuel von Wittelsbach, Elector of Bavaria, and his brother Joseph Clemens, Elector and Archbishop of Cologne. German princes generally were infatuated with France and French culture. Stimulated by the example of Louis XIV and Versailles, they commissioned lavish palace architecture, furnishings, and decorative-arts objects as important propaganda tools for self-glorification. In terms of new construction, they sought to imitate smaller retreats like Marly or the Grand Trianon for summer palaces, hunting lodges, or hermitages for falconry. The architects and designers they hired were either French-born or Paris-trained. In the case of the Wittelsbachs, their French connection was solidified through a family marriage with the French royal house and from periods of exile in the Netherlands and France during the War of the Spanish Succession. Both Wittelsbach brothers, well acquainted with Parisian architecture and design during the seminal period of rococo's development, consulted with French architect Robert de Cotte about the completion of their

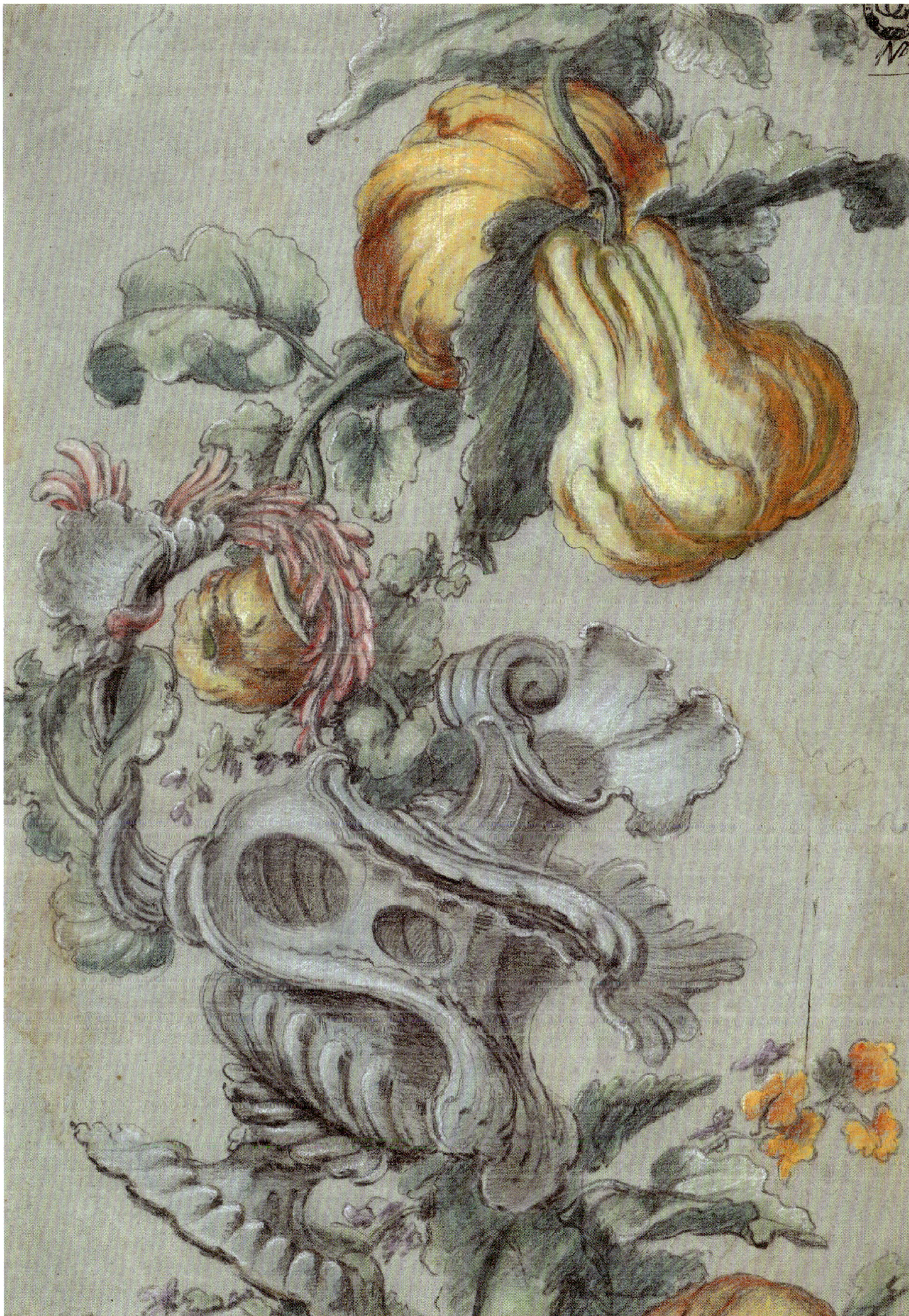

FIG. 23 *Ornament Design with a Squash Vine and Rocaille Urn.* Alexis Peyrotte (French, 1699–1769). Paris, France, ca. 1749. Black chalk, pastel on blue laid paper. The Metropolitan Museum of Art, The Elisha Whittelsey Collection, The Elisha Whittelsey Fund, 1961, 61.557.3

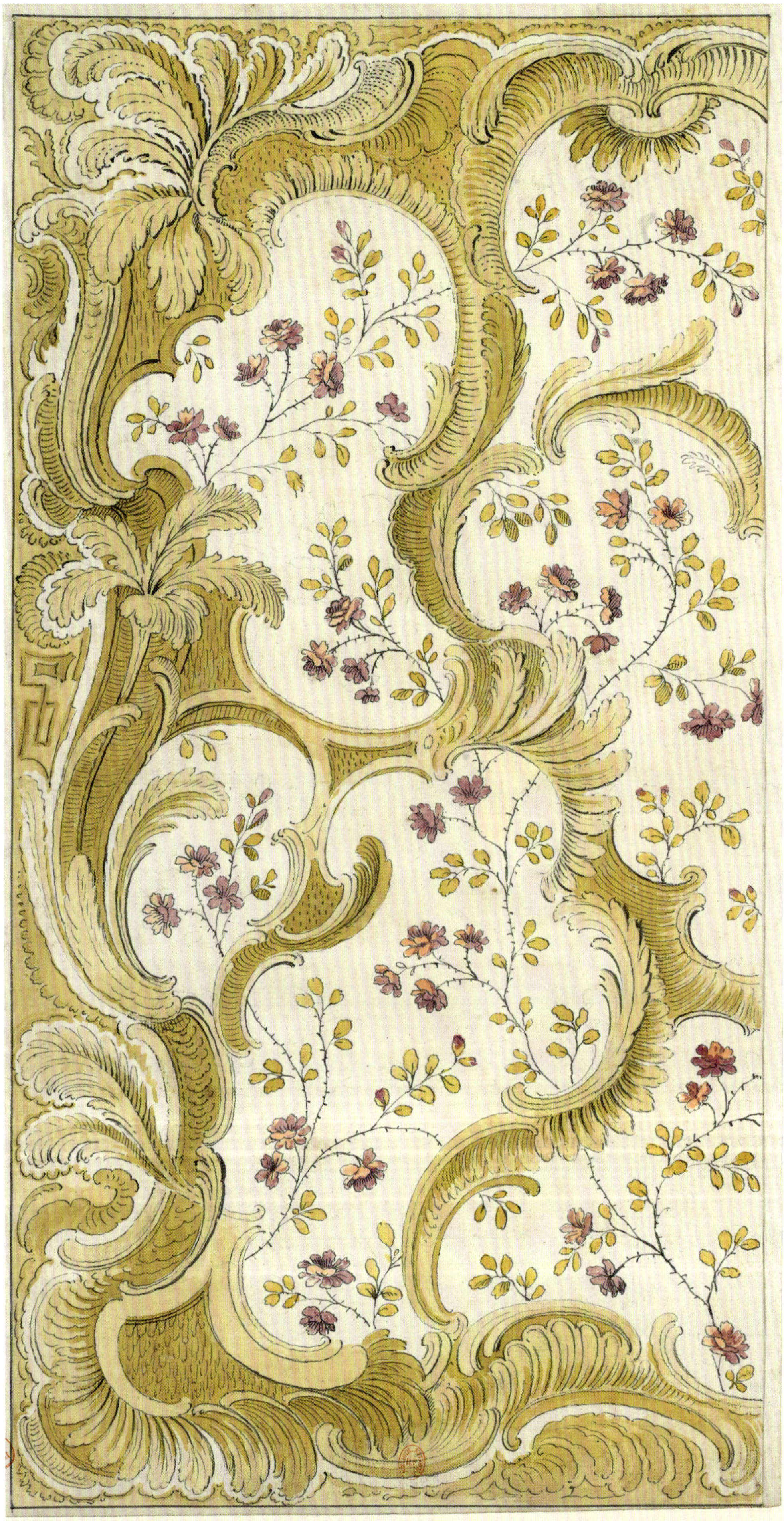

FIG. 24 *Ornament* Design. Alexis Peyrotte (French, 1699–1769). Paris, France, ca. 1749. Brush and watercolor on off-white paper, lined, framing line on three sides in pen and purple-gray ink, on mounting paper. La Bibliothèque Nationale de France, Cabinet des Estampes et Photographie, Le 39 Reserve, Fol. 20

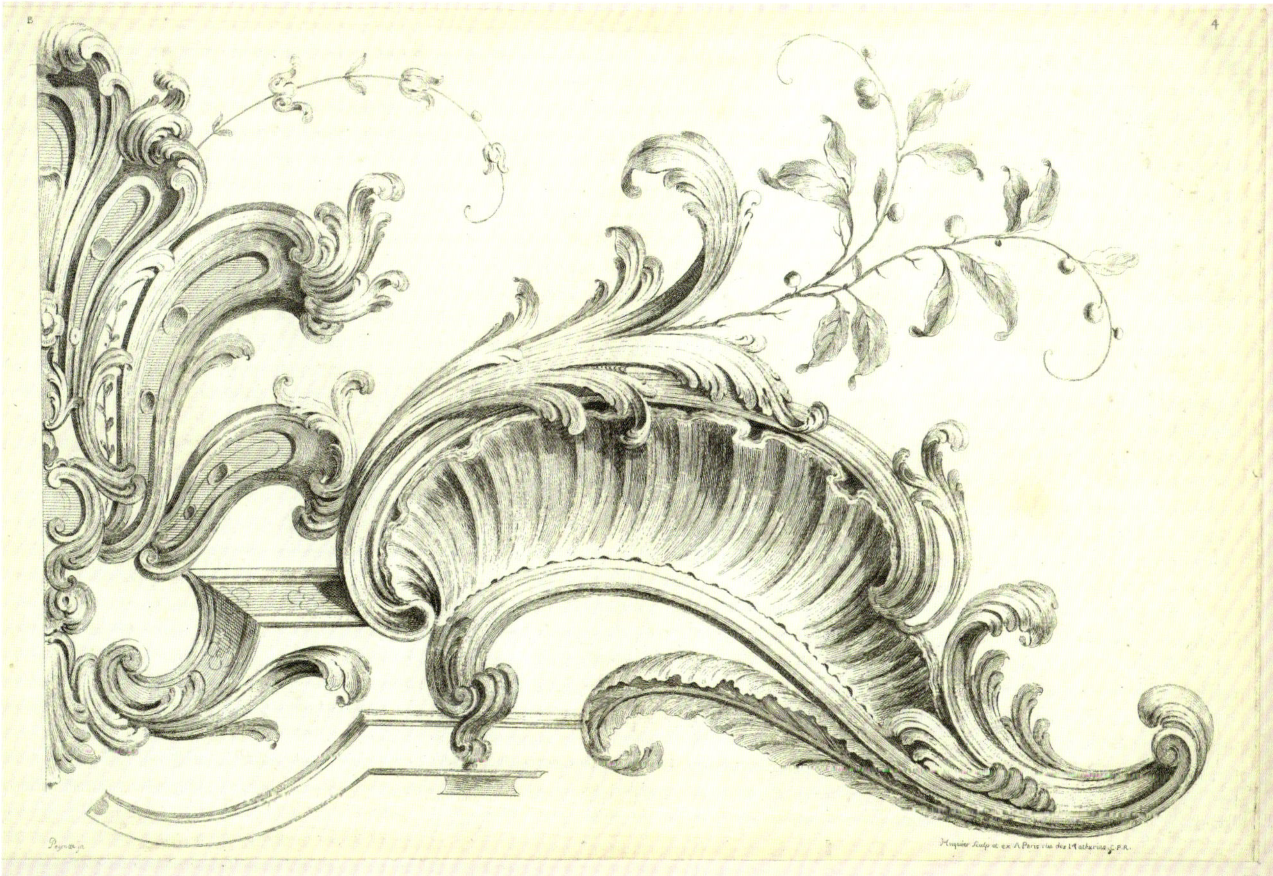

FIG. 25 Design for *Rocaille Decoration*, plate 4 in *Seconde Partie de divers Ornements*. Alexis Peyrotte (French, 1699–1769). Etched by Gabriel Huquier (French, 1695–1772). Paris, France, ca. 1745. Etching on white laid paper. Cooper-Hewitt, National Design Museum, Smithsonian Institution, Purchased for the Museum by the Advisory Council, 1921-6-213-10

respective German palaces. Maximillian II Emanuel had hired Germain Boffrand to design a hunting pavilion in the Netherlands and to redecorate his house at Saint-Cloud. And both brothers turned to the elder Cuvilliés to create new interiors in the latest French fashion for their residences in Germany.

Born in Flanders in 1695, then controlled by the Maximillian II, Cuvilliés entered the elector's service at the age of eleven.[48] Maximillian, recognizing Cuvilliés's artistic talent, brought him to Munich in 1715 and then sent him to Paris for architectural training (1720–24), where the young designer became familiar with Nicolas Pineau's emerging rocaille interior decoration. In 1725, Maximillian appointed Cuvilliés court architect of Bavaria under Josef Effner, who was also Paris-trained. Cuvilliés rose through the ranks during the succeeding reign of Elector Charles-Albert to become chief court architect in 1763, acquiring a noble title along the way. Through his many commissions in and around Munich, Cuvilliés introduced rococo style to Bavaria.

His major early commissions (1729–40) for the Wittelsbach courts encompassed the palace interiors at Brühl, including the pleasure palace dedicated to falconry, Falkenlust (1729–40), for Joseph Clemens's successor Clemens August; the renovation of the state apartments (Reiche Zimmer) in the royal palace in Munich, known as the Residenz (1730–37), for Charles Albert; and the architecture and interiors of the small pleasure retreat for pheasant hunting in the park of Nymphenburg palace, Amalienberg Pavilion (1734–39), for Charles Albert, considered one of the masterpieces of rococo decoration. Ten years later, in the declining years of rococo, he designed and constructed the Residenz Theater (1751–55) for the succeeding Bavarian elector Maximillian III Josef.

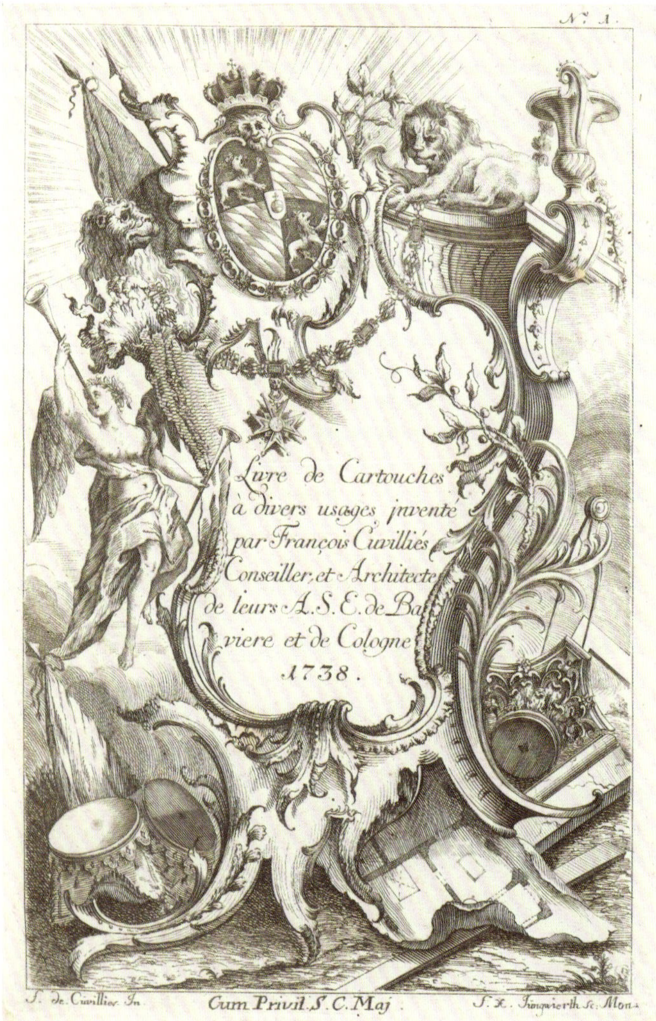

FIG. 26 Title page, *Livre de Cartouches à divers usages*. Jean-François Cuvilliés (Flemish, active Germany, 1695–1768). Etched and engraved by Franz-Xavier Jungwierth (German, 1720–1790). Munich, Germany, 1738. Etching and engraving on white laid paper. Cooper-Hewitt, National Design Museum, Smithsonian Institution, Purchased for the Museum by the Advisory Council, 1921-6-281-2

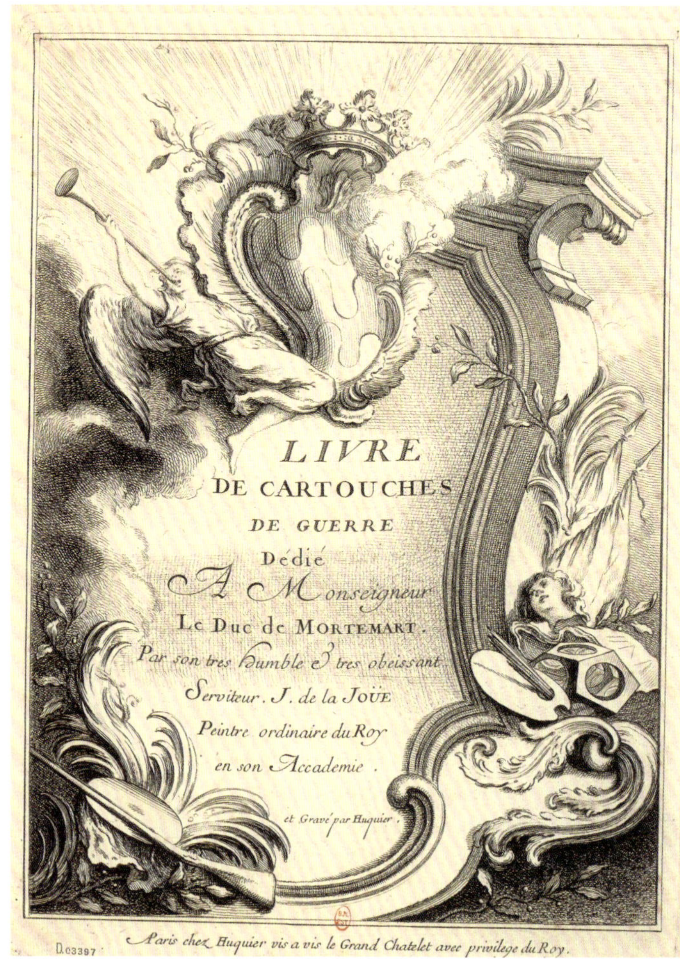

FIG. 27 Title page, *Livre de cartouches de Guerre*. Jacques de Lajoüe (French, 1687–1761). Etched by Gabriel Huquier (French, 1695–1772). Paris, France, 1736. Etching on white laid paper. Bibliothèque Nationale de France, Cabinet des Estampes et Photographie, Hd 64 b rés petit folio

With the dual goals of impressing the Wittelsbach electors with his genius and advancing his status in their courts, Cuvilliés turned out an extraordinary number of designs for ornament, totaling seventy-five series, published in Munich between 1738 and 1756. These included designs for cartouches, interior decoration, wall paneling, ceilings, furniture, wrought-iron work, and other decorative fantasies. Most of the 400 to 500 sheets were engraved by Cuvilliés's pupil, friend, and collaborator Charles-Albert de Lespilliez. Other interpreters of his designs included Franz-Xavier Jungwierth, Balthazar Sigmond Zedletzky (Sedlesky), Georges Sigmond Roesch, Joseph Kaltner, and his son, Cuvilliés the Younger. The two Cuvilliés must have been particular favorites of Léon Decloux, as he created or commissioned elaborate hand-drawn title pages for each of his seven albums devoted to their work.

Cuvilliés had no qualms about mining the printed designs of other French rococo designers who preceded had him. He would have had access to the original prints as well as pirated German editions of French prints published in Augsburg. A good number of the designer's prints elaborated on models by Jacques de Lajoüe. Cuvilliés's first series, *Livres de Cartouches propres à divers usages* (1738), devoted to the theme of battle, borrowed liberally from Lajoüe's highly successful *Livre de cartouches de Guerre*, published three years earlier.[49] (figs. 26, 27) Plates in Cuvilliés's *Livre Nouveau de Morceaux de Fantaisie* similarly derived from Lajoüe's variations on the fantasy theme in *Livre Nouveau de Douze Morceaux de Fantaisie* (figs. 28, 29).

Cuvilliés also appropriated ideas for furniture and metal objects from Meissonnier's *Oeuvre*. His design for a small sofa (*canapé*) with pineapple-motif upholstery beneath a wall mirror from *Dessins de lambris nouvellement inventés* (fig. 30) evolved directly from Meissonnier's upholstered canapé created for Count Bielinski (Fuhring, fig. 8), although Cuvilliés's design lightened and flattened the sculptural exuberance of Meissonnier's model. So too Cuvilliés' rocaille fireplace chenets in the *Livre de decoration de Lambris* (fig. 31) took their inspiration from Meissonnier's irregularly shaped chenets in Count Bielenski's cabinet.[50] (Fuhring, fig. 6) Characteristically, Cuvilliés lightened and upended the firedogs and placed them parallel to the picture plane—totally ignoring Meissonnier's foreshortened objects in space—and relied on the plan

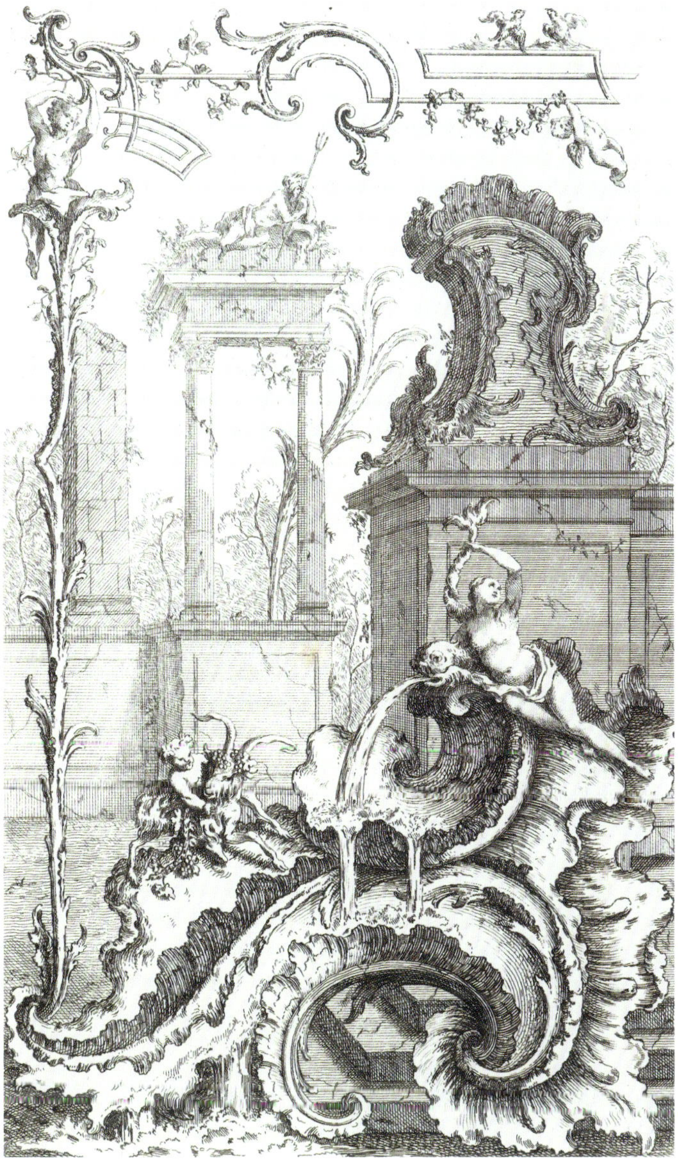

FIG. 28 *Rococo Cartouche*, in *Livre Nouveau de Morceaux de Fantaisie*. Jean-François Cuvilliés (Flemish, active Germany, 1695–1768). Etched and engraved by Charles-Albert de Lespilliez (Flemish, active Germany, 1723–1796). Munich, Germany, 1738–45. Etching and engraving on white laid paper. Cooper-Hewitt, National Design Museum, Smithsonian Institution, Purchased for the Museum by the Advisory Council, 1921-6-282-22

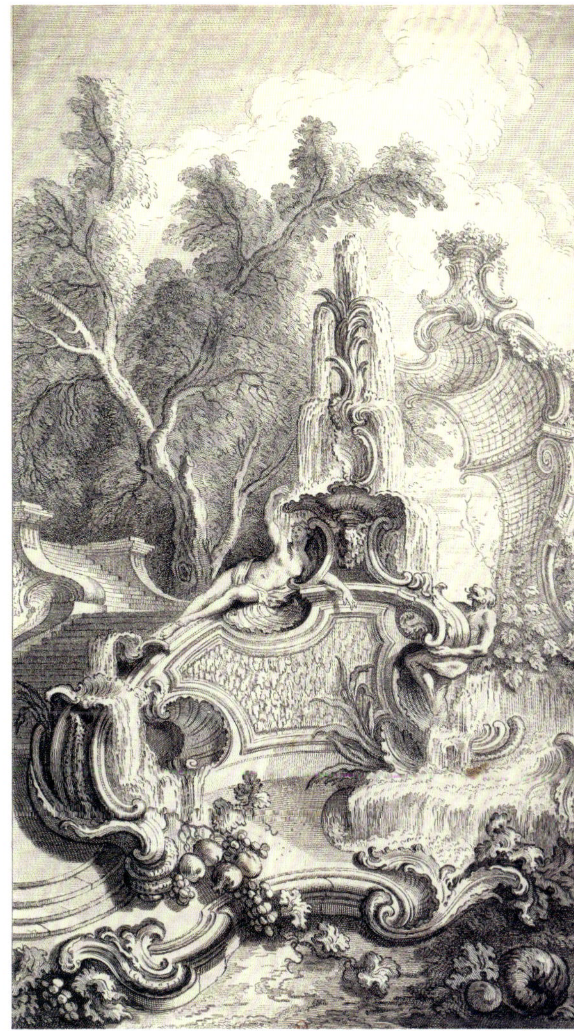

FIG. 29 *Fontaine et Bosquet*, in *Livre Nouveau de Douze Morceaux de Fantaisie*. Jacques de Lajoüe (French, 1687–1761). Etched and engraved by Philippe-Louis Compagnon-Desplaces (French, 1682–1739). Paris, France, 1737. Etching and engraving on white laid paper. Bibliothèque Nationale de France, Cabinet des Estampes et Photographie, Hd 64 Fol. rés./80

diagram to indicate the spatial depth of the chimney.

Cuvilliés's decorative brilliance truly resided in his creations for stucco-decorated ceilings and for decorative wall panels, both of which took advantage of the decorative traditions of stucco and carved gesso ornament in southern Germany. A talented group of craftsmen, including the stuccoist J. B. Zimmerman and wood-carvers Adam Pichler, Wenzel Mirofsky, and Joachim Dietrich, formed Cuvilliés's team of specialists, who executed his wild design ideas. His elaborate creations for stucco ceilings incorporating fountain motifs in the corners would never have been conceived in France (fig. 32). In the area of wall-panel decorations, Cuvilliés was especially prolific, producing two series of elaborate grotesques (fig. 33) to be interpreted in gesso on the interiors of state rooms, replacing the wall paintings in French interiors. Designs like these were used in the Residenz and at Amalienburg. One of these grotesques, revised in a smaller format, also found its way onto furniture, including a gilt-wood commode in the Getty Museum (similar pieces are in the Metropolitan Museum and in the Residenz) attributed to Dietrich.[51] (figs. 34, 35) Due to the sculpted-wood and gesso traditions in Germany, carved and gilded ornament sometimes replaced the gilt-bronze orna-

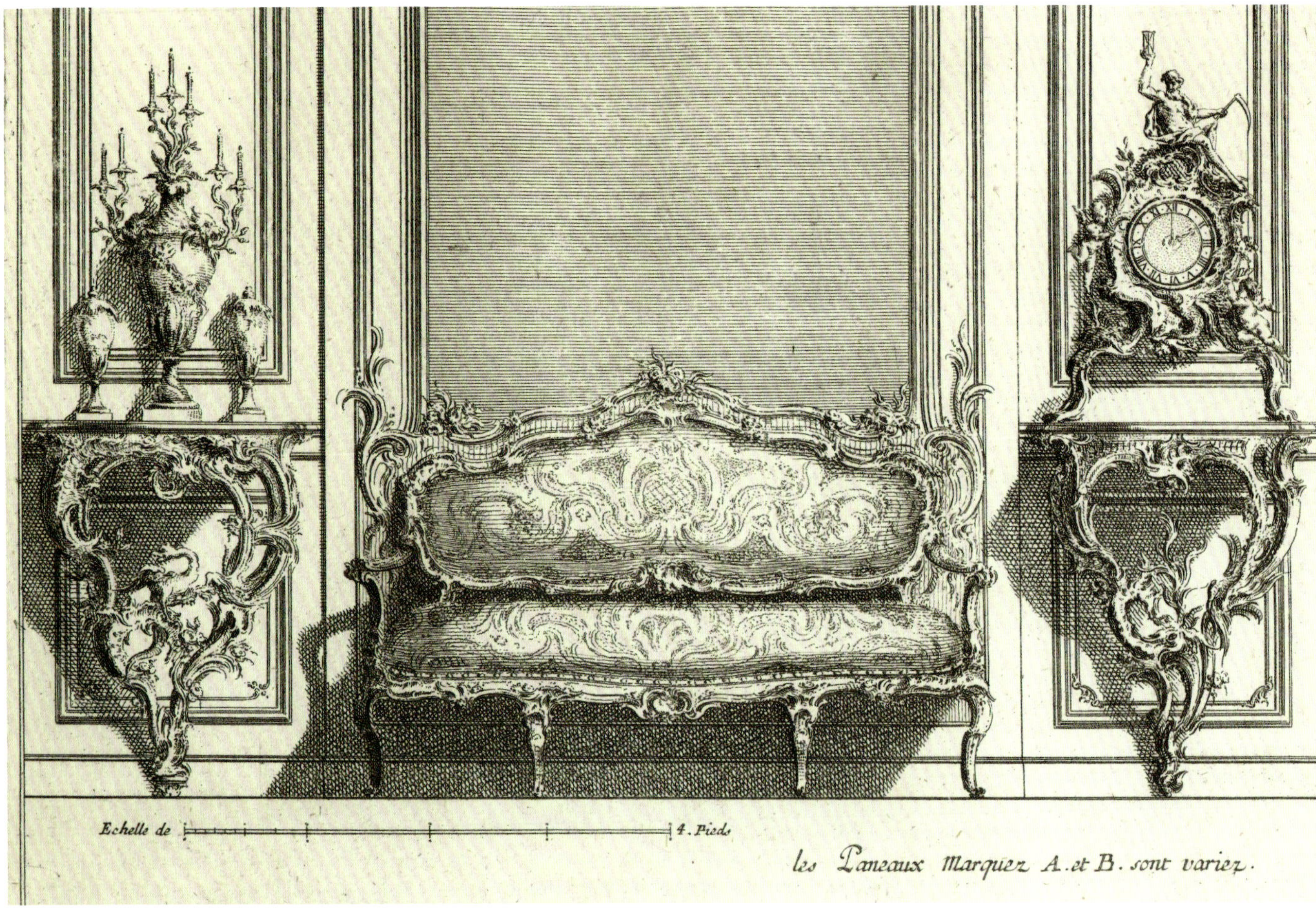

FIG. 30 *Decoration de Lambris pour un Cabinet, in Dessins de Lambris nouvellement inventés.* (detail). Jean-François Cuvilliés (Flemish, active Germany, 1695–1768). Etched and engraved by Charles-Albert de Lespilliez (Flemish, active Germany, 1723–1796). Munich, Germany, 1745–55. Etching and engraving on white laid paper. Cooper-Hewitt, National Design Museum, Smithsonian Institution, Purchased for the Museum by the Advisory Council, 1921-6-283-88

ment that prevailed in France. Another one of Cuvilliés's designs for a more German-style bombé commode appears to have served as inspiration for a commode from the Schloss Seehof, in the Sheafer collection at the Metropolitan Museum of Art (figs. 36, 37).

All of the Cuvilliés team's efforts crystallized in the lavish interiors of Amalienburg Pavilion, considered the designer's masterpiece (fig. 38). The resplendent blue and silver circular Mirror Room had an undulating coved cornice, derived from Boffrand's influential Salon de la Princesse of 1738–40 in the Hôtel de Soubise, which displayed three levels of silvered gesso natural motifs—birds, animals, fountains, trees, and nymphs—that spill onto the stucco ceiling itself. The mirrored walls multiplied and reflected the richness of Cuvilliés's personal design vision.

While Cuvilliés's interpretation of French rococo dominated design in southern Germany, another group of architects, designers, woodcarvers, and stuccoists worked in northern Germany, in and around Berlin. They included Johann August Nahl the Elder (1710–1785)[52]; Johann Michael Hoppenhaupt II (1709–1778-86) and his brother Johann Christian Hoppenhaupt (active 1742–ca. 1778-86)[53]; and architect Georg Wenzeslaus von Knobelsdorff (1699–1753), who worked for Frederick II von Hohenzollern (the Great), King of Prussia.

Upon acceeding to the throne in 1740, Frederick began a series of rococo additions or renovations to existing palaces, including Charlottenburg and the Königliches Schloss (never executed) in Berlin and the Stadtschloss in Potsdam. The rococo style of the day dovetailed perfectly with his pursuit of pleasure, sensual enjoyment, literature, music, and stimulating conversation. Built from scratch according to Frederick's plans by Knobelsdorff, his much-beloved Schloss Sanssouci

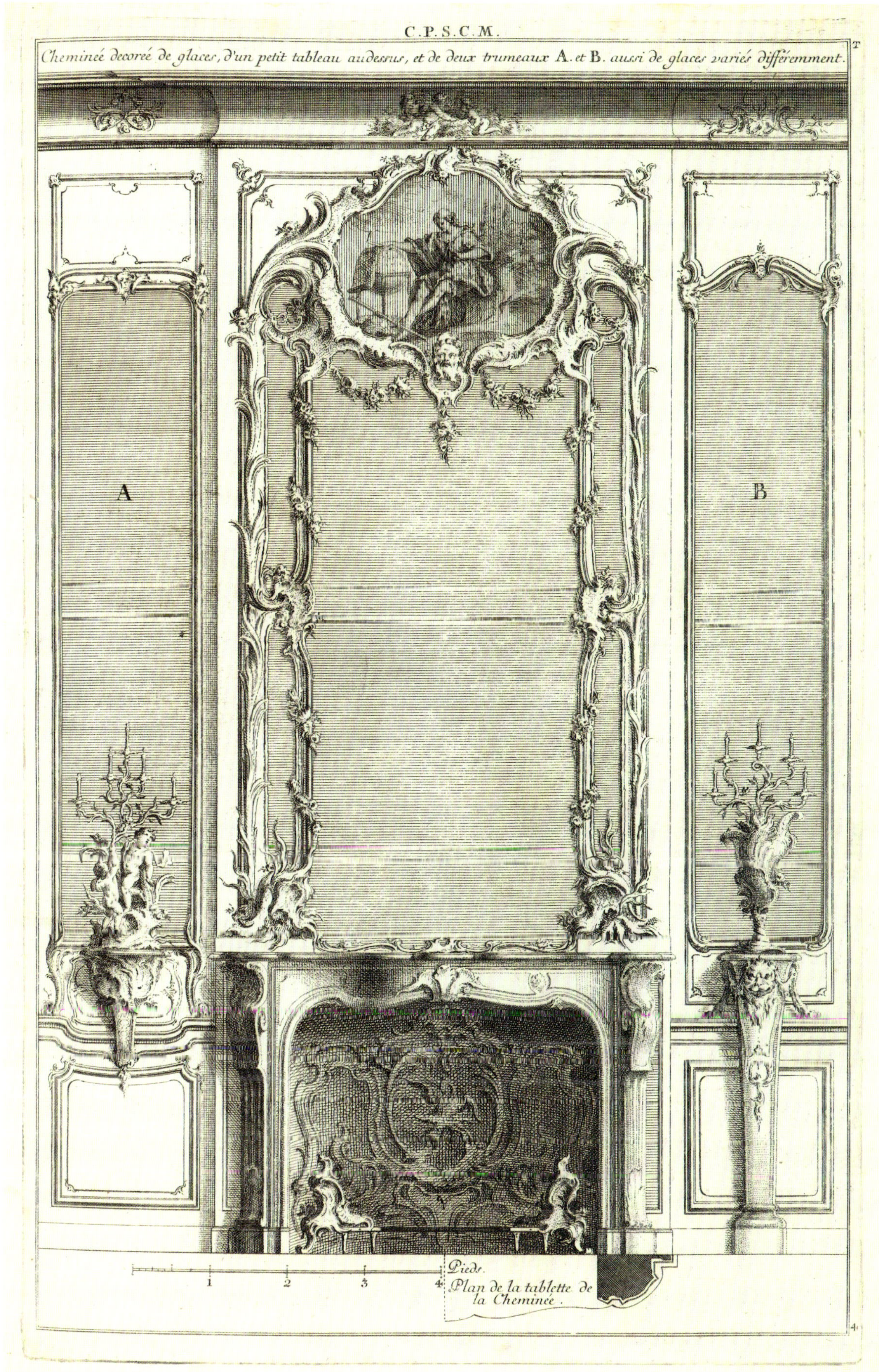

FIG. 31 *Cheminée decorée de glaces*, in *Livre de décorations de lambris*. Jean-François Cuvilliés (Flemish, active Germany, 1695–1768). Etched and engraved by Charles-Albert de Lespilliez (Flemish, active Germany, 1723–1796). Munich, Germany, 1745–55. Etching and engraving on white laid paper. Cooper-Hewitt, National Design Museum, Smithsonian Institution, Purchased for the Museum by the Advisory Council, 1921-6-283-108

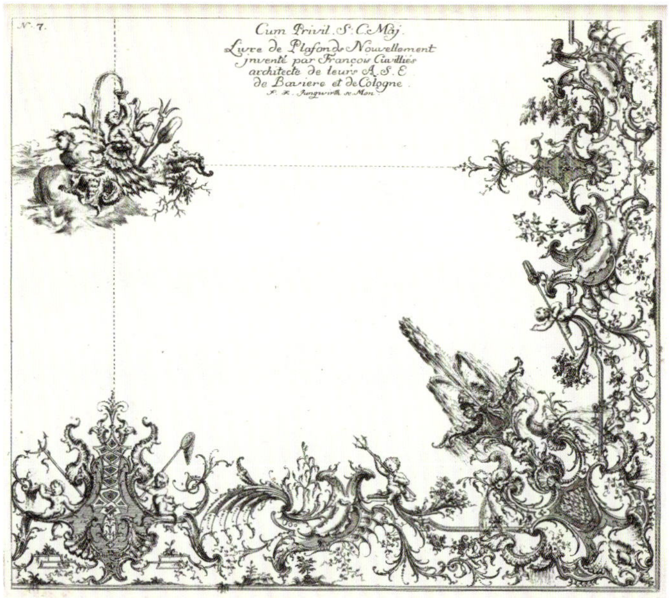

FIG. 32 Ceiling Design, in *Livre de Plafonds nouvellement inventés*. Jean-François Cuvilliés (Flemish, active Germany, 1695–1768). Engraved by Franz-Xavier Jungwierth (German, 1720–1790). Munich, Germany, 1738–45. Etching and engraving on white laid paper. Cooper-Hewitt, National Design Museum, Smithsonian Institution, Purchased for the Museum by the Advisory Council, 1921-6-282-9

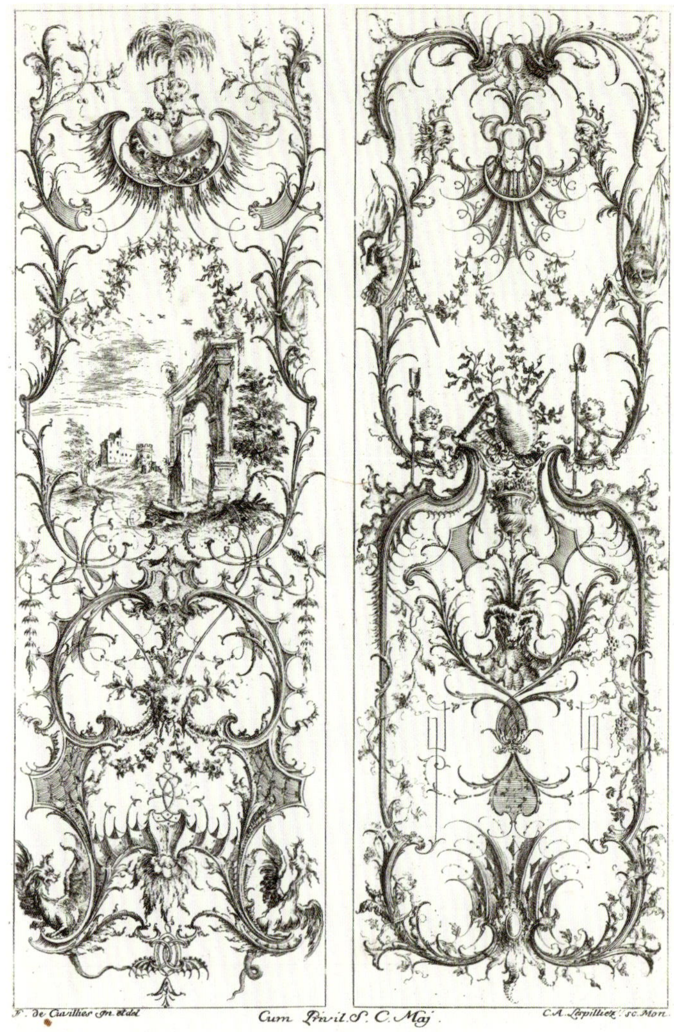

FIG. 33 Design for Two Panels of Grotesques, in *Livre Nouveau de paneaux à divers usages*. Jean-François Cuvilliés (Flemish, active Germany 1695–1768). Engraved by Charles-Albert de Lespilliez (Flemish, 1723–1796). Munich, Germany, 1738–45. Etching and engraving on off-white laid paper. Cooper-Hewitt, National Design Museum, Smithsonian Institution, Purchased for the Museum by the Advisory Council, 1921-6-282-4

(1745–47) is universally recognized—particularly after its latest renovation in the 1980s—as the finest flowering of the Federician rococo style. Modeled on the single-story Grand Trianon at Versailles, Sanssouci served as a carefree retreat from Berlin and the War of the Austrian Succession, where the king relaxed among his vineyards and entertained the likes of Voltaire.

Frederick turned to Nahl (whom he appointed *directeur des ornements* in 1744) to handle the interiors of Sanssouci after the designer had supervised renovation designs for the king's apartment in Charlottenburg and created the royal apartments in Potsdam's Stadtschloss (destroyed after World War II). For Sanssouci, Nahl designed the Library and the Concert Room (Leben, fig. 13). His drawing from the Decloux collection *Design for a Wall Panel with Fireplace* (fig. 39) shows his light and airy interpretation of rococo ornament in comparison to Cuvilliés's more dense and exuberant decoration. The feathery plant ornament framing the central painting sprouts graceful raffle leaves that curve over the central field and onto the chimney panel; a floral vine dips down in a graceful, asymmetrical loop over the central painting; pastoral-themed trophies are incorporated into the framing decoration and the rocaille ornament on the pilasters echoes and harmonizes with the framing decoration. These elements all recall Nahl's designs for the chimney wall in the Bronzesaal of the Potsdam Stadtschloss, as well as the Library and Concert Room at Sanssouci. The Cooper-Hewitt drawing could have been connected to one of these projects or a similar commission.[54]

Finding Frederick's demands too oppressive, Nahl fled Berlin for Strasbourg, later settling in Bern. The completion of his Sanssouci interiors fell to Johann Michael Hoppenhaupt II and his brother. The Hoppenhaupts also designed interiors in Frederick's last architectural project, the Neues Palais (1763–69), in the park near Sanssouci. Some Neues Palais interiors by Hoppenhaupt, in the print series *Wandfüllungen nebst Kaminen, Türen, Spiegeln*, and coach designs are in the Decloux col-

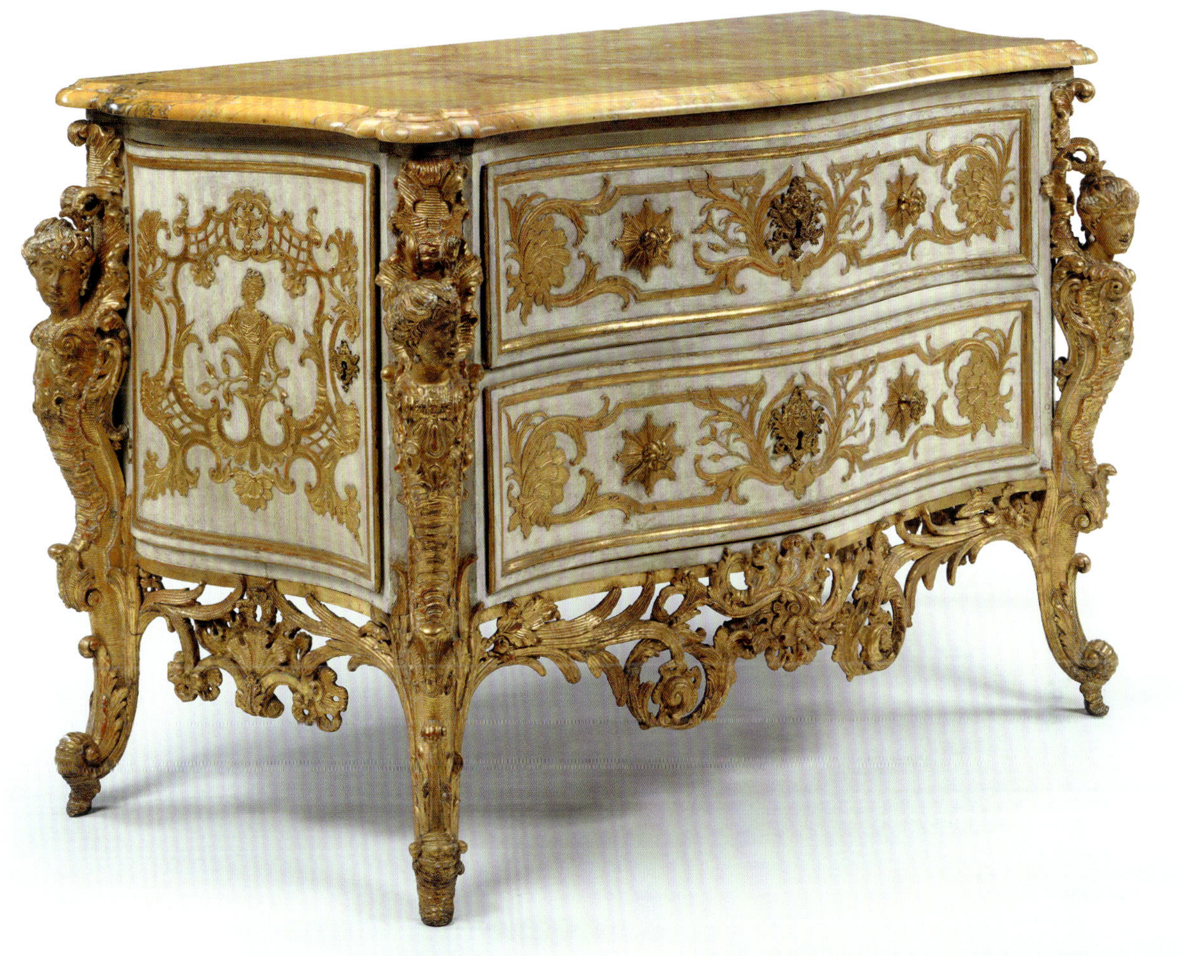

FIG. 35 Commode. Attributed to Joachim Dietrich (German, 1690–1753) after Jean-François Cuvilliés (Flemish, active Germany, 1695–1768). Munich, Germany, ca. 1745. Pine, gilt-bronze, jaune rosé de Brignolles marble, paint. The J. Paul Getty Museum, 72.DA.63

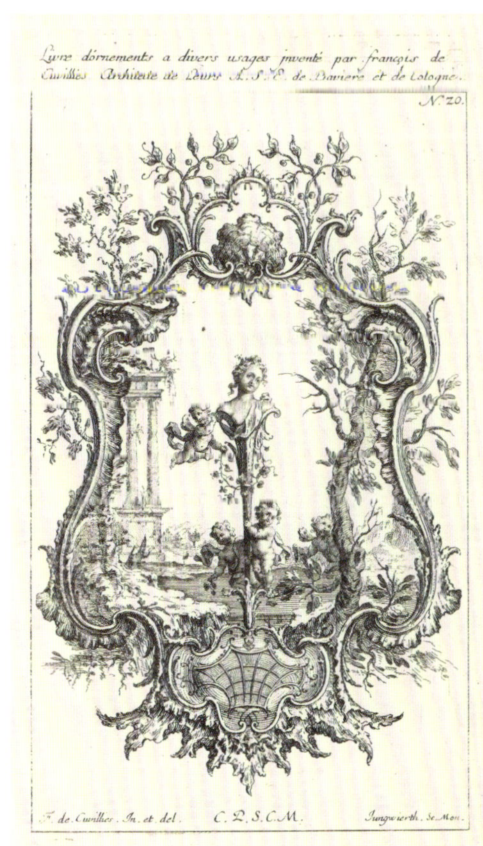

FIG. 34 Cartouche Design, in *Livre d'ornemens à divers usages*. Jean-François Cuvilliés (Flemish, active Germany, 1695–1768). Etched and engraved by Franz-Xaver Jungwierth (German, 1720–1790). Munich, Germany, 1738. Etching and engraving on cream laid paper. Cooper-Hewitt, National Design Museum, Smithsonian Institution, Purchased for the Museum by the Advisory Council, 1921-6-281-86

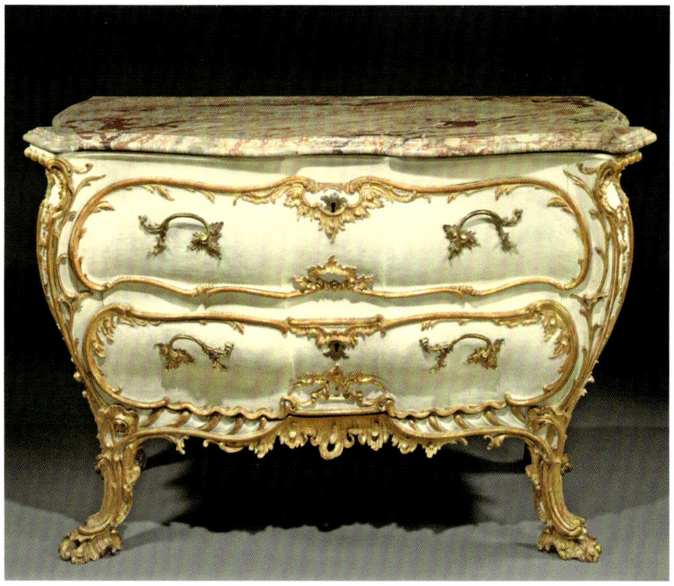

FIG. 37 Commode. The manner of Jean-François Cuvilliés (Flemish, active in Germany, 1695–1758). Franconia, Germany, ca. 1765. Painted and gilded pine, gilt bronze, marble. The Metropolitan Museum of Art, The Lesley and Emma Sheafer Collection, Bequest of Emma A. Sheafer; 1973, 74.356.129

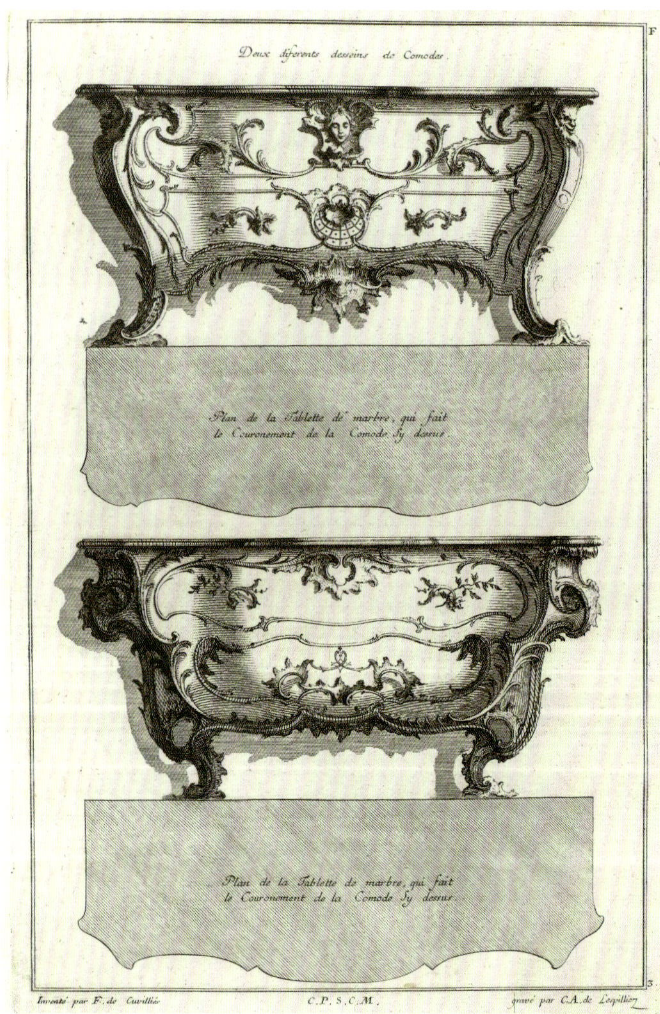

FIG. 36 Deux diférents desseins de Comodes, in *Livre de diférents desseins de Comodes*. Jean-François Cuvilliés (Flemish, active Germany, 1695–1768). Etched and engraved by Charles-Albert de Lespilliez (Flemish, active Germany, 1723–1796). Munich, Germany, 1745–55. Etching and engraving on off-white laid paper. Cooper-Hewitt, National Design Museum, Smithsonian Institution, Purchased for the Museum by the Advisory Council, 1921-6-285-35

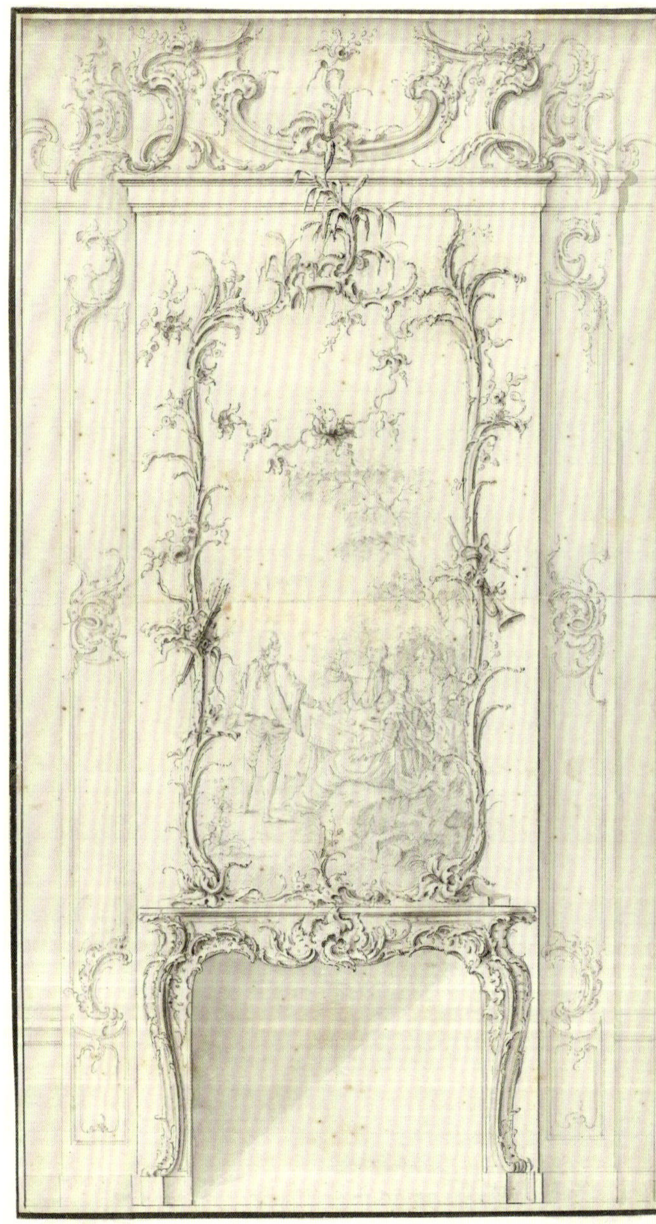

FIG. 39 *Design for a Wall Panel with Fireplace*. Johann August Nahl the Elder (German, 1710–1785). Berlin, Germany, 1745. Pen and black ink, brush and gray and light violet wash, graphite on white laid paper, ruled border in pen and black ink. Cooper-Hewitt, National Design Museum, Smithsonian Institution, Purchased for the Museum by the Advisory Council, 1911-28-36

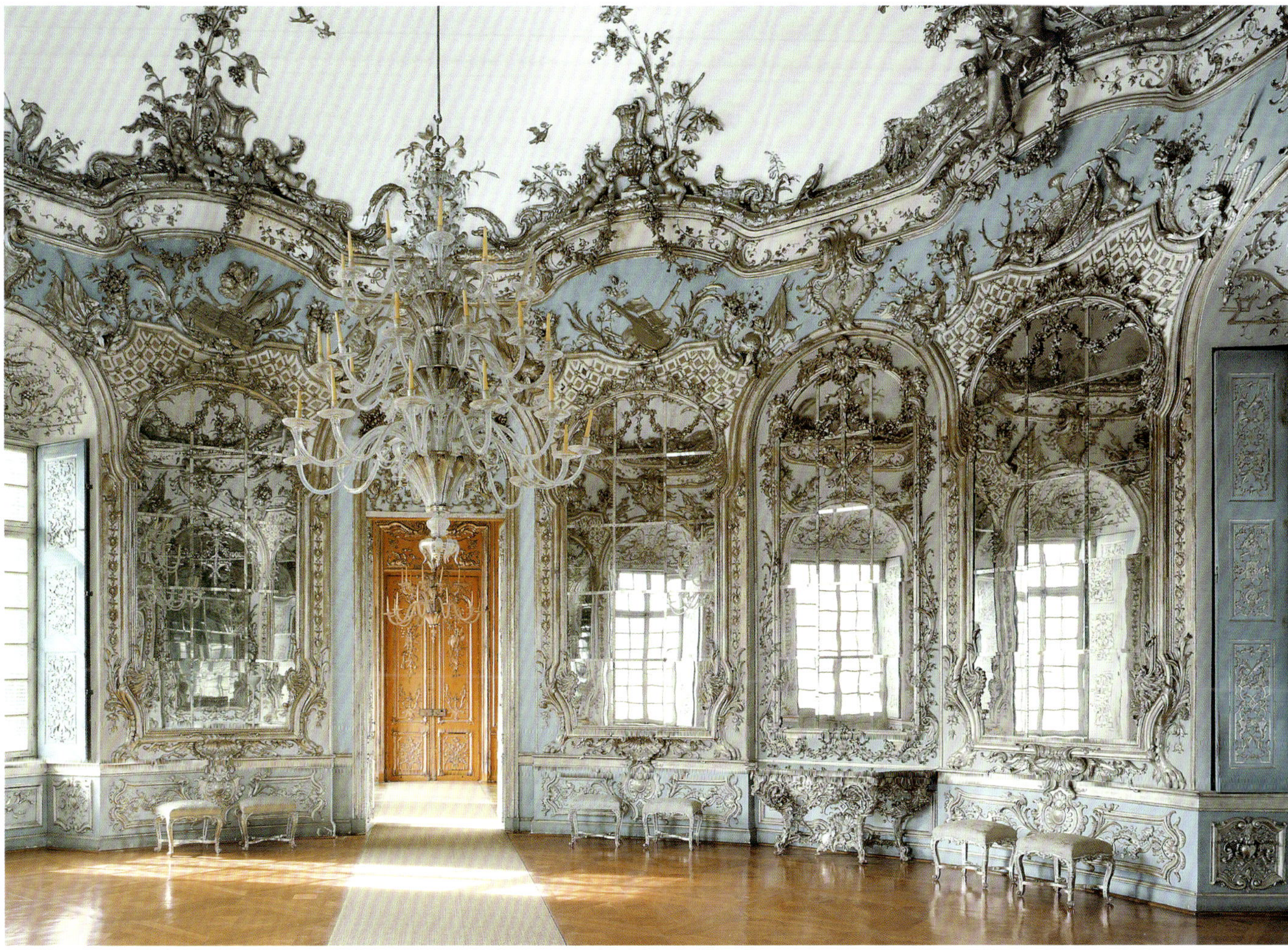

FIG. 38 Mirror Room, Amalienberg Pavilion, Nymphenburg Palace. Jean-François Cuvilliés (Flemish, active Germany, 1695–1768). Nymphenburg, Germany, 1734–39

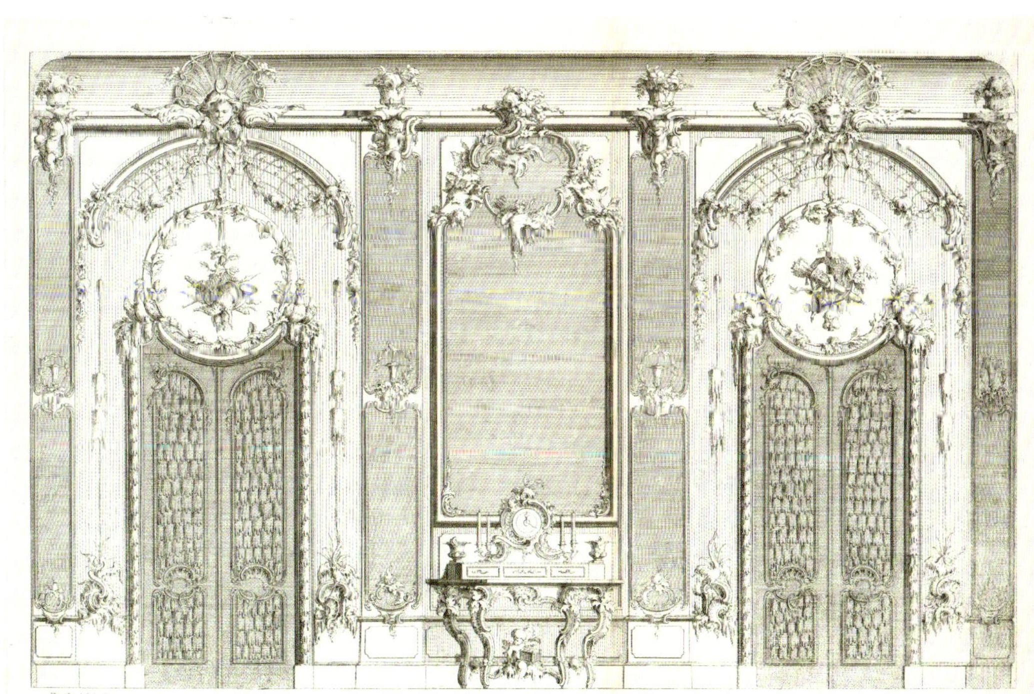

FIG. 40 Design for a Wall Elevation, in *WandFüllungen nebst Kaminen, Türen, Spiegeln*. Johann Michael Hoppenhaupt II (German, 1709–1778–86). Engraved by Johann Wilhelm Meil (German, 1733–1805). Berlin, Germany, 1753. Etching and engraving on white laid paper. Cooper-Hewitt, National Design Museum, Smithsonian Institution, Purchased for the Museum by the Advisory Council, 1921-6-221-5

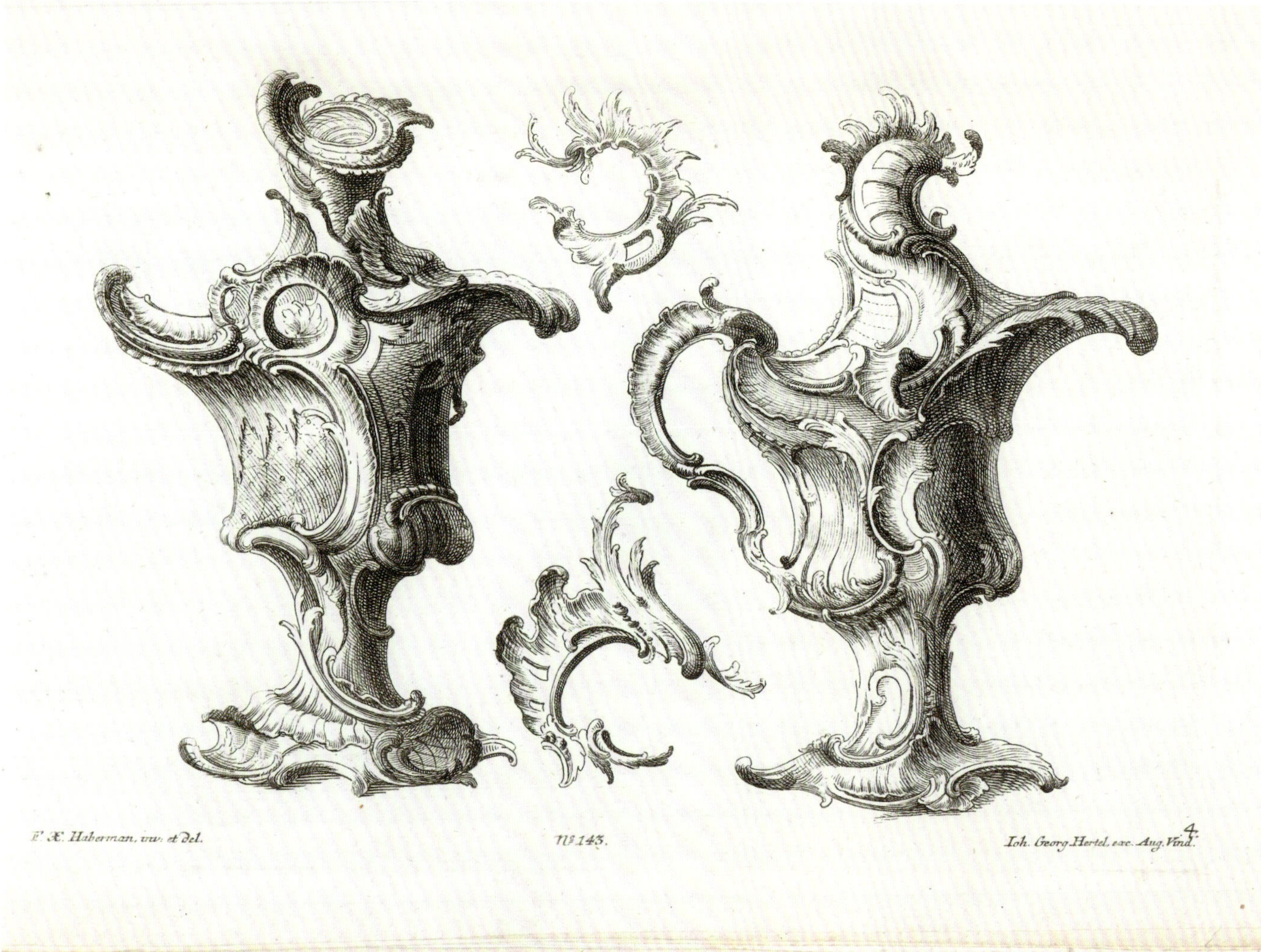

FIG. 42 *Two Designs for Ewer-shaped Ornaments.* Franz Xaver Habermann (German, 1721–1796). Etched and engraved by Johann Georg Hertel (German, ca. 1700–1776). Augsburg, Germany, ca. 1750. Etching and engraving on white laid paper. Cooper-Hewitt, National Design Museum, Smithsonian Institution, Purchased for the Museum by the Advisory Council, 1921-6-317-28

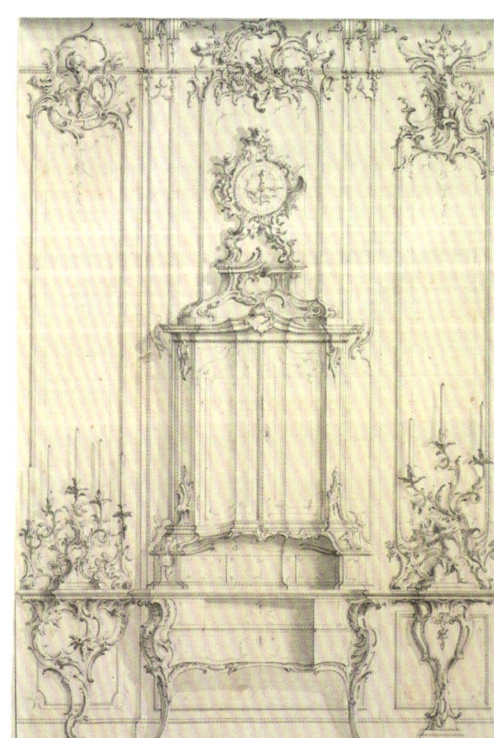

FIG. 41 *Design for an Interior Elevation, for Bureaux sur Fond de Lambris.* Franz Xaver Habermann (German, 1721–1796). Augsburg, Germany, ca. 1760. Pen and black ink, brush and gray wash, graphite on cream laid paper, red chalk on verso. Museum of Art, Rhode Island School of Design, Museum Works of Art Fund, 46.535

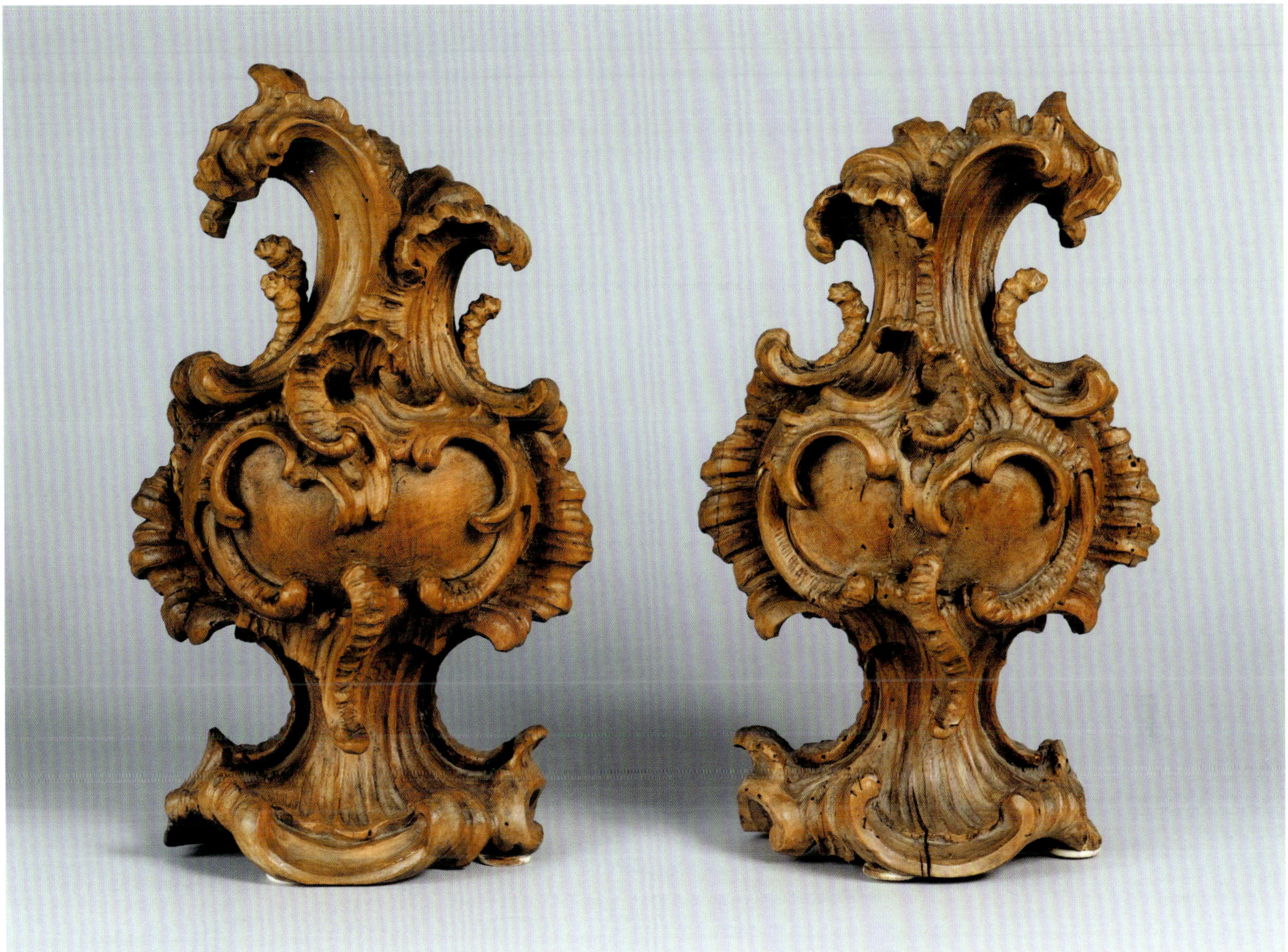

FIG. 43 Wall ornaments or finials. Southern Germany, ca. 1760. Linden wood. Courtesy of L'Antiquaire and The Connoisseur, Inc.

lection. *Design for a Wall Elevation (Upper Concert Room, Neues Palais)* (fig. 40) suggests, particularly in the abstract depiction of shellwork on the doors, Hoppenhaupt's aesthetic sensibility, which, though influenced by Nahl's naturalism, tended toward a heavier, more stylized depiction of nature.

Another designer whose creative ideas percolated through the design community by way of numerous pattern prints was the sculptor, designer, and printmaker Franz Xaver Habermann (1721–1796). Living in Augsburg, a center for metalwork and related graphic arts, Habermann turned to publishing his designs when commissions for wood sculptural decorations became scarce. Between 500 and 600 ornament prints of his design ideas, covering a broad range of decorative-arts objects and ornamental motifs, were produced by two Augsburg publishers, Johann Georg Hertel (1700/01–1776) and Martin Engelbrecht (ca. 1684–1756). Habermann's design influence was also spread by the school of design that he founded in 1781, where he taught architecture and perspective until his death.

About thirty-three of Habermann's designs fill most of one ornament-print album from the Decloux collection. These prints, which were published in a series of four plates each, include designs for rococo cartouches framed or intertwined with raffle leaves, ivy, flowers, and putti; designs for rococo ornament framed mirrors, console tables, candelabra, and sconces; as well as wall elevations with stoves, fireplaces, and mirrors over console tables. A group of autograph drawings for wall elevations with furniture is connected to Habermann's folio *Bureaux sur fond de lambris*.[55] His *Design for an Interior Elevation* (fig. 41), delicately and deftly rendered in pen and black ink and gray wash, shows a secretary with a clock above it, framed by two console tables supporting girandoles. The fact that nothing in the drawing is symmetrical indicates that this design presented two examples of each category of object to be selected by a wood-carver, metalworker, or client to fabricate into three-dimensional objects. The designs on the right side of the drawing appear to be slightly more neoclassical in spirit than those on the left, suggesting the direction in which design was moving after the middle of the century.

Habermann showed his training as a sculptor to dazzling effect in his suite of printed designs for ewer-like ornaments (fig. 42). These totally fantastic, "boisterous rococo"[56] forms would have enabled a silversmith or wood-carver to demonstrate his talent for replicating cartouches, flowers, icicles, and other forms of rococo ornament. As outrageous as these designs may seem, they could have inspired a pair of carved wood ornaments, possibly intended for wall ornaments resting on brackets or as finials on domestic or eccelesiastical furniture, since

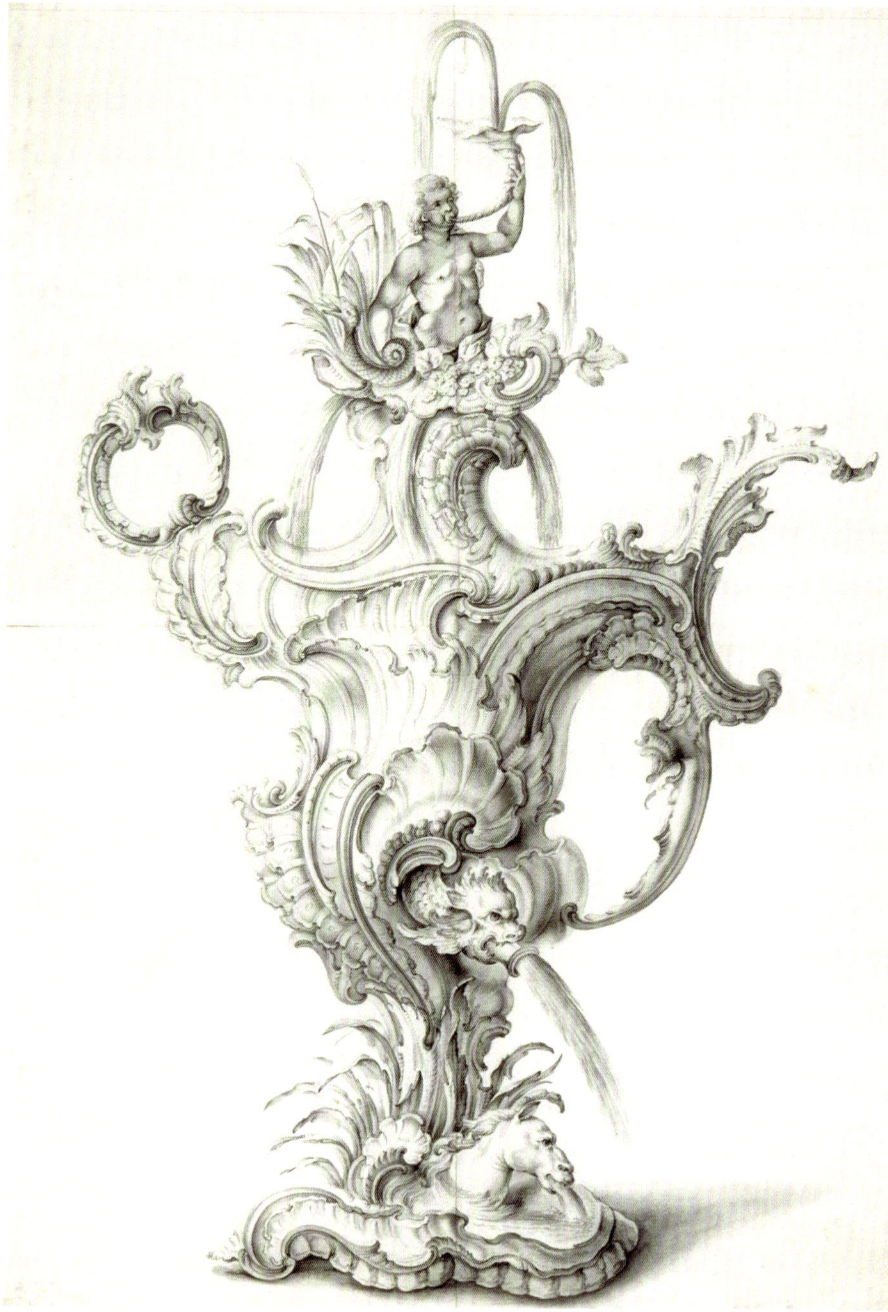

FIG. 44 Design for *Ornament*. Circle of Franz Xaver Habermann (German, 1721–1796). Augsburg, Germany, ca. 1750. Pen and black ink, brush and wash on white laid paper. Collection of Horace Wood Brock

they are not hollow and therefore could not have held anything.[57] (fig. 43) These prints, or something very close to them, may have prompted the Design for *Ornament* in the form of a ewer with a triton blowing a horn spouting water (fig. 44). While the function of this drawing remains a mystery (its current designation as a design for a table fountain seems doubtful), its execution appears to be close to the detailed, punctilious hand of Habermann's wall elevation discussed above.

Like Habermann, Johann Wolfgang Baumgartner (1712–1761) was based in Augsburg, where he supplied preparatory drawings for print publishers in addition to painting in oil and fresco.[58] His drawings are particularly noteworthy for their large scale and their combination of narrative and rococo ornamental elements elaborated with fluid gray washes and white gouache highlighting on blue paper. An unpublished series of four interiors (figs. 45–48)—a dining room, bedroom, cellar, and kitchen—probably executed as book illustrations, provides stunning examples of Baumgartner's unique integration of figures, landscape, architecture, and ornament in a unified, sinuous rococo composition.

This essay has looked at examples of rococo ornament prints and drawings, focusing on Cooper-Hewitt's Decloux collection. The *Rococo: The Continuing Curve* exhibition and book provide a much-needed examination of these holdings, one of the world's major deposits of rococo (and neoclassical) works on paper for the decorative arts. Our hope is that the entire collection will be catalogued and published on the Web for scholarly use and public enjoyment in the near future.

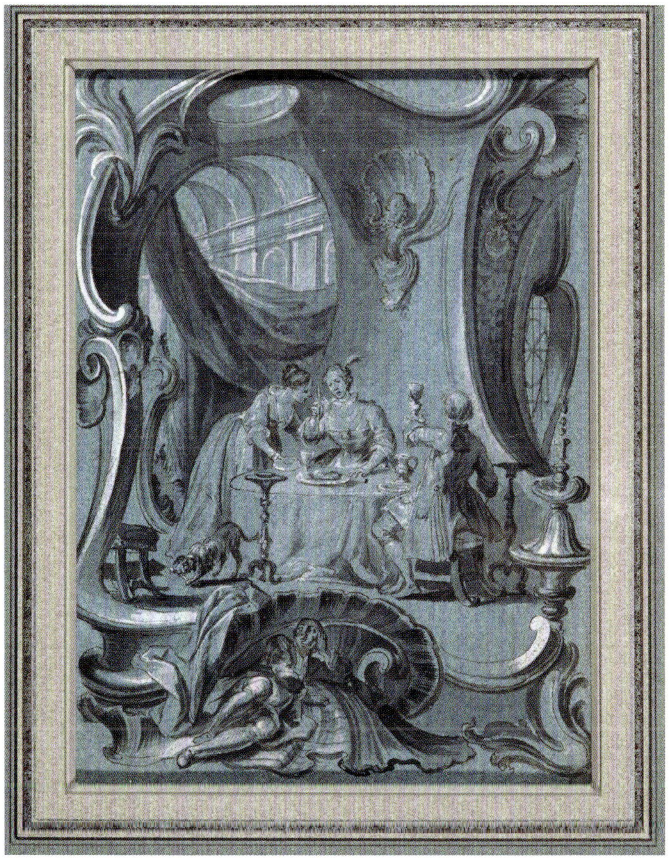

FIG. 45 Design for Illustration: *Dining Room*. Johann Wolfgang Baumgartner (German, 1712–1761). Augsburg, Germany, 1740s. Pen and black ink, brush and wash, white gouache on blue laid paper. Collection of Horace Wood Brock

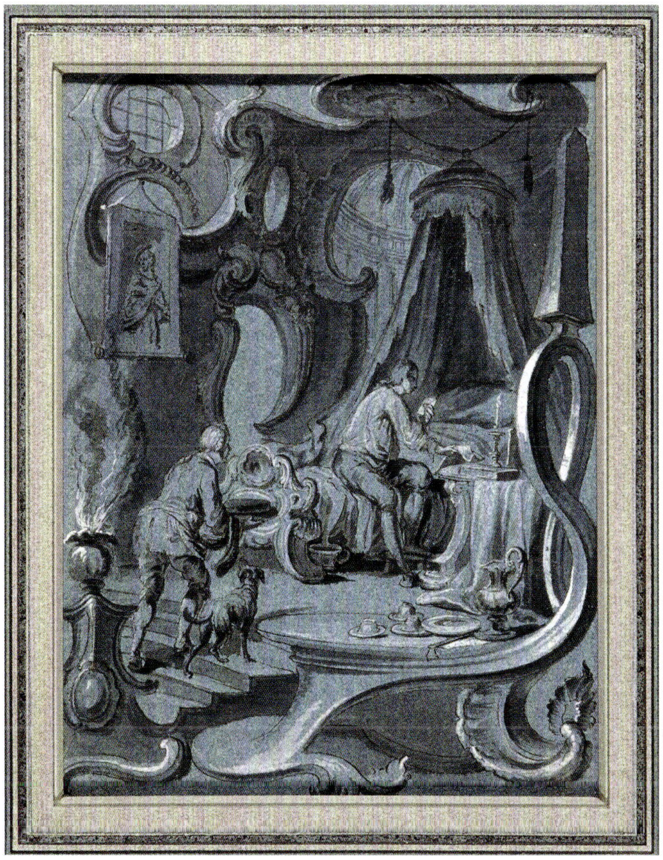

FIG. 46 Design for Illustration: *Bedroom*. Johann Wolfgang Baumgartner (German, 1712–1761). Augsburg, Germany, 1740s. Pen and black ink, brush and wash, white gouache on blue laid paper. Collection of Horace Wood Brock

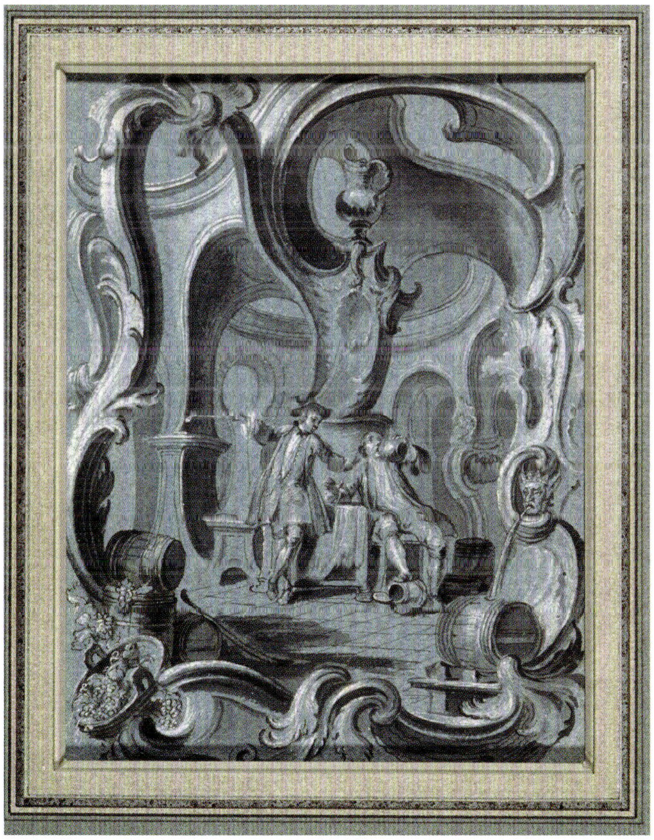

FIG. 47 Design for Illustration: *Cellar*. Johann Wolfgang Baumgartner (German, 1712–1761). Augsburg, Germany, 1740s. Pen and black ink, brush and wash, white gouache on blue laid paper. Collection of Horace Wood Brock

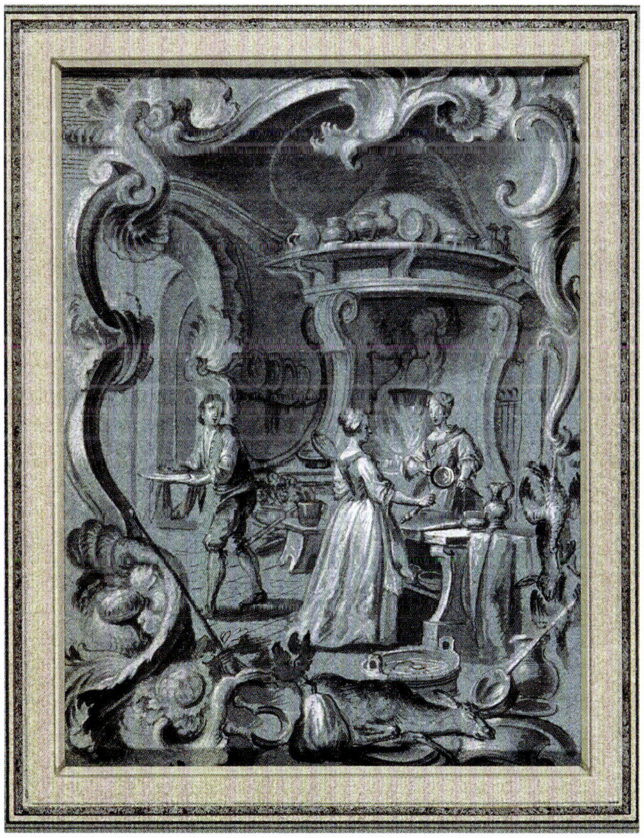

FIG. 48 Design for Illustration: *Kitchen*. Johann Wolfgang Baumgartner (German, 1712–1761). Augsburg, Germany, 1740s. Pen and black ink, brush and wash, white gouache on blue laid paper. Collection of Horace Wood Brock

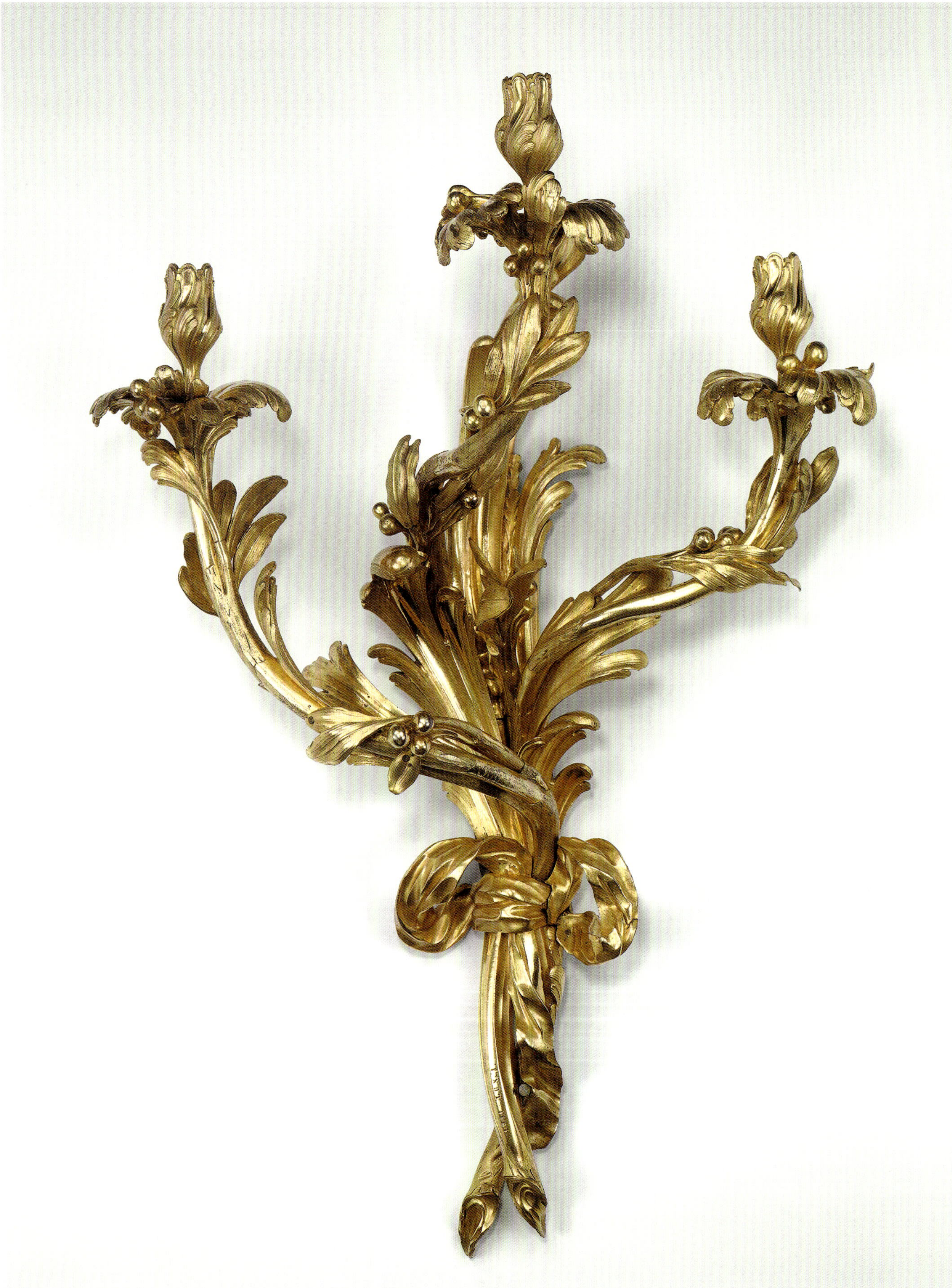

fig. 15 Wall light (one of a pair). François-Thomas Germain (French, 1726–1791). Paris, France, 1756. Gilt bronze. The J. Paul Getty Museum, 81.DF.96

Louis XV Style

Penelope Hunter-Stiebel

In France, rococo style is termed *style Louis XV* or *style Pompadour*, for the Marquise de Pompadour (née Jeanne-Antoinette Poisson, 1721–1764), also known as Madame de Pompadour, the king's official mistress from 1745 until her death. Informality eroded the grandeur of Versailles during the minority of Louis XV, while the libertine regent, Philippe, duc d'Orléans, held court in Paris. The taste for private environments of sensuous appeal received royal sanction in 1738, when the young Louis XV himself banished the formal trappings of his apartments at Versailles to assert his own preference for intimacy through the renovation of his surroundings.[1] Decorating with sinuous, organic designs became a major hobby for the king and Madame de Pompadour. Her successor, Madame du Barry, favored neoclassical novelty, but Louis XV remained faithful to the curvilinear comforts of the style identified with his reign.

MENUISERIE

Furniture was a major form of aesthetic expression in eighteenth-century France. Furniture-making was divided into two branches: carved wood furniture (*menuiserie*) and veneered furniture or cabinetwork (*ébénisterie*). The medieval Paris guild of *menuisiers*, which covered several specialties including coach makers, was dominated by the joiners who made seat furniture, frames, and consoles. Silver lay at the source of innovation in this conservative group, which was called upon to follow the sculptural forms of the cast-silver furniture that Louis XIV had commissioned for Versailles but later melted down to pay for his wars. Most menuiserie was considered part of the architecture of an interior: seating furniture was ordered in sets with settees and chairs to stand against the walls, and console tables were designed to be the climactic statement of the ornament carved in the wall paneling of a room. Thus the menuisiers had to accommodate the innovations of the architects and designers that clients hired for interior renovations. The unified concept was short-lived, however, as sets were broken up and components reused in different contexts when rooms were redone.

It is difficult to give exact dates for the evolution of baroque forms, which began to soften during the regency to become the full-blown Louis XV style. However, Pierre Verlet's study of the meticulous documentation of acquisitions that passed through the royal furniture warehouse (*Gardemeuble*) provided invaluable benchmarks in a series of five consoles made to support stucco tabletops illustrating the royal forests. Two consoles delivered in 1730 and 1731 established the basic model of S- and C-scroll legs and a central cartouche for the royal coat of arms. By 1737, the scrolls became sinuous, with embellishments carved to evoke

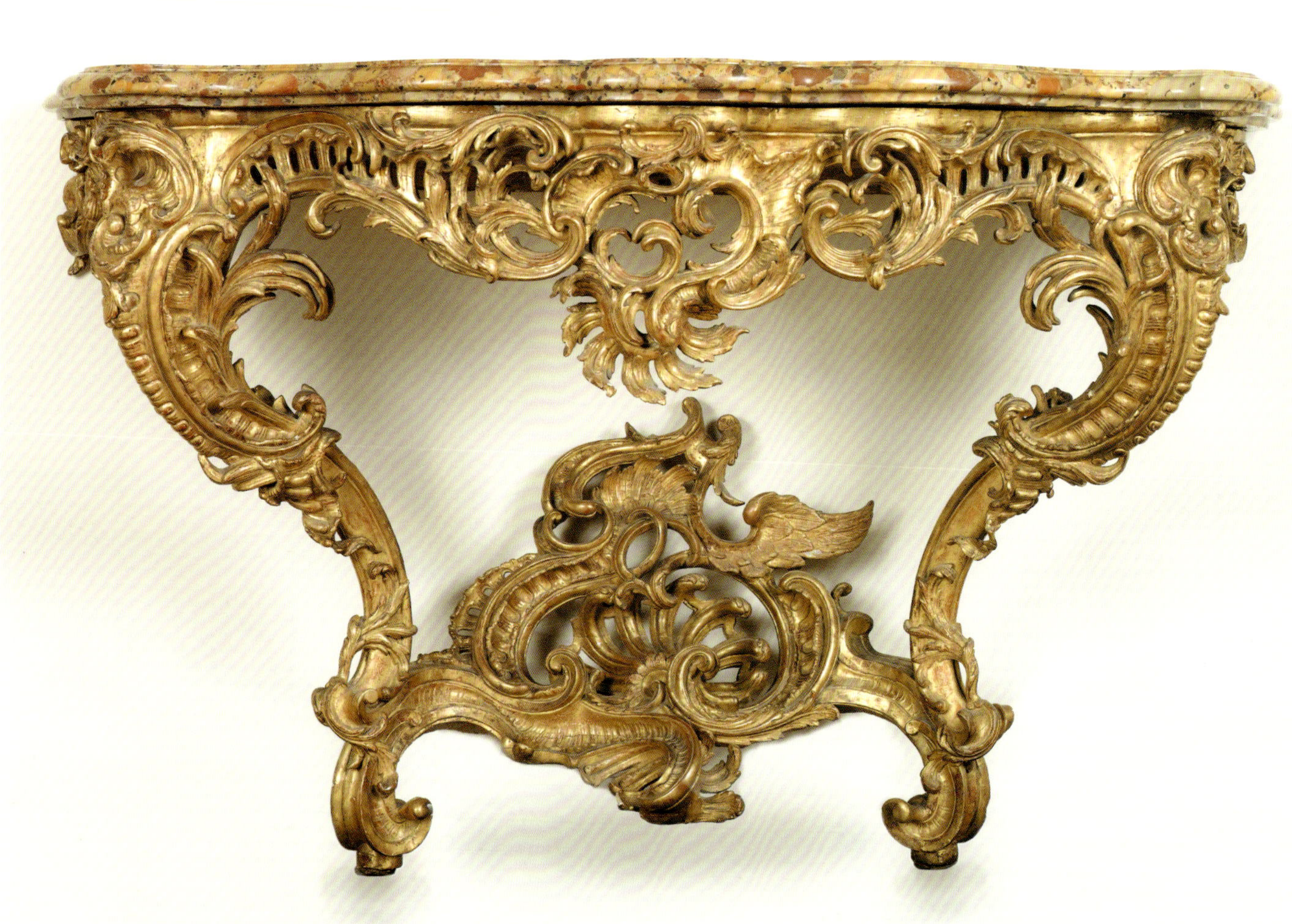

FIG. 1 Console table. France, ca. 1735. Gilt wood, marble. Collection of Horace Wood Brock

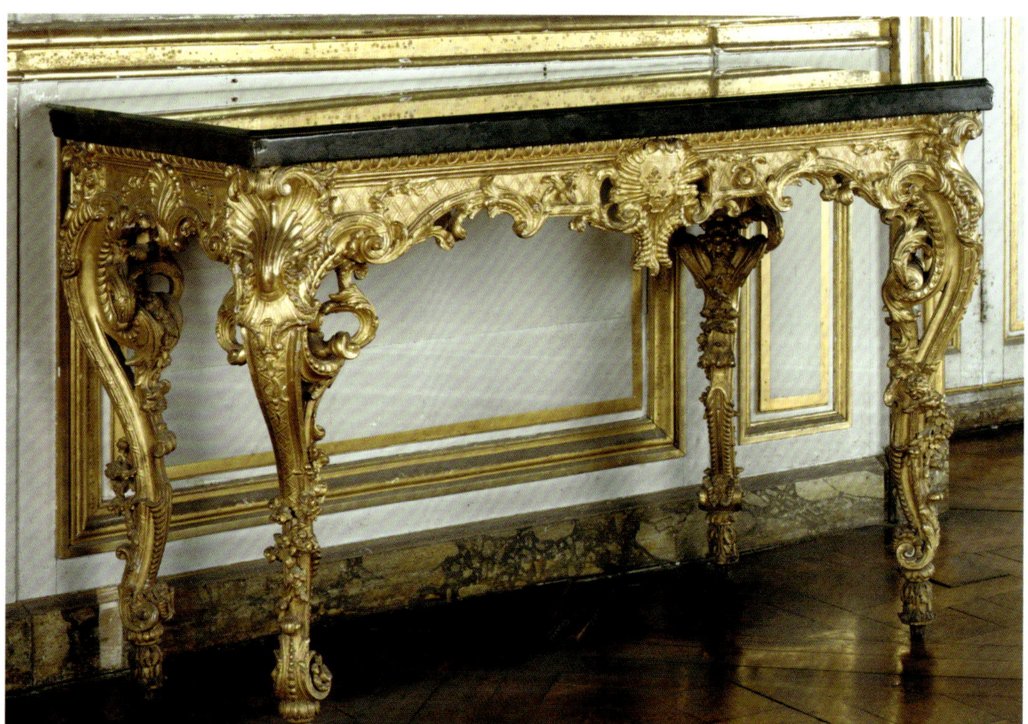

FIG. 2 Console table delivered to the French royal *garde-meuble*. France, 1730–31. Gilded wood. Versailles, Châteaux de Versailles et Trianon, Vmb 1024-2

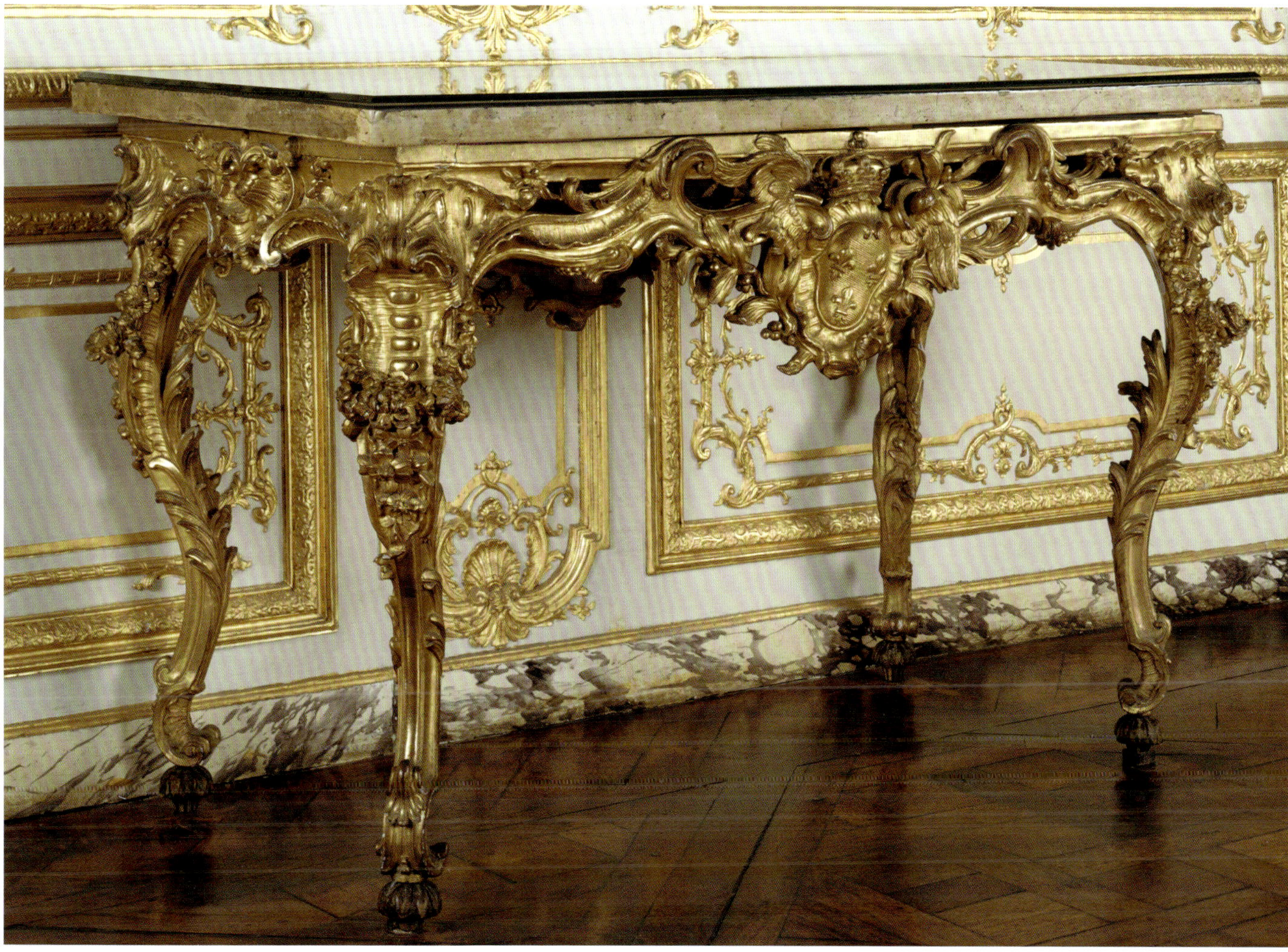

FIG. 3 Console table delivered to the French royal *garde-meuble*. France, 1737. Gilded wood. Versailles, Châteaux de Versailles et Trianon, Vmb 1024-4

cartilaginous material, and the winged cartouche thrust at a perilous angle. By 1739, a pair of only slightly tipped wings held the cartouche upright. In the final console, delivered in 1757, a symmetrical design enclosed the armorial in smooth openwork contours entwined with flower garlands.[2] (figs. 2-6)

The console's basic function of support was put to the test in an example that pushed the envelope of structural logic in a feverish flight of ornamental daring. The apron was voided with openwork carvings of windswept asymmetry, and the stretcher was mounted high with a skeletal shell in a surround of entwined scrolls tipped by a single wing (fig. 1).

The proliferation of intimate apartments inspired a myriad of new contoured seating forms, which were often given exotic names. A lady could read while reclining in the latest fashion on the silken pillows of a *veilleuse à la turque*,[3] a sofa-cum-daybed that conformed to popular harem fantasies. A rare surviving example features leafy moldings cascading from the rounded head to the contoured return at the foot, and flowers exploding on the seat rail above scrolling feet variously angled to support the kidney-shaped bed (fig. 7). Court etiquette still demanded sets of formal stools, but the anachronism was countered by carving the traditional X supports in sinuous foliate scrolls (fig. 8). At the practical end of the spectrum, caning replaced straw or fabric upholstery for seats with specific uses, such as a coiffeuse with a scooped-out back to facilitate hair

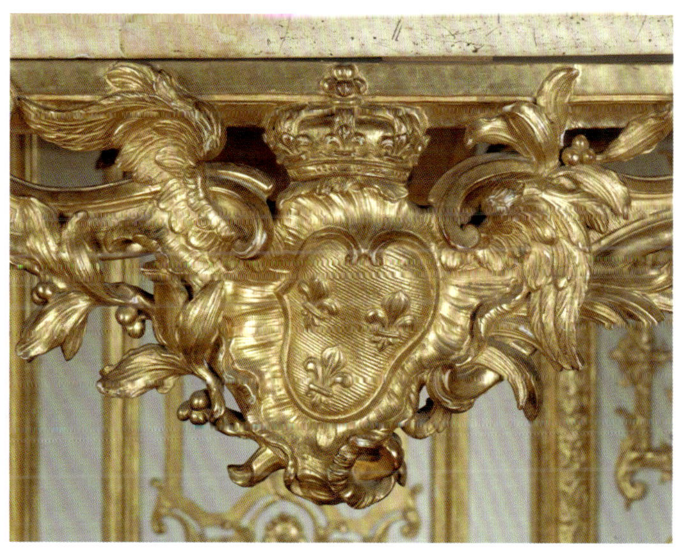

FIG. 4 Detail of Fig. 3

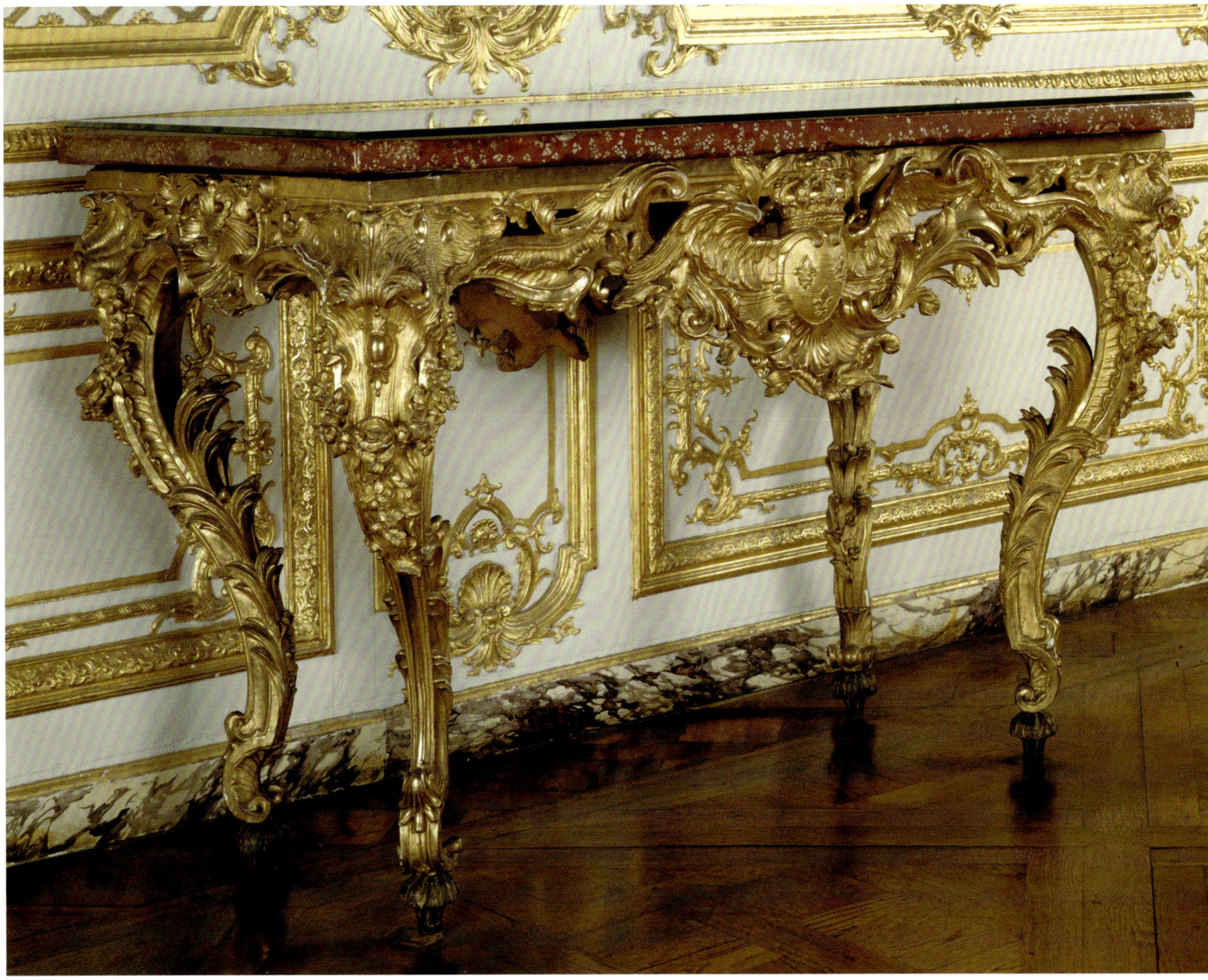

FIG. 5 Console table delivered to the French royal *garde-meuble*. France, 1739. Gilded wood. Versailles, Châteaux de Versailles et Trianon, Vmb 1024-5

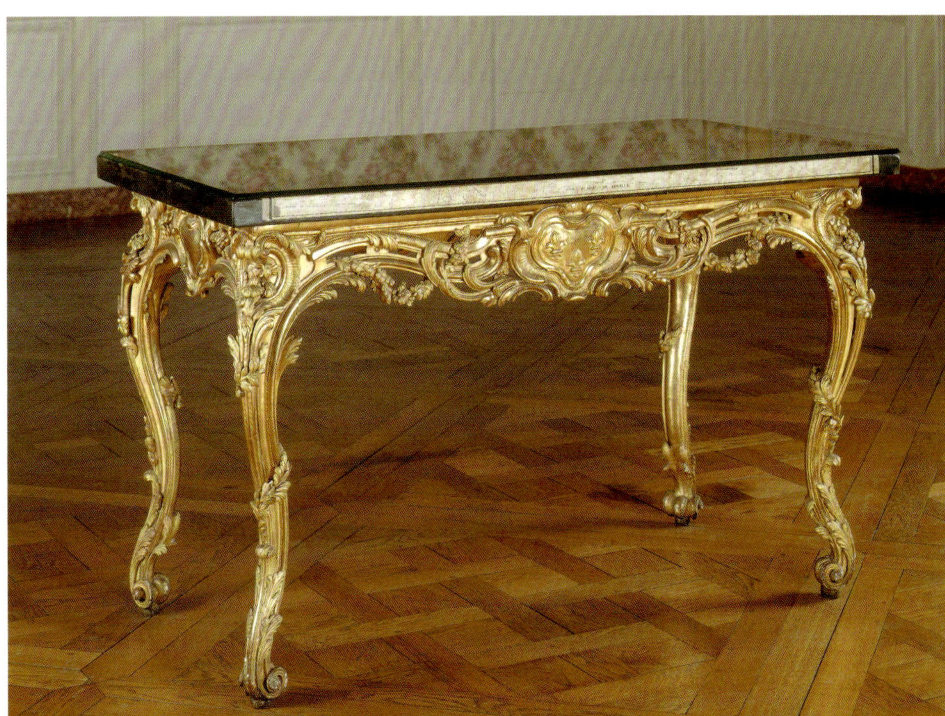

FIG. 6 Console table delivered to the French royal *garde-meuble*. France, 1757. Gilded wood. Versailles, Châteaux de Versailles et Trianon, Vmb 1024-1

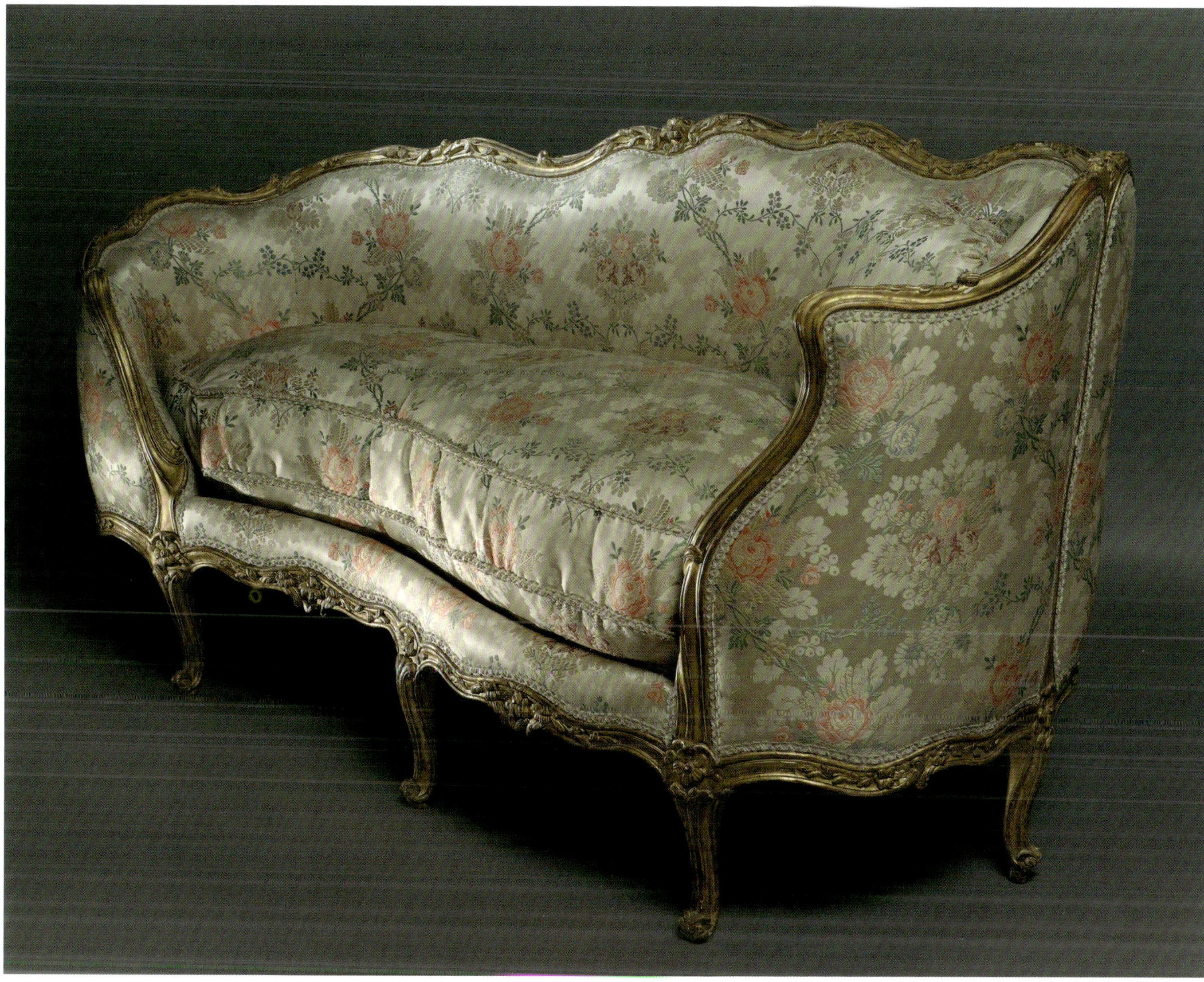

FIG. 7 Veilleuse à la turque (sofa). French, ca. 1750–60. Gilt wood, upholstery (replaced). Private collection

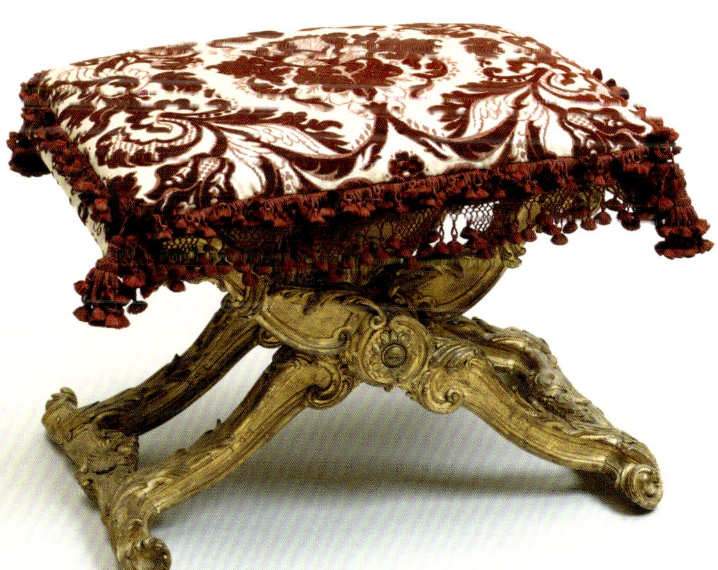

FIG. 8 Pliant (folding stool). France, ca. 1740. Gilt, walnut. Hillwood Estate, Museum & Gardens; bequest of Marjorie Merriweather Post, 31.105.4

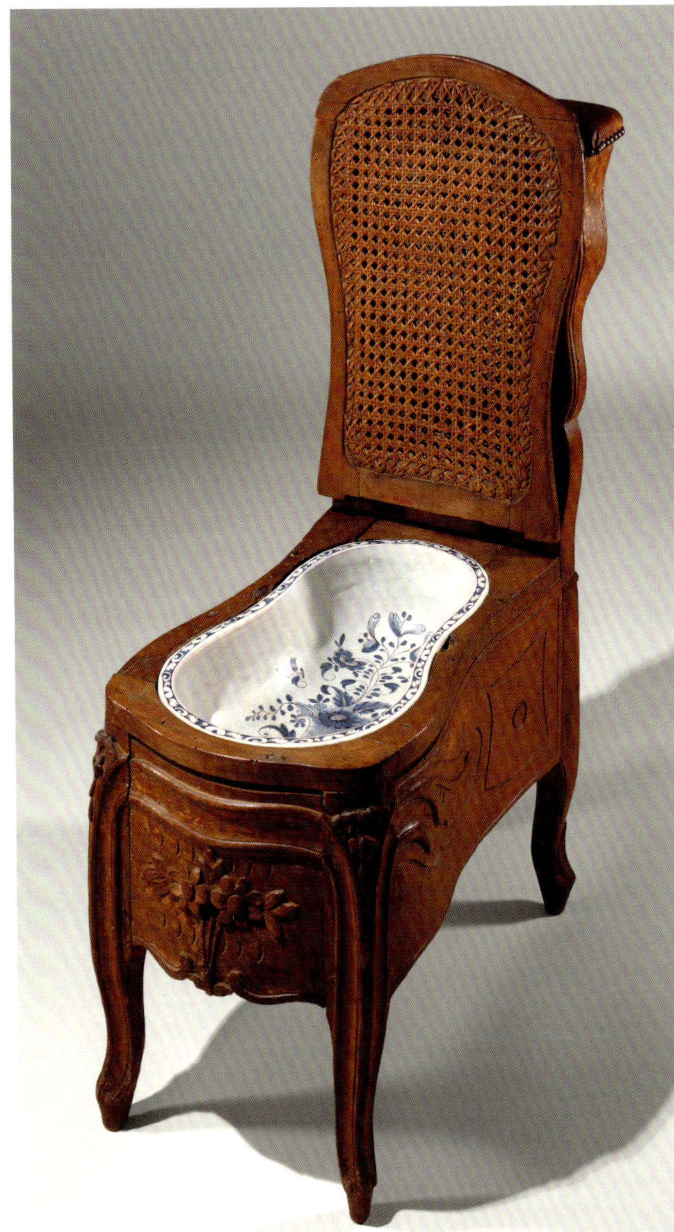

FIG. 9 Bidet. France, ca. 1750. Fruitwood, caning, leather, glazed earthenware. Cooper-Hewitt, National Design Museum, Smithsonian Institution, Gift of Mrs. W. G. Dunnington, Jr., 1968-114-1a/c

dressing, or a desk chair with the legs rotated ninety degrees to provide extra support at the front and back. The sophisticated contouring of the wood frames made these models as strong as they were visually appealing.

Ergonomics combined with style in a bidet by Noel Baudin (1719–1784, master 1763) in Cooper-Hewitt's collection, in which the carved moldings emphasized the contouring. Practical above all, it was designed to be straddled, with the caned chair back actually serving as an armrest, and equipped with compartments under a leather-covered hinged top. The seat was double-caned for strength. A floral spray is carved on the front, and single wing-like leaves embrace the sides of the cavity that contains the faience bowl (fig. 9).

EBÉNISTERIE

Ebénisterie was regarded more as art than as furniture, and individual pieces were avidly collected. Even though the originality of design and technical invention in Louis XV cabinet work were admired for centuries to come, little was known about the ébénistes themselves. Only in 1743 was a regulation passed that all furniture on the Paris market had to bear a maker's stamp. Further muddying the waters was the fact that many ébénistes sold their furniture through colleagues or through *marchands merciers*, purveyors of luxury goods who became increasingly important in setting the fashion of the day.[4] Moreover, cabinetmakers affixed their stamps to furniture they restored.

Eighteenth-century ébénistes developed a new furniture type dubbed the *commode*—meaning commodious and useful—a chest of drawers raised on a stand, with a sinuous, sculptural form. It became the most valuable showpiece of a stylish Parisian residence during the reign of Louis XV. Exotic lacquer commodes became the ne plus ultra of furniture under Louis XV, selling for several times the price of wood-veneered commodes.[5] Lacquer screens and cabinets imported from the East were purchased by Paris marchands merciers and entrusted to the most skilled ébénistes. The lacquer had to be cut, shaved thin, and weighted in hot sand until the panels could be adhered to the bowed surfaces of the commodes. Japanning, or covering with a coat of varnish, was also done in imitation of true lacquer, often to cover surfaces beyond the panels or add motifs to harmonize assorted panels. The oriental subjects depicted in the lacquer were dramatically set off as pictures on the front and sides of commodes by glittering frames composed of connected leafy scrolls

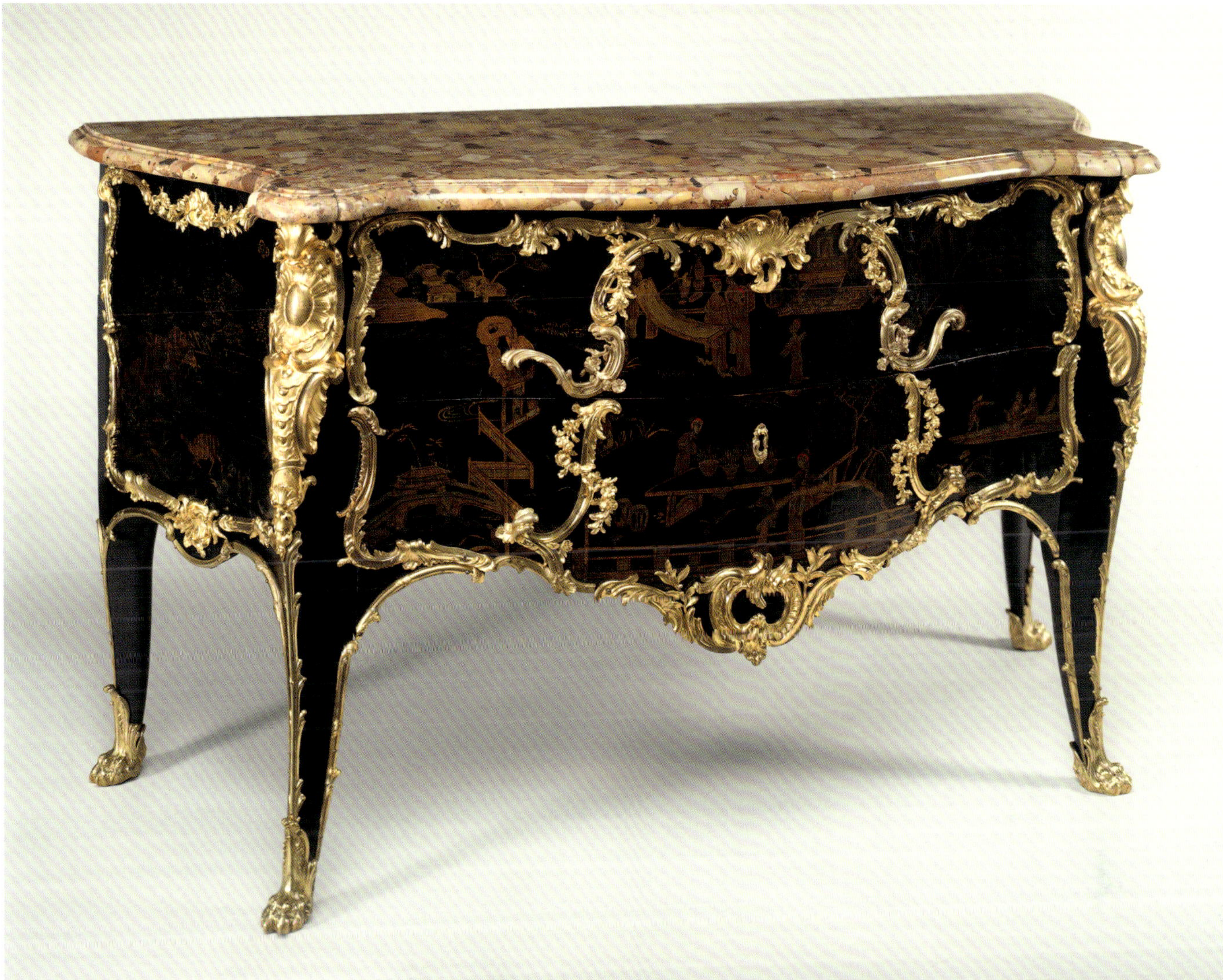

FIG. 10 Commode (chest of drawers). Jean Desforges (French, active ca. 1739). France, 1745–49. Oak, togidashi lacquer, gilt bronze, marble. National Gallery of Art, Widener Collection, 1942.9.408

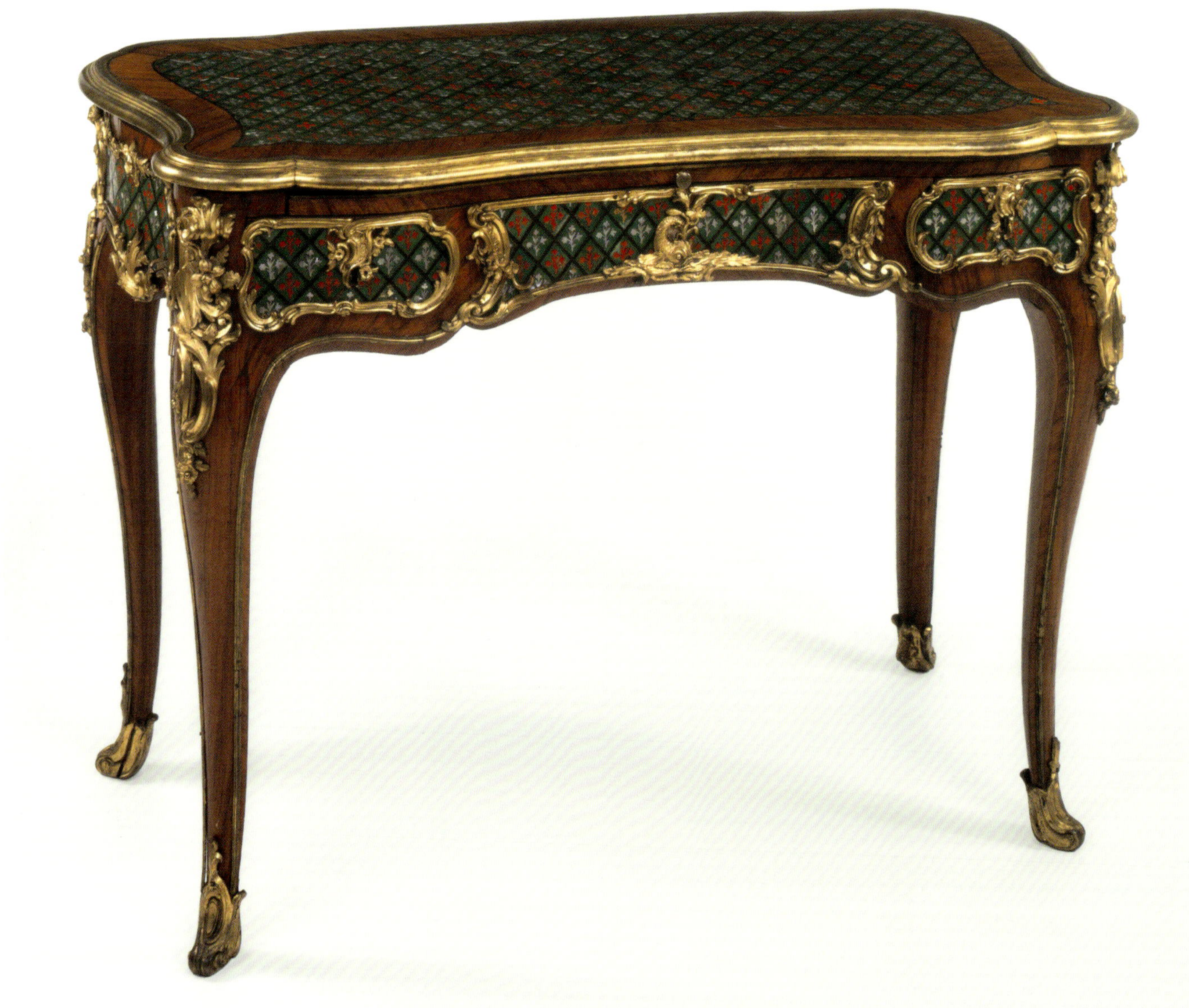

FIG. 11 Table à écrire (writing table). Bernard II van Risenburgh (French, active 1700–49). France, 1745–49. Mahogany, tulipwood veneer, mother-of-pearl and horn marquetry, gilt bronze. Fine Arts Museums of San Francisco, Gift of Archer M. Huntington, 1926.115

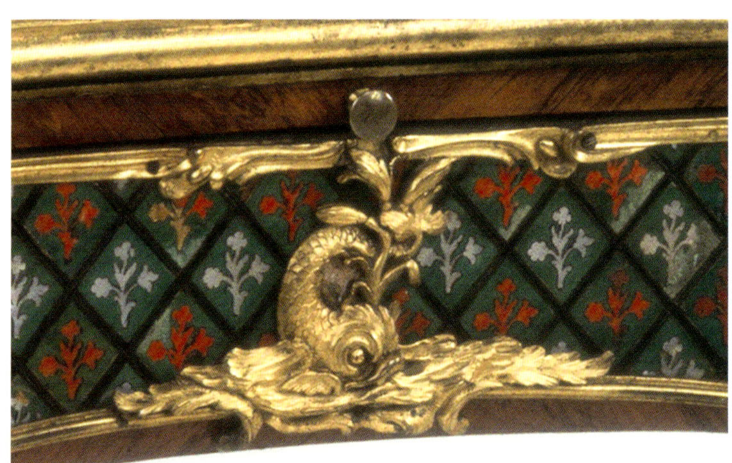

FIG. 12 Table à écrire (detail)

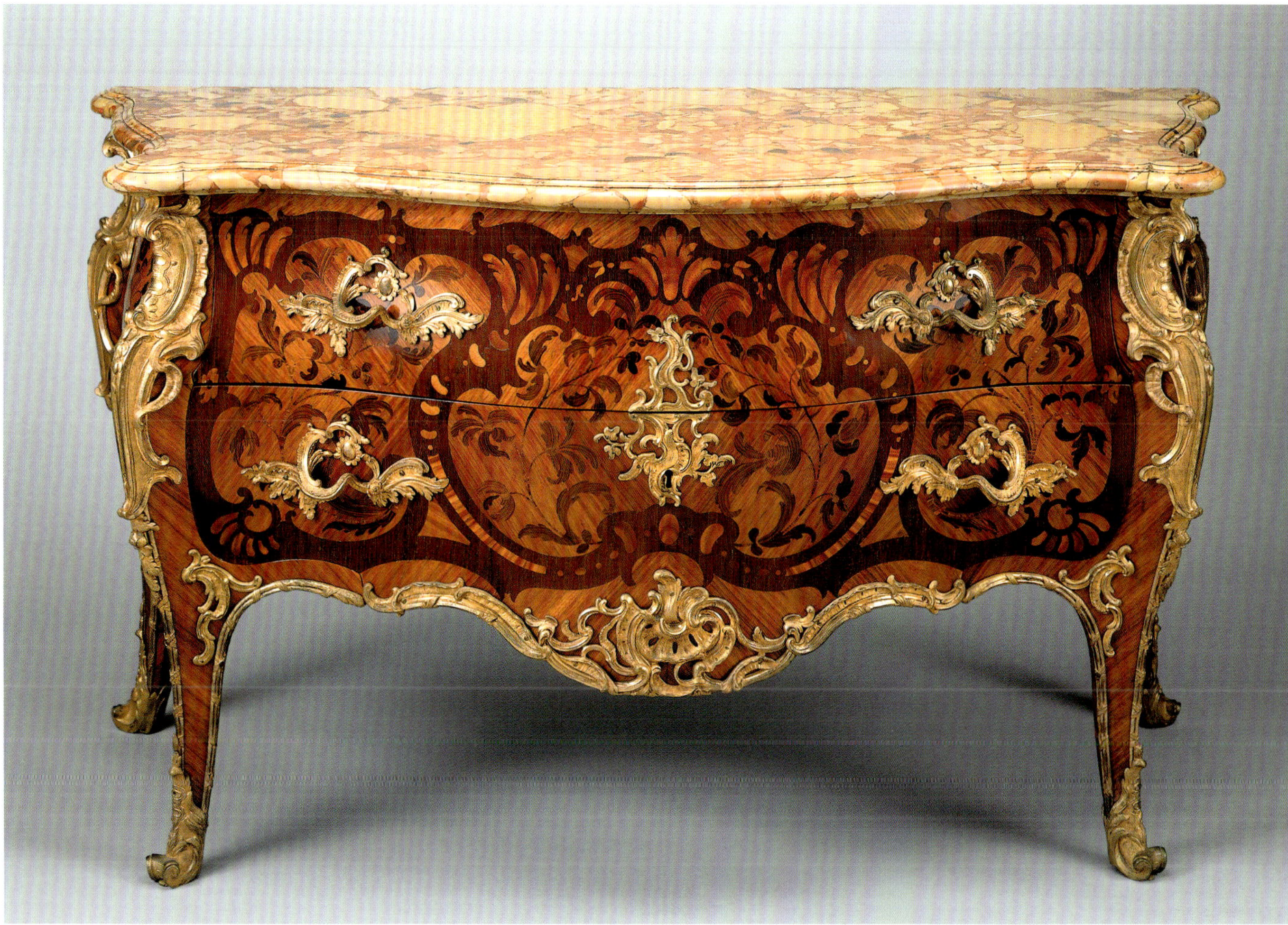

FIG. 13 Commode (chest of drawers). Jean-Pierre Latz (French, 1691–1754). Paris, France, ca. 1745. Oak, marquetry of tulipwood, breche d'Alep marble, gilt bronze. Cincinnati Art Museum, Museum Purchase, by exchange, and with assistance of funds and gifts from A.J. Howe, Henry Meis, Phyllis H.Thayer Purchase Fund, Gloria W. Thomson Fund for Decorative Arts, Israel and Caroline Wilson, John J. Emery, Dr. and Mrs. Martin Macht, Robert Dechant, George Toewater, in memory of Jan Thomson Herschede, and Mr. and Mrs. Daniel Ransohoff, 1976.435

in gilt bronze. Some of the most sumptuous examples were signed DF, a specialist in this genre whose identity has been debated. Recent scholarship supports his identification as Jean Desforges, born into a dynasty of Parisian furniture makers.[6] His tour-de-force commode, now in the National Gallery in Washington, D.C., can be dated because the mounts were stamped with the crowned C signifying payment of a tax on bronzes in effect between 1745 and 1749. Drawer handles spring directly from the bell-form cartouche formed by connected gilt-bronze mounts. This inner frame serves as a visual bridge, making three assorted Chinese lacquer panels appear to be a single continuous scene enclosed by an outer gilt-bronze frame (fig. 10).

Furniture signed B.V.R.B. has long been appreciated as the height of rococo sophistication, but the author behind the initials remained a mystery until the mid-twentieth century. Archival research revealed this maker to be Bernard van Riesamburgh, the second generation of a dynasty of cabinetmakers bearing the name.[7] Bernard II (ca. 1696–1766) used the most advanced decorations of end-cut wood marquetry, lacquer, porcelain plaques, and, in the rarest cases, stained horn and mother-of-pearl. The eloquent gilt-bronze flourishes on B.V.R.B. pieces appear to have been his own exclusive designs. His structures achieved a level of lyricism that belied their sturdy functionalism, particularly evident in his writing tables and desks. Such pieces served as pivotal communications centers in a sophisticated society dependent on letter-writing (figs. 11, 12).

The most extreme rococo expressions in French furniture bore the stamp of Jean-Pierre Latz (ca. 1691–1754). In a 1970 publication, Henry Hawley established the oeuvre and identified Latz as a German who worked in Paris from 1719 and became a French citizen in 1736.[8] Latz covered every surface of his bulbous designs with extravagant marquetry, whether floral, pictorial, or Boullework.[9] (fig. 13) His gilt-bronze mounts brought his pieces to a pitch of exuberance. They were so distinctive that, in 1749, the guild of Paris metalworkers raided his atelier for evidence that he was defying their exclusive prerogative of making and applying bronzes.[10] Not surprisingly, Latz had many foreign clients, including Frederick the Great of Prussia and Augustus III of Saxony, who sought to transplant to their courts the most emphatic statements of Paris rococo.

GILT BRONZE

Gilt bronze played an autonomous role as a primary vehicle for high rococo style beyond the furniture mounts that provided gleaming outlines and accents for cabinetry. The medium gained popularity as a glamorous substitute for the precious metals of silver and gold in which the style was first defined. Bronze was more practical and less expensive than precious metal, and multiple examples could be obtained by casting from a single model. Once gilding was applied, the object assumed a graphic value, catching and channeling light across its contours. This was ideal for lighting fixtures. The silver candlesticks Juste-Aurèle Meissonnier designed for the Duke of Kingston were almost immediately reproduced and adapted in gilt bronze, and continued to be produced through the nineteenth century. Gilt-bronze wall lights with arms spiraling to different levels were set in balanced pairs on either side of mirrors to amplify the effect. Gilded andirons provided a sculptural, curvilinear frame to the hearth and could withstand the heat.

Timepieces were a source of intellectual pride in eighteenth-century homes. In France, gilt-bronze clock cases featuring figures in swirling surrounds, attached to the wall or centered on a mantelpiece, became sculptural exclamation marks. One lavish gilt-bronze cartel (fig. 14) conveyed the triumph of love over time: a winged Father Time rests on his protractor and dividers amid palm branches and clouds, as cupids taunt him from above. The composition relates to Meissonnier's designs of the 1720s and 1730s, published in engravings by Gabriel Huquier around 1750.

An exceptionally massive set of gilt-bronze wall lights (figs. 15, 16), now in the J. Paul Getty Museum[11], reveals the direct connection between silver and bronze, as the metal was stamped by François-Thomas Germain (1726–1791) with his title as sculptor and goldsmith to the King and the date 1756. Primarily known as the author of some of the greatest examples of French rococo silver, Germain followed his father Thomas Germain in supplying silver to the court of Portugal. The Getty wall lights were an exceptional commission from the Duke of Orléans for a room designed by Pierre Constant d'Ivry in the Palais Royal, and were illustrated *in situ* in two plates of Denis Diderot's *Encylopédie*. Even though the sweeping, naturalistic form of three laurel branches would have been out of style in 1783 when the duke's possessions were sold, the quality was such that the wall lights were purchased by Louis XVI and hung at the château in Compiègne.

Only a few bronze makers' names are known, as their guild did not require signatures. Jacques Caffieri (1678–1755) was the most celebrated member of his profession. The son of a sculptor, he was a bronze caster, chaser, and gilder, furnishing gilt bronzes to the administration of royal buildings. He occasionally signed his robust rococo creations, like the andirons, now in the Cleveland Museum of Art, in which the head of a lion is couched in massive scrolls on one while that of a snarling boar appears on the other (fig. 17). [12]

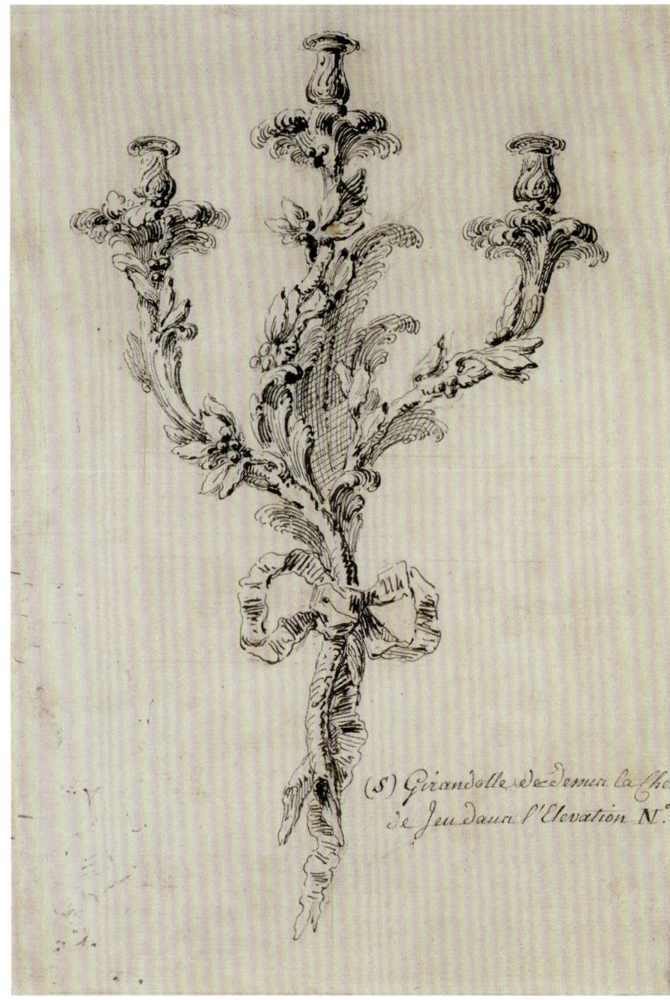

FIG. 16 *Drawing of a Wall Light.* Attributed to Pierre-Constant d'Ivry (French, 1698–1777). Paris, France, ca. 1760. Ink on paper. The J. Paul Getty Museum, 86.GA.692

Gilt-bronze mounts transformed exotic items into works of French art. A long tradition of setting precious antiquities or stonework in metal mounts was taken up by the marchands merciers, who employed bronze workers to mount the prized oriental porcelains they marketed. An ingenious foot, rim, and handle could turn a Chinese porcelain vase into a ewer; a base, collar, and finial could make a covered vase into a *pot pourri*. Even figural Meissen porcelains from Saxony were set in lavish gilt-bronze foliate scrolls to create watch stands, clocks, or candelabra that brought high prices (figs. 18–20).

Illustrations of porcelains with flamboyant rococo gilt-bronze mounts appear among the pen-and-wash colored drawings in the album of Albert of Sachsen-Teschen (fig. 21). The sheets represent an illustrated inventory of marchand-mercier wares used by the duke and his consort Maria-Christina to decorate their palace in Laeken, near Brussels, which was built for them as joint governors of the Low Countries between 1780 and 1785.[13] They were discerning clients: Maria Christina was the sister of Marie-Antoinette. The album illustrated of the latest neoclassical furniture, and the surprising inclusion of the rococo mounted porcelains meant they had not yet lost their appeal.

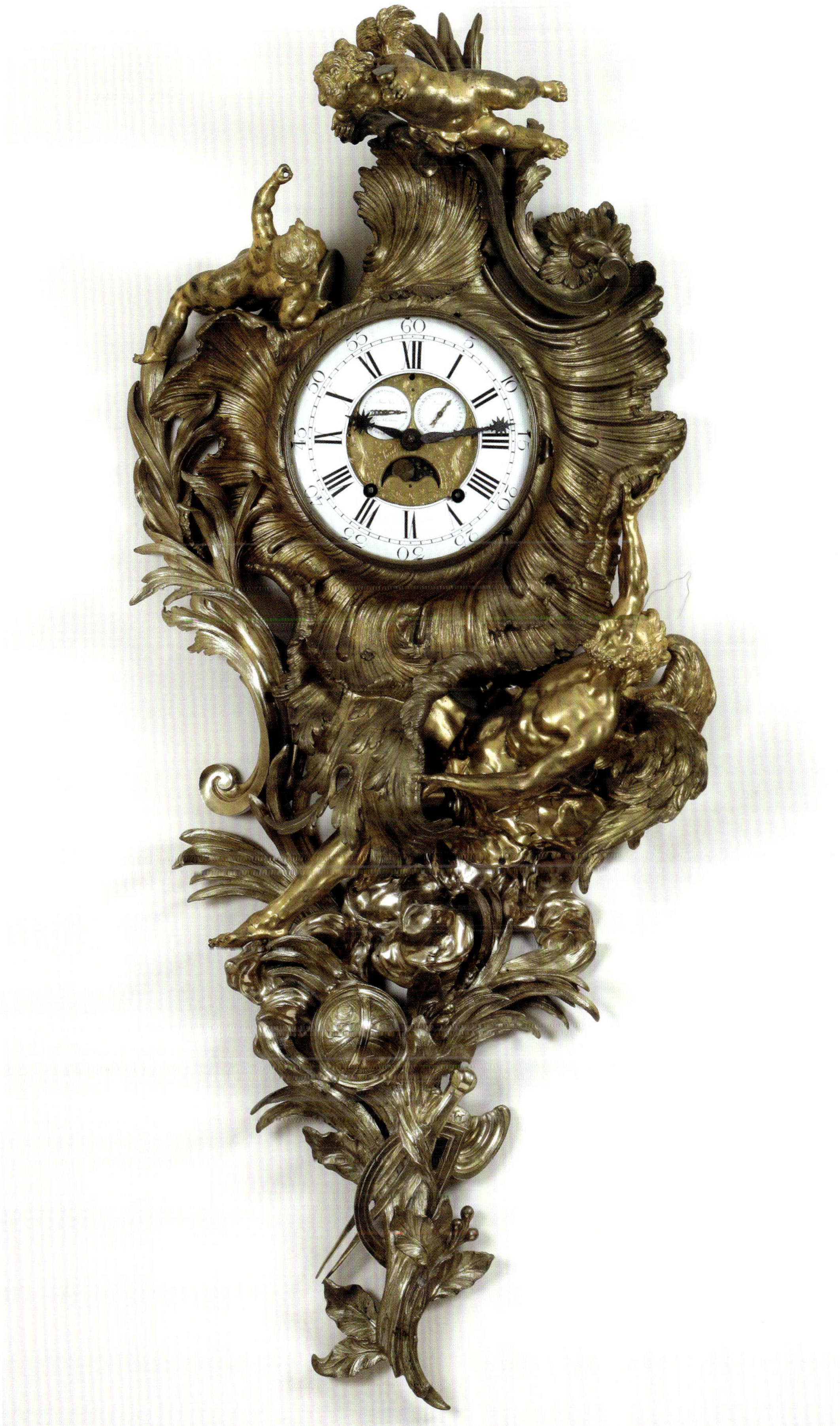

FIG. 14 Wall clock: "Victory of Love over Time." France, ca. 1750. Gilt, varnished bronze. Dalva Brothers

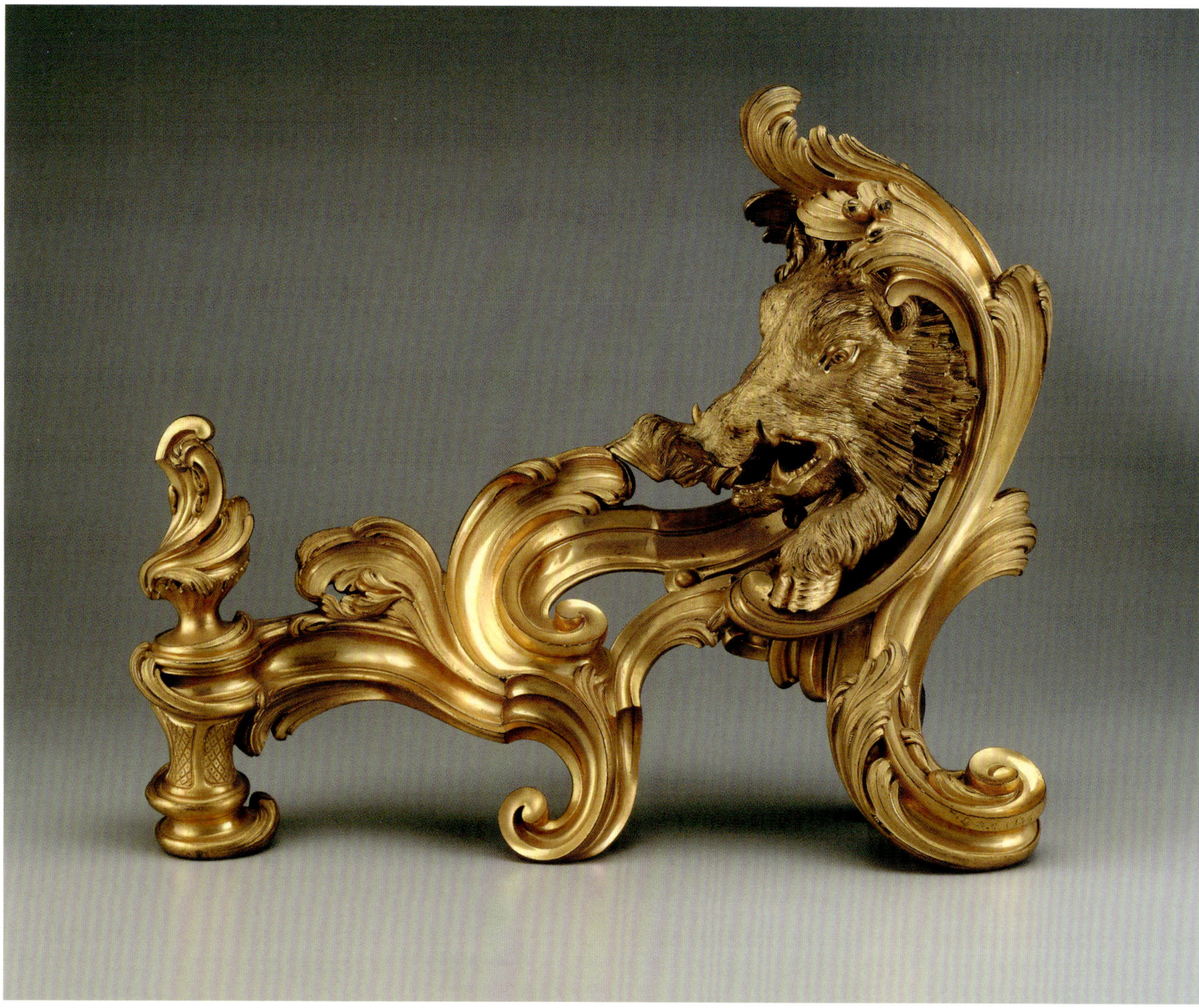

FIG. 17 Chenet (andiron) (one of a pair). Jacques Caffieri (French, 1678–1755). France, 1752. Gilt bronze. The Cleveland Museum of Art, Bequest of John L. Severance, 1942.799.2

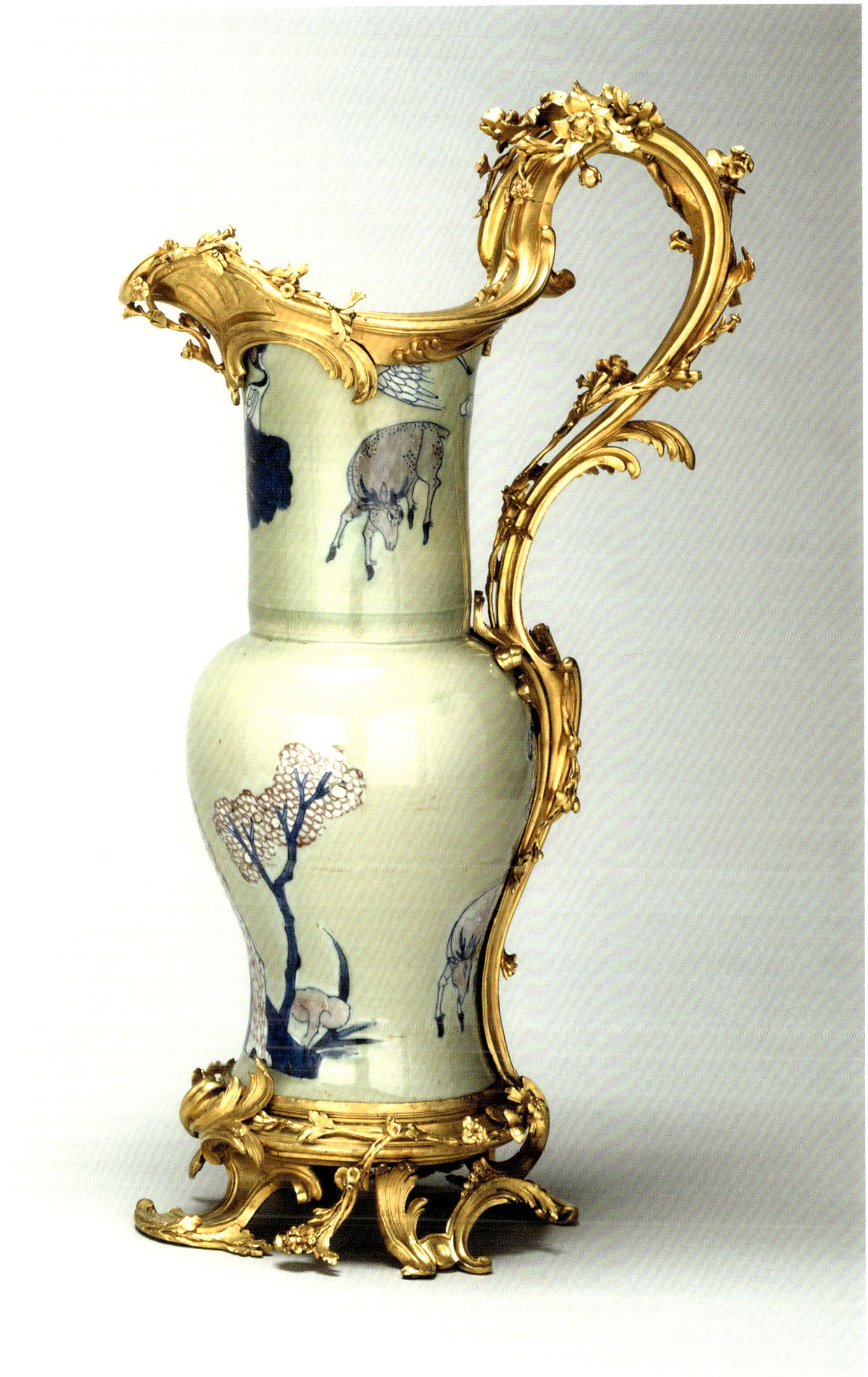

FIG. 18 Mounted ewer (one of a pair). China, 1736–95 (ewer); Paris, France, 1745–49 (mounts). Hard-paste porcelain, underglaze, gilt bronze. The J. Paul Getty Museum, 78.DI.9.1

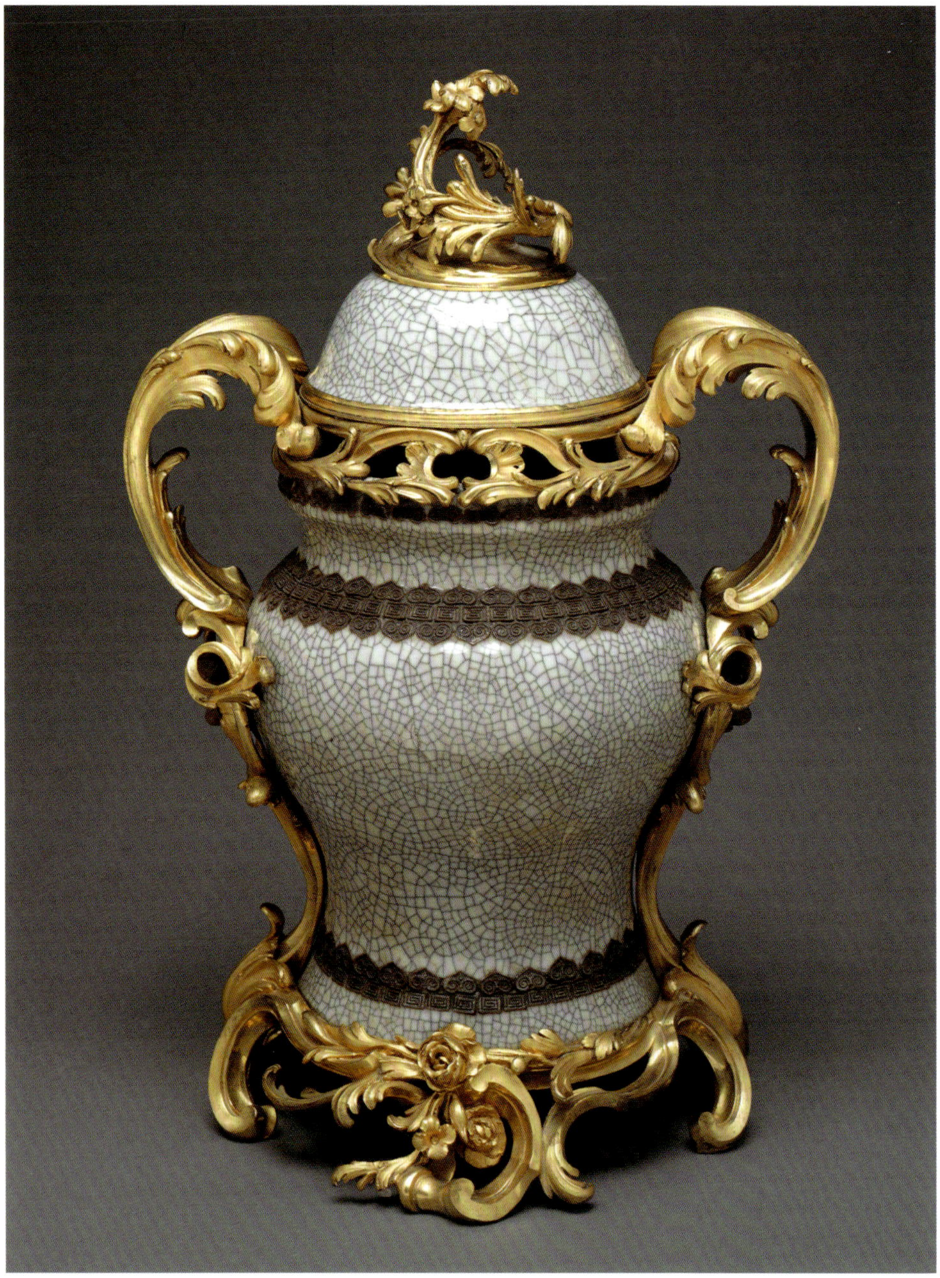

FIG. 19 Pot pourri vase. China, ca. 1700 (vase); France, ca. 1730 (mounts). Crackleware, gilt bronze. San Francisco Fine Arts Museum, Gift of Archer M. Huntington, 1927.168a-b

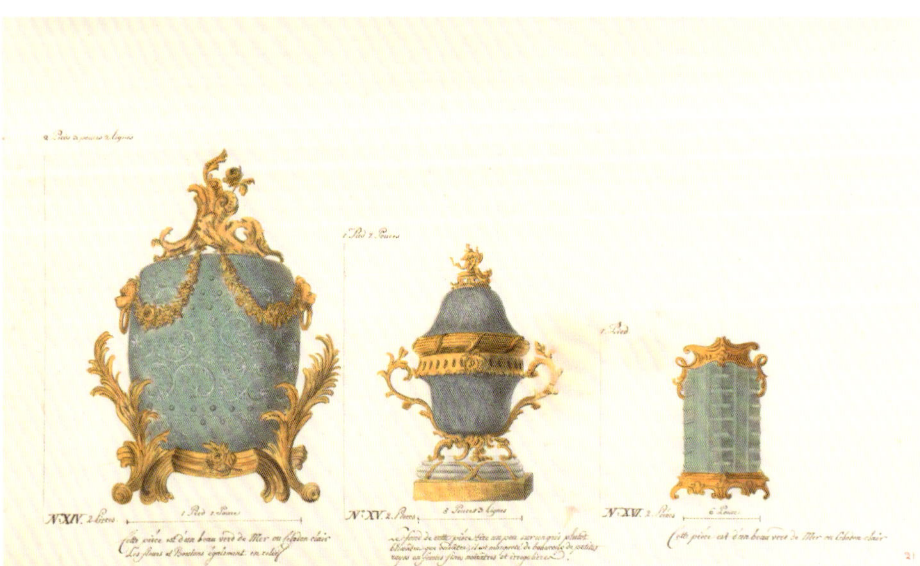

FIG. 21 *Three Drawings of Mounted Porcelains*. France, ca. 1770–85. Brush and brown and grey wash, watercolor, gouache over pen and brown ink, traces of black chalk on off-white laid paper. Metropolitan Museum of Art, Gift of Ralph Esmerian, 1961, 61.680.1.7,.8,.9

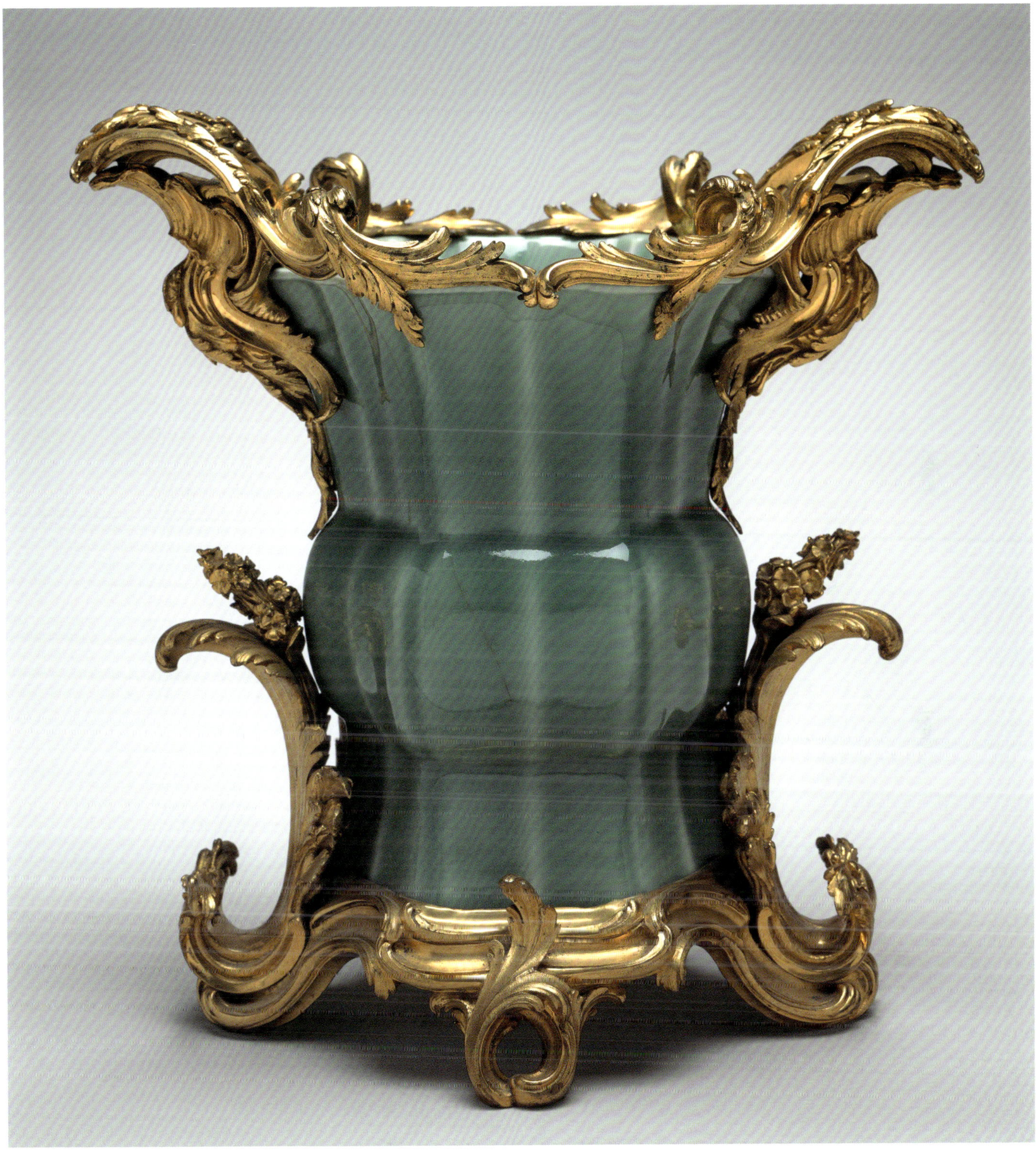

FIG. 20 Mounted vase. China, ca. 1700; France, ca. 1730 (mounts). Celadon porcelain, gilt bronze. San Francisco Fine Arts Museum, Gift of Archer M. Huntington, 1927.175

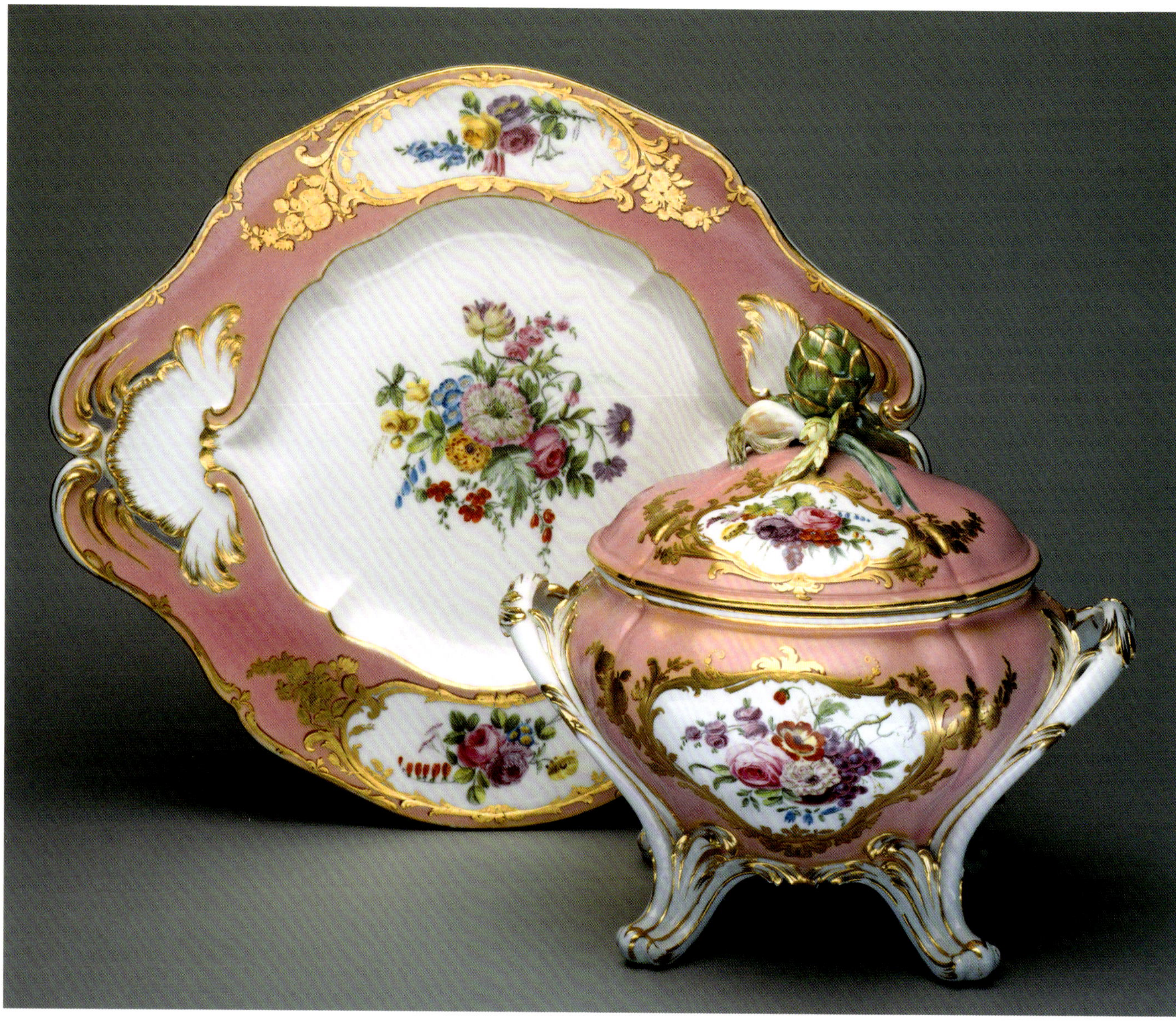

FIG. 23 Covered tureen with stand. Manufactured by the Manufacture Royale de Sèvres. Sèvres, France, ca. 1757. Soft-paste porcelain, gilding. The Philadelphia Museum of Art, Bequest of Eleanore Elkins Rice, 1939; Purchased with funds contributed by Mr. and Mrs. Fitz Eugene Dixon, Jr., 1999, 1939-41-40a,b;1999-132-1

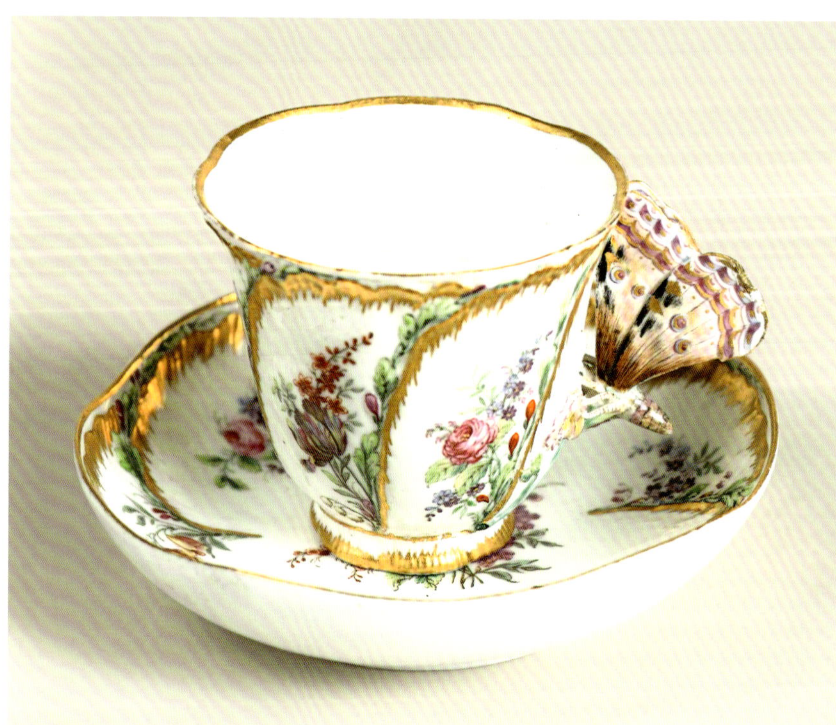

FIG. 22 Teacup and saucer. Manufactured by the Manufacture Royale de Sèvres. Sèvres, France, ca. 1755. Soft-paste porcelain, gilding. Private collection

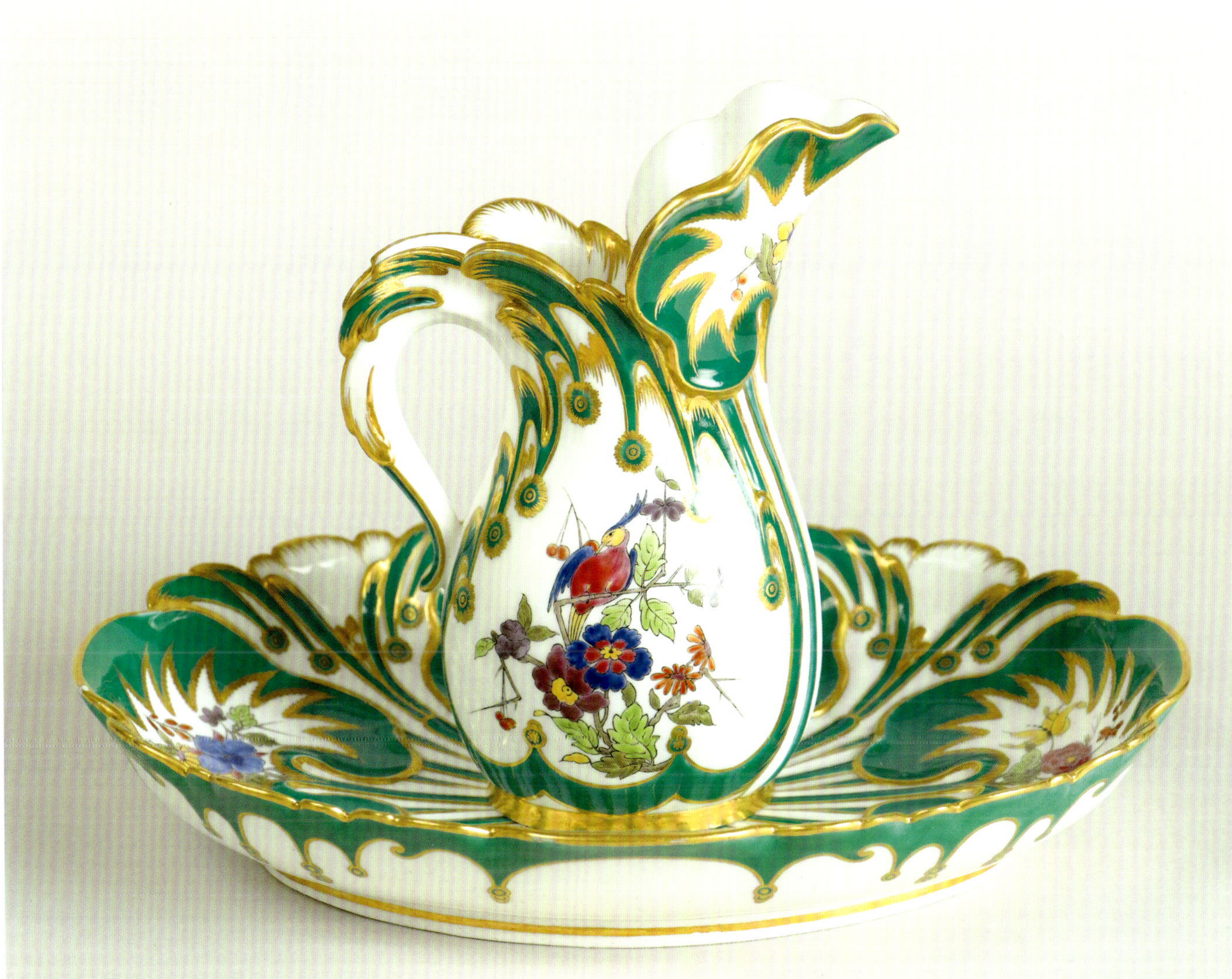

FIG. 24 "Water Leaf" ewer and basin. Manufactured by the Manufacture Royale de Sèvres. Sèvres, France, 1756–57. Soft-paste porcelain, gilding. Private collection

PORCELAIN

The medium of porcelain became a focus of French rococo thanks to the enthusiasm of Madame de Pompadour. Among her first concerns after becoming the official mistress of Louis XV was gaining his support for a fledgling porcelain factory located in the abandoned fortress of Vincennes. Seeing the potential of international prestige if a French manufactory could overtake the production of the Saxon court at Meissen, she had her royal paramour construct the factory at Sèvres, near her château in Bellevue, and finally buy the enterprise outright in 1759. To counter Meissen's technical advantage of having the secret ingredient for true hard-paste porcelain, Pompadour pushed the French factory toward artistic invention (figs 22, 23).[14] While Meissen's wares continued to reflect the baroque character of the Dresden court, Sèvres enlisted masters of the new rococo style. When a new management team drawn from Pompadour's entourage took over the operation in 1751, the goldsmith Jean-Claude Duplessis (ca. 1695–1774) advised on new shapes. Duplessis was responsible for the most audacious rococo models produced at Sèvres, including a wash basin and ewer which combined the three-dimensional rendering of a splash of water with a relief decoration of water-lily pads (fig. 24). Rococo forms were so eminently suited to porcelain tablewares that models such as the verrière with its undulating edge and cresting wave handles stayed in production through the triumph of neoclassicism in the 1780s (see Davidson, p. 44, fig. 4).

THE TEST OF TIME

The achievements of mid-eighteenth-century Parisian designers and craftsmen have outlived fashion. A 1791 painting by Henri-Pierre Danloux, now in the National Gallery, London, portrays a renowned aesthete of his time, Baron de Besenval, contemplating his collection. Dutch paintings cover his walls. Neoclassical andirons stand before the fire; but celadon vases with rococo gilt-bronze mounts grace the mantel, and his seat is a *bergère*, one of the sinuous, form-embracing inventions of the Louis XV era. Even after it was outmoded by neoclassicism, the genius of French rococo was still admired, and that appreciation has remained a constant in French culture.

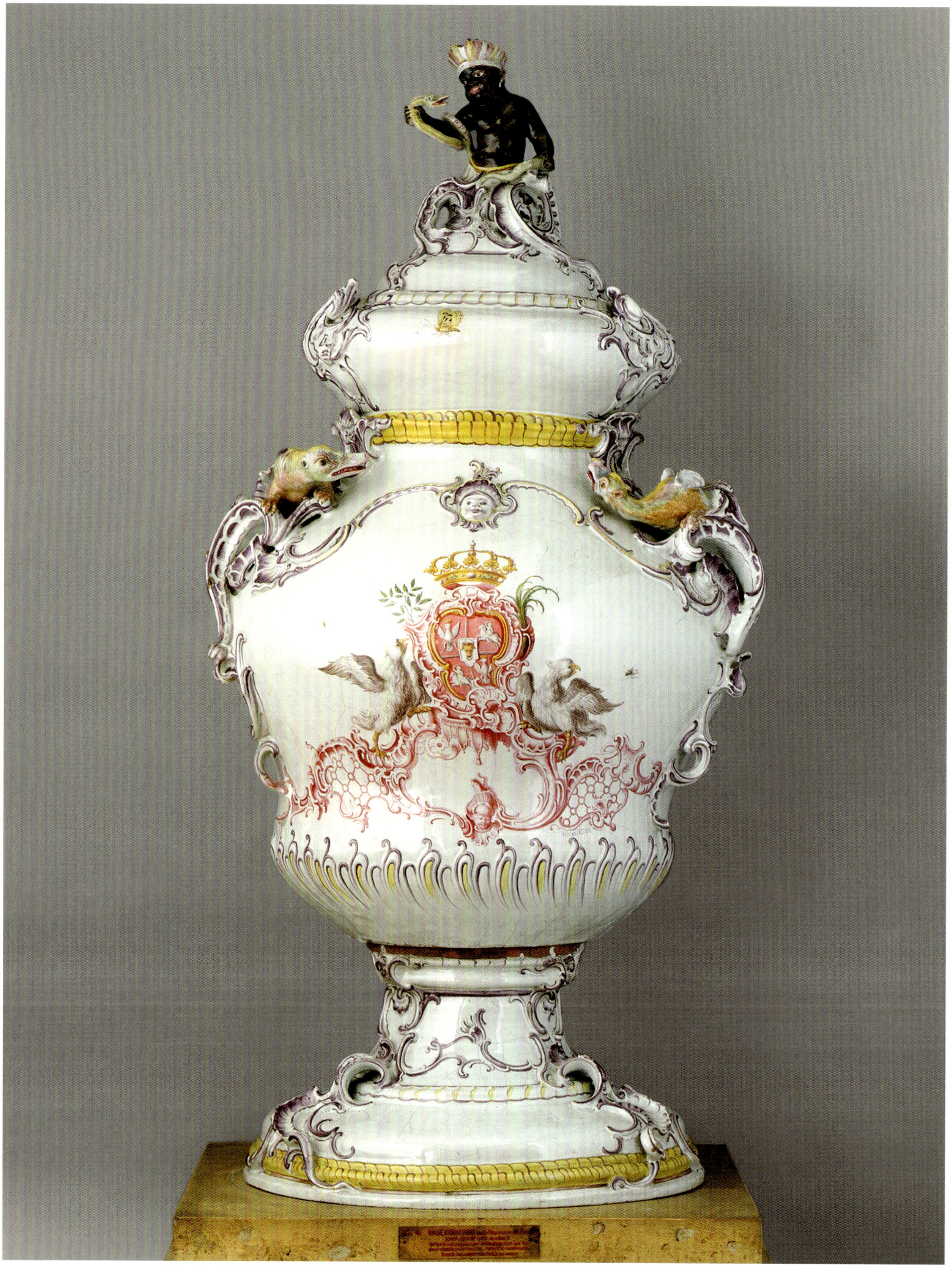

FIG. 5 Monumental pharmacy jar with the arms of Stanislas Lesczynski. Manufactured by the Manufacture de Niderviller. Nancy, France, ca. 1750. Tin-glazed earthenware. Musée Lorrain, Nancy, dépôt de l'Hôpital de Nancy, D. 2007.0.21

Eighteenth-century Nancy: The Good King and the Blacksmith

Penelope Hunter-Stiebel

In 1983, UNESCO added the great public spaces of the city of Nancy, in eastern France, to the World Heritage List in order to honor and preserve this unique expression of eighteenth-century rococo.

STANISLAS LESCZYNSKI

Geopolitics brought a patron of rococo, Stanislas Lesczynski (1677–1766), to the duchy of Lorraine. He was twice elected king of Poland—with the backing of Sweden in 1704, and that of France in 1733—and twice had the throne wrested from him. He retained one claim to fame in the person of his daughter Maria Lesczynska, who became the bride of Louis XV in 1725. In a settlement negotiated between Austria and France to end the War of Polish Succession in 1737, Stanislas was allowed to retain the title of king, but ceded Poland to rule Lorraine under French protection.

During his years of exile in France, Stanislas witnessed the birth of high rococo. He commissioned Meissonnier to make sword hilts for his entourage at his daughter's marriage to Louis XV. At Versailles, he likely appreciated the spectacular mirror on his daughter's dressing table, which Louis XV commissioned from Meissonnier.[1] He was also well acquainted with the extravagant rococo interior Meissonnier created for Catherine Bielinska, a Polish compatriot whom Stanislas repeatedly visited in Paris.[2] Even when ensconced in the Lorraine, he regularly visited his daughter, and decorated his Lorraine residence at Lunéville with such opulence that Voltaire, one of his distinguished guests, declared, "Transported from Versailles to Lunéville, one would be unable to tell the difference."[3]

After Stanislas's death, Louis XV systematically destroyed the splendor of his châteaux to expunge any symbols of regional independence when the duchy was absorbed into France. The only furnishings known to survive are a series of andirons, of which two are preserved in the Musée lorrain.[4] (fig. 1) In this light hearted rococo model, a pair of children cast as Flora and Zephyr sit atop assemblages of cartilaginous scrolls, and cartouches bearing the arms of Lorraine are tucked at a jaunty angle between the waves and scrolls. The andirons can be dated between 1745 and 1749, as they bear the crowned C mark.[5] Four pair appear in the 1753 inventory of Chanteheux, a grandiose pavilion for entertainments constructed in 1742–43 on the grounds of the château of Lunéville. They embellished the four fireplaces of its three-story *salon italien*.[6]

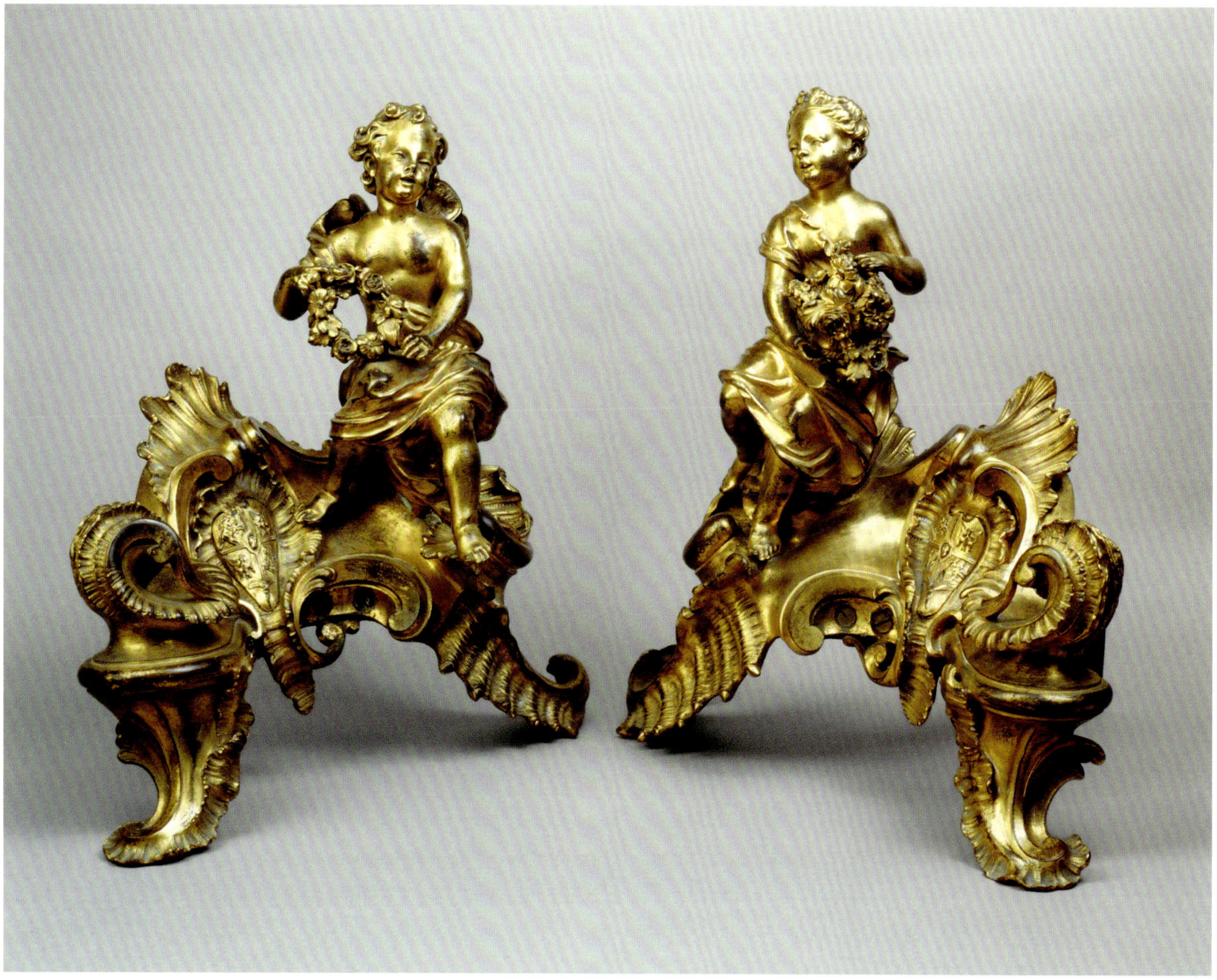

FIG. 1 Pair of chenets (andirons) with the arms of Stanislas Lesczynski, from the Pavilion of Chanteheux, Château of Lunéville. France, ca. 1745. Gilt bronze. Musée Lorrain, Nancy, dépôt du Musée du Louvre, D. 72.2.5.1/2,OAP184/5

As a ruler, Stanislas was a model of the Enlightenment. A philosophical essayist and painter in pastels, he was an active protector of the arts and sciences and patron of local talent. Solicitous of the welfare of his subjects, he founded free schools, a public library, an orphanage, and several hospitals, and supported regional industry and commerce (fig. 2). A precious document of his benefactions survives in the apothecary jars he commissioned for the hospital of the Brothers of Charity of the order of Saint-Jean-de-Dieu, which he founded in Nancy in 1750. From the nearby faience factory of Niderviller, he ordered a set of more than 300 practical vessels for the hospital pharmacy between 1750 and 1755. The original commission, with fanciful animal finials and spouts, was supplemented with additions of more advanced, abstract rococo form.[7] Two extravagant and exotic vases announced the importance of the benefaction. Their monumental size (43 1/4 in., or 110 cm.), which surpassed that of any porcelain creation in the West, was achieved by making each vase in three parts. In a merry medley of references to far-off continents, a boy on the lid wears a feathered headdress (associated with America) and seems to engage in cheerful conversation with a serpent (associated with Africa), whose head he holds at arm's length as it coils around his body. He emerges from a pile of scrolls in relief, which cascade down the vase and offer perches to a crocodile (associated with America) and a dragon before descending to the foot. Even the painted armorial decoration introduces an element of exoticism, harboring the head of a Chinese figure at the bottom of a scrolling plinth (figs. 3–5).

Stanislas thrust Nancy into the movement of urban planning and beautification initiated in Paris. The local architect Emmanuel Héré (1705–1763), who had worked under Germain Boffrand (1667–1754) for previous dukes of Lorraine, was retained; but it was the new ruler's vision that transformed Lorraine's capital. After protracted negotiations with the French minister of war, Stanislas won permission to breach the fortifications between the old and new city with a triumphal arch. On one side, he created a spacious square, Place Royale (now Place Stanislas), anchored by a massive new Hôtel de Ville and centered by a statue of Louis XV—choosing not to placing a monument to himself at the hub of his civic center, but rather to focus the attention of his people on their future ruler, Louis XV.[8] The elaborate iron gateways, grilles, and balconies brought unique character to the project. Beyond the archway, he lined an existing boulevard with unified façades and completed it with a

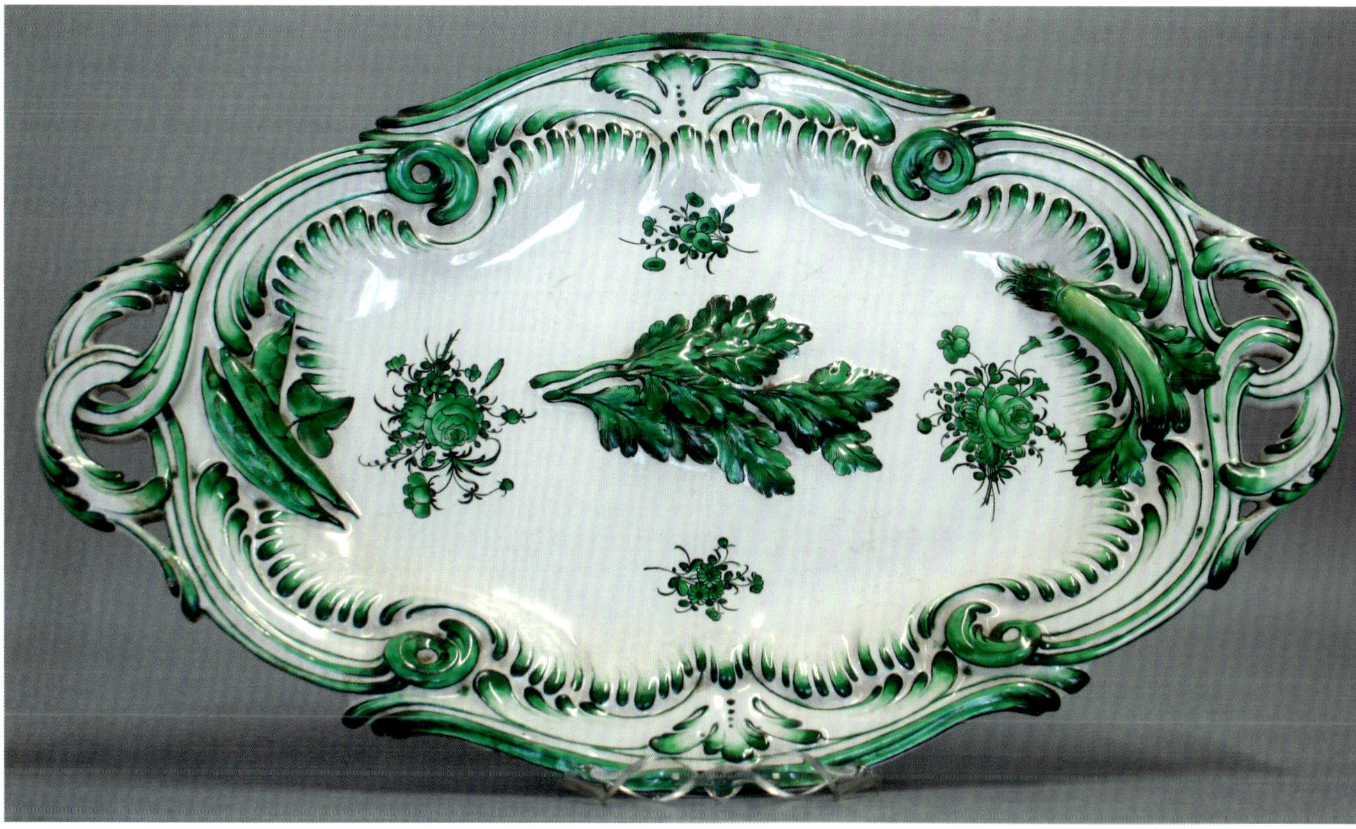

FIG. 2 Tray from the service of Stanislas Leszcynski, Château of Commercy. Manufactured by the Manufacture de Lunéville. Lorraine, France, ca. 1750. Tin-glazed earthenware. Musée Lorrain, Nancy, 97.798.1

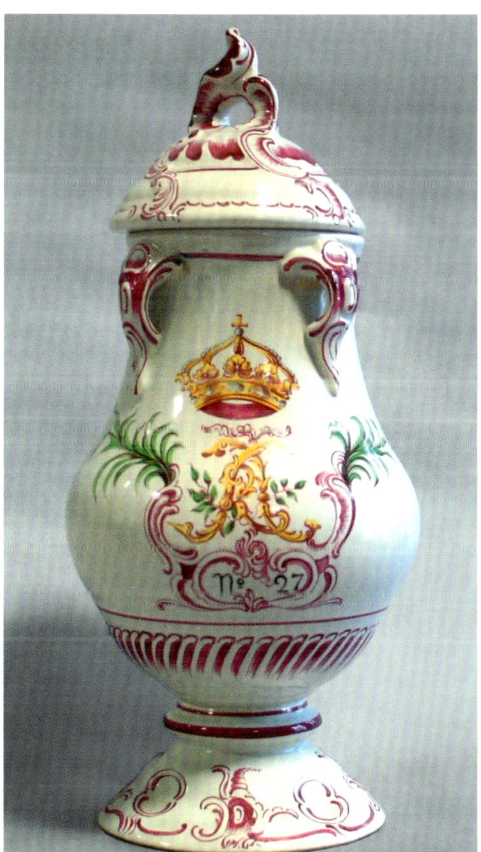

FIG. 4 Pot cannon (pharmacy jar). Manufactured by the Manufacture de Niderviller. Nancy, France, ca. 1755. Tin glazed earthenware. Musée Lorrain, Nancy, 2004.4.2

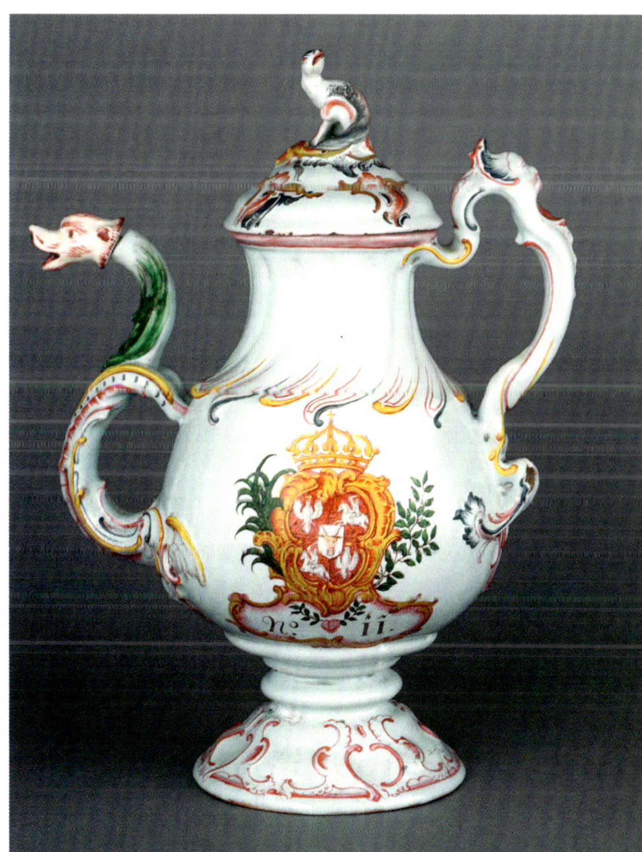

FIG. 3 Chevrette (wet-drug jar) with the arms of Stanislas Lesczynski. Manufactured by the Manufacture de Niderviller. Nancy, France, ca. 1750. Tin-glazed earthenware. Musée Lorrain, Nancy, dépôt de l'Hôpital de Nancy, 2007.0.33

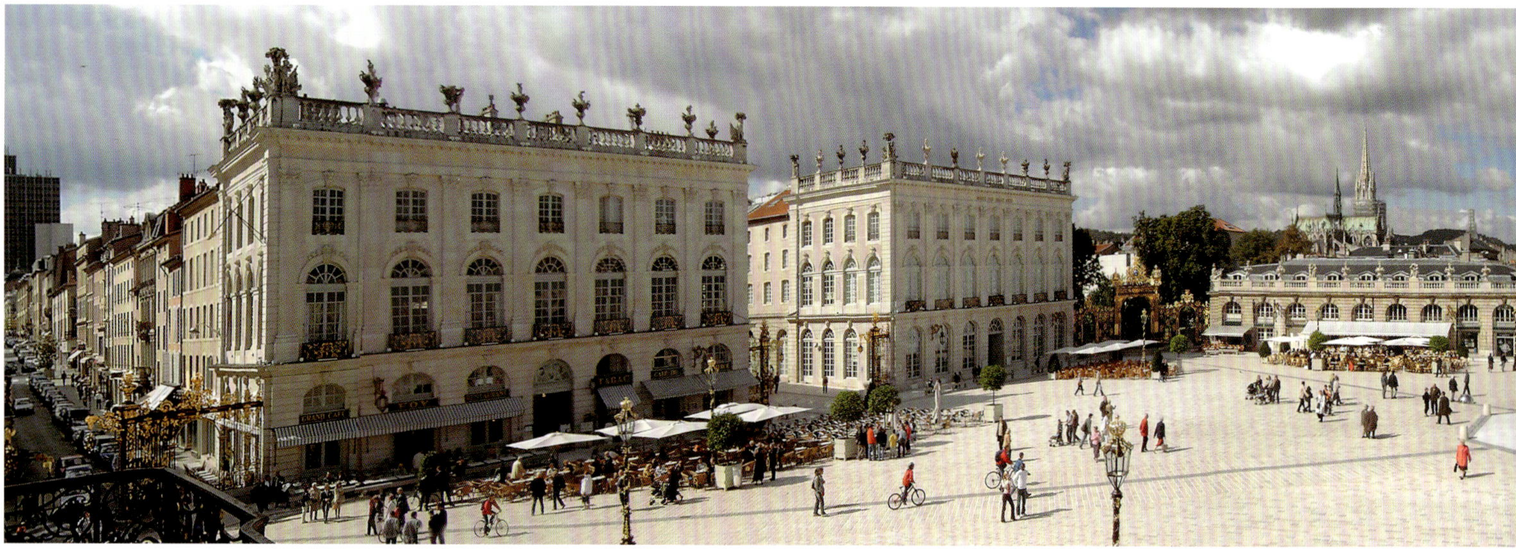

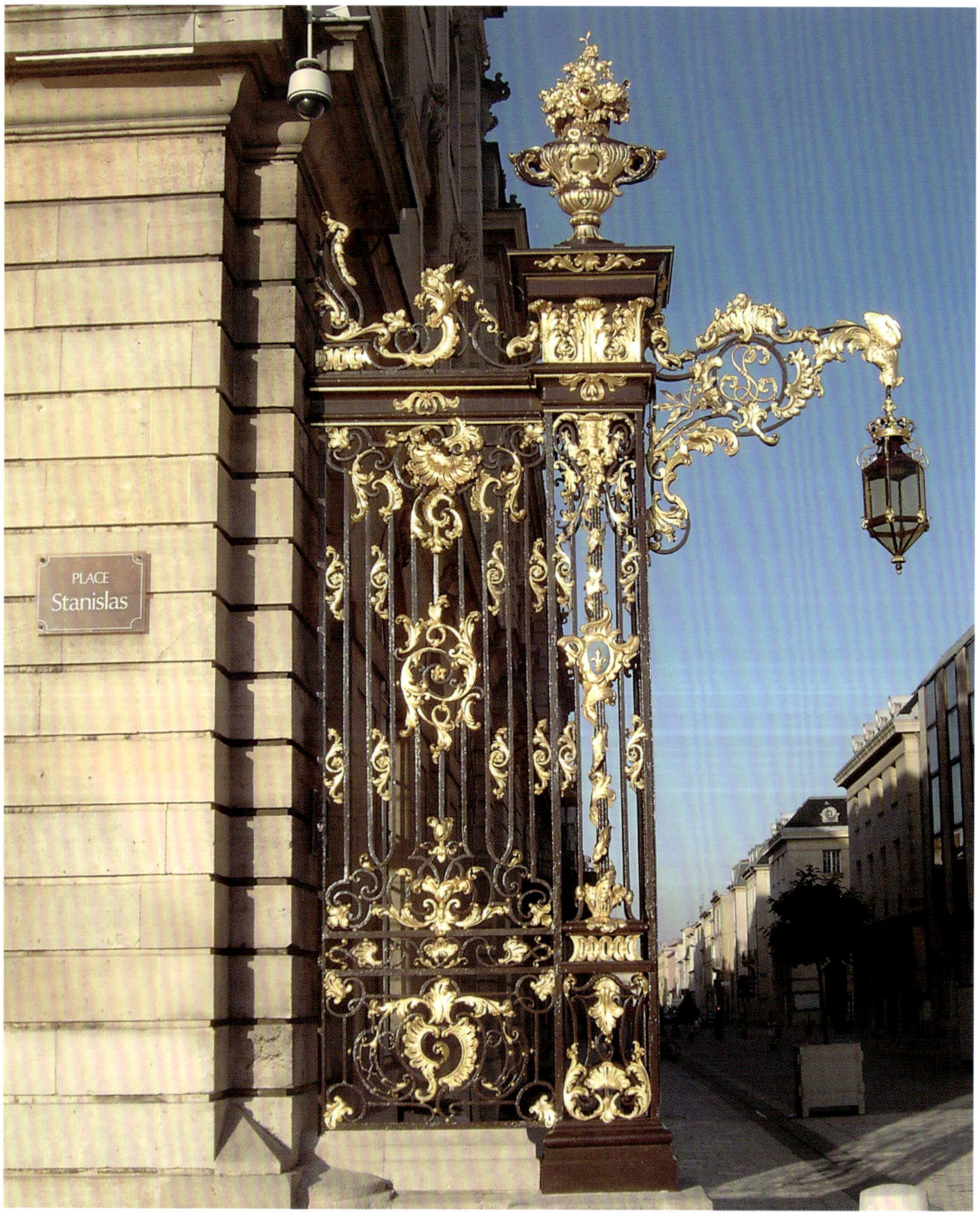

FIG. 6 Place Stanislas, Nancy, France

FIG. 7 View of entrance gate to Place Stanislas. Nancy, France

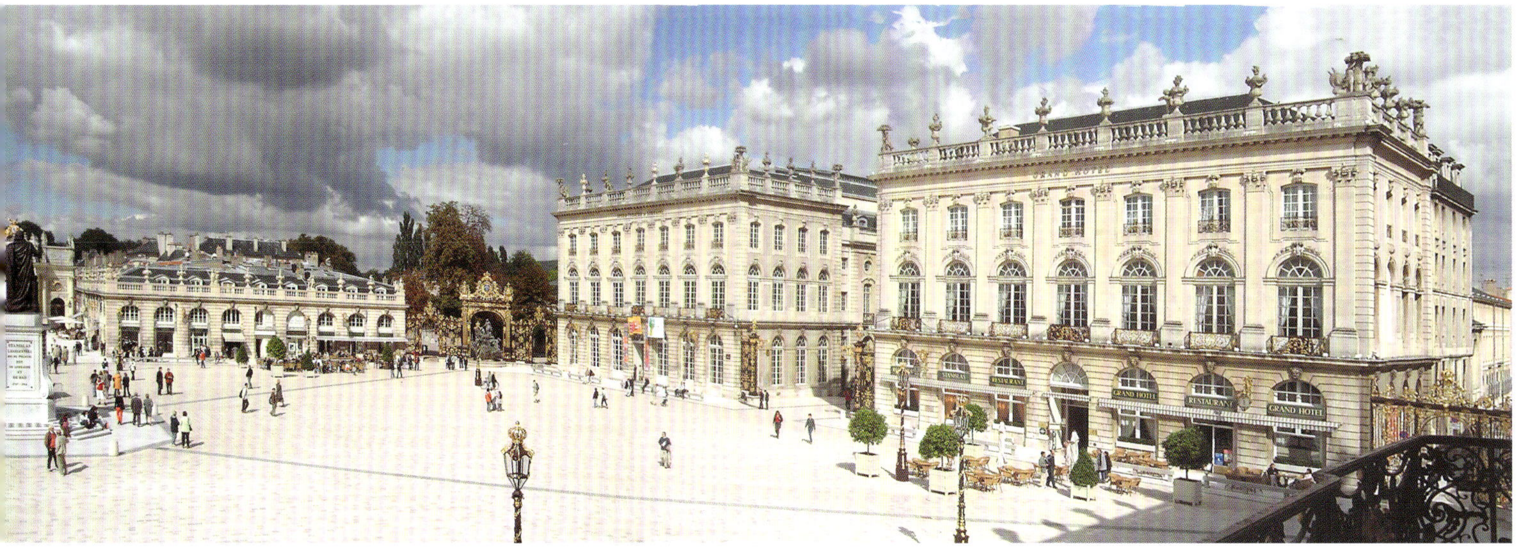

hemicycle colonnade (Place Carrière) embracing another new government building, the Palais de l'Intendance. Stanislas devoted his attention and finances to the exterior space and façades, leaving the buildings' interiors to their owners (figs. 6, 7).

JEAN LAMOUR

The artist responsible for Nancy's distinction was the blacksmith Jean Lamour (1698–1771). A native of Nancy, he followed his father to become a *serrurier* and *taillandier*, making locks and forging tools, knives, pots, and pans. He mastered the techniques of blacksmithing in his father's workshop before extending his studies between 1715 and 1719 in Metz and Paris, where it is believed that he also learned architectural design.[9] A city appointment in 1724 burdened him with mundane duties like the repair of street lights, but, two years later, he received the title of *serrurier de la ville*, or city locksmith, which helped him gain opportunities to display his creative abilities. The grille he executed with the arms of the city for the church of Saint-Epvre in 1728 has been lost. However, two elements of a balustrade in full asymmetrical rococo style, preserved in the Musée lorrain, must have been executed shortly thereafter, as they were identified as coming from the *ancienne Intendance*,[10] (fig. 8) a wing of the ducal palace renovated in 1729 to accommodate Duke François III, the remains of which have been incorporated in the present museum complex. Lamour balustrades were part of the renovation that was inspected and paid in 1730.[11] Their asymmetrical riffs on the established vocabulary of scrolls and cartouches place Lamour's designs alongside the Paris works whose similar liberties marked the commencement of high rococo.

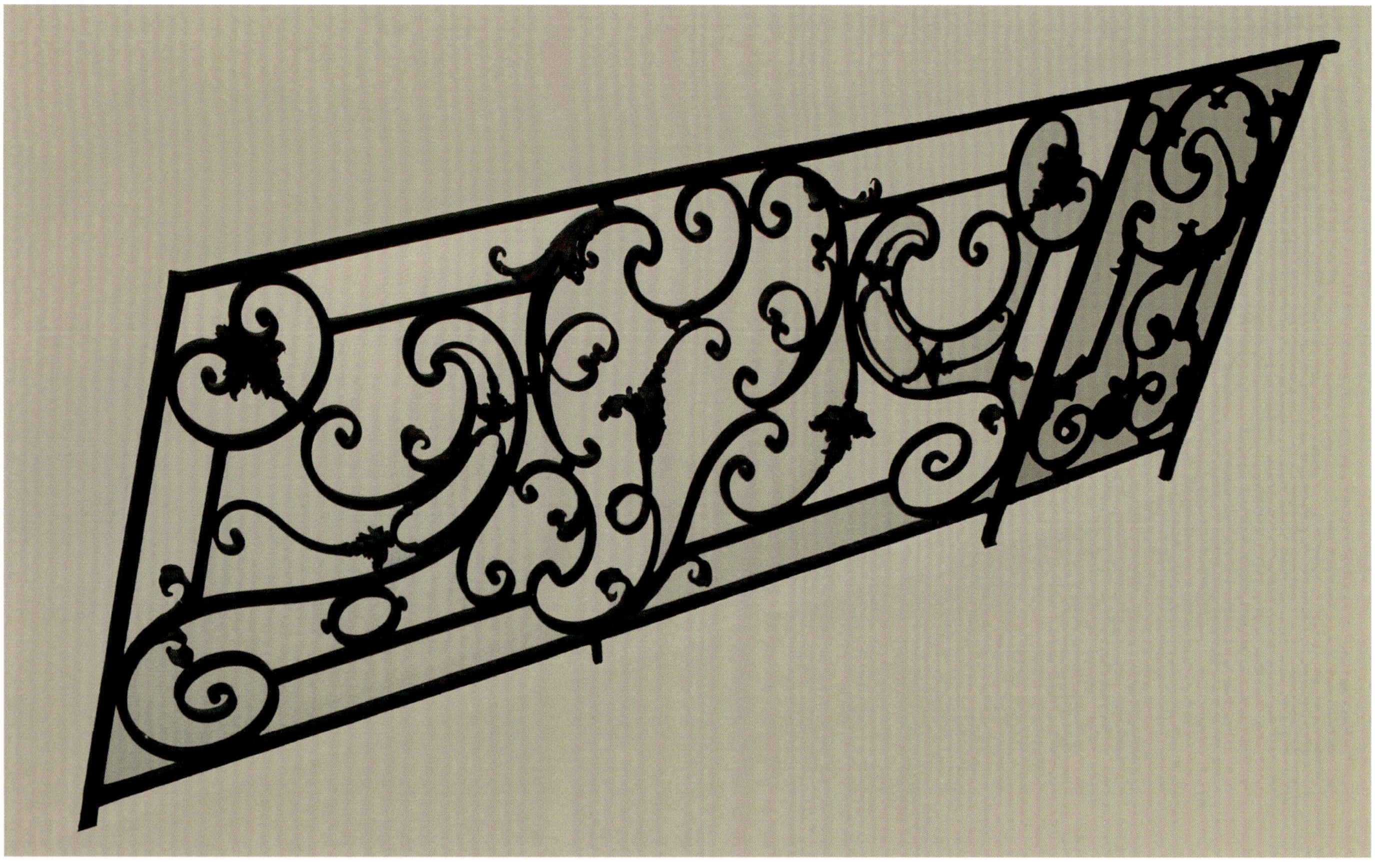

FIG. 8 Balustrade from the Ancienne Intendance. Jean Lamour (French, 1698–1771). Nancy, France, 1729. Forged iron. Musée Lorrain, Nancy, 07.04.25.314

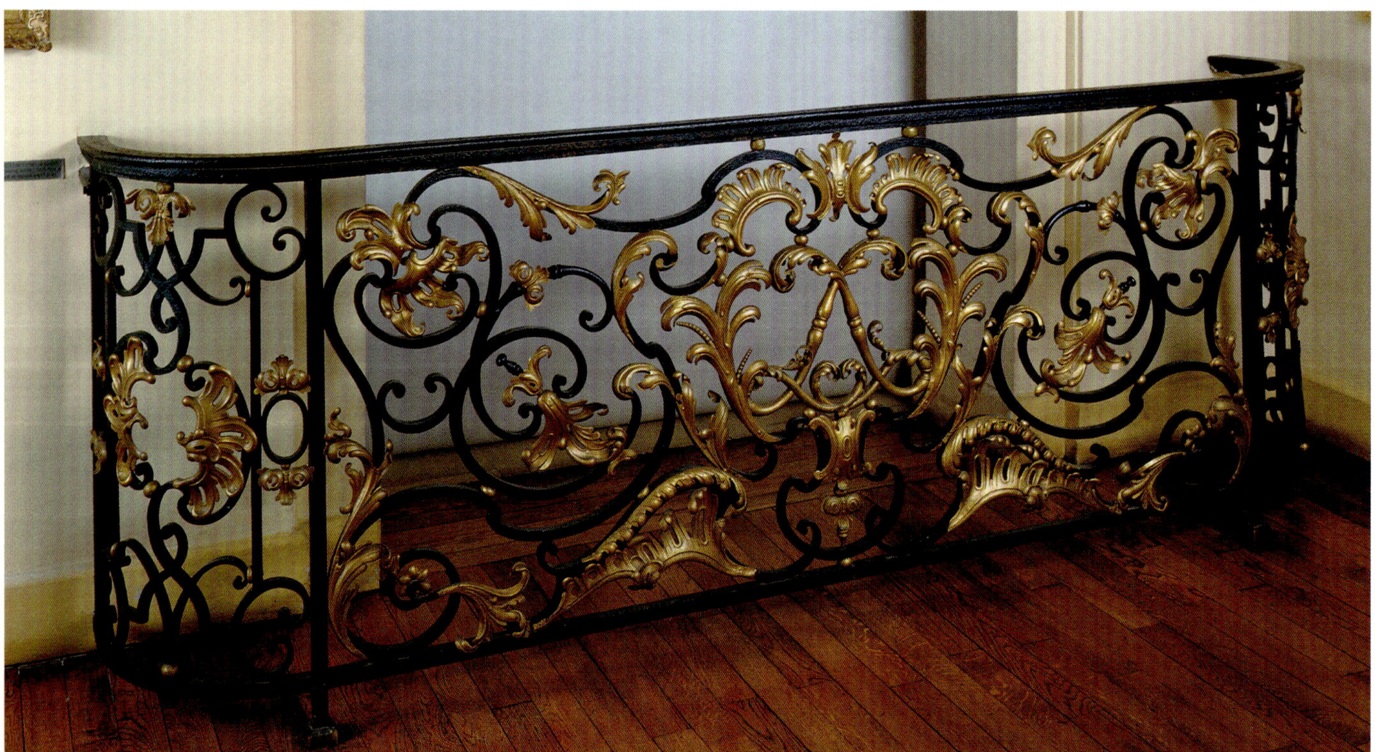

FIG. 9 Balcony from the Hôtel de Ville. Jean Lamour (French, 1698–1771). Nancy, France, 1752–55. Gilded, forged iron. Musée Lorrain, Nancy, 69.4.3

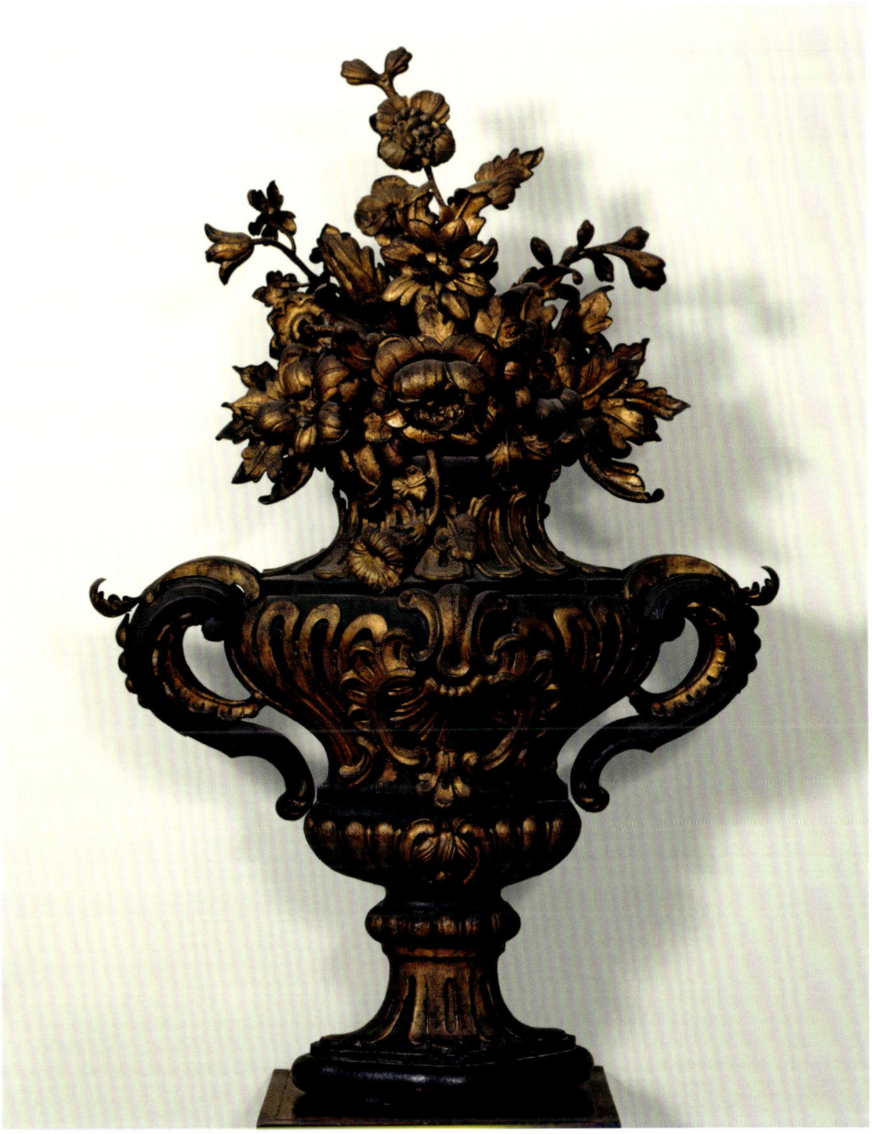

FIG. 10 Vase. Jean Lamour (French, 1698–1771). French, 1752–55. Gilded, forged iron. Musée Lorrain, Nancy, D. III-198

Héré took Lamour as a collaborator in his architectural commissions even before the arrival of Stanislas, who immediately perceived his outstanding talent. Lamour was appointed *serrurier du roi* in 1738, and his ironwork was prominently featured in all of Stanislas's subsequent architectural commissions[12] leading up to the monumental project for the Place Stanislas, which occupied him from 1752 to its inauguration in 1755. As many as two hundred workers were employed under Lamour's direction for this unprecedented ironwork commission. They made innumerable balconies of different design, ranging from the sumptuous splendor of the Hôtel de Ville (figs. 9) to the simpler inventions along the Place Carrière; brackets for street lamps hanging from the beaks of roosters; and gateways for the streets emptying onto the Place Royale (fig. 7). The ultimate triumph lay in framing the fountains by the local sculptor Barthélémy Guibal (1699–1757) in two corners of the square (figs. 11, 12). Lamour had to engineer a novel support system for the towering, transparent architecture, set against newly planted trees to mask the fortifications of the old town. Gilding was lavished on decorative elements made

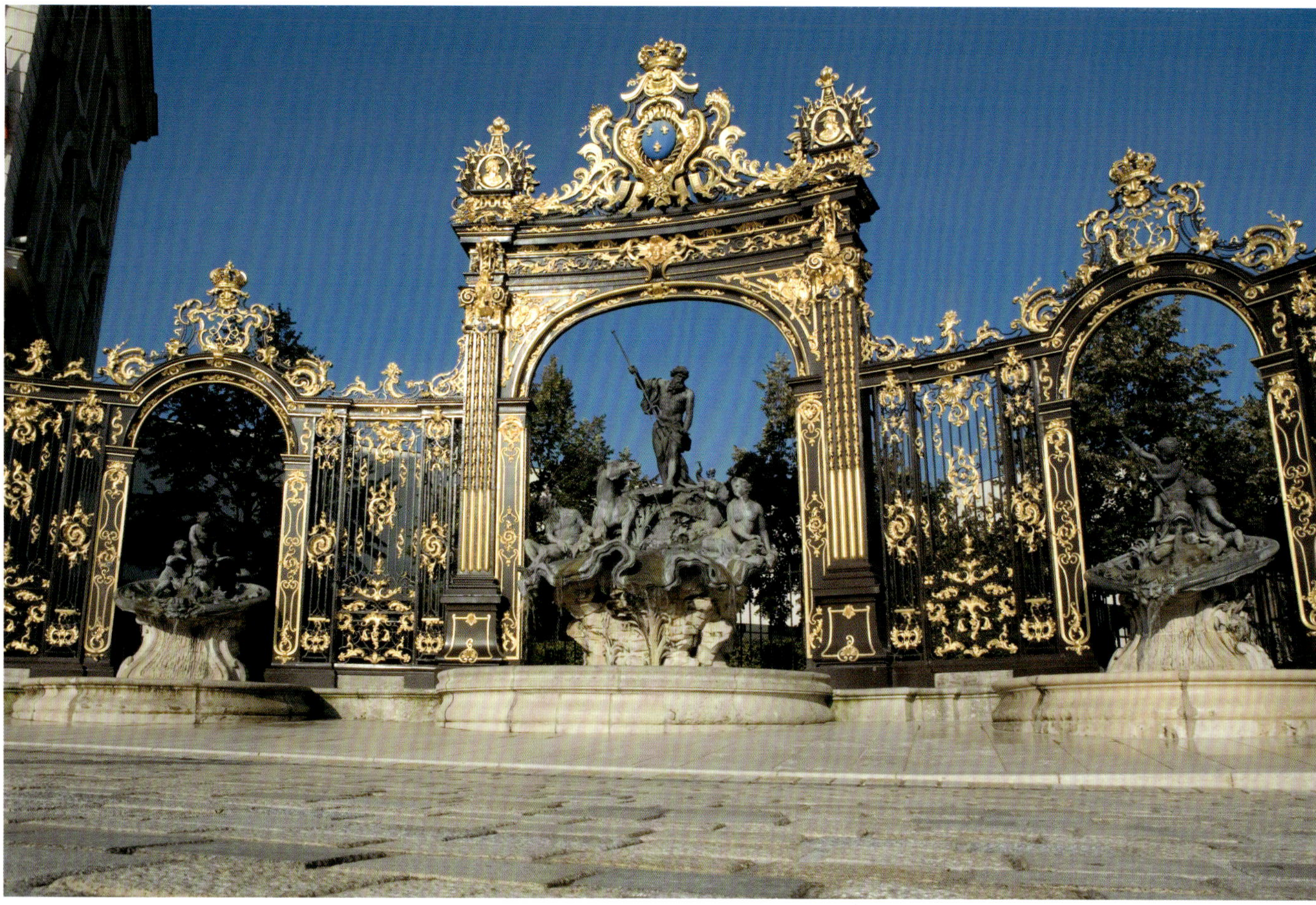

FIG. 11 View of the Neptune Fountain, Place Stanislas. Designed by Jean Lamour (French, 1698–1771)

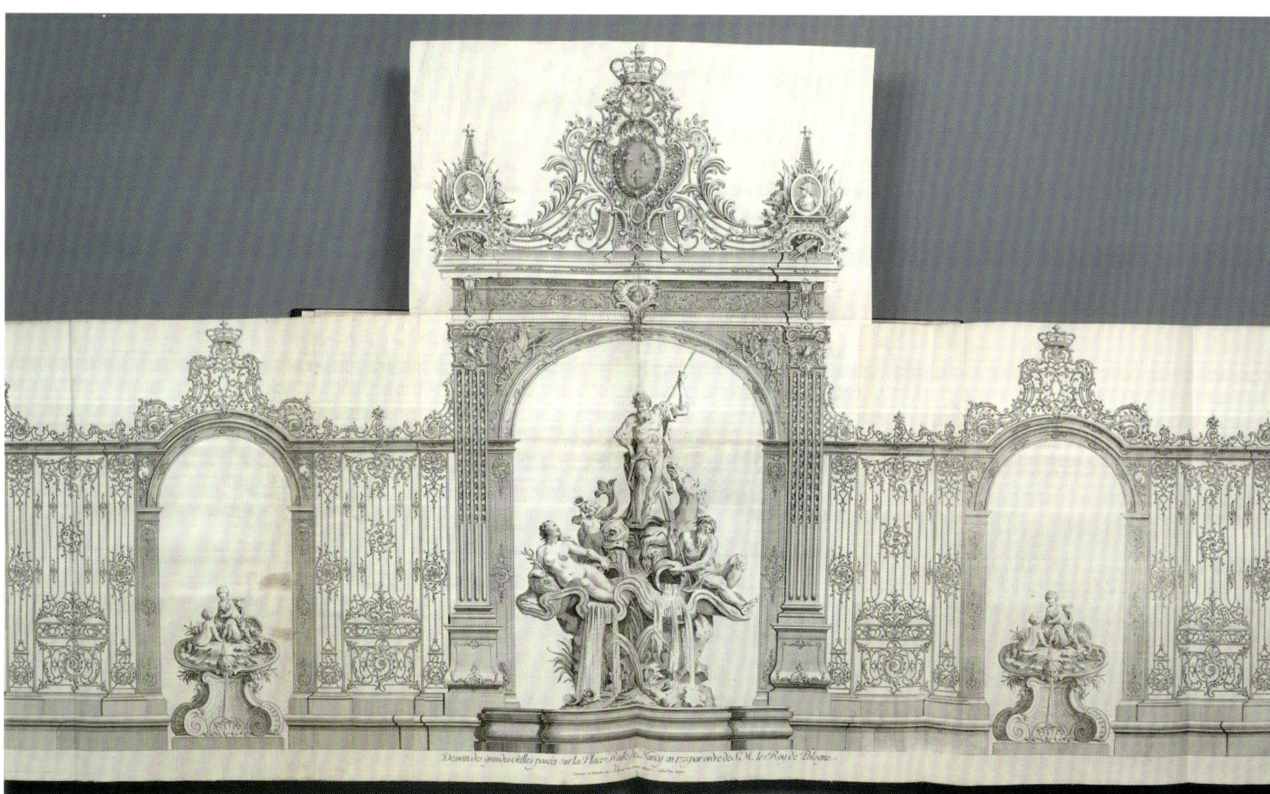

FIG. 12 Designs for the Neptune Fountain, Place Stanislas. Jean Lamour (French, 1698–1771). Engraved by Nicolas Collin. France, 1763. Engraving on heavy cream laid paper. Cooper-Hewitt, National Design Museum, Smithsonian Institution, Purchased for the Museum by the Advisory Council, 1921-6-210-3

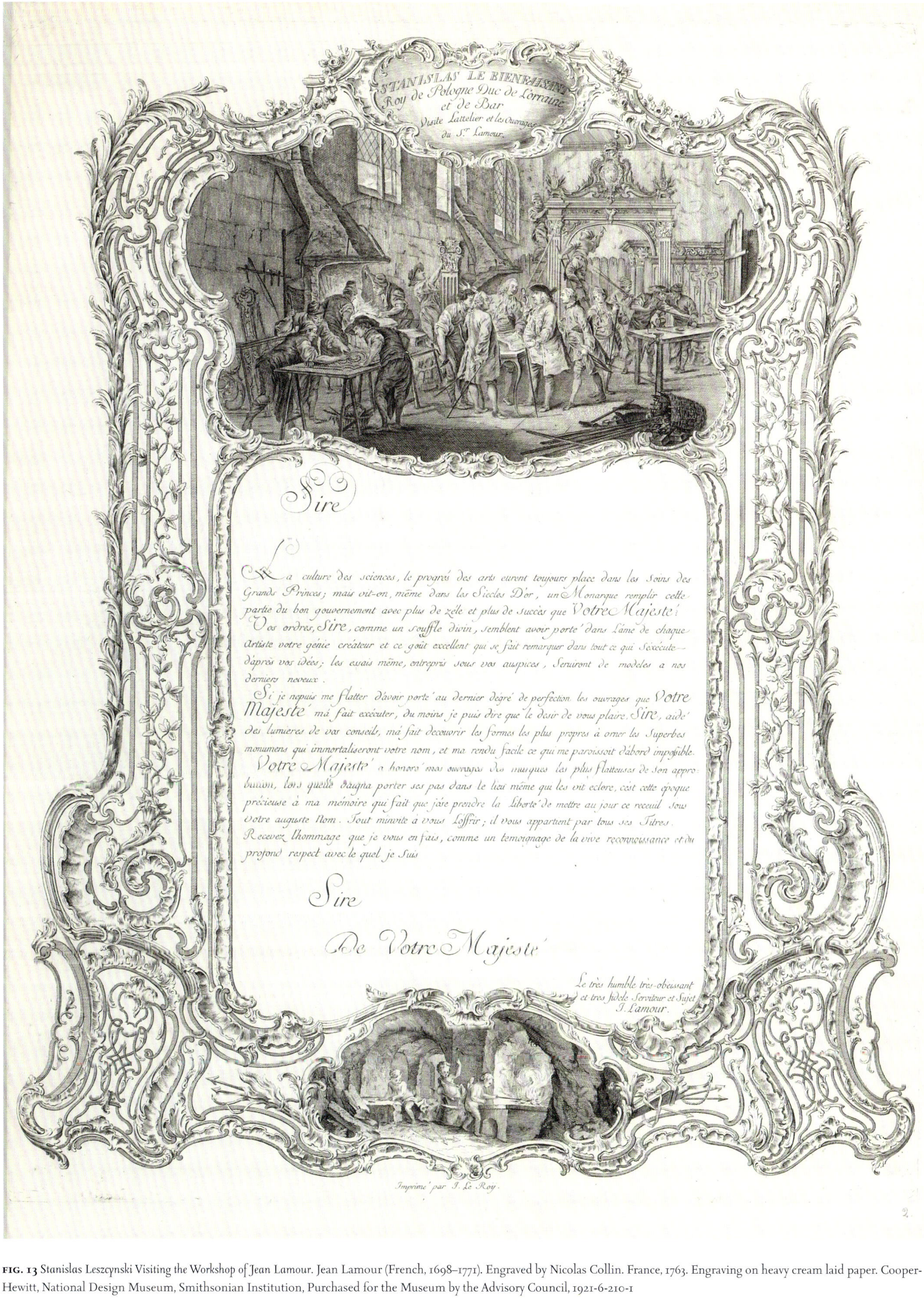

FIG. 13 Stanislas Leszcynski Visiting the Workshop of Jean Lamour. Jean Lamour (French, 1698–1771). Engraved by Nicolas Collin. France, 1763. Engraving on heavy cream laid paper. Cooper-Hewitt, National Design Museum, Smithsonian Institution, Purchased for the Museum by the Advisory Council, 1921-6-210-1

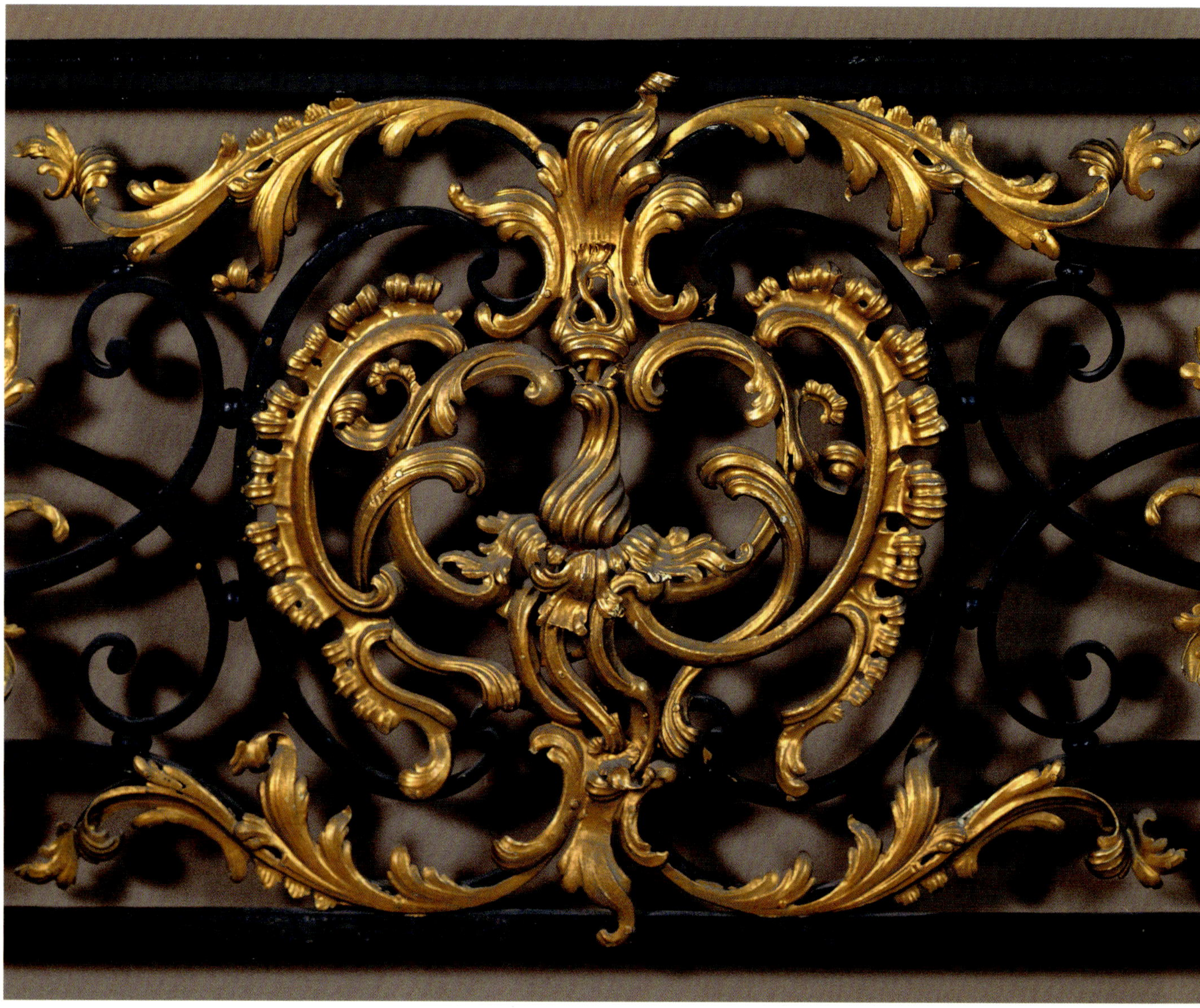

FIG. 14 Window grill from the residence of Jean Lamour. Jean Lamour (French, 1698–1771). Nancy, France, ca. 1766. Gilded, forged iron. Musée Lorrain, Nancy, D.70.7.8.A

of tole and attached to the iron members. Golden flourishes and asymmetrical eddies danced across the darkly painted iron bars, transforming their forbidding monumentality into a *capriccio*, or fantasy.

In 1767, a year after Stanisas's death, Lamour published at his own expense his *Recueil*, an album of engravings of the work he had done for his great patron. A vignette in the preface depicts Stanislas visiting Lamour in the deconsecrated Primatiale church that was made available to him as an atelier (fig. 14). Lamour is shown presenting for his patron's inspection a pilaster being executed after the drawing on the table before them. The huge archway that will span one of the fountains rises behind them. The blacksmith wears the wig and attire of a gentleman, appropriate to his role as the entrepreneur, designer, and engineer who realized what became Stanislas's lasting legacy.

Lamour accrued no great fortune, but did have a simple country retreat, a library of more than 200 volumes, and a collection of eighty-three paintings, drawings, and prints. He spent the last decade of his life in a modest four-story townhouse he constructed around 1766. (The building was demolished in 1970, but salvaged ironwork elements are preserved in the Musée lorrain.) Lamour presented the distillation of his art in the rococo essays of the window grilles (figs. 15, 16). In each of the second-floor windows, different gilded, asymmetrical eddies floated in a framework of iron bars enlivened by gilded scrolling leaves. Inside his home, however, Lamour acknowledged the onset of the new style. The simple scrolls of his staircase balustrade were encased in a frame whose only ornaments were circles and squares, which presaged neoclassicism (fig. 17).

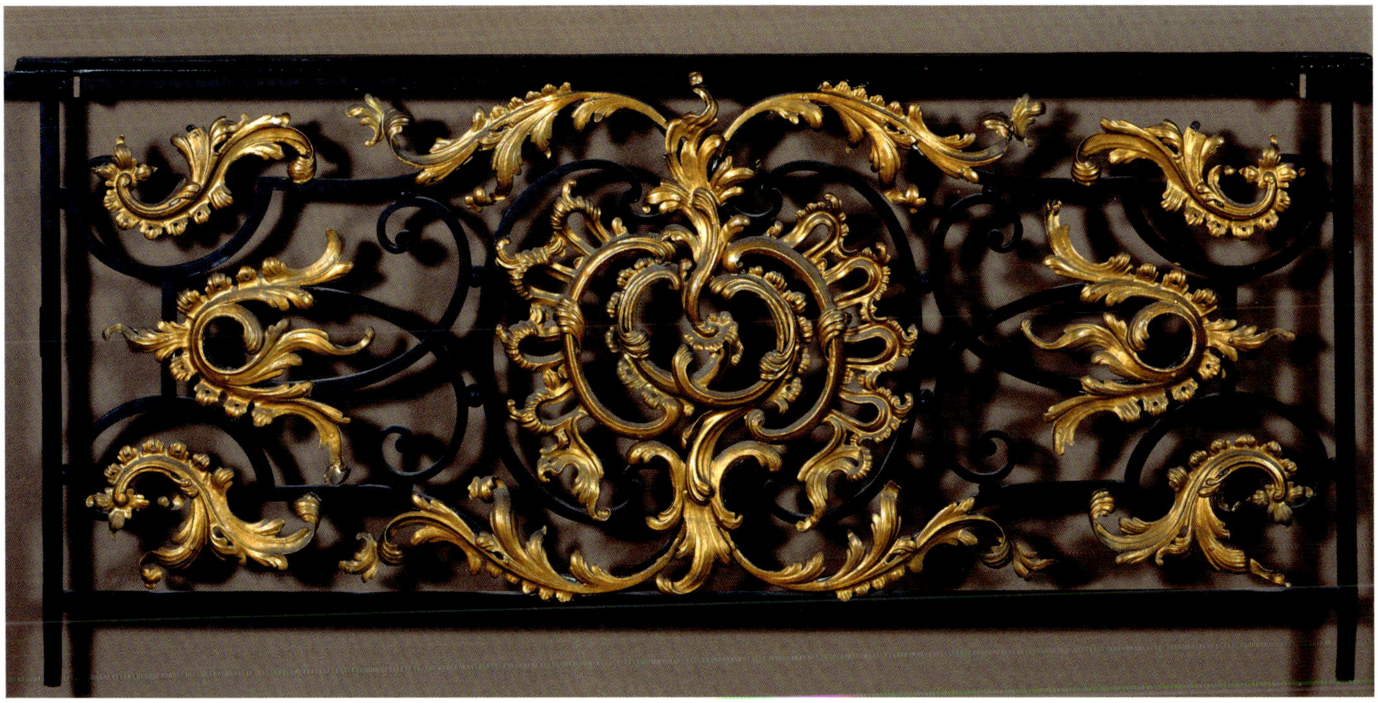

FIG. 15 Window grill from the residence of Jean Lamour. Jean Lamour (French, 1698–1771). Nancy, France, ca. 1766. Gilded, forged iron. Musée Lorrain, Nancy, D.70.7.8.B

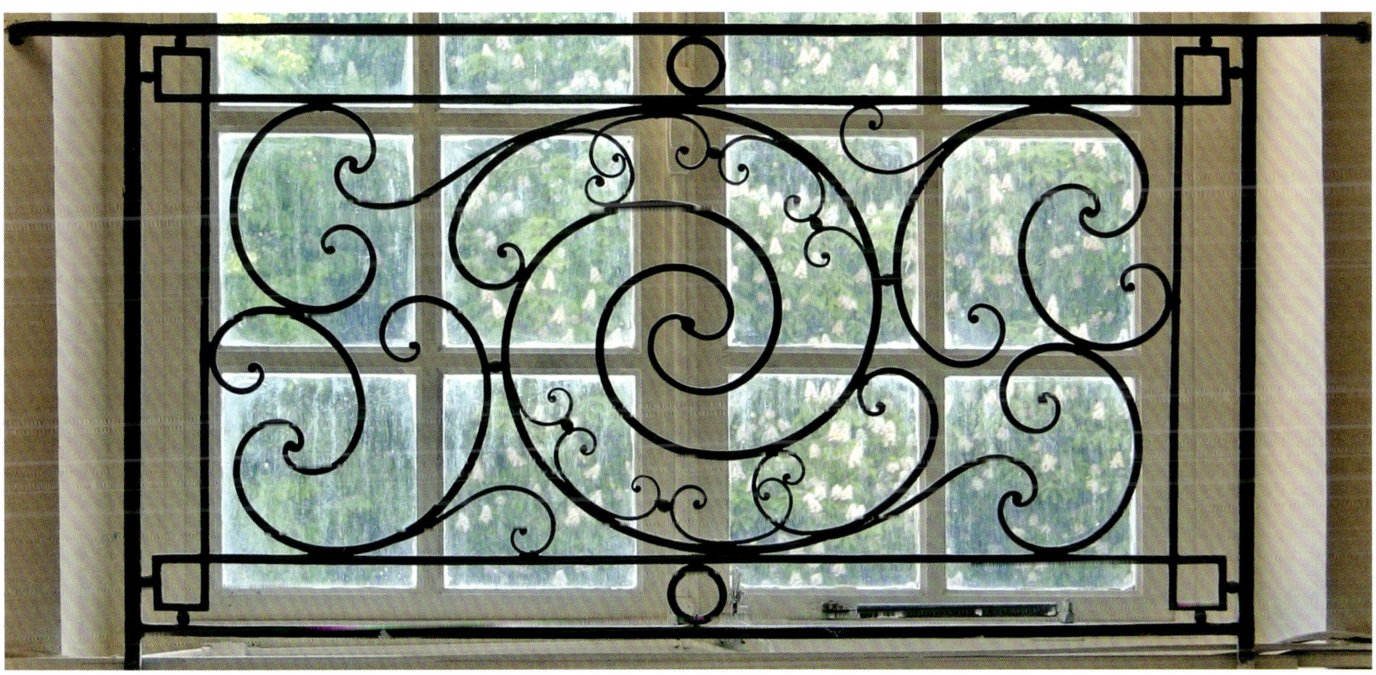

FIG. 16 Balustrade from the residence of Jean Lamour. Jean Lamour (French, 1698–1771). Nancy, France, ca. 1766. Forged iron. Musée Lorrain, Nancy, D. 70.7.10.1

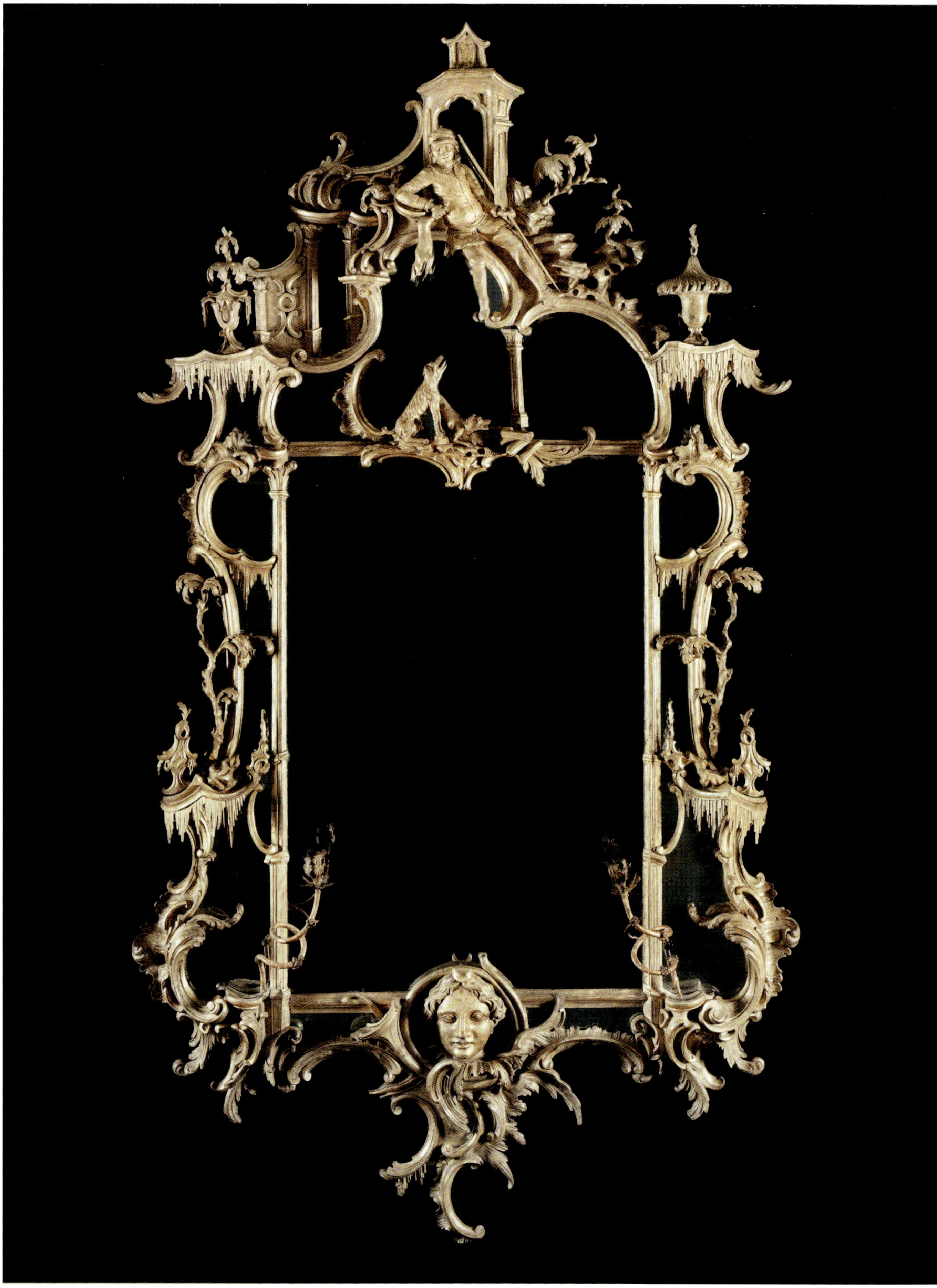

FIG. 44 Mirror. After a design by Thomas Johnson (English, 1714–ca. 1778). England, ca. 1755. Carlton Hobbs LLC

Radiating Rococo

THE DISSEMINATION OF STYLE THROUGH MIGRATING DESIGNERS, CRAFTSMEN, AND OBJECTS IN THE EIGHTEENTH CENTURY

Sarah D. Coffin

Patronage is key to the blossoming of a style from artist's fancy to its articulation in accepted forms. The craftsmen and objects that spread rococo were encouraged by patrons who were of lively, and sometimes slightly rebellious, spirit. Rococo style is sinuous, organic, and sensuous, and often asymmetrical. It is much like a newly nubile teenager showing off to provoke parental disapproval. The spirit of the rebellion, embodied in the work of Juste-Aurèle Meissonnier (1695–1750) and Thomas Germain (1673–1745), enchanted the court of young Louis XV and his Polish bride Maria Lesczynska in the late 1720s. It was later exported to foreign patrons, many of whom can be described as *bon vivants*, enjoyers of life with an eye for something new. One ambassador of taste, the snuffbox, carried rococo style to much of Europe. Indeed, the snuffbox is, in many ways, the embodiment of rococo style and its associations with pleasure and fantasy (fig. 1).

OBJECTS OF UNVIRTUOUS VERTU: WHERE VIRTUOSITY REIGNED OVER FUNCTIONALITY

Snuffboxes were vanity objects, often designed by the top goldsmiths, and given as royal or aristocratic presentations to ambassadors and loved ones to hold snuff, the newly fashionable powdered tobacco. The spread of rococo fashion in Europe started in full force by the 1730s, corresponding to a great rise in the consumption of snuff and the parallel increase in the number of snuffboxes that transported not only snuff but taste and style. It is no coincidence that these boxes—made for something nonessential, whose use was strictly for pleasure, an addictive and slightly naughty fashion—were the most outré displays of the new style.

The rococo snuffbox of Paris that inspired many of these creations may have owed its forms—the shell, cartouche, and other shaped variants which fit into one's palm—to Juste Aurèle Meissonnier's designs. Many of the boxes made in Paris that most closely reflected Meissonnier's designs or spirit were created by Daniel Govaers (or Gouers, as he signed in Paris). Of Dutch or Flemish origin, Govaers, accepted as a master in Paris in 1717, was patronized by the young Louis XV. He contributed jewelry for the *corbeille*, or basket, for the new Queen Marie Leczinscka[1] in 1725; that same year, he made a diamond-encrusted sword handle, whose design is attributed to Meissonnier, presented to the Elector of Bavaria.[2] He made eleven snuffboxes for Louis XV to give as diplomatic gifts, as well as others for the Queen of Spain, the Elector of Saxony, and the Duke of Bavaria.[3]

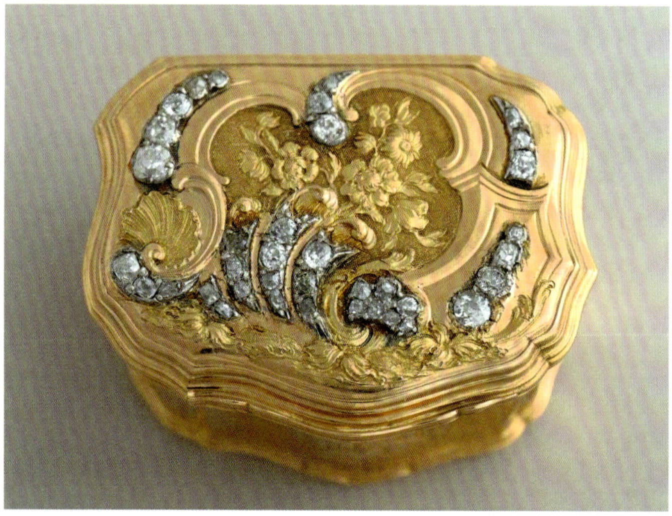

FIG. 1 Snuffbox. Daniel Govaers (Flemish, active Paris ca. 1717–54). Paris, France, ca. 1735. Gold, diamonds. Private collection

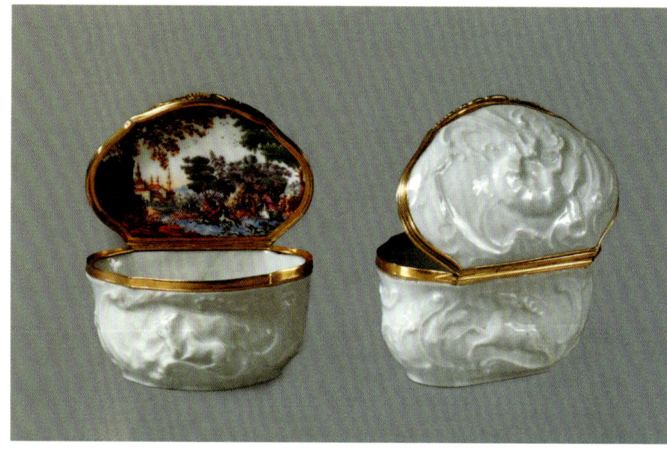

FIG. 2 Snuffbox. Modeled by Johann Joachim Kändler. Meissen Porcelain Manufactory. Meissen, Germany, 1737–40. Porcelain, enamel, gold. Private collection

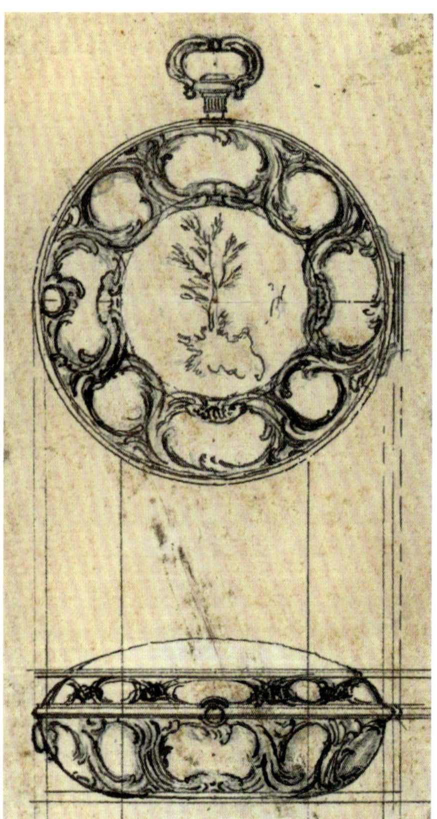

FIG. 3 *Design for a Gold Watchcase Showing Front and Elevation.* Hubert-François Gravelot (French, 1699–1773). England, 1745. Pen and grey ink over graphite; smudge of brown wash. The Metropolitan Museum of Art, Gift of A.S.W. Rosenbach, 1944.66.1

His works are characterized by an innate sense of the curvilinear and the sophisticated integration of jewels into rococo design.

It is hard to know whether the brevity of the fashion for the most organic elements of rococo design or financial reasons led to Govaers's bankruptcy. He fled Paris for Brussels in 1736, while retaining his title as *orfèvre ordinaire de la Reine* (Goldsmith in Ordinary to the Queen). However, most of the modified shell-form snuffboxes made in France date to the 1730s. Some examples of this form in porcelain, enamel, and hardstone were still produced for another twenty years, but primarily in other countries and in decreasing numbers.

The inroads of snuff into European society bear some resemblance to those of rococo style. Earlier trade between Spain and Portugal and the Western hemisphere in tobacco brought its uses and fashions, including snuff-taking, to southern Europe, working its way north through France in the mid-seventeenth century and on to northern Europe in the late seventeenth century. While Spain is not generally thought of as a source of rococo, Spanish architect Francisco Juvarra flirted with rococo style when he designed parts of the royal palace in Turin, the birthplace of Meissonnier. The trajectory of snuff through France is also relevant because the Edict of Nantes, which protected French Huguenots, was revoked in 1685. Many of the French goldsmiths who made fine snuffboxes were Huguenots who migrated to parts of Germany, Holland, and England. There, they and their progeny, along with other artisans seeking patronage, became some of the finest goldsmiths in those countries, producing snuffboxes of a caliber made in Paris but adapted to local taste. One such example made in Amsterdam in 1739 by Jean Saint, originally from St. Lo, in Normandy, was inspired by Meissonnier's designs (see Baarsen, fig. 14). These emigrant masters often inspired local talent with their craftsmanship and style, the results incorporating both local and foreign design sources.

Another snuff route followed Italian-controlled tobacco monopolies in Bavaria and other German states. Similar routes were taken by Italian stuccoists and modelers who added rococo ornament to buildings and worked for porcelain manufacturers, silversmiths, and bronze casters. The flow helped create, in a variety of media, a rococo style very different from that in France, even when works were inspired by French engravings. Augustus the Strong of Saxony, who long had the secret of porcelain locked up at Meissen, used porcelain for top ambassadorial gifts, although not much of it was rococo in spirit, in part a reflection of his taste. However, porcelain snuffboxes, highly prized, were occasionally made in rococo style and shape (fig. 2).

During the 1740s, rococo decoration of snuffboxes was increasingly limited to geometric shapes, such as the oval. The style manifested itself in the surface treatment, created by gold chasing and enameling, which added festive color in much the way polychrome decoration was enlivening porcelain (fig. 3). England and some of the German states also produced original as well as French-inspired snuffboxes and other objects of vertu,[4] some of which combined local preferences with French designs. Objects based on French design sources were often later and larger than the originals. Good examples are Meissonnier-inspired scent bottles (figs. 4–6) made in London, from 1740 to 1760. A major source of French design was the former student of Boucher, Parisian engraver and drawing instructor Hubert-François (Bourguignon) Gravelot (1699–1773), in London from 1732/3 to 1746, who produced designs for snuffboxes, watchcases, etuis, frames, and other objects. More important, he taught drawing first at his own school and, by 1745, at the St. Martin's Lane Academy, founded by William Hogarth. Many talented modelers and craftsmen studied design drawing together there, unhampered by the restrictions on apprenticeship to one trade. Gravelot's engraved book illustrations also disseminated rococo style.

Among the group of goldworkers associated with the academy was another key figure in the transmission of rococo to England, the Swiss goldsmith George Michael Moser, from Schaffhausen, who came to England via Geneva by 1730. In 1731–32, he and the medalist James (Jacques) Röettiers lived at the same address. Moser worked for John Haidt, a Berlin-trained goldsmith who let him run a drawing school in his house.[5] Like Gravelot, Moser was teaching at Hogarth's academy by 1746. He was not only an accomplished enamelist, but also a gold chaser of considerable talent, which reflected his strong skills as a draftsman (figs. 7–9). Moser, who combined enamel and gold work in watchcases and snuffboxes, was not the only Swiss artist in London to combine these materials, a Swiss specialty. Jean-André Rouquet, born of French Huguenot refugees in Geneva, painted enamel miniatures, some of which were incorporated into snuffboxes, as well as full-scale works. Like Moser, he was considered an artist and was a friend of Hogarth, a

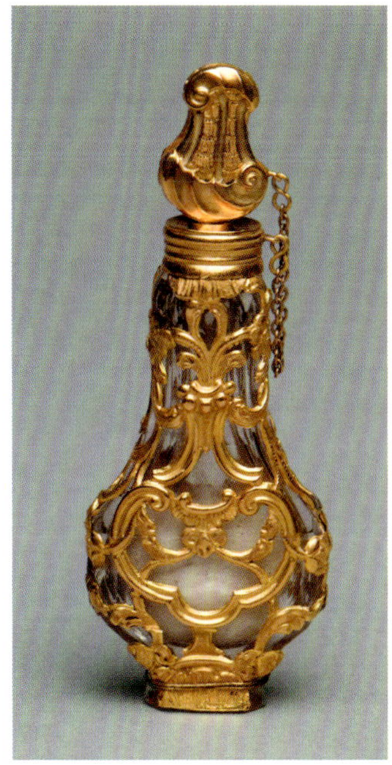

FIG. 4 Scent bottle. Probably England, ca. 1745. Glass, gold. Cleveland Museum of Art, Gift of Mr. and Mrs. J. H. Wade, 1916.315

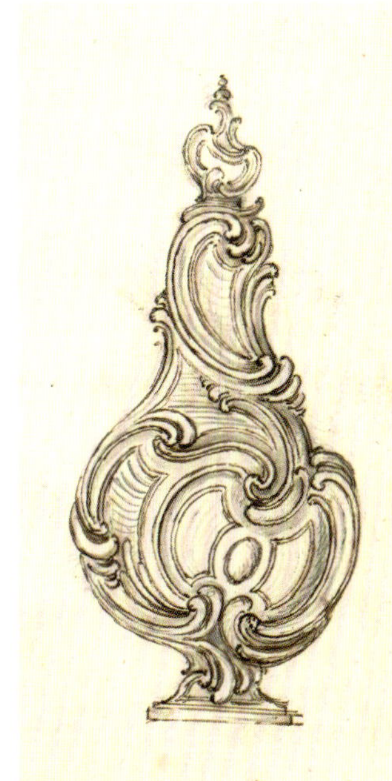

FIG. 5 *Ornament Design*. Juste-Aurèle Meissonnier (French, 1695–1750). France, ca. 1735. Pen and brown ink, brush and gray wash, graphite underdrawing. The Metropolitan Museum of Art, Rogers Fund, 1986.1032.1

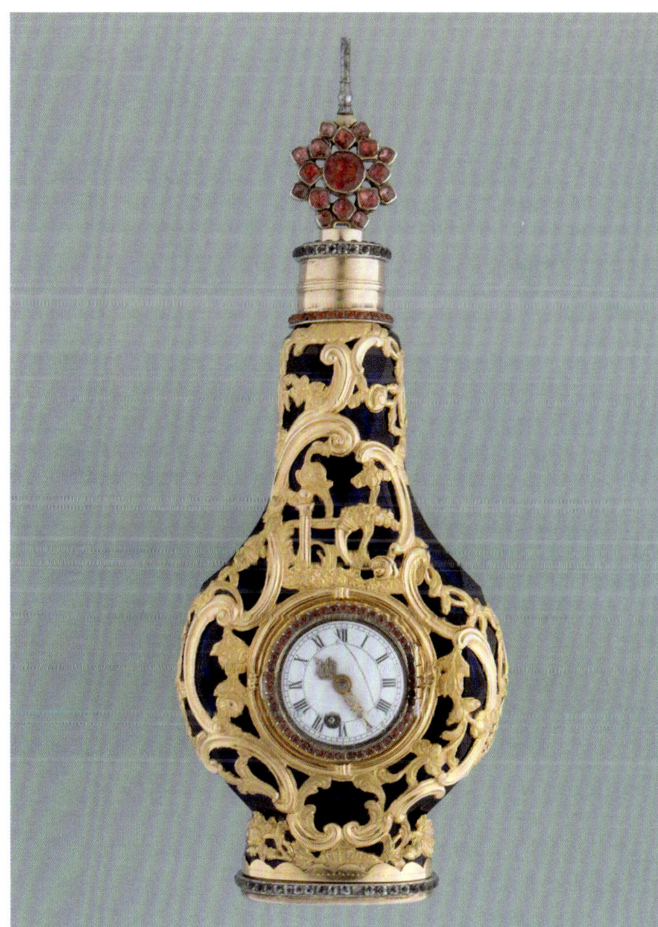

FIG. 6 Scent bottle with mounted clock. James Cox (English, ca. 1723–1800). London, England, ca. 1760. Brass, brillant, clockworks, colored glass, garnet, gold. Musée du Louvre, OA8024

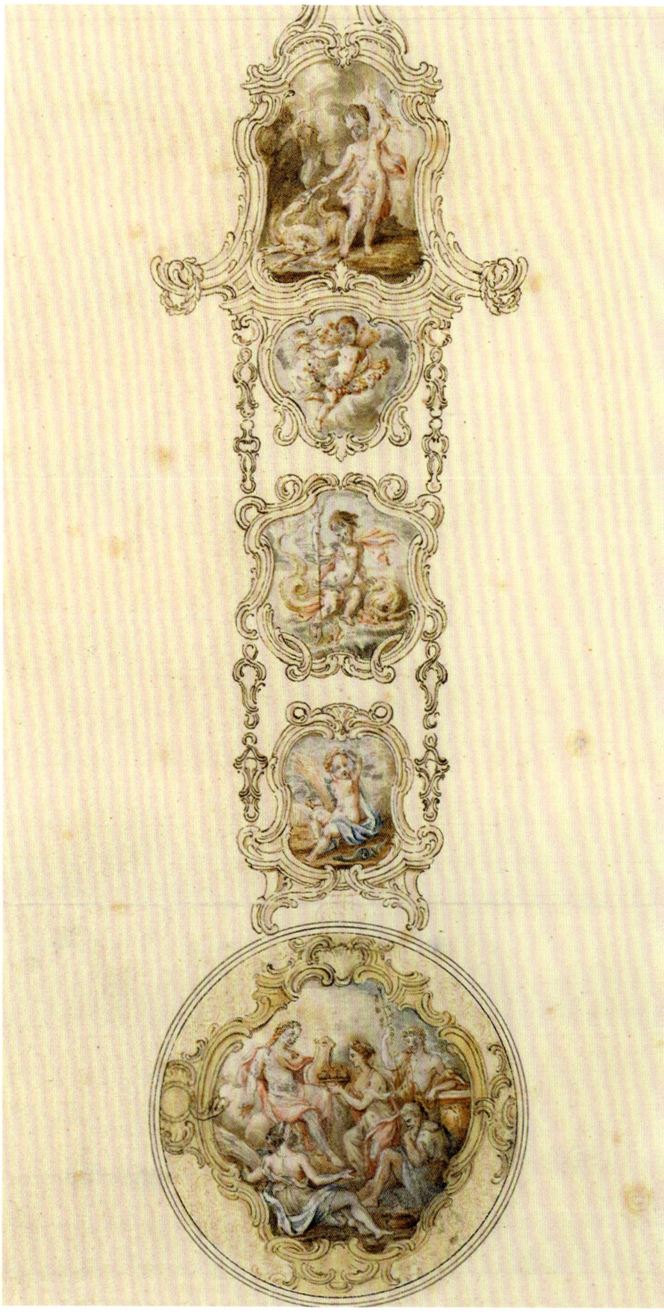

FIG. 7 *Design for Watchcase and Chatelaine*. George Michael Moser (Swiss, 1706–1783, active London 1736–79). England, ca. 1760. Pen and ink and gouache on paper. The Metropolitan Museum of Art, Gift of Janos Scholz, 49.93.9

The watchcase depicts Apollo and the Four Seasons, the chatelaine with the Four Elements, to be executed in enamel, of which Moser was an adept practitioner.

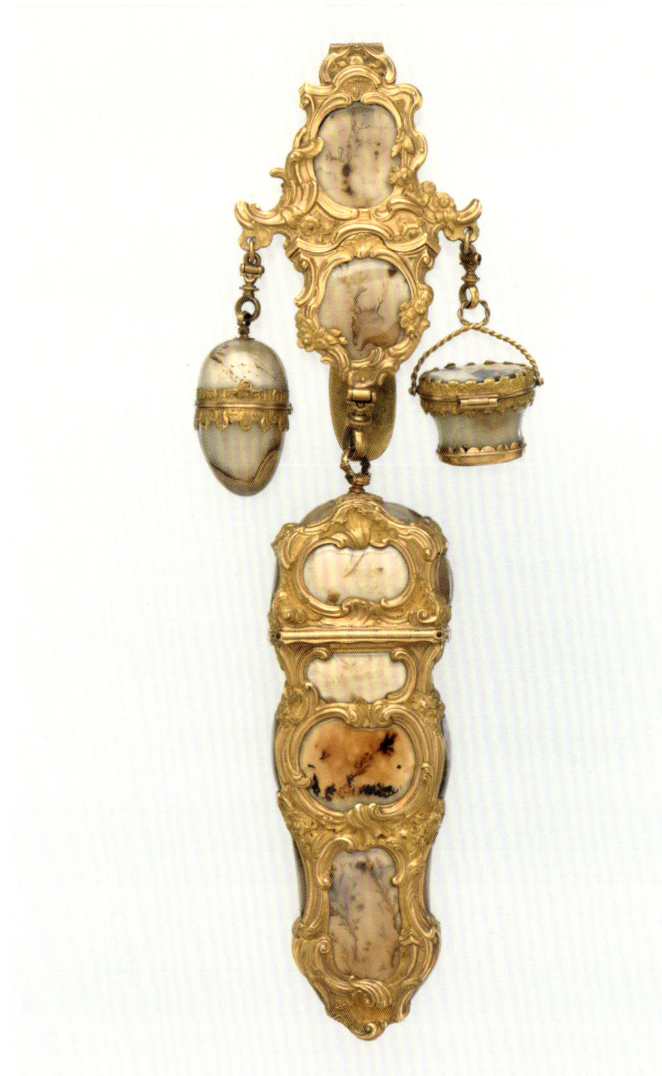

FIG. 8 Chatelaine. England, 1750–60. Gold, moss and variegated agate. The Metropolitan Museum of Art, Rogers Fund, 35.102

The use of variegated agate, which allowed the creation of a pictorial element in hardstone, was especially popular with English and German makers.

common denominator with most of the rococo artists of the day. Moser eventually became a founding member of the Royal Academy at its inception in 1768.[6]

Critical to the integration of the arts and of rococo style in England is an understanding of gold chasing, which required a combination of skills—of draftsman, sculptor-modeler, and goldsmith. Chasing sometimes refers to the process, also called repoussé work, whereby gold (or other metal) is raised from the reverse with a hammer or punch to create decoration in relief. It also can refer, without the raising, to the tooling and engraving of a surface to refine and add detail to the decoration. The latter refinements can also be applied to raised decoration created by casting in the *cire perdu*, or lost wax, process, which starts with sculpting in wax. It is not surprising that sculpture and engraving were so integrated with the gold chasing of this period, and it also explains the crossover of talented carvers and sculptors from one medium to another, as well as the higher status those who chased and sculpted enjoyed over most other goldsmiths. St. Martin's Lane and other drawing academies

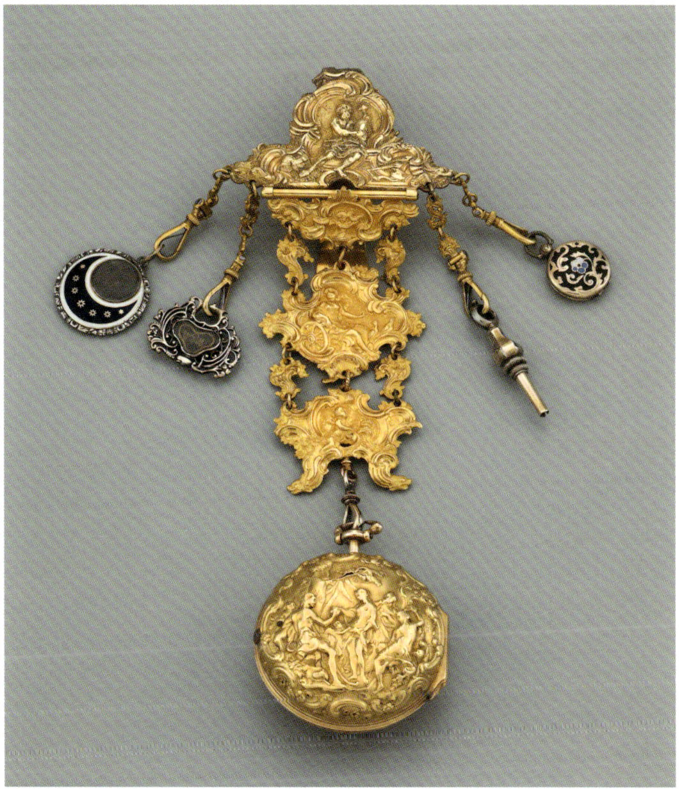

FIG. 9 Chatelaine watch. Retailed by Thomas Gordon, New York, NY. London, England, 1759–60. Gold, silver, enamel, glass, porcelain, hair. Yale University Art Gallery, Mabel Brady Garvan, 1948.224a-f

This watch is an example of great rococo chasing for the American market. Few, if any, chasers of this caliber were working in the colonies at this time.

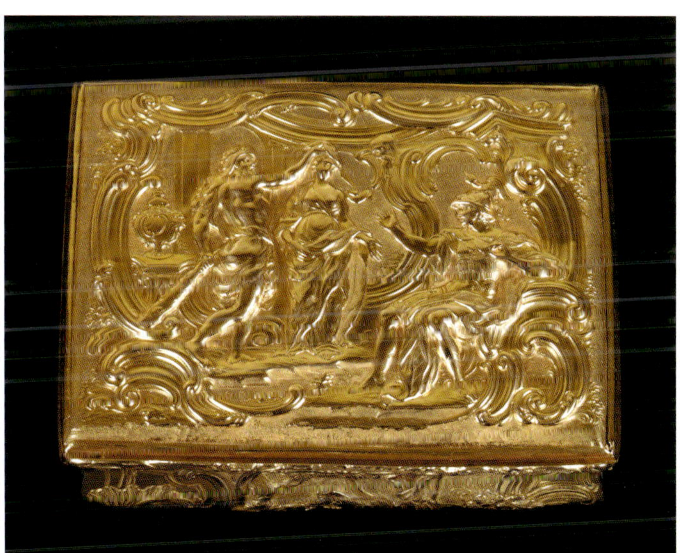

FIG. 10 Snuffbox. Francis Harache (English, active ca. 1738–58). Chasing signed by Thomas Burges (English, active ca. 1731–82). London, England, ca. 1750. Gold. A la Vieille Russie

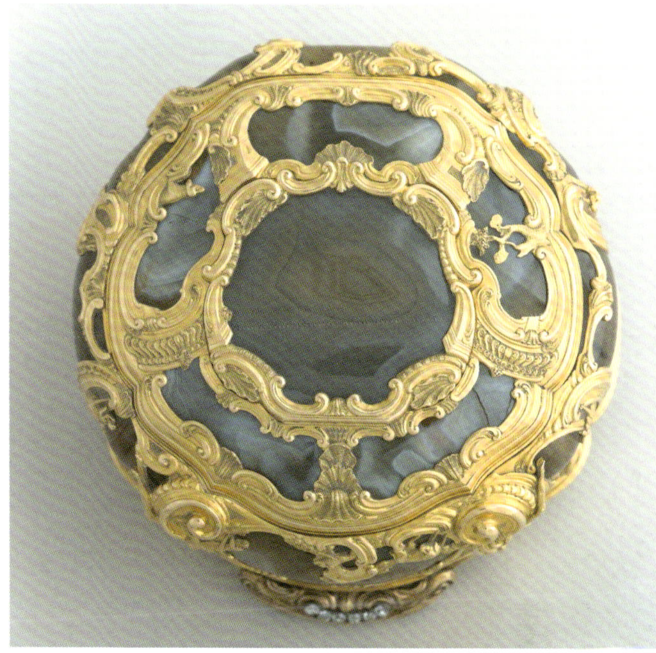

FIG. 11 Watch and snuffbox. London, England, ca. 1760. Agate, gold, enamel, metal. Private collection

This box in the manner of James Cox was the type of object often exported from London to foreign courts, as Cox's delicate use of gold cagework on hardstone combined with high-level watch-making made this a desirable import.

fostered the multinational talents of rococo, enhancing the skills of goldsmiths, chasers, and modelers with instruction in drafting and sculpting. Moser's drawing skills certainly led to his inclusion in the Royal Academy. Another artist whose drawing skills may have enabled him to switch professionally from chasing to full-time drawing was Thomas Burges(s), who signed the chasing of the lid of a box by Francis Har(r)ache.[7] (fig. 10)

Some of the most skilled practitioners of gold chasing were trained in Germany, especially Augsburg, a center for refined engraving and gold-work. Augustin Heckel (ca. 1690–1770) was a renowned chaser whose gold boxes and watchcases showcased his skill. Heckel's career began in Augsburg,[8] after which, according to George Vertue (1684–1756), chronicler of the London art scene of the period,[9] he traveled through "most of the capital cities in Germany and France"[10] before appearing in London by the early 1720s.[11] That he was accomplished in figure drawing was apparent in his gold chasing. However, his only known portrait engraving was published in Nuremberg in 1750–73, after he had retired from gold chasing in 1746.[12] Other works published during the 1750s included a set of cartouches and two sets of flowers.[13] Geographical proximity must have encouraged further connections. Richmond, including Twickenham, was also home to Horace Walpole, who collected Heckel's and Gravelot's work, and to various members of the "Rococo Set" in addition to Heckel.[14]

London also boasted local talent, such as James Cox, also a jeweler, who created elaborate mechanical objects such as watches, automata, and clocks in cases with gold casework over hardstone, which were sought

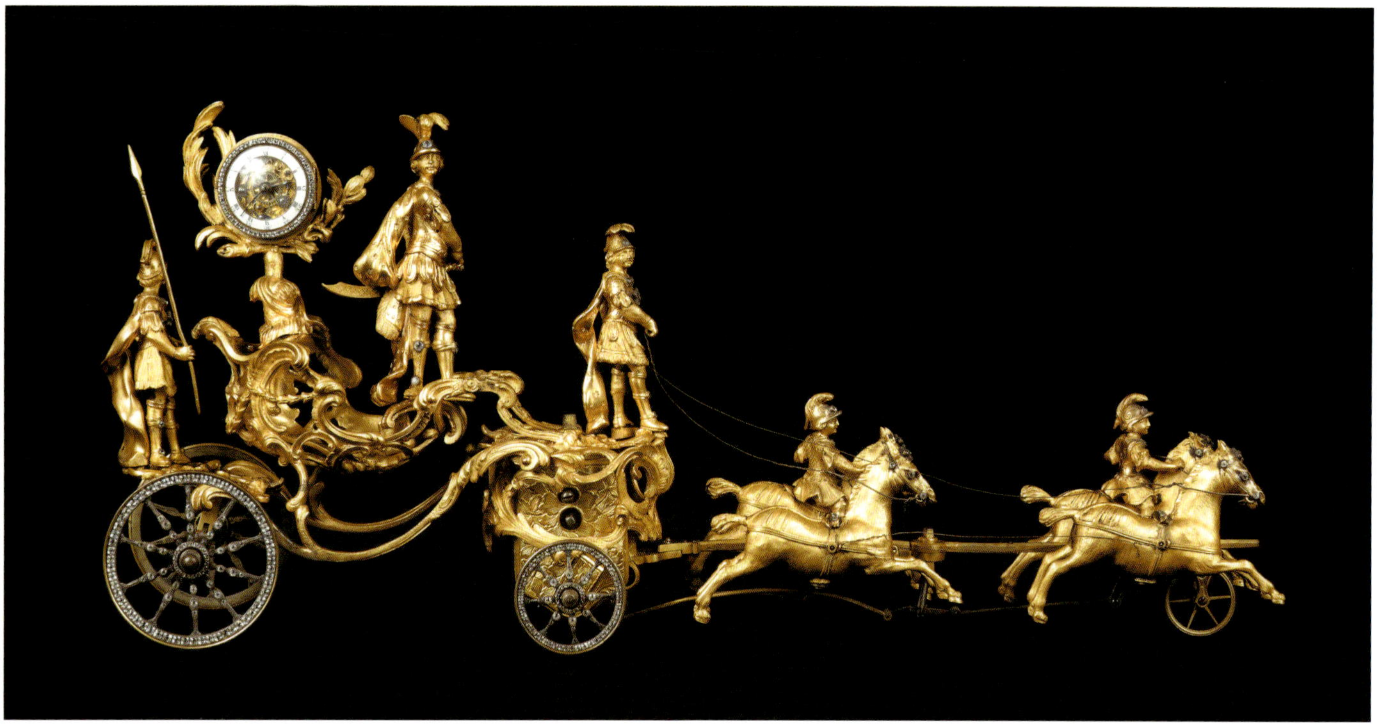

FIG. 12 Automaton. Movement by James Upjohn (English, active ca. 1760). England, ca. 1760. Gilt bronze, diamonds, paste, enamel clockworks. A la Vieille Russie

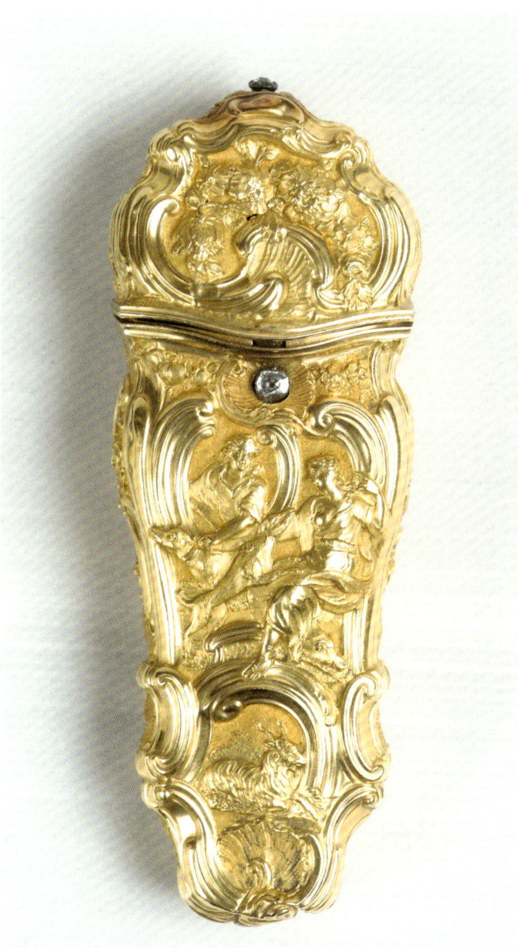

FIG. 13 Nécessaire: "Meleager and Atalanta with Their Hunting Dogs and the Head of the Calydonian Boar." London, England, ca. 1755. Gold, diamonds, metal. Horace Wood Brock

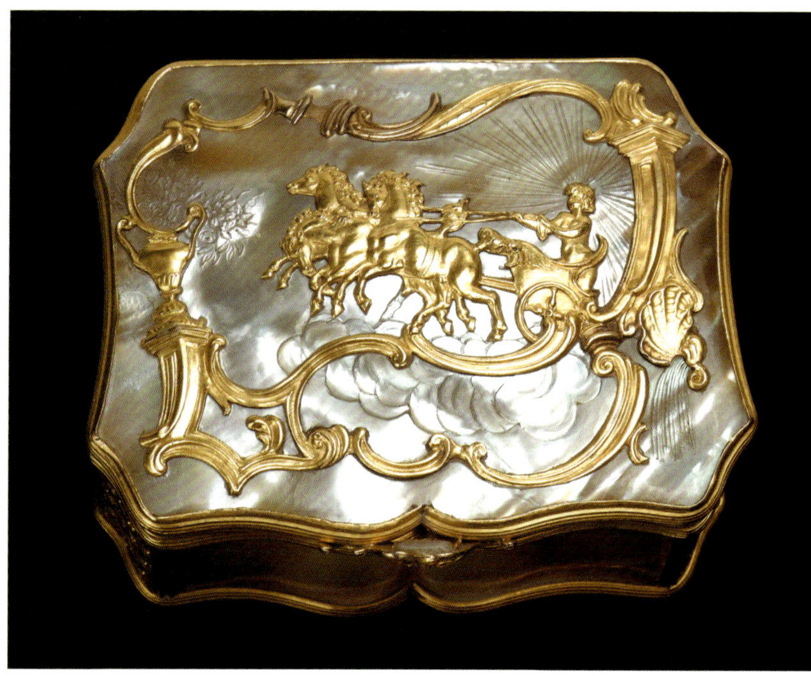

FIG. 14 Snuffbox. Probably Dresden, Germany, ca. 1745. Mother-of-pearl, gold. Horace Wood Brock
The gold scrolls are reminiscent of the designs of Hoppenhaupt.

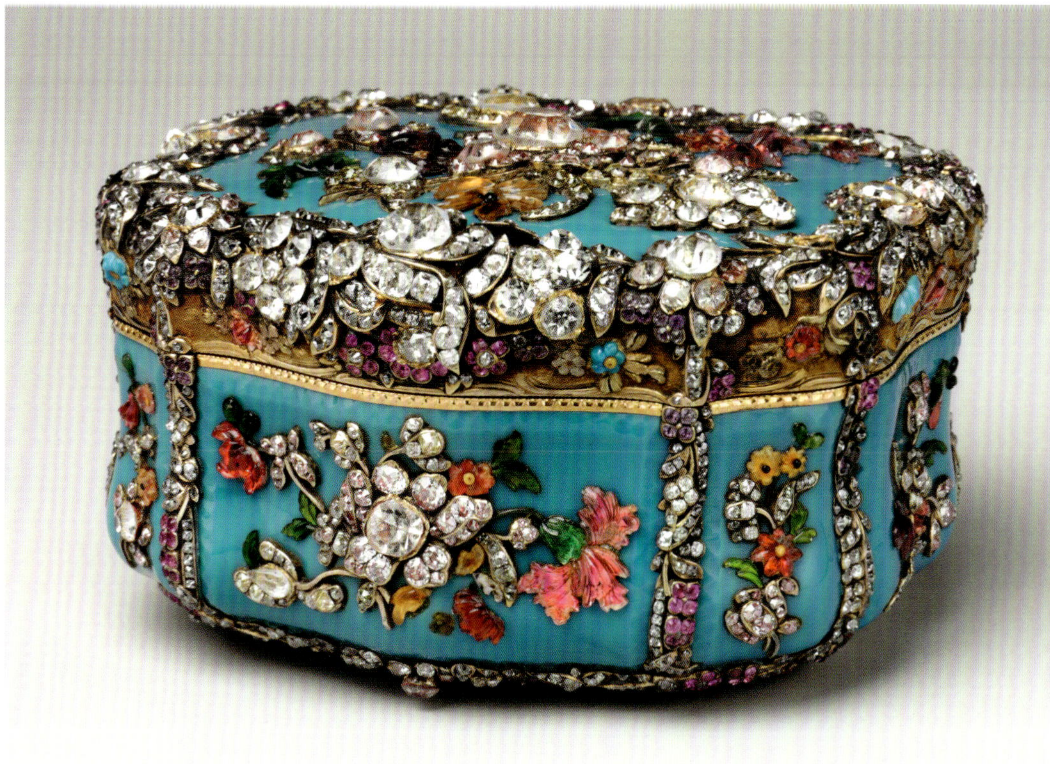

FIG. 15 Snuffbox made for Frederick the Great. Berlin, Germany, ca. 1765. Jewels, glass, and gold-mounted vitreous composition. The Metropolitan Museum of Art, Robert Lehman Collection, 1975, 1975-1-1536

One of four known apparently vitreous composition boxes for Frederick the Great, this box exemplifies the rich colors, encrustations, and large size so appealing to Frederick.

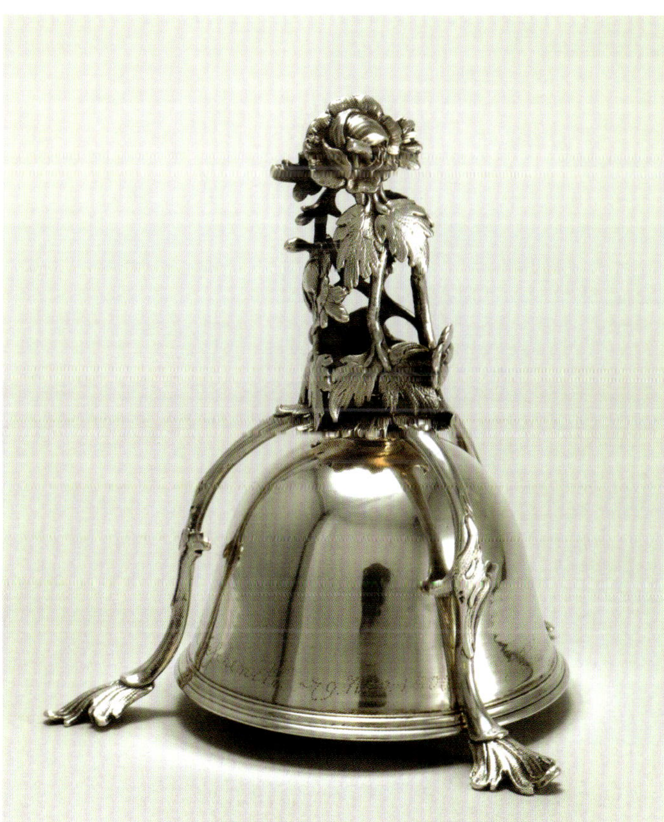

FIG. 16 Tripod table bell from Sanssouci. Hermann Neupert II (German, 1727–1807). Berlin, Germany, ca. 1765. Silver. Private collection

for the skill of the watchmaking and the casework. His success included exports to the Turkish market as well as continental Europe, including Russia, stimulating local production of snuffboxes and other objects in this style (fig. 11). Others in London produced similar and even more rococo works such as the robustly scrolled coach automaton by James Upjohn (fig. 12). The ormolu scrolls of the coach are similar to those in a design for the side of a coach by Charles Crace of 1754, in Cooper-Hewitt's collection.[15]

By mid-century, the English, with a German component, were considered a source of cartouche-form rococo gold boxes. This is evident from a gold box by Laurence Ham(m)ond from about 1750 for retailer Frederick de Veer of London, who presumably exported it around 1756 to relatives who were jewelers in Amsterdam, where it was marked for that year. While the scrolls on the base are like Meissonnier's, the lid shows a plastic figural modeling characteristic of London work, often executed by Swiss- or German-born chasers such as Moser, Heckel, and others (fig. 13).

Many of these artists had previous exposure to Italy and the works of Italian Gaetano Brunetti, who worked in Germany and London producing a variety of designs. These artists were also familiar with the great engravers and chasers of Augsburg. Thus Italy provided a second, more sculptural, source of inspiration for English and other northern rococo design, an influence that usually went through Germany to England but also in the other direction.

The American colonies did not consume much snuff until after the rococo period. Although tobacco was plentiful, most producers considered it a product to be exported in trade for other goods. As they grew

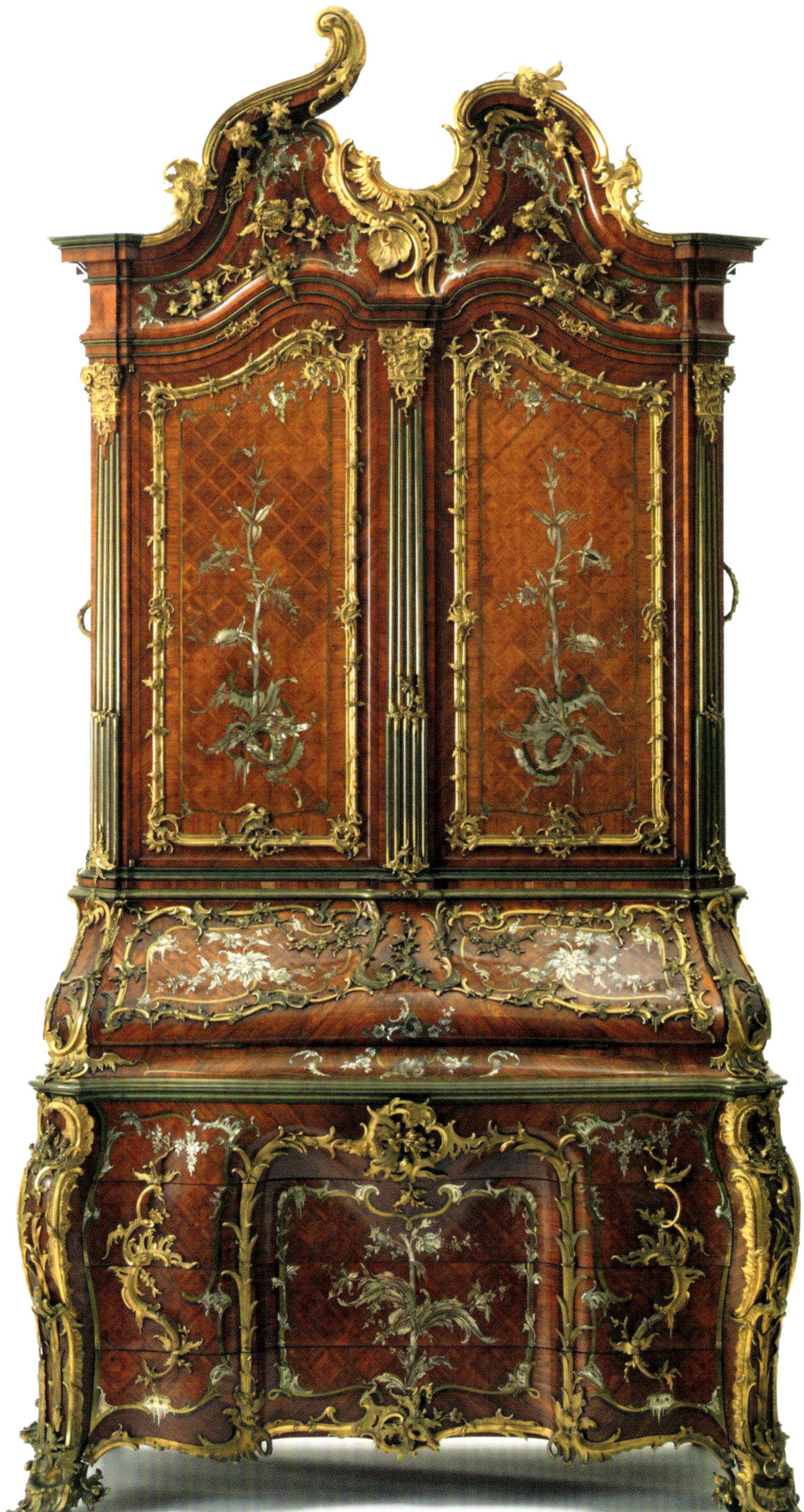

FIG. 17 Bureau cabinet. Michael Kümmel (German, active ca. 1750). Dresden, Germany, ca. 1750–55. Kingwood, mother-of-pearl, brass, ivory, ormolu, gilding. Victoria & Albert Museum, 63-1977

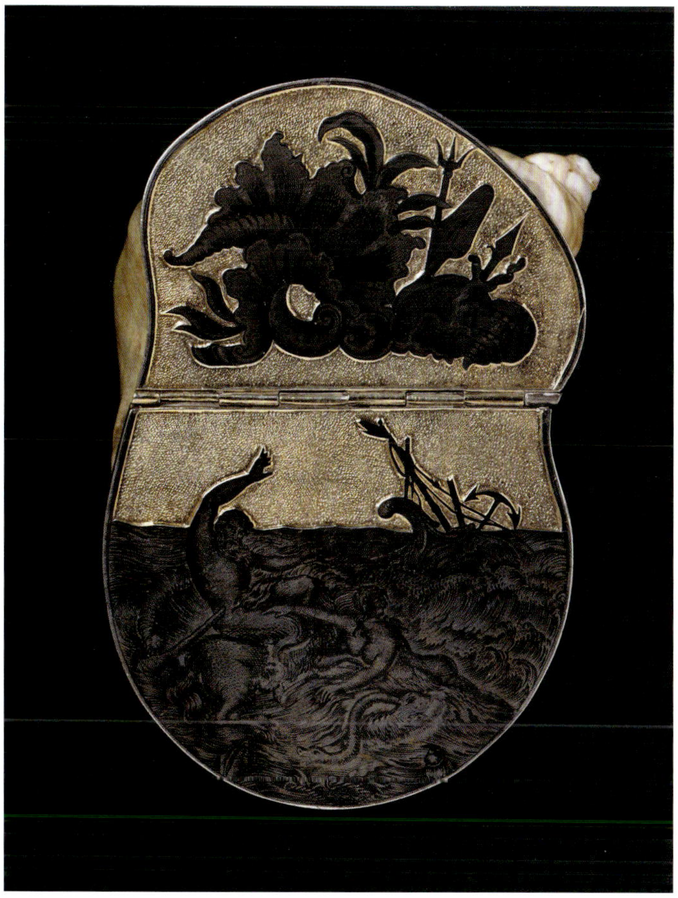

FIG. 18 Table snuffbox. Decoration after *Naufrage* by Jacques de Lajoüe (French, 1687–1761). Possibly by Aleksei Ignatiev Moshnin (Russian, b. 1721). Velikii Ustiug, Russia, 1740–50. Silver, gilt, niello, turban snail shell. Hillwood Estate, Museum & Gardens; bequest of Marjorie Merriweather Post, 1973, 13.5

This is one of a small group of boxes of expensive turban snail shells with niello-decorated lids after Lajoüe engravings. Although not made in St. Petersburg, it may have been an imperial commission from Tsarina Elizabeth, as some are unmarked.

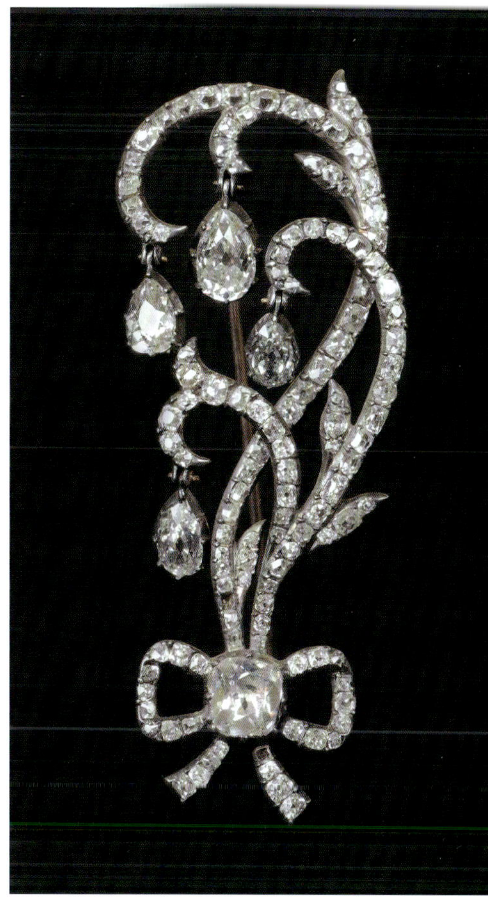

FIG. 19 Brooch. St. Petersburg, Russia, ca. 1770. Diamonds, gold. A la Vieille Russie

One of the few rococo-style pieces of jewelry in the eighteenth century, this brooch was probably originally made to fasten into a support in the bouffant powdered hair, a style which continued to the end of the century.

in wealth, the more Anglophilic and less puritanical colonists added snuffboxes to their accessories. Some were imported from England; a few, emulating their styles, were made in New York and Philadelphia. Joseph Richardson of Philadelphia imported and made silver in the English taste. His snuffbox of about 1760 was in cartouche shape, with chasing reminiscent of English examples.

German snuffboxes and other goldsmiths' work also included some elaborate gold chasing, reminding one of the origins of many of the chasers who moved to London for the patronage of the Hanoverian court, particularly of King George II of England and the more free-spirited taste of his son Frederick, Prince of Wales. In Prussia and Saxony, the combination of hardstone and gold, as well as the use of hardstones alone, was popular (fig. 14).

Frederick the Great of Prussia (1712–1786), more than anyone else, brings forth images of snuffboxes, one type in particular, an unusually large cushion-form box with shaped edges, decorated with various hardstones in a colorful interplay and encrusted with diamonds (fig. 15). A bachelor, Frederick lived in Potsdam and at his pleasure palace Sanssouci, whose name, French for "without cares," sums up rococo playfulness. More than a hundred of his boxes can be documented; although he may well have owned several hundred, some of which were from France. No doubt he acquired still more, as he gave many snuffboxes as presents. According to accounts by Voltaire and others, every cushion had grains of snuff on it. It was Voltaire who noted, when at Sanssouci, in 1750, "I am in France here. Only my own tongue is spoken. German is reserved for addressing soldiers and horses."[16] Frederick created the Fabrique Royale de Berlin, where he employed French goldsmiths such as Daniel Baudesson, a Huguenot whose work often incorporated pastel-toned enamels. Much of the finest enamel painting on Frederick's boxes was by Daniel Chodowiecki, of Polish origin, who also worked in Paris. In addition, André and Jean-Louis Jordan, along with Jean-Guillaume George Krüger, all Huguenots, were key figures working in Germany. The latter's drawings for the *friderizianisch*, or "Frederick style," of large boxes still survive. Krüger's mixed name evokes the essence of rococo internationalism; he was probably born in London in 1728, moving to Berlin in 1753. He left for Paris by 1774, when he was registered at the Académie St. Luc, later returning to Berlin, where he died in 1791.[17] His designs for the rococo boxes of chrysoprase, other hardstones, jewels, glass, and gold, probably dating to before his visit to Paris, are rather late manifestations of rococo idiom. Snuffboxes, furniture, silver, and porcelain contributed to a total rococo environment at Sanssouci, which was far more flamboyant than any French interior (fig. 16).

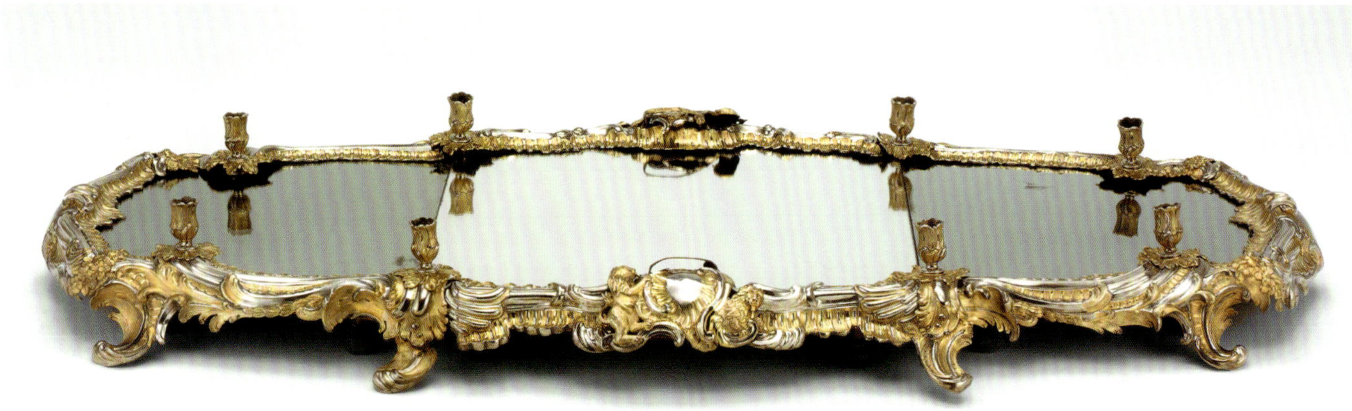

FIG. 20 Surtout de table (table centerpiece). Bartolomeo Pagliani (Italian, active 1754–75). Turin, Italy, 1754–75. Silver, silver-gilt, mirror glass, wood. The Art Institute of Chicago, Gift of the Antiquarian Society, 2001.112

In Scandinavia, Swedish court goldsmith Franz Bergs created boxes of very high caliber of craftsmanship and design, which, along with French boxes imported into Sweden, demonstrated its consuming interest in French fashion in the 1750s and later. However, silver hollow wares such as coffeepots are closer to German examples than French. In the same period, French-style rococo boxes were produced in Denmark, but by the 1760s, the work of the Danish Frederick Fabritius reflected the popularity of James Cox's English exports using hardstone in gold cage style. Germany was also represented in decorative arts imported into Denmark; one of the outstanding pieces of rococo furniture made in Dresden was for the Danish court (fig. 17).

Empress Elizabeth of Russia (r. 1741–62), daughter of Peter the Great, was known to be a fun-loving Francophile; her predecessor Anne had been dour and autocratic. Pretty and fashion-conscious, Elizabeth, who loved music and dancing, introduced French as the primary language of the Russian imperial court along with French fashions. The taking of snuff—and the creation of boxes with Govaers- or Meissonnier-like designs—appeared during her reign. Many of the boxes made were among the most rococo objects produced in Russia, and most were made in St. Petersburg, where the aristocracy was more Western-oriented than their Moscow counterparts. A large box made from an actual shell employed the technique of niello work, popular in Russia but not the West, and featured a scene based on an engraving by Jacques de Lajoüe called *The Shipwreck* on its silver lid (fig. 18). With foreign craftsmen the norm in St. Petersburg, determining the geographical origin of some snuffboxes is sometimes difficult, as imported pieces coexisted with those made in Russia by foreign-born masters. One was Jérémie Pauzié, born in Geneva in 1716, who immigrated to the St. Petersburg court by 1731, where he apprenticed to Gravelot, who would later exert great influence in England. Pauzié created jeweled snuffboxes and bouquets of flowers made of precious stones set in "vases of water." The bouquets were somewhat similar to those mounted on some of James Cox's works. Pauzié's and Cox's sumptuous pieces were undoubtedly an inspiration much later for another artist of Swiss origin, Carl Fabergé.[18] Boxes in Germanic taste with larger jewels and hardstones, a style more characteristic of the 1760s, and diamond-studded spray brooches (fig. 19) were made during the reign of German-born Sophie von Anhalt-Zerbst, known as Catherine the Great, who also appreciated and acquired the English-made silver of Paul de Lamerie.

ROCOCO'S CONTINUOUS CURVE THROUGH VARIOUS MEDIA

Silver in Russia was rarely in rococo form, but did feature rococo decoration, which persisted on traditional beaker and baluster pot forms throughout the second half of the eighteenth century. The importation of Italian architects, such as Rastrelli, along with carvers to execute their interior designs meant that some giltwood furniture was created in Russia in the rococo mode, but, for the most part, aristocratic Russia imported Western fashion. This included large shipments of furniture from Paris in the Louis XV taste, shipped via Le Havre and Rouen, including works by Bernard van Riesenburgh and others. The degree to which this happened can be gauged by the fact that the first French trading houses appeared in Russia in the late 1740s and that, in 1746, sales of French furniture reached 36,000 rubles, excluding diplomatic gifts.[19] With the advent of Catherine the Great, more was locally produced, especially with the increase in foreign, often German, workmen. Only in the nineteenth century did Russia's non-aristocratic, indigenous styles get taken up by the aristocracy and combined with foreign elements such as rococo.

In Italy, the snuffbox did not play the important role it did in the north. Despite the usage of snuff, a habit which even some clergy indulged during services, snuffboxes did not become a primary art form there. However, larger sculptural traditions merged with rococo design. The debate about what is late Italian baroque and what is rococo has been argued extensively by art historians, most significantly by Fiske Kimball's seminal 1943 work *The Creation of the Rococo*. The rococo style focused on here burst as a new breath into the regency and early years of Louis

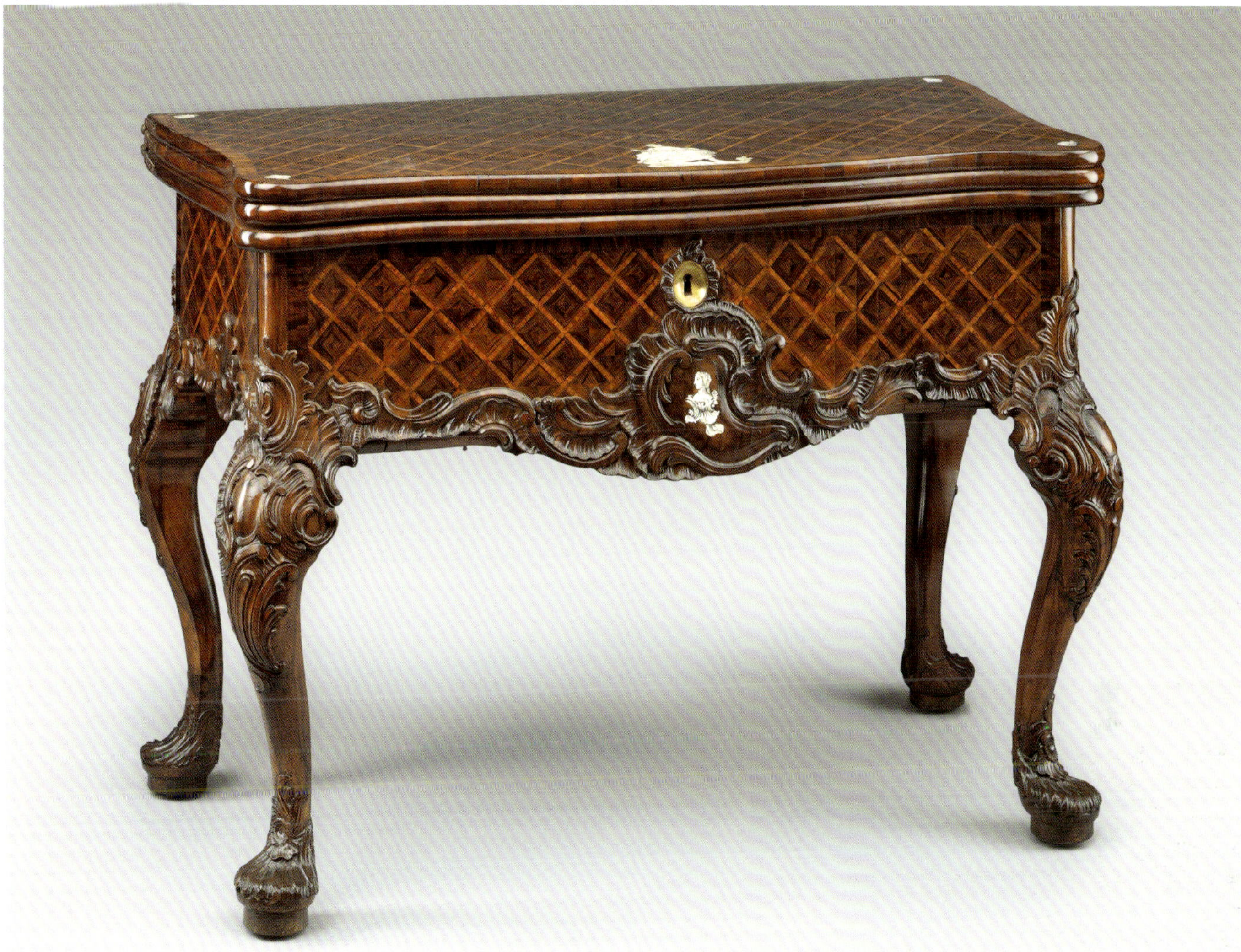

FIG. 21 Gaming table. Abraham Roentgen (German, 1711–1793). Neuwied, Germany, ca. 1755–58. Walnut, yew, rosewood, palissander, mahogany, brass, ivory. Private collection

One of a group of pieces commissioned from Roentgen by Johann Philipp von Walderdorff, Archbishop of Trier, this table opens to reveal gaming and desk functions with a raised "cartonnier," or compartments for papers.

XV's reign in France, primarily through the designs of Meissonnier and Thomas Germain. While this put Paris at the epicenter, reverberations to and from Italy, especially Turin, did exist. Meissonnier was born in Turin in 1695 to a Provençal father,[20] living there in an era when the House of Savoy and kingdom of Sicily (exchanged for the kingdom of Sardinia in 1720) was active in architecture and the decorative arts. The son of a French court goldsmith, Germain, born in 1673, spent time in Rome before returning to Paris in 1706. Meissonnier moved to Paris from Turin around 1715, not long after the 1713 Treaty of Utrecht reconciled France and the Duchy of Savoy from the War of Spanish Succession. Subsequent activity between Turin and Paris was centered on Andrea Boucheron, appointed Savoy court silversmith in 1737, who apprenticed with Thomas Germain in Paris.[21] As Germain and Meissonnier both had commissions from the French court, Meissonnier might have helped secure the apprenticeship with Germain for his fellow Torinese, who had worked with his father on a project in 1727 in Turin.

With the recent ascription of the mark on the inkstand at the Metropolitan Museum to Boucheron, a group of silver for the chapel of the Sardinian Embassy in London, fitted out by the Comte de Viry between 1756 and 1763, should now also be regarded as by him.[22] By adopting the existing chapel in Lincoln's Inn Fields, the House of Savoy gave the local Catholic community a focal point and sought to make it a showplace. While the censer, incense boat, and crucifix are rather more baroque than rococo, the cruets and their salver, which have no specific ecclesiastical features and hence are also domestic objects, are more rococo.[23] What is significant is that these pieces, commissioned by the House of Savoy, were sent to England.

As much of the Savoy royal silver is no longer extant, it is hard to judge the taste of the era from this medium. A rare surviving example of court-level silver shows rich rococo ornament on a parcel-gilt surtout de table of courtly proportions. While the original patron is unknown, it shows a sculptural enlivening of the tabletop in silver (fig. 20). In other media, decorative elements in the interiors of the Palazzo Reale and other palaces in Turin show it to be one of the centers of rococo style in Italy. In cabinetry, the work of the ebenist Pietro Piffetti (1705–1770) and Luigi Prinotto (1712–1780) show the use of ivory inlay with fantastically sculptured shapes to create truly rococo objects. Piffetti's use of ivory and metal inlays in the mid-eighteenth century has a parallel in the pieces the

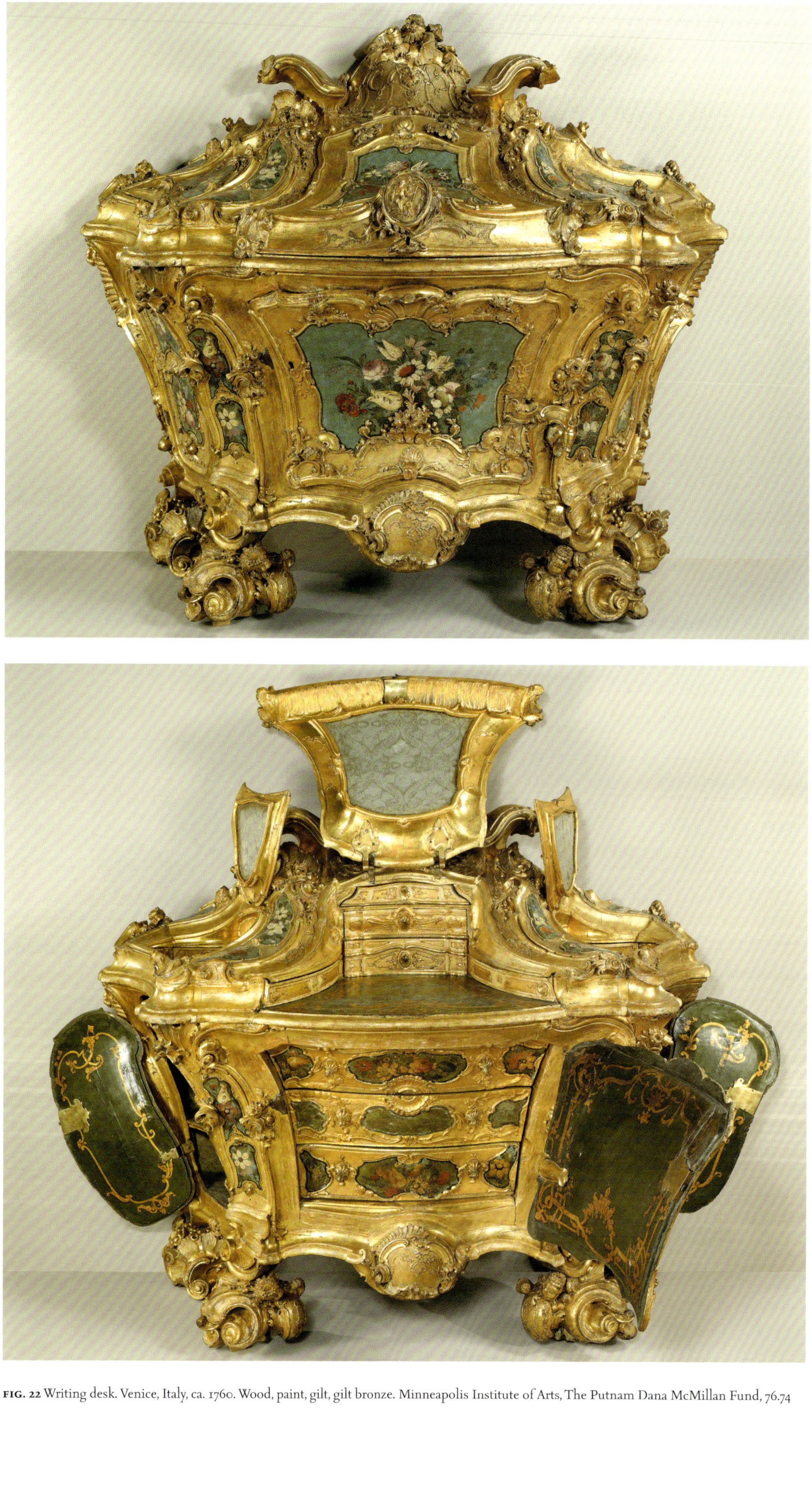

FIG. 22 Writing desk. Venice, Italy, ca. 1760. Wood, paint, gilt, gilt bronze. Minneapolis Institute of Arts, The Putnam Dana McMillan Fund, 76.74

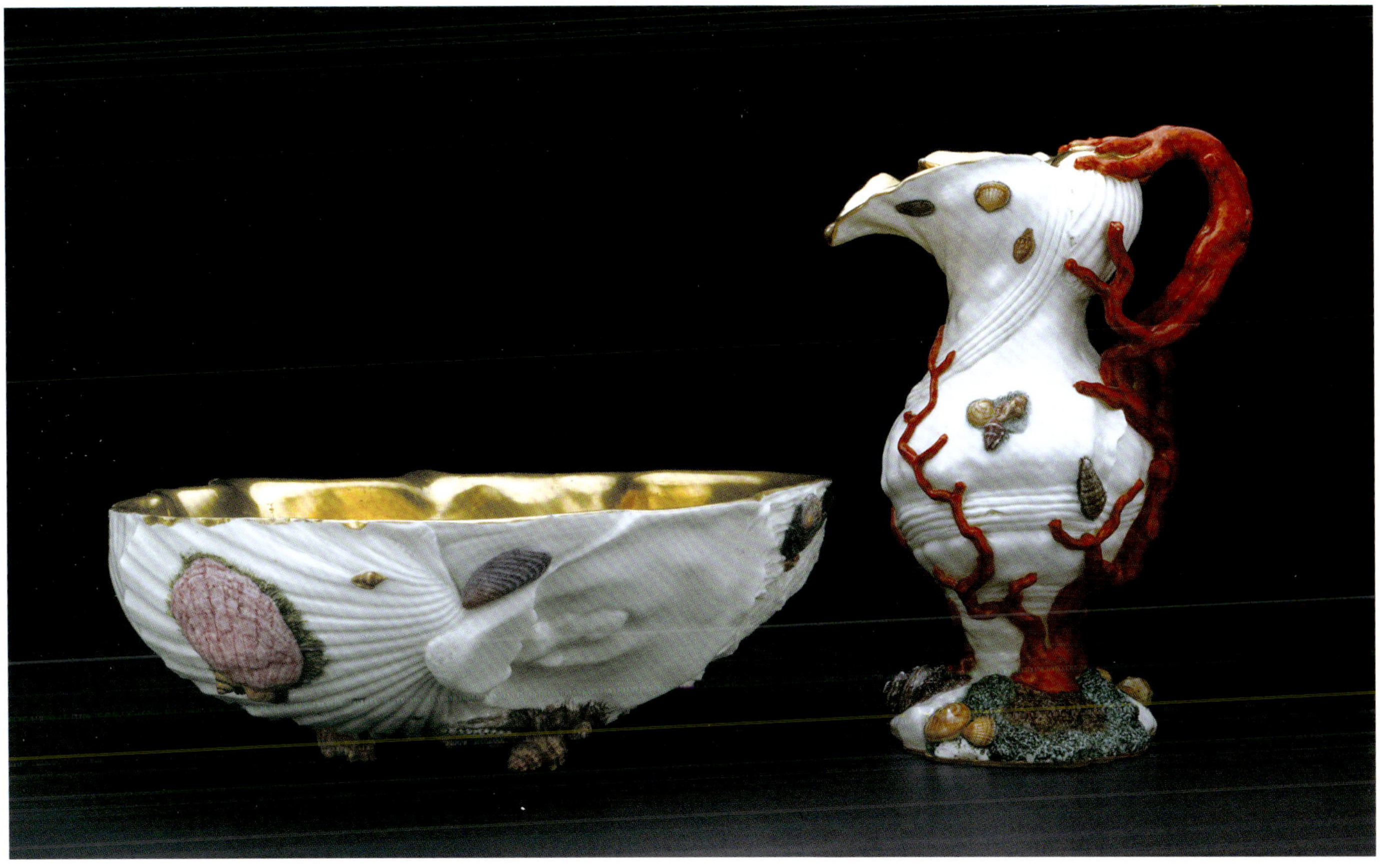

FIG. 23 Ewer and basin. Capodimonte Porcelain Manufactory. Italy, ca. 1745. Soft-paste porcelain, shells, enamel, gilding. Art Institute of Chicago, Gift of Mr.and Mrs. Robert Norman Chatain in memory of Professor Alfred Chatain, 1957.490a-b

These pieces incorporate real shells with the porcelain versions, reflecting the Italian preoccupation with water and the sea.

German Abraham Roentgen created in Neuwied for Archbishop Johann Philippe von Walderdorff of Trier (fig. 21). However, the Roentgen table also reflects techniques Roentgen learned in London, combined with German engraving sources. In London, his use of various inlays, especially brass, influenced such makers as John Channon and Frederick Hintz.

In northern Italy in general, and in Venice and Piedmont in particular, rich gilding or painted and gilt decoration on exuberantly carved scrolling forms epitomized rococo style during the middle of the century to as late as 1770, especially in lavish Venetian interiors (fig. 22). In Parma, where the eldest daughter of Louis XV had married the Duke of Parma, considerable furniture was ordered from Paris for the couple, but local makers learned the style from the imports and added their own touches as well. The Marches too produced rococo furniture, but Tuscany stayed with the baroque. Rome was divided, with late baroque dominating, but some rococo in the form of a few energetically carved pier tables and mirrors was made. Most of the rest of Italy did not respond to the style except in the ceramics of Doccia, Capodimonte, Venice, and a few small factories. Capodimonte, in Naples,[24] produced porcelain objects that sometimes featured shells and scrolls (fig. 23), including shell-form snuffboxes. By the time the factory principals moved to Spain, taste had turned to a neoclassical mode.

Spain was not a stronghold for rococo, preferring the baroque in many areas as a counterbalance to the heavily ornamented designs of its Moorish heritage. There were some major exceptions. One is the sedan chair of a type known in eighteenth-century Andalucia.[25] A rare example for ecclesiastical use, at the Hispanic Society in New York, probably made around 1760, would have been considered the height of fashion and glory.

Spanish rococo silver existed along with French imports. A probable example of the latter is a pair of candelabra made in Paris in 1739–40 by Claude II Ballin (ca. 1661–1754), now in Cooper-Hewitt's collection (fig. 24). While their bases suggest the more restrained early rococo design, the branches are flamboyantly rococo. Possibly made for the king of Spain, they were "copied" by the court silversmith Juan de San Fauri in Madrid in 1761, receiving a slightly less reserved interpretation (fig. 25).

Ballin's obituary referred to his work being well known outside France, stating that he worked mainly for the courts of Spain, Portugal, and Italy, the Electors of Saxony and Bavaria, a great number of princes and noblemen of Germany, the Czar, Prince Eugene of Savoy (for whom he made a much-admired silver candelabrum), and the Padishah, or Ottoman emperor. The candelabrum shown here was also the source for pieces by Carl Ingermann of Berlin for Augustus emperor III of Saxony

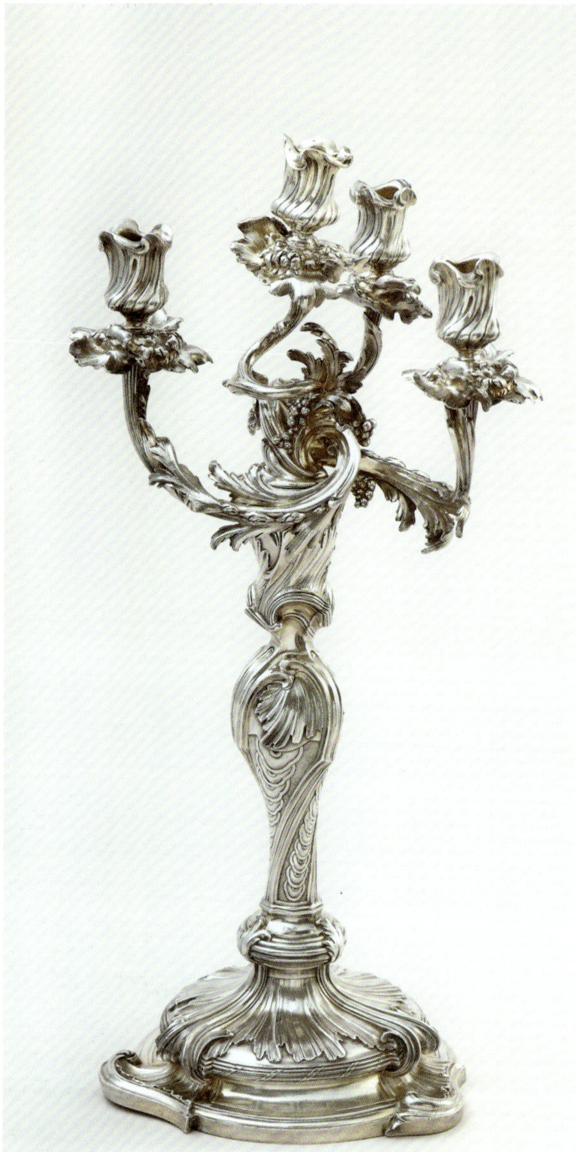

FIG. 24 Candelabrum (one of a pair). Claude de Ballin II (French, 1661–1754). France, 1739–40. Silver. Cooper-Hewitt, National Design Museum, Smithsonian Institution, Gift of Anonymous Donor, 1949-131-2 a/f

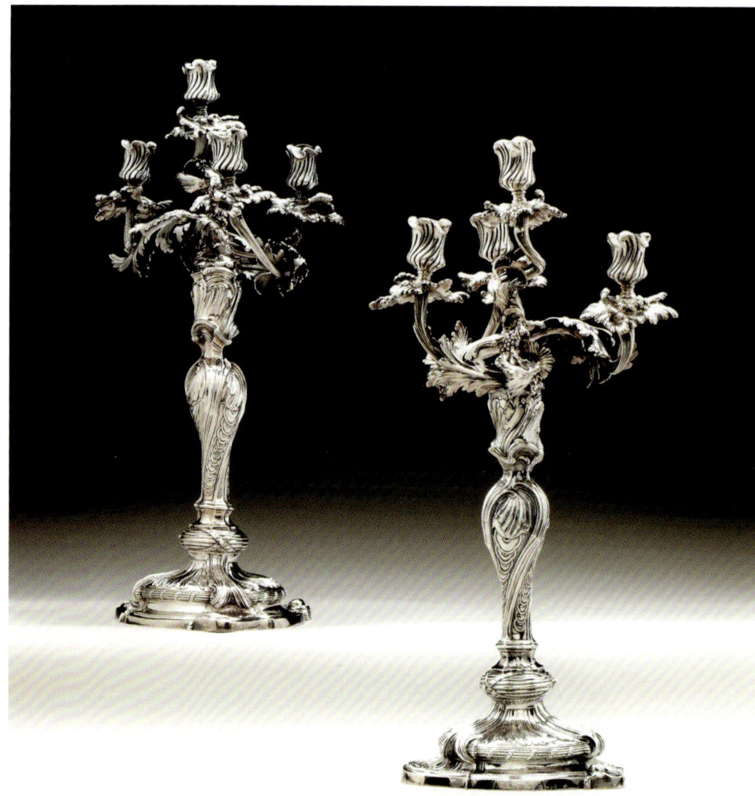

FIG. 25 Four-light candelabrum (one of a pair). Juan de San Fauri (Spanish, active ca. 1740–70). Madrid, Spain, 1762. Silver. Private collection

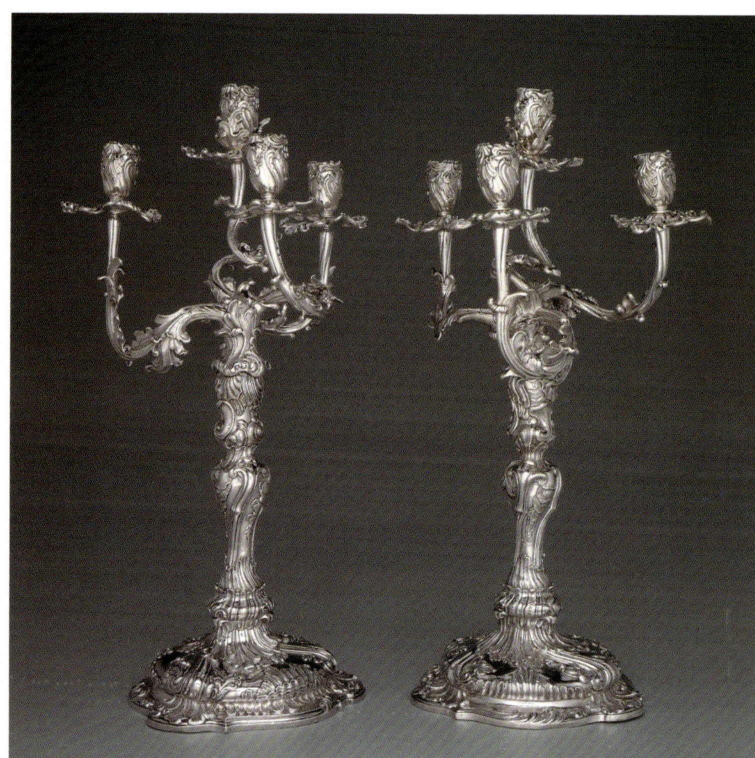

FIG. 26 Candelabrum (one of a pair). Christian Heinrich Ingermann (German, active 1732–98). Dresden, Germany, ca. 1750. Silver. Museum of Fine Arts, Boston, Gift of William A. Coolidge, 1984.186

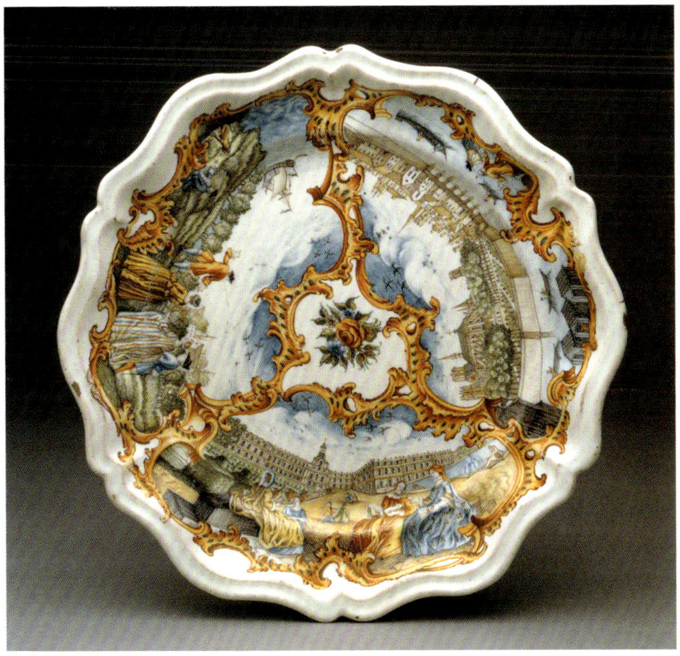

FIG. 27 Plate. Manufactured by Alcora Porcelain Factory. Spain, 1773–84. Tin-glazed earthenware. Hispanic Society of America, LE 1893

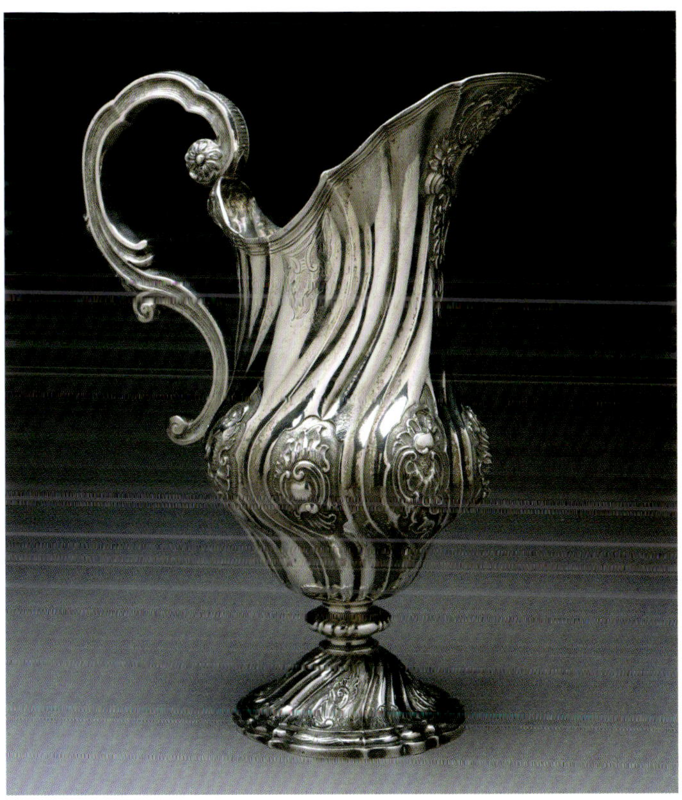

FIG. 28 Ewer. Lisbon, Portugal, ca. 1770. Silver. Hispanic Society of America, R3086

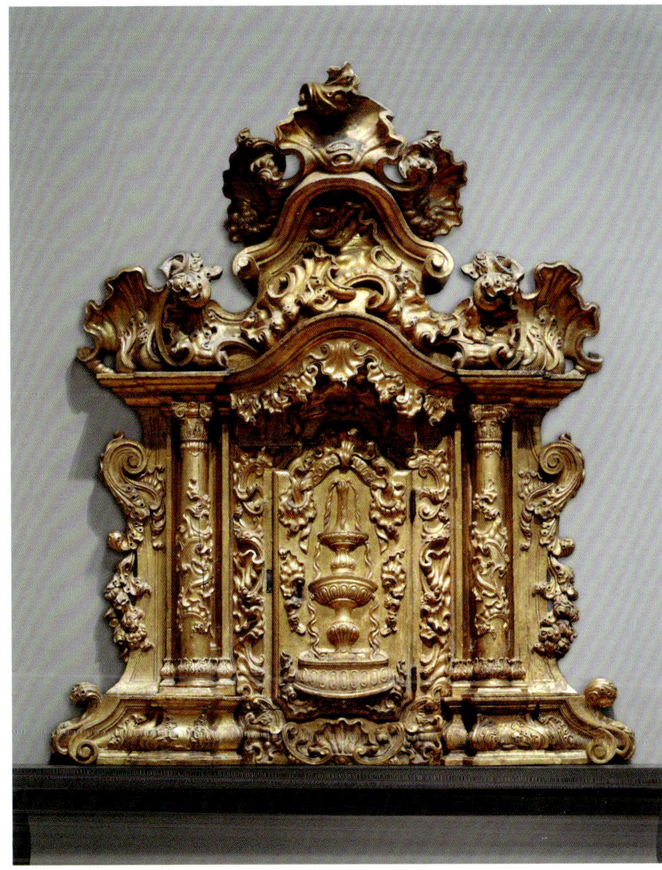

FIG. 29 Altarpiece. Northern Portugal, 1740–60. Chestnut, gilding. Samuel S. Fleisher Art Memorial

(fig. 26),[26] thus showing the wide appeal of this form. In addition, good Spanish gilt-metal objects were made, including for ecclesiastical use, as well as a few pieces of silver in Spanish Latin America; but most remained baroque. Individual patrons were the key, and for such patrons, the Alcora ceramics factory took up the style with gusto, importing French ceramicists to help start the factory (fig. 27).

PORTUGAL

The Portuguese monarchy was a major patron of French rococo silver, but it also patronized Huguenot Paul Crespin and others in London. The 1755 earthquake in Lisbon resulted in much rebuilding at a time when rococo was fashionable, and many furnishings were made in this style, including replacement objects such as the services commissioned by King Jose I from François-Thomas Germain (see Hyde, fig. 3). From the presence of pieces by Germain, Meissonnier, and others, local silversmiths adopted swirling forms on ewers and other vessels (fig. 28). Churches were built and rebuilt as well, and many contained sumptuous giltwood structures (fig. 29). Plentiful rosewoods from its Brazilian colony were used for carved serpentine-backed chairs and undulating, often ormolu-mounted commodes in both Portugal and colonial Brazil. Ceramics, a major industry, specialized in *azulejos*, tiles that were often used in mural panels with rococo borders as wall decoration in both domestic and ecclesiastic surroundings.

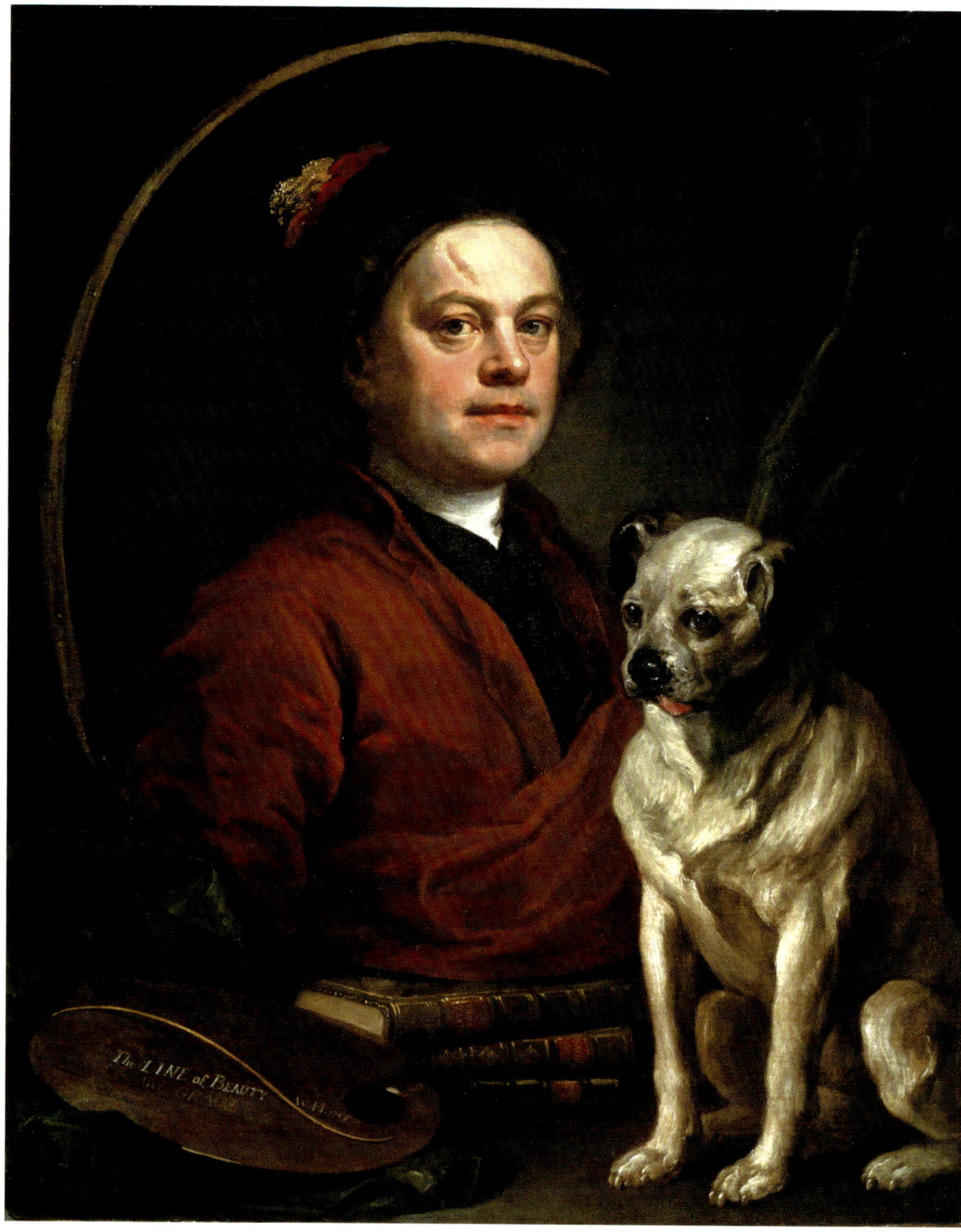

FIG. 30 *The Painter and His Pug.* William Hogarth (British, 1697–1764). England, 1745. Oil on canvas. Tate Britain, N00112
The S-curve, touted by Hogarth as the "line of beauty," is visible on the artist's palette—a clear message to his students and followers at St. Martin's Lane Academy.

ENGLISH ROCOCO

Nowhere was the leading stylistic edge more apparent in silver- and goldwork than in England, where numerous examples of rococo silver were produced. A leading advocate of rococo style was William Hogarth (1697–1764), a skilled painter and engraver who promoted artists and designers from a variety of countries. His 1745 self-portrait includes a palette with an S-curve and the moniker "The Line of Beauty and Grace," the rococo "line of beauty" he later codified in his 1753 *Analysis of Beauty* (fig. 30). He engraved the arms[27] of Sir Robert Walpole on a salver made in London in 1727 by the great Huguenot silversmith Paul de Lamerie (1688–1751), who created some of the most rococo objects in English silver.[28] Hogarth was a leading member and instructor at the St. Martin's Lane Academy, which he founded in 1735. The academy also counted among its instructors Gravelot, George Moser, the French sculptor and medallist André Roubiliac, painters Thomas Gainsborough and Francis Hayman, and the architect James Paine, a good friend of Thomas Chippendale's.

It is no coincidence that the real move toward rococo in England started just after the accession to the throne of George II in 1727 and the subsequent arrival from Hanover of his eldest son Frederick, Prince of Wales (1707–1751). Frederick had remained in Hanover as family representative upon the accession to the throne of his grandfather George I in 1714 and had grown up with continental taste, but, as Prince of Wales and presumed heir to the throne, he heeded his father's call to England. Artists and craftsmen followed in their wake. The king continued to spend the

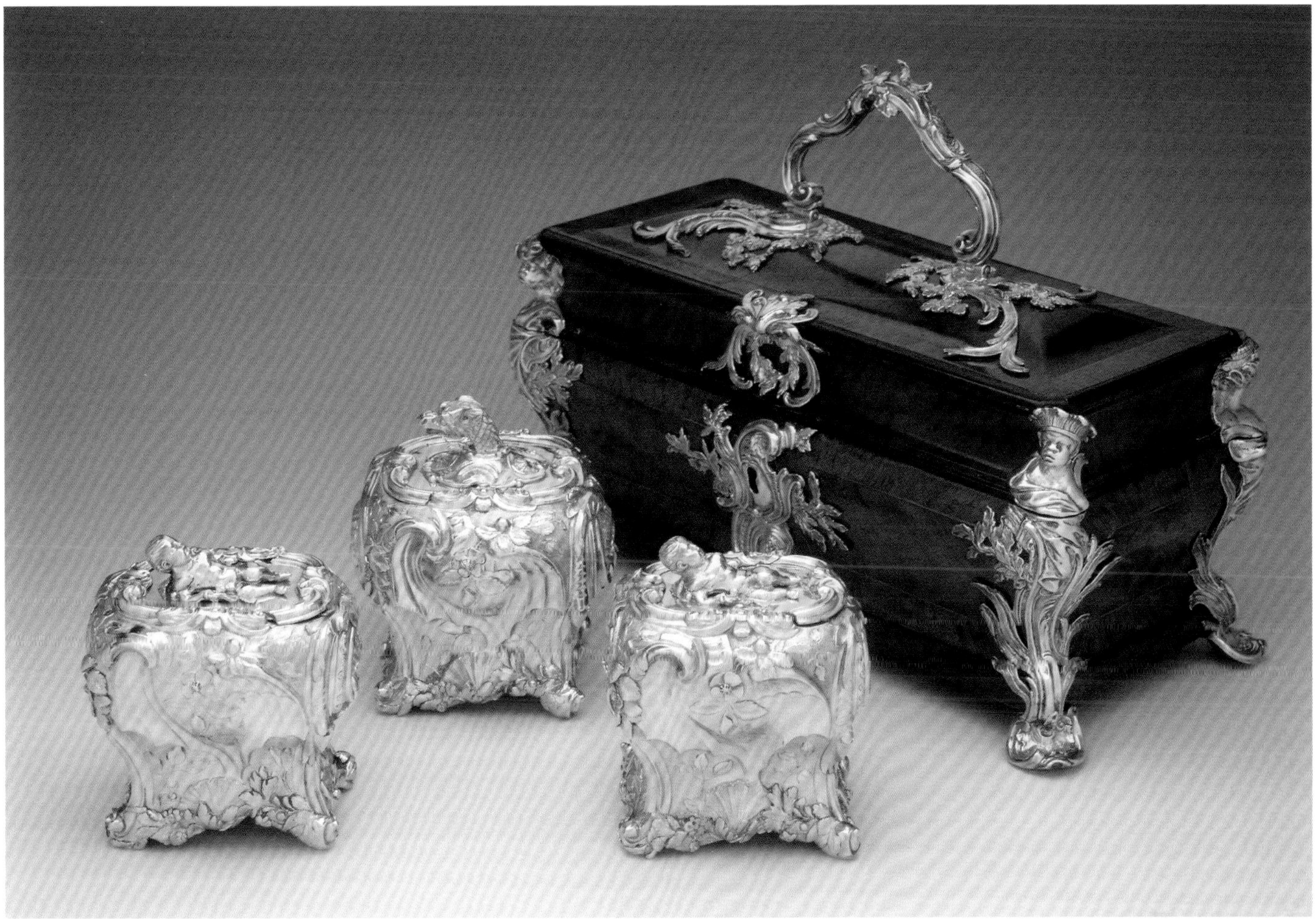

FIG. 31 Set of tea caddies and sugar box in case. Lewis Pantin I (English, active ca. 1734–44). London, England, 1739–40. Silver, mahogany. Museum of Fine Arts, Boston, Gift of Alan and Simone Hartman and Harriet J. Bradbury Fund, 2001, 2001.97.1-4

summer months in Hanover even after being crowned. George II never learned to speak English well and patronized German-speaking artists when possible. His composer of choice was Handel, and he preferred to sit for the Dresden-born goldsmith and enamelist Christian Zincke.[29]

While George II was not a strong patron of rococo style, Frederick, a bon vivant who rebelled against his father's strictures, often was. However, his patronage was seemingly more a result of an interest in a "new" style and adventures than in a committed aesthetic policy; he commissioned works in more classical taste as well. Nonetheless, his affinity for a group of artists and artisans who were often employed by Jacobite sympathizers has led to some discussion as to whether his rebelliousness and stylistic preferences might have had political overtones.

The antagonism between George II and Frederick and the latter's corresponding espousal of French rococo were echoed in the politics of the day, when the Palladian architecture and interiors of William Kent were approved by various governmental figures, most especially Lord Burlington and Sir Robert Walpole. The former was the object of a caricature called "Man of Taste" by Hogarth.[30] Frederick patronized a tight-knit group of artists, many of whom were teachers at St. Martin's Lane Academy, who frequented Slaughter's Coffee House in St. Martin's Lane. These artists collaborated on the decoration of the Vauxhall Gardens, whose owner was a friend of Hogarth's. The project included a pavilion and tent erected in 1738–42. The academy, coffeehouse, and their denizens were an international mix, where the teaching of drawing and design that could be applied to multiple uses prevailed. The fact that the drinking of coffee, tea, and hot chocolate was expensive led to the creation of some of the most fashionable objects of their period to serve them. A dynamic example of the involvement of a variety of creators working in mixed media with the latest rococo fashion is seen in Lewis Pantin I's tea and sugar caddies and box (fig. 31).

Since records of Gravelot's and Moser's drawing schools are virtually nonexistent, and those of St. Martin's Lane Academy show no distinction between students and teachers, it is difficult to tell if any of the silversmiths or furniture makers enrolled, other than cabinetmaker John Linnell, who attended in the 1740s.[31] However, Vertue refers to Gravelot's drawings for engravings, which with "other kinds of Gold and Silver works

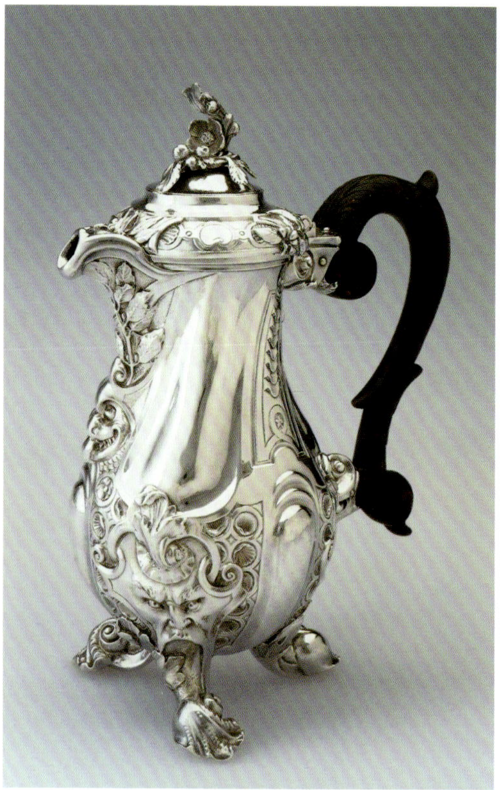

FIG. 32 Coffee jug. Paul de Lamerie (English, 1688–1751). London, England, 1738. Silver. Cincinnati Art Museum, The Folgers Coffee Silver Collection, Gift of Procter and Gamble, 1999.659

This boldly modeled jug embodies English early organic rococo through its references to seventeenth-century Dutch auricular ornament, with grotesque masks mixed with shells and naturalistic plant elements.

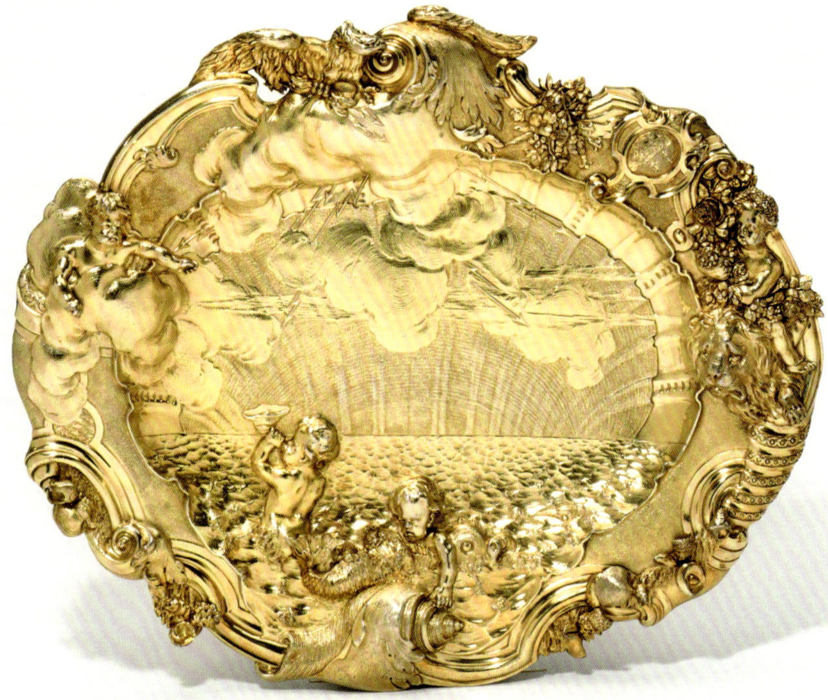

FIG. 33 "Ilchester" basin. Attributed to Paul de Lamerie (English, 1688–1751). London, England, ca. 1740. Silver, gilt. Private collection

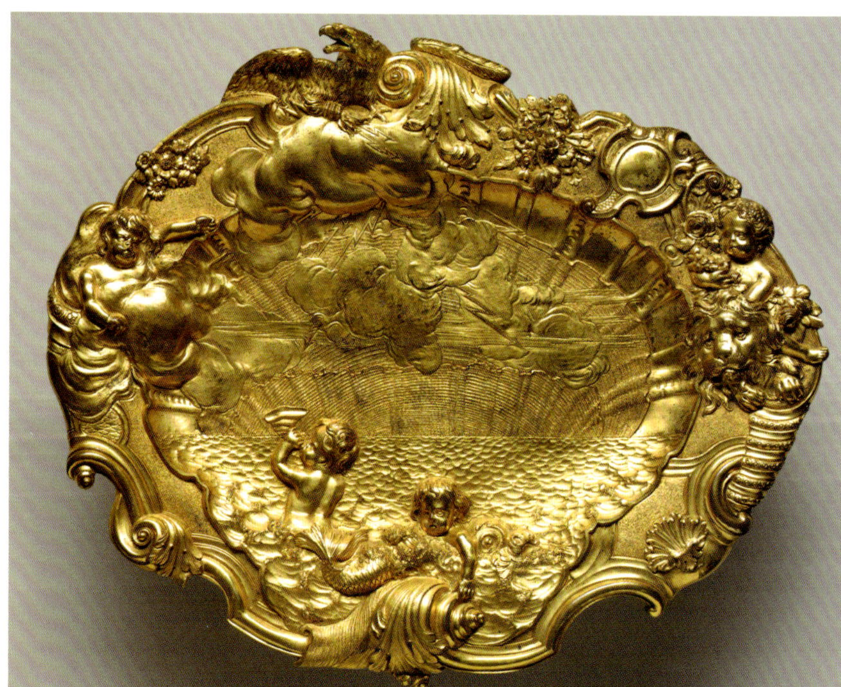

FIG. 34 Basin. Probably England, 1725–40. Gilt bronze. Cleveland Museum of Art, John L. Severance Fund, 1955.69

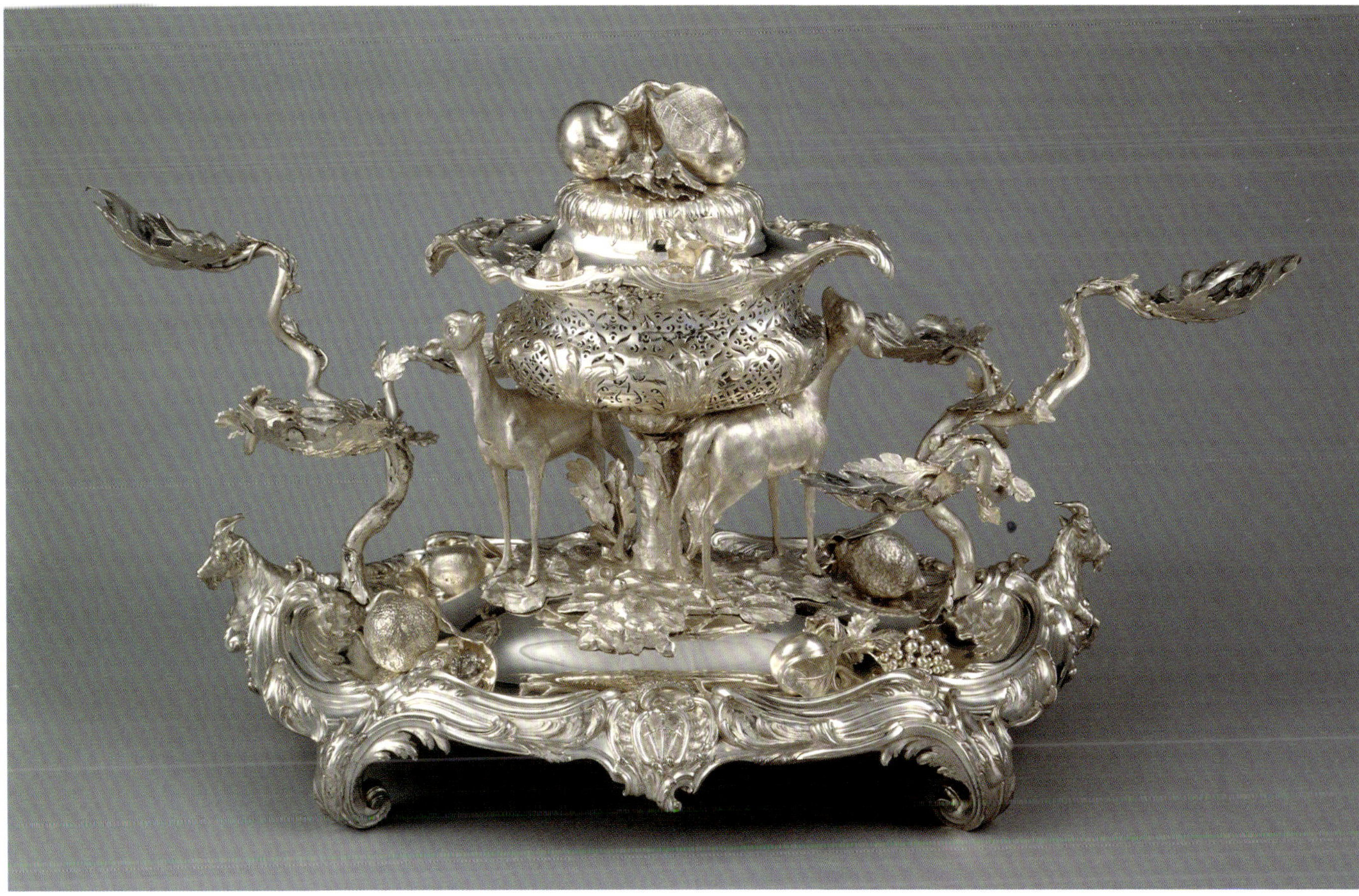

FIG. 35 Epergne. John Parker (English, free 1762) and Edward Wakelin (English, free 1748). London, England, ca. 1760. Silver. Museum of Fine Arts Boston, Theodora Wilbur Fund in Memory of Charlotte Beebe Wilbour, 65.915

shows he is endowed with a great and fruitful genius for designs, inventions of history and ornaments." (See Hunter-Stiebel, p. 4, fig. 1) Although written in 1741, the comment reflected Gravelot's activity after his arrival in England in 1732, a date which corresponds to Paul de Lamerie's turn to truly rococo forms (See Hunter-Stiebel, p. 6, fig. 8).

While de Lamerie's origins were French Huguenot via Holland, his work showed a strong connection to that of German immigrant silversmiths in London, as well as to some aspects of Dutch design (fig. 32). His engraving showed a marked improvement around this date, suggesting the hiring of a new specialist engraver familiar with rococo design,[32] and the modeling of his pieces became more rococo and plastic, also implying the arrival of a specific modeler or modelers. While the Ilchester basin (fig. 33) was not marked by de Lamerie, it shows his style and has been attributed to him.[33] As with a number of pieces of important English silver of this period, multiple specialists were undoubtedly involved, such as the example cited above of the Crespin, de Lamerie, Sprimont collaboration. Modeling in wax and other media including possibly papier-mâché, chasing, engraving, and casting were skills necessary to produce a final product. Presumably an important maker like de Lamerie would have been able to retain artists of the highest skill for an important commission, some of whom may well have had experience in Germany and the Low Countries either as engravers or even porcelain modelers. The German connection becomes more evident in a gilt-bronze version, with some differences in the border (fig. 34), which appears close to German engravings, including some by the Augsburg engraver Johann Haidt. While its origins in both England and Germany can be considered, the basin could show one of the modelers of the Ilchester basin working in another medium. Haidt's presumed relative, the London chaser John Haidt, may have played a role in its creation. The variations indicate that it was not a slavish copy; they may be accounted for if the maker of this basin was not the modeler de Lamerie asked to execute the variant parts of the Ilchester example. In sum, the basin appears to have been made in London by someone with strong connections to Augsburg, possibly in concert with someone with more of a background in Dutch design. Another piece for which a group of modelers, casters, and chasers must have been needed was an elaborate centerpiece made for the fifth Duke of Bolton by Parker and Wakelin of about 1760. With its deer and goat heads, fruit, vine leaves, and pierced basket, it is a technically difficult work of sculpture (fig. 35). A candlestick marked by David Willaume II may indeed have been a production of de Lamerie's shop, as this model exists with his mark at an earlier date and Willaume is thought to have been primarily a retailer (fig. 36).

It has been suggested that the silversmith James Shruder (a presumed Anglicization of Schroeder) was a modeler for de Lamerie.[34] A hot-water kettle by him from 1750 (fig. 37) shows the influence of Meissen teapots and sculpture in its figural areas. It is similar in style to a London-made silver example by Charles Kändler of 1730–32, which, not surprisingly, is closer in date to the Meissen examples.

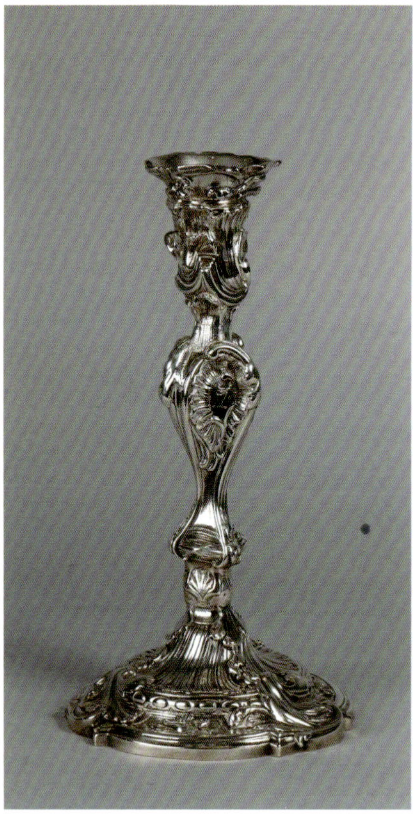

FIG. 36 Candlestick. David Willaume II (English, 1693–1761). London, England, 1740. Silver. Laurence N. Strenger, Los Angeles, California

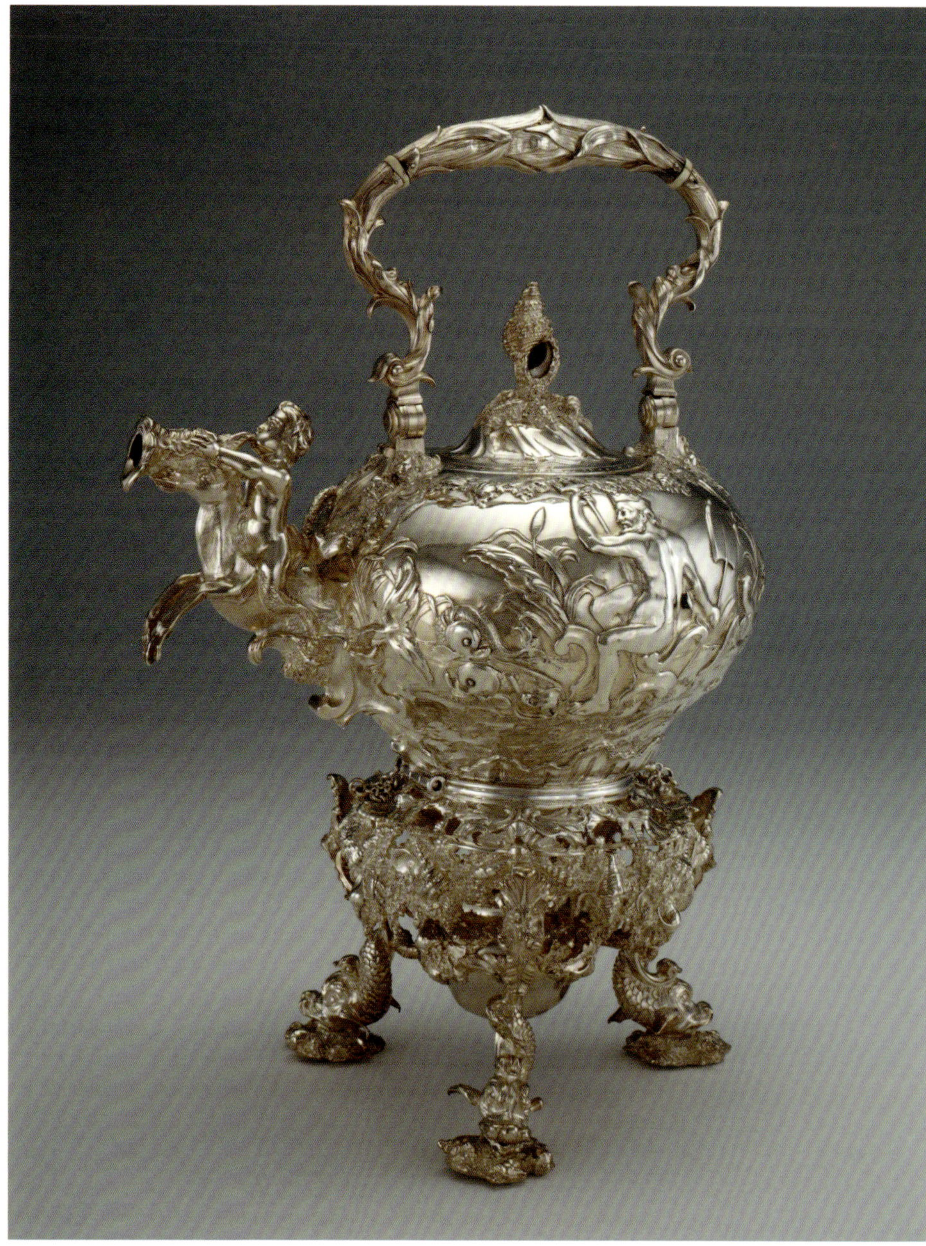

FIG. 37 Teakettle, stand, and lamp. James Shruder (British, active 1737–49). London, England, 1749–50. Silver, ivory. Virginia Museum of Fine Arts, Richmond. The Jerome and Rita Gans Collection of English Silver. 97.29a-d.

Kändler was an important German silversmith who, recent scholarship suggests, was the younger brother of the famous Meissen modeler Johann Joachim Kändler. Charles Kändler's known work in England demonstrated considerable skill. He appears to have returned to Germany around 1735, when he visited the Meissen factory, and was probably not the same person as Charles Frederick Kändler, who appeared in London a few years later.[35] The strong correlation between Kändler's silver forms and porcelain reinforces the idea of the family connection (figs. 38, 39). In any case, the flow between Germany and London was extensive, and the Kändlers' time in London was characterized by contact with those hailing from a variety of countries to create an English style. Frederick Kändler's cistern for Henry Jernegan to offer by lottery included figural handles modeled by Rysbrack, and Gravelot engraved the winner's certificate.[36]

In 1747, Count Brühl, who commissioned the great "Swan" Service from Meissen (see Leben, fig. 10), wrote to the ambassador of Saxony to London for designs for a toilet service, which needed to be commissioned and made in only four months for the double wedding of the daughters of Augustus the Strong in 1747.[37] The drawing shows similarity with the style of the Maynard Master dish by de Lamerie in the Cahn collection.[38] It shows again a German style, although the hand of Nicholas Sprimont has also been suggested.

Sprimont (1716–1770), a silversmith from Liège, a prince-bishopric in the Holy Roman Empire where influences flowed from Flanders, France, and Germany, arrived in London by 1742. Almost immediately, he was commissioned to produce some major pieces of silver (figs. 40, 41), and soon became involved in a newly formed Chelsea porcelain

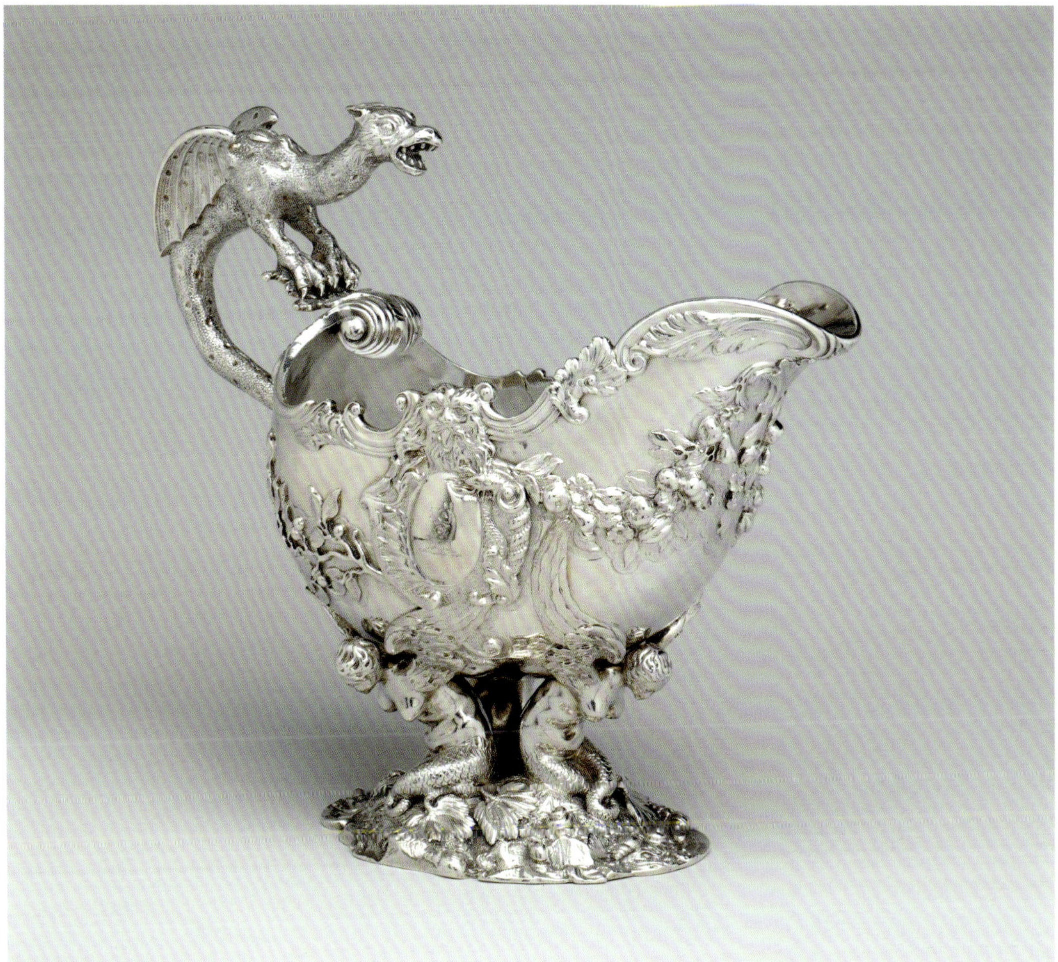

FIG. 38 Sauceboat. Charles Frederich Kändler (German, active in England 1727–73). London, England, 1742. Silver. The Metropolitan Museum of Art, Bequest of Irwin Untermeyer, 1973, 1974.28.181

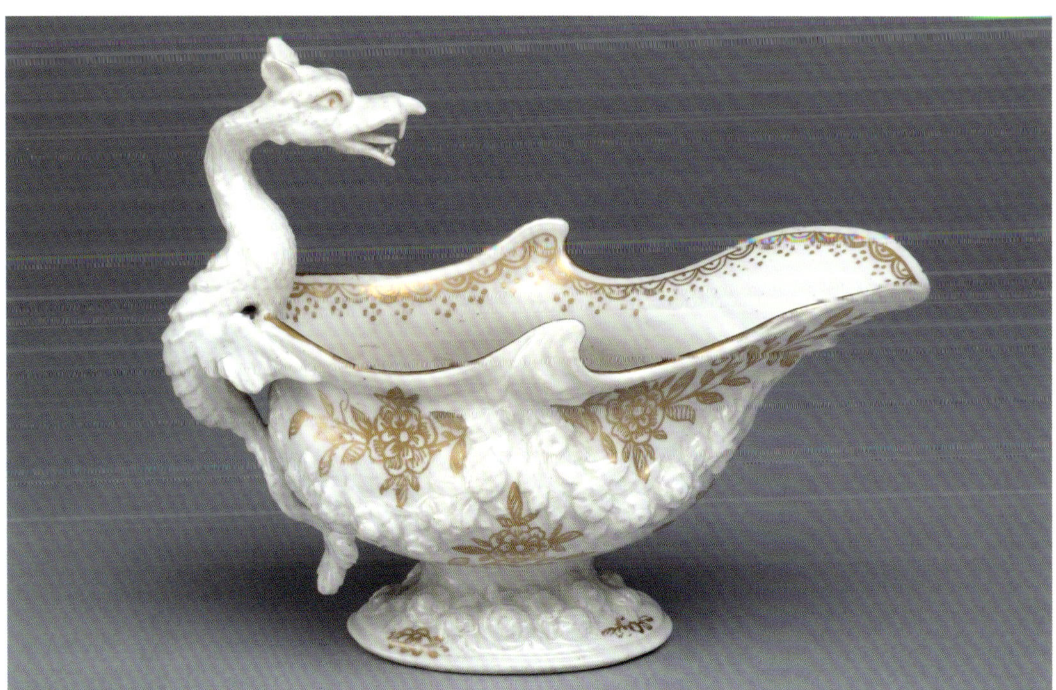

FIG. 39 Sauce boat. Manufactured by Bow Factory. London, England, ca. 1750. Glazed porcelain, gilding. Cooper-Hewitt, National Design Museum, Smithsonian Institution, Museum purchase from Charles E. Sampson Memorial Fund, 1979-18-1

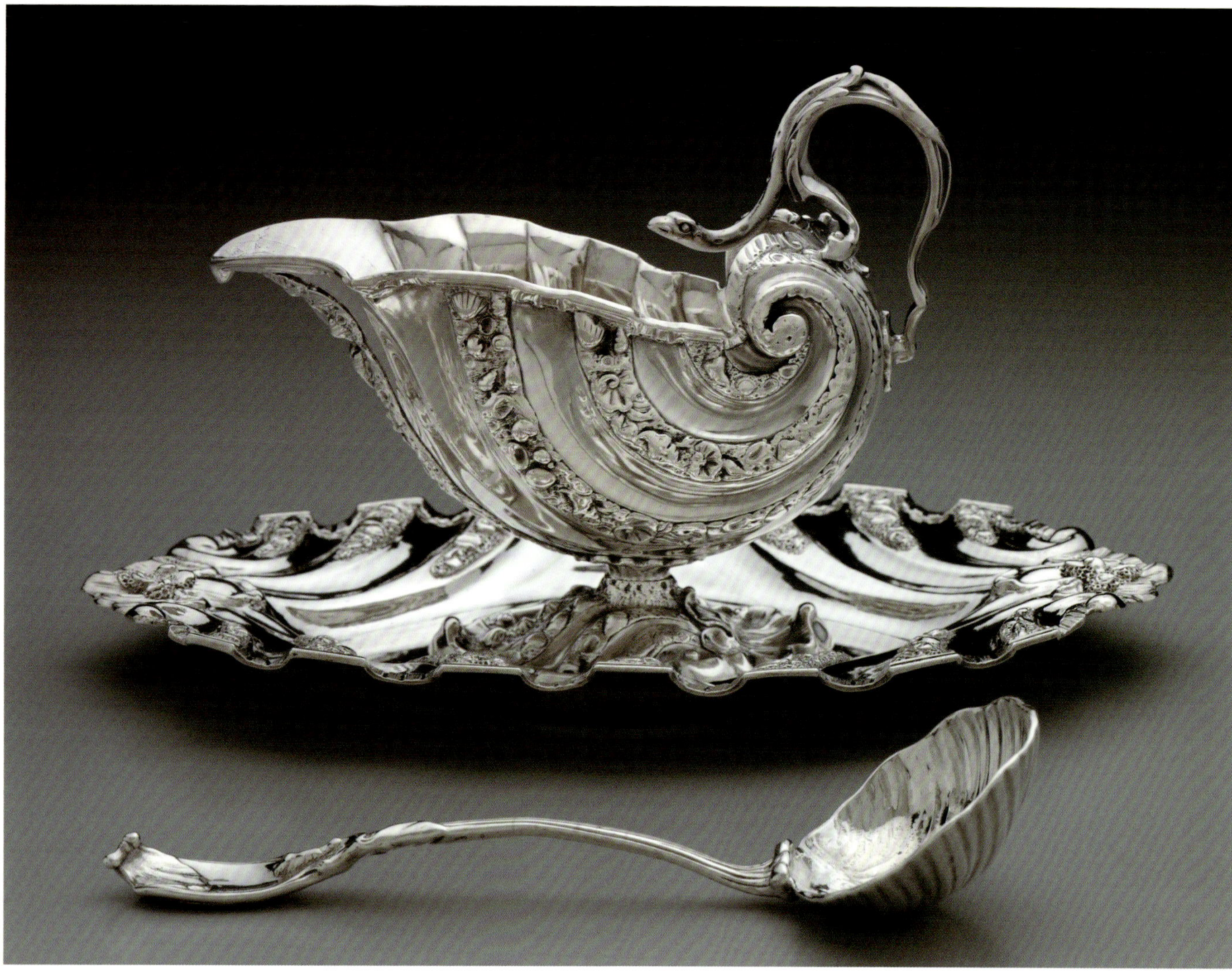

FIG. 40 Sauceboat, stand, and ladle. Nicholas Sprimont (active in England ca. 1742–70). London, England, 1746–47. Silver. Museum of Fine Arts, Boston, Gift of Alan and Simone Hartman and Harriet J. Bradbury Fund, 2001.68

factory. Almost all of his known silver is from the years 1742–47, after which it appears that the Chelsea factory took up his whole time. One of his small productions at the factory was a porcelain copy after a model by Roubiliac of Hogarth's favorite pug, showing his connection to the St. Martin's Lane group.[39] The primary modeler from around 1748 to 1766 at Chelsea was the Fleming Joseph Willems.[40]

In Europe, toilet services were wedding *trousseau* items in silver and, when available, porcelain, which makes Sprimont a reasonable candidate as the designer of the mixed porcelain and silver example requested for Augustus the Strong. It also shows that the ability to model could be applied to more than one medium, a possibility that may relate to the Kändlers' work as well. There is a mirror for an imperial toilet service in Russia by Charles Kändler of somewhat similar design to the drawing for the Saxon service. While the Saxon service does not appear to exist, it is interesting to note that Charles Gouyn (d. 1785), Sprimont's former partner at Chelsea, who left the factory around 1748 to go out on his own, did produce one in mixed media. Gouyn, a Huguenot jeweler, was born in Dieppe and had a German named d'Ostermann compounding his paste when he was at Chelsea. Gouyn produced his independent productions, known as "Girl in a Swing," which mixed, gold, silver, and other

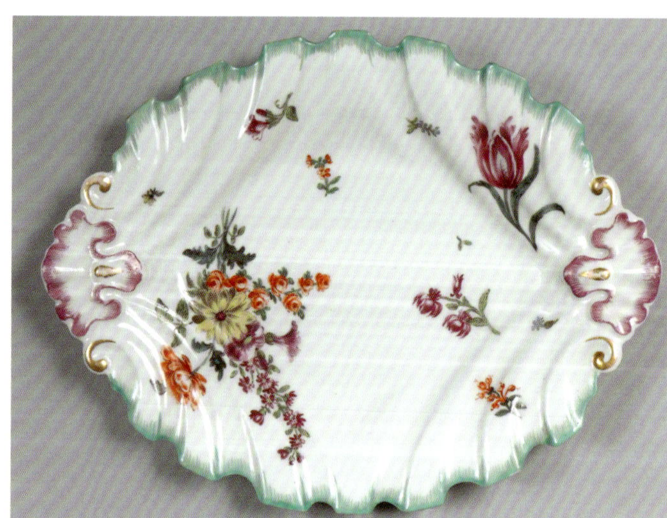

FIG. 41 "Silvershape" dish. Nicholas Sprimont (active in England ca. 1742–70). Chelsea Porcelain Manufactory. London, England, 1753–56. Laurence N. Strenger, Los Angeles, California

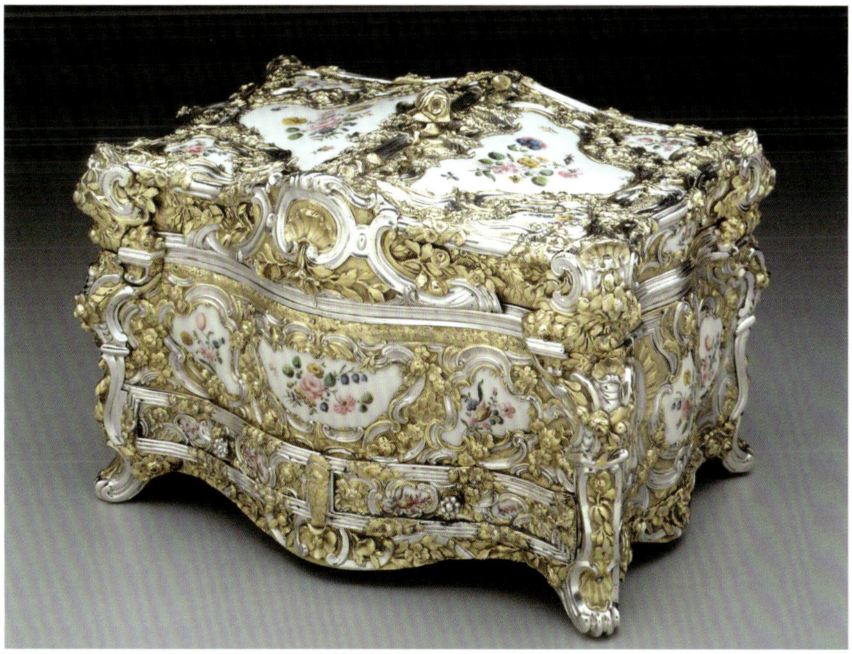

FIG. 42 Toilet service. Attributed to Charles Gouyn (English, active 1749–59). St. James' Factory. London, England, ca. 1755. Silver, Silver-gilt, porcelain, enamel, glass, garnets, velvet. Dallas Museum of Art, The Esther and Karl Hoblitzelle Collection, gift of the Hoblitzelle Foundation by exchange, 1995.22.1/21

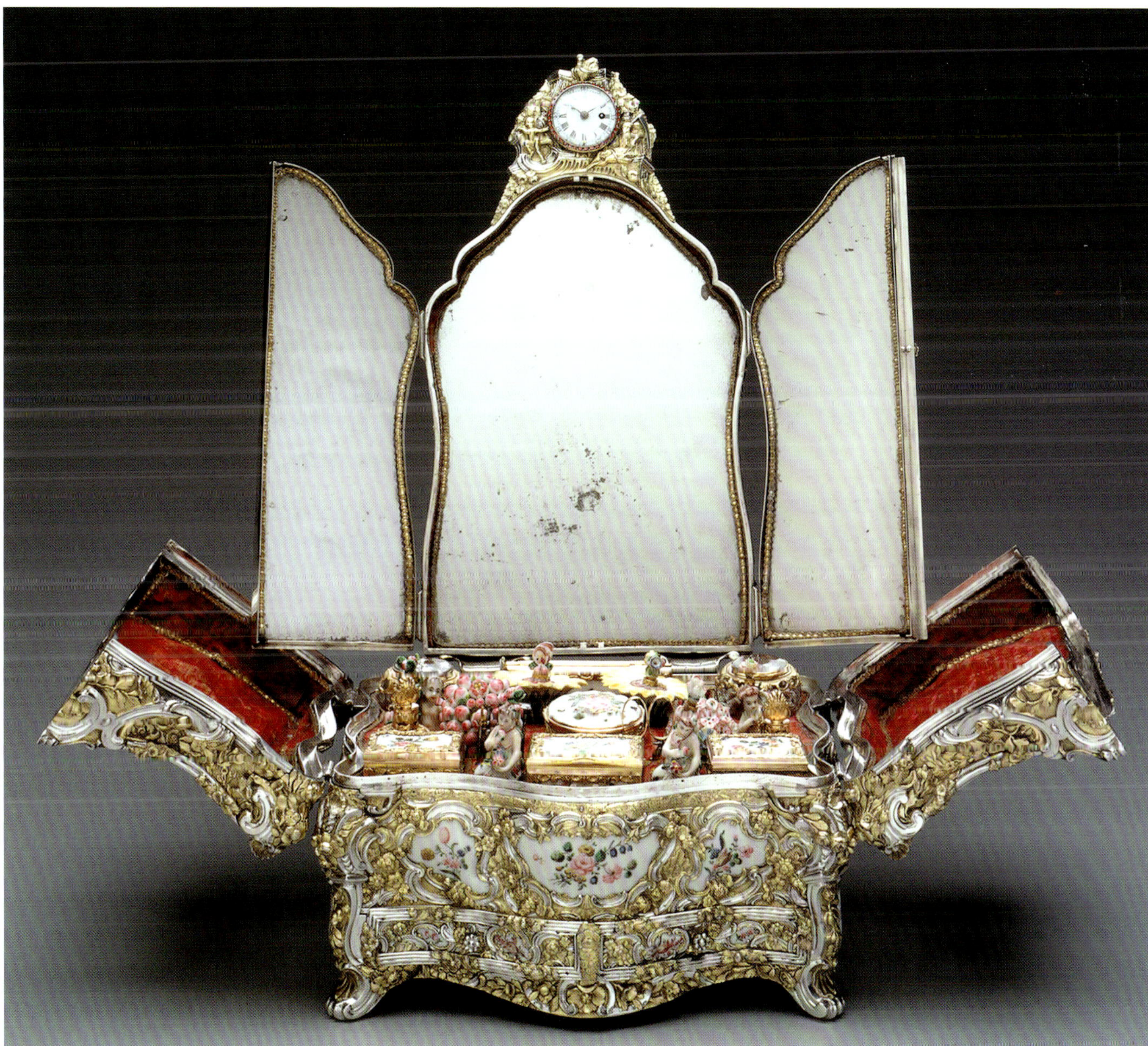

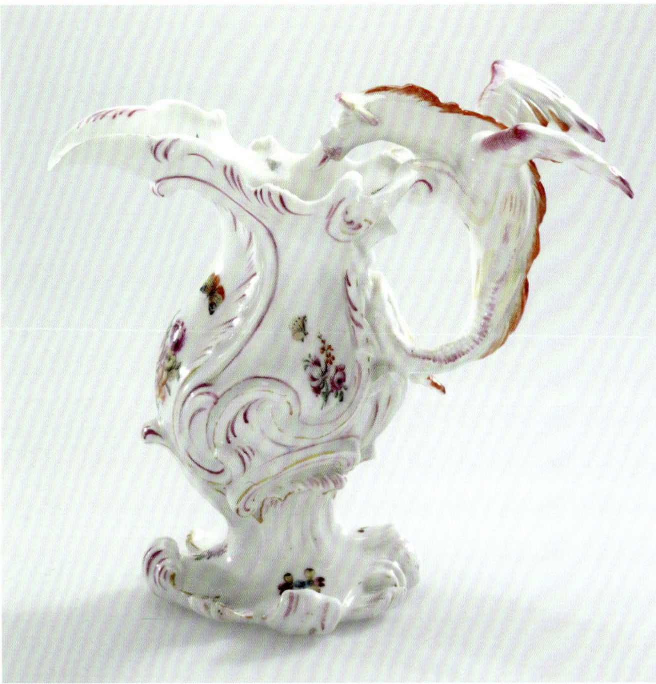

FIG. 43 Ewer. Vauxhall China Works. Lambeth, England ca. 1760. Porcelain. Minneapolis Institute of Arts. Gift of Leo and Doris Hodroff, 2005.159.3

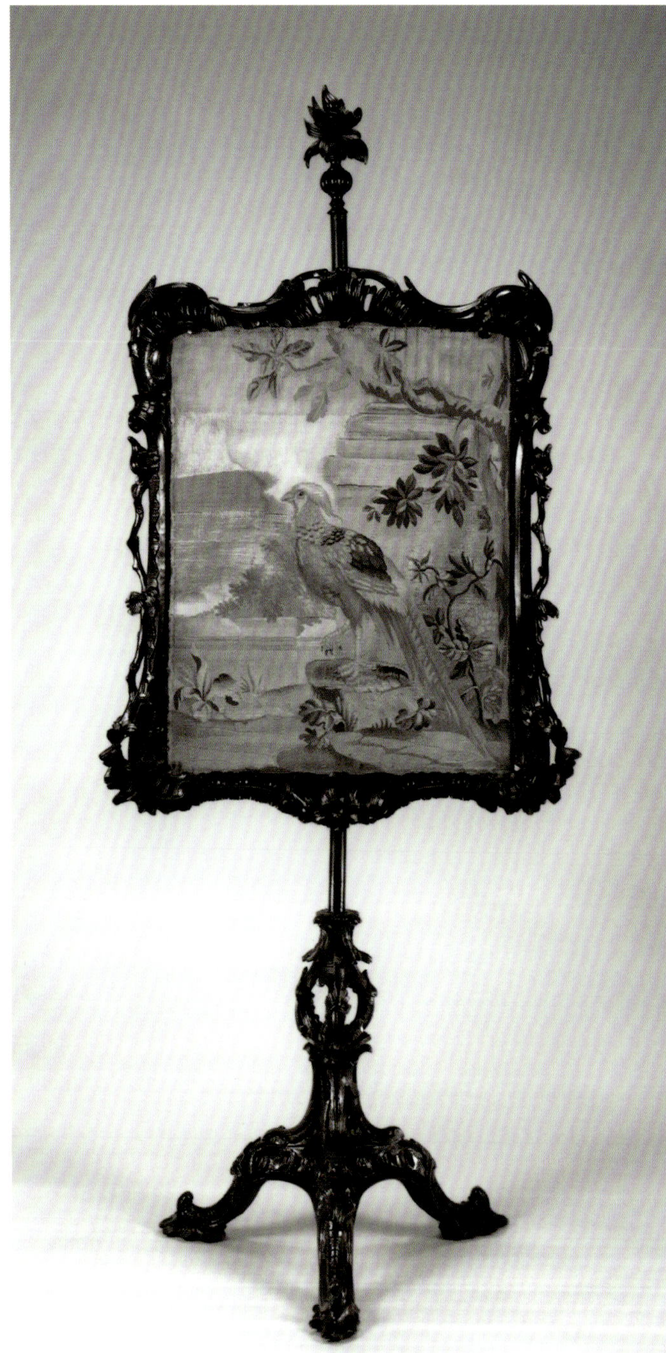

FIG. 45 Fire screen. England, ca. 1755. Mahogany, tapestry. The Gerstenfeld Collection

metalwork with porcelain, in St. James's Street.[41] (fig. 42) Other foreign-born and -trained ceramic artists included some who worked at Tournai, Derby modeler Nicholas Gauron, Chelsea painters William and Fidelle Duvivier, and a Chelsea modeler named Flanchet, a pupil of Joseph Duplessis.[42] The similarity of some rococo pieces of Derby porcelain to ones created in French faience speaks to that connection. A flamboyant ewer made at Vauxhall is in a similar spirit (fig. 43).

Modeling and, by extension, carving came to the fore in Britain as well as a major conduit of rococo in a trail of decorative schemes in stucco, initially and primarily by Italian stuccoists such as Giuseppe Artari and Giovanni Bagutti, who produced some of the most rococo decoration. The flow started before the rococo era with the architect James Gibbes, a Catholic who was patronized by many of his co-religionists such as the Dukes of Norfolk. After such examples as Ditchley Park, Oxfordshire, the use of rococo stuccowork became popular in the north, especially in Yorkshire, as well as in Scotland and Ireland. A superb example of this type of work, dating from the 1750s, was at Hagley Hall, Yorkshire, where torchères and girandoles designed by Thomas Johnson (1723–1799) were used as part of the furnishings. Johnson had met Matthias Lock around 1744 and copied his drawings when both worked, the former as an apprentice, for the carver and gilder James Whittle.[43] While the English cabinetmakers had a hard time being truly rococo in spirit, the carvers of giltwood mirrors and pier and console tables were the most able practitioners of the style (fig. 44). In these objects and others, such as fire screens and smaller objects (fig. 45), the virtuosity of the carving was less in opposition to the structure than in case pieces, such as

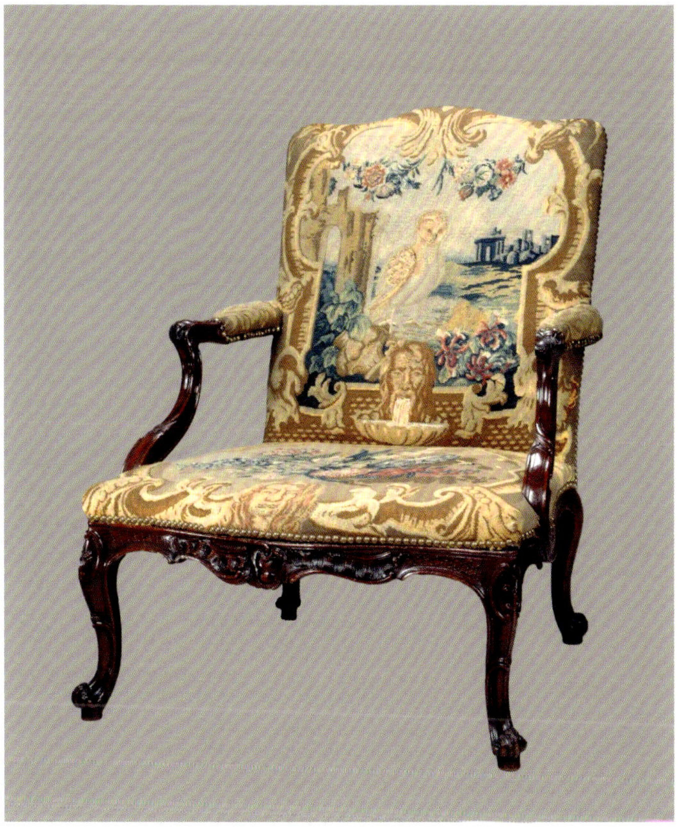

FIG. 46 Library chair for Glemham Hall. England, ca. 1755. Mahogany, gros point needlework upholstery. The Gerstenfeld Collection

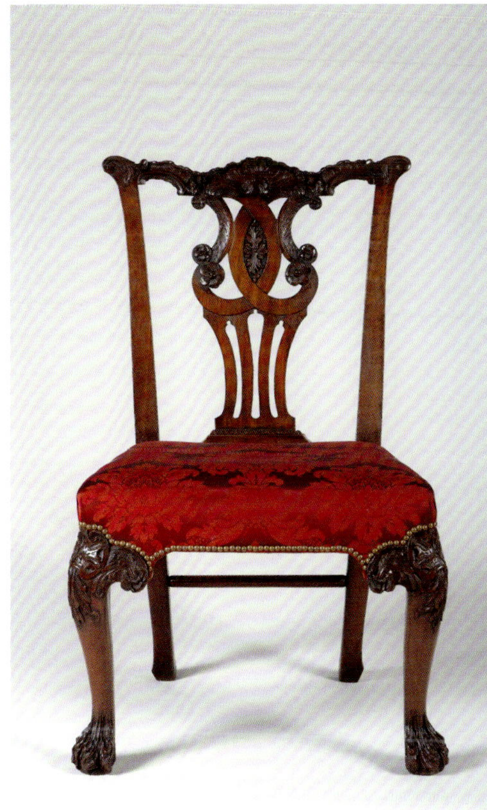

FIG. 47 Chair (one of a pair). England, ca. 1750–60. Red walnut, silk damask (reproduction). Cooper-Hewitt, National Design Museum, Smithsonian Institution, Museum purchase from General Acquisitions Endowment Fund, 2006-5-1

chests of drawers. In Scotland, Thomas Chippendale's large commission from the Earl of Dumfries for Dumfries House was unusual because it included some major rococo pieces made by him and some commissions for rococo mirrors to Edinburgh makers such as Allen Mathie. Yorkshire was Chippendale's home and the site of many of his great commissions, such as Nostell Priory. Chippendale made specially designed furniture and produced the *Gentleman and Cabinetmaker's Director* (first edition 1754), both of which resonated throughout much of the British Empire and elsewhere. One of a series of armchairs that relate to Chippendale's designs for "French Chairs" came from Glemham Hall, Suffolk, and has its original needlework with different birds in rococo cartouches (fig. 46).

The earliest example of the pattern books of designs produced at this time was in England, for furniture with organic rococo designs, which reflected French and other continental designs. Designs by the carver Matthias Lock appeared in his *Six Tables* (1744),[44] which was produced in the heyday of Gravelot and St. Martin's Lane. It also cribbed quite closely from extant French designs. Another pattern book, by Robert Manwaring,[45] contained designs for chairs that may be the closest to Cooper-Hewitt's example (fig. 47). Many of these books portrayed the author's specific variations on styles already in existence. The one furniture maker known to have been at St. Martin's Lane, John Linnell, was a fine draftsman and designer of rococo furniture (fig. 48). However, it is certain that others who went to work for furniture makers studied design drawing at St. Martin's Lane. There is no firm evidence that Chippendale studied there, despite his friendship with Paine and the proximity of his shop. If he did not attend the academy, the increased emphasis on

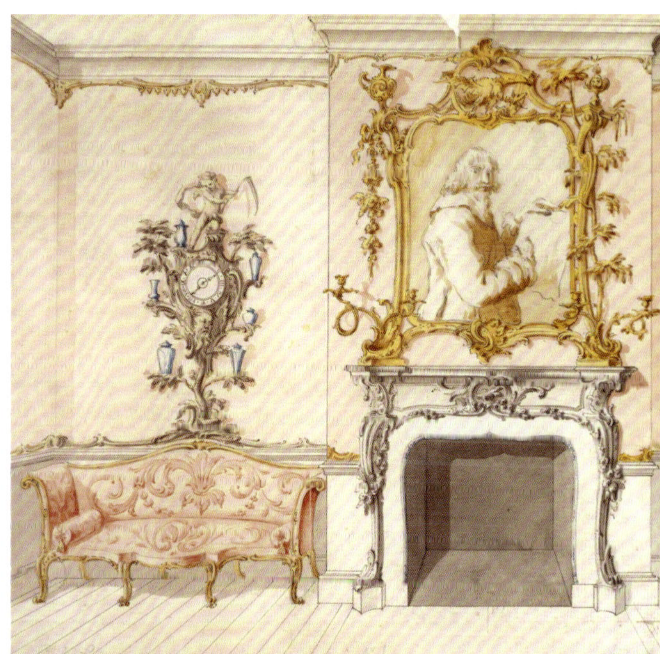

FIG. 48 *Design for the Side of a Room*. John Linnell (English, 1723–1796). England, ca. 1755. Pen, ink, and watercolor. Victoria and Albert Museum, E.263-1929

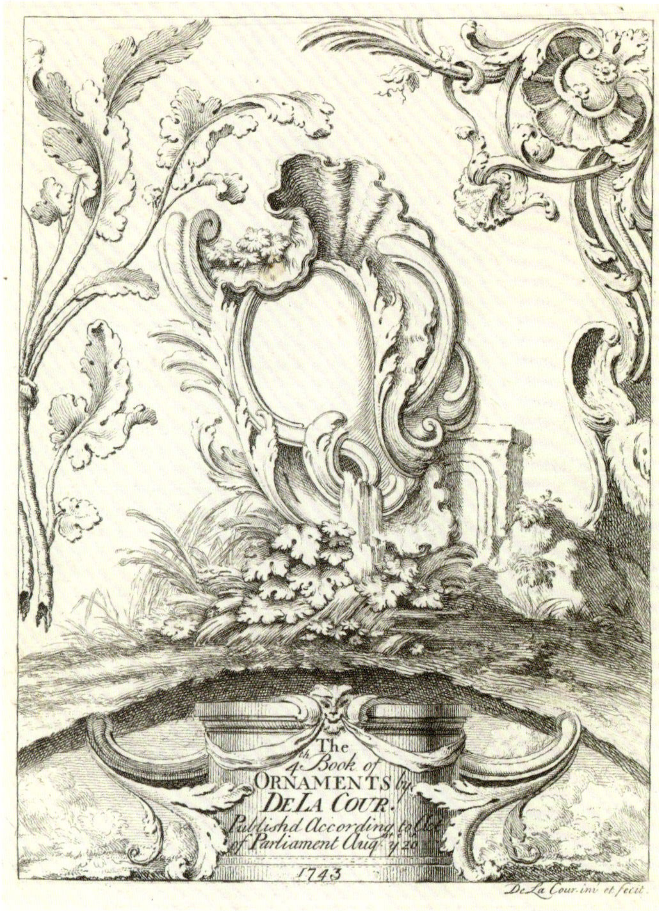

FIG. 49 Frontispiece, Book 4, *Eight Books of Ornament* (bound together). William Delacour, (French, 1741–1767). Engraved by François Vivares (French, 1709–1782). Designed in Paris, France, published in England, 1741–47. Engravings, bound in half-calf and marbled boards. Cooper-Hewitt, National Design Museum, Smithsonian Institution, Purchased for the Museum by the Advisory Council, 1962-126-1

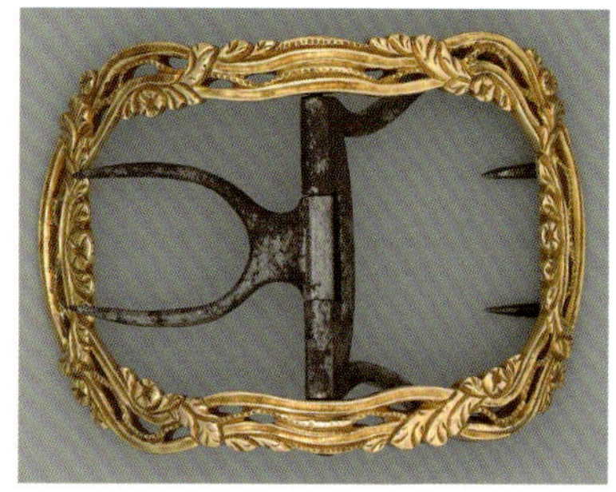

FIG. 50 Shoe buckle. Myer Myers (American, 1723–1795). New York, NY, ca. 1765–70. Gold, iron. Yale University Art Gallery, Gift of Mr. and Mrs. Phillip Holzer, 1989.77.1

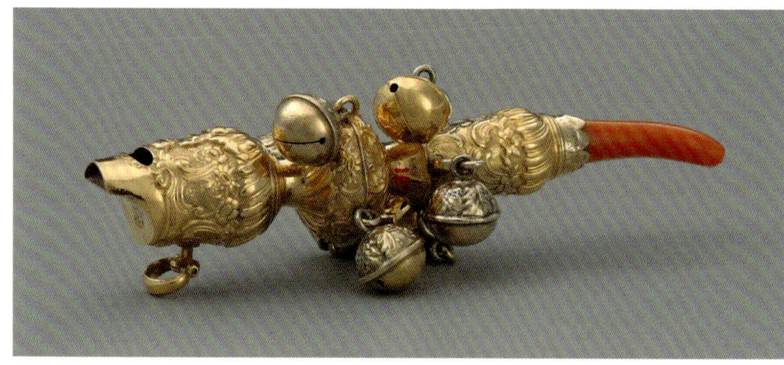

FIG. 51 Whistle and bells. Daniel Christian Fueter (Swiss, 1720–1785, active in New York 1754–69). New York, NY, 1761–65. Gold, coral. Yale University Art Gallery, Mabel Brady Garvan Collection, 1942.91

drawing skills there must have led him to learn, as his drawings are very accomplished. William Delacour, of French birth, published a series of books of ornament, cartouche, mirror, furniture, and snuffbox designs in London starting in 1741 (fig. 49). He advertised on the title page of the 1743 volume that he "designs for all Sorts of Trades, & teaches to Draw."

Rococo style continued to be popular, especially for carved ornament in wood furniture, in northern England, Scotland, and Ireland through the third quarter of the eighteenth century. In addition to Chippendale from Yorkshire, Johnson worked for a year in Dublin and about seven years in Liverpool. William Delacour was hired around 1760 by the trustees of the Edinburgh Society for Encouraging Arts, Sciences, Manufactures and Agriculture in Scotland, founded in 1755. His role was master of its school of design, which produced patterns for making "Damask, printed linen, carpets and other flowered goods."[46] These fabrics almost certainly found their way to the American colonies. Delacour's principal influence, however, or that of similar designs by Gravelot, may be seen in chairs with interlaced backs made in Newport, Rhode Island.[47]

THE AMERICAN COLONIES

The tobacco trade is one way through which rococo style found its patrons in America. Glasgow was a primary trading port with the American South, and many Scots in the tobacco trade moved to southern port

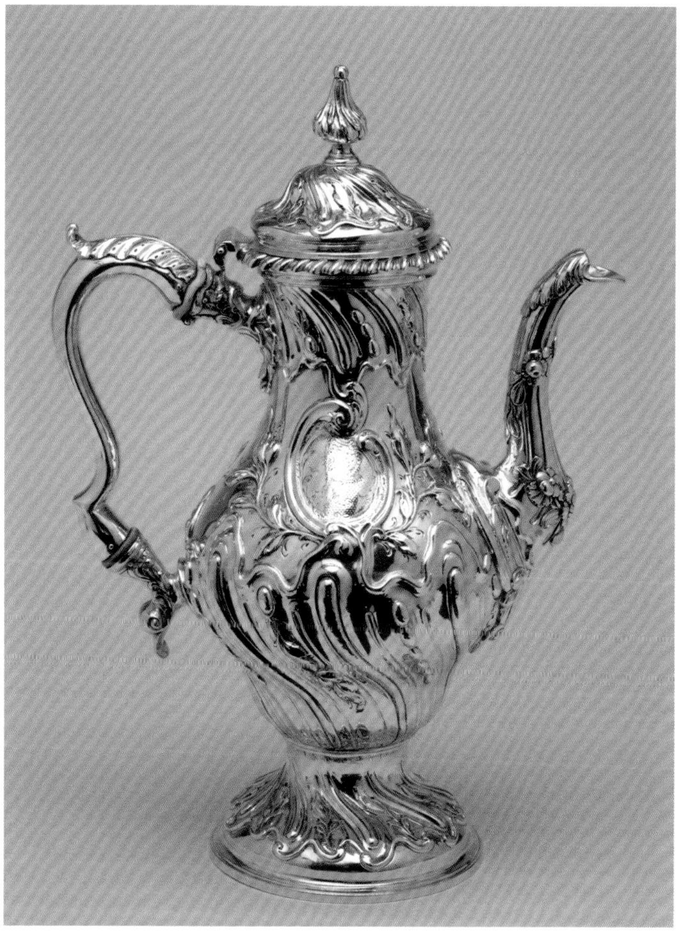

FIG. 52 Coffeepot. Thomas Whipham II and Charles Wright (English, active in partnership 1757–75). London, England, 1763. Silver, ivory. Philadelphia Museum of Art, Purchased with the John D. McIlhenny Fund, 1988.35.1a/b

cities to facilitate the trade, bringing possessions with them. Certainly those who were getting rich from tobacco sent to Glasgow, and elsewhere, used their gains in trade for acquisitions of silver and furniture. But in general, the main introduction of rococo design, which never took hold to a wide extent in the American colonies, was through imported silver, furniture, and craftsmen, especially foreign-trained silversmiths, chasers, and carvers. They came primarily to the major port cities of Boston, Newport, New York, Philadelphia, Norfolk, and Charleston; the primary consumers of rococo were in Philadelphia. In addition, books like Chippendale's *Director* were sold or brought over by craftsmen such as Thomas Affleck, the Edinburgh-trained furniture maker who worked in London before moving to Philadelphia in 1763, where he produced chairs in the Chippendale mode, responding to the widespread demand created by the *Director*'s publication.

By 1765, the Non-Importation Acts resulted in patrons needing to acquire American-made goods, increasing the demand for specialized workers such as chasers and carvers from Europe. Conveniently, this coincided with the decline of rococo in England. Several immigrant carvers impacted rococo style dramatically.[48] Boston, generally more conservative in taste, produced little rococo work, though Paul Revere (anglicized from Rivoire), son of a French Huguenot silversmith, clearly had the skills for it, and did execute a few scalloped-edge pieces.

In New York, Henry Hardcastle was particularly influential in interior architectural carving and decoration; James Strachan, a carver and gilder, supplied picture and mirror frames; and John Brinner, a cabinet- and chair maker imported six specialists as he advertised a broad range of goods, including carving and girandoles.[49] However, beyond architectural, picture, and mirror frames, rococo design was less pronounced than in the furniture and woodwork in Philadelphia.

By contrast, Myer Myers used and creatively adapted English models for some of the most sophisticated rococo silver produced in the American colonies.[50] That a set of snuffers on stand by Myers is almost identical to some made by Philadelphia silversmith Phillip Syng implies an English model was the design source. Robert and Catherine Livingston, for whom Myers made it, had opulent taste in table silver, and owned a substantial amount of English silver. Myers also produced some skilled goldwork, including a pair of buckles (fig. 50) whose chasing is much more fluid and sophisticated than his earlier snuffbox.[51] The other primary silversmith of New York rococo was Daniel Christian Fueter, who was born and apprenticed in Switzerland before moving to London in 1742. There he may have been exposed to a fellow Swiss, the gold chaser George Moser, before coming to New York in 1754, where he stayed until he returned to Switzerland in 1767. His gold and coral baby's whistle and bells of around 1761–65 has very sophisticated rococo chasing (fig. 51), possibly reflecting the work of a chaser from Geneva whose presence in New York he advertised in 1769.[52]

In Philadelphia, James Reynolds (ca. 1736–1794), Nicholas Bernard, and Martin Jugiez (d. 1815), who were in partnership from around 1762 to 1783; and Hercules Courtenay, who apprenticed with Thomas Johnson from 1756 to 1760,[53] were all skilled carvers from London who contributed to the particularly elaborately carved works made in the city. In addition, the carver John Pollard, who, like Courtenay, may have carved some of the pieces for the Cadwalader house, was working in London before Courtenay and he had their way paid by Benjamin Randolph to come to Philadelphia.[54] Courtenay arrived just before the 1765 Non-Importation Act, as his name appears in agreement to it.

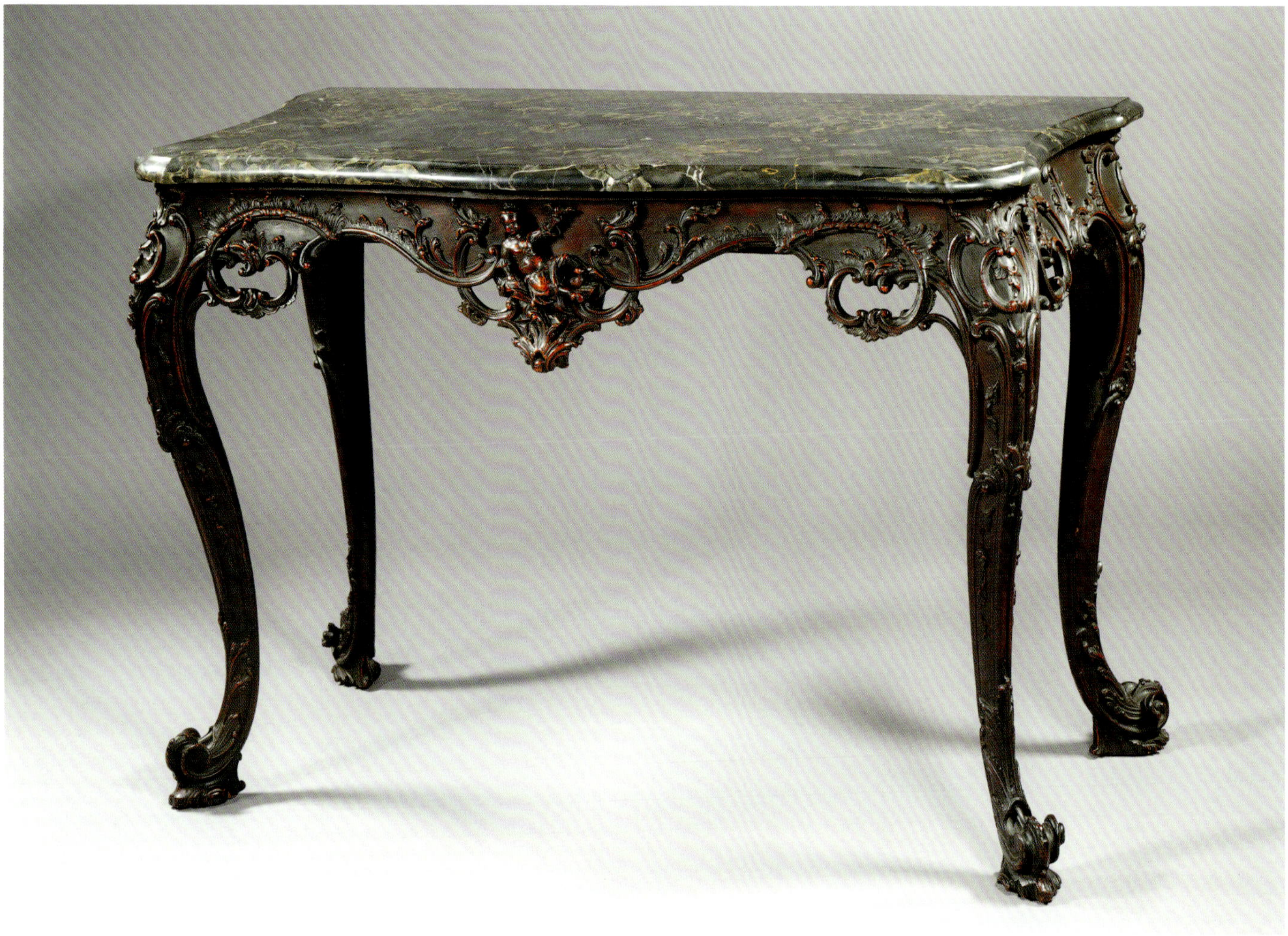

FIG. 53 Pier table. Philadelphia, PA, ca. 1770. Mahogany, marble, yellow pine, walnut. The Metropolitan Museum of Art, John Stewart Kennedy Fund, 18.110.27

The Cadwalader commissions for their house on Second Street in Philadelphia resulted in the truest rococo furniture produced in the American colonies, although the impetus appears to have come from the direct purchase from England of significant silver and furniture by Elizabeth Cadwalader's father, Edward Lloyd III of Wye Plantation, in Maryland. Among his purchases was a tea and coffee set (fig. 52), which he presented to his daughter and son-in-law and which inspired some of the decoration of the house.[55] James Reynolds received payment for frames for family portraits and for a "Pier glass…party gold" in rococo style.[56] Bernard and Jugiez, who were first recorded as partners in Philadelphia in 1762,[57] provided rococo architectural carving for Cliveden and for the Cadwaladers as well as furniture for Thomas Affleck and Benjamin Randolph for the latter's house in the early 1770s. Their fire screens for this and other houses were covered with rich rococo carving. They also advertised in Boston, New York, and Charleston, for, among other goods, gilt and painted glasses and papier-mâché for ceilings.[58]

Courtenay, who described himself as a carver and gilder, may have brought a copy of Thomas Johnson's *New Book of Ornaments* (1762) with him when he came, as Johnson's interpretation of Aesop's fables appear in the carving of several pieces of Philadelphia woodwork, most notably the marble-topped table for the Cadwaladers of around 1769, the most fully realized piece of rococo furniture made in America (fig. 53). A gilt painted wall bracket, made in Philadelphia, also was modeled on Johnson's designs (fig. 54). Other pieces had extremely rococo carving on less rococo forms. Scottish-born Thomas Affleck (1740–1795) made an undulating carved card table and a set of side chairs for General Cadwalader in 1770–71, which reflect the type of rococo seen in northern England and Scotland at about the time he emigrated (fig. 55).

Philadelphia was also the sole location in the colonies where porcelain was made in the eighteenth century. British-born Gousse Bonnin and George Morris created a factory in 1770, which mainly emulated dessert tablewares based on similar types from Bow (fig. 56),Worcester, and Plymouth. There is archaeological evidence in Williamsburg, Virginia, of a Bow example from colonial times.[59] The Cadwaladers ordered a pair from Bonnin and Morris. Despite this patronage, the factory did not survive the 1770 resumption of trade with England and the subsequent ease of importing ceramic goods, closing in 1772.

Philadelphians possessed great examples of English silver, including a very rococo tea set by Paul de Lamerie owned by the David Franks family (fig. 57). They also bought rococo pieces from a handful of silversmiths, most notably Joseph Richardson, who produced a teakettle of similar quality and appearance to London models (fig. 58). Among those working in rococo style were the Irish-born Philip Syng and Philip Hulbeart. As with carving in furniture, doing the repoussé work, or

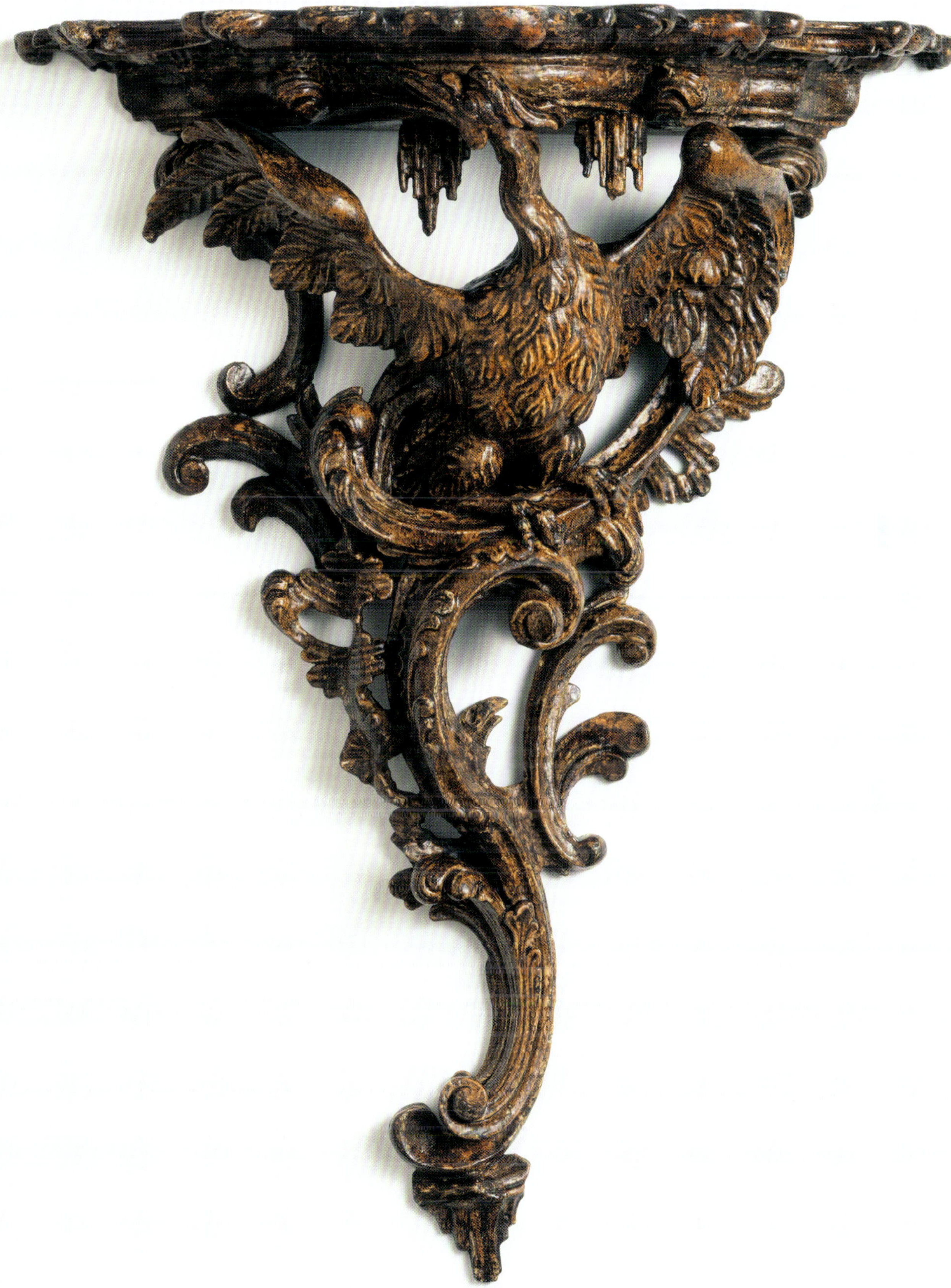

FIG. 54 Wall bracket. James Reynolds (American, 1736–1794). Philadelphia, PA, ca. 1760–85. Yellow pine, gilding, paint. Winterthur Gardens, Museum, and Library, 58.2242

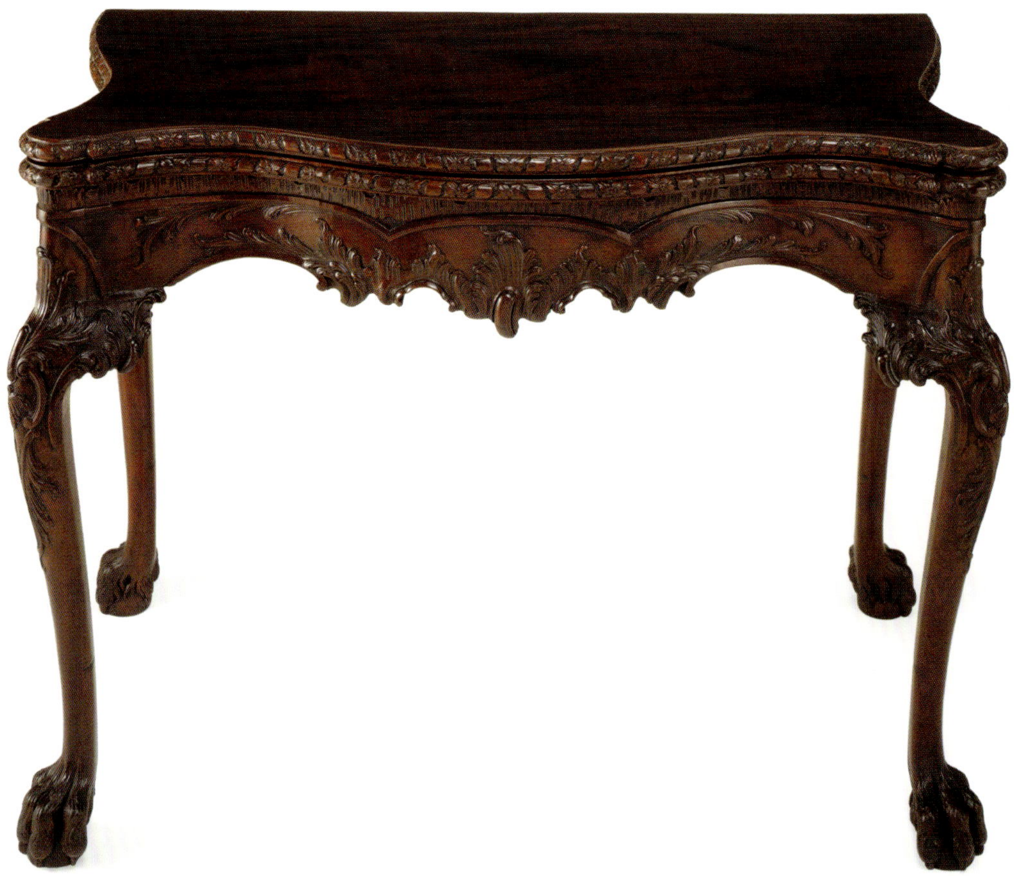

FIG. 55 Card table. Workshop of Thomas Affleck (American, born Scotland, 1740–1795). Philadelphia, PA, 1770–71. Mahogany, yellow pine, yellow poplar oak. Philadelphia Museum of Art, 1984-6-1

pushing out from the back, was a special talent, and the finishing by chasing even more so. Not surprisingly, there was a very limited number of chased pieces of American silver. One rare example is a teapot by the little known Gabriel Lewyn of Baltimore (fig. 59). Another is a coffeepot from Charleston around 1750–60 by Scottish-born Alexander Petrie, who made a number of plain-bodied coffeepots (fig. 60). Only one survives with elaborate rococo chasing, and that remained in his estate—either because it was a prized object, or perhaps it was too ornate for his market. Ironically, Charleston, which was very sophisticated, wealthy, and up to date on things English (fig. 61), including emulating the Anglo-Irish style, also had a community of German-born immigrant craftsmen. One of them was Martin Pfenninger, who incorporated German rococo marquetry techniques into the pediment of an early Federal breakfront bookcase.[60] It is interesting to consider whether Abraham Roentgen, who headed out on a Moravian mission to South Carolina in 1740, was headed to join this community, or whether Pfenninger might have learned his marquetry skills in Neuwied.[61]

The Scotland-Virginia tobacco connections mentioned earlier[62] extended to the furniture trade as well. Most notable was Scottish-born Robert Walker (ca. 1710–1777) in King George County, Virginia, who mainly produced chairs, but a group of well-carved tables has recently been attributed to him by Robert Leath. One made for the Carter

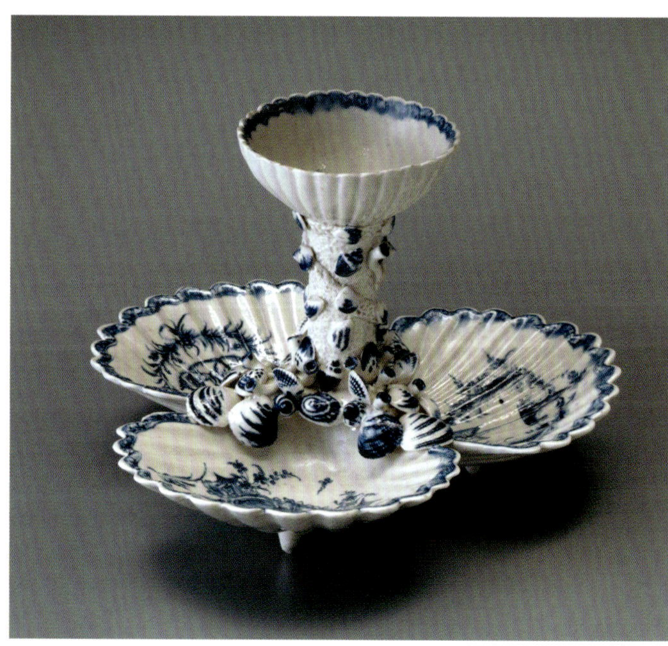

FIG. 56 Pickle stand/sweetmeat dish (one of a pair). Manufactured by American China Manufactory (Bonnin and Morris). Philadelphia, PA, 1770–72. Soft-paste porcelain. Collection of Mrs. George Kaufman

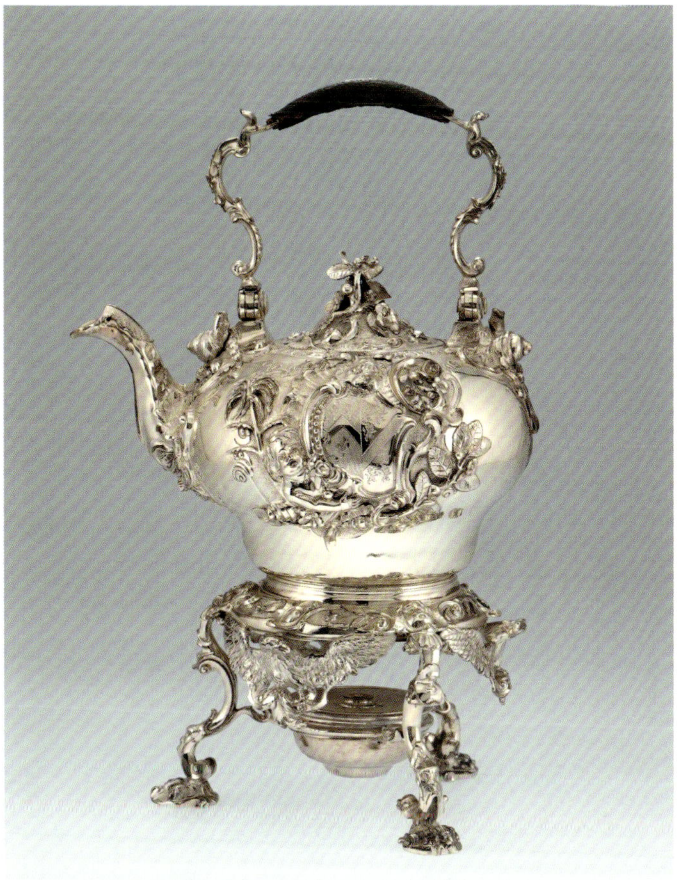

FIG. 57 Teakettle (with spirit lamp and pedestal). Paul de Lamerie (English, 1688–1751). London, England, 1744–45. Silver. The Metropolitan Museum of Art, Gift of George D. Widener and Mrs. Eleanor Widener Dixon, 58.9.19a/c

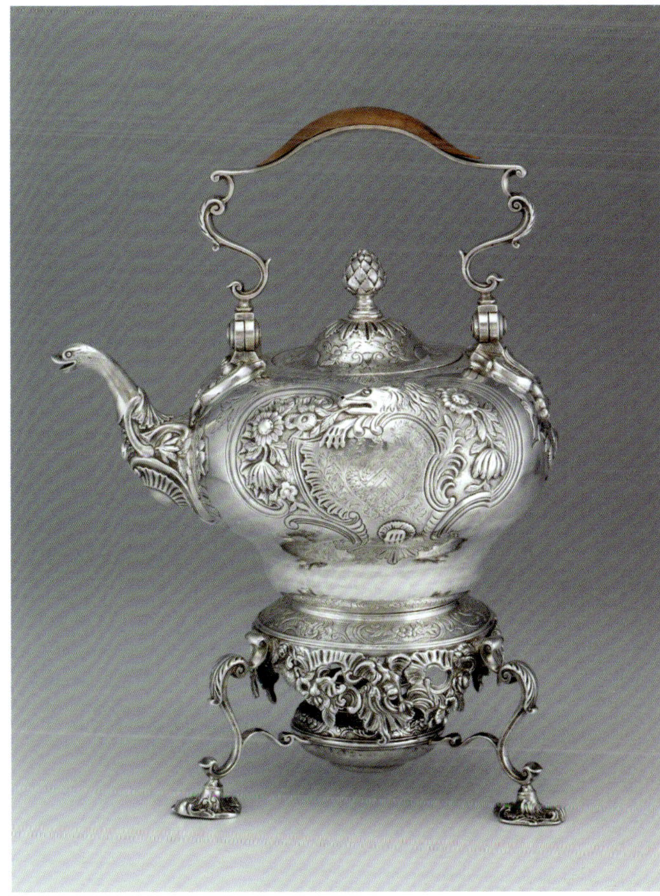

FIG. 58 Teakettle and stand. Joseph Richardson, Sr. (American, 1711–1784). Philadelphia, PA, 1745–55. Silver. Yale University Art Gallery, Mabel Brady Garvan Collection, 1932.93

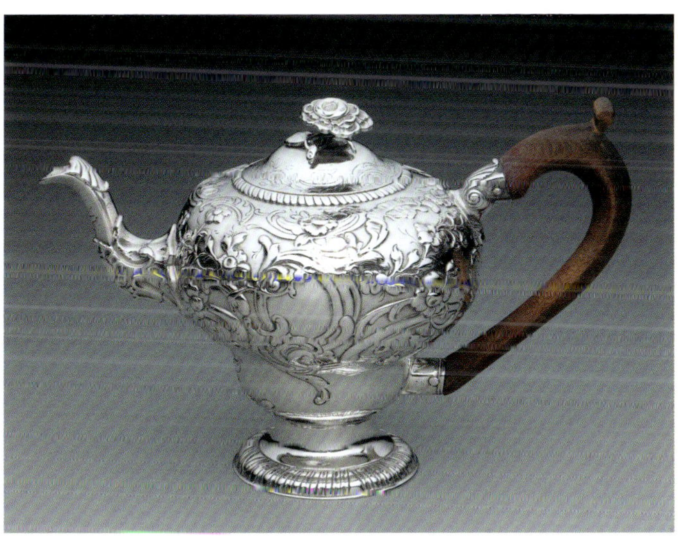

FIG. 59 Teapot. Gabriel Lewyn (American, active ca. 1768–80). Baltimore, MD, ca. 1760–70. Silver, wood. Yale University Art Gallery, John Marshall Phillps Collection, 1955.10.4

Little is known about Lewyn, but his name implies a Huguenot orgin, probably based on Leuven in Flanders via England.

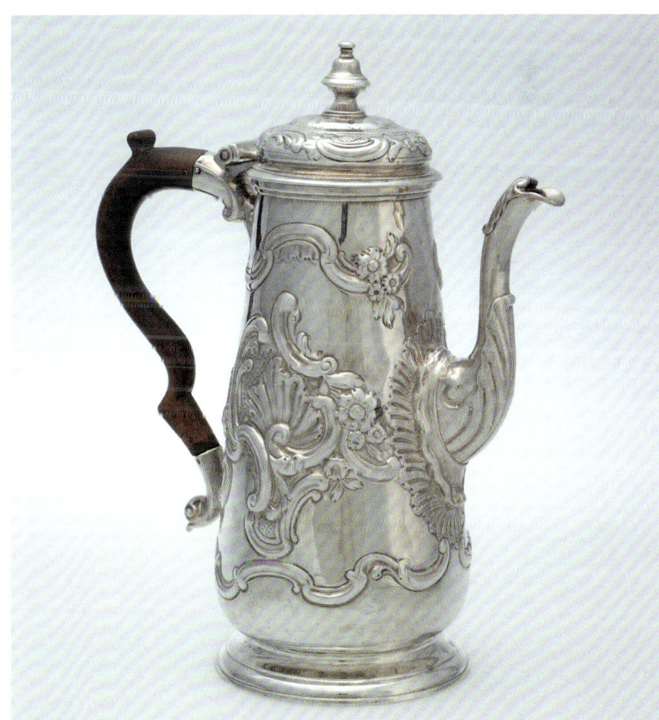

FIG. 60 Coffeepot. Alexander Petrie (American, active ca. 1742–68). Charleston, SC, ca. 1750–60. Silver, wood. Collection of the Museum of Early Southern Decorative Arts, Old Salem Museums & Gardens, 3996

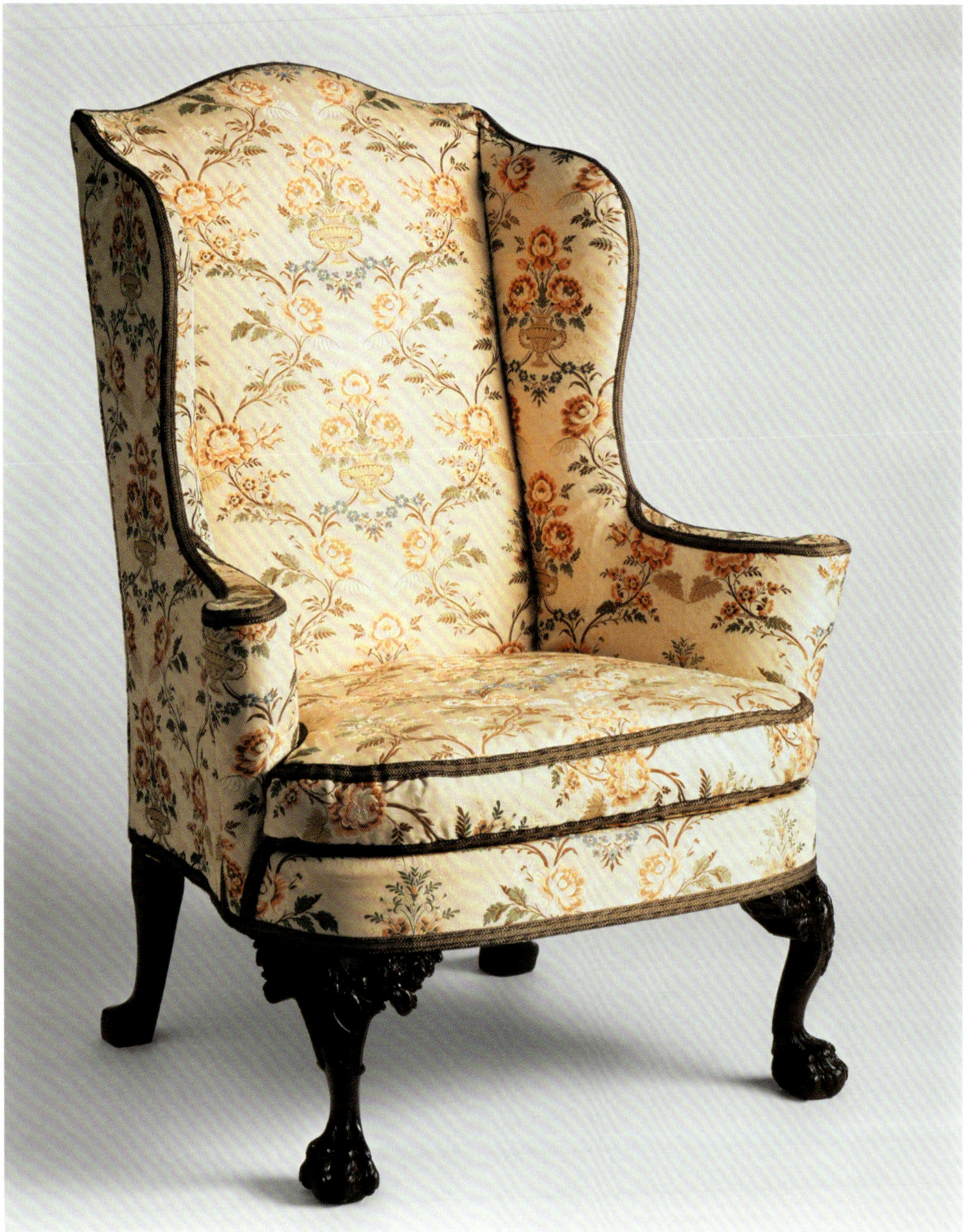

FIG. 61 Easy chair. Charleston, SC, ca. 1765–75. Mahogany, cypress, tulip poplar, upholstery. Winterthur Gardens, Museum, and Library, 60.1058

family (fig. 62) featured a top possibly based on a silver salver owned by the Spottiswoode family, which was made in London by John Swift in 1733–34.[63] Walker was either a superb carver himself, or retained one throughout the period of his business.

James Allan (1716–1789) immigrated to Fredericksburg, Virginia, from Hamilton, Scotland, in 1739 to join his brother, who was in the mercantile trade. George Washington acquired from him in 1759 a pair of candlestands that were almost identical to those published in the London Society of Upholsterers *Genteel Household Furniture* of about that date and similar to ones in Chippendale's 1754 *Director*. As Washington ordered the needlework screens through Philip Bell of London, but paid Allan less for these,[64] Allan likely had a British-trained carver working for him to attract Washington away from his London orders.

William Buckland (1734–1774), the English-born architect and furniture designer who trained with his uncle, architect William Buckland, in London, was an important figure in the transmission of rococo and other styles to Virginia. He was responsible for the rococo carving, including chinoiserie, in George Mason's House, Gunston Hall, begun in 1755.[65] This carving is similar to that found in various publications, which show the sure hand of someone able to invent within an accepted vocabulary.

From silver- and goldsmiths who needed modelers, chasers, and draftsmen to furniture and other woodworking shops that needed carvers who were sculptors, rococo design of the eighteenth century, which seems so "sanssouci," required virtuoso performances and discipline from artists and a sense of fantasy from both patrons and artisans.

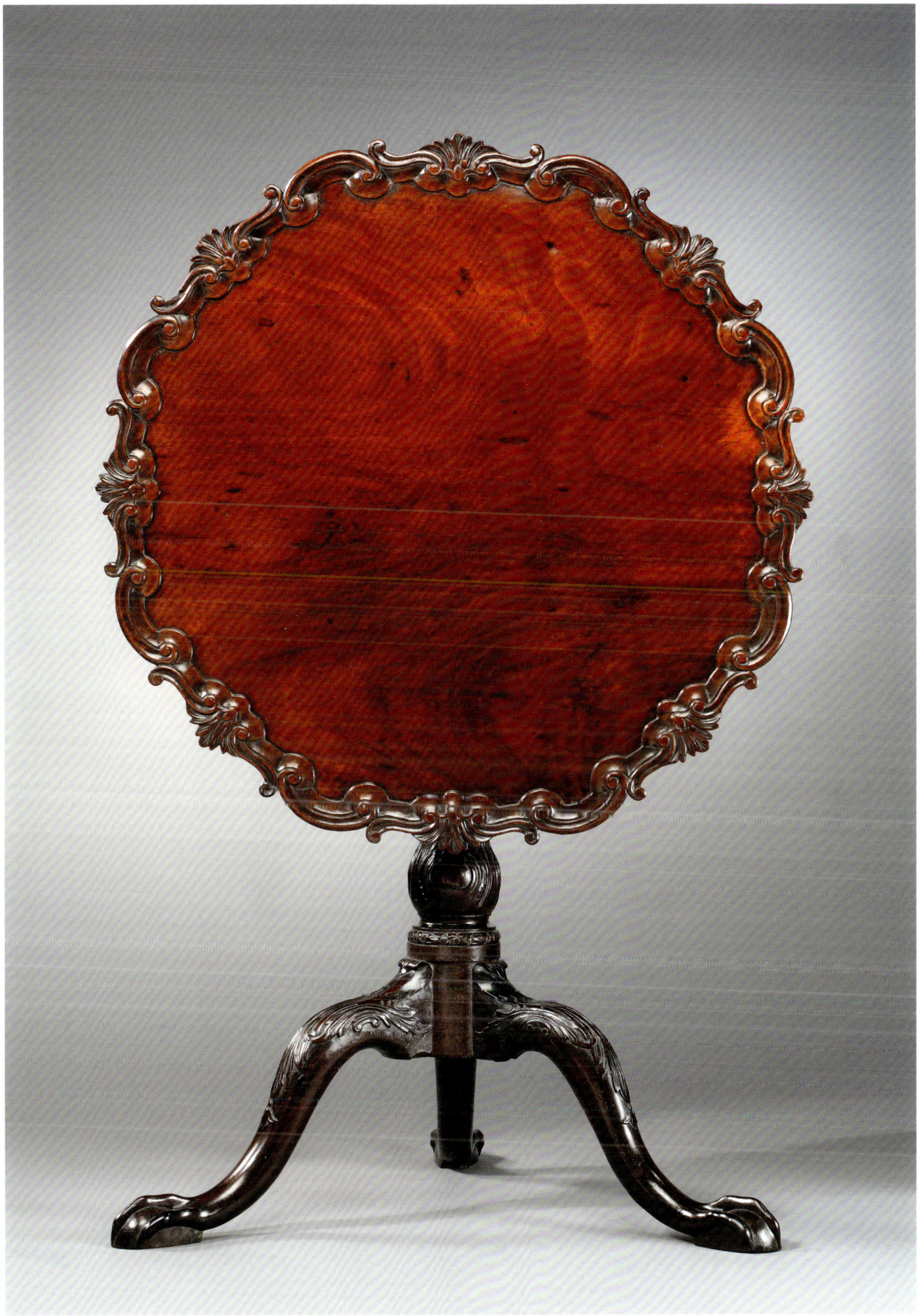

FIG. 62 Tea table. Attributed to Robert Walker (American, ca. 1710–1770). King George County, VA, 1750–60. Mahogany, cherry. Collection of the Museum of Early Southern Decorative Arts, Old Salem Museums & Gardens 3992

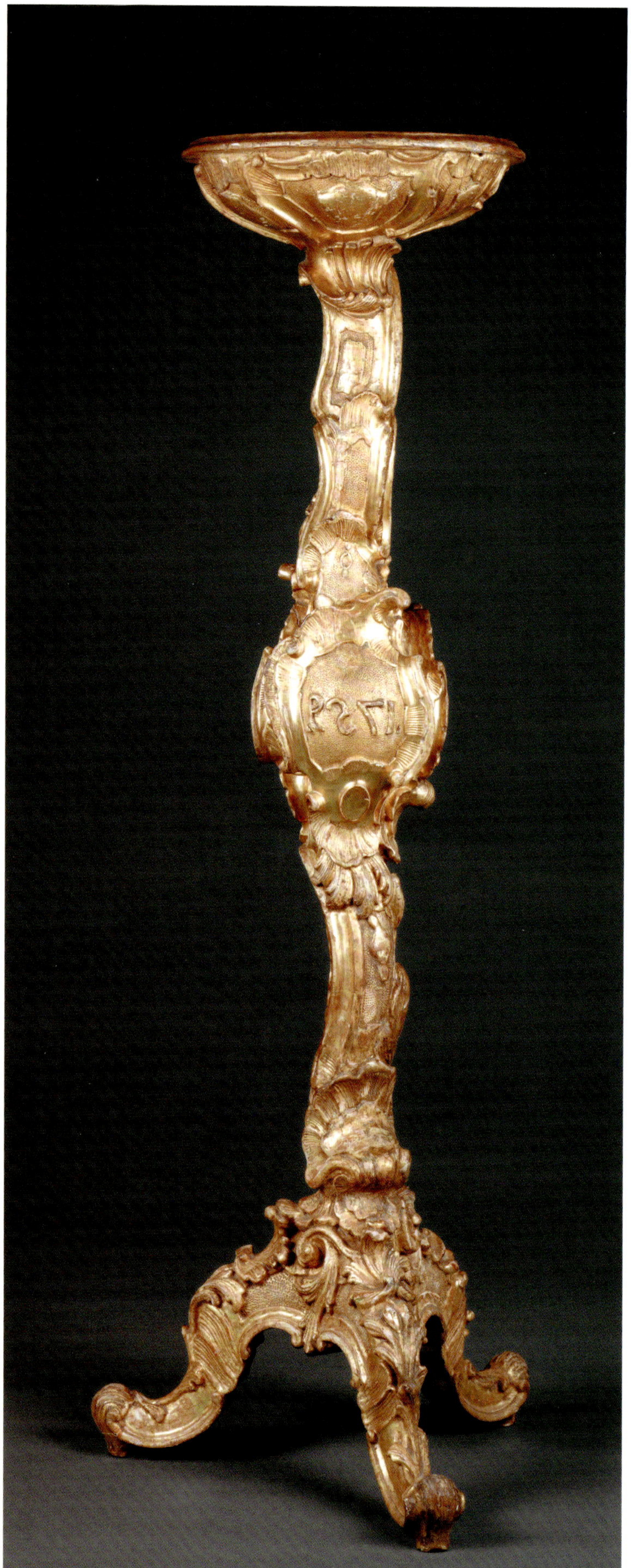

FIG. 7 Torchère (one of a pair). Southern Germany, ca. 1755. Gilt wood. Collection of Horace Wood Brock

German Rococo

FROM CUVILLIÉS IN MUNICH TO NAHL IN POTSDAM

Ulrich Leben

The style generally known today as rococo was very fashionable all over Germany in the eighteenth century, and engaged at least one generation of artists and craftsmen in a prolific period of creativity in architecture and the applied arts. By studying the phenomenon of rococo in certain geographic and religious segments of Germany, it is possible to see a number of variations in the style.

The idea of rococo, characterized by curvilinear lines, sinuous shapes, and asymmetry, was originally invented and launched by Italian and French architects, designers, and craftsmen. When rococo objects found their way into Germany, local artists familiar with the formal repertory happily assimilated and created their own interpretations of the new design language. German rococo often exceeded French models in fantasy and extravagance and extended into built architecture.

The geographic entity of what now forms Germany was, in the 1700s, a patchwork of many different counties, principalities, and kingdoms—a diversity which makes it more complex to analyze German rococo as a proper national interpretation of the style than in countries with one centralized capital, such as France and England. Every region had its key figures, in most cases an architect, who took the lead in its adaptation of the style: the architect Mathäus Daniel Pöppelmann (1662–1732) and sculptor Johann Joachim Kändler (1706–1775) in Dresden; Jean-François Cuvilliés (1695–1768) in Munich; the architect Johann Balthasar Neumann (1687–1753) in Würzburg, Georg Wenceslaus Knobelsdorff (1699–1753) in Potsdam; and an ingenious collaboration between Cuvilliés and Johann August Nahl (1710–1773) in Schloss Wilhelmsthal, near Kassel. There was also great creativity in smaller cities and regions.[1]

After the cataclysm of the Thirty Years' War (1608–43), rococo was the first style to unify Germany, at least aesthetically. In this respect, rococo could be called a style with a democratic dimension. Originally created for nobility, it easily reached, through the success and popularity of its repertory, all levels of the social scale. German rococo also enjoyed a longevity that was remarkable in comparison with other European countries. Through public architecture and monuments, distribution of rococo language was ensured, and, in the end, it became equally as valuable for a teapot or stove in a humble cottage as in a scheme for a nobleman's palace.

FROM PARIS TO GERMANY: THE TRANSIT OF ROCOCO

Physically, the idea of rococo was imported to Germany by traveling nobility, who returned from abroad with works of art and furniture and even invited artists and craftsmen to come with them. In addition, migrating craftsmen and

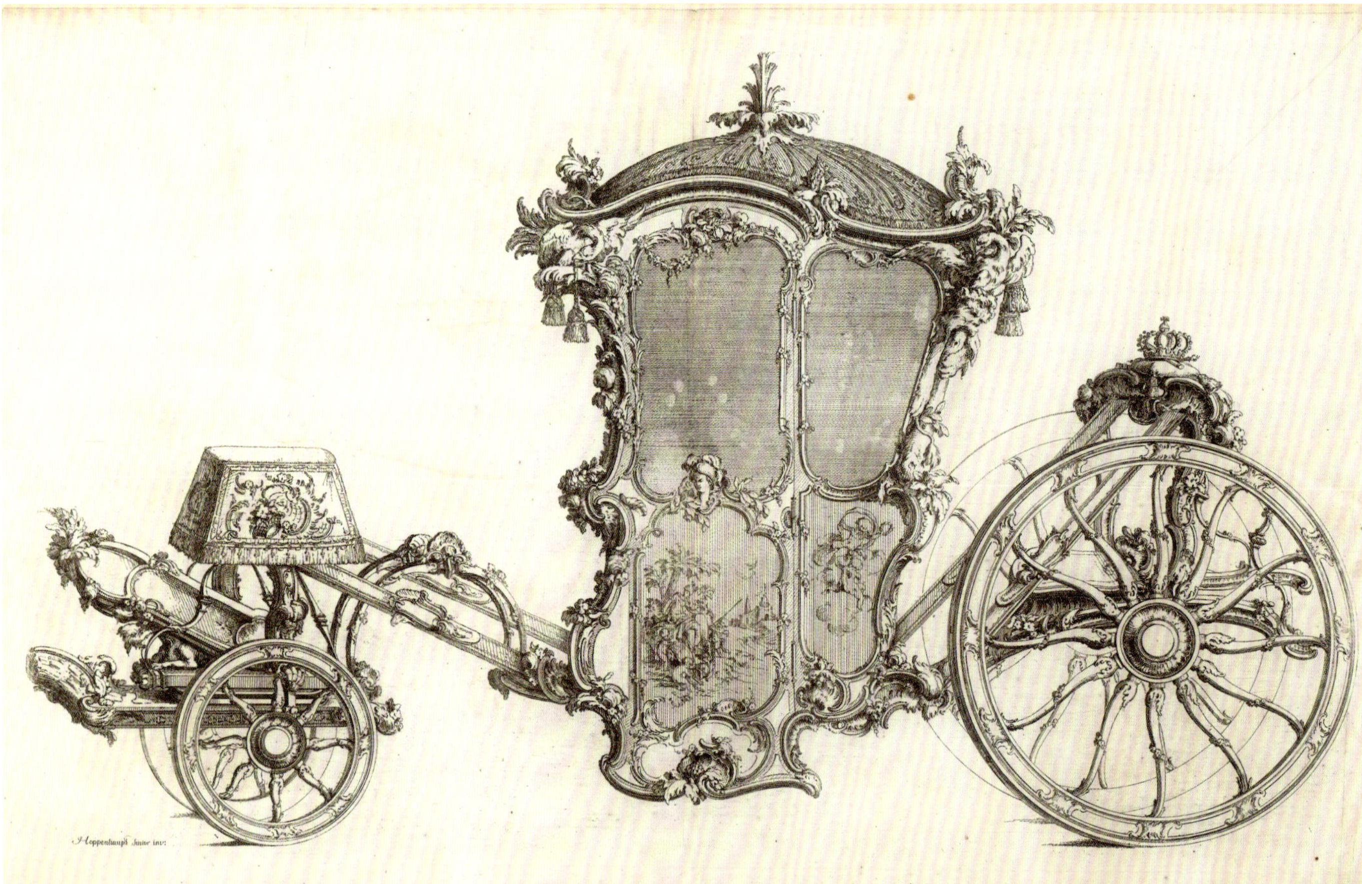

FIG. 1 *Design for a Carriage.* Johann Michael Hoppenhaupt II (German, 1709–1778-86). Berlin, Germany, 1753. Etching on off-white laid paper. Cooper-Hewitt, National Design Museum, Smithsonian Institution, Purchased for the Museum by the Advisory Council, 1921-6-221-2

artists from the centers of creativity brought the new ideas with them. The transit of taste was not new; Huguenots, who were obliged to leave France due to religious persecution, found refuge in the Netherlands, England, and Germany, and brought French style with them.[2]

The new style in France was instigated by the death of King Louis XIV in 1715 and the resulting desire for a change in lifestyle among the young elite, who systematically commissioned work from young artists who set the trends in Paris. Model engravings made after French designs were widely exported to Germany. The model plates were often pirated in the German printmaking centers of Augsburg and Nürnberg, whose specialized workshops helped distribute them. There were very few original print series actually designed in Germany, such as those by Jean-François Cuvilliés (fig. 2); Johann Michael Hoppenhaupt II (1709–ca. 1755) (fig. 1); the lesser known but very prolific designer Johann Wolfgang Baumgartner (1712–1761), published by Johann Georg Hertel in Augsburg; the vivid designs with eccentric, asymmetrical scrolls by Karl Puer Elvaci (active 1745) engraved by Jakob Gottlieb Thelott (1708–1761); and those by Johann Esaias Nilson (1721–1788).

The regions on the western border of the Rhine River were exceptional in Germany since, due to their geographical proximity with the kingdom of France, Paris had always been the city of reference. The prince electors from these regions regularly commissioned work or consulted with French architects in order to build in authentic French style and follow standards set by the authorities of the French Royal Academy of Architecture. This seemed to be easier for them to do than to find local artists who were able to realize their ambitious commissions.[3]

FROM ORNAMENTAL PLATE TO OBJECT: FORMAL SPECIFICITIES OF GERMAN ROCOCO

In spite of regional differences, a number of general observations concerning German rococo can be made. The love of rich ornament is one; the moderate balance between ornament and structure characteristic of French rococo was lacking in Germany, where ornament often dominated the design of an object or an entire room. Much German rococo also featured lavish finishes, silvered or gilt or painted in very bright colors. The color conceptions of the period might sometimes astonish, but they matched the textile design of the period and were representative of a positive attitude toward bright color schemes.

The production of German silver and *objets de vertu* was prolific in Augsburg, a center for the production of silver flatware, whose extensive distribution across the country is illustrated by a toilet box and dish dating from about 1750 (fig. 3). Due to the high cost of the material, German silverware was often thinner than in other countries, even though the same rococo ornamentation as in other fields of the decorative arts was applied. In Berlin, the gold boxes made for Frederick II by Huguenot immigrant goldsmiths such as Samuel Colliveaux (1669–1736), Pierre Boquet (1692–1763), and Jean-Louis Jordan (1712–1759) were examples of excellence in this art with royal patronage.[4]

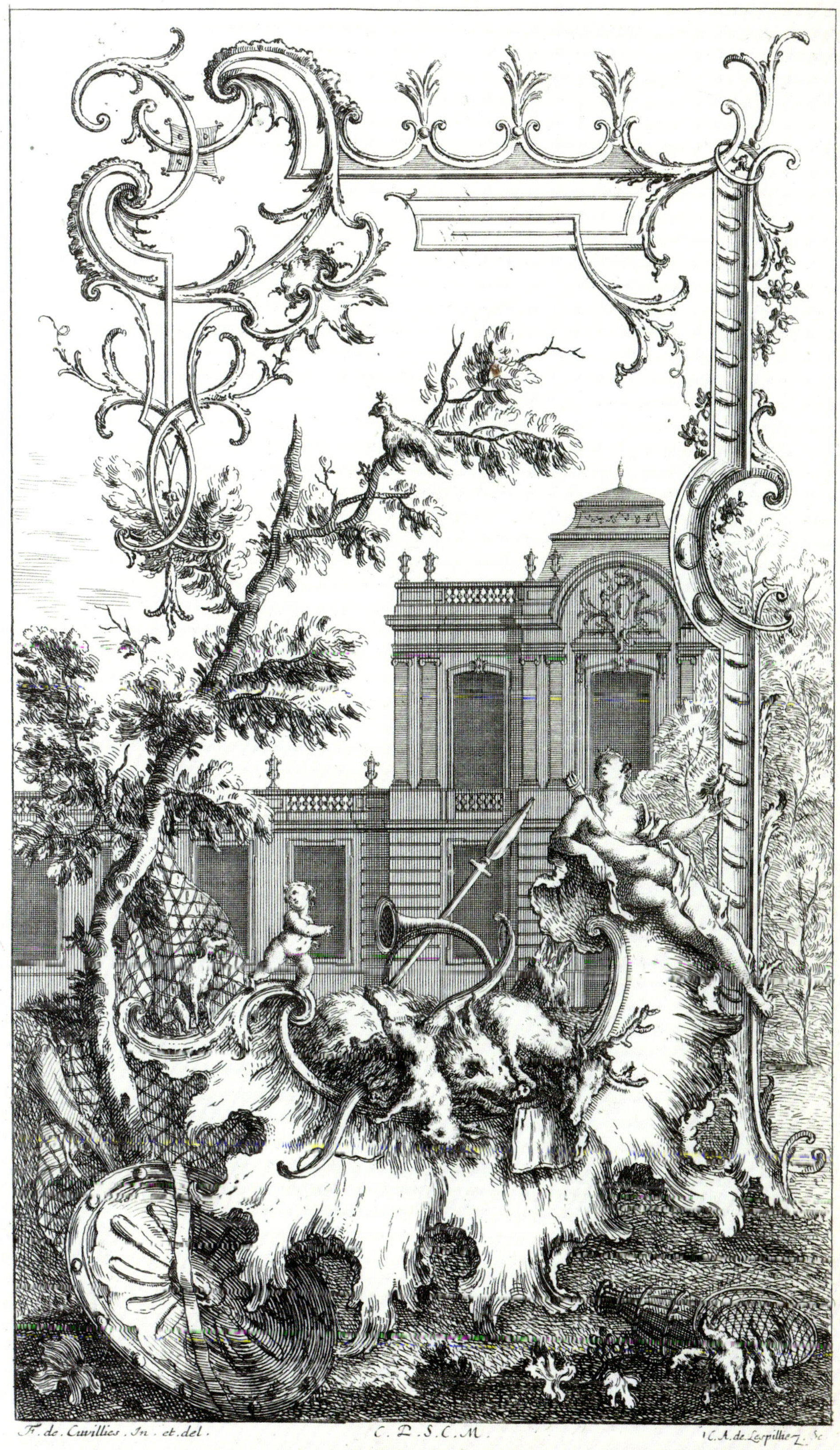

FIG. 2 *Cartouche with Hunting Motifs, from Livre Nouveau de Morceaux de Fantaisie.* Jean-François Cuvilliés (Flemish, active Germany, 1695–1768). Engraved by Charles-Albert de Lespilliez (Flemish, active Germany, 1723–1796). Munich, Germany, 1738–45. Engraving on off-white laid paper. Cooper-Hewitt, National Design Museum, Smithsonian Institution, Purchased for the Museum by the Advisory Council, 1921-6-282-21

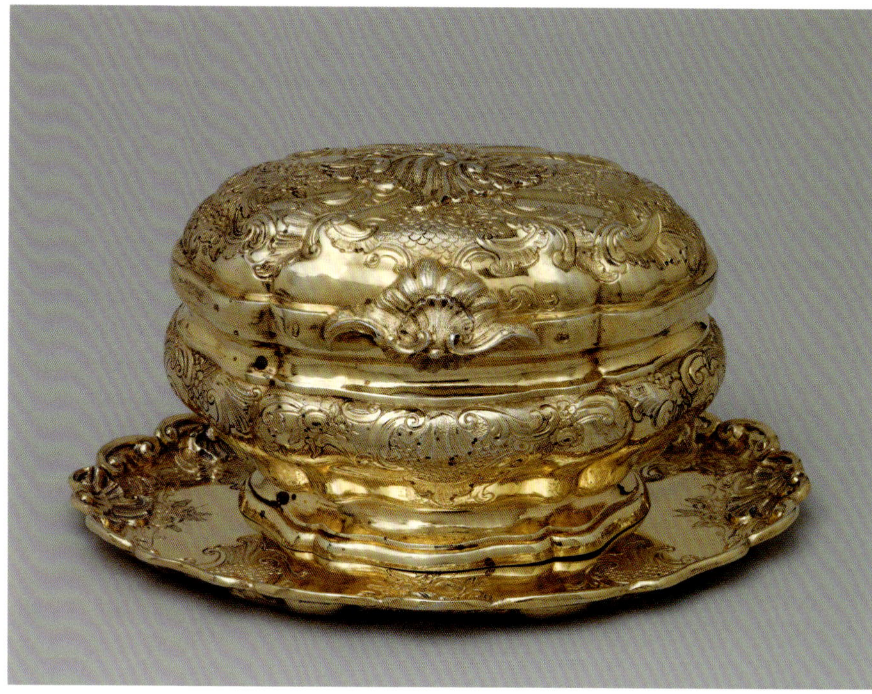

FIG. 3 Oval box and cover on matching salver. Gottlieb Satzger (German, ca. 1709–1783). Augsburg, Germany, ca. 1749–51. Silver. The Metropolitan Museum of Art, The Lesley and Emma Sheafer Collection, Bequest of Emma A. Sheafer, 1973, 1974.356.717/8

While ornamentation on French furniture was applied in gilt bronze, ornaments were more commonly carved in Germany, and carving can sometimes explain the change of scale and enlargement of a motif. In Germany, few pieces had ormolu mounts, and those, as with silverware, were often extremely lightweight compared with their French prototypes. The very refined lace-like stucco work or wood carvings seen in Munich buildings or at the Sanssouci Palace in Potsdam prove the ability of the craftsmen who executed them. Thus extremely high material prices and comparatively affordable manpower were likely the determining factors in the choice of material in Germany. While imported model plates inspired ornament in all regions of Germany, the changes of scale and free combination of various elements transformed the final product.[5]

Three-dimensional ornaments in German decorative arts owe much of their character to the French designers Jacques de Lajoüe, Juste-Aurèle Meissonnier, Gabriel Huquier, Pierre-Edmé Babel (1720–1775), and Alexis Peyrotte. Their projects, originally intended for execution in relief at the most, were at times interpreted as three-dimensional creations in Germany, especially as monumental cipher escutcheons on the tops of buildings. In the field of porcelain figurines, these ornaments presented extreme shapes as accessory elements or pedestals behind the figures, which took their inspiration straight from the model plates.

Pure rococo ornament never succeeded fully and the exuberance of asymmetric rococo was unknown in French society, with the exception of engravings and commissions for foreign clients, and the style was soon supplanted by a revival of the classicism favored under Louis XIV. However, in Germany, unbound by the laws of academic tendency in favor of classicism, rococo bloomed and developed its own language. When one looks at some of the most extravagant German objects from the rococo period, such as the monumental bronze chandelier by Johann August Nahl in Charlottenburg, the porcelain chandeliers of the Meissen manufactory, the outrageous and ambitious carvings of Paul Egell (1691–1752) in Mannheim, or the delightful sconces made by the Berlin porcelain manufactory, one can understand how far the enthusiasm for ornament became in its own right the main feature which determined the structure, form, and shape of objects (fig. 7). The same applied for two-dimensional objects, such as the Savonnerie-style carpets by Charles Vigne (d. 1751) in Berlin, in which an asymmetrical central cartouche dominates the composition in the center of a framework of S- and C-curves adorned with flower petals. This simple structural difference is what made the style look wilder and less contrived than in other countries, as in the designs for wall elevations by Simon Gehle (active 1760–81) for the Schloss Mirow and the Schloss Neustrelitz.[6] (figs. 4, 5)

The exotic look of chinoiserie schemes, favored by many artists in Germany, constitutes a specific element within rococo style. Elements from Jean-Baptiste Pillement's (1728–1808) published series of engravings were combined to design new compositions, such as Friedrich Wilhelm Höder's (d. 1761) lofty pastel-colored, partially gilded murals in Potsdam and Charlottenburg. Pillement's German interpretation of chinoiserie was later picked up as a favorite style for conceptions during the rococo revival of the early twentieth century.[7]

The exuberance of ornament was a specifically German characteristic that could also be found in other periods such as the Renaissance, when ornament was particularly preferred by artists. Different regions had different avenues for expressing ornament. In the Catholic south, where Italian influence and an established tradition of carved decoration and plasterwork were present, it was popularized through public buildings, churches, and places of pilgrimage. In Berlin, Frederick's support of the style led to the creation of Potsdam rococo. It is interesting to note that the style spread through a wide range of secular and religious

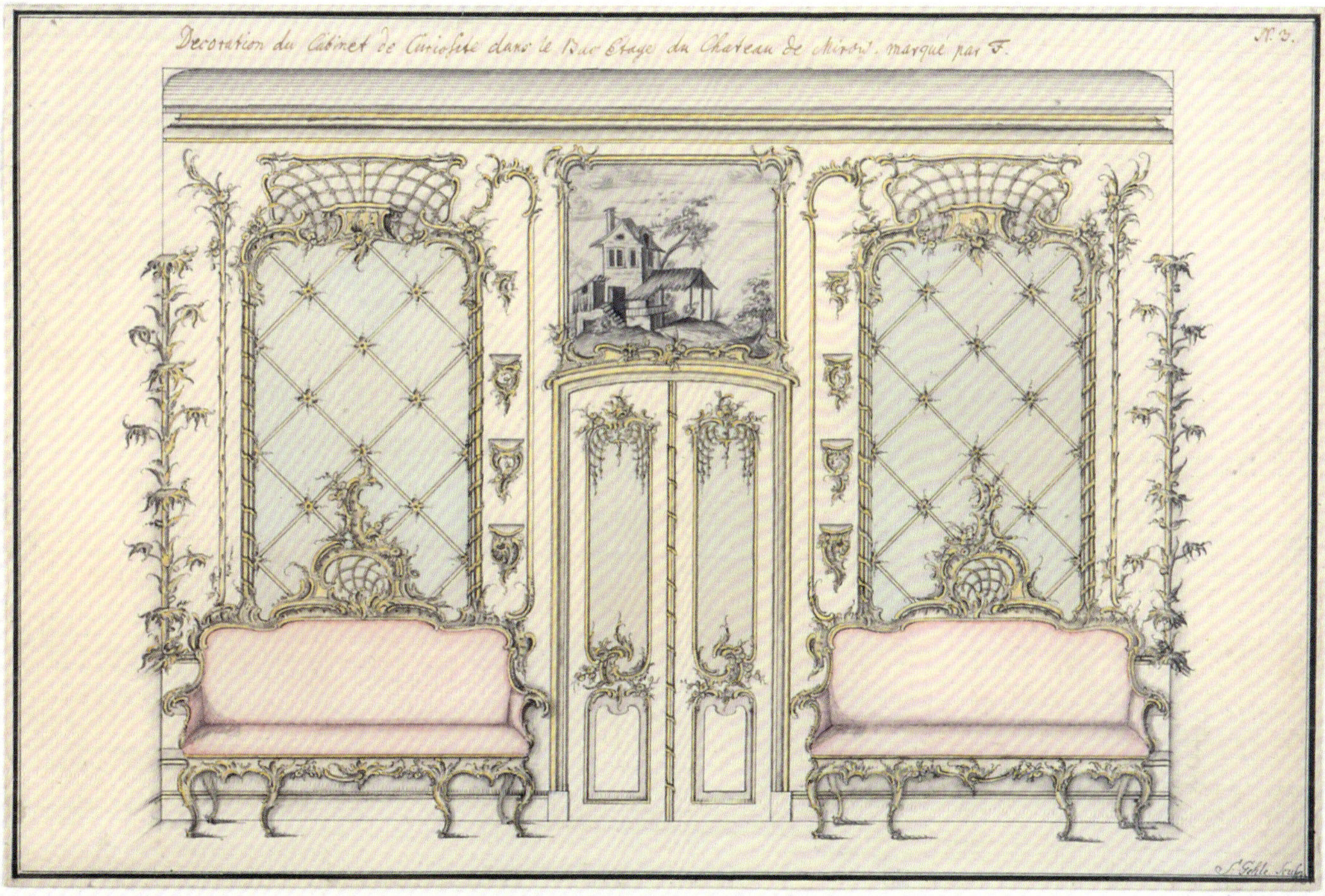

FIG. 4 Design for the Long Wall of the Cabinet of Curiosity, Schloss Mirow, Mecklenburg-Strelitz. Simon Gehle (German, active 1760–81). Germany, ca. 1760–65. Pen and gray ink, brush and wash, watercolor, ruled border on laid paper. Waddesdon Manor, The Rothschild Collection, The National Trust, Inv. no. 227/8-Acc. no. 1661

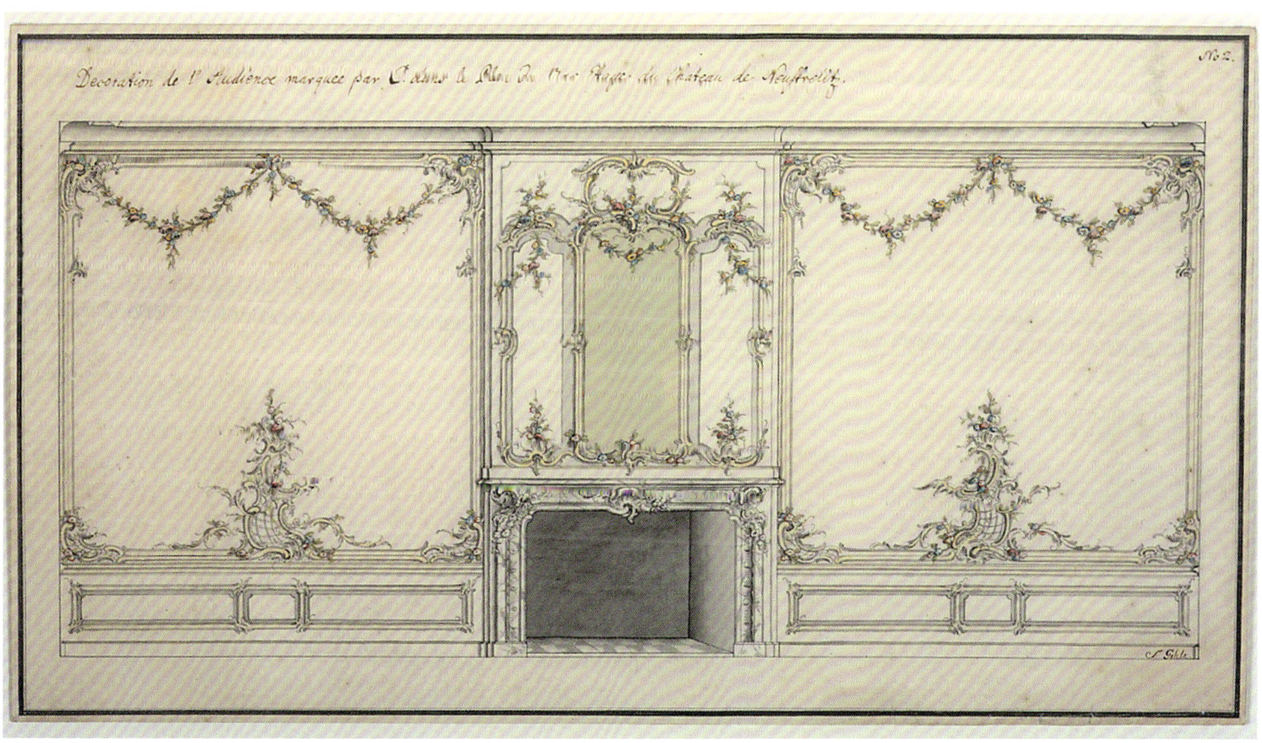

FIG. 5 Design for the Chimneypiece Wall of the Audience Chamber, Schloss Neustrelitz, Mecklenburg-Strelitz. Simon Gehle (German, active 1760–81). Germany, ca. 1760–65. Pen and gray ink, brush and watercolor, ruled border on laid paper. The Rothschild Collection, The National Trust, Waddesdon Manor, Inv. no. 226/6-Acc. no. 1649

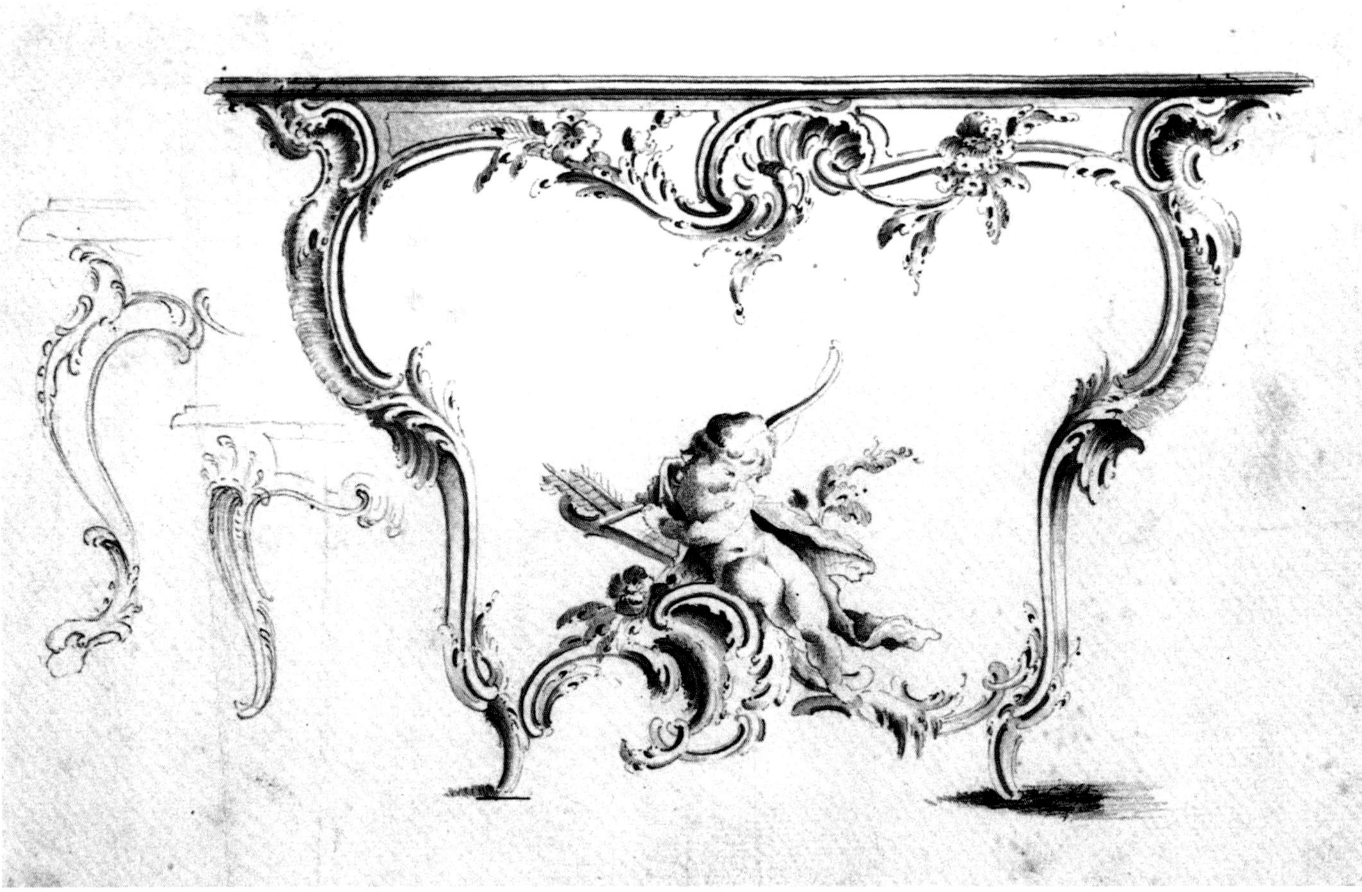

FIG. 6 *Design for a Console Table*. Johann Michael Hoppenhaupt II (German, 1709–1778-86). Berlin, Germany, ca. 1750. Pen and gray ink, wash, black chalk on laid paper. Waddesdon Manor, The Rothschild Collection, The National Trust, Inv. no. 75-Acc. no. 1671

schemes in the south, where it was easily adopted by local craftsmen, while in Würzburg, Berlin, and Potsdam, it remained reserved to a very small fraction of society, as court society was limited to the archbishop, the king, and their respective circles (fig. 6).

THE EVOLUTION OF ROCOCO IN GERMANY

The most significant building in the preliminary phase of rococo style was the Zwinger in Dresden, built 1711–18 by Daniel Pöppelmann for the Saxon king August the Strong, whose lofty and airy structure is flooded with light. The forms and ornament of the building were indebted to late baroque as designed by the Roman baroque architect Francesco Borromini (1599–1677). Yet the dynamic swinging lines and the sculptures by Balthasar Permoser (1651–1732) displayed rococo spirit on a large scale, casting an ephemeral *Festarchitektur* into stone and thus giving it a solidity intended to last for eternity. Pöppelmann's design related also to Italian garden architecture, which he studied on his journeys to Italy, Paris, and Vienna.

One of the earliest manifestations of a truly identifiable rococo architecture can be found in Munich, where one person was responsible for importing the new trend, Prince Elector Max II Emmanuel (1679–1726), who, after defeat at the battle of Höchstedt in the War of Succession, lived in exile in Paris between 1704 and 1715. While there, he established himself in high society and became familiar with French art, style, and craft. He sent for his court architect Joseph Effner (1687–1745) to join him in Paris to train with the famous architect Germain Boffrand (1667–1754). Effner was not the only architect to get the privilege of French studies in his art; in 1720, Francois Cuvilliés also went to Paris to study architecture, and later become Effner's successor in Munich, working mainly for the Elector Charles Albert (1726–45). The stylistic influence in Munich shifted from Italy to France as soon as the architect returned home. Once the elector was able to move back to Munich, he not only had Paris-trained architects at his service, but also brought back with him an important amount of art and furniture that had significant impact on local production, style, and materials. If one looks at architecture as the frame in which artworks and objects are displayed, Munich rococo was the first significant manifestation of rococo in Germany. Its introduction can be found in work by Effner, who used ornament with filigree lace–like networks in stucco decorations on the ceilings in Schleissheim castle, outside Munich. Before really starting his career in Munich, Cuvilliés was sent for by the elector of Cologne, Clemens August, to help out with the interiors of the Gelbe Zimmer in the Castle at Brühl (1728–33) and the construction of the Falkenlust hunting lodge (1733) in the park of Brühl.

The first building conceived completely in rococo style was the hunting lodge at Amalienburg, built in 1734–39. Built as a *maison de plaisance*, a model defined by French architecture manuals, Amalienburg was built for Electress Maria Amalia in the gardens of Nymphenburg castle, on the outskirts of Munich. The interior architectural organization followed the French model, with parquet floors, lower dado, and mirrors above the cornice and on the ceiling. The circular drawing room in the center (see Davidson, fig. 38) displayed a particular wealth of

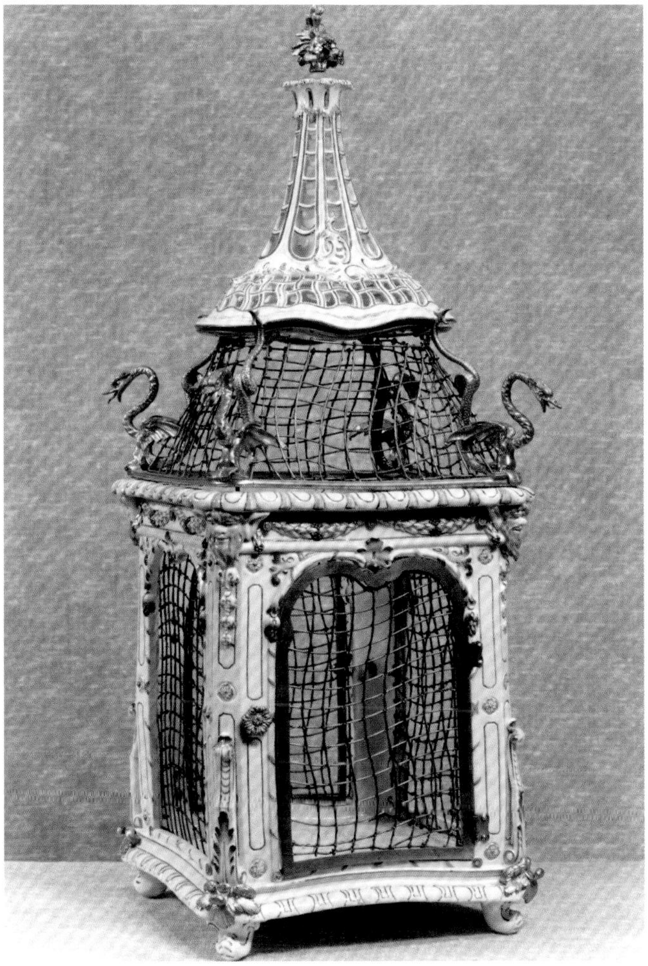

FIG. 8 Birdcage in the form of a pagoda. Manufactured by Frankenthal Porcelain Factory. Frankenthal, Germany, 1765–70. Porcelain, gilt bronze. Waddesdon Manor, The Rothschild Collection, The National Trust, Inv. P/2522–3162

ornament, and the way it connected the different levels of the architecture was particular to Cuvilliés's interpretation of the French prototypes he had studied in Paris. The dense rococo ornament harmoniously interwove abstract and naturalistic elements, C- and S-scrolls, plant stems, trelliswork, fountains, fishing nets, fish, shells, cranes, children, and various forms of hunting and fishing. The figurative motifs in relief were silvered and placed against a pale blue background. The mirror-covered walls gave a magnificent effect of endless reflections, and the numerous French windows created stunning views of the surrounding grounds.[8] (fig. 7) The architect of Amalienburg designed the overall scheme, including the plasterwork, light fittings, and even the furniture, and local craftsmen ably realized the design. The brothers Johann Baptist (1680–1766) and Domenikus (1685–1766) Zimmerman became renowned for their ambitious rococo schemes of plaster ornament for royal and private patrons in Bavaria.

New architecture in Berlin and Potsdam was also strongly influenced by rococo style. The Prussian King Frederick II (1712–1786) strongly favored rococo architecture, and continued to commission works even as neoclassicism came to maturity in France and England. Frederick at first encountered rococo in Strasbourg in 1740 during an incognito journey into the territory of the French king. Work at the archbishop's palace, built after designs by Robert de Cotte (1656–1735), was underway, and Frederick met the young Berlin-born sculptor August Nahl (1710–1785), whose father, the sculptor Johann Samuel Nahl, was originally from Bayreuth, in Franconia. August Nahl trained with his father and the architect Andreas Schlüter (ca. 1660–1714), and later left Berlin for a "Grand Tour" to Italy and Paris. Frederick immediately enticed Nahl away from the project at the archbishop's residence and hired him to be the main ornamental sculptor for his ambitious building projects in Berlin and Potsdam.[9]

Nahl thus became the interpreter of rococo style, which was very much shaped by the ornamental models of the French architects and designers Nicolas Pineau, Meissonnier, Gilles-Marie Oppenord, Jean Mondon (active 1736–45), Lajoüe, and Pillement. Through his collaboration with the king's favorite architect Knobelsdorff, Nahl developed a very personalized vision of French rococo, which had a profound impact on rococo style in Berlin and Potsdam. Between 1740 and 1746, Nahl and his workshop worked simultaneously on several commissions in the residences of Charlottenburg, the Potsdam Stadtschloss, and Sanssouci. Frederick admired Nahl's work and was eager to build ever bigger and more ambitious schemes very quickly. In the end, the exhausted sculptor asked permission to work less. Frederick opposed this demand, and Nahl secretly left Potsdam with his family to get away from his insatiable patron. Nahl was chased by the king's police, but managed to escape. After some time, during which he worked in Switzerland, he happily settled as court sculptor for Duke Frederick II of Hessen in Kassel.[10]

In Potsdam, Nahl was replaced by two other south German artists, the brothers Johann Michael II and Johann Christian Hoppenhaupt, who had been working in various places as ornament designers and sculptors. One of the most intriguing creations by the Hoppenhaupts

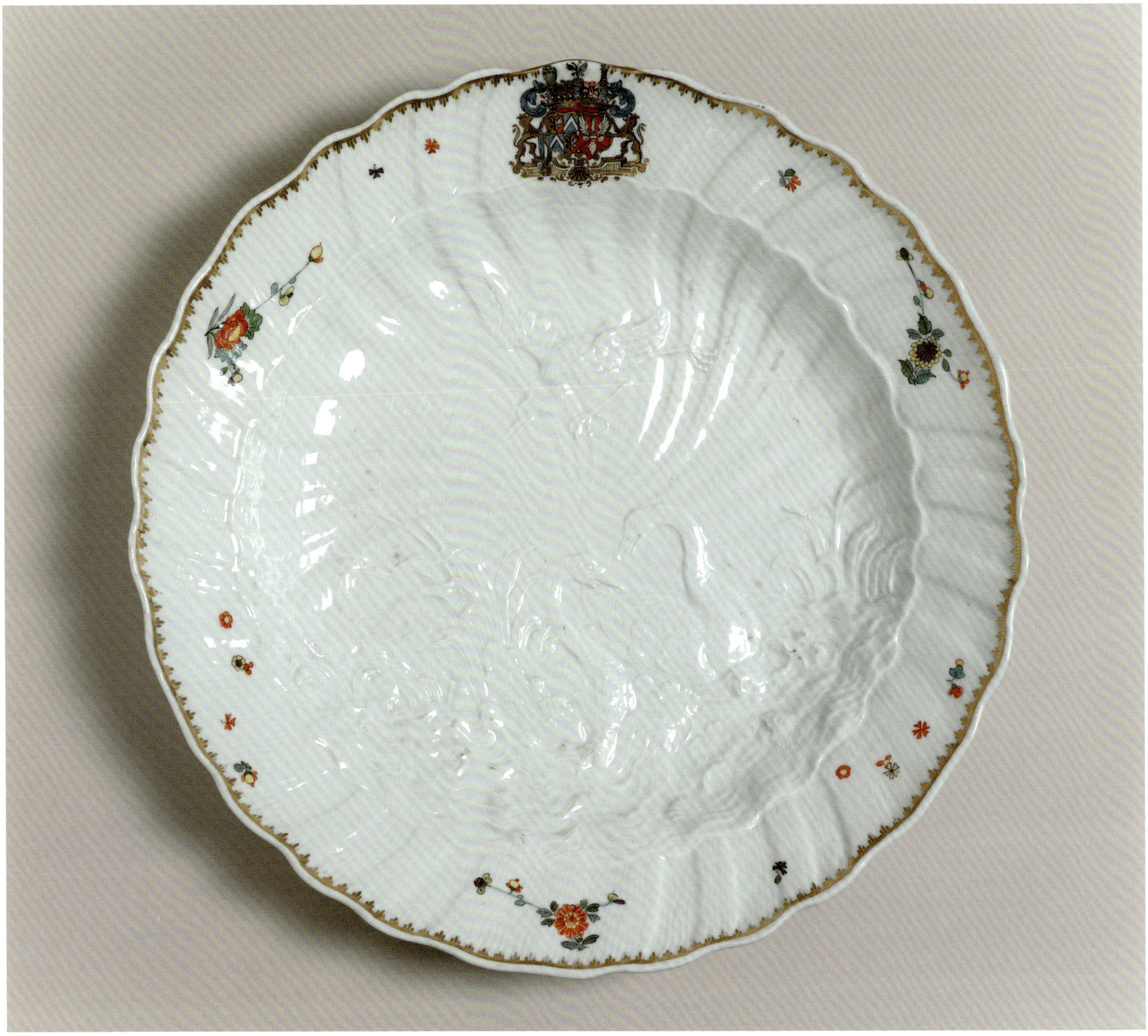

FIG. 9 Plate from the "Swan" service for Count Heinrich von Brühl. Modeled by Joachim Kändler (German, 1706–1775). Manufactured by Meissen Porcelain Manufactory. Meissen. Germany, 1737–41. Hard-paste porcelain, enamel, gilding. Cooper-Hewitt, National Design Museum, Smithsonian Institution, Museum purchase through gift of Commander Henry H. Gorringe, 1950-130-1

before arriving in Berlin was the creation of the Merseburg mirror cabinet, which combined ornamental and figurative sculpture with mirrors to an amazing effect.[11]

Once they accepted Frederick's invitation to settle in Potsdam, they were happy to find a patron who constantly provided them with projects. Their adaptation of Nahl's vision of rococo was to introduce naturalistic elements into the intricate webs of asymmetrical ornament so desired by their royal patron. While their motifs recalled French model plates, the ornament was bigger, and slightly more abstract, extreme, and airy. In Frederick's library at Sanssouci, a circular room with cedar wall paneling and bronze mounts; the music room; and the Voltaire room, with its painted chinoiserie scenes and cheerful colored lacquer, are probably the most refined of the early creations which can still be seen in Potsdam, after the demolition of the Potsdam Stadtschloss in the 1950s. The asymmetrical ornament formed by escutcheons and C- and S-curves covers the walls and ceilings in organic overgrowth. Motifs were also taken from nature: trelliswork richly adorned with children flowers and fruit, leafy garlands, birds, monkeys, cranes, pouring water fountains, and grotto work were some of the favorites, and become the trademark of Frederician rococo.[12]

Near Kassel, in the geographic center of Germany, one finds the climactic achievement of rococo in Germany in the genius conjunction of the architect Cuvilliés and the sculptor Nahl, who combined to conceive and decorate the country house of Wilhelmsthal (1749–65) for Duke Frederick II, a French *maison de plaisance* in the model published by Cuvilliés's teacher Jacques-François Blondel. As Duke Frederick of Hessen was a friend of Frederick II, he knew the Potsdam palaces from his visits, and one easily sees the influence in rooms such as the

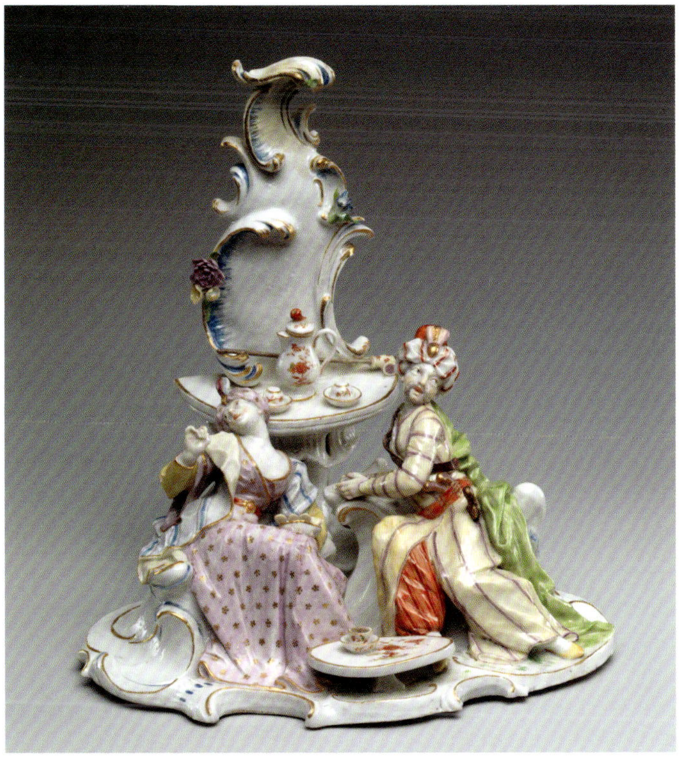

FIG. 10 Figural group, "Turkish Couple at Coffee." Franz Bustelli (d. 1763). Manufactured by Nymphenburg Porcelain Manufactory. Nymphenburg, Germany, ca. 1763. Hard-paste porcelain. The Metropolitan Museum of Art, The Lesley and Emma Sheafer Collection, Bequest of Emma A. Sheafer, 1973, 1974.356.528

Papageienkabinett, whose three-dimensional carved birds sitting in cages clearly imitate the Voltaire room at Sanssoucci. As in Munich, no expense was spared, and some very fine pieces of French marquetry and lacquer furniture were imported directly from Paris.

PORCELAIN PRODUCTION AS A CATALYST FOR A NEW STYLE

One of rococo's greatest success stories was the making of hard porcelain in Europe. For generations, unlocking the secret to China's "white gold" had eluded alchemists and princes alike. But through a combination of science, economics, and artistic creativity, many of the most wonderful creations during the rococo period were made in porcelain, and this industry deserves special attention. Numerous porcelain manufactories founded at the time successfully adhered to the style, such as Meissen manufactory (1710), which represented the German style to the whole of Europe; and followed much later, at the peak of rococo, by Höchst (1746), Nymphenburg (1747), Fürstenberg (1747), Frankenthal (1751) (fig. 8), Ludwigsburg (1758), and Berlin (1763), as well as a number of smaller manufactories. The art of making porcelain was one of the best-kept public secrets of industrial culture during the eighteenth century. Although porcelain makers tried to hold on to their workers, makers, modelers, and painters migrated constantly among the various centers of production, thus insuring the spread of techniques, colors, models, and design trends.[13]

In Dresden, Meissen porcelain set the tone for rococo. The extreme flexibility of the material and new coloring techniques led to creations of refined and delicate expression. Under the supervision of the sculptor Johann Joachim Kändler, the painter Höroldt, and their workshop, luxurious utility objects and complete table services were created, such as the Swan service for Count Heinrich von Brühl (1737–41) (fig. 9), as well as figurines and other purely decorative pieces. For many of these pieces, ornamental model plates from France were used, and due to recent research it is now known how far Paris had its place as a reference for modernity of the style.[14] The delicate porcelain figurines of Meissen, Nymphenburg, and Ludwigsburg were created as ornaments or as table decorations. Those made by Franz Antoine Bustelli (1723–1763) at Nymphenburg, with their often twisting poses, expressive faces and gestures, and bright-colored costumes, embodied the full flourishing of rococo (fig. 10). Far from being the merely decorative items or whimsical toys that their multiple copies from later revival periods were, these figurines were representative of a very lucky moment when scientific research, technical achievements, and new trends in the decorative arts were articulated by brilliant designers.

The most interesting thing is how purely ornamental forms, which originated in engravings, were created in three dimensions in order to serve as objects or props in a figurine group. This was a particular invention of German rococo, visible in the oversized escutcheons displaying the coats of arms on the pediments of royal buildings in Berlin, in small objects with figure groups by the sculptor Bustelli in Nymphenburg, or in other German works. Meissen and Berlin also excelled in the creation of grand-scale furnishing objects, such as mirrors with porcelain frames, sconces, or chandeliers.[15]

THE NEW TREND IN FURNITURE

The exuberant *bombé* shapes of commodes resting on cabriolet legs represent perfectly the interpretation and materialization of French rococo in Germany (see Davidson p. 66, fig. 37). Such ambitious designs were often realized in solid softwood, which allowed easy carving of the ornament. These pieces were executed by sculptors rather than cabinetmakers. Because of their extreme sinuous shapes, it would have been difficult to apply veneer, and these pieces were either painted, partially or completely gilded, or silvered. The extremely high prices for materials such as exotic veneers, cast-metal furniture mounts, and fire gilding were other factors for the use of cheaper carving for furniture ornament.

The idea of bringing nature into the interior inspired a suite of furniture, comprising two settees and six chairs, from the Seehof castle in Franconia, today divided between The Metropolitan Museum of Art in New York and the residence at Würzburg. The general shape of the chair followed the model for a rococo dining-room chair, with a high backrest on cabriolet legs (fig. 11). Its particularity stems from the fact that these

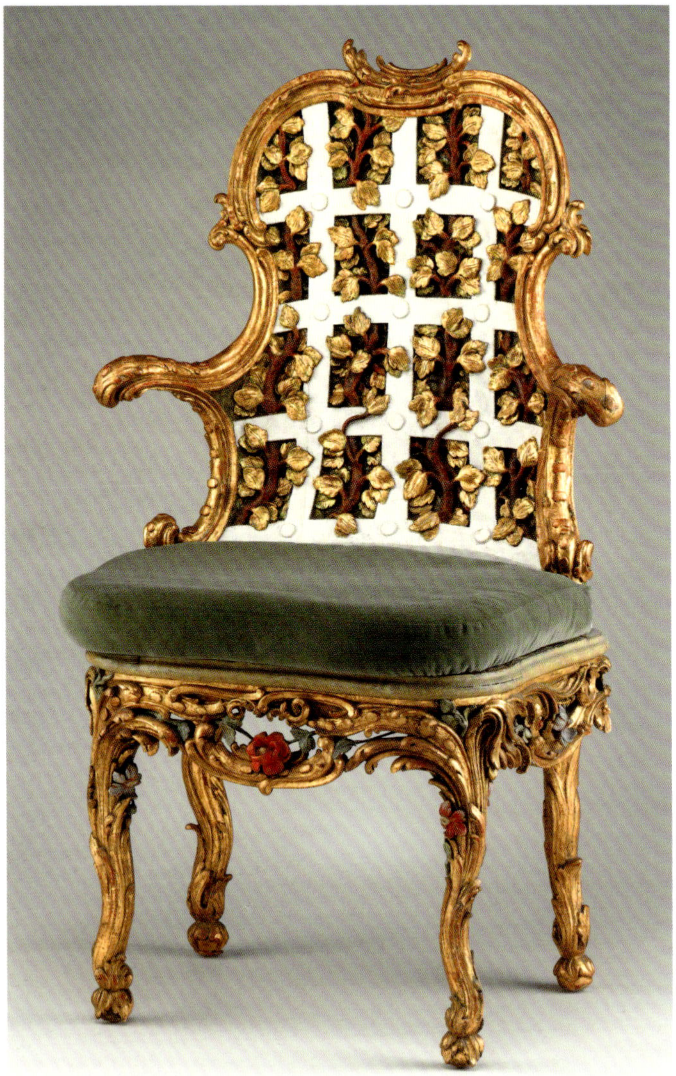

FIG. 11 Armchair (part of a set). Probably Bamberg, Germany, ca. 1761–68. Linden wood, paint, gilding. The Metropolitan Museum of Art, The Lesley and Emma Sheafer Collection, Bequest of Emma A. Sheafer, 1973, 1974.356.119a

naturalistic elements seem to have completely taken over the structure of the piece: The backrests show trelliswork interlaced with flower petals. Between the chair's legs are swags of petals of flowers and leaves. The basic structure of the chairs is gilded. The figurative elements are not accurate naturalistic depictions, but are painted. The result is a cheerful allusion to, rather than a precise copy of, nature. The curvilinear carved frame of the settee realized in three dimensions the most audacious of rococo schemes engraved by Hoppenhaupt or the French designers. This design is daring for its extreme outline but less intrepid in its figurative ornamentation. In the residence of Bamberg, the sculptor Adam Ferdinand Tietz (1708–1777) created a style for bombé-shaped furniture and console tables with elaborate carvings.

Farther north, in Potsdam, Knobelsdorff, Nahl, and the brothers Hoppenhaupt all created projects for interior architecture as well as furniture. As the king was the main patron for the local production, many of the pieces which survive today were somehow connected to a royal commission. Potsdam rococo corpus furniture was often characterized by extremely bombé-shaped volumes with delicate ornament added in carved wood. More rare are pieces with ormolu mounts, such as a chest of drawers by J. A. Hülsmann (dates unknown), which is the most significant surviving example from the early years of the king's reign in the 1740s. Frederick occasionally acquired pieces of luxury furniture with gilt bronze mounts in Paris, which were then copied exactly or used as models. The local production for elaborate case furniture with gilt mounts stayed relatively modest, although productivity increased in the latter part of his reign, after the Seven Years' War. Among those projects, probably the most significant are mirror frames and armchairs designed by Nahl and the Hoppenhaupts. Their organically curvilinear outlines, armrests, and cabriolet legs followed French prototypes, transformed in scale and design. Sometimes the flamboyant curvilinear structures were decorated with carved and flowers painted in lively colors, which gave an even richer appearance to the furniture. These models are among the most extraordinary achievements in European rococo furniture, and deserve much more research so that we may more fully understand their originality.[16]

Potsdam rococo's distinguished individual character would become the reference for the various revivals in the nineteenth and twentieth centuries, when the models created for Frederick became the prototypes for a kind of national style of Frederician rococo.

When Frederick's sister, the Markgräfin Wilhelmine von Bayreuth, died in 1758 at the age of forty-nine, the king knew where to find new teams of skilled craftsmen. After the first generation of artists who built the Sanssouci palace and the Stadtschloss in Potsdam either died or returned to their homelands, there was need for a change.[17] In the period following the Seven Years' War, Frederick continued his ambitious building schemes with plans for the construction of the imposing Neues Palais, for which he needed new artists. In order to entice more craftsmen, he made potential workers promising offers if they settled in Berlin. After a number of moves, the Spindler brothers settled in Prussia, setting up cabinetmakers' workshops in Potsdam and Berlin. Johann Friedrich (1726–after 1793) and his younger brother Heinrich Wilhelm (1738–1788) were known for producing fine cabinetry, paneling, and furniture. They started their career as court artisans while working for Wilhelmine, creating elaborate marquetry designs (fig. 12) made in precious materials, including mother-of-pearl, ivory, and tortoiseshell, which became their trademark. The bronze and hardstone tops for these were provided by Johann Melchior Kambly (1713–1783). Of Swiss origin, Kambly had trained in Paris, possibly at the Royal Workshop of the Gobelins, where he would have learned to work with hardstone and bronze.

While Frederick occasionally bought pieces in Paris, in Dresden, the King of Saxony and Poland was wealthy enough to have furniture directly

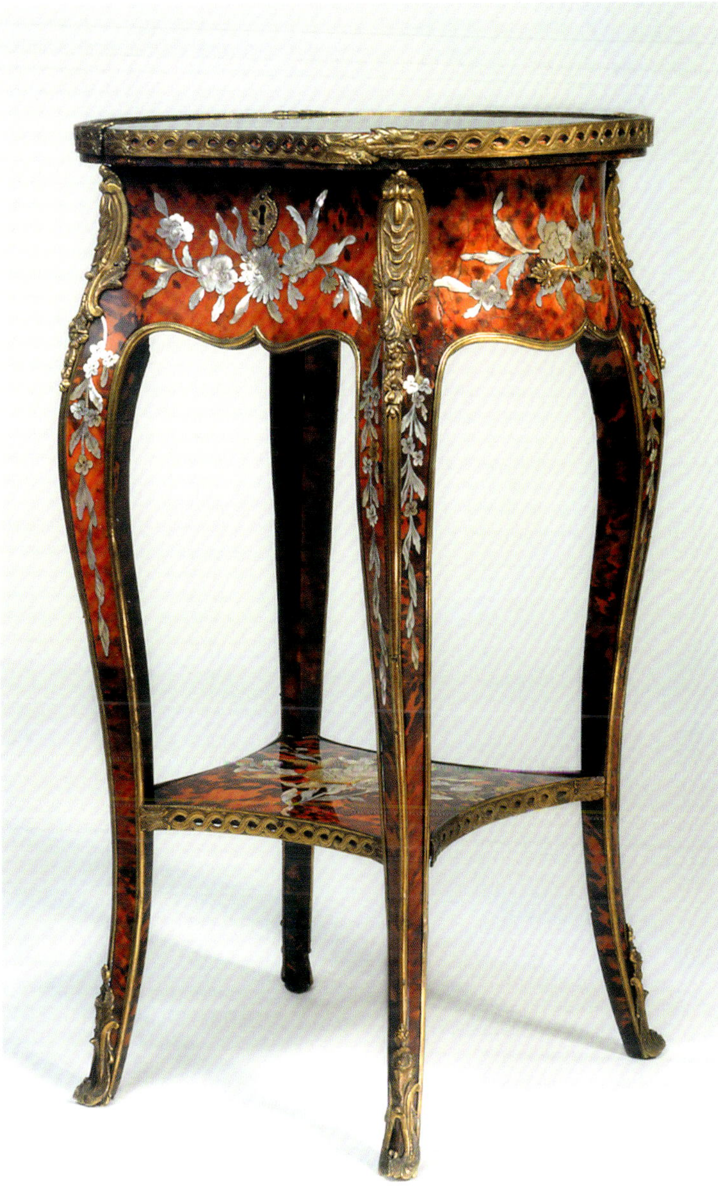

FIG. 12 Table for Frederic II at the Neues Palais. Johann Friedrich Spindler (German, 1726–ca. 1799) and Heinrich Wilhelm Spindler (German, 1730–1788). Germany, ca. 1770–85. Wood, mother-of-pearl, brass. Waddesdon Manor, The Rothschild Collection (Rothschild Family Trust), Inv. 19/ 1997

commissioned in Paris by Jean-Pierre Latz, and a number of French pieces can still be seen in the Saxon collections today (see Hunter-Stiebel, p. 81, fig. 13).[18] These seem to have been used as models by local craftsmen, and only in recent years has the very high level of craft of Dresden cabinetmakers been recognized through newly discovered pieces. Pieces of that standing would have been made by craftsmen such as Johann Gottfried Leuchte (d. 1759), Michael Kimmel (1715–1794), and Johann Christoph Hesse. For these pieces, the finest craftsmanship was employed, using rare imported woods, brass sheet, and mother-of-pearl or tortoiseshell, often enriched with mirrors and gilt mounts. With respect to the rarity of these pieces in Dresden, it is obvious that these were all *pièces uniques* made for the crown or a client in the direct orbit of the king.[19]

ROCOCO REVIVALS IN GERMANY, 1840–1930

After a period of disdain for rococo, a new perception and interest in the style began in the 1820s. In the revivals of the early nineteenth century, rococo was reconceived as a romantic, ludicrous, and somewhat erotically charged image of the previous century, when courtesans and shepherdesses reigned in Versailles boudoirs and bosquets, as interpreted in the engravings of such cabinetmakers as Wilhelm Kimbel (1786–1869) and his sons.[20] Nevertheless, later in the century, some remarkable designs appeared, and the interior decorations and furnishings of the Bavarian King Louis II were probably the best witnesses of that revival style. The revival had its repercussions on private apartments of the period. The most typical German furnishings in neo-rococo style can be seen at Linderhof castle. Ludwig II bought a number of fine copies of historic cabinetmakers' pieces in Paris, but the most original German designs were furnishings by the firm of Anton Pössenbacher (1842–1920) and made in the workshop of the cabinetmaker brothers Jakob and Gutbert Pfister. The carved or veneered case furniture was often oversized and heavily decorated with opulent ormolu mounts. The inspiration came from Munich rococo prototypes as well as from French models and ornamental engravings from the eighteenth century. Also at Linderhof are sets of console tables and chandeliers which were made in Meissen. They followed the taste in Germany for porcelain and, in that respect, are the logical descendants of the decorative objects

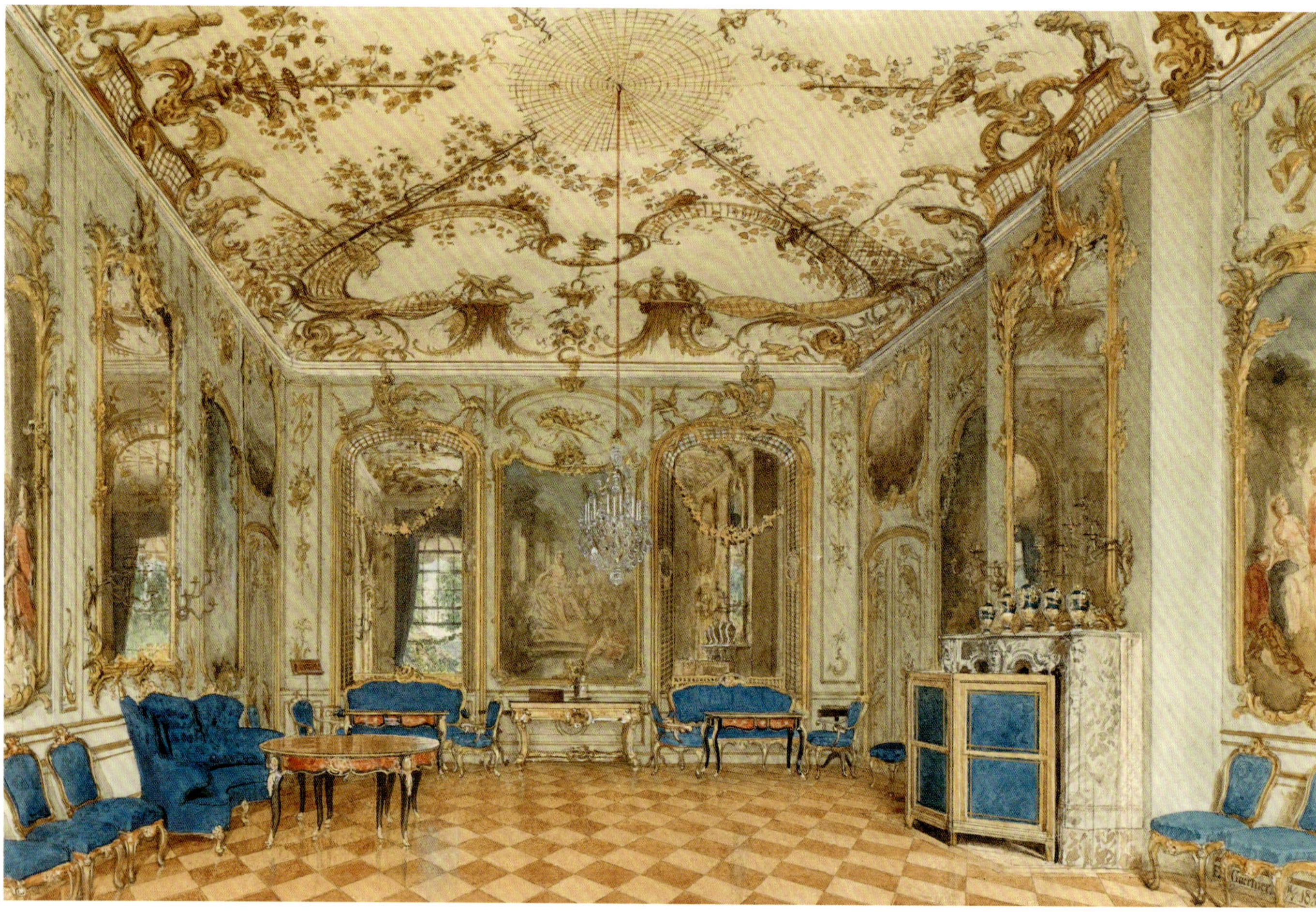

FIG. 13 *Concert Room of Sanssouci Palace, Potsdam, Germany.* Eduard Gaertner (German, 1801–1877). Berlin, Germany, 1852. Brush and watercolor, gouache on paper. Cooper-Hewitt, National Design Museum, Smithsonian Institution, Thaw Collection, 2007-27-51

made in the eighteenth century. The other noticeable difference for all these pieces is their larger scale in comparison to the eighteenth-century models.[21] In Berlin, copies were made of the famous Nahl armchairs as sets with matching pieces, which would not have existed in the eighteenth century (fig. 13). A bedroom suite in neo-rococo style bought by Emperor Wilhelm II was modeled after French period prototypes by the famous Parisian cabinetmaker Bernard Van Risembourgh (master before 1730). This set of furniture was made in Berlin by Paris-trained Julius Zwiener (active 1895).[22]

In the early twentieth century, the revival of rococo was in opposition to the sometimes dogmatic sobriety and frosty chill of the *Neue Sachlichkeit* and to the Bauhaus movement. Some lavish and elegant interior designs which made reference to historic styles were published in specialized publications such as *Farbige Raumkunst* or *Moderne Bauformen* between 1910 and 1935.[23] (figs. 14, 15) After World War II, the so-called *Gelsenkirchener Barock*, with its curvilinear lines, became a style with a historic reference. Having already existed as a more conservative style before the war, it was now particularly appreciated because it had no connotation of classicism, which had been instrumentalized as the official style of the Nazi government through its main architect, Albert Speer (1905–1981), and thus was completely out of favor after 1945.[24]

The variety of revivals in Germany reflected the sometimes drastic changes in matters of aesthetic appreciation, and the fact that the *Rococo: The Continuing Curve* exhibition at Cooper-Hewitt is happening right now seems to be an affirmative indicator for yet another rediscovery of that style. In this context, it is very interesting to see that, in the current period of distrust of historic styles, contemporary designers see apparently no problem in designing furniture which combines industrial materials and cabriolet legs or a curvilinear mirror frame, as if to hint at a bygone time, whose gaiety and daring may bring it back once more.

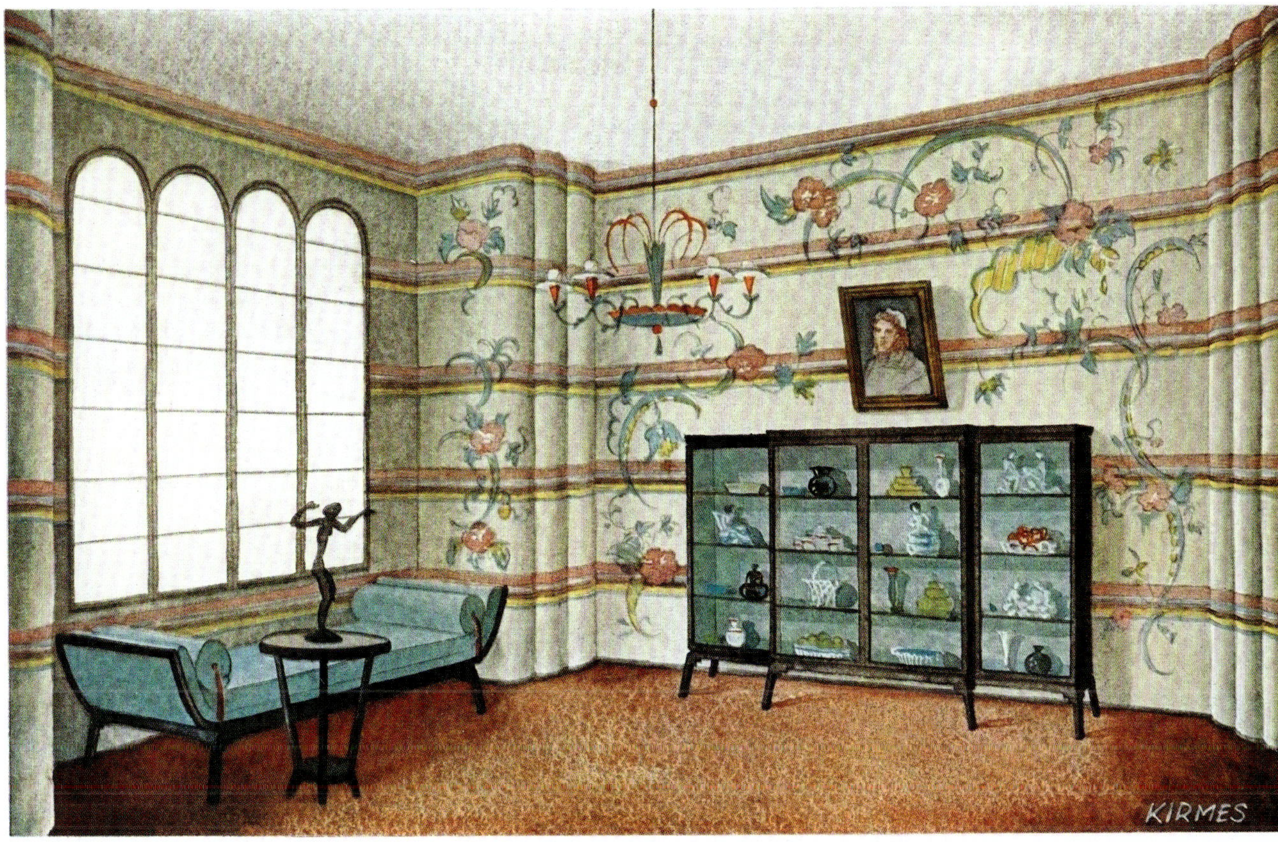

K. Kirmes, Munich
Boudoir

FIG. 14 *Drawing Room for a Lady* by Karl Kirmes, Munich, before 1927, figure 35 from *Decoration in Colour; 100 Modern Interiors in Colour* (English translation of *Farbige Raumkunst*, vol. 4), Stuttgart: Julius Hoffman, 1927 Smithsonian Institution Libraries, Cooper-Hewitt, National Design Museum

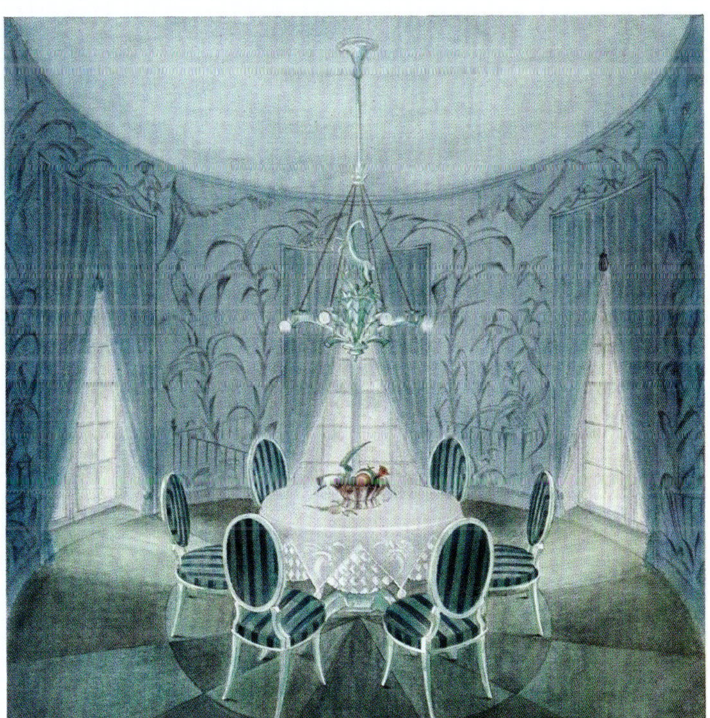

E. Fahrenkamp, Düsseldorf
Dining-Room

FIG. 15 *Dining Room* by E. Fahrenkamp in Düsseldorf, before 1927, figure 58 from *Decoration in Colour; 100 Modern Interiors in Colour* (English translation of *Farbige Raumkunst*, vol. 4). Published by Julius Hoffman. Stuttgart, Germany, 1927. Smithsonian Institution Libraries, Cooper-Hewitt, National Design Museum

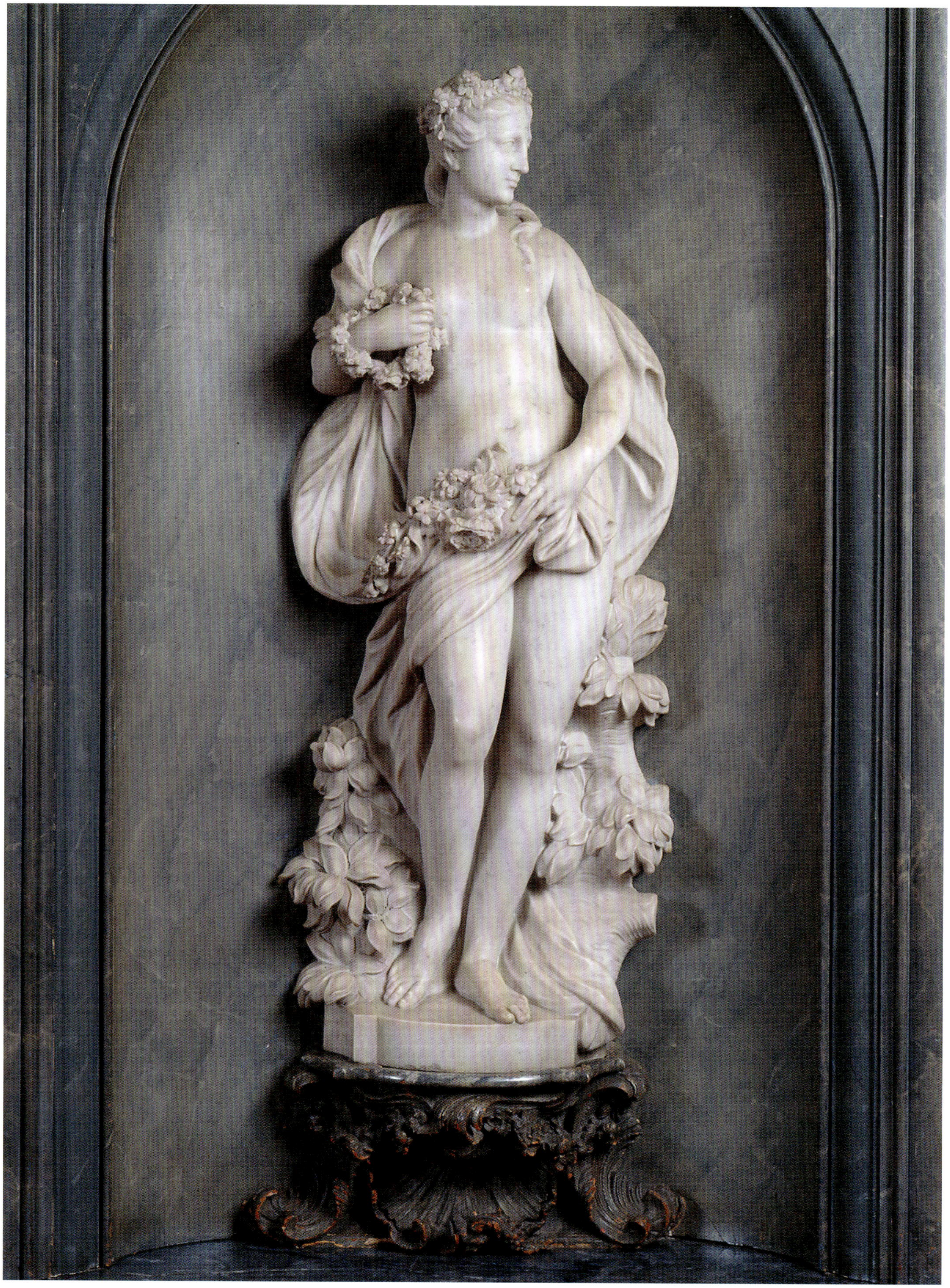

FIG. 2 *Flora*. Jan Baptist Xavery (Dutch, 1697–1742). The Hague, the Netherlands, 1742. Marble, painted lime wood. The National Trust, Waddesdon Manor, Buckinghamshire

Rococo in Holland

THE ASSIMILATION OF A FOREIGN STYLE

Reinier Baarsen

Although the Dutch Republic was not one of the main centers of rococo in comparison to, say, Paris or southern Germany, its version of the style was characterized by vigor and originality, with an appealing character of its own. This small nation presents an excellent opportunity to study the wider implications of rococo in Europe. Holland was a small, highly developed country in the eighteenth century, but its greatest prosperity and cultural preeminence—the seventeenth century, its so-called Golden Age—lay firmly in the past. It was no longer a source but a recipient of major artistic innovations, which, through the impact of the country's cultural legacy and social and political conditions, were transformed into an individual expression of rococo style. Holland was exceptional in being a republic; however, near-hereditary rulers, the Princes of Orange, had held the leading position of stadholder and chief commander of the army and navy since the founding of the nation in the late sixteenth century, and had firm aspirations to be regarded on a par with the ruling houses of Europe. The introduction and development of rococo in Holland, situated between France, Germany, and England, have recently been the subject of extensive research, and much new material has come to light.[1]

A CRAFTSMAN'S STYLE

For the Dutch Republic, the first half of the eighteenth century was a period of calm. The extraordinary expansion it witnessed during the seventeenth century was at an end; its foremost rivals, France and England, had, in the course of a protracted series of wars, established the superiority befitting their much larger size. The country was still extremely prosperous, but its citizens enjoyed and invested the wealth accumulated by earlier generations, rather than reaching further into world trade and territorial expansion. Culturally, the remarkable assertion of a national identity during the Golden Age had been followed by a period of cosmopolitan splendor dominated by the court of Stadholder William III, who, together with his consort, Mary Stuart, had also ruled as King and Queen of Great Britain from 1689 onward.[2] Upon William's death without issue in 1702, the States-General, the central body of government, decided not to appoint his cousin, who was next in line, as stadholder, but to do without one—beginning what is known as the Second Stadholderless Period. There was no longer a court to grant new commissions for palaces or other grand buildings. At the same time, the population stagnated, and cities that had grown dramatically during the previous century turned out to be sufficiently large for eighteenth-century needs. With no promising prospects for young, ambitious architects, the field was

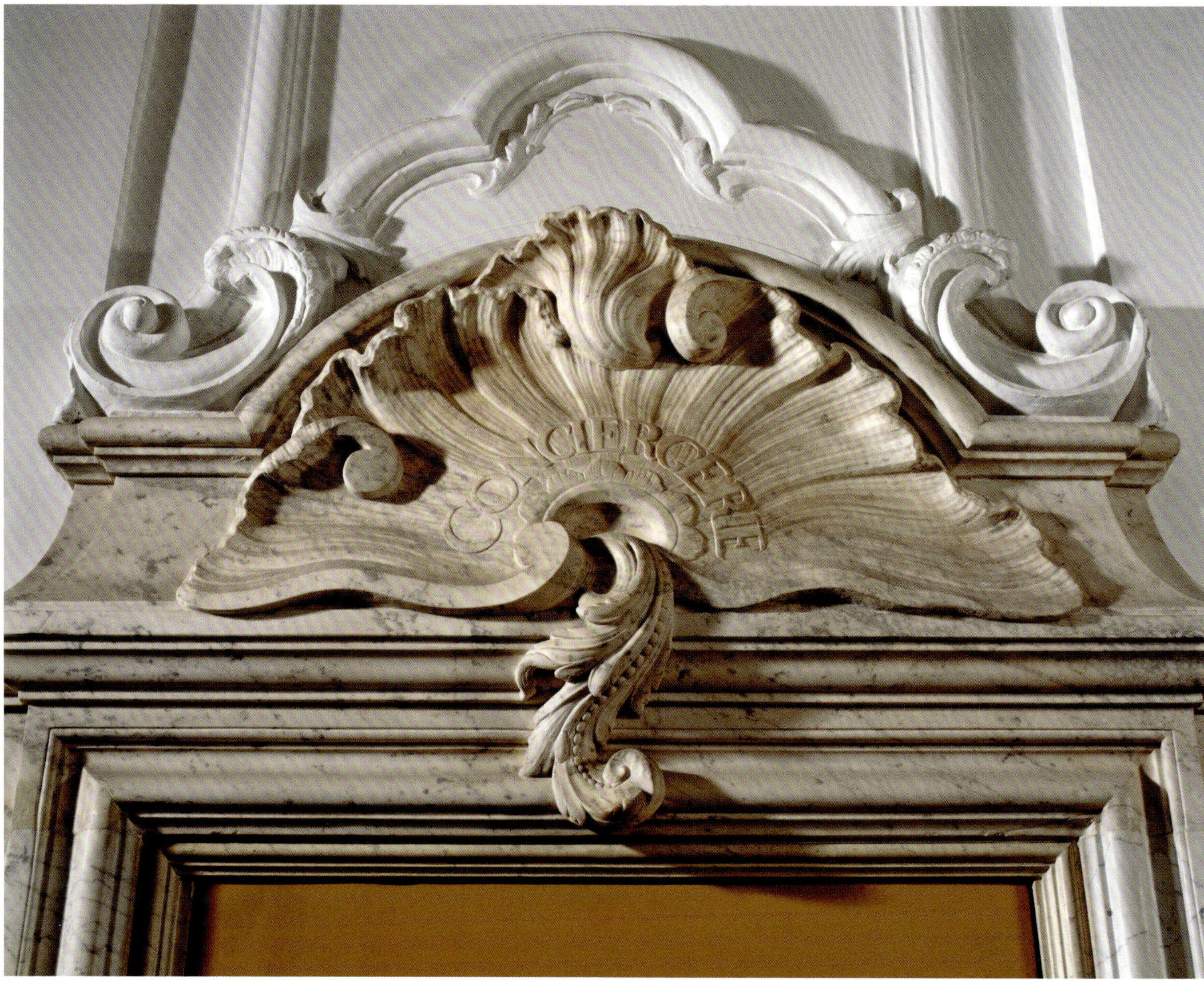

FIG. 1 Overdoor of the Conciergerie in the Hague Town Hall. Jan Baptist Xavery (Dutch, 1697–1742). The Hague, the Netherlands, 1734–36. Marble.

left to the aging Daniel Marot (1661–1752), the French-born architect and designer who had been responsible for most of the buildings constructed and decorated for William III and his court.[3] Although Marot continued to receive a variety of commissions, his manner became increasingly ponderous and old-fashioned. He died in 1752 never having adopted any elements of true rococo style.

Artists and craftsmen, sculptors foremost among them, effected the introduction of the new, foreign manner. In 1784, when rococo was all but a thing of the past and classicism had reasserted itself in a novel guise in Europe, the Dutch author Rhijnvis Feith looked back on it in the following terms: "It is not long ago that we thought the most tortuous ornaments to be beautiful. The sculptor who could work the most curious and misshapen forms into frames and chimneypieces was considered the greatest artist."[4] Generally speaking, rococo as an irrational, anti-classical style came into being despite, rather than through, architects and theoreticians, and the prominence of goldsmiths, carvers, ornamental designers, and other craftsmen was also characteristic of the genesis of rococo style elsewhere. In Holland, this tendency was especially marked due to the absence of any innovative architect working in the country.

The first recorded use of veritable rocaille ornament is a case in point. For a new wing added to the town hall of The Hague in 1736, the Antwerp-born sculptor Jan Baptist Xavery (1697–1742), carved a series of marble overdoors featuring large, shell-like rocailles.[5] (fig. 1) Xavery first designed them in 1734, the year of the publication in Paris of a revolutionary series of ornamental engravings in the early rococo manner, the *genre pittoresque*. Xavery was directly influenced by these engravings, and the abrupt way he applied an isolated, novel ornament within a conventional architectural framework showed his reaction to the shock of the new. He soon developed a more integrated adaptation of rococo, firmly based in his generous naturalism, as seen in the beautiful carved wooden base of his marble *Flora* of 1742.[6] (fig. 2) Xavery was also active as a designer for the decorative arts, ranging from plasterwork to furniture and embroidery patterns, and he undoubtedly influenced the evolution of early rococo in The Hague.

Rococo ornament was introduced in Amsterdam by the sculptor and stuccoist Jan van Logteren (1709–1745), who was born in the city and trained with his father Ignatius, also a sculptor.[7] His 1737 frame for the board recording the names of the governors of the city orphanage

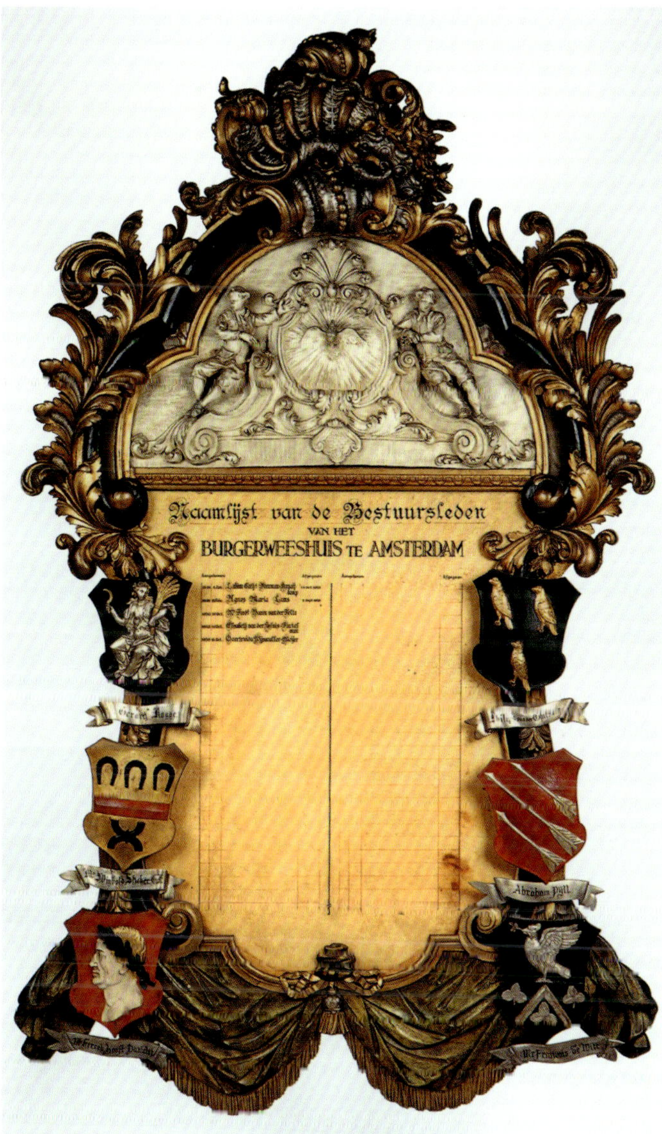

FIG. 3 Frame. Jan van Logteren (Dutch, 1709–1745). Amsterdam, the Netherlands, 1737. Lime wood, gilt, paint, terra-cotta. Amsterdams Historisch Museum, KB 745

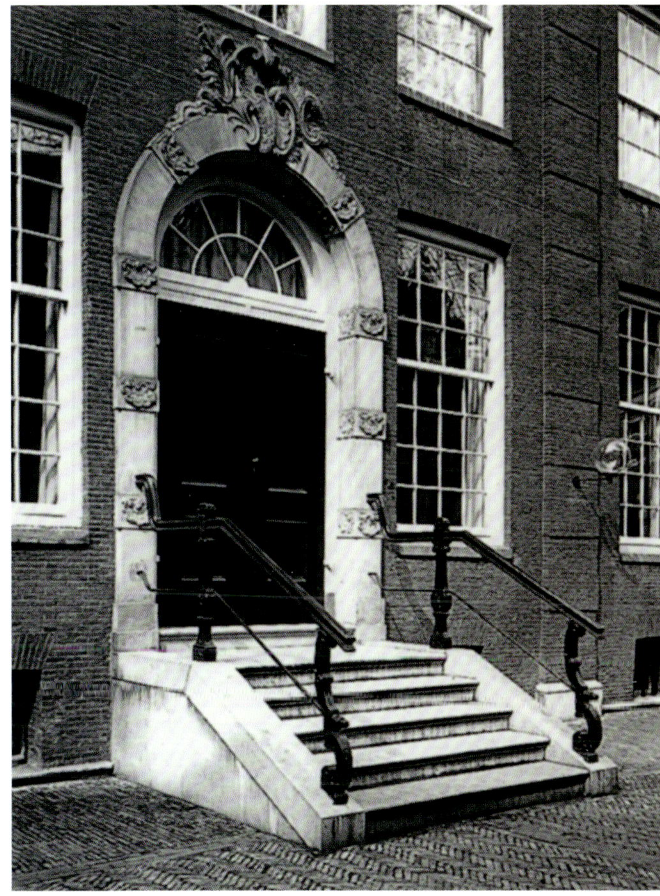

FIG. 4 Door surround, Amsterdam Orphanage. Jan van Logteren (Dutch, 1709–1745). Amsterdam, the Netherlands, 1739. Hardstone. Rijksdienst voor de Monumentenzorg, Zeist

(startlingly repainted at a later date) is in a heavy, late Marot-esque style, but its crowning feature is a full-blown rocaille, centered on a shell- or wave-like form, but more crowded and contorted than Xavery's version.[8] (fig. 3) On the exterior of the orphanage, Van Logteren employed a comparable composition atop a rusticated door surround (fig. 4), probably the first appearance of the new ornament on an Amsterdam façade.[9] In the ensuing decades, rocailles proliferated in Amsterdam, dominating to this day the appearance of many otherwise traditional houses on the city's canals.

A surprisingly early set of rococo chairs was made in Amsterdam in 1738–39 and delivered for the newly built town hall of the small nearby city of Edam.[10] (fig. 5) The chairs may be attributed to Jan Ermans (ca. 170?–1761), a newly established, ambitious young chairmaker who announced in a 1737 newspaper advertisement that he made "French" armchairs in the newest and most modern manner. The model of the Edam chairs is indeed heavily indebted to contemporary Parisian examples, but the openwork back, with its asymmetrically carved splat, is highly idiosyncratic—its overcrowded, charged appearance is related in feeling to van Logteren's ornament. Ermans likely engaged a carver to execute this prominent feature, possibly Asmus Frauen (1707–1779), who originally came from Craiova, in present-day Romania, settled in Amsterdam in

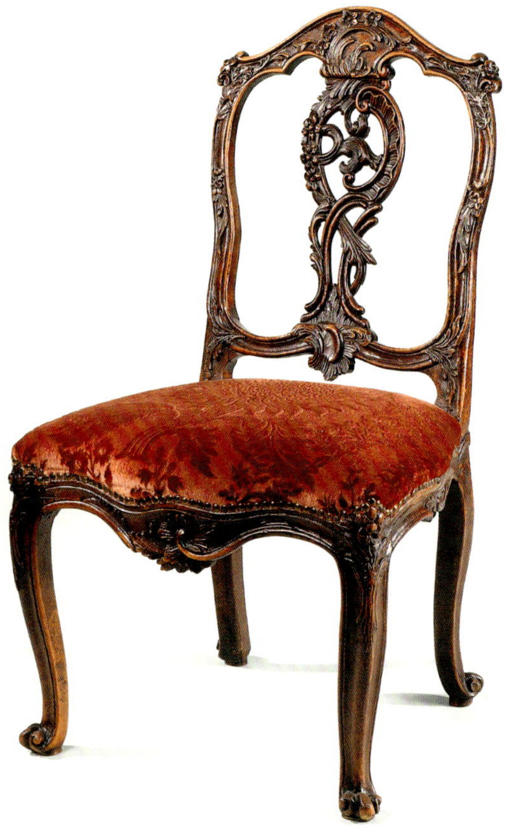

FIG. 5 Chair. Attributed to Jan Ermans (Dutch, ca. 1702–1761). Amsterdam, the Netherlands, 1738–39. Walnut, renewed upholstery. Rijksmuseum, Amsterdam, BK-1976-206

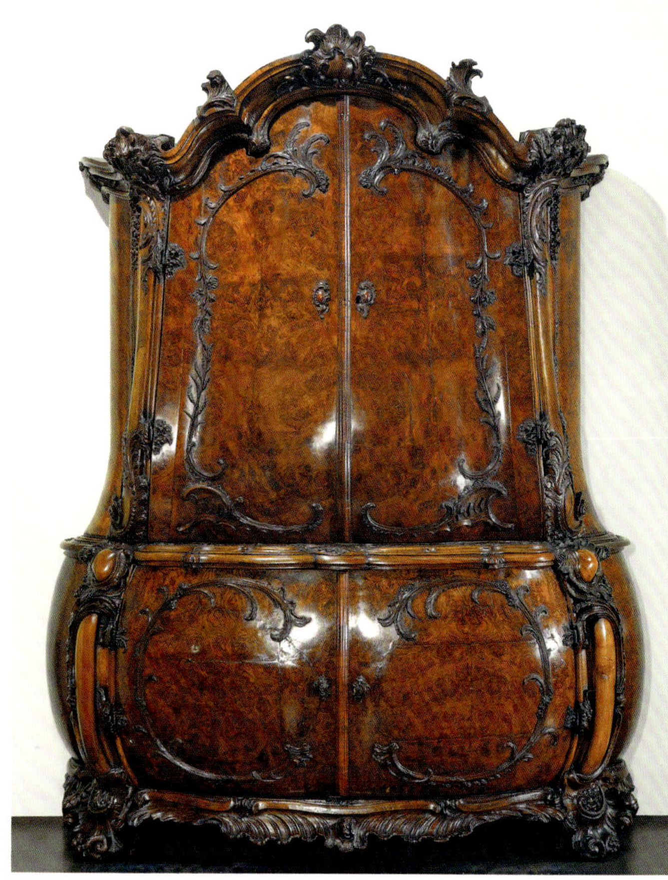

FIG. 6 Buffet cabinet. Amsterdam, the Netherlands, ca. 1755–65. Walnut and oak, veneered with burr walnut. Rijksmuseum, Amsterdam, BK-1989-16

the mid-1730s, and went on to become the foremost sculptor of the generation succeeding Van Logteren. Frauen, who excelled in both figurative and ornamental carving, may have contributed significantly to the pronouncedly sculptural rococo paneling and furniture that flourished in Amsterdam. A good example is a buffet cabinet from about 1755–65. A striking interpretation of a conventional type of "clothes-press," it features undulating surfaces punctuated by boldly carved vegetal ornament instead of the ubiquitous metal mounts and fittings.[11] (fig. 6) The sculptor must have contributed the outline and overall appearance of such a piece, while the cabinetmaker played a subordinate role. A huge and overpowering buffet of roughly the same date evinces the preponderance of the carver's work even more conspicuously in the two tigers supporting it and the figures of Neptune and two tritons on its cornice.[12] (fig. 7) This monumental piece was sold in 1776 as part of the renowned art collection of Anthony Grill, who lived in a great seventeenth-century house on Keizersgracht in Amsterdam. At that time, its doors opened to reveal a carved fountain featuring Silenus on a donkey, Apollo playing a cither, Bacchus riding a chariot, and many other creatures, which has since been removed; clearly, the work of the sculptor figured even more prominently when the piece was in its original condition. In furniture that was the exclusive province of carvers, the artist was able to create objects that were free of any conventional, tectonic structure—quintessential expressions of pure rococo. A number of such console tables are known, but there is also a rare gilt-wood chandelier of a kind evoked by

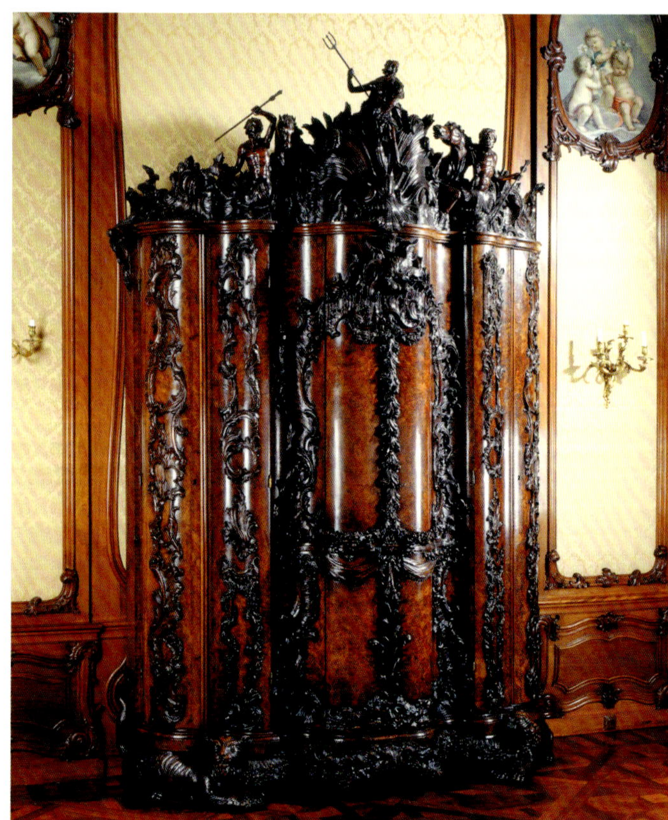

FIG. 7 Buffet cabinet. Amsterdam, the Netherlands, ca. 1755–65. Walnut and oak, veneered with burr walnut. Private collection

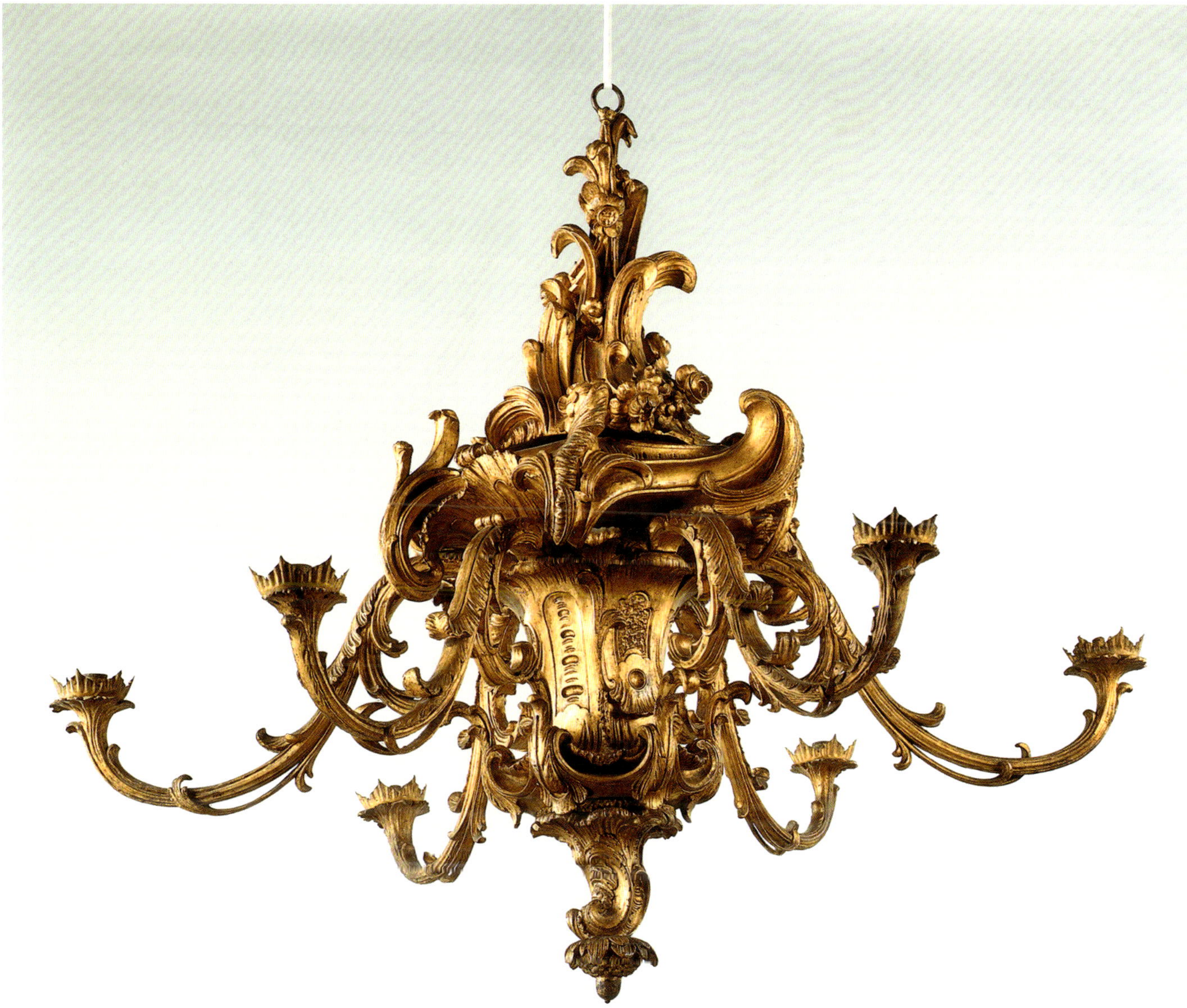

FIG. 8 Chandelier. The Netherlands, ca. 1750–70. Gilded lime wood. Rijksmuseum, BK-16035

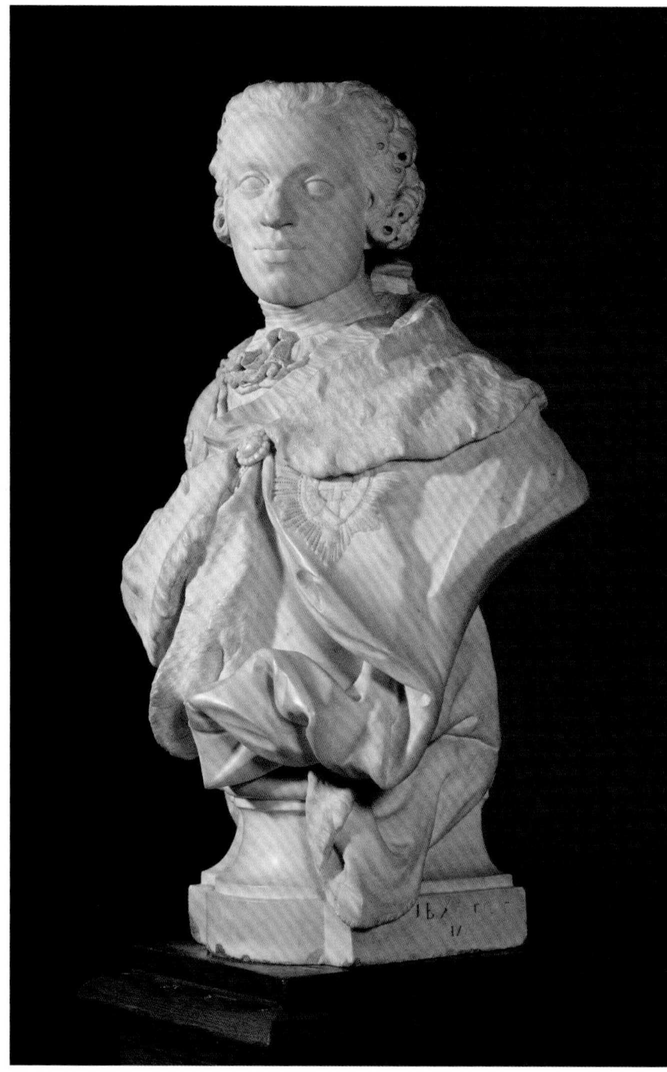

FIG. 9 *Prince* William IV. Jan Baptist Xavery (Dutch, 1697–1742). The Hague, the Netherlands, 1733. Marble. Koninklijk Kabinet van Schilderijen Mauritshuis, 0371

the Amsterdam carver Assueris van Weeghel (master sculptor, 1755) in a 1765 description of his wares: "modern gilded chandeliers with double-triple twisted branches."[13] (fig. 8)

WILLIAM IV, PRINCE OF ROCOCO

Significantly, the works of art described so far did not function within major rococo buildings. The town halls of The Hague and Edam and the Amsterdam Orphanage were fairly conventional edifices in which the application of rocaille ornament was restricted to certain areas, and Anthony Grill's house was a venerable old structure in which he had assembled many art treasures from the past. Furnishings such as buffet cupboards and chandeliers were individually advertised for sale and could be acquired separately in order to add a contemporary, "modern" element to an existing interior. The patrons involved were obviously attracted to the new style, but they were not in a position, or did not feel the desire, to commission a great *Gesamtkunstwerk* that would be a supreme realization of it.

In Holland, the solitary exception to this rule was Prince William IV of Orange, whose political ambitions were realized in 1747 when he was appointed stadholder, bringing the Second Stadholderless Period to a close (fig. 9). Having married Princess Anne of Hanover, the eldest daughter of King George II of Great Britain, in 1734, he was the brother-in-law of Frederick, Prince of Wales (1701–1751), a young patron of progressive artists across the Channel. Another contemporary of his was his cousin Frederick the Great (1712–1786), King of Prussia, who from the moment of his accession to the throne in 1740 was embellishing his kingdom with masterpieces of French-inspired rococo architecture.[14] Prince William must have been eager to emulate his peers: in 1745, he sent the promising Dutch master mason Pieter De Swart (1709–1773) to Paris to train as an architect with the famous Jacques-François Blondel. Upon his appointment as stadholder, he immediately recalled him, and together the two set out to devise a series of buildings that would transform The Hague into a dazzling, modern, princely city. De Swart designed a huge palace for William entirely in the grand manner taught by Blondel,[15] but the States-General could not be persuaded to allocate funds for such an enormous project, and it remained a dream on paper. At Huis ten Bosch, his private country residence in the vicinity of The Hague, the prince was at greater liberty to realize his vision; several of the main spaces were transformed into rococo paneled rooms according to designs by De Swart.[16] In him, Holland at last had a modern architect capable of designing every feature of a building,[17] (fig. 10) including fully integrated interiors. At the same time as De Swart, and possibly in his wake, Agostino Carlini (ca. 1718–1790), a sculptor from Genoa, arrived in The Hague to

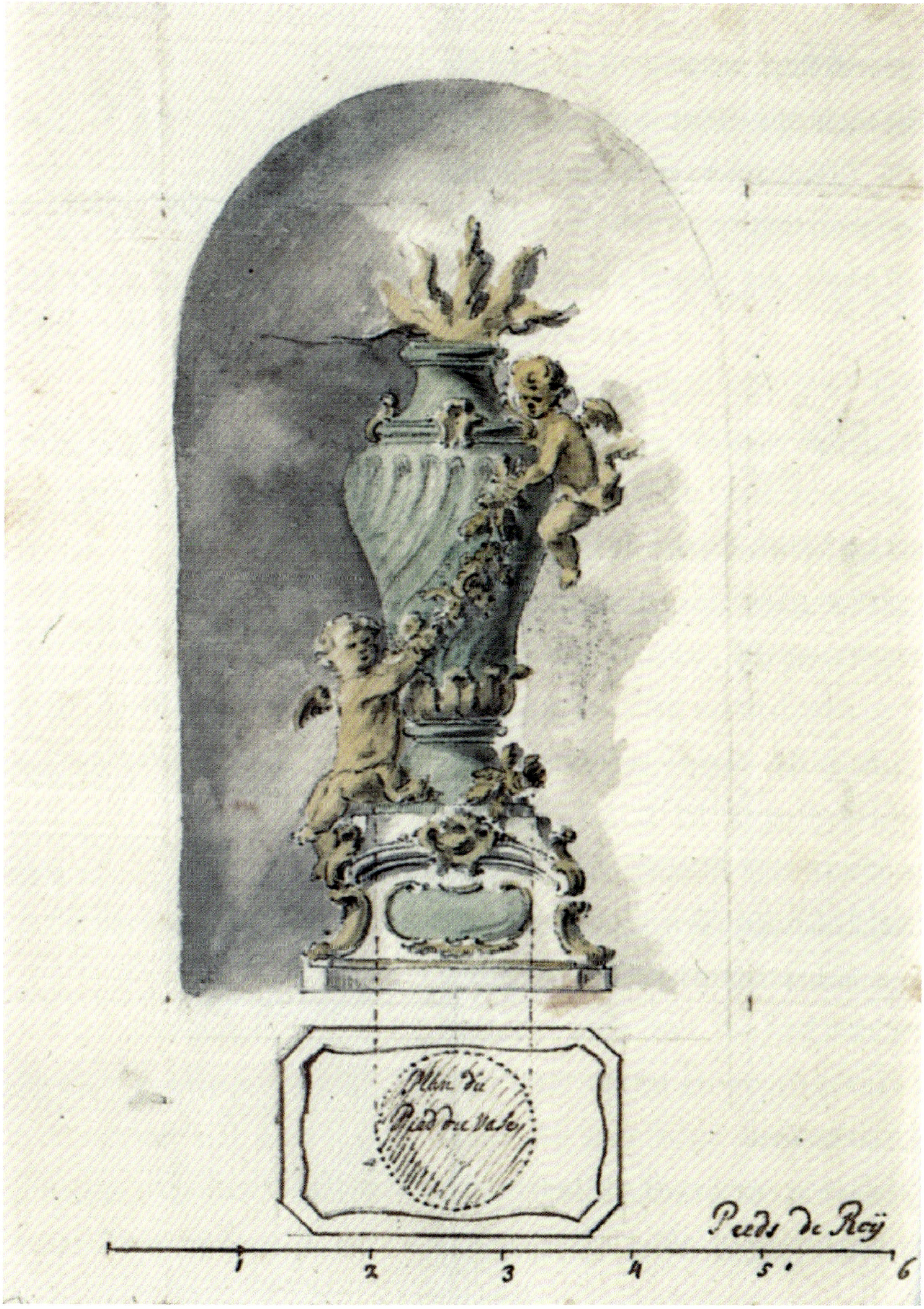

FIG. 10 *Design for a Ceramic Stove for the Town Hall in Leewarden.* Pieter de Swart (Dutch, 1709–1772). The Hague, the Netherlands, 1763. Pen and ink, brush with wash. Historisch Centrum, Leeuwarden, Singels 371

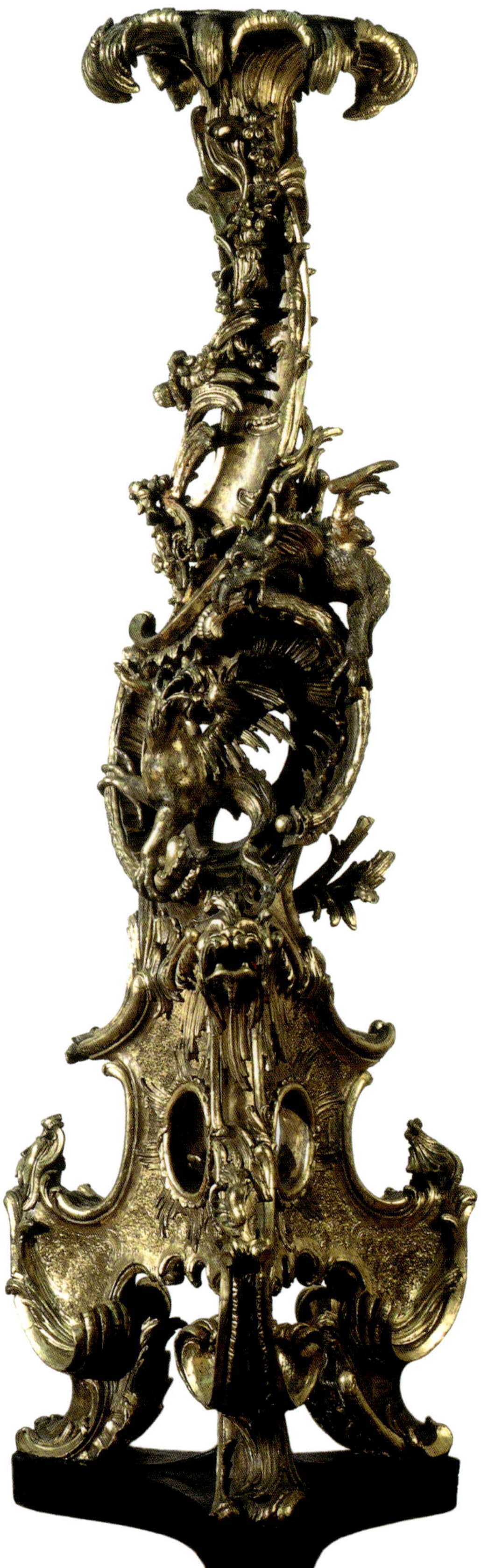

FIG. 11 Candle stand. Agostino Carlini (Italian, ca. 1718–1790). The Hague, the Netherlands, 1749–51. Lime wood, gilded with a black marbleized base. Dutch Royal Collections, The Hague

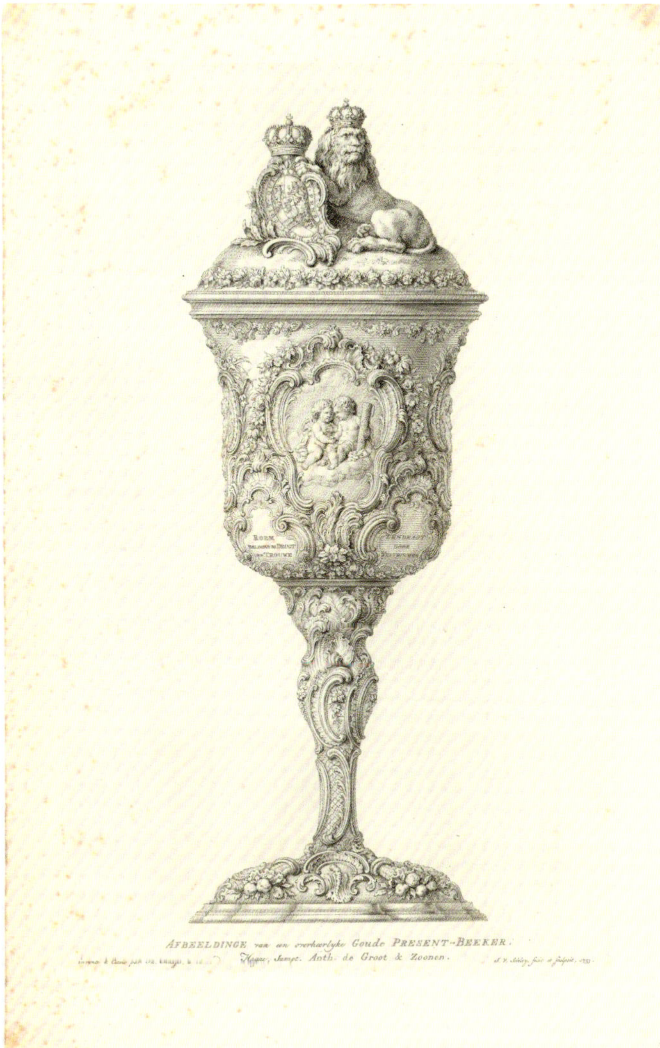

FIG. 12 Design for a Gold Cup. Jan van Schley (Dutch, 1715–1779) after Philippe Metayer. Engraving. Rijksmuseum, Amsterdam, RP-P-1964-4502

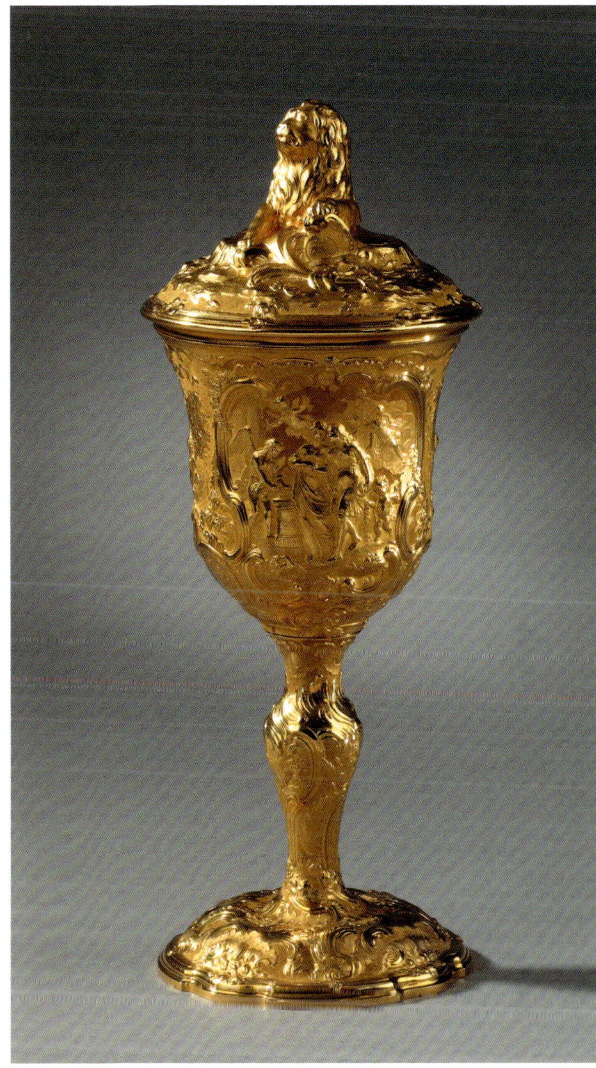

FIG. 13 Cup. Louis Metayer (French, active in the Netherlands ca. 1730–74) and Philippe Metayer (French, active in the Netherlands ca.1726–63). Amsterdam, the Netherlands, 1754. Gold. Rijksmuseum, Amsterdam, BK-1981-51

work for Willliam IV. He executed much of the carving to De Swart's designs, but also produced extravagant items of furniture such as a series of four enormous candlestands for the large central painted hall at Huis ten Bosch.[18] (fig. 11) These did not reflect the restrained manner dictated by French architectural theory and advocated by Blondel for such major pieces of representational court furniture. They may be characterized as transformations on a giant scale of the most fantastic inventions proposed by Parisian ornamentalists merely as fanciful engravings. Here, the initiative appears to have been Carlini's rather than De Swart's.

Although William IV desired to commission all kinds of fashionable court art, The Hague did not have the artists steeped in the most up-to-date rococo to execute them at the highest level. When he wished to have a gold cup made to present to the local archers' corporation, he turned to two French-born immigrants working in Amsterdam, the goldsmith Louis Metayer (d. 1774) and his brother, the gold chaser Philippe Metayer (d. 1763). This cup does not survive, but was recorded in two engravings (fig. 12); and a similar piece, clearly inspired by it and created by the same makers for one of the stadholder's closest associates, is now in the collection of the Rijksmuseum.[19] (fig. 13) It adheres to the long-established model used in Holland for such presentation pieces, but its outline and superb chasing of human figures and rocailles emulate the finest contemporary Parisian work.

The small group of goldsmiths working in Amsterdam, most of them of Huguenot descent, may actually vie with sculptors such as Xavery and Van Logteren as the forerunners of rococo in Holland. A 1736 gold watchcase by Louis Metayer shows a mythological scene framed by asymmetrical scrolls linked by rocaille ornament.[20] Another French-born goldsmith, Jean Saint (ca. 1698–after 1769), made a snuffbox in 1739, the lid of which is chased with an asymmetrical cartouche framing a view of a garden with buildings and a fountain, reminiscent of Jacques de Lajoüe's

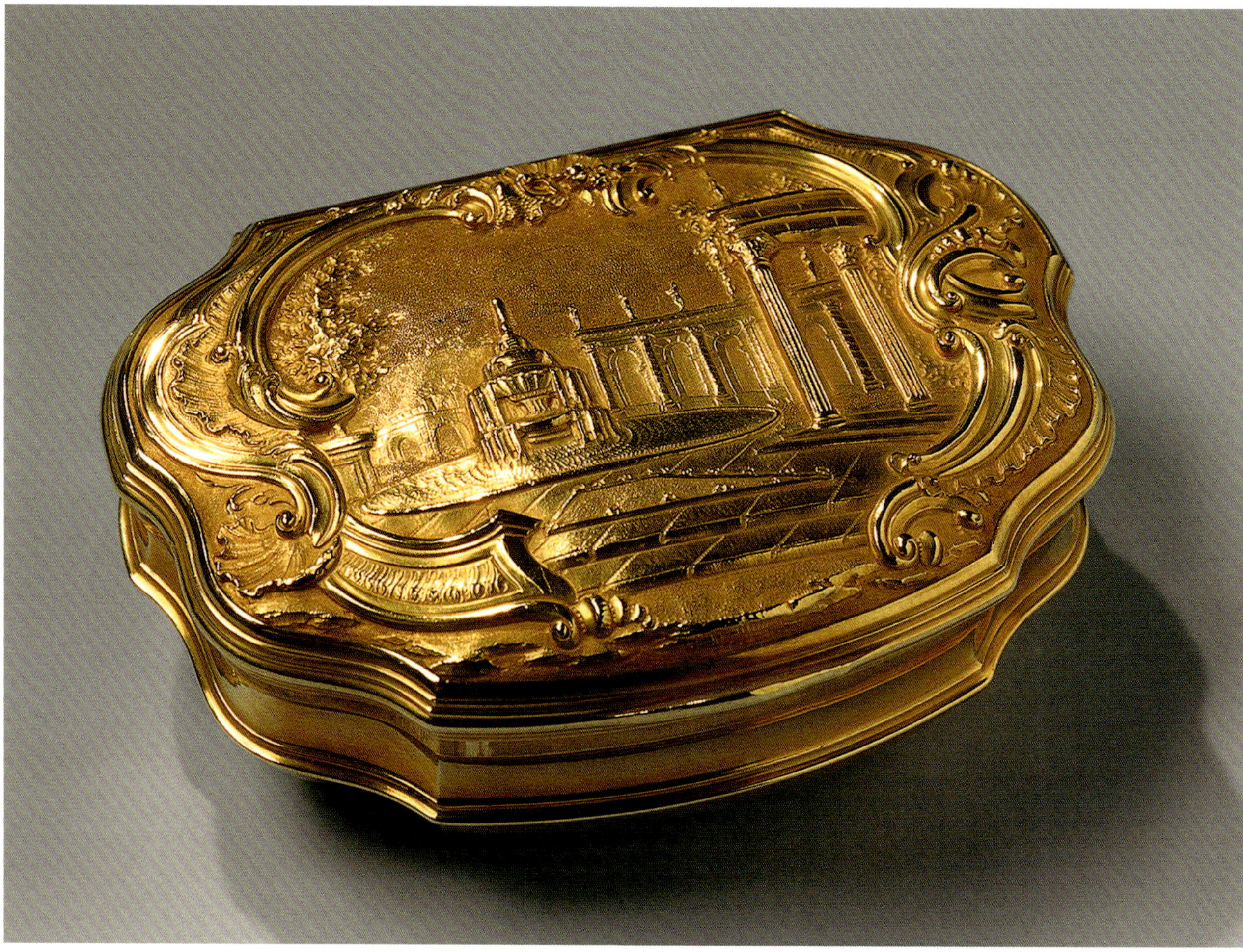

FIG. 14 Snuffbox. Jean Saint (French, ca. 1698–1769). The Hague, the Netherlands, 1739. Gold. Rijksmuseum, Amsterdam, BK-1959-19

most fanciful inventions (fig. 14); a somewhat later cane handle by Louis Metayer is clearly indebted to Meissonnier's designs.[21] (fig. 15) These artists were obviously conversant with the latest developments in their country of origin, which in part explains the avant-garde nature of their productions. On a more general level, many works by Metayer and Saint were costume accessories, dictated more than any other aspect of fashion by swift changes in taste. Along with the visionary activity of the foremost designers and architects, fashion has often been one of the prime agents of stylistic innovation.

It is of particular import that, in the case of the gold cup, William IV went to a great deal of trouble to commission an unprecedented masterpiece destined not for his own use, but as a public presentation piece. He clearly set great store on being considered an enterprising patron of innovation and excellence in all artistic endeavors, a role befitting a true ruler. As rococo deviated so willfully from the classical rules that had dominated architecture and the decorative arts since the advent of the Renaissance, it was immediately recognizable as a novel style to a larger audience than the various forms of classicism. Thus, paradoxically, the frivolous and extravagant rococo idiom, which had originated in the private whims of artists and connoisseurs, took on rhetorical and propagandist overtones. In unusually straightforward fashion, it proclaimed to the multitudes that their prince was an enthusiastic protector of the arts. One of the most expensive works of art ordered by William IV at the time of his marriage in 1734 was a gilded carriage, supplied by the French royal coachmaker La Fontaine, executed in the very latest style and featuring elements of rocaille. What more public way for the prince to demonstrate his artistic inclinations?[22] (fig. 16)

The stadholder's preference for the most outspoken rococo style amounted to something of a policy, as nearly all those who commissioned works of art for him adhered to it. In the numerous institutions over which he presided, the stadholder had a special throne, and many were ordered upon William's appointment in 1747. The Amsterdam Admiralty, for example, had one made in The Hague—probably in the workshop of Xavery run by his widow after his death—a vigorous example of early rococo at its most sculptural.[23] (fig. 17) Even his new throne in the Council Chamber of the Court of Justice in The Hague, a venerable symbol of the stadholder's authority at the very heart of the country's political structure, was couched in an exaggerated, modish idiom.[24] (fig. 18) A specialist carver named Pieter van Dijck was commissioned to execute the sculptural decoration adorning the frame made by the chairmaker Gerrit Hutte, and he smothered it in a profusion of rocailles and foliage.

William IV died in 1751, only four years after his appointment, leaving a three-year-old son, Prince William V (1748–1806), to succeed him. Faced with manifold difficulties and precarious circumstances, his widow Princess Anne immediately put a stop to all building activities. After lingering for a few more years in The Hague, Agostino Carlini,

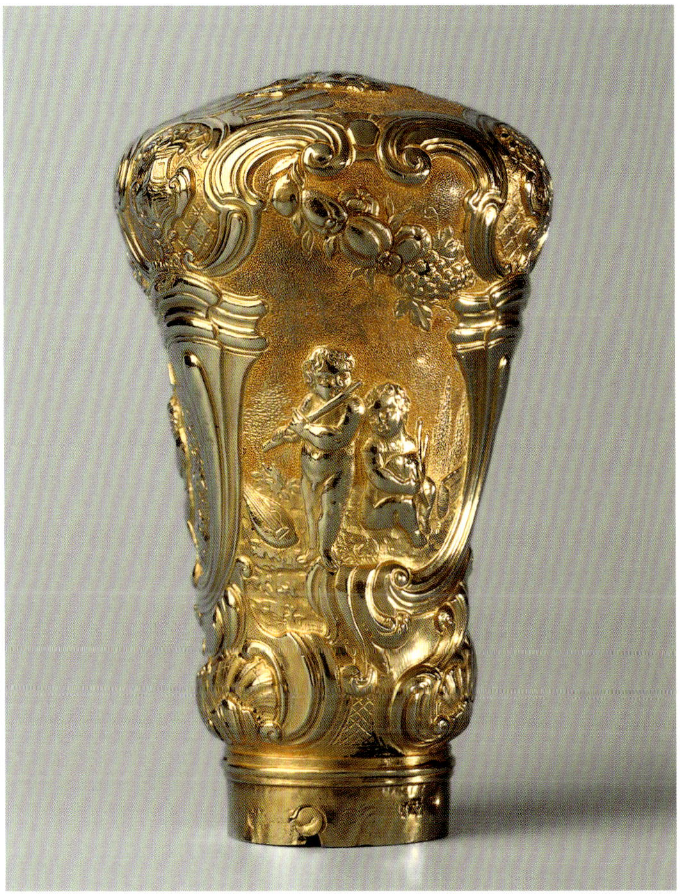

FIG. 15 Cane handle. Louis Metayer (French, active in the Netherlands ca. 1730–74). Amsterdam, the Netherlands, 1750. Gold. Rijksmuseum, Amsterdam, BK-VBR-395

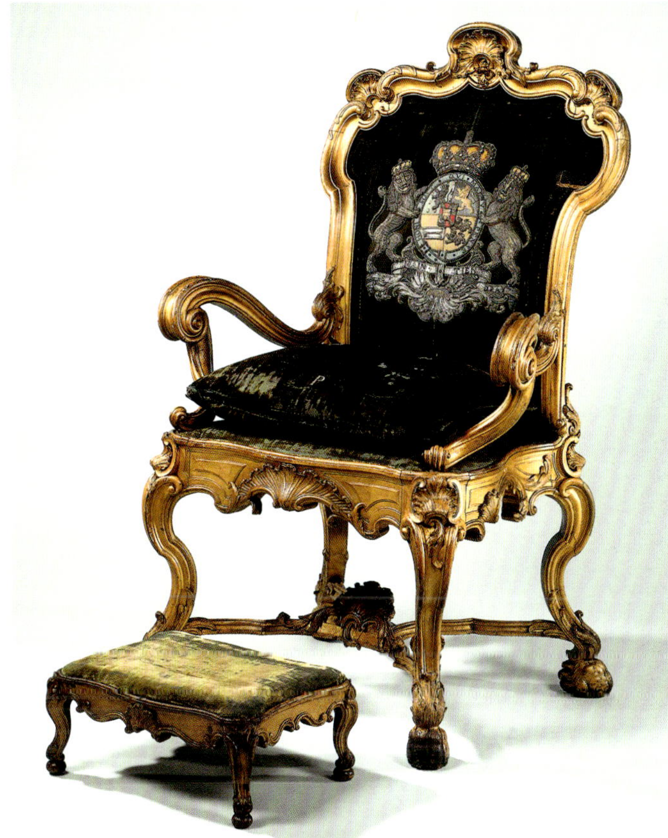

FIG. 17 Stadholder's chair and footstool. Attributed to the workshop of Jan Baptist Xavery (Dutch, 1697–1742). The Hague, the Netherlands, 1747–48. Gilded elm wood, upholstered in embroidered velvet. Rijksmuseum, Amsterdam. BK-NM-3559-3560

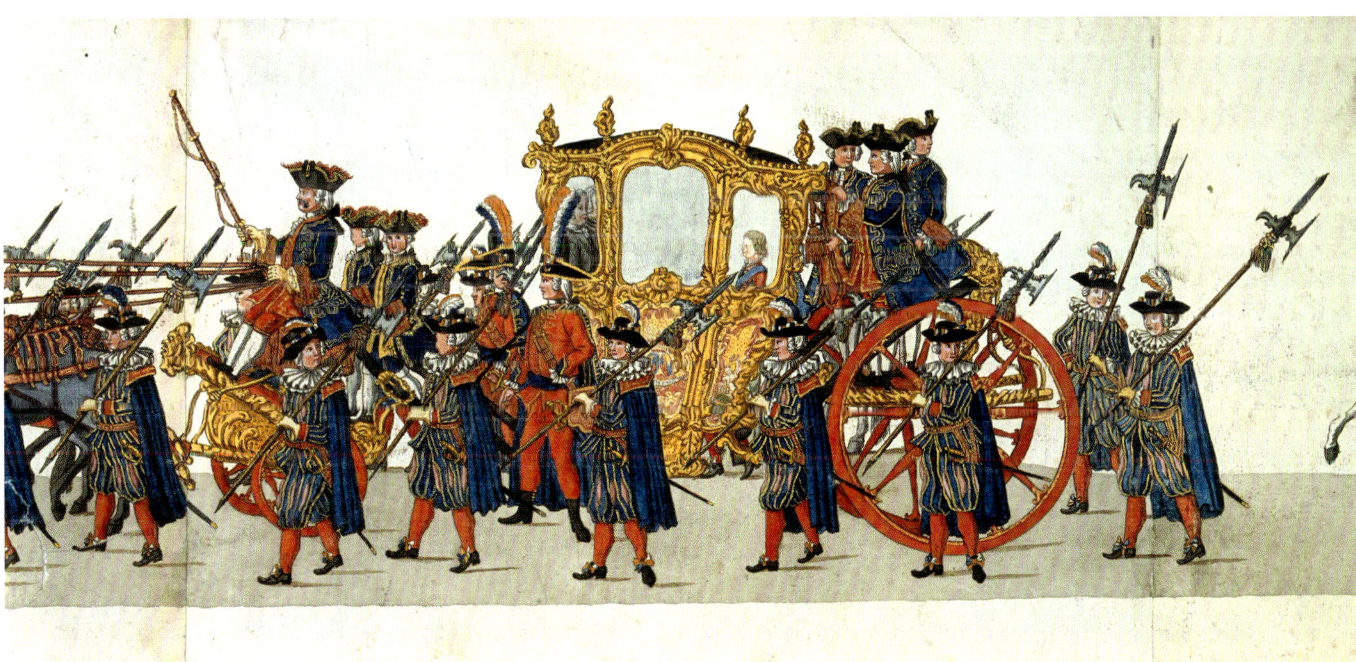

FIG. 16 *Prince William V on His Way to Visit the French Ambassador*. Attributed to Tethart Philip Haag (Dutch, 1737–1812). The Netherlands, 1752. Pen and ink color, brush with wash. Stichting Historische Verzamelingen van het Huis Oranje-Nassau, The Hague. AT/0079

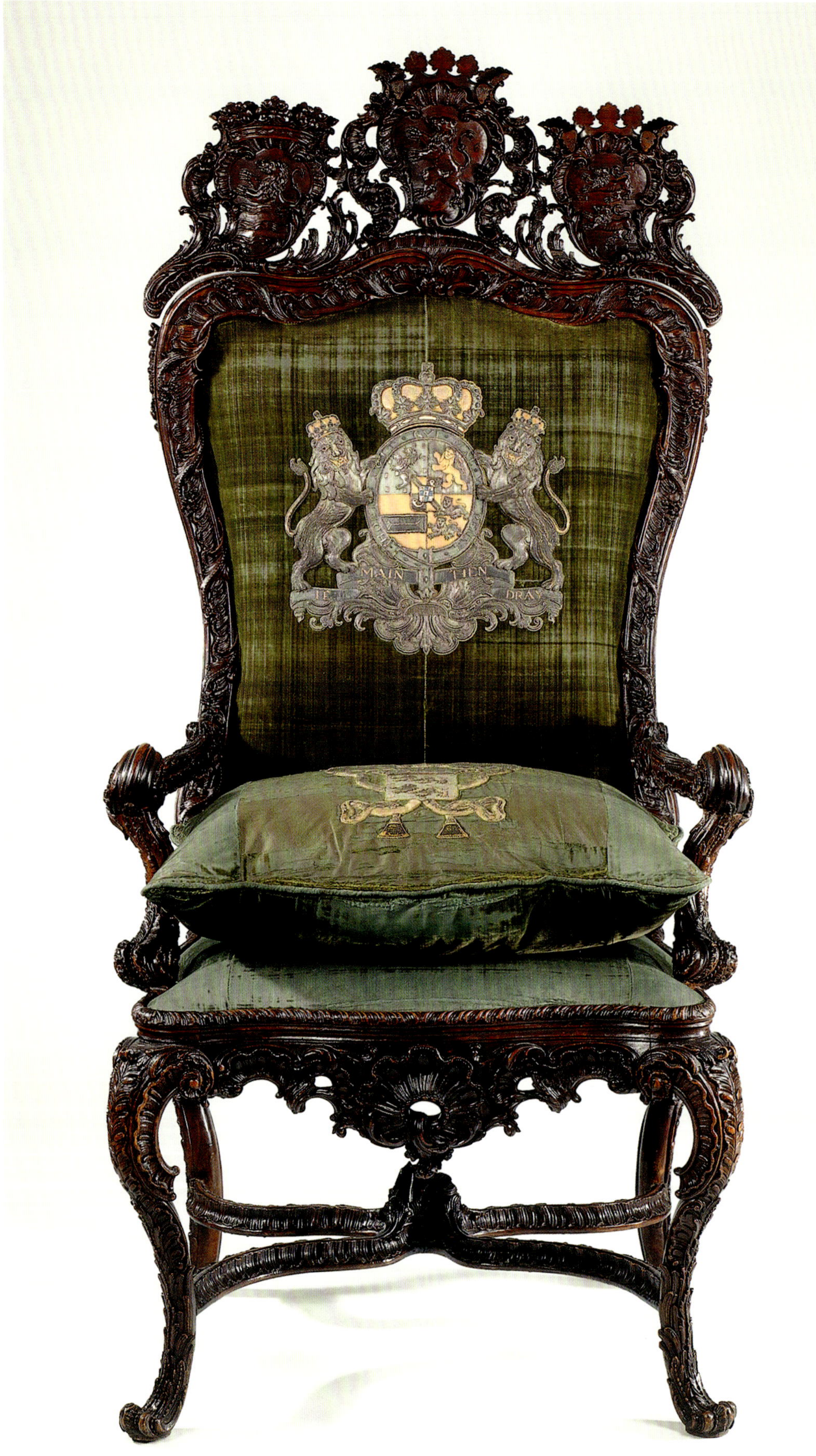

FIG. 20 Stadholder's chair. Gerrit Hutte (Dutch, active ca. 1747) and Pieter van Dijck (Dutch, d. 1757). The Hague, the Netherlands, 1747. Walnut upholstered in silk velvet embroidered in silver thread and silk. Rijkmuseum, Amsterdam, BK-NM-1315

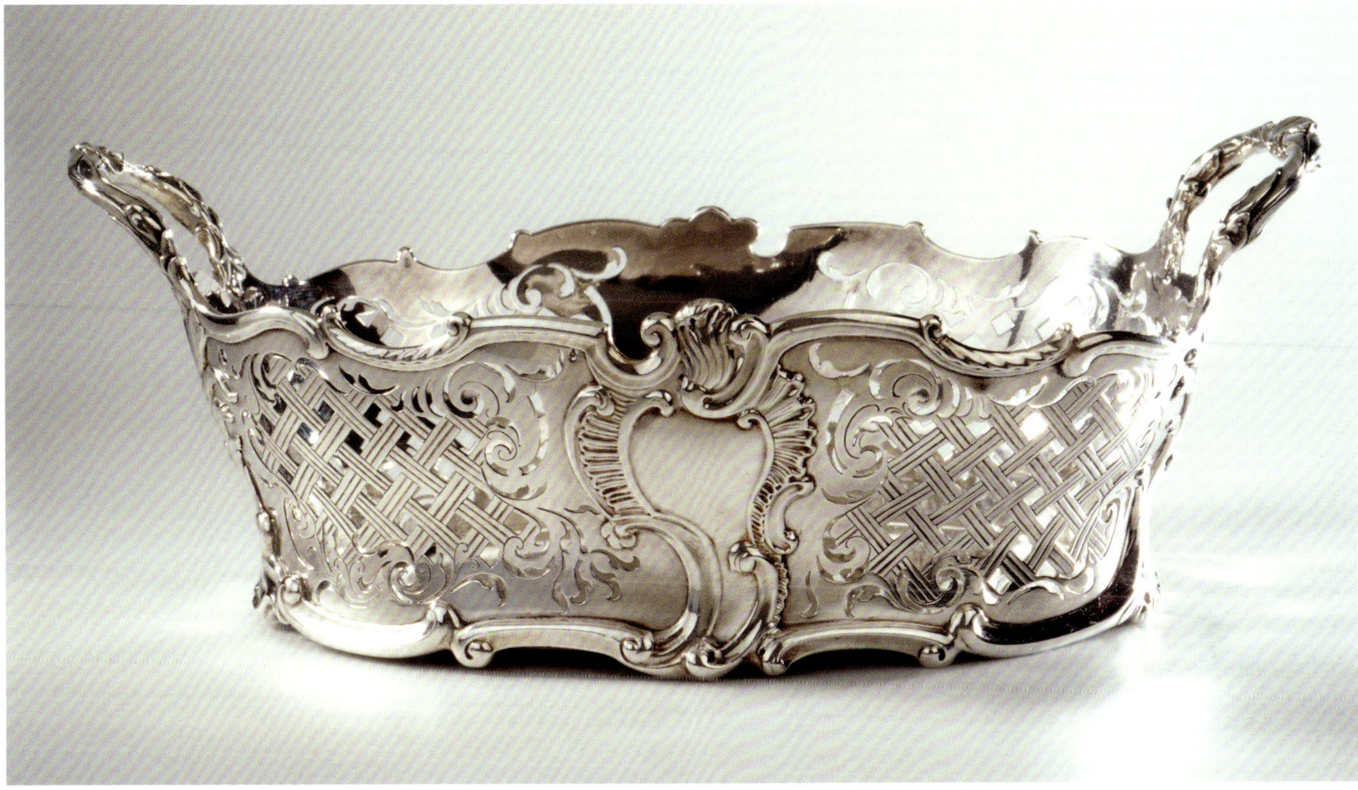

FIG. 19 Basket. François van Stapele (Dutch, 1698–1775). The Hague, the Netherlands, 1747. Silver. Private collection

sensing there were no other patrons in Holland for his ambitious high rococo confections, moved to London, where he acquired considerable fame as a sculptor of large-scale works in marble. With the death of the Dutch prince of rococo, the fullest and most glorious flowering of the style in Holland met an untimely end.

FROM CITY TO CITY

Alongside the short-lived fireworks of princely patronage, rococo style gradually pervaded all different branches of the decorative arts in Holland, a process that continued to be punctuated by occasional outbursts. However small the country, there was no such thing as a unified Dutch rococo. In the Dutch Republic, the major cities traditionally enjoyed a large measure of independence, infusing them with their own artistic personality, and each city developed its individual version of the style. The two main centres, The Hague and Amsterdam, provided inspiration to craftsmen in many smaller towns. The picture was complicated by patrons in one city turning to artists in another, the free flow of journeymen and works of art between cities, and the all-pervading influence from abroad. This complex pattern was in no way unique to the Dutch Republic: all over Europe, rococo style gave rise to a delightful multitude of interrelated local variations.

The art of the silversmith lends itself particularly well to the study of this phenomenon. As objects made of silver and gold were habitually hallmarked, their place of origin, date, and maker can be established. Our

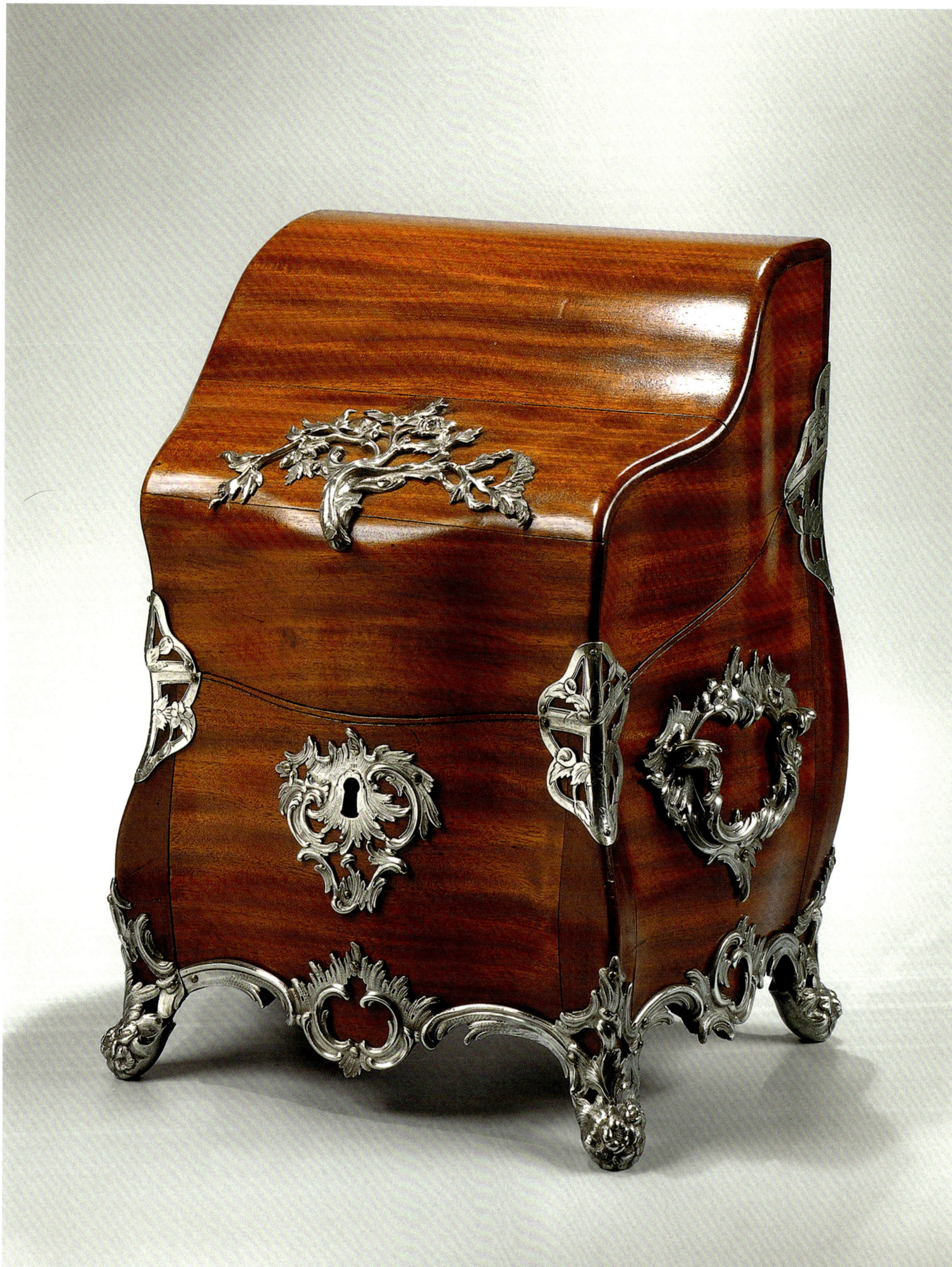

FIG. 20 Knife box. Johannes Schiotling (Swedish, active the Netherlands, 1730–1799). Amsterdam, the Netherlands, 1772. Mahogany mounted in silver. Rijksmuseum, Amsterdam, BK-1964-13

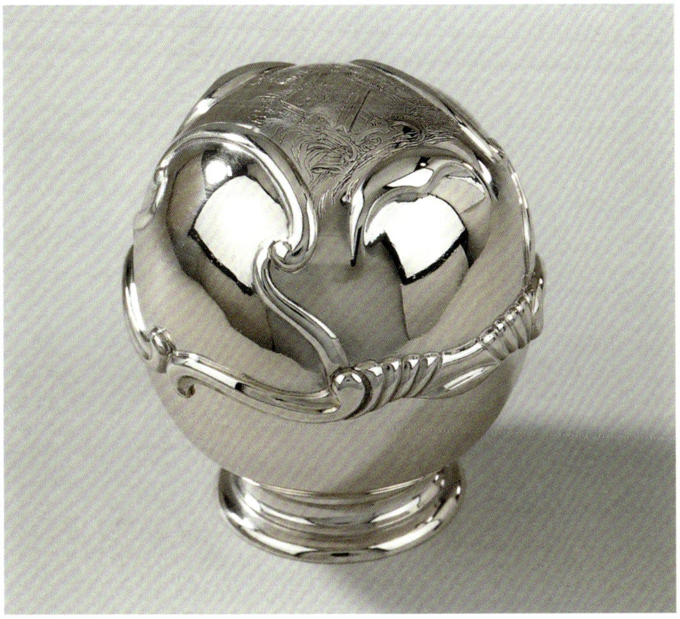

FIG. 22 Soap box. Reynier Brandt (Dutch, 1707–1788). Amsterdam, the Netherlands, 1753. Silver, partly gilded. Rijksmuseum, Amsterdam, BK-16041

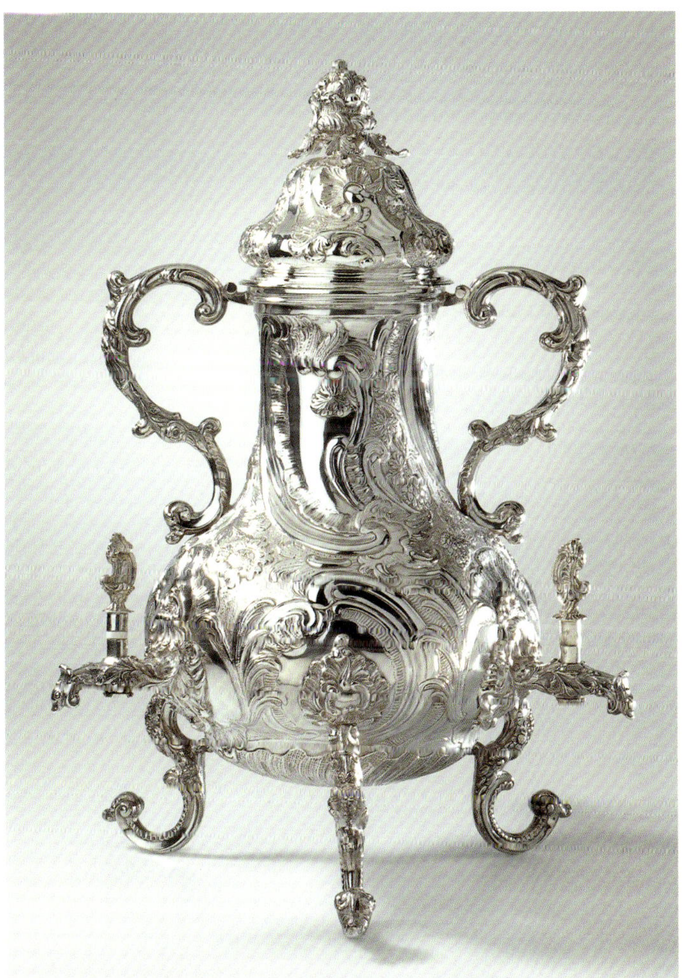

FIG. 21 Coffee urn. Jacobus Rensing (Dutch, b. 1723). Amsterdam, the Netherlands, 1761. Silver. Rijksmuseum, Amsterdam, BK-1958-23

knowledge of silver is severely impeded by the relatively small number of surviving artifacts. However, the existing material suggests that, in contrast to the pattern observed in France, rococo style conquered Dutch silversmithing considerably later than ornamental carving or goldsmithing. The earliest known examples of silver in this style date from the mid-1740s.[25] (fig. 19) Very soon afterward, the new manner gained general acceptance, and a striking distinction developed between silver from Amsterdam and The Hague, illustrating some fundamental differences between the two cities.

Since the late sixteenth century, Amsterdam was a hub of world commerce, and it continued to function as both a major port and one of the foremost centers of finance and trade. Naturally, it had always attracted a varied international population, although the principal local families jealously guarded their position of power. Amsterdam's wealth acted as a magnet for a constant stream of foreign craftsmen who came to work in the city. It was no different in the middle of the eighteenth century, and silversmiths from abroad greatly contributed to the impact of rococo style. For instance, the Swedish-born Johannes Schiotling (1730–1799), who set up as an independent master in 1762, brought a distinctive Stockholm style with him, which was only gradually amalgamated into a recognizably Dutch manner.[26] (fig. 20) As a result, it may be argued that there was no one true Amsterdam version of rococo silver, but rather multiple variations that coexisted. The wealthy merchant population generally preferred objects richly embellished with applied, chased, and engraved ornament, such as the overpowering coffee urn made by Jacobus Rensing (1723–ca. 1772) in 1761, which is clearly indebted to Danish or south German examples.[27] (fig. 21) Such items proclaimed their owners' affluence and adherence to the new style, without perhaps always being entirely successful as expressions of that style's fundamental characteristics. But exceptions prove the rule, as is demonstrated by an effortlessly sophisticated and restrained soap box by the well-known maker Reynier Brandt (ca. 1707–1788).[28] (fig. 22)

The Hague, a much smaller city, housed the court of the stadholder, the bodies of national government, and the foreign embassies. It was cosmopolitan rather than international, and advocated a restrained, elegant rococo, which was nowhere more eloquently realized than in its silver.[29] (fig. 23) True rocaille ornament rarely occurred; in an original interpretation of the style, its place was taken by naturalistic twigs of foliage and floral sprays. Various silversmiths worked in this manner, their work displaying a remarkable stylistic unity. Thus a tureen by Engelbart Joosten[30] (fig. 24) could easily be combined with candlesticks, sauceboats, and baskets by other makers. These objects have a quiet distinctiveness which addressed a different audience than the more showy pieces from Amsterdam.

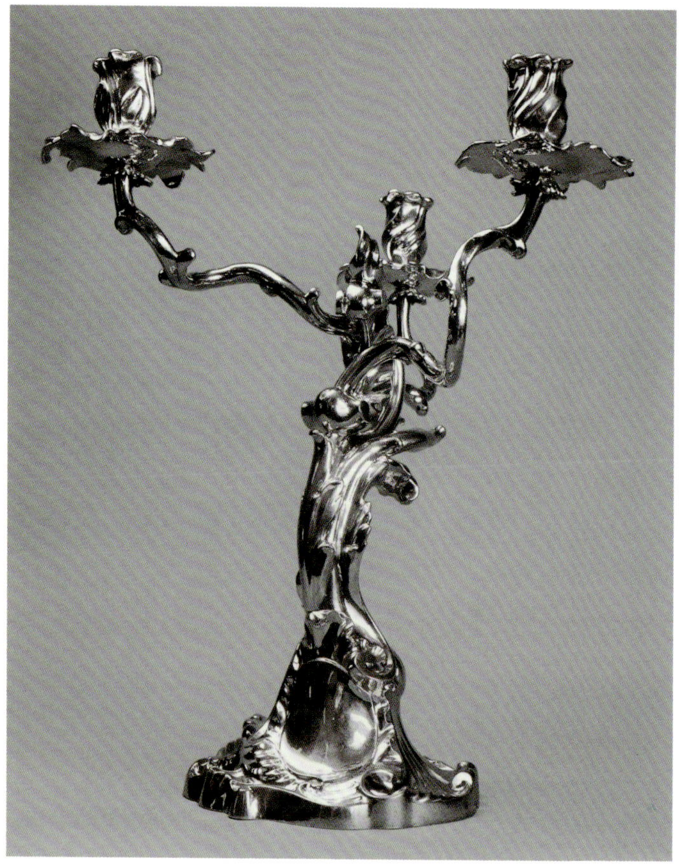

FIG. 23 Candelabrum. Jan Willem Burger (Dutch, master 1739). The Hague, the Netherlands, 1757. Silver. Collection of His Royal Highness the Grand-Duke of Luxemburg

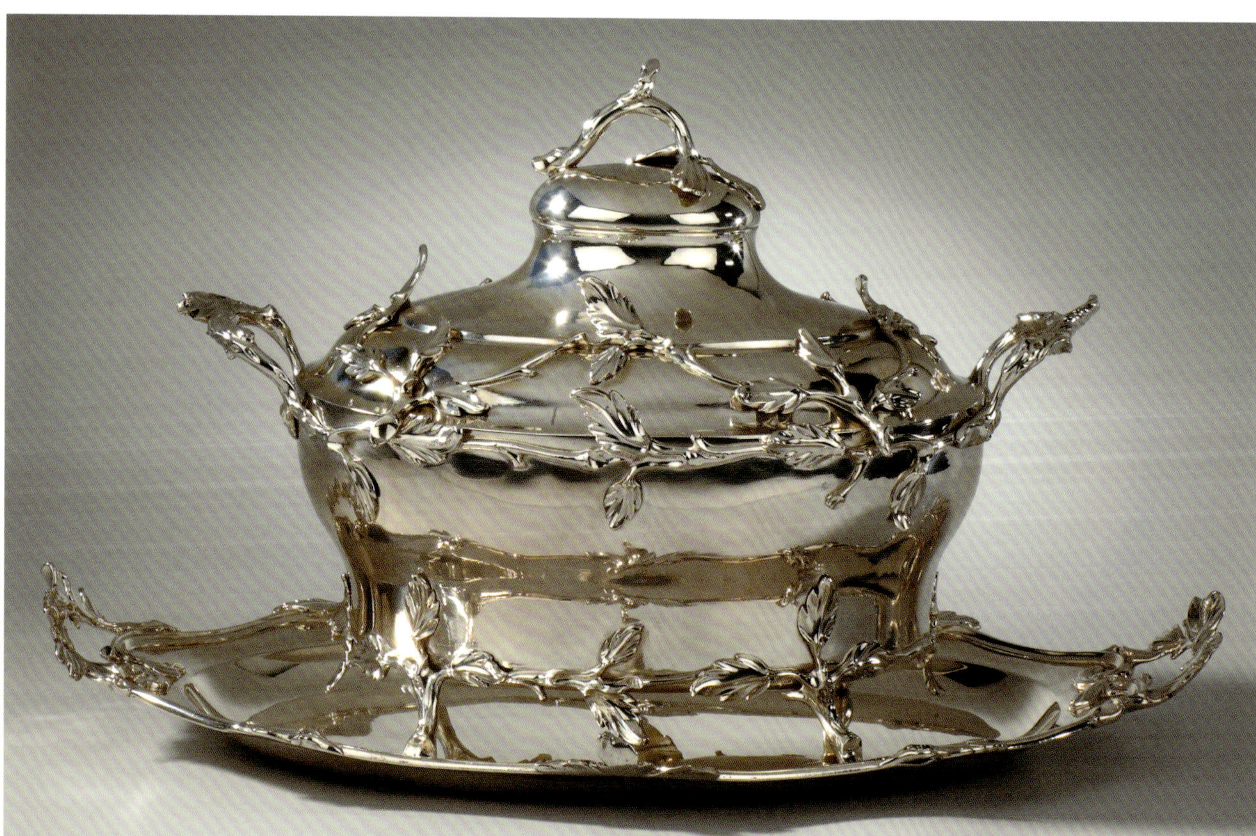

FIG. 24 Tureen and stand. Engelbart Joosten (Dutch, 1717–1789). The Hague, the Netherlands, 1763 (tureen), 1764 (stand). Silver. Rijksmuseum, Amsterdam, BK-1982-1

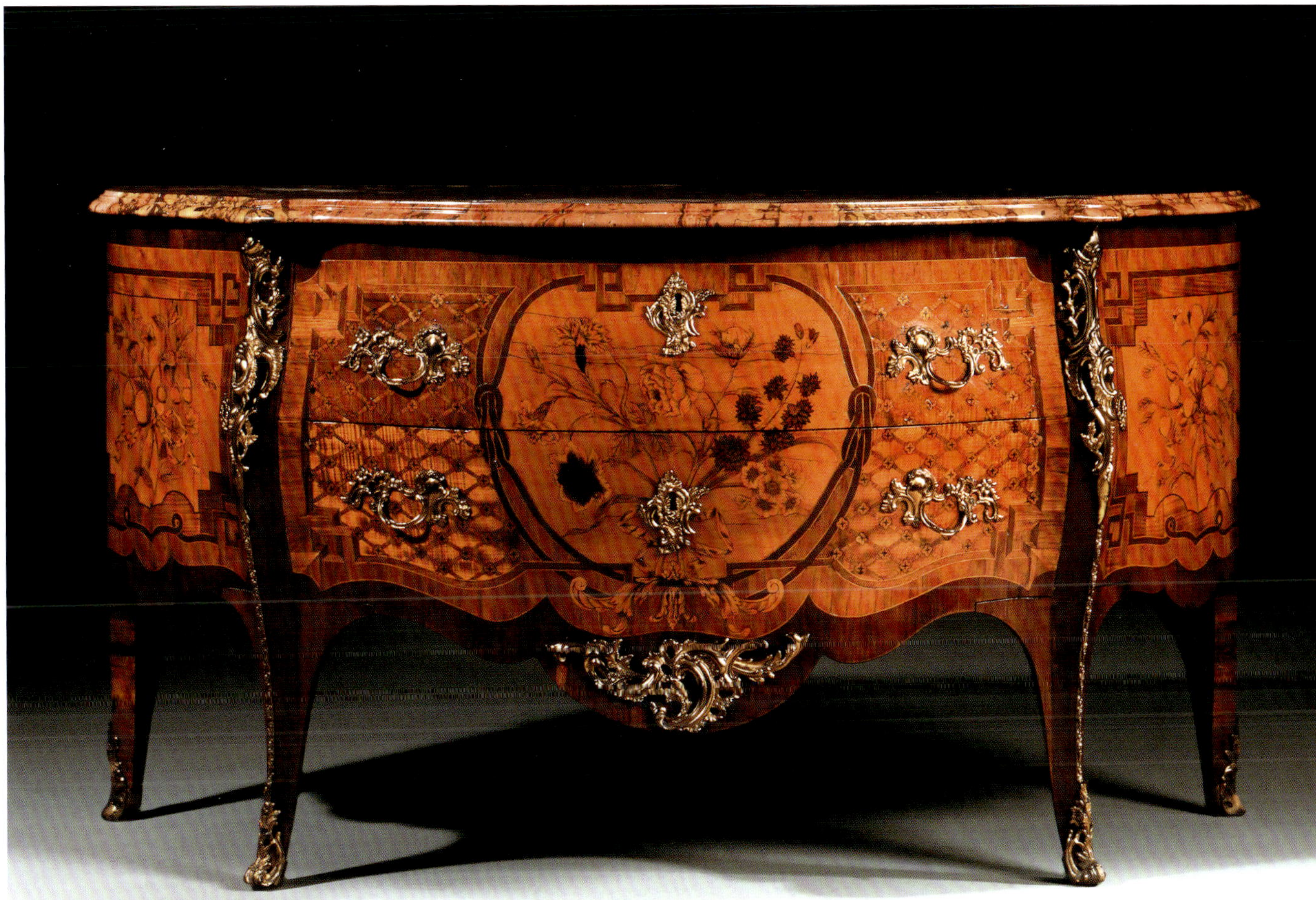

FIG. 25 Commode. Attributed to Matthijs Horrix (German, 1735–1809). The Hague, the Netherlands, ca. 1765–70. Oak, wood veneer, marble top, gilded brass mounts. Private collection

A LATE ROCOCO COURT

Court life in The Hague gradually gathered momentum again as Prince William V grew into young adulthood, and greatly intensified upon his marriage in 1767 to Princess Wilhelmina of Prussia (1751–1812). A favorite niece of King Frederick the Great, she was raised among the splendors of his palaces in Berlin and Potsdam. In order to receive her, the stadholder's residences were modernized and refurbished. Rococo was still the dominant style, but a change had taken place, prefigured in The Hague's distinctive silver. The fantastic, sometimes even unsettling, ornament of early rocaille had given way to an elegant and naturalistic manner. Flowers were omnipresent, and an airy lightness pervaded interiors and works of art alike. Among the new fashions imported from Paris, *bombé* furniture veneered with floral marquetry figured prominently. The German-born cabinetmaker Matthijs Horrix (1735–1809) established himself in The Hague in 1764, where from his shop, "in the commode from Paris," he supplied an enthusiastic clientele with up-to-date pieces.[31] (fig. 25) Soon, the stadholder and his consort were among his most fervent admirers.

This graceful phase had a sophisticated appeal of its own, but it lacked the powerful vigor and revolutionary boldness of early rococo. There is an elegiac quality, a hint even of a certain tiredness. On Horrix's commode, the floral marquetry is combined with intertwined ribbons, which, at the corners, form angular shapes called *grecques*, with a trellis pattern and rosettes. These motifs herald the new neoclassicism that, again inspired by Paris, had started its triumphant ascent by the mid-1760s. It soon superseded rococo entirely, bringing to an end an exciting period that, in Holland as elsewhere, stands like no other artistic movement for the unique qualities of the ancien régime.

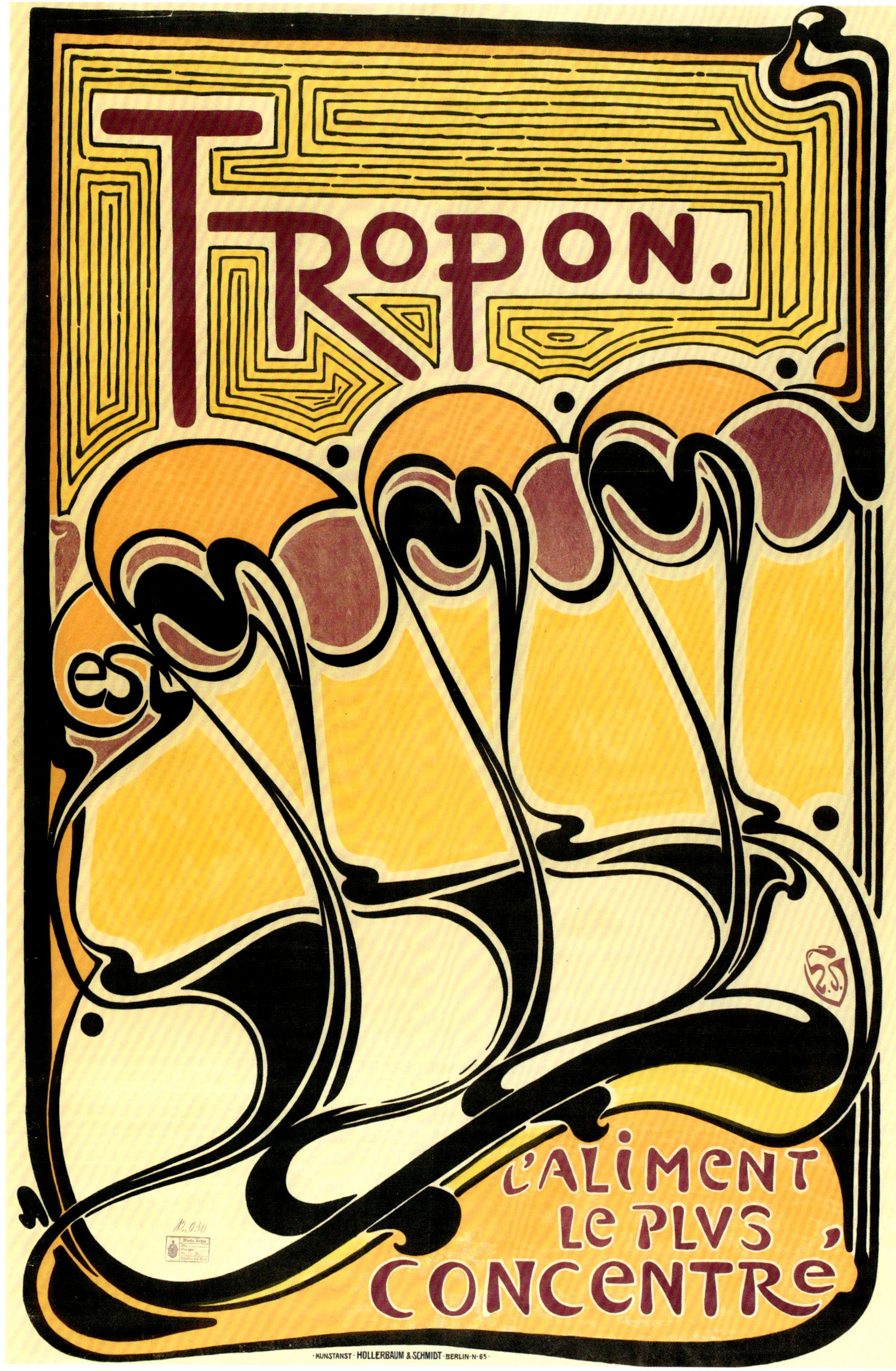

FIG. 7 Tropon est L'Aliment le Plus Concentré (Tropon, the Most Concentrated Food Supplement). Henry van de Velde (Belgian, 1863–1957). Printed by Hollerbaum and Schmidt. Berlin, Germany, 1898. Lithograph on wove paper, lined. Cooper-Hewitt, National Design Museum, Smithsonian Institution, Museum purchase through gift of Mr. and Mrs. Lee S. Ainslie II, Marilyn Friedman, and Nancy Marks; General Acquisitions Endowment; Drawings & Prints Council Fund, 2007-2-1

Emulation and Subversion

NINETEENTH-CENTURY ROCOCO REVIVALS IN THE GRAPHIC ARTS

Gail S. Davidson

In 1902, after Art Nouveau design had reached its apogee, J. H. Elder-Duncan, a British writer on household decoration, issued a scathing criticism of the style: "The chaos in design has spread all over France, Germany, Austria, and Italy....There, all respect for natural limitations in the materials has been cast to the winds. Wood is cut as though it were a grainless and fibreless substance like cheese; metal is twisted into the most weird and unnatural shapes.... In no case is this ghastly riot of form more marked than in Germany and Austria, where ingenious fancy, a craze for novelty, and a certain morbid strain in the Teutonic temperament have combined with the most unhappy results."[1] This anti–Art Nouveau diatribe recalls Jacques-François Blondel's critique of rocaille decoration 120 years earlier.

While Art Nouveau may have been the most significant rococo revival in the nineteenth century, the glorification of rococo occurred in several waves. After its banishment by neoclassicism during the late eighteenth and early nineteenth centuries, rococo design regained a foothold in France during the reign of Louis-Philippe (1830–48) and was adopted as one of the court styles under the Second Empire (1852–70). In England, rococo was revived during the reign of George IV (1811–30); while in Germany, it returned around the time of Napoleon's defeat by Prussia in 1815 (fig. 1). As noted by Paul Greenhalgh, by the middle of the century, "rocaille forms were stamped, pressed, moulded and stenciled onto middleclass domestic objects everywhere."[2]

In England, the Crace firm of decorators, famous for its chinoiserie interiors for the Royal Pavilion at Brighton (1801–ca. 1827), also worked in an "old French" manner, combining features of baroque, rococo, and neoclassical styles, beginning in 1829, after John Gregory Crace returned from a study trip to France and the Netherlands. Crace's most famous project in rococo-revival style was the Lower Library at Chatsworth for the Duke of Devonshire in 1840. Among Cooper-Hewitt's Crace works on paper is a *Design for a Rocaille Ornament* from about 1839 (fig. 2), which elaborated on the eighteenth century rococo cartouche form, adding a nineteenth-century color palate of rose and gold against the dark blue paper and a broader, more swashbuckling bravura paint handling.[3]

The great demand for rococo decorative-arts objects in France paralleled the rising bourgeoisie, whose status rested on money and possessions. Consumers purchased objects and furnishings in a variety of revival styles including rococo, choosing what was opulent and comfortable. Alfred de Musset wrote shortly after 1830 in *Confession d'un enfant du siècle* that "one found, assembled and confused, the furniture of every age and

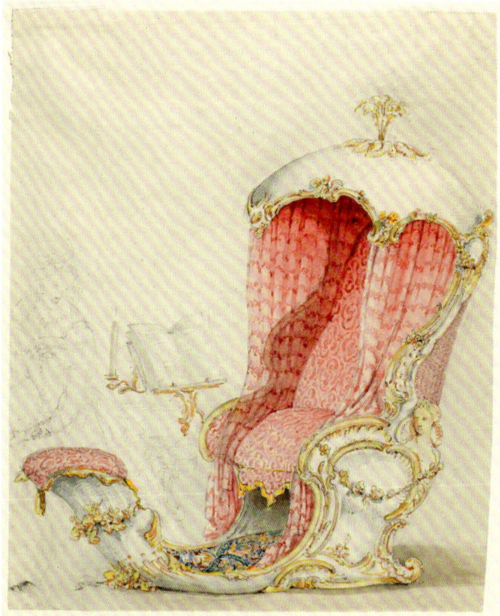

FIG. 1 *Design for a Chaise Longue.* Germany, ca. 1810. Brush and watercolor, graphite on white laid paper. Cooper-Hewitt, National Design Museum, Smithsonian Institution, Museum purchase through gift of Jacques Seligmann, 1948-24-1

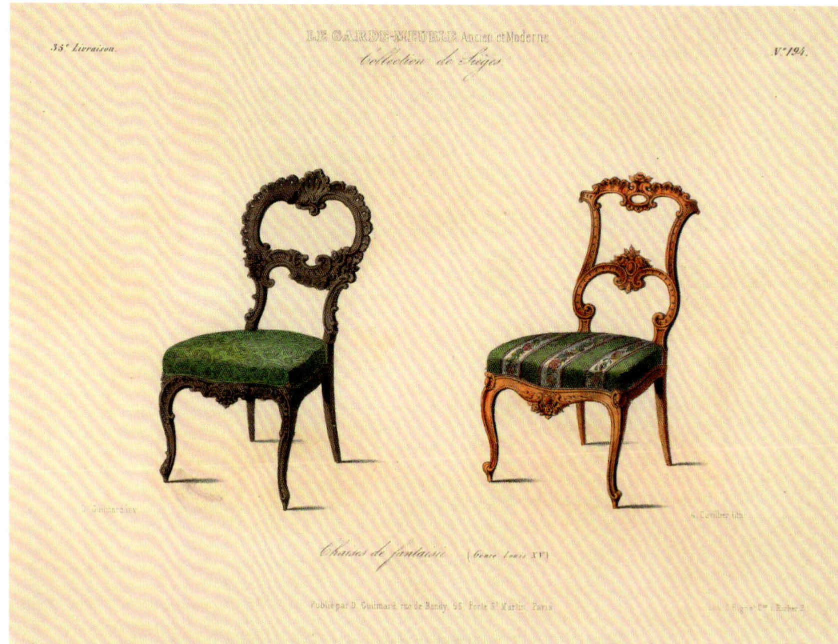

FIG. 3 *Chaise de Fantaisie*, from *Le Garde-meuble, ancien et moderne*, livre 35, no. 194. Désiré Guilmard (French, ca. 1810–1885). Paris, France, 1844. Lithograph, brush and watercolor, gouache on wove paper. Smithsonian Institution Libraries, Cooper-Hewitt, National Design Museum

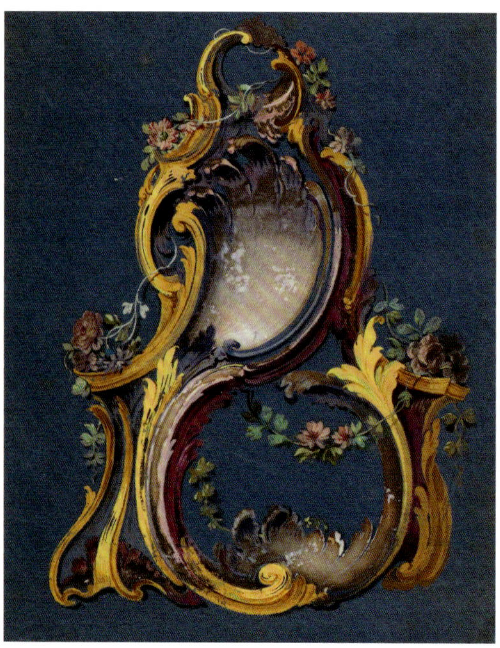

FIG. 2 *Design for a Rocaille Ornament.* Frederick Crace and Son. England, ca. 1839. Brush and gouache, gold paint on dark blue wove paper. Cooper-Hewitt, National Design Museum, Smithsonian Institution, Museum purchase through gift of Mrs. John Innes Kane, 1948-40-186

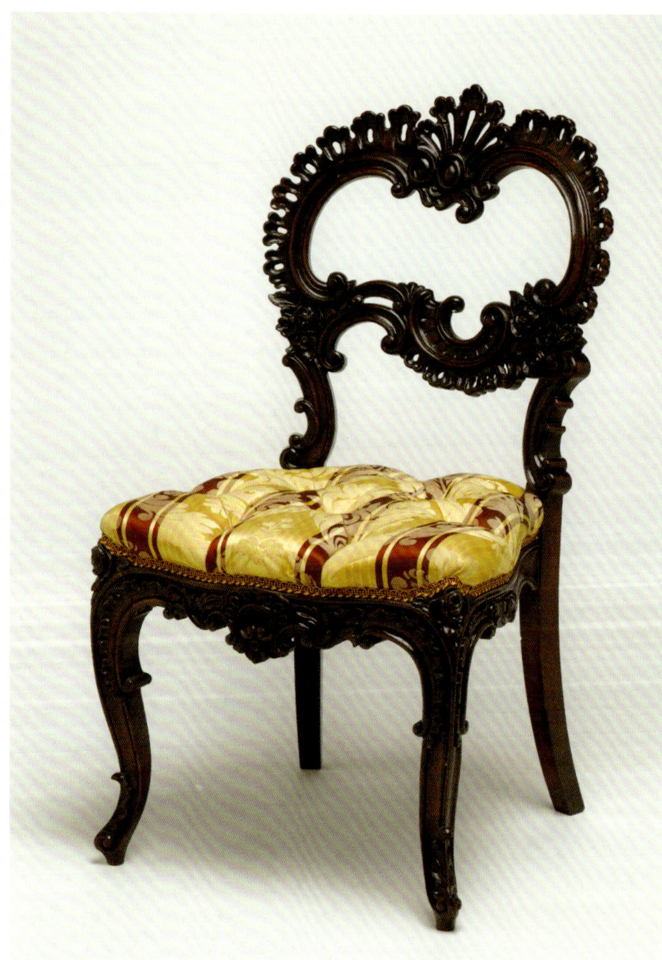

FIG. 4 Side chair. Désiré Guilmard (French, ca. 1810–1885). Possibly manufactured by Bembé and Kimbel. France or United States, ca. 1855. Rosewood, modern upholstery. Brooklyn Museum, Alfred T. and Caroline S. Zoebisch Fund, 1992.42

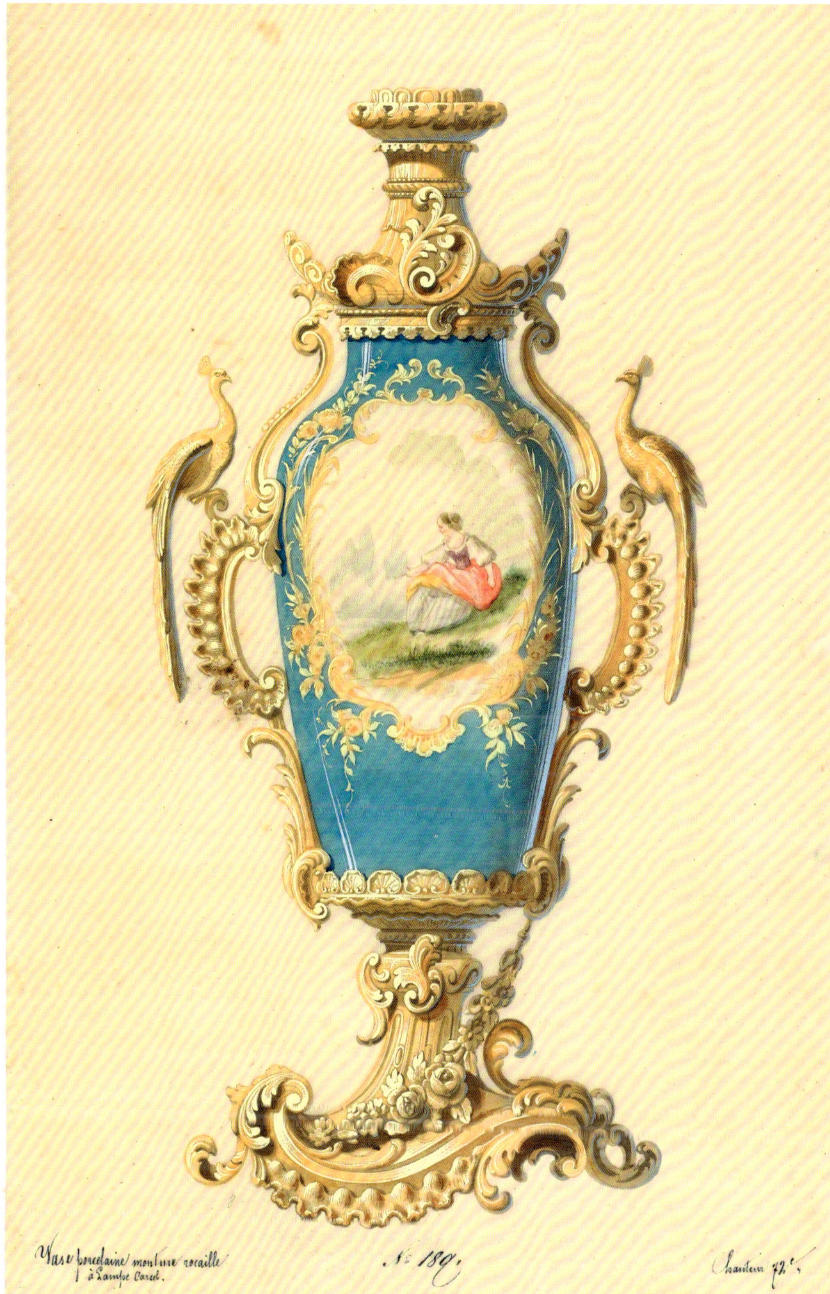

FIG. 5 *Design for the Base of an Oil Lamp.* France, ca. 1855. Brush and gouache and watercolor, graphite, and pen and brown ink on cream tracing paper mounted on white laid paper. Cooper-Hewitt, National Design Museum, Smithsonian Institution, Museum purchase from Pauline Riggs Noyes Fund, 1953-206-8

every country.... The apartments of the rich are cabinets of curios: the ancient, the Gothic, the taste of the Renaissance, of Louis XIII, all jumbled together. In short, we have something from every century except our own."[4]

Many nineteenth-century decorators, fabricators, and consumers relied on *Le Garde-meuble, ancien et moderne* as a design resource. Published by Désiré Guilmard from 1839 through 1935, this bimonthly serial contained images of furniture, window treatments, and room settings, in folios of up to nine hand-colored, exquisitely detailed lithographs, many bearing a stylistic label, such as Louis XIV, Louis XV, or Louis XVI.[5] The *Garde-meuble* provided models for craftsmen in Europe as well as the United States for fabricating rococo-revival furniture (figs. 3, 4). This kind of eclectic source material, where designers could dip here and there for various furnishings objects, may have contributed to the intermingling of styles in nineteenth-century interiors.

Individual objects frequently incorporated more than one style. *Design for the Base of an Oil Lamp* (fig. 5), from an unknown French firm, echoes eighteenth-century gilt-bronze mounted Japanese and French porcelains in its pseudo-Boucher scene in the central cartouche and mounts incorporating C-curves and shell motifs for the neck and asymmetrical bronze mounted base. Yet the elongated urn shape, symmetrical handles ornamented with double-facing peacocks, and suspended rose garland on the base reflect the late eighteenth-century neoclassical manner of the Second Empire. *Cartoon for a Woven Carpet* (fig. 6) shows richly colored floral sprays framed by heavy foliate cartouches, in bright

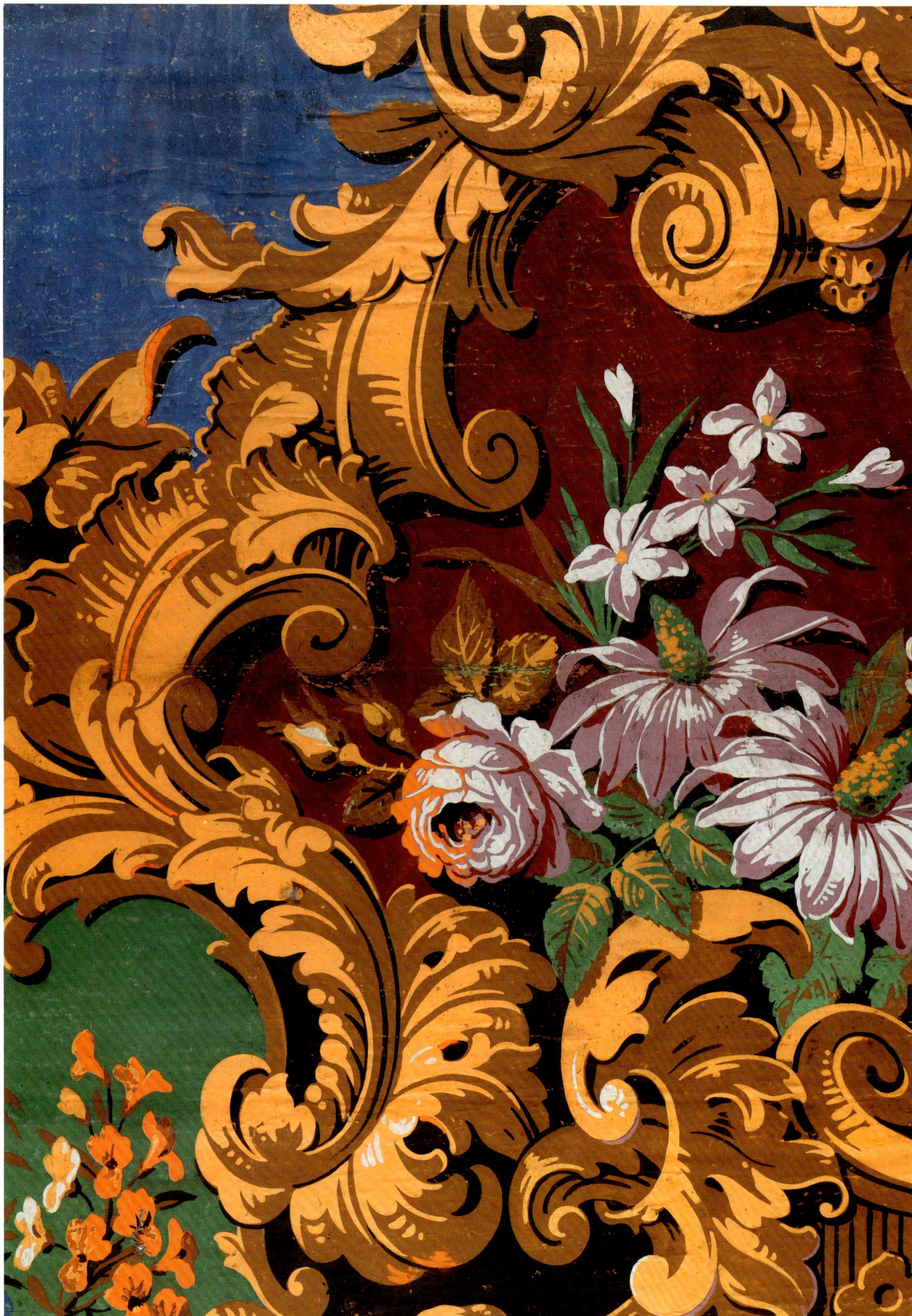

FIG. 6 *Cartoon for a Woven Carpet*. France, ca. 1848. Brush and gouache on heavy wove paper, lined. Cooper-Hewitt, National Design Museum, Smithsonian Institution, Gift of John Judkyn, 1954-23-12

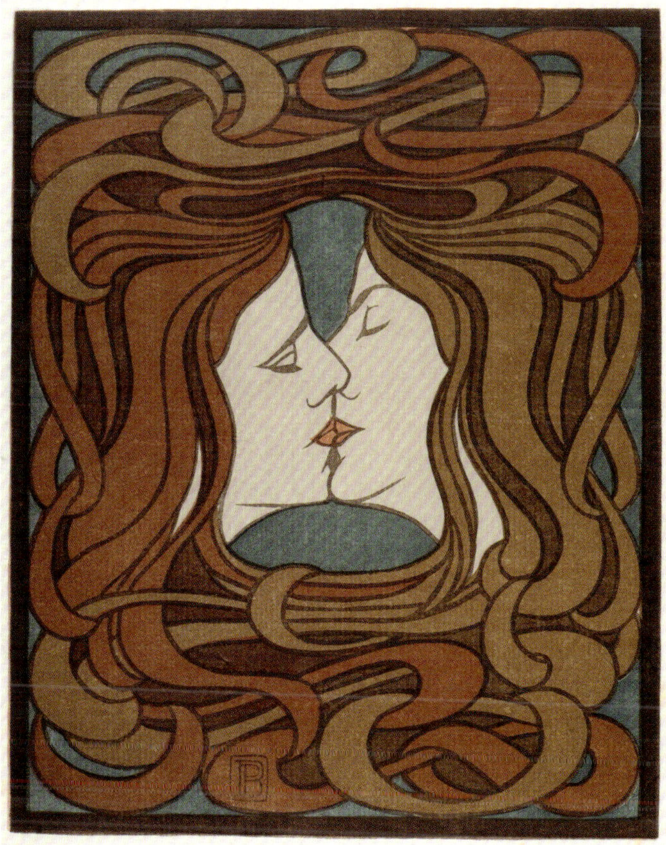

FIG. 8 Der Küss (The Kiss), from *Pan*, vol. 4, no. 2. Peter Behrens (German, 1868–1940). Germany, 1898. Woodcut on thin buff Japan paper. Cooper-Hewitt, National Design Museum, Smithsonian Institution, Museum purchase from the General Acquisitions Endowment, 2005-13-1

orange-gold on a blue and green ground. Such over-scaled floral patterns were commonly used for public reception rooms from about 1845 to 1870.[6]

Rococo, Gothic, Renaissance, and other decorative-arts revivals generated the "historicist" label for this period. Against this prevailing "sterile" eclecticism, designers including John Ruskin in Britain and theorists such as Eugène Viollet-le-Duc in France began to argue for equality among the "major" (fine) and "minor" (decorative) arts, and for a new style that embraced all of the arts in a single, unified design aesthetic—what the German-speaking world referred to as *Gesamtkunstwerk*.

A major theorist of this "new art" in Belgium and Germany during the 1890s was designer Henry van de Velde (1863–1957). Starting his career as a painter in Antwerp and Brussels, Van de Velde, increasingly influenced by the British Arts and Crafts reformers Ruskin and William Morris, abandoned painting to design interiors and objects. Following Ruskin and Morris, he argued that all branches of art shared a common language of form and were equally important to human existence. He also shared the Arts and Crafts ideal that design serve humanity; but rejected the British revival of pre-industrial handcraftsmanship, maintaining that design should reflect new machine processes, technological achievements, and modern engineering. Van de Velde's emphasis on technology, structure, and energy connected him with the technologists, a group of designers including Victor Horta and Hector Guimard which formed one branch of Art Nouveau (*Jugendstil*) design.[7]

Van de Velde incorporated the technologists' ideas into his theory of line as the creative force. Inspired by the recently discovered paleolithic cave paintings at Altimira, he argued in an unpublished manuscript (1916–18) that line, rather than geometry, was the basic component of all art because it was the instinctive manner of describing and was the expression of creative energy.[8] The designer's iconic *Tropon est l'aliment le plus concentré* poster, advertising a food supplement made from eggs for the Tropon-Werke company, illustrated this concept (fig. 7). The poster's visual power—its curving, spiraling, intertwining lines, its bright colors appearing at times to be brushed in by hand—rested on the relatively new technique of chromolithography, allowing the designer or printmaker to draw directly on a lithographic stone and layer bright colors over large areas. Chromolithography was responsible for the enormous production of posters at the end of the century, which lined the walls and kiosks of major European cities and inserted the Art Nouveau graphic style into the consciousness of consumers, who acquired them to create personal collections.

A reduced image of the *Tropon* poster accompanied Van de Velde's 1898 article on modern furniture in the influential periodical *Pan*.[9] Founded in 1895 by Otto Bierbaum and Julius Meier-Graefe as the German response to Britain's *The Studio*, *Pan* showcased articles on avant-garde art and design. Peter Behrens's color woodcut *Der Küss* (*The Kiss*) was incorporated in the November 1899 issue (fig. 8). Influenced by the flat patterning and expressive outlines of Japanese woodcuts, *The Kiss* depicted a couple kissing, their faces framed and joined by the undulating curves of their locks. These androgynous faces floating in a sea of hair suggested illicit gay sex and the use of opiates, undercurrents in turn-of-the-century art and literature. Although Van de Velde later refused to be identified with Art Nouveau as the roots and concerns of his aesthetic were distinct from someone like René Lalique, he gladly accepted a commission from Sigfried Bing to design rooms and furnishings for the opening of Bing's Paris shop, L'Art Nouveau. He also allowed Bing to install the rooms again, along with a newly designed fourth room, at the 1897 international art exhibition in Dresden.[10]

Bing was one of many individuals and forces that led to the development of Art Nouveau style, as discussed in Deborah Silverman's seminal book *Art Nouveau in Fin-de-Siècle France*.[11] Other commercial entrepreneurs and producers of objects, such as Emile Gallé in Nancy, who founded the Ecole de Nancy in 1901 to promote the arts in industry, certainly had an impact in "liberating taste from the imitation of old styles by a new principle, that is the observation of living models." Additional influences included contemporary psychological discourse, which considered a new cult of the self and the study of the irrational in human behavior, and the emergence of the Symbolist movement in painting and sculpture.

Perhaps more important was the role of the French state in the aftermath of the Franco-Prussian War. Suffering a wound in the national pride after its defeat, the Third Republic, seeking to promote national patrimony, heavily invested in rococo style. In 1889, the government began sponsoring renovations of eighteenth-century palaces and interiors at Versailles, Chantilly, and elsewhere. A plethora of articles and books on

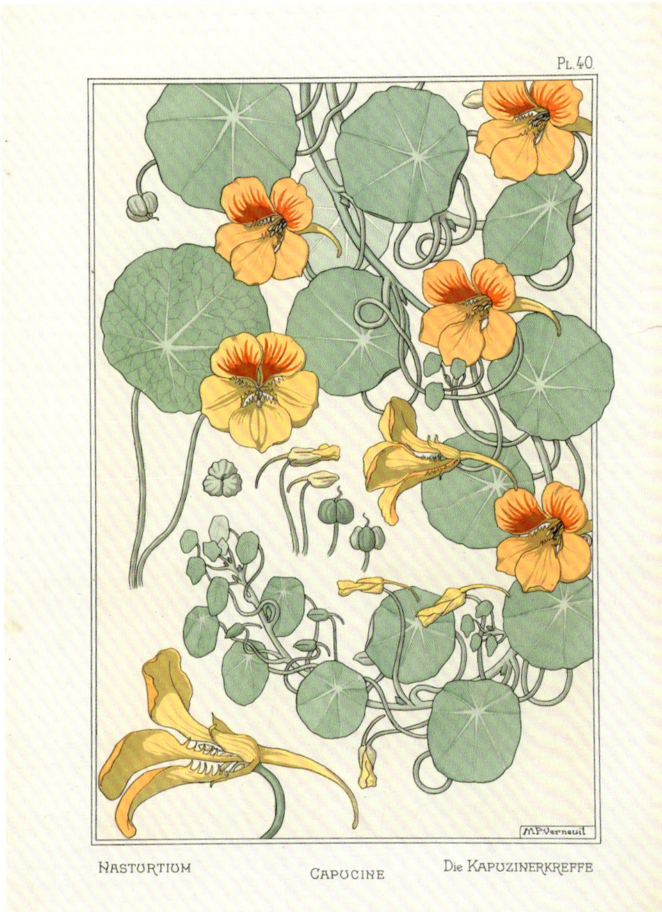

FIG. 9 *Capucine*, plate 40 from *La Plante et ses applications ornementales*. Eugène-Samuel Grasset (Swiss, 1841–1917). Published by Librairie Centrale des Beaux-Arts. Paris, France, 1897. Smithsonian Institution Libraries, Cooper-Hewitt, National Design Museum

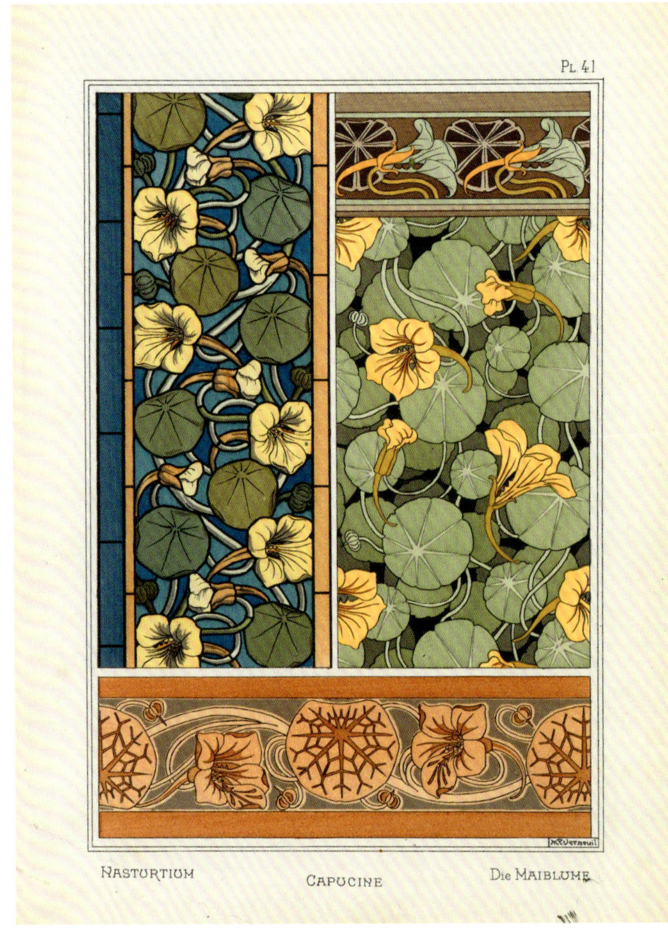

FIG. 10 *Capucine*, plate 41 from *La Plante et ses applications ornementales*

eighteenth-century art and republications of prints by rococo designers also appeared.[12] Individual collectors and social arbiters of taste further impacted the revival in the last quarter of the nineteenth century, the most compelling of whom were Edmond and Jules de Goncourt. The Goncourt brothers have been called "the bridge" between the intimate, organic rococo style of the eighteenth and the emerging *style moderne* of the late nineteenth century.[13] In their home in Auteuil, which housed their collection of eighteenth-century decorative arts in recreated interiors, they wrote their homages to such significant figures as Madame de Pompadour ("the godmother and queen of rococo") and Marie-Antoinette, and offered "primers of rococo design principles" in their "model home."[14] In their fiction writing, the Goncourts reinterpreted France's rococo patrimony in terms of the Romantic ideas of their time and of their own neuroses. They stressed the idea of the artist/designer as the creative genius with a "hyper-refined," visual, and nervous sensibility. They also subverted the elite, pleasure-seeking, charming rococo woman into an insatiable, greedy, and egotistical bourgeoise consumer.[15]

Edmond de Goncourt was among the aristocratic and middle-class collectors and amateurs in Paris who united to form the Society for the Decorative Arts Museum in 1877. Goncourt's friend Philippe de Chennevières was the president of the society, which sponsored a series of exhibitions from private collections of decorative-arts objects in the late 1870s and early 1880s. With the Central Union of Fine Arts Applied to Industry, it also published the *Revue des arts décoratifs* from 1880. The two organizations joined to become the Central Union of the Decorative Arts in 1882.[16]

The single most important influence in the development of Art Nouveau graphics was Japanese prints and their glorification of the natural world. Encouraged by the Japanese government, foreign travelers, and traders, Louis Comfort Tiffany and Arthur Liberty imported Japanese decorative arts and prints and showed them in their respective shops. Japanese crafts and prints were featured in the *Revue des arts décoratifs* and in *Le Japon artistique*, a journal founded by Bing in 1888. Writing for these journals and the *Gazette des Beaux-Arts*, Philippe Burty, a drawings and prints collector, urged the French to follow the Japanese example. By cultivating their own garden, refocusing on their native plants and flowers, and joining this study with their tradition of rococo organicism, the French could invent a new French style based on nature rather than historical models.[17]

For the designer Eugène Grasset (1841–1917), nature was a key element in his work. Grasset, like Lalique, built upon the ideas of Eugène Viollet-le-Duc, who, as chair of ornamental composition at the Ecole des arts décoratifs from 1834 on, advised designers to turn to nature for guidance concerning the structure of objects made of new materials.[18] In turn, Grasset exerted his own influence teaching at the Ecole normale d'enseignement du dessin in Paris and through his publications.

In *La Plante et ses applications ornementales*, produced by Grasset with the help of his students, the designer wrote that the "anemic" state of contemporary design rested on the "ruins of imitating the past," and that ornamentation based on natural forms was the path to achieving a new style.[19] Departing from the mid-century naturalists, however, he cautioned that nature should not be copied slavishly. It was necessary, he stated in *Méthode de composition ornementale*, that artisans understand natural phenomena and "extract a simplified principle whose clarity, stripped of all accessories, coincides with something in the brain."[20]

La Plante comprised seventy-two lithographic plates organized in suites, showing a flower or plant first as it appeared in nature then stylized into different motifs, such as a nasturtium along with two prints of the flower abstracted into a repetitive pattern (figs. 9, 10). In this book, Grasset and his publisher took advantage of color-printed photo relief printing, a new process which offered quicker, less costly production than straight lithography. It was one among many such European and North American publications from the last quarter of the century, including German Ernst Haeckle's *Kunstformen der Natur* (1899–1904).[21]

Grasset's designs for jewelry reflected his association with the French Symbolists. He was commissioned by the jewelry firm Maison Vever to design a series of brooches, combs, and buckles in which he incorporated the symbolic motifs of the time—peacocks, fish, snakes—for the 1900 Paris *Exposition Universelle*. Drawings for a number of these designs are in Cooper-Hewitt's collection, such as a brooch design of a woman swimming (or drawing) in the waves (fig. 11). The female figure in relation to water was a frequent rococo motif, suggesting sexual fertility and abundance;[22] but in the late nineteenth century, these elements were subverted to express a darker meaning. The woman's eyes and gaunt body implied something terrifying or malevolent rather than titillating—a benign rococo sea nymph became a tortured goddess or demon. Another drawing for a comb with a nymph rising from the waves played on the same haunting imagery (fig. 12). This sinister element of Grasset's designs affected at least one reviewer of the jewelry displays, Charles Saunier, who wrote that Grasset "has designed a series of jewels...which appear somewhat grim at first sight, but which obviously respond to a private and well thought out conception by that eminent artist."[23]

Grasset's contemporary Alphonse Mucha (1860–1939) was tapped by the Maison Fouquet jewelry firm to create attention-grabbing jewelry for the 1900 exposition. Mucha had already made his reputation as a popular poster designer for Sarah Bernhardt (for whom he designed nine posters between 1894–95 and 1900) and the *Salons des Cent* exhibitions (fig. 13), as well as for commercial enterprises. Most of his designs, which were published by F. Champenois,[24] featured a sensual, languid woman whose abundant hair, often decorated with flowers or jewelry, formed stylized spirals later derided as "macaroni."[25] For the display, Mucha developed a unique type of ornament, worn or wrapped around the chest, from which dangled enamel pendants, the largest of which often featured Mucha's classic female. One such piece (fig. 14) displayed a woman similar to her counterpart in Mucha's *Salons des Cent* poster. Henri Vever wrote that

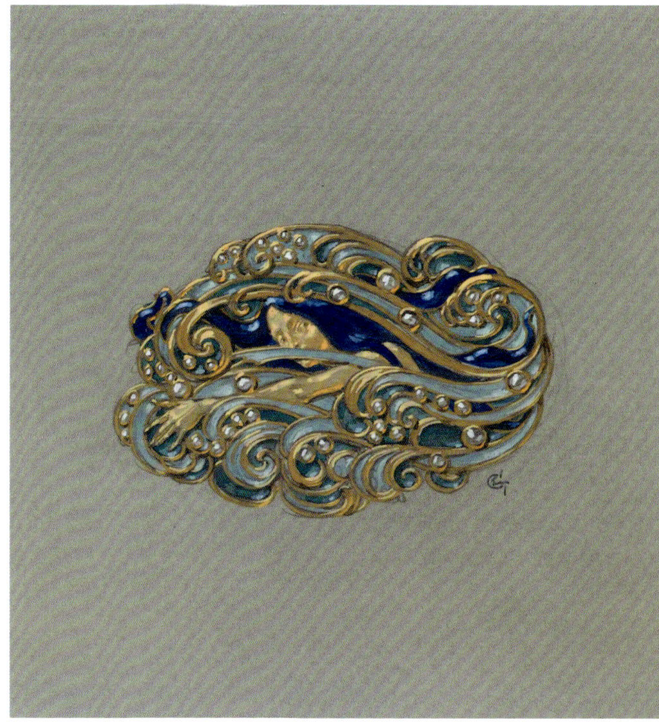

FIG. 11 *Design for a Brooch.* Eugène-Samuel Grasset (Swiss, active Paris, France, 1841–1917). France, ca. 1900. Brush and gouache, watercolor, graphite on blue-gray wove paper. Cooper-Hewitt, National Design Museum, Smithsonian Institution, Museum purchase through gift of Mrs. Henry B. du Pont, 1954-41-1

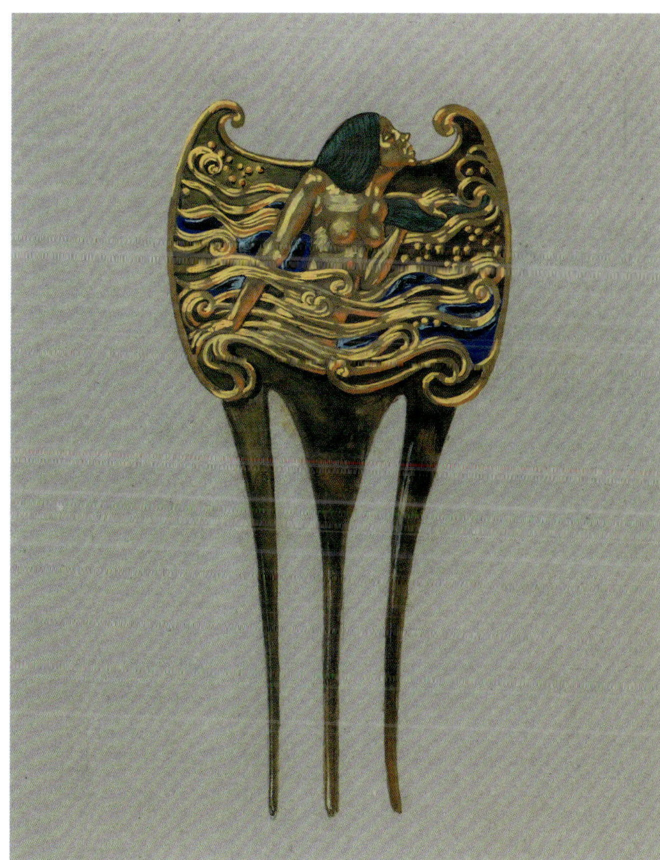

FIG. 12 *Design for a Nymph Comb.* Eugène-Samuel Grasset (Swiss, active Paris, France, 1841–1917). France, ca. 1900. Brush and gouache, watercolor, graphite on gray wove paper. Cooper-Hewitt, National Design Museum, Smithsonian Institution, Museum purchase through gift of Mrs. Gustav E. Kissel, 1950-6-5

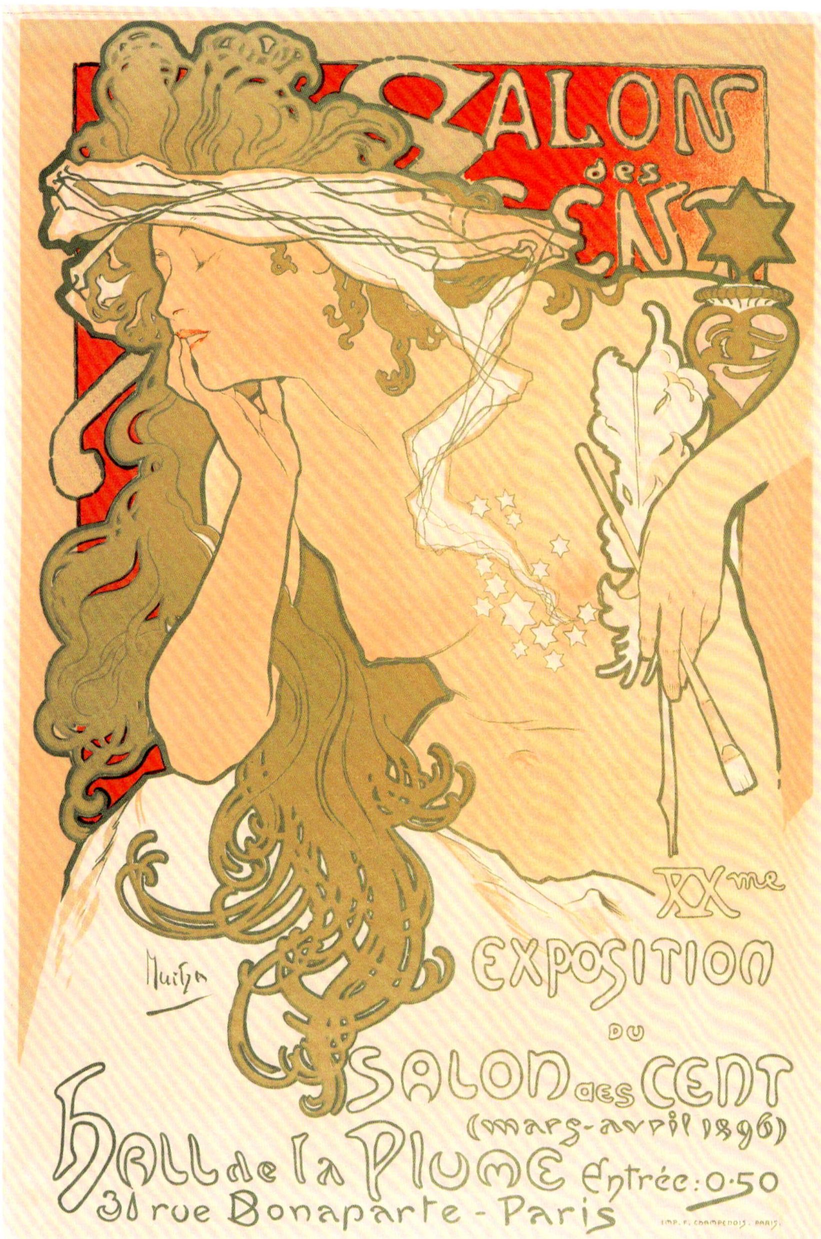

FIG. 13 *XXème Exposition du Salon des Cent.* Alphonse Maria Mucha (Czech, 1860–1939). Printed by F. Champenois. Paris, France, 1896. Lithograph, printed in gold metallic ink, dark gray-green, light olive gray, light yellow brown, deep red. The Museum of Modern Art, Gift of Ludwig Charell, 170.1956

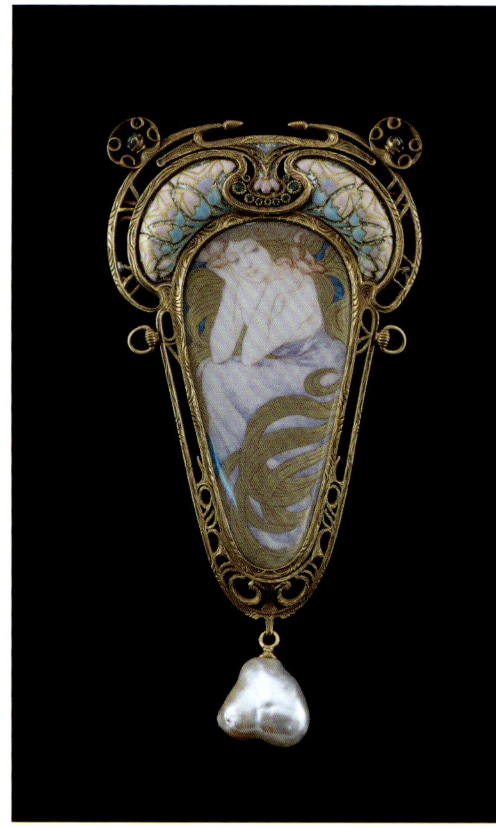

FIG. 14 Bodice adornment. Alphonse Maria Mucha (Czech, 1860–1939). Georges Fouquet. France, ca. 1900. Gold, enamel, emeralds, baroque pearl, watercolor and metallic paint, mother-of-pearl. Virginia Museum of Fine Arts, Richmond. Gift of Syndey and Frances Lewis, 85.253

these elaborate jewels, "although thought slightly eccentric...justifiably attracted a good deal of attention."[26]

Two years later, Mucha produced a design-pattern portfolio similar to Grasset's entitled *Documents décoratifs*. Comprising seventy-two lithographic plates, it was a visual encyclopedia of his designs for furniture, metalwork, and other objects (fig. 15), as well as studies on abstracting or stylizing flowers into designs.[27] Mucha's textile designs for the fabric manufacturer C.-G. Forrer applied his abstractions from nature to flat patterning. One Mucha textile design in Cooper-Hewitt's collection uses meandering sprays of anemones, apple blossoms, and narcissi with a generic vine in background.[28] (fig. 16) A similar design, *Femme à Marguerite*, was produced by the major Alsatian firm Scheurer, Lauth & Cie in velveteen (fig. 17), cotton sateen, and ribbed cotton in several different colorways; the fabric was used to make pillows or applied to screens.[29] Mucha left Paris in 1904 for the United States, where he produced several posters, the most famous of which employed his iconic female to advertise the 1904 Saint Louis Exposition.

Mucha and Grasset's contemporary René Lalique (1860–1945) far exceeded them in originality and brilliance as a designer of Art Nouveau jewelry. Having apprenticed with a jeweler and studied ornamental composition, he also pursued a lifelong study of nature in drawings and photographs. His observations of the wildflowers in his native Champagne and rarer floral species and of animals and insects such as swans, bats, birds, and dragonflies provided the unusual repertory for his jewelry.

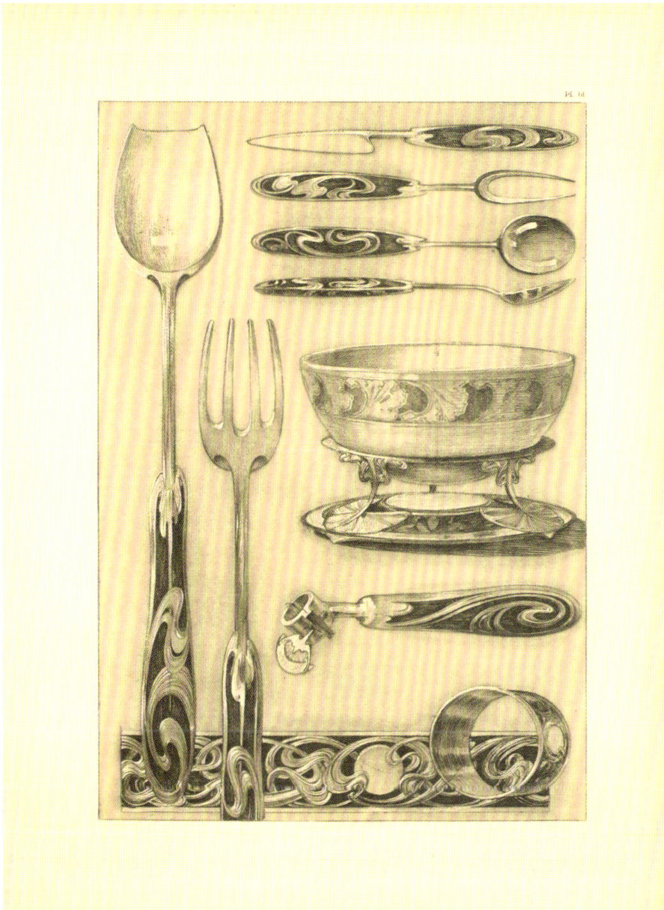

FIG. 15 *Silverware*, plate 61 from *Documents décoratifs*. Alphonse Maria Mucha (Czech, 1860–1939). Published by Librairie Centrale des Beaux-Arts. Paris, France, 1902. General Research Division, The New York Public Library, Astor, Lenox, and Tilden Foundations

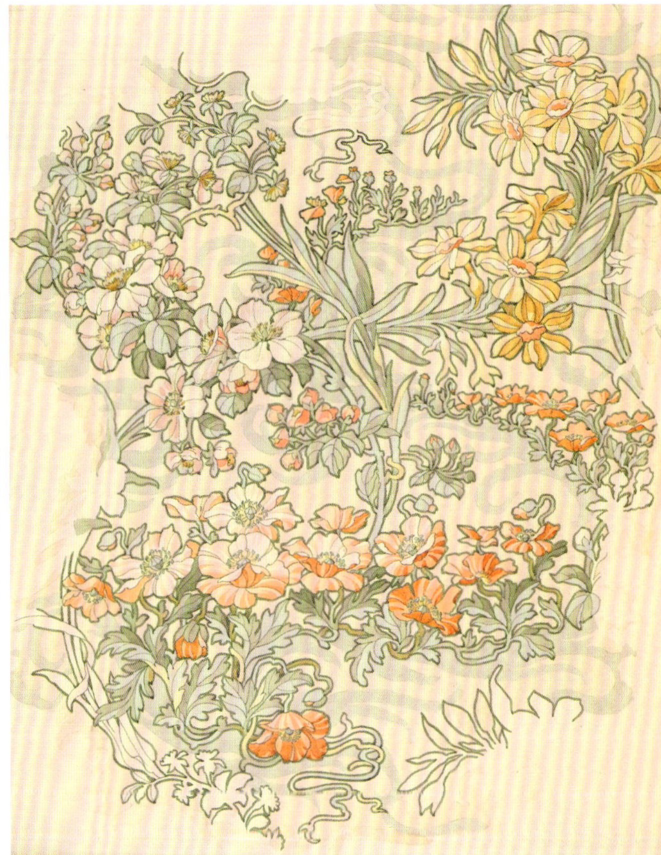

FIG. 16 *Anemones, Apple Blossoms, and Narcissi*. Alphonse Maria Mucha (Czech, 1860–1939). France, 1897–98. Brush and watercolor, graphite on dark cream wove paper. Cooper-Hewitt, National Design Museum, Smithsonian Institution, Museum purchase from Drawings and Prints Council Fund, 1999-58-1

By 1887, Lalique set up his own business, producing jewels and supplying designs for firms such as Boucheron and Vever. His fascination with cloisonné and pliqué-à-jour enameling, which he adopted in place of traditional gemstones, as well as non-precious stones like opals and new materials such as ivory and horn, completely changed the look of late nineteenth-century jewelry.[30] His *Design for a Diadem*, with its band of rococo cartouches in silver against a gold diaper-patterned ground, shows that he was also conversant with rococo (and gothic) design.[31]

An important feature of Lalique's jewelry was the comb. In his article "On Combs" in *Le Japon Artistique*, Théodore Duret described and illustrated a variety of Japanese combs, bringing this aspect of Japanese design to the attention of receptive Paris jewelers and their clientele.[32] Lalique featured nine large tortoiseshell, ivory, and horn combs in his display in the 1898 Salon, which were "very Japanese in flavor.[33]

One comb with a fish motif (fig. 18) particularly attracted the attention of Raitif de la Bretonne (Jean Lorrain), who wrote in the May 22 *Journal* about "the large fins and the head with gaping gills...whose twisted body resembles images in Japanese prints. The animal arches its back and twists in the transparent horn captured in the vitrified lacquer...It is the subject of the decoration itself, the blue-green life of water frozen in the material of the comb."[34] This description corresponds to a Lalique drawing in Cooper-Hewitt's collection, *Comb Design with "Flying Fish" Motif* (fig. 19), a spectacular watercolor and gouache study (which

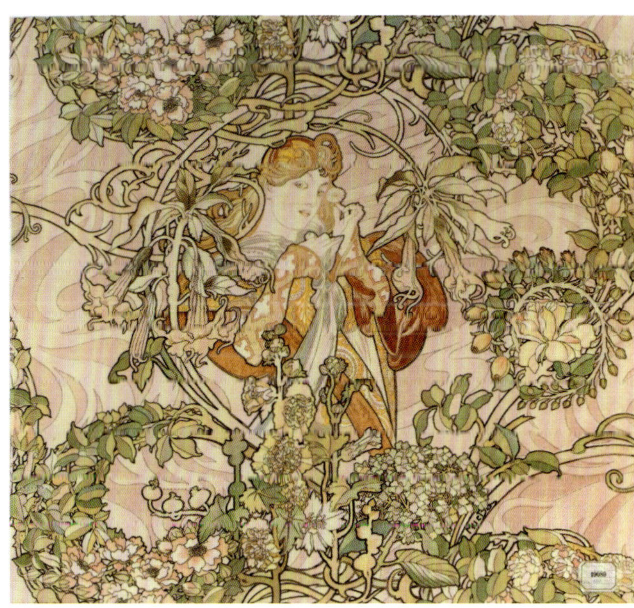

FIG. 17 *Femme à Marguerite*. Alphonse Maria Mucha (Czech, 1860–1939). Manufactured by Scheurer, Lauth & Cie. Thann, France, ca. 1898–1900. Printed cotton velvet. Cooper-Hewitt, National Design Museum, Smithsonian Institution, Museum purchase from General Acquisitions Endowment Fund, 2004-6-2

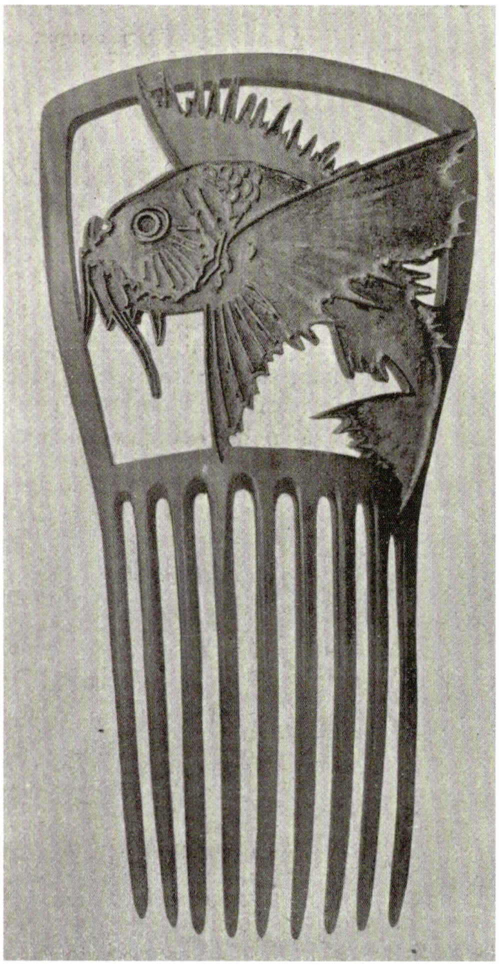

FIG. 18 Comb, page 170 from *Art et Décoration*, vol. 3. René Lalique (French, 1860–1945). Published by Editions Albert Lévy. Paris, France, 1898. General Research Division, The New York Public Library, Astor, Lenox, and Tilden Foundations

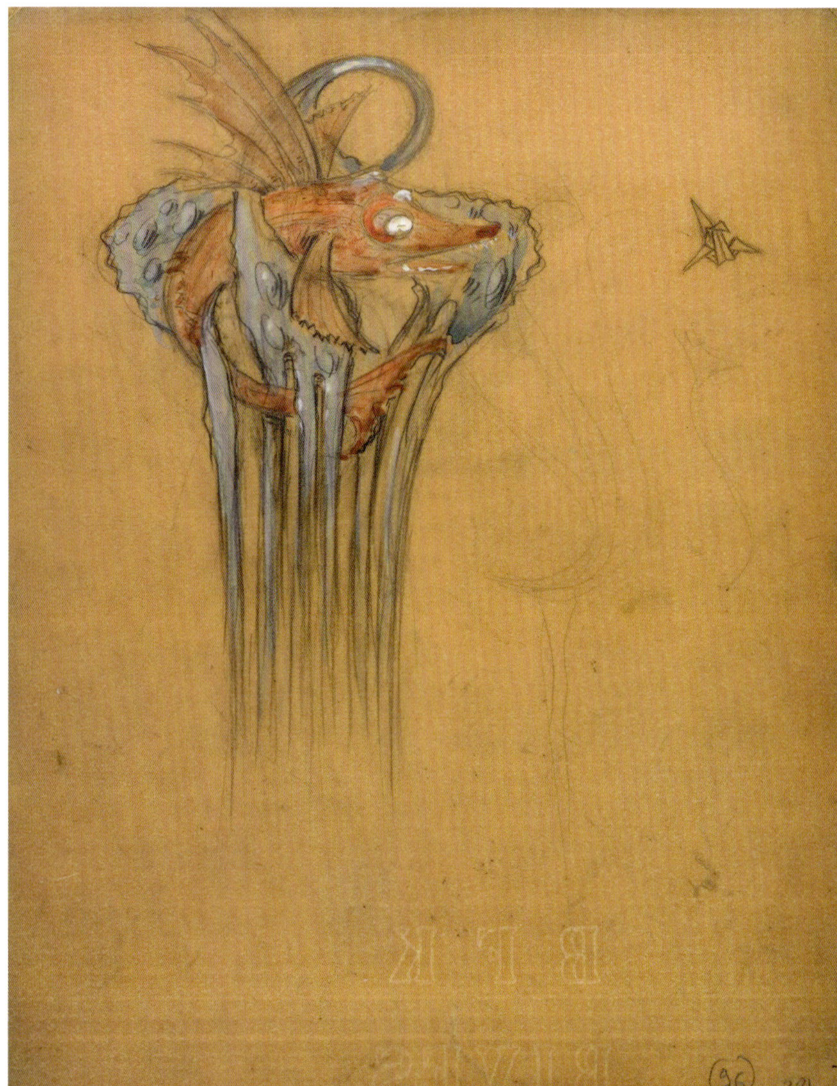

FIG. 19 *Design for a Comb with "Flying Fish" Motif.* René Lalique (French, 1860–1945). France, 1904–06. Graphite, brush, and watercolor, white gouache on brown wove paper, possibly coated with resin. Cooper-Hewitt, National Design Museum, Smithsonian Institution, Museum purchase from General Acquisitions Endowment and Smithsonian Institution Collections Acquisition Funds, 1998-10-1

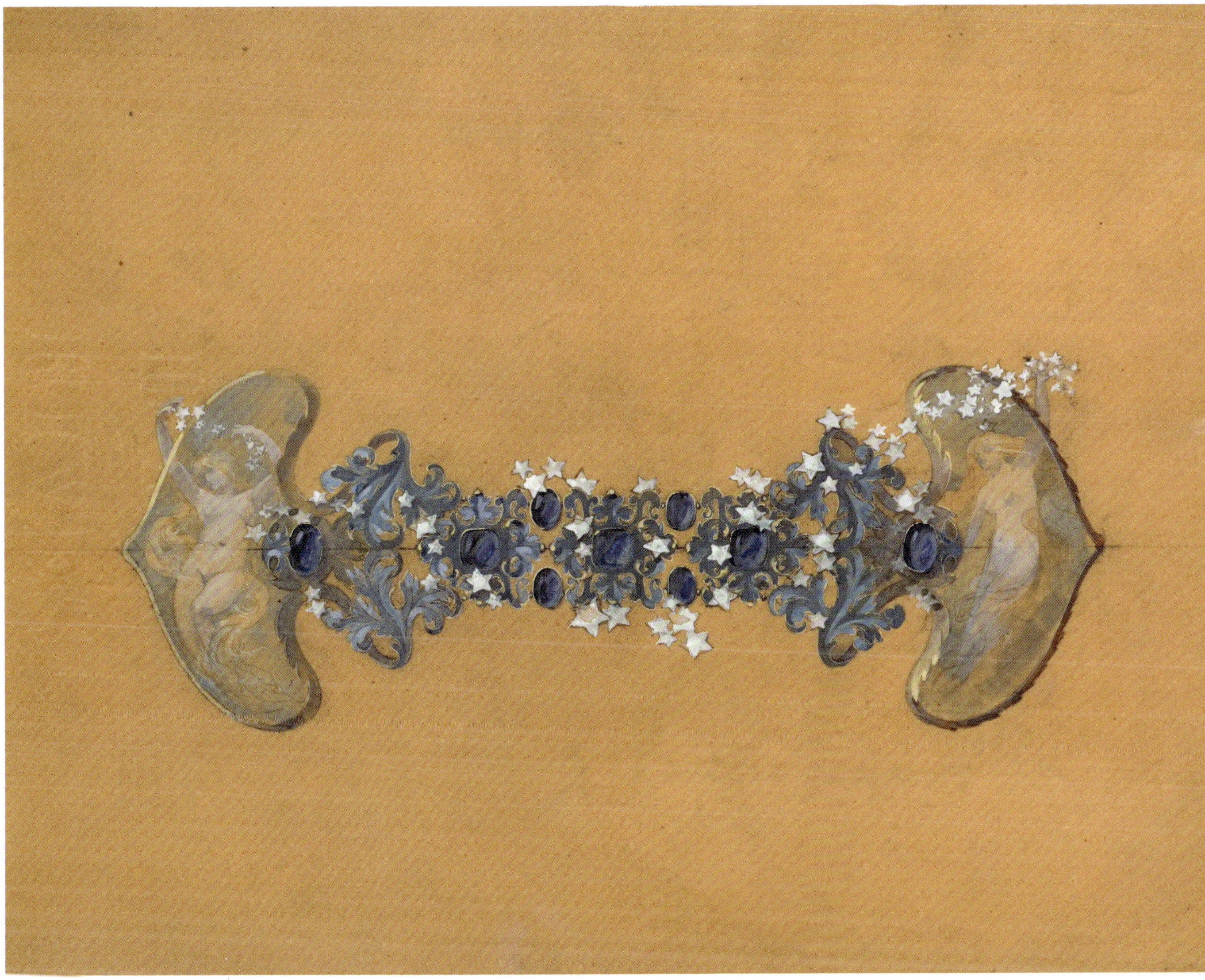

FIG. 20 *Design for a Corsage Ornament: Night.* René Lalique (French, 1860–1945). France, before 1900. Brush and watercolor, graphite, brush and gouache on brown wove paper, possibly coated with resin. Cooper-Hewitt, National Design Museum, Smithsonian Institution, Museum purchase from Drawings and Prints Council Fund through gift of The Florence Gould Foundation, 1998-50-1

includes a sketch of an origami bird in the upper right corner) on the Rives paper Lalique used for all of his drawings. The design has characteristically darkened considerably due to a coating (possibly resin) to make the paper translucent, heightening the design's impact. While the drawing could date from the 1898 exhibition but deemed too difficult to execute, it might also come from a later point in Lalique's career, around 1904–06, when the designer was creating a series of adornments using the fish motif.[35]

The rare and important *Design for a Corsage Ornament*, known as the "Night Brooch," represents another category Lalique treated in his jewelry, the expression of literary ideas—in this case, the drama of light and darkness and the passage of time (fig. 20). Created for his fabulous display at the Paris 1900 World Exposition,[36] the Night Brooch showed in enamel two sinuous female nudes (personifications of Night) tossing a shower of stars into the azure blue evening sky, while the Milky Way, a curving line of shimmering diamonds, sparkles in the heavens. Enchanted by this allegory and the magical bijou, the critic Pol Neveux commented that "no work of symbolism of finer and more eloquent execution has been produced for many centuries in the history of the goldsmith's art."[37] According to Vever, Lalique's exposition display "gained a victory without equal; an avid and tight crowd jostles to see his work…critics of art hostile to the new genre of which Lalique was one of the creators are rare, and many are considered absolute enthusiasts."[38]

As in the eighteenth century, nineteenth-century works on paper served as transmitters of design concepts and models to people in the design professions and to consumers. With new printing technologies came new forms of communication to disseminate the style, and Art Nouveau converted an unprecedented audience to the spirit and charms of rococo.

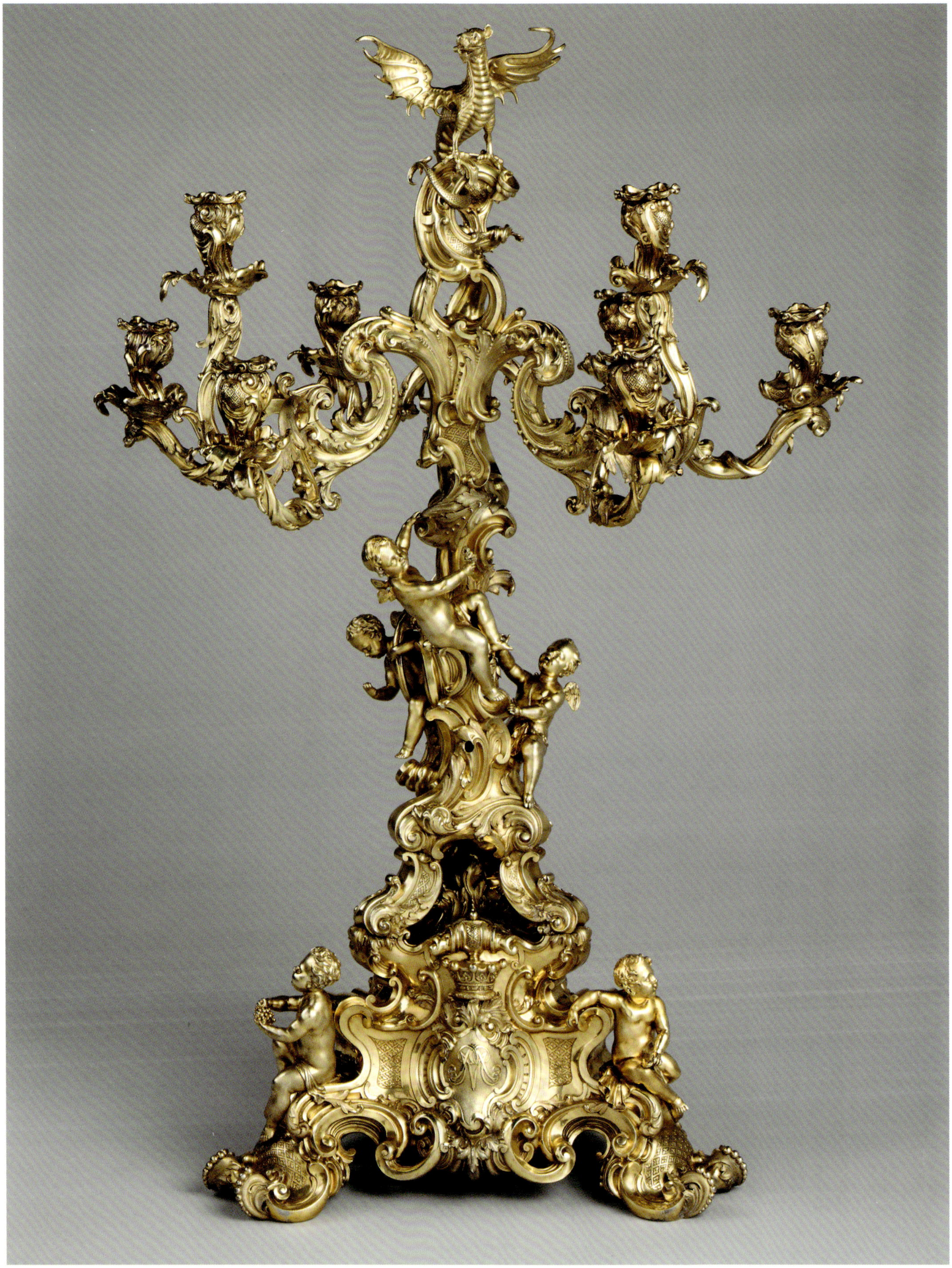

fig. 4 Candelabrum centerpiece, engraved with the intials "P" and "M" and an earl's coronet for Robert Herbert, twelfth Earl of Pembroke and Montgomery. Paul Storr (English, 1771–1844). England, 1835–36. Silver gilt. Metropolitan Museum of Art, Bequest of Rupert L. Joseph, 60.55.10a-s

The Rococo Revival in English and American Nineteenth-century Silver

Sarah D. Coffin

Rococo design enjoyed revivals in England earlier in the nineteenth century than in other countries. Rundell, Bridge & Rundell,[1] goldsmiths to the Crown, filled a royal commission in 1803 to augment pieces made in a rococo marine style by Nicholas Sprimont in 1742. While these represented reproductions or extensions of existing sets, that objects in rococo style were commissioned indicates a revival of interest and use. In addition to apparent revival works, which may have differed subtly from their eighteenth-century forebears, especially in weight, there were original designs with rococo elements from this period (fig. 1).

Much of the enthusiasm for the rococo-revival spirit in England could be ascribed to the taste of the Prince of Wales, later Prince Regent and George IV (1762–1830), a flamboyant character who loved French decorative objects, especially Sèvres porcelain, which he imported even after his father George III imposed a trade embargo with France and the two countries were at war.

The prince regent's decadent nature gravitated to the sensuous scrolls of early Louis XV rococo, but the continued interest in classical antiquity in England created an environment where the two styles mixed. In the case of the prince regent and his brothers, the favored neoclassical elements related more to luxurious interpretations of the late Louis XV and Louis XVI periods (ca. 1760–89) than to pared-down versions of anti-monarchist Empire France. During the Regency (1810–20), George and his brother Frederick Augustus, Duke of York, patronized makers of high-quality, robust works of rococo silver.

Like Frederick, Prince of Wales, eldest son of George II, before him, Frederick Augustus was a profligate spender and an enthusiast of rococo. He did much to foster historicism in silver design, under the influence of Kensington Lewis,[2] an antiquarian, retailer, and purveyor of designs of all periods. Lewis channeled the Duke of York's spending to Edward Farrell (ca. 1775/81–1850) (fig. 2), a London goldsmith of enormous talent but less renown than Paul Storr, Benjamin Smith, Benjamin Rundell, John Bridge, or Robert Garrard I and II, whose firms enjoyed more extensive royal patronage. Much of Farrell's production included marine motifs, often as part of elaborate concoctions which referenced rococo design both in details and spirit. These motifs and related rockwork, or rocaille, were popular in the 1740s, as demonstrated in the work of Nicholas Sprimont, the Liège-born silversmith who later headed the Chelsea porcelain manufactory (See Coffin, p. 124, figs. 40, 41). A variety of early nineteenth-century English silversmiths employed them, though not always in a rococo context.

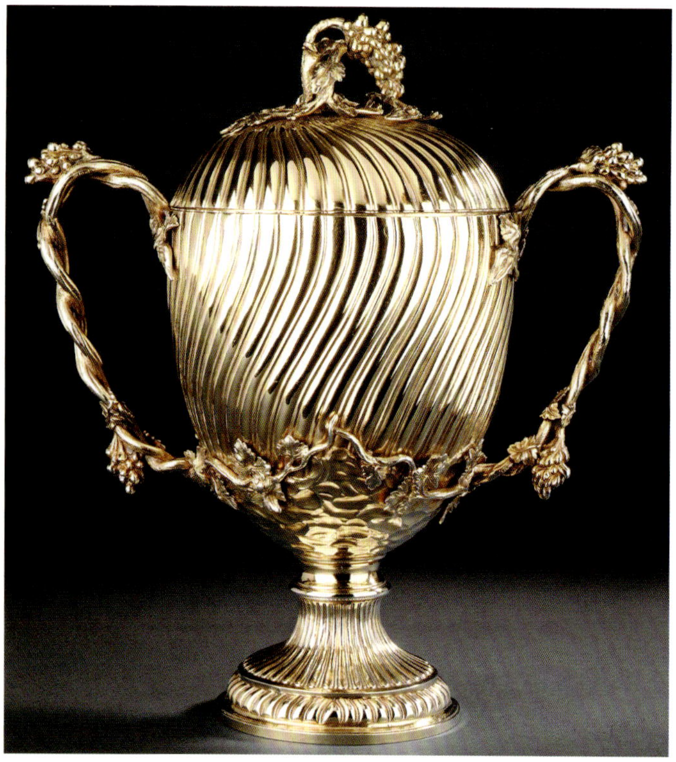

FIG. 1 Wine cooler. William, William, and John Frisbee (English, active in partnership 1811–20). London, England, 1810–11. Silver, gilt. A. M. Marks Ltd., London, England

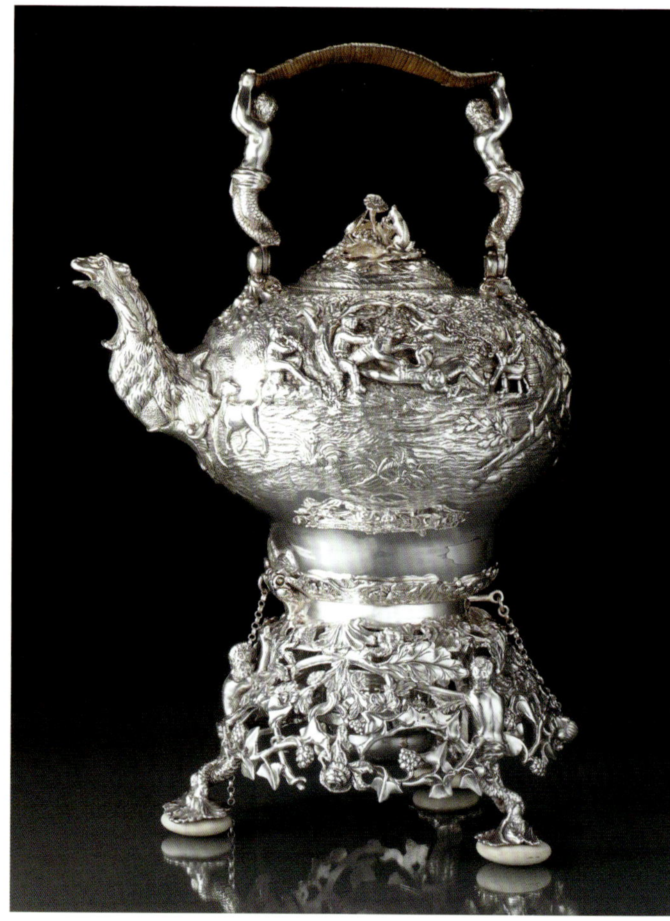

FIG. 2 Kettle on lamp stand. Edward Farrell (English, active 1813–22). London, England, 1817. Silver. Sotheby's

Arguably the most widely recognized and important English silversmith of the era was Paul Storr (1771–1844),[3] whose quality of workmanship and versatility enabled him to create works that suited any taste. It is not surprising, therefore, that extraordinary rococo creations could be found among his oeuvre, though he was best known for his classically inspired pieces. Storr's salver (fig. 3), featuring signs of the Zodiac, had a border cast and chased with rococo scrolls, further rococo decoration on the surface, and feet in rococo-cartouche form. A remarkably pure grouping of rococo motifs, this salver nonetheless had its feet firmly set in the nineteenth century.

The arrival to the throne of William IV (r. 1830–37), younger brother of George IV, did not create a radical change in style, but the tendency toward opulent forms grew. The end of his reign and the arrival of the young Victoria as queen in 1837 caused a flowering, in almost literal terms, of the arts, as the sentimental and curvilinear prevailed. Among the most monumental of works created in the rococo idiom of this era was Storr's large candelabrum (fig. 4), whose flowing branches and undulating surfaces were completely rococo in feeling without being a direct quotation of the eighteenth century.

By the late 1820s, there developed, alongside commissions for the aristocracy, a broader market for an anti-classical style, which produced a rather different expression of rococo in England and the United States. Manufacturers in Birmingham and Sheffield became mass-producers not only of Sheffield plate, a layered combination of silver and copper, but also of silver with embossed scrolls, flowers, and foliage, all of which was created cheaply by steam presses on thin silver. These wares were made to imply a luxury not previously available on thin-sheeted silver, and were broadly marketed at home as well as exported to the United States. Ironically, this style, which used scrolls and other rococo characteristics, often did not comprise as much rococo spirit as other pieces in which rococo was used in an eclectic mix. Instead, it took the enthusiasm for naturalism and equated it with rococo, producing decoration which gave new meaning to *horror vacui*. However, some of the silver produced in these cities aimed to compete for London's clientele by including more informed decoration and heavier-gauge silver (fig. 5).

In the United States, Samuel Kirk (1792–1872) of Baltimore was an exception to the declining caliber of works often represented by rococo style. His earlier pieces, in particular of the 1820s and 1830s, showed an

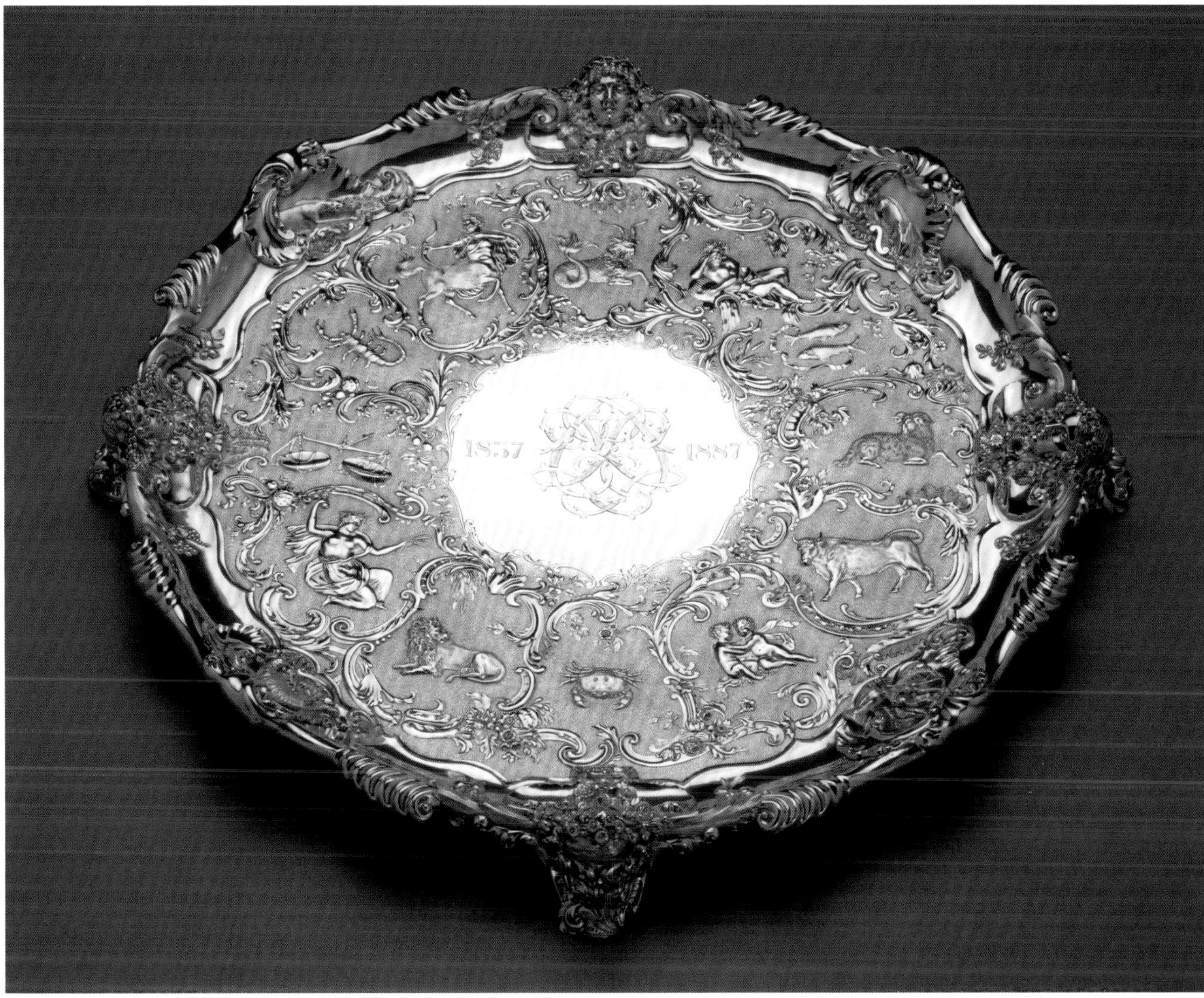

FIG. 3 Salver with signs of the zodiac. Paul Storr (English, 1771–1844). London, England, 1827. Silver. Hillwood Estate, Museum & Gardens; Gift of Mrs. Augustus Riggs, 1974.12.408

understanding of the eighteenth-century sources (fig. 6). Unlike some early nineteenth-century American silversmiths who allowed their work to dip below sterling standard, or others who stuck with classical motifs, Kirk used, along with Andrew Warner, also of Baltimore, a hallmarking system for sterling-standard silver while incorporating free-spirited rococo motifs on silver of heavier gauge. A few others, such as Osmon Reed of Philadelphia, adopted a similar style (fig. 7). Bailey and Kitchen, a Philadelphia firm, used a much more restrained rococo in the 1830s when it created a silver tureen (fig. 8) in the year of Victoria's accession in England.

The decline in quality of the decorative arts in England, whether through shoddy workmanship or confused design, was the main inspiration for the organization of major art and design fairs, most notably the 1851 *Great Exhibition of the Works of Industry of All Nations*, also known as the Crystal Palace exhibition, in London. Prince Albert, who saw the need to bring the kind of high-quality English craftsmanship patronized by foreign courts to a broader, domestic base, instigated a move to establish exhibitions, museums, schools, and discourse to better educate people about design. That rococo eventually filtered to all levels of society is evident in the numerous card cases by Nathaniel Mills & Sons from Birmingham (fig. 9). Their mixed use of rococo scrolls with popular Gothic motifs was typical not only of nineteenth-century English objects but also of some eighteenth-century English rococo designs as well.

An example of the objects of quality sought from abroad is an 1841 wine cooler by Mortimer and Hunt, successors to Paul Storr, commissioned for the Russian Prince Worontsov-Dashkov (fig. 10). It shows familiarity with the firm's collection of sixteenth- to eighteenth-century engravings, including one for a vase by the French artist Jean-François Saly (1717–1776) (fig. 11), a version of which was owned by Storr and Mortimer.[4]

The Crystal Palace exhibition and its offspring in New York in 1853 were occasions for which many firms created bold displays of their craftsmanship and design. The illustrated Crystal Palace catalogue featured a candelabrum by Hunt and Roskell for the Marquess of Tweeddale, which comprised a scene from Scottish history surrounded by rococo scrolls (fig. 12); the firm produced a simpler, but more completely rococo, variant of the candelabrum, with six lights, in 1852 (fig. 13). Another exhibition piece, a ewer depicting Andromeda and sea nymphs with Neptune and

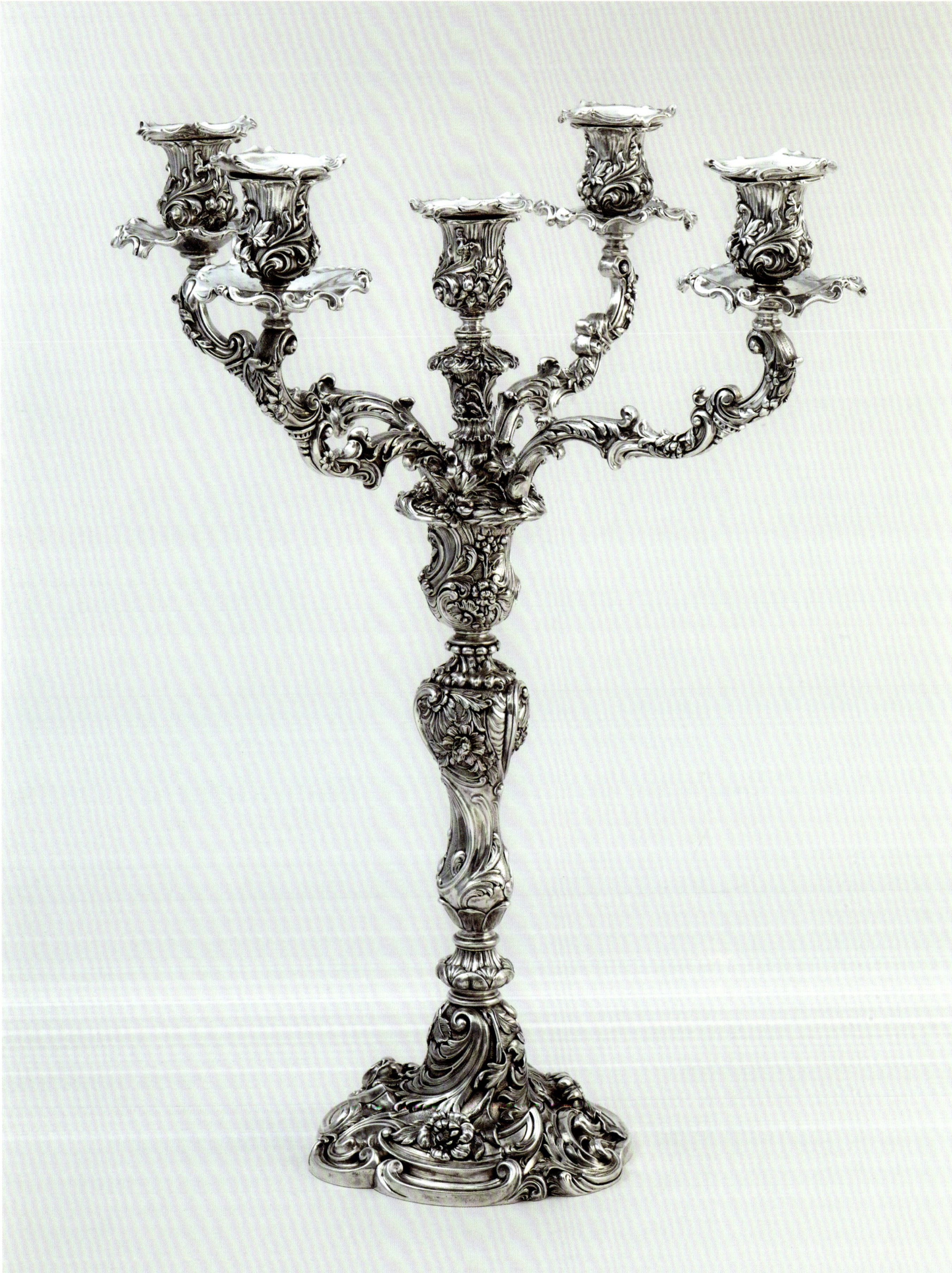

FIG. 5 Candelabrum. Edward, Edward Jr., John, and William Barnard (English, active in partnership 1829–ca. 1853). London, England, 1832–33. Silver. Cooper-Hewitt, National Design Museum, Smithsonian Institution, Gift of anonymous donor, 1952-166-99-a/c

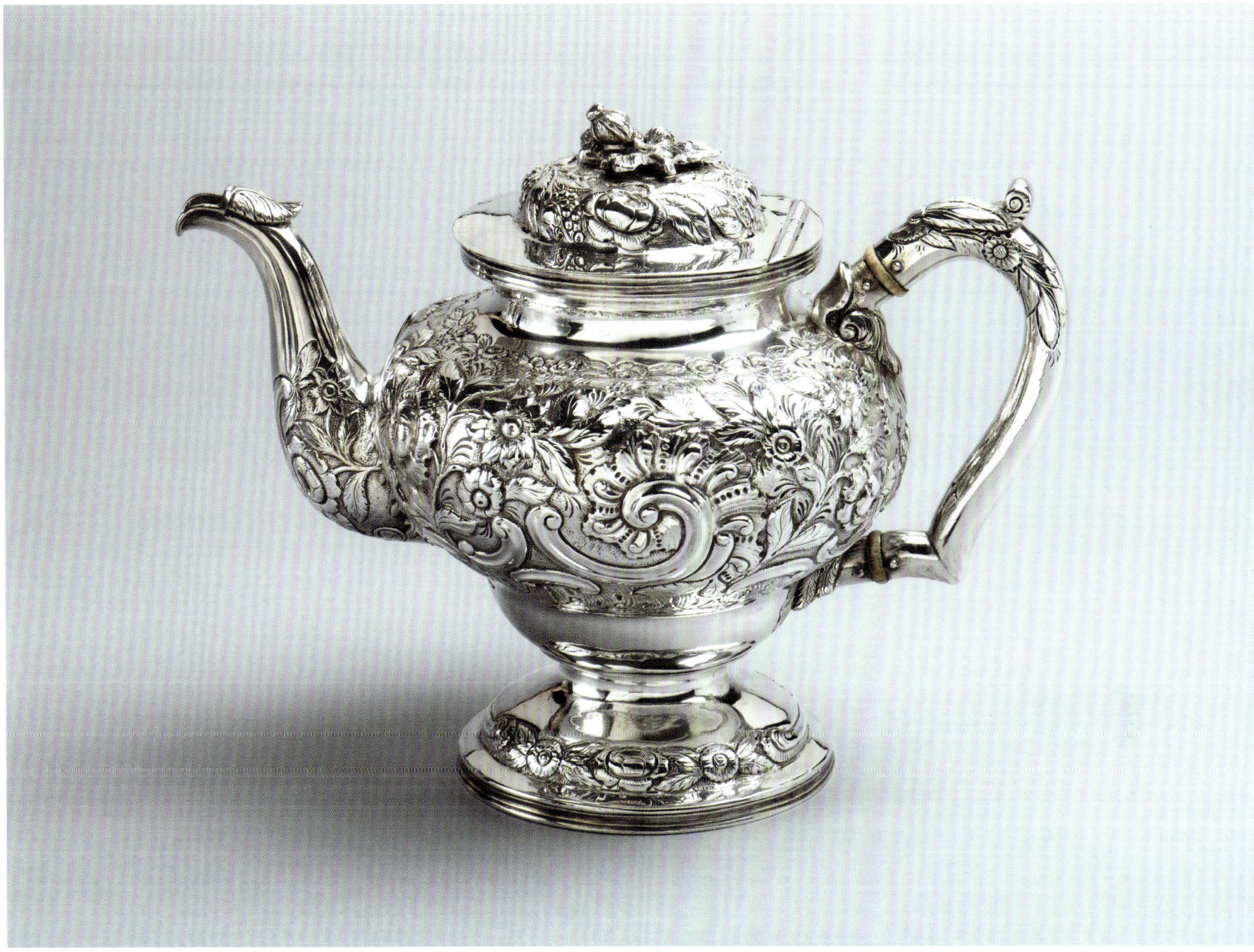

FIG. 6 Teapot. Samuel Kirk (American, active 1821–72). Baltimore, MD, 1830–46. Silver, ivory. Cooper-Hewitt, National Design Museum, Smithsonian Institution, Gift of Allyn Cox, 1976-109-1-a/e

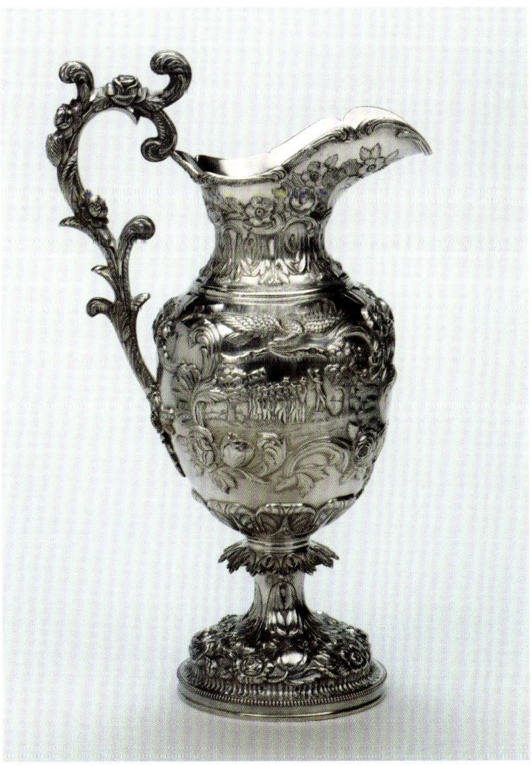

FIG. 7 Presentation ewer. Osmon Reed (American, active 1833–63). United States, 1843. Silver. Philadelphia Museum, Purchased with the Joseph E. Temple Fund, 1902-6

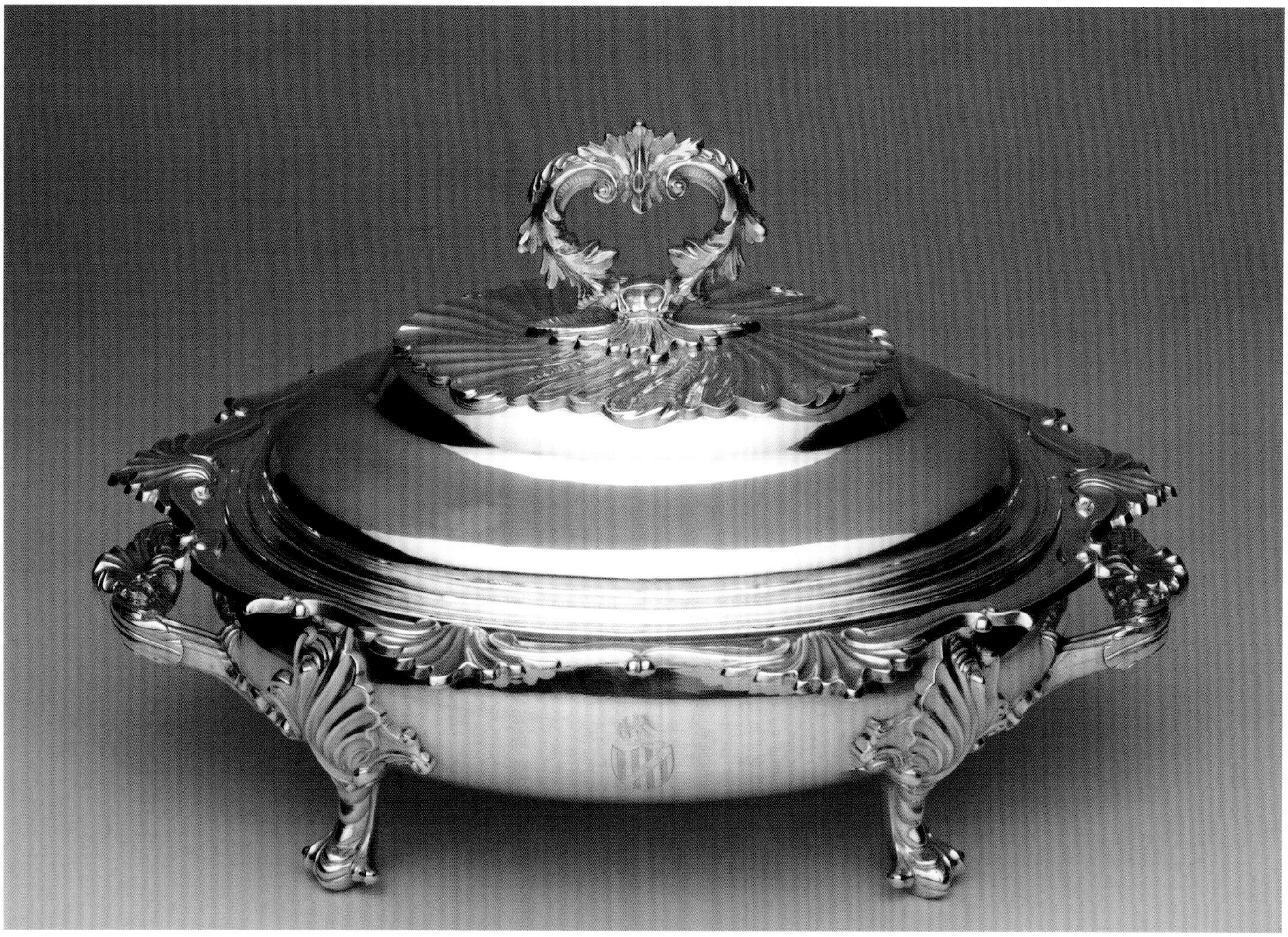

FIG. 8 Entrée dish and cover. Bailey & Kitchen. United States, ca. 1837. Silver. The Metropolitan Museum of Art, Purchase, Edward and Kathleen Scheider Gift, 2003.382a-c

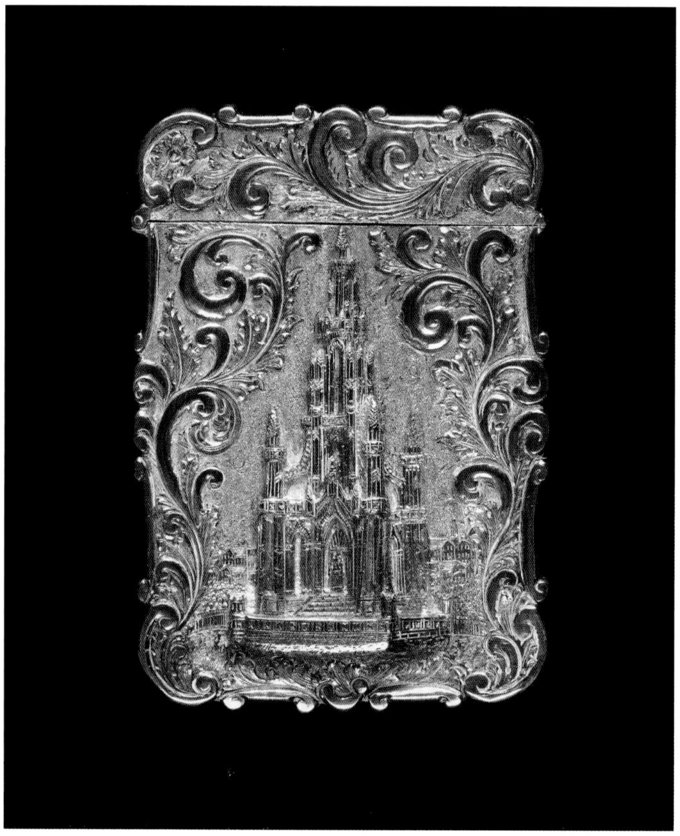

FIG. 9 Card case. Nathaniel Mills & Sons. Birmingham, England, 1845–46. Silver. Cooper-Hewitt, National Design Museum, Smithsonian Institution, Gift of Sarah and Eleanor Hewitt, 1931-48-97

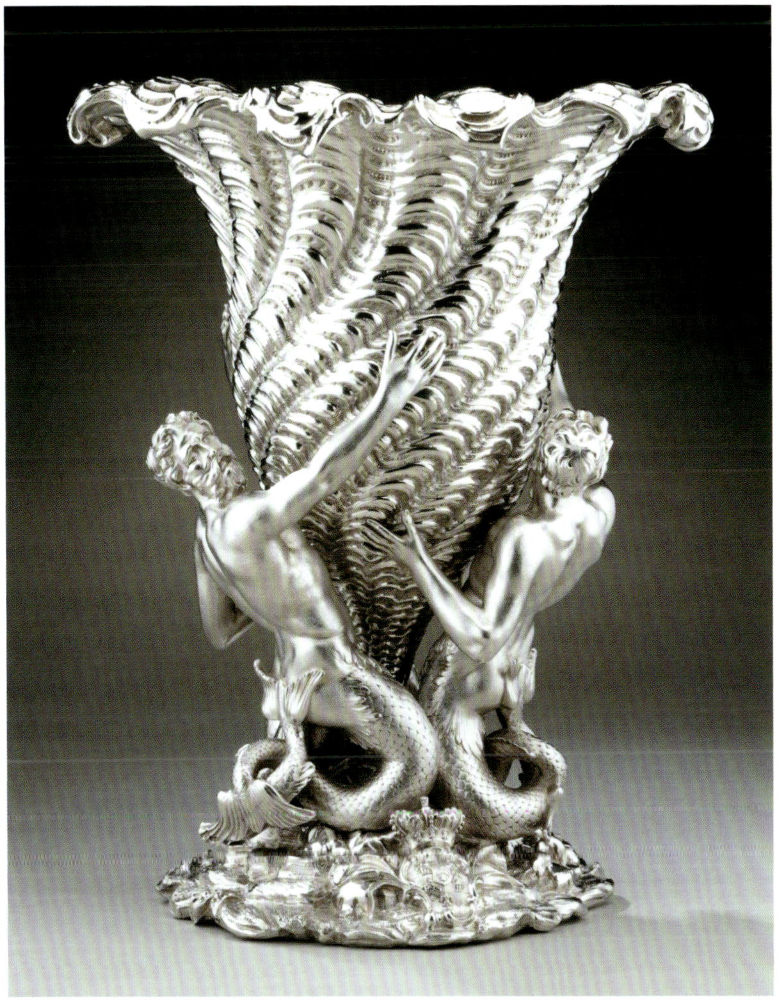

FIG. 10 Wine cooler/caviar pail. Edward Hodges Baily (English, 1788–1867). Made by John Mortimer and John Samuel Hunt (English, active 1839–42). England, 1841. Silver. Carnegie Museum of Art, Bequest of Joan B. Lappe-Bowman, 94.24.A-B

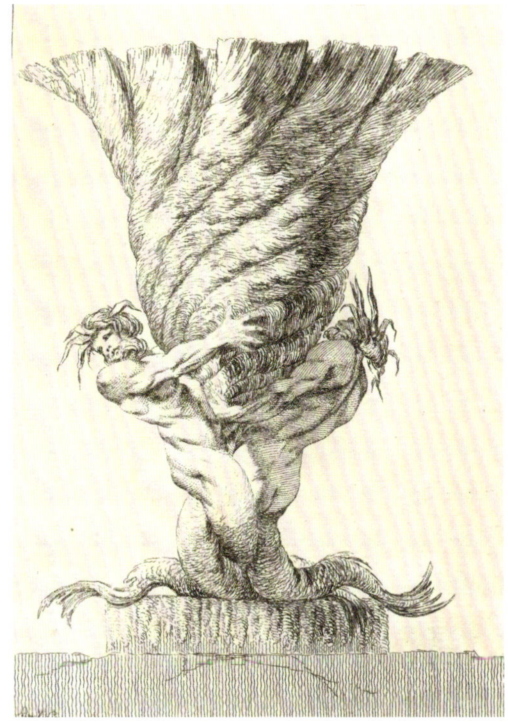

FIG. 11 *Première Suite de Vases Antiques d'après Saly et autres.* After Jacques-François-Joseph Saly (French, 1717–1776). Paris, France, 1746. Etching on off-white laid paper. Cooper-Hewitt, National Design Museum, Smithsonian Institution, Purchased for the Museum by the Advisory Council, 1921-6-478-1

sea horses (fig. 14), combined rococo and marine elements with earlier design sources.

Many of the most truly rococo works in metal from French firms, or based on Parisian designs, were in ormolu, or bronze covered in finely ground gold. Parisian designers responded to the desire of Napoleon III and his wife Eugénie to lend legitimacy to their court through stylistic references to the ancien régime, in the forms of the Louis XV style and its use of ormolu. In addition, Frenchmen were employed by Elkington and other British firms to bring French designs to English silver and silver-plate.

The discovery of the Comstock lode in Nevada in 1862 made silver plentiful in the United States. This abundance, combined with the creative energies of Edward C. Moore (1827–1891) and others at Tiffany & Company and the Gorham Company, helped American silver design come into its own at a time when rococo style was part of the design vocabulary. While continuing to find sources in England and continental Europe, American designers also led stylistic innovations such as Japonism, although many foreign-born designers or craftsmen led the initiative. Among other original concepts was the rococo-style overlaying of silver onto ceramic and glass objects (fig. 15).

The early Arts and Crafts aesthetic did not have much in common with rococo design, and did not lead to much English silver made in Art Nouveau style. There were some vivid exceptions, however. An English charger by Latino Movio incorporated seventeenth-century-style naturalism with rococo's organic, wavy designs (fig. 16). In addition to buckles by Archibald Knox for Liberty (See Hunter-Stiebel, p. 208, fig. 1), there was also some rococo-spirited Art Nouveau American silver and gold jewelry and British Aesthetic moment silver at the end of the century (fig. 17). Englishman William Christmas Codman (1831–1921) designed and supervised the production of a line of limited-edition silver called "Martelé" ("hammered" in French) for the Gorham Company (fig. 18). Their sensuous, flowing motifs, such as waves, female forms, and fish, embodied rococo spirit in the way they shook off all the historicism and classicism of late nineteenth- and early twentieth-century Beaux-Arts style. The dressing table, with its mirror and stool reflect the feminine form, as the ewer and basin reflect water, both so much a part of rococo spirit (See Stiebel, p. 209, fig. 2). For the dressing table and stool, the silver was used in new and exciting ways, creating an eighteenth-century rococo furniture type which dared to seduce its user and onlooker with sumptuous curves.

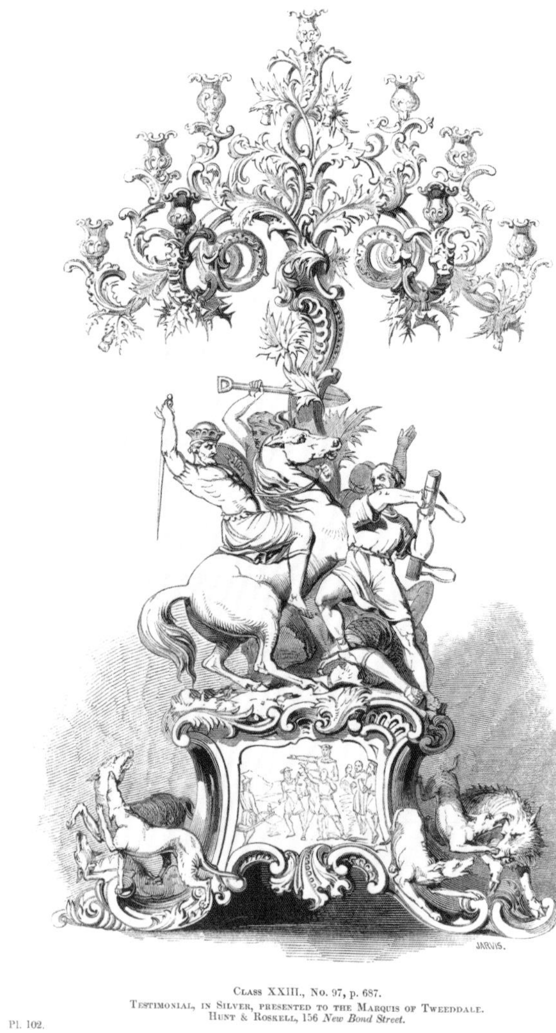

FIG. 12 Testimonial in Silver Presented to the Marquis of Tweedale, plate 102 from *Official Descriptive and Illustrated Catalogue / by authority of the Royal Commission*, vol. 2. Hunt & Roskell late Storr & Mortimer. Published by Spicer. England, before 1851. Bound volume. Smithsonian Institution Libraries, Cooper-Hewitt, National Design Museum, f T690 .D62 1851

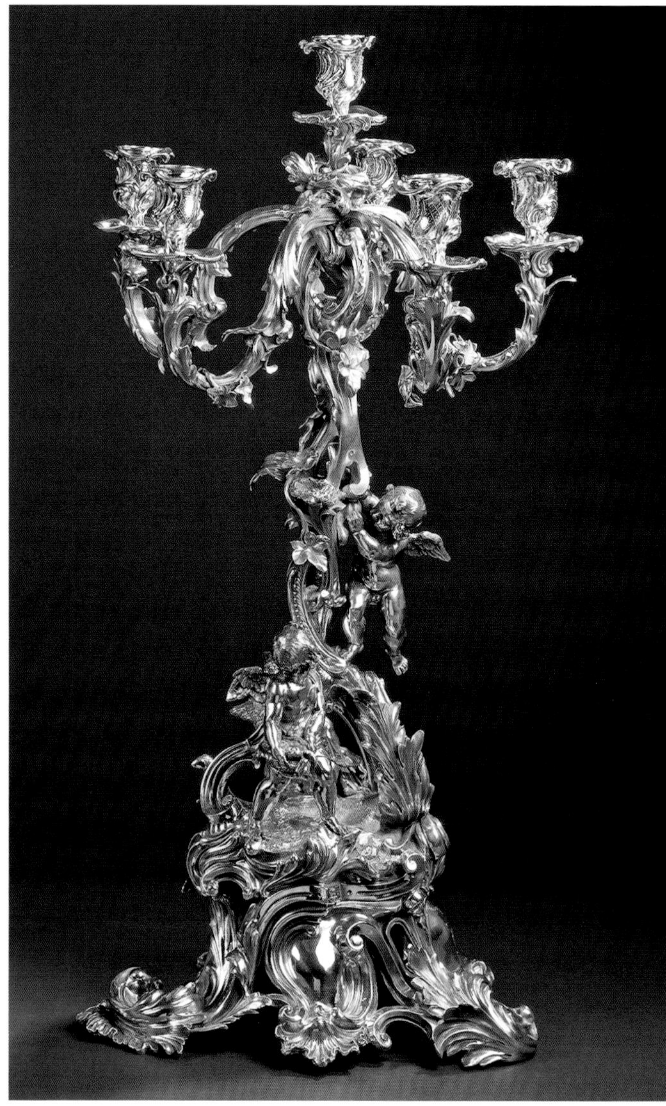

FIG. 13 Candelabrum. John Samuel Hunt, John Hunt & Robert Roskell. London, England, 1852. Silver. A. M. Marks Ltd., London, England

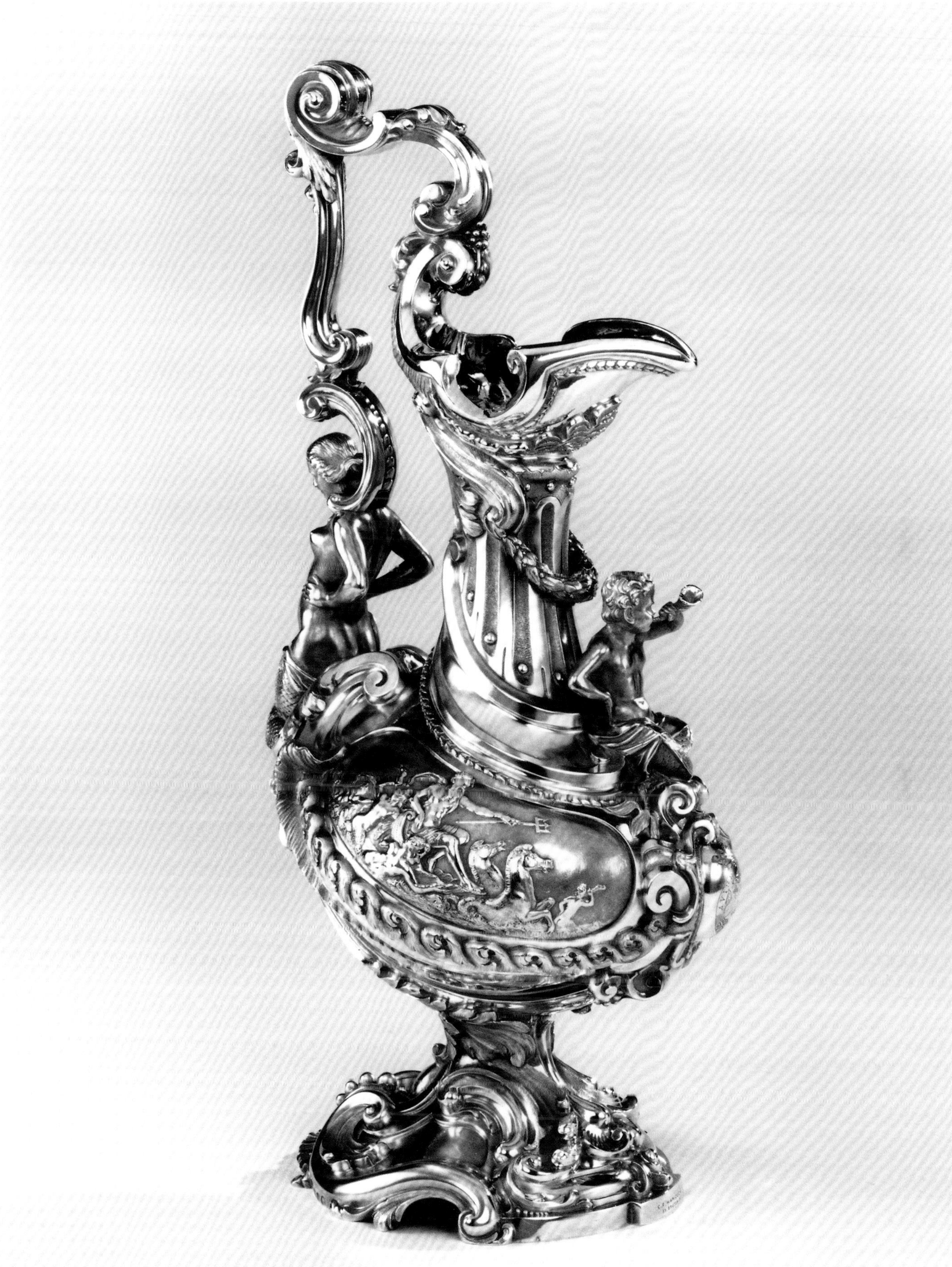

FIG. 14 Ewer. Samuel Hayne and Dudley Cater (English, active in partnership 1836–64). London, England, 1854. Silver. J. H. Bourdon-Smith Ltd.

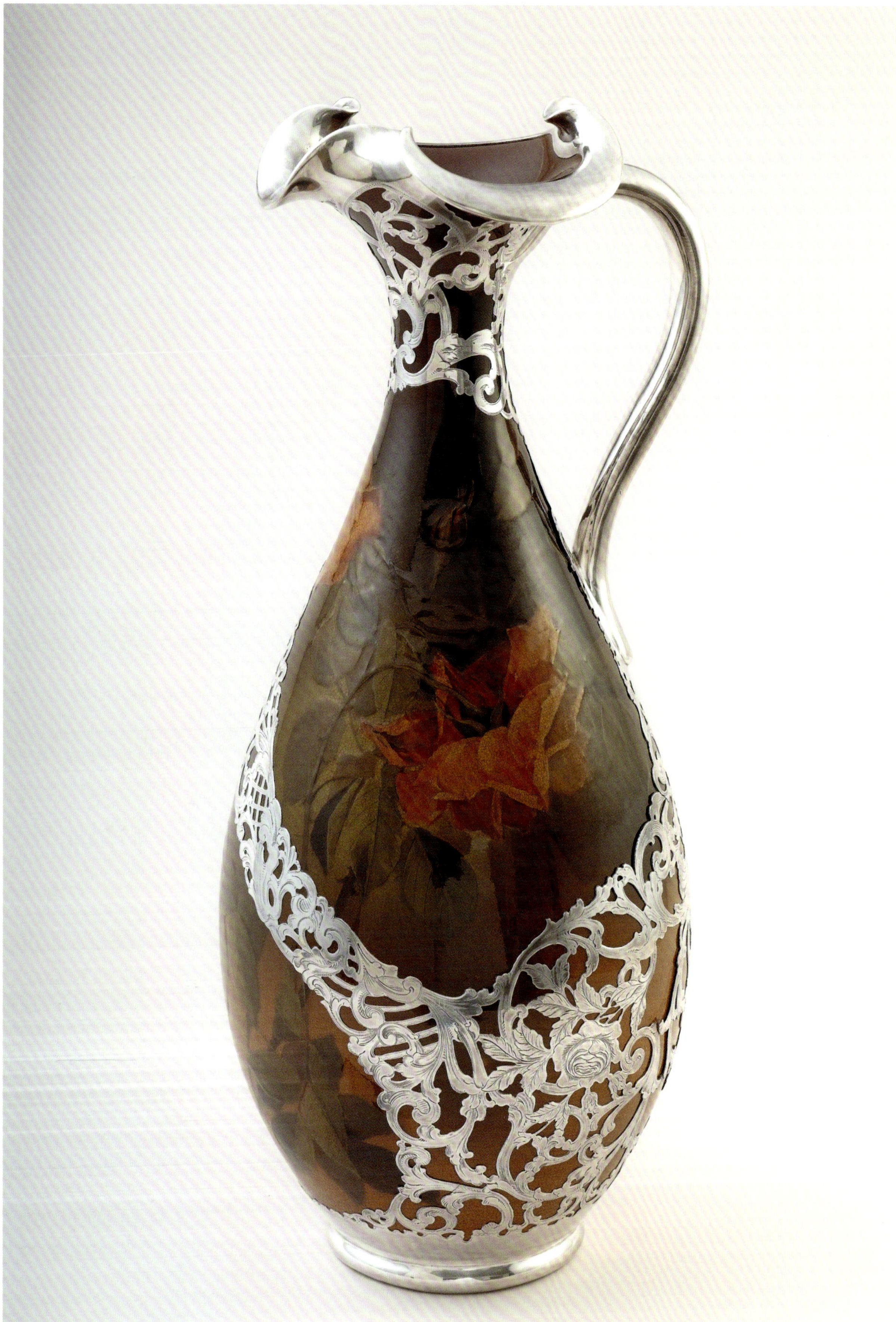

FIG. 15 Ewer. Matthew Andrew Daly (American, 1860–1937). Produced by Rookwood Pottery, Cincinnati, OH, 1894, silver overlay by Gorham Manufacturing Company, Providence, RI, 1984. White earthenware, glazed decoration with silver overlay. Cooper-Hewitt, National Design Museum, Smithsonian Institution, Gift of Marcia and William Goodman, 1984-84-9

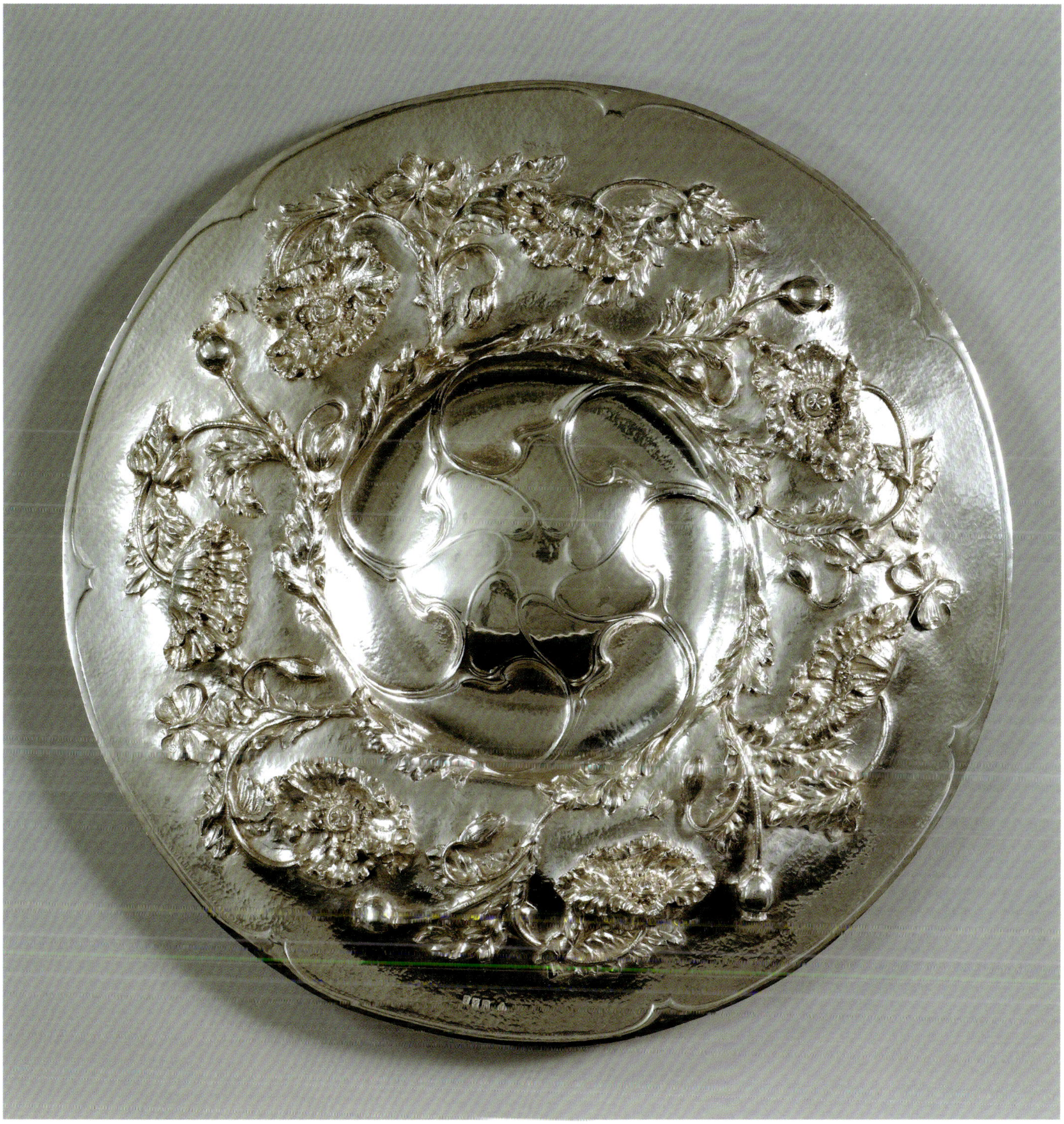

FIG. 16 Dish. Latino Movio (English, active from ca. 1900). Produced by Holland, Aldwinkle & Slater. London, England, 1907–08. Silver. Cooper-Hewitt, National Design Museum, Smithsonian Institution, Museum purchase from General Acquisitions Endowment Fund, 1985-64-1

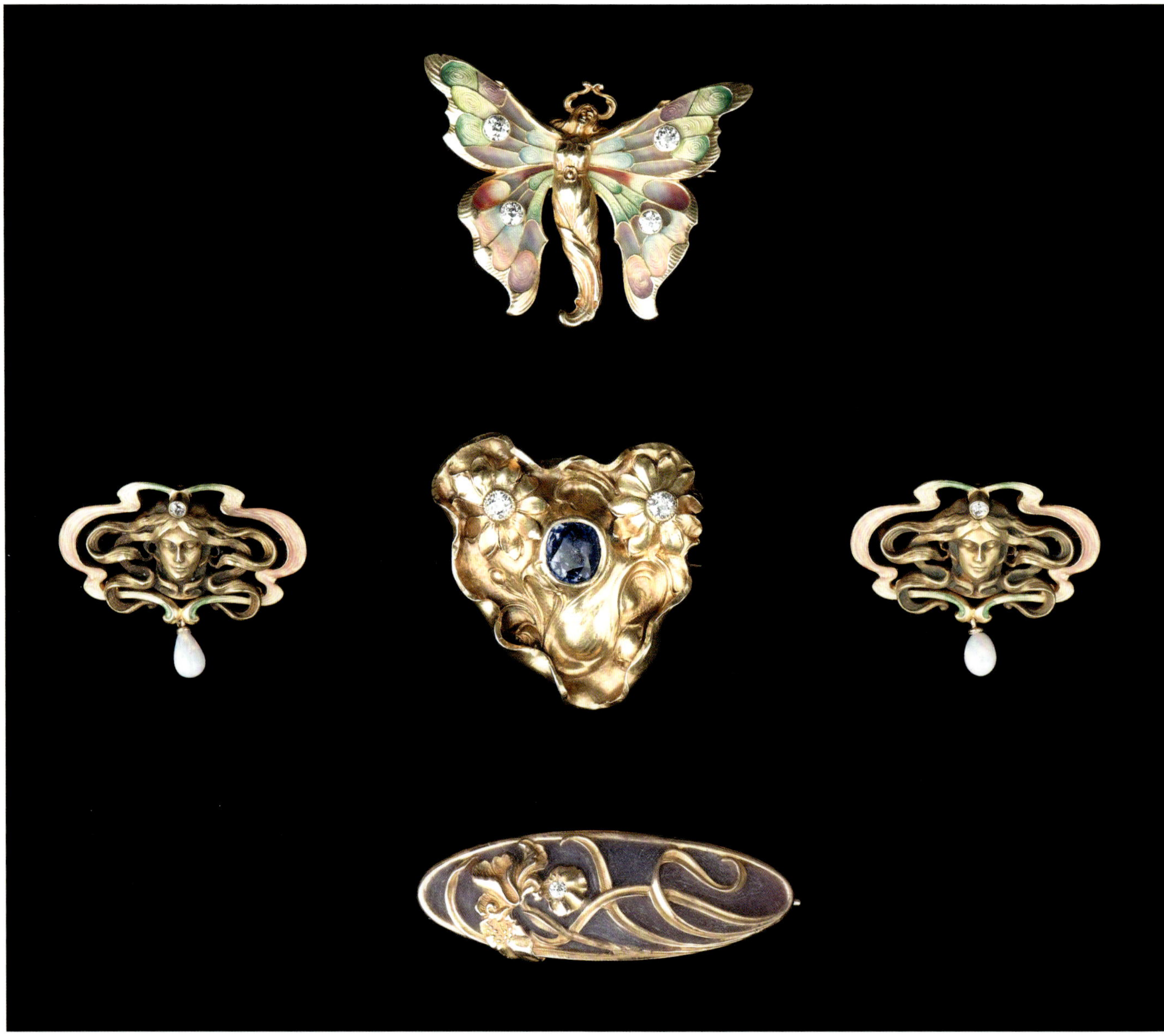

FIG. 17 (top) Butterfly with nymph brooch. Whiteside and Blank. Newark, NJ, ca. 1905. Gold, enamel, diamond. (middle left and right) Pair of brooches. Probably Newark, NJ, ca. 1905. Gold enamel, diamonds. (bottom) Brooch. William Riker & Sons. Newark, NJ, ca. 1900. Gold, enamel. (center) Brooch. Gorham Manufacturing Company. United States, ca. 1905. Diamonds, gold, sapphires. All the collection of Eric Streiner.

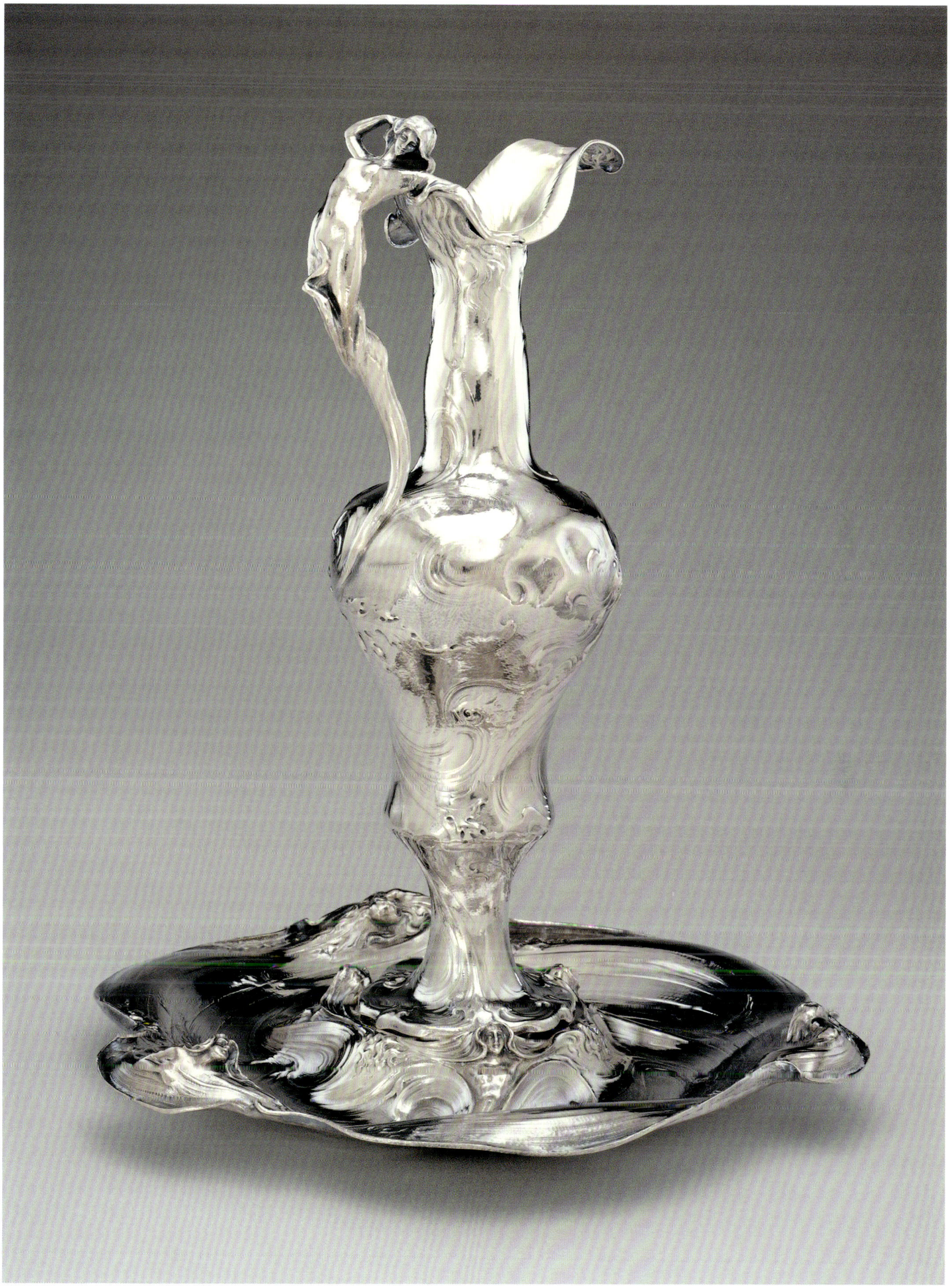

FIG. 18 Ewer and plateau: "Martelé." Gorham Manufacturing Company. Providence, RI, 1901. Silver. The Metropolitan Museum of Art, Gift of Mr. and Mrs. Hugh J. Grant, 1974.214.26a,b

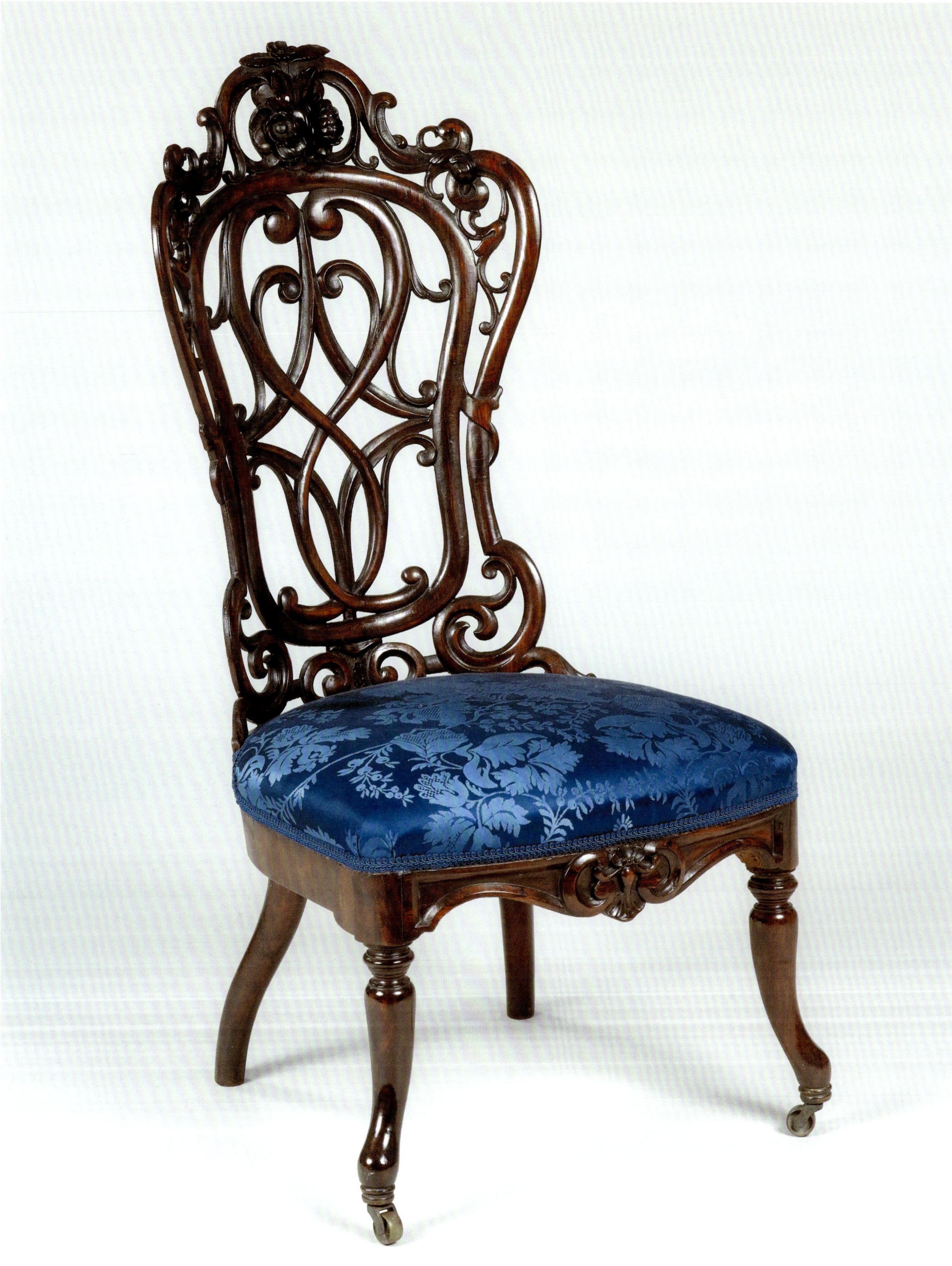

FIG. 1 Side chair. Attributed to John Henry Belter (American, born Ulm, Germany, active ca. 1844–63). New York, NY, ca. 1855. Rosewood veneer, oak (frame), silk upholstery (replaced). Cooper-Hewitt National Design Museum, Smithsonian Institution, Gift of Mrs. Edwin Gould, 1937-4-2

"Equal to Any in the World"

ROCOCO-REVIVAL FURNITURE IN AMERICA

Jason T. Busch

The World of Science, Art, and Industry/Illustrated from Examples in the New-York Exhibition, 1853–54, the unofficial guide to the first world's fair in America, reported:

We (Americans) have a furniture style of our own, which, though not original, bears yet the marks of our utilitarian age. It is a modification and a moderation of the style of Louis XIV.; and while it assumes the graceful motives of that style, it also reduces them to greater simplicity, and moulds them into forms more consistent with comfort and constructive truth.[1]

This enlightened interpretation describes the florid, often asymmetrical rococo-revival style pervasive in furniture and furnishings throughout America in the 1840s and 1850s, reaching its apogee before the Civil War (1861–65). From New York to New Orleans, New England to the Mississippi Valley, rococo revival became a favored style among status-conscious Americans, proven through the writings, receipts, and actual objects that survive from this brief moment in design history.[2] Some of the most notable American furniture in this style, like the rosewood chair illustrated here (fig. 1), is profusely decorated with undulating lines, bold, overlapping curves, lush carving, and pierced surfaces, veneered or laminated. With a rounded seat and splayed legs reminiscent of eighteenth-century rococo and a sinuous, interlaced back suggestive of the late nineteenth-century Art Nouveau movement, the chair epitomizes how rococo revival was as much looking forward as it was looking back. According to the 1845 *Encyclopedia of Domestic Economy*, "Certainly no kind of furniture equals it in the general splendour of appearance."[3]

While the origins of rococo-revival furniture were in English designs of the 1820s and 1830s,[4] the manifestation of the style in America was predominantly influenced by German and especially French pattern books and furniture. Indeed, in America during the mid-nineteenth century, it was varyingly referred to as "Louis Quatorze," "modern French," and even "antique French," reinforcing its connections with the curvilinear, naturalistic designs associated with the reigns of Louis XIV (r. 1643–1715) and particularly Louis XV (r. 1715–74). American architect Samuel Sloan mused about the confusion of names and origin for the revival in his *Sloan's Homestead Architecture* (1861): "The styles of Louis XIV., Louis XV., and Louis XVI…are so similar that it is difficult to say where one left off and where the other began.… In fact, neither purchasers nor cabinet-makers in this country (America) know what is the distinctive feature of either style; and even the French themselves admit that the form was the same in each style, and the difference was only in the character of the ornament."[5]

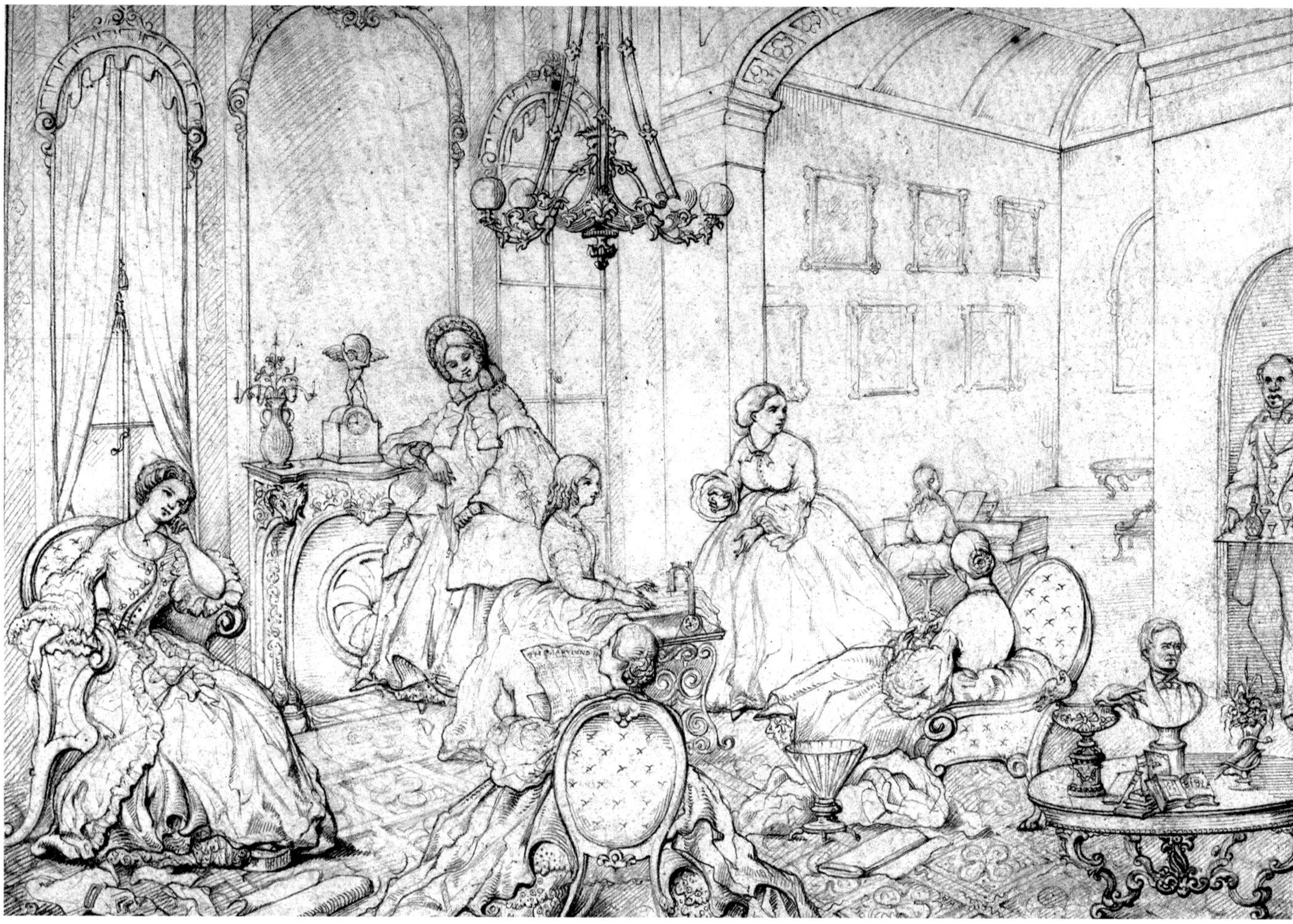

FIG. 2 *Entertaining in the Parlor.* Attributed to Adalbert John Volck (American, born in Bavaria, 1828–1912). Baltimore, MD, ca. 1863. Pen and graphite on paper. The Maryland Historical Society, Baltimore

The modern connoisseur of mid-nineteenth-century decorative arts is faced with the same dilemma of defining a style that in essence eschews precise definition. Rococo revival was at once plagued and enhanced by the layering of motifs from the Elizabethan, Renaissance, and rococo epochs. This idea is crystallized in the images of furniture in contemporaneous texts, including Sloan's *Homestead Architecture*, which includes an appendix on furniture complete with prints of rococo-revival bedroom, dining-room, and parlor suites, all based upon those offered by the much-advertised Philadelphia furniture retailer George J. Henkels (active ca. 1843–77). Rococo revival in America existed among a proliferation of revivals, including the Grecian and Gothic, each with symbolic associations that supposedly made it appropriate for specific types of rooms, such as halls or libraries. Rococo revival was a preferred choice for parlors, or "a drawing room where a lady of elegant manners and educated tastes might appropriately receive her guests,"[6] as depicted in a rare drawing of a Baltimore parlor in rococo-revival style (fig. 2). Sumptuously decorated objects of furniture—tables, chairs, sofas, and étagères—assumed almost a theatrical role in the staging of a rococo-revival parlor.

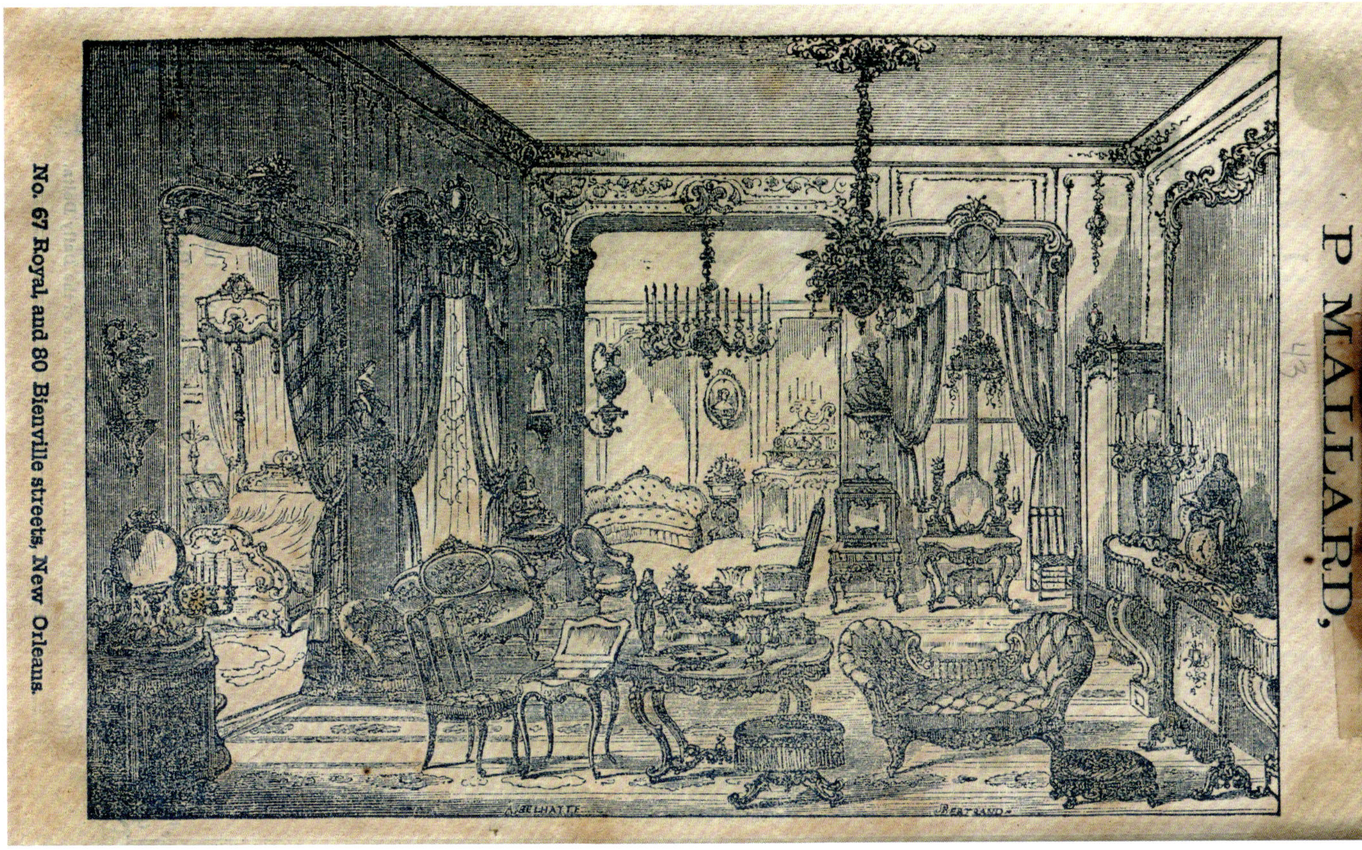

FIG. 3 Advertisement for the Gallery of Prudent Mallard, in A. Mygatt & Co.'s New Orleans Business Directory. Published by A. Mygatt & Co. New Orleans, LA, 1857. Printed paper. Louisiana State Museum, New Orleans

The noteworthy American tastemaker Andrew Jackson Downing (1815–1852) stated, in his influential 1850 guide *Architecture of Country Houses*, "There is, at the present moment, almost a mania in the cities for expensive French furniture and decorations.... Modern French furniture, and especially that in the style of Louis Quatorze, stands much higher in general estimation in this country than in any other."[7] During the mid-nineteenth century, France was seen as the undisputed center of decorative style for American consumers, and Louis XIV or XV–style objects were considered status symbols. Samuel Sloan quipped in 1861 that Paris was "where the congregated taste and wealth of the world expect to find everything that human nature requires or fancy can conceive."[8] Francophilia was definitely fashionable. Interest in Parisian rococo-revival wares was spawned from exposure to the material for those who could afford to travel to Europe, such as Henry Shaw, who purchased directly from Parisian cabinetmakers and upholsterers in the 1840s and 1850s furnishings for his Italianate villa called Tower Grove, located today in the Missouri Botanical Garden.[9] Equally ambitious consumers undertook the Grand Tour of Europe, similar to their counterparts in the eighteenth century. As part of their six-month tour of Western Europe in 1851, the Turnbulls of St. Francisville, Louisiana, shopped in Paris and toured the Gobelins factory.[10]

Whether a rococo-revival object was actually made in France or America apparently mattered, as recorded in the advertisements of furniture makers and retailers of the period. Edwin A. Smallwood, who operated a large furniture factory in Newton Center, Massachusetts, and a warehouse and showroom in Boston, took out several rococo-revival parlor-furniture patents and employed artisans who "evinced their ability to produce workmanship, in their line, equal to any in the world, of the most elaborate, costly, and luxurious descriptions."[11] Meanwhile, the most successful purveyor of furnishings on the Mississippi River, Prudent Mallard of New Orleans, filled his showroom (fig. 3) with expensive rococo-revival French furnishings and advertised his buying trips to Europe to his regular patrons. Mallard imported furniture from Parisian furniture makers such as Jean Baptiste-Abeillard Marchand & César-Aimé Bastard and Frédéric Roux, brother of the famous New York furniture maker Alexander Roux, whom Mallard also patronized.[12] Much of

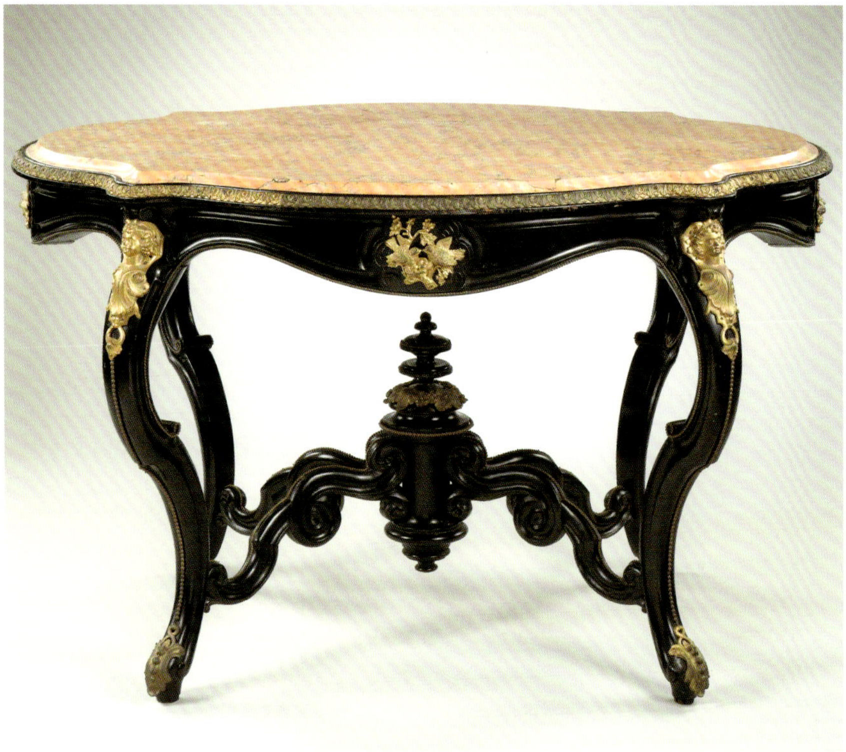

FIG. 4 Center table. Probably New York, NY, ca. 1860. Ebonized American black walnut, cherry, Siena marble, gilt-bronze mounts. Carnegie Museum of Art, Pittsburgh, Dupuy Fund, 82.30.1

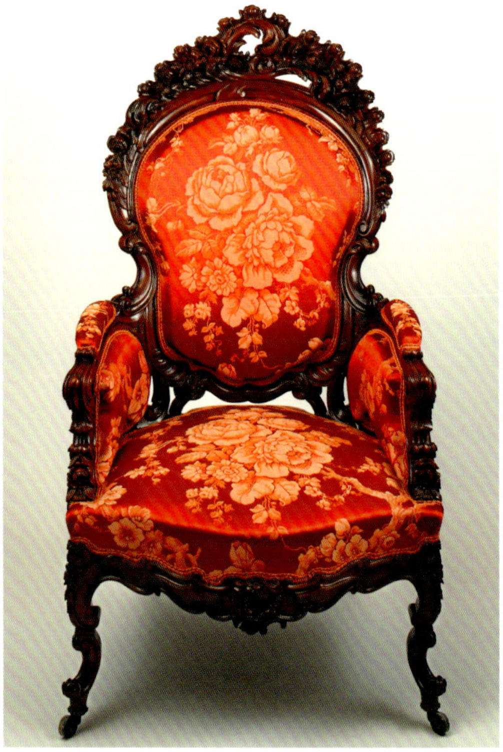

FIG. 5 Armchair. Paris, France, or New York, NY, ca. 1858. Rosewood, silk upholstery (replaced). Stanton Hall, Pilgrimage Garden Club, Natchez

the French furniture sent to New Orleans remains today, unsigned, in the plantation homes and suburban villas of the Mississippi Valley.

Regardless of varying levels of quality in design and execution, unsigned rococo-revival furniture with a mid-nineteenth-century provenance in the United States could have been made in Europe or America. The table illustrated here (fig. 4) is composed of American black walnut and cherry, yet its appearance is very similar to objects advertised and sold by Ringuet Leprince and L. Marcotte, the Parisian firm that had a branch in New York.[13] The table has an ebonized surface, perhaps inspired by objects with ebony created by André-Charles Boulle (1642–1732)[14] and his circle during the reign of Louis XIV, although similar rococo-revival center tables of ebony or ebonized woods were made in America at the time.[15] The table is handsomely ornamented with gilded-bronze mounts of female busts, kissing birds, and foliage; gilded beading along the sensually curved sides, legs, and stretchers; and a salmon-colored Siena marble top, all corresponding to rococo and early neoclassical traditions. Tables of comparable form and mounts could be found in period French pattern books, including *Le garde-meuble, ancien et moderne* by Désiré Guilmard (1839–1935).[16]

The furniture catalogue of George Henkels identifies him as an importer of French furniture and fancy goods, and seller of American-made parlor furniture in the style of Louis XIV, "of the Latest French Designs which are regularly received from Paris. Purchasers can have made to order without delay, any selections from the book of Patterns."[17] Henkels's admission provides evidence of American makers' use of French pattern guides, which were distributed in Western Europe as well as in American cities on the East Coast. Michel Jansen's *Ouvrage sur L'Ébénisterie, Dédié aux Fabricants* (Paris), *Neues Journal für Möbelschreiner* (Mainz, Germany), and others often included exquisite hand-colored images showing ideal surface pattern and decoration, accompanied by construction diagrams with dimensions.[18]

Jansen's *Le Guide du Fabricant de Meubles et du Décorateur. Album de sièges et de Teintures…* (Paris, 1852) and Victor Quétin's *Le Magasin de Meubles* (Paris, ca. 1860) include designs similar to the rosewood chair illustrated in figure 5, which was procured by the New Orleans interior decorator Henry Siebrecht for Belfast, now called Stanton Hall, the grand Italianate town house in Natchez, Mississippi, of planter and commission merchant Frederick Stanton (1794–1859).[19] The armchair, loosely based on eighteenth-century prototypes, features ornate floral carving, a broad seat, and cartouche-shaped back, adapted to mid-nineteenth-century levels of comfort through a curved spring seat and generously padded arms. The graceful curves and cabriole legs of rococo are replaced by bold, exaggerated C- and S-shapes—a recurring motif in American rococo-revival furniture—which form the front legs and visually elevate the armchair. The high-relief, densely carved scallops, shellwork, rosebuds, and overlapping acanthus leaves are quite similar in quality to a

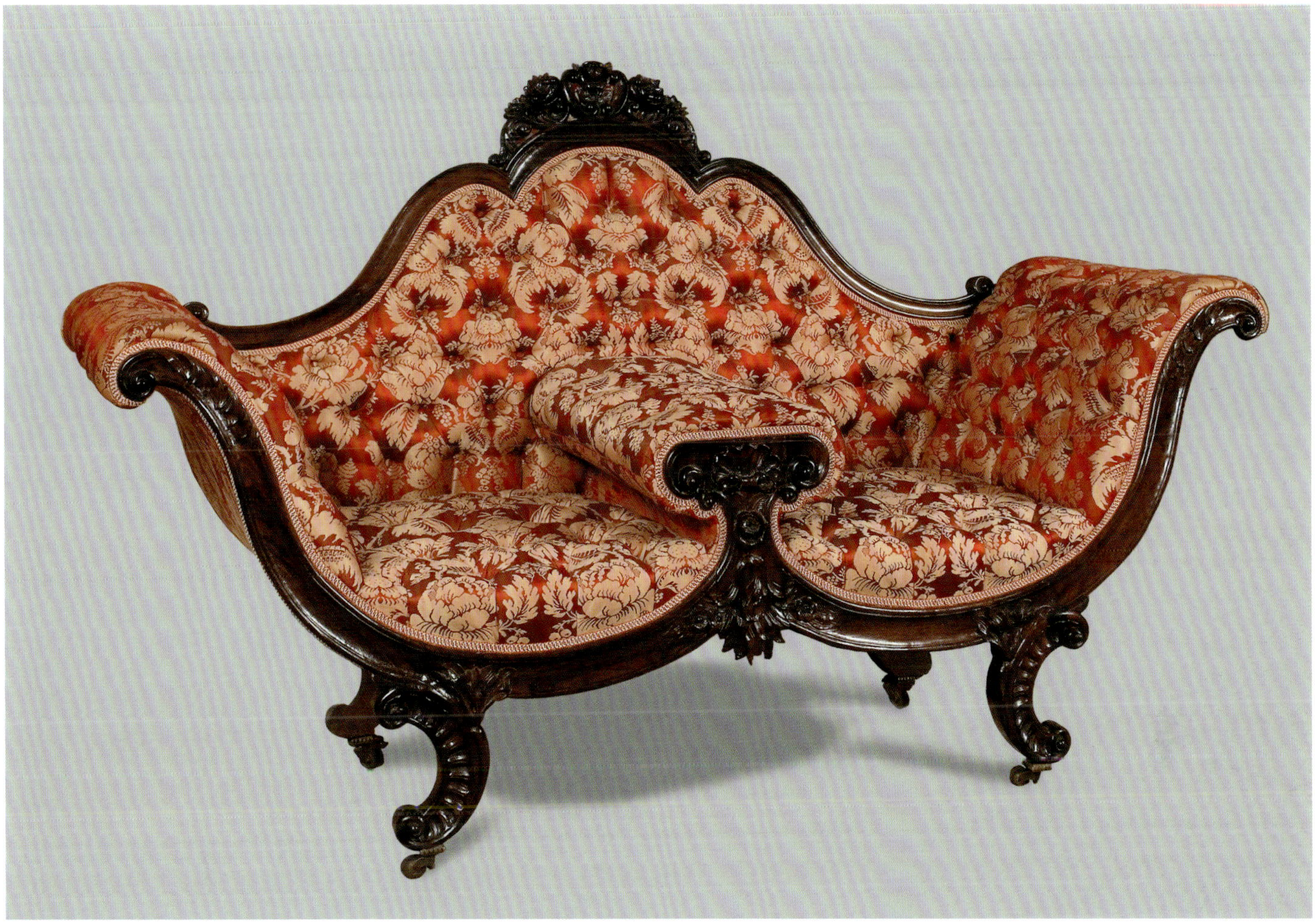

FIG. 6 Causeuse. Probably United States, ca. 1855. Rosewood, silk upholstery (replaced). Natchez National Historical Park, Melrose

rosewood chair, which is directly based on the *Chaise de fantaisie* illustrated in an 1844 issue of Désiré Guilmard's *Le garde meuble, ancien et moderne*. Likewise, the heretofore unpublished *causeuse* (loveseat) (fig. 6), which has a nineteenth-century provenance in Melrose, a suburban villa in Natchez, is nearly identical in form and decoration to a *Causeuse fantaisie* (fig. 7) depicted in Guilmard's book. While it is probable that all of these objects were made in America, none have a known history of manufacture in the United States, which leaves their origin open to speculation. A thorough examination of customs manifests from European ports, like Le Havre, Nantes, and Marseille in France and Hamburg in Germany, and a systematic comparison of documented rococo-revival furniture in Europe and America could shed more light on networks of furniture importation and exportation.

The great international expositions or world's fairs of the 1850s in London, New York, and Paris[20] exposed furniture makers and patrons to a veritable bazaar of avante-garde rococo-revival designs. Their direct influence on American furniture production is demonstrated in the rare 1854 trade catalogue of Philadelphia furniture maker Charles H. White. The cover of the catalogue shows a line-for-line engraving of a rococo-revival console glass and table made by the London firm Lecand and originally illustrated in the *Art Journal Illustrated Catalogue / The Industry of All Nations 1851*, the exhibition catalogue of the Crystal Palace, the first world's fair in London (fig. 8). Charles White's description of the

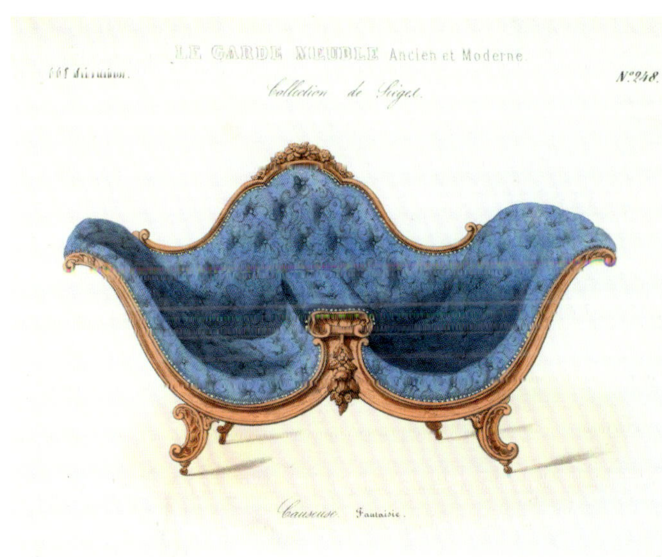

FIG. 7 *Causeuse Fantaisie*, no. 248 from *Le garde-meuble, ancien et moderne*. Désiré Guilmard (French, 1839–ca. 1889). France, ca. 1841–51. Lithograph with hand coloring. Smithsonian Institution Libraries, Cooper-Hewitt, National Design Museum, NK2547 .Z8G96

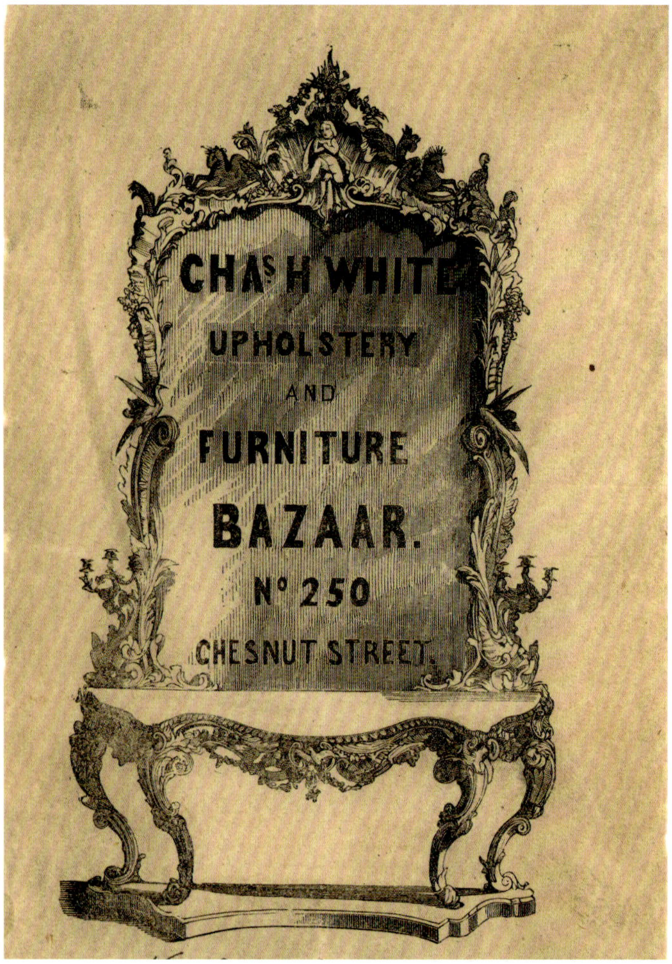

FIG. 8 Console glass and table, in *Chas H White/ Upholstery and Furniture Bazaar* (cover). Charles H. White (American, 1796–1876). Published by Sickles & Reading. Philadelphia, PA, 1854.

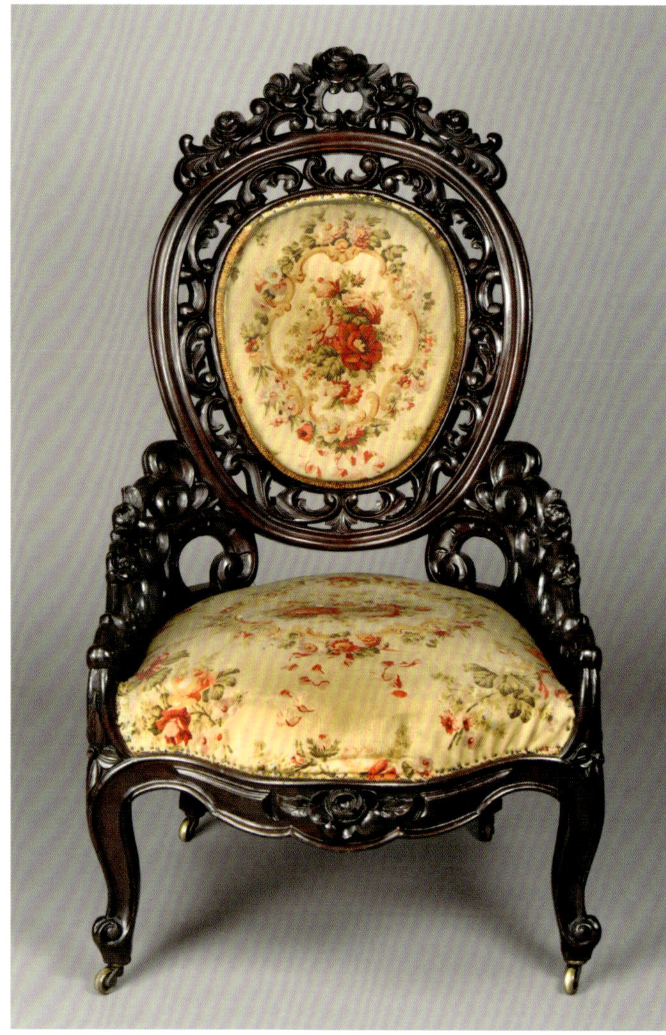

FIG. 9 Armchair. Charles H. White (American, 1796–1876). Philadelphia, PA, 1853. Walnut, wool block-printed upholstery. Carnegie Museum of Art, Pittsburgh, Richard L. Simmons Acquisition Fund, 2007.59.1

console, "The frames are carved in American pine and Lime tree Woods, and double gilt in matted and burnished gold, the style is a variation of the Louis Quatorze,"[21] implies that it was made in Philadelphia during the mid-nineteenth century, though no documented American gilded rococo-revival furniture has emerged.

White's catalogue is peppered with other images of rococo-revival furniture included in the *Art Journal* catalogue and made by manufacturers from all over Europe.[22] An exhaustive essay on the history of styles, including rococo, lifted almost verbatim from the *Art Journal*, accompanies the prints. Interestingly, White did not reveal the origin of his essay or illustrations, but instead championed his "large Assortment of all the late STYLES OF FRENCH FURNITURE, got to stand this climate...better than the Imported."[23] One of the few rococo-revival objects presumably made and sold by White that have come to light is an armchair (fig. 9), one of a pair, made in about 1853 for the Philadelphia lawyer Richard Rush (1780–1859), son of Dr. Benjamin Rush, an American founding father.[24] Similar chairs are listed at twenty-five to thirty-five dollars in White's price list.[25] The raised, medallion-shaped back is undoubtedly inspired by eighteenth-century French chairs favored during the ancien régime, and one of many designs revived during the Second Empire in France (1852–70) under Empress Eugénie and Emperor Napoleon III. However, the revival chair's proportions, particularly the back, are enlarged, and the arms are purposely low to accommodate copious female costumes. The pierced back and arms allow light to pass through, suggesting a sense of delicacy that belie the heaviness of the walnut wood. The walnut is manipulated with surface coatings to suggest the appearance of mahogany.

Most extraordinary about the Charles White chair is that it is one of the relatively few mid-nineteenth century rococo-revival objects in America that retains its original upholstery—in this case, a wool rep upholstery, decorated with block-printed floral designs in vivid hues and galloon trims of the same color palette.[26] The upholstery echoes the

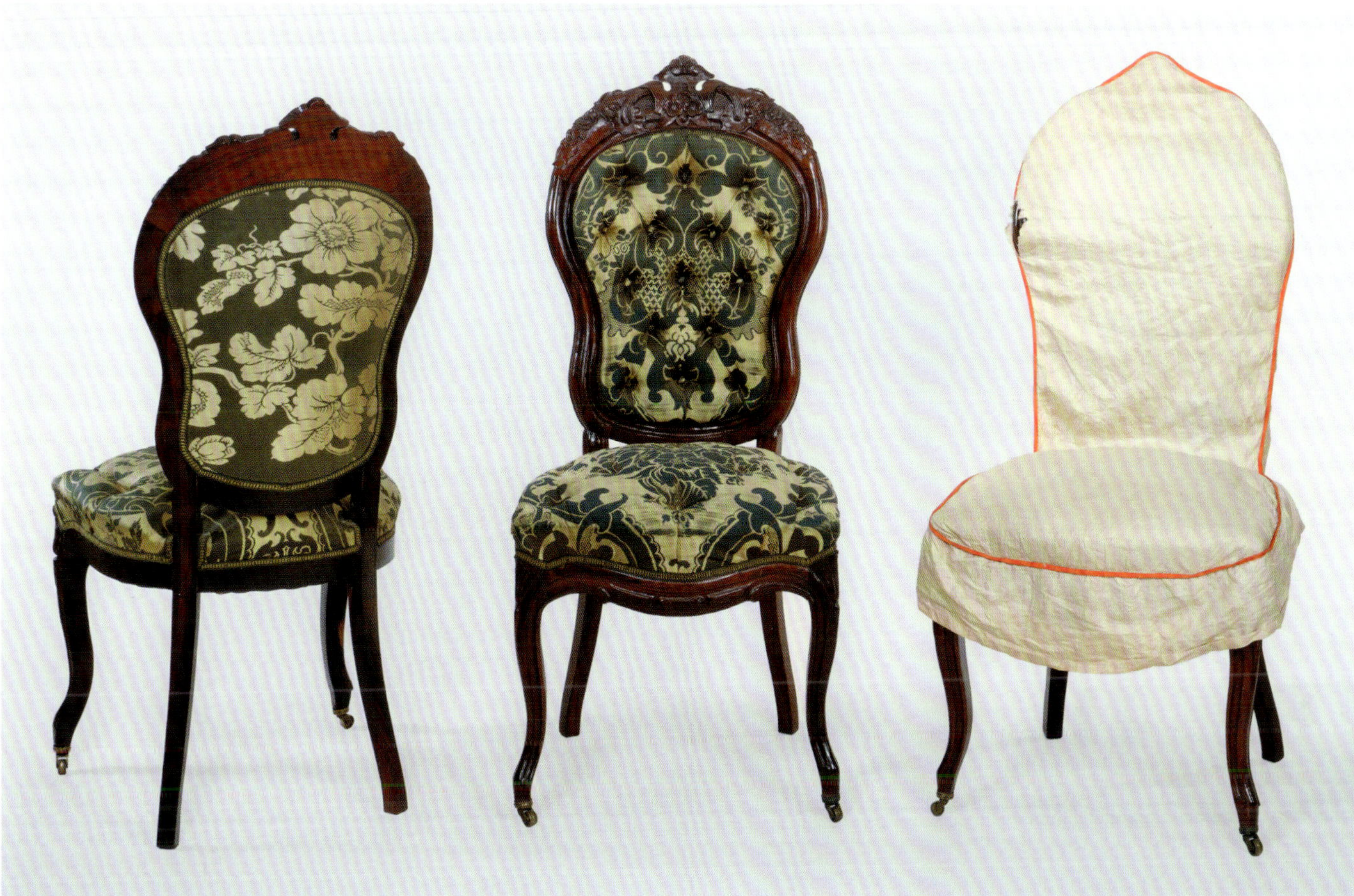

FIG. 10 Side chairs. Probably Boston, MA, ca. 1863. Rosewood, silk lampas (upholstery), linen (dust covers). Wadsworth Atheneum Museum of Art, Hartford, CT. Gift of Mrs. Horace B. Clark and Thomas L. Cox by exchange, 1985.2.2-5

naturalistic carving and interwoven scrolls on the back, crest, and arms. Other popular choices for rococo-revival partial parlor-furniture show-covers included silk damask and lampas with large, brilliantly rendered floral motifs. These patterns were often cleverly arranged to produce a depth of perspective, similar to looking through a kaleidoscope. A good example is the original upholstery on the illustrated rosewood rococo-revival parlor suite (fig. 10), which lived most of its life under original linen dustcovers in a Vermont parlor.[27] It was probably made in Boston in 1863; the date is reflected in the design of the chairs, each of which is a form commonly seen in American rococo-revival furniture from the mid-nineteenth century. The shallow carved decoration, primarily confined to the crest, interweaves rococo-revival flowers and foliage and Renaissance-revival strapwork and triangular pediment.

Parlor tables were made *en suite* with seating furniture, substantiated through those few that retain upholstered panels.[28] (fig. 11) The table illustrated here was made in Cincinnati about 1859 by the firm of Squire James John and F. Weber; the former was acknowledged by Cincinnati census taker Charles Cist in *Sketches and Statistics of Cincinnati* in 1851: "There are no finer articles made in Cincinnati than [John's] pier and sofa tables, covered with Egyptian marble…among the variety of fine furniture, are sure to catch the visitor's eye, and to open the visitor's purse."[29] The table appears to spring upward, elevated by animated, tightly rolled scrolls and leaves, carved roses, and machine-cut ripple molding that follows the shape of the oblong Egyptian marble top. The pierced, organically rendered fretwork on the sides of the table shields the patterned silk panels, which could have been changed out depending on the upholstery of other objects in the room.[30] The absence of such upholstered panels on the vast majority of rococo-revival center tables suggests that the panels, if used, were a novelty, and not often replaced when worn and faded textile was removed.

Consumers in the American furniture-production centers at the time, Cincinnati, Boston, Philadelphia, and New York, as well as regional distribution cities, such as St. Louis, Memphis, and New Orleans, were well served by manufacturers and retailers who stocked their showrooms with imported and domestic furniture and fancy goods.[31] Contemporaneous writings and advertisements, like those depicting the showrooms of George Henkels (fig. 12) and Prudent Mallard in New Orleans, featured wares arranged to inspire, if not to instruct, patrons in decorating their own homes. This early version of one-stop shopping was a relatively novel American concept in comparison to France; divisions among the trades in Paris resulted in separate and distinct shops for *passementerie*, *ébénisterie*, and so forth. Samuel Sloan commented in 1861 that "many Americans, who had expected to purchase their whole furnishing in Paris, have returned home with only a few fancy articles…causing them to

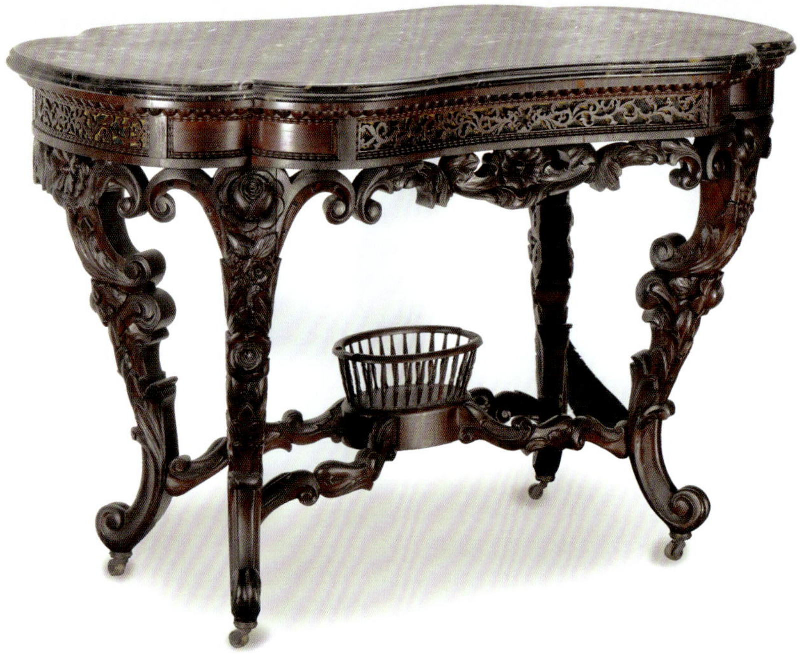

FIG. 11 Center table. Squire James John (active 1838–59) and F. Weber (active ca. 1859). Cincinnati, OH, ca. 1859. Rosewood, satin damask (behind fretwork). Cincinnati Art Museum, Gift of Polly Whittaker in memory of her mother's parents and the Wilby family, 2002.92

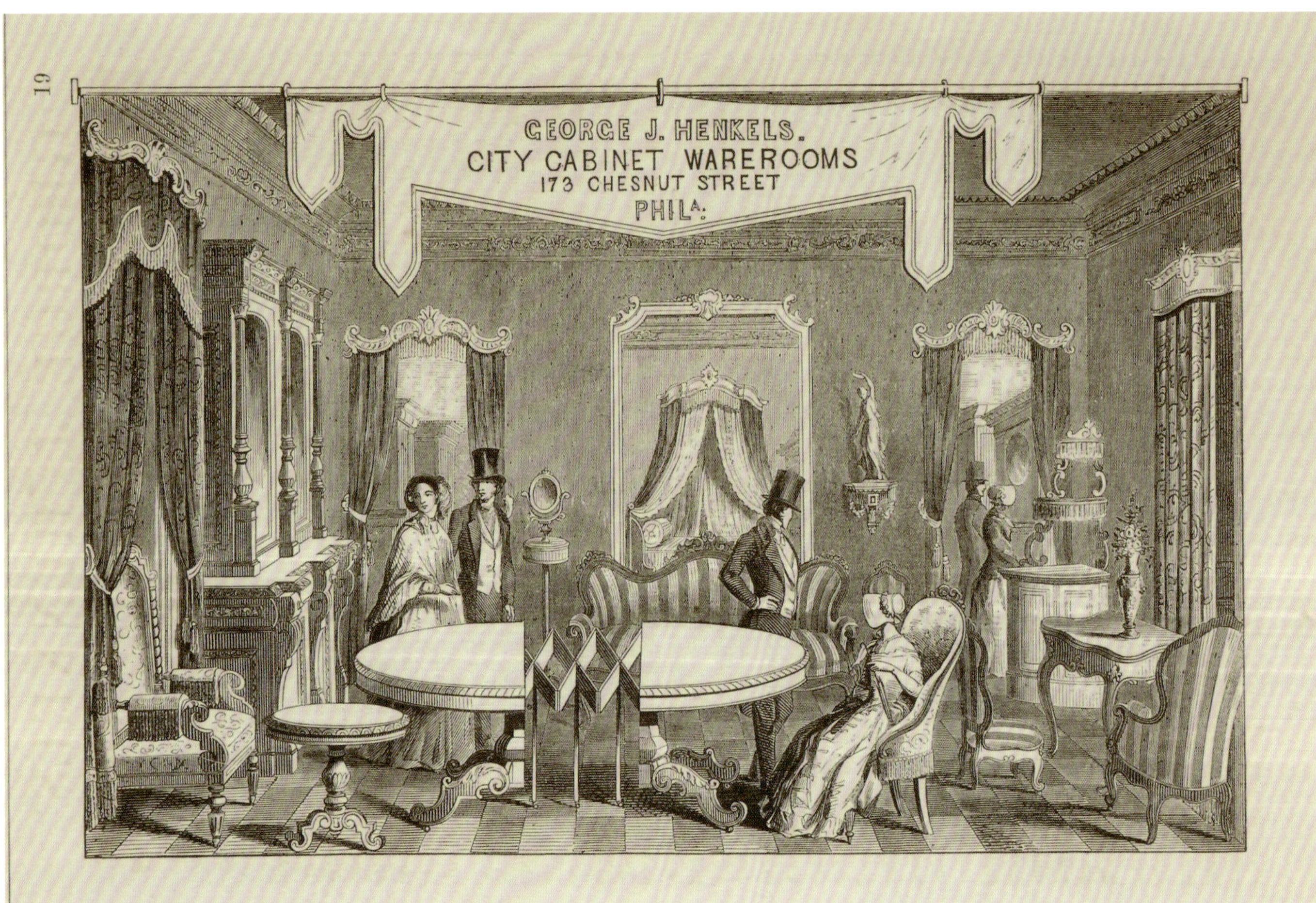

FIG. 12 Advertisement for Philadelphia Warerooms of George J. Henkels, page 19 from *History of Prominent Mercantile and Manufacturing Firms in the United States*, vol. 6. Published by David Bigelow. Boston, MA, 1857. Winterthur Library, RBR HD9723 B59

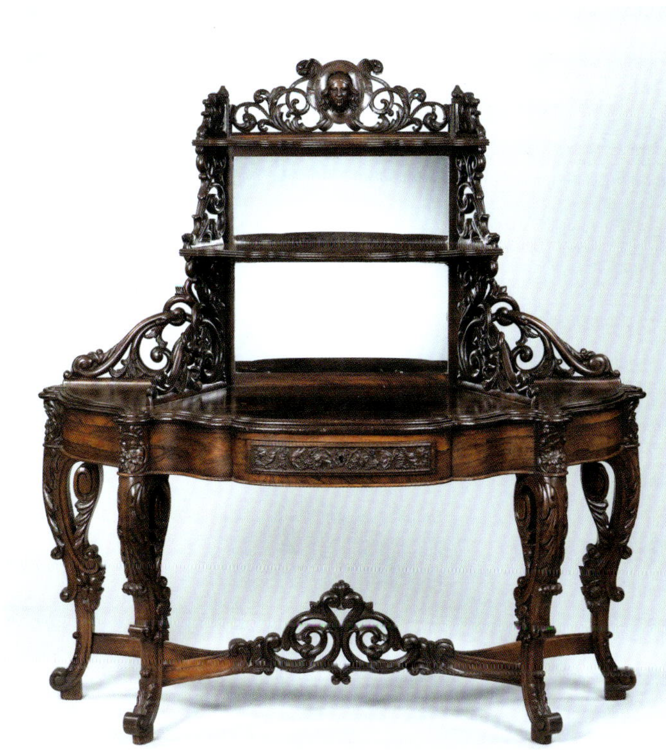

FIG. 13 Etagère. Julius Dessoir (American, born Germany, active 1842–65). New York, NY, ca. 1855. Rosewood, maple, mirrored glass, brass. Cooper-Hewitt National Design Museum, Smithsonian Institution, Gift of Anonymous Donor, 1937-45-6

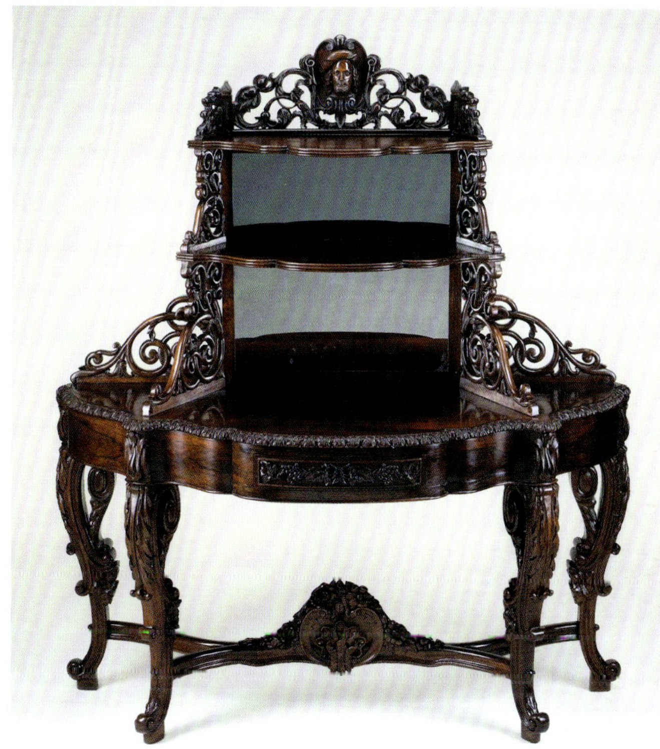

FIG. 14 Etagère. Julius Dessoir (American, born Germany, active 1842–65). New York, NY, ca. 1855. Rosewood, satinwood, maple, mirrored glass. Minneapolis Institute of Arts, Gift of funds from Sandra and Peter Butler, 2000.167 a,b

appreciate the enterprise of our own countrymen, who keep assortments of everything required in house furnishing...as cannot be obtained in Paris."[32] *Godey's Magazine and Lady's Book*, *Gleason's Pictorial*, and other publications advised consumers on decorating parlors and bedrooms, types of "New Furniture," and complicated French names, such as *Chaises légères* (reception chairs) and *Canapés à trois dossiers* (sofa with three backs), and recommended particular purveyors of fine furnishings.[33]

Yet despite the convenience of local retailers and manufacturers, patrons from all over America, particularly the South and West, came to or bought through New York. Cosmopolitan New York had ready access to imported furniture and the latest European fashions, some brought with immigrant craftsmen like Alexander Roux. Roux, along with fellow immigrants Julius Dessoir and Johann Heinrich (John Henry) Belter from Germany, made furniture in New York by the 1840s, occupied neighboring showrooms on fashionable Broadway in the early 1850s, and were sought out for their work in rococo-revival style into the 1860s. Roux and Dessoir in particular made their reputations early on through their successful exhibition of furniture at the 1853 World's Fair in New York, and examples of their ambitiously carved rococo-revival furniture, particularly étagères, are amply documented.[34]

In his 1850 *Architecture of Country Houses*, Andrew Jackson Downing described the étagère as a "what not" with "shelves for articles of vertu—bouquets of flowers, scientific curiosities, or whatever else of this kind

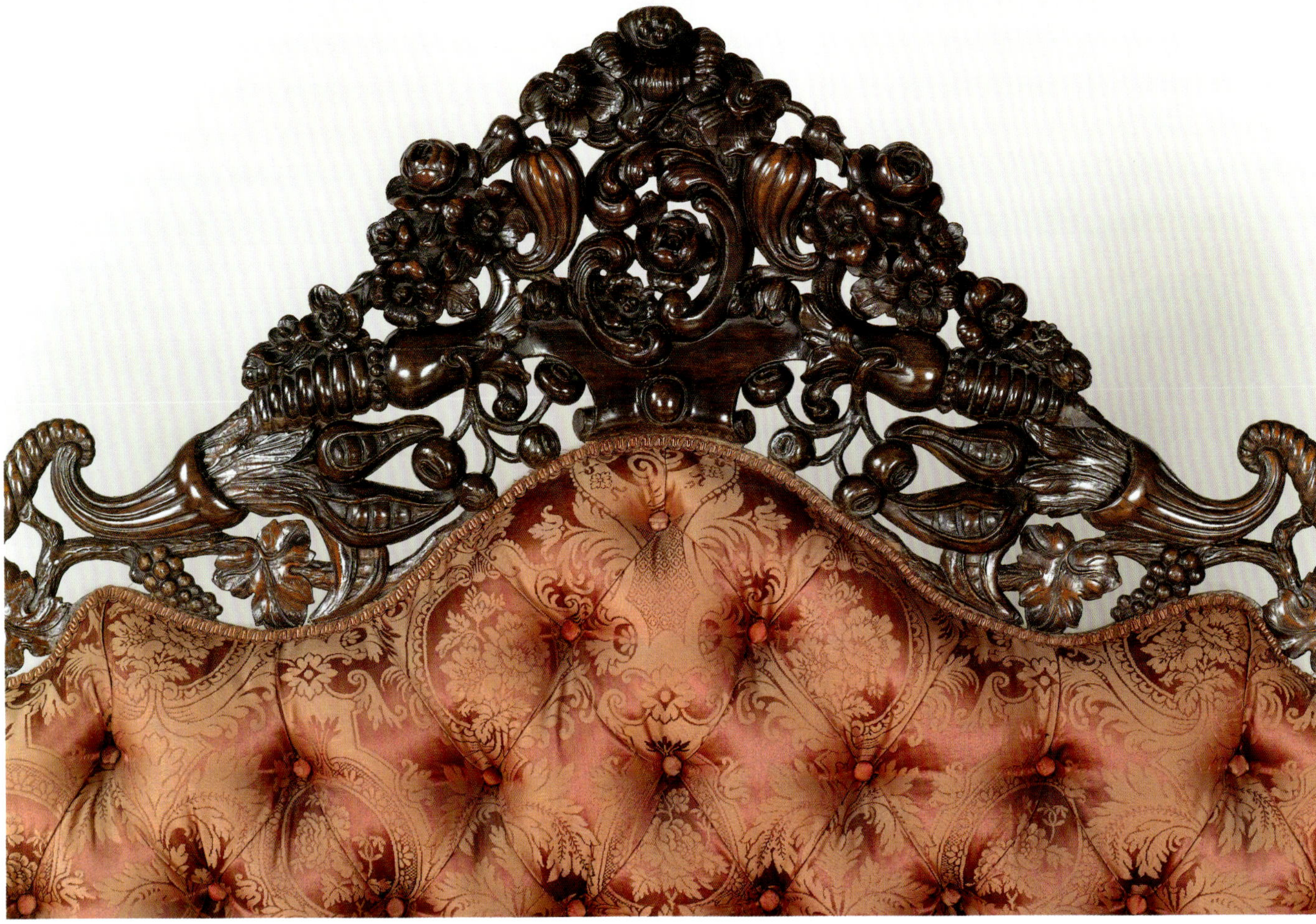

FIG. 15 Sofa (detail)

the owner may indulge his taste in."[35] An étagère provided a focal point in a rococo-revival parlor, displaying marble, glass, and porcelain from all sides, on mirrored shelves. In describing his experiences working in the mid-nineteenth-century New York furniture industry, Ernest Hagen stated that his employer, furniture maker Charles Baudouine, "made very large etageres...with glass back and small shelves on bracketts [sic] and any amount of gorgeous heavy carvings. This was the style about 1855–56."[36] Appropriate to their function, the particularly fine étagères made by Julius Dessoir (figs. 13, 14) are composed of richly grained and imported rosewood and rosewood veneer, favored for rococo-revival objects in part because the grain of the wood corresponded to the lines of carved decoration.[37] Each object conveys a sense of overstated embellishment. The complex network of arabesques, cascading along the crest and down the upper sides of each étagère, is punctuated by masks, perhaps taken from romantic literature, and snarling hounds, possibly derived from Désiré Guilmard's *Ornements d'appartements* or other pattern books.

Perhaps more than any other furniture maker in America, John Henry Belter is synonymous with rococo-revival parlors, reflected today in numerous attributions for objects at auction or in museum collections. A diminutive sofa (fig. 15), part of a suite of furniture including a signed Belter center table, is decorated in a vocabulary of rococo-revival motifs: cornucopia, floral and foliage bouquets, cabriole legs. During the mid-nineteenth century, Belter sold suites of parlor furniture to patrons as far from New York as Milledgeville, Georgia; Lexington, Kentucky; and Natchez, Mississippi.[38] These suites, or the receipts from their original sale, provide a treasure trove of information on Belter's various patterns for parlor sofas, chairs, tables, and étagères. Belter's success undoubtedly stemmed from his patent for steam-bending and laminating wood with alternating grains, producing curvaceous seat backs of several layers of wood that were often pierced in a complex openwork of interlaced scrolls, leaves, and flowers.[39] Through his technique and quality of ornamentation, Belter made a lasting contribution to bentwood and laminated furniture in rococo-revival style.[40]

Complex, if not at times convoluted, rococo-revival style served as a transitional bridge between eighteenth-century rococo and late nineteenth- and early twentieth-century Art Nouveau. Introduced to America in the 1830s, it persisted well into the 1870s, as evidenced in trade catalogues that juxtapose heavily carved rococo-revival furniture alongside bentwood objects composed of Art Nouveau whiplash lines *à la* Michael Thonet.[41] Inspired by the taste of eighteenth-century France, which was revived by sovereigns in the nineteenth century, rococo revival found its way into nearly every American home, and, as stated at the time, "its abundance of light, ornamental scroll-work, and foliage...admirably adapt it for the modern drawing-room."[42]

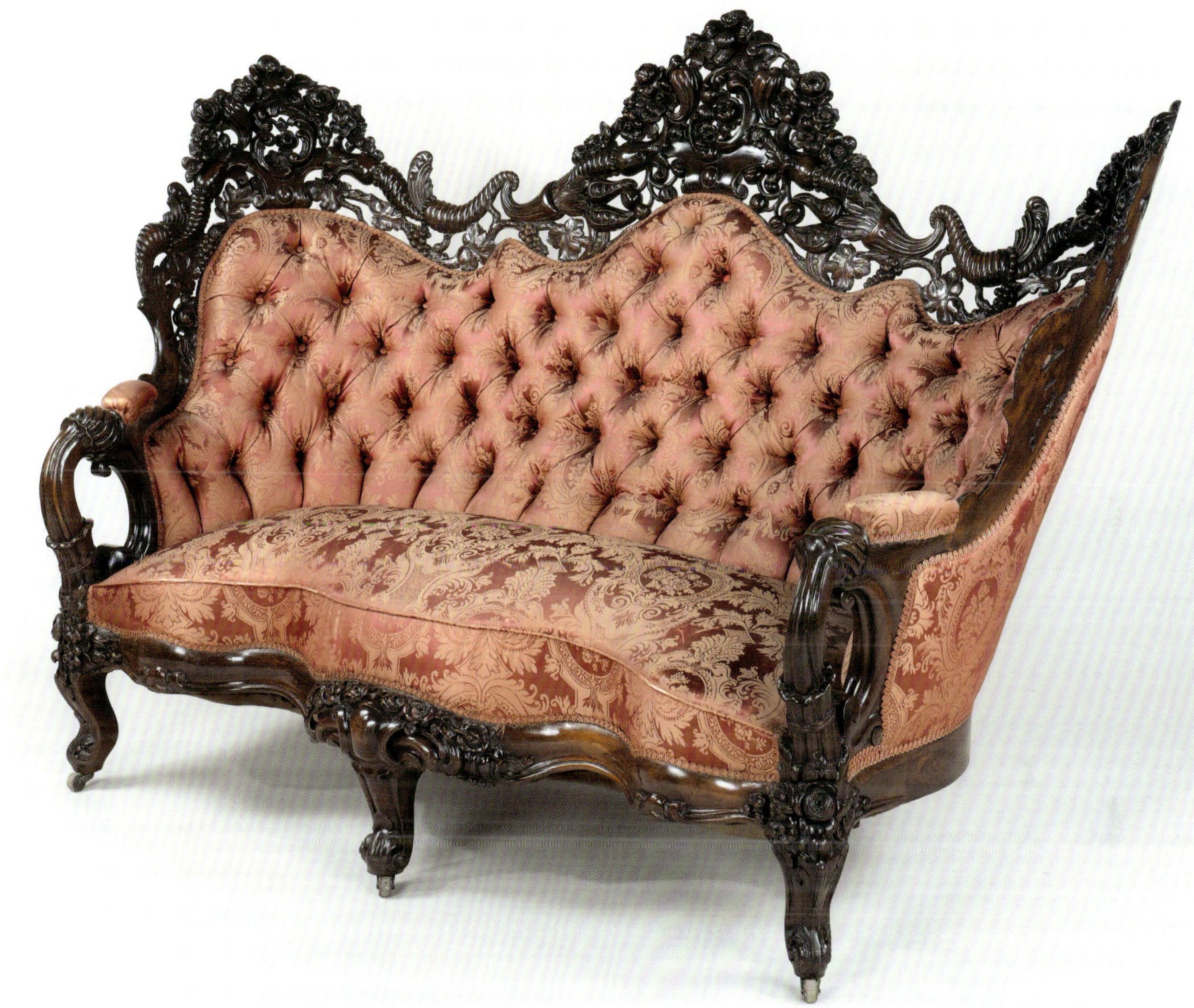

FIG. 15 Sofa. Attributed to John Henry Belter (American, born Ulm, Germany, active ca. 1844–63). New York, NY, ca. 1855. Rosewood, silk upholstery (replaced). Museum of the City of New York, Gift of Mr. and Mrs. Ernest Gunther Victor, 38.53.1

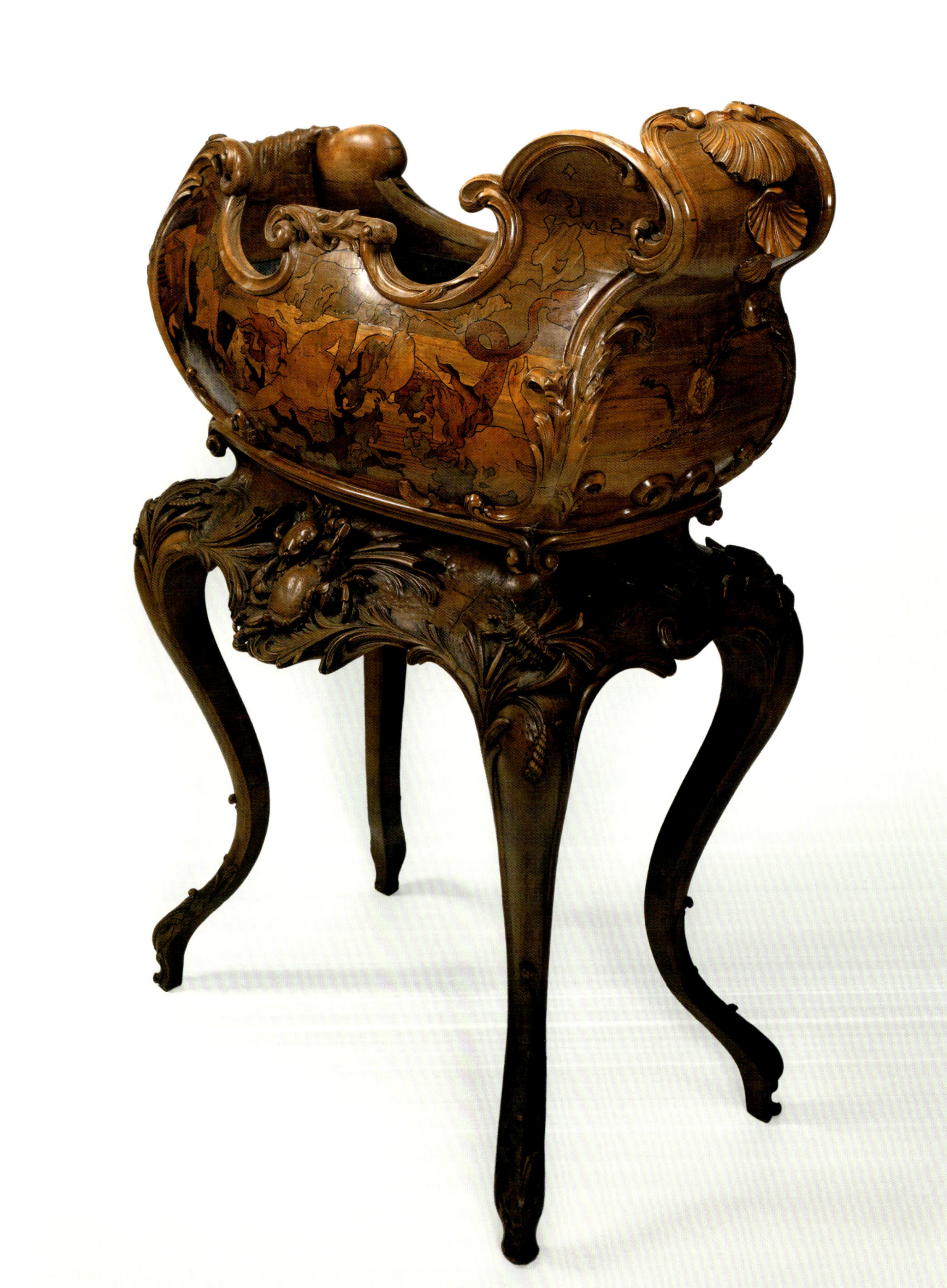

FIG. 10 "Flora Marina, Flora Exotica" jardinière. Émile Gallé (French, 1846–1904). Marquetry designed by Victor Prouvé (French, 1858–1943). Carvings by Louis Hestaux (French, 1858–1919). France, 1889. Pearwood and marquetry of various woods. Musée de l'Ecole de Nancy, NV76

Art Nouveau

Penelope Hunter-Stiebel

The term Art Nouveau has been broadly applied to the outbursts of original design across Europe and America that began in the 1880s and terminated in 1914 with the cataclysm of World War I. Exuberant, curvilinear, organic form and sensuous ornament characterize some of its most memorable expressions. Although a more geometric discipline would eventually triumph, most turn-of-the-twentieth-century innovations began with the principles that branded Art Nouveau style.

As the nineteenth century drew to a close, the desire to break free from historical formulas took on an aspect of nationalist competition. The leadership of France in matters of style no longer went unchallenged, as genius seemed to spring up everywhere.

In England, Art Nouveau devolved from the Arts and Crafts style. Invention and promotion were personified by Arthur Lasenby Liberty (1843–1917), founder of the Liberty store, and Archibald Knox (1864–1933), who provided designs to the firm from 1893 to 1912. Knox employed the entwined, curvilinear designs found on Celtic antiquities on his native island of Man, giving Britain its own line of Art Nouveau (fig. 1). America's most important contribution to the style was the glass of Louis Comfort Tiffany (1848–1933). In addition, several American silver manufactories seized on French imagery of sirens and plants to produce jewelry and bibelots. Gorham developed showpieces in the distinctive "Martelé" line, combining Arts and Crafts historicizing and Art Nouveau floral themes (fig. 2). In Spain, the surreal, organic vision of Antonio Gaudí (1852–1926) inspired other Catalan architects (fig. 3). Italy was jolted into innovation for the 1902 *International Exposition* in Turin. Carlo Zen (1851–1918) used floral and whiplash motifs in inlays of precious materials for the refined products of his Milan furniture factory (fig. 4). In Germany, the early works of the Munich Secession demonstrated the curvilinear impulse, as did early Austrian pieces, but this initial tendency was soon curbed by the Jugendstil and Vienna Secession styles.

ECOLE DE NANCY

The earliest of the localized Art Nouveau movements makes an interesting case study with direct connections to the eighteenth century. It occurred in Nancy, the capital of the province of Lorraine, which had enjoyed a golden age during the reign of Stanislas Leczynski. Following Germany's defeat of France in 1870, Nancy became the locus of regional patriotism. It stood at the new German border of a diminished

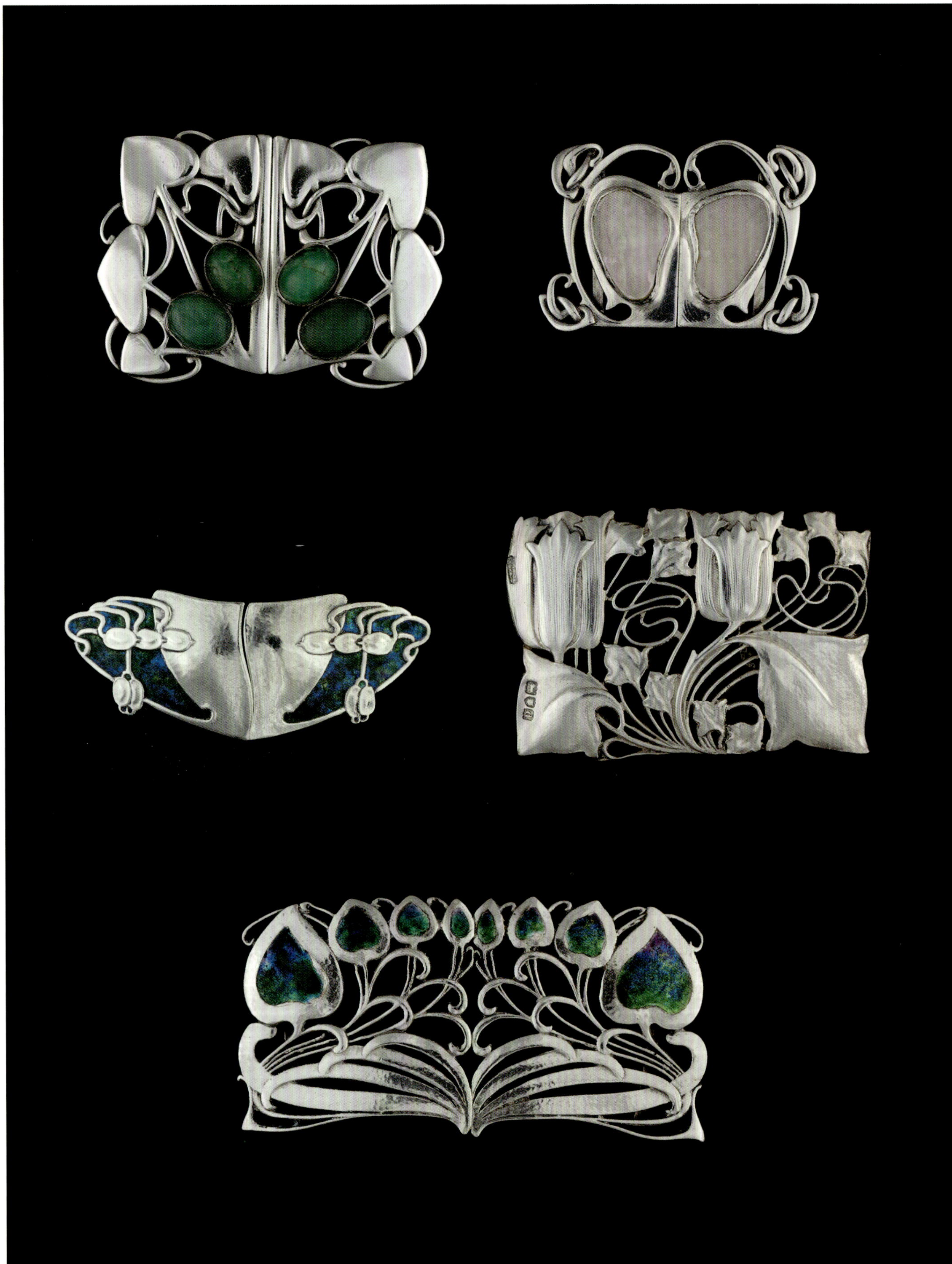

FIG. 1 Five buckles. Archibald Knox (English, 1864–1933). Liberty & Co. England, ca. 1899–1906. Silver, enamel. Virginia Museum of Fine Arts, Richmond. The Adolph D. and Wilkins C. Williams Fund, 2002.39. 2002.42a-b, 2002.46a-b, 2002.47; Gift of Dr. Karl and Gisela Kreuzer, 2002.178a-b

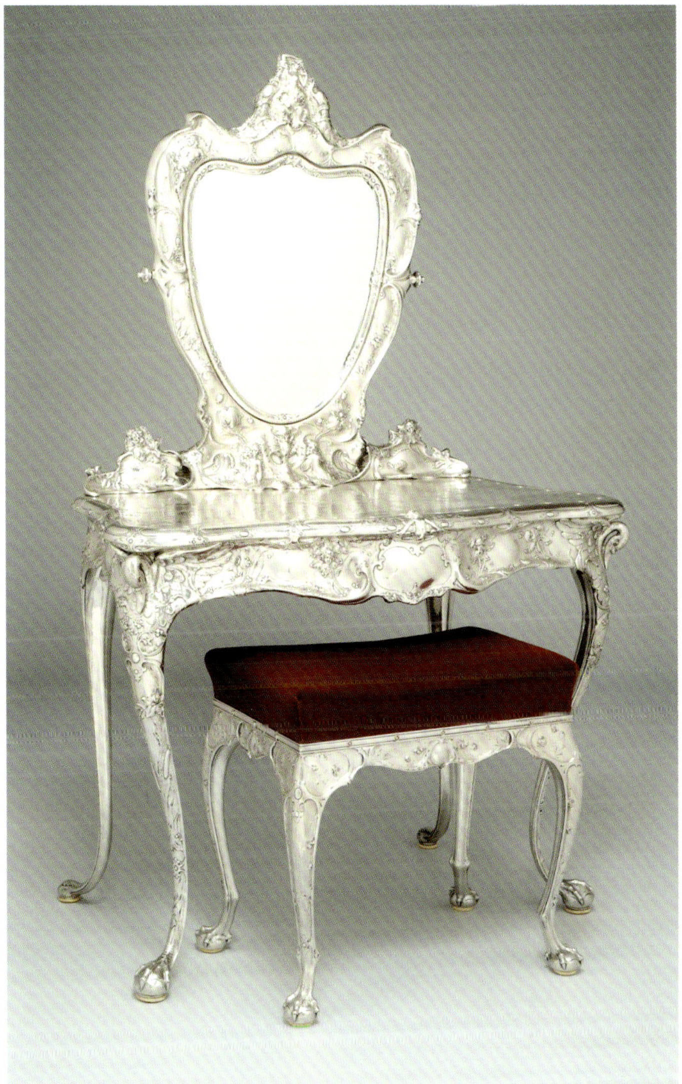

FIG. 2 "Martelé" dressing table and stool. William C. Codman (English, 1839–1921). Manufactured by Gorham Manufacturing Company. Providence, RI, 1899. Silver, glass, fabric, ivory. Dallas Museum of Art, The Eugene and Margaret McDermott Art Fund, Inc., in honor of Dr. Charles L. Venable, 2000.356.a–b

This eye-popping showpiece is rife with eighteenth-century references.

France, which had also lost the neighboring province of Alsace. Alsatians fleeing German annexation augmented the region's population as well as its growing mining and metallurgical industries. The mid-eighteenth century Place Stanislas symbolized the pride of a burgeoning city. Local periodicals published studies of traditional arts alongside documentation of contemporary work, which was depicted as the renewal of a regional heritage.

GALLÉ THE INDUSTRIALIST

The talents and energy of Emile Gallé (1846–1904) propelled a regional movement already underway in the 1880s. His passionate advocacy inspired artists and architects to collaborate and industrialists to patronize and provide financial support. The alliance formed around him was known as the Ecole de Nancy, or School of Nancy, well before its official statutes were written in 1901.[1] Gallé brought current theories of the unity of art and industry for the betterment of society to a community steeped in eighteenth-century precedent. His rallying cry of nature as a source of inspiration put him on the same aesthetic track as Meissonnier a century earlier. Whereas the latter was a designer/craftsman and royal appointee functioning in the structure of the ancien régime, Gallé was a designer/activist functioning in the modern commercial world.

In 1877, Gallé took over the family firm; his father, Charles Gallé-Reinemer, had achieved distinction as a supplier of glasswares and ceramics to the court of Napoleon II. Designs were realized at factories outside Nancy until 1885, when Emile built his own factory near the family's home to produce ceramics and furniture. By the turn of the twentieth century, he had one hundred employees in his design, modeling, ceramic, woodwork, and glass workshops and chemistry laboratory.[2] He developed a sales network across thirteen countries and had his own stores in Paris, London, and Frankfurt.[3] The products bearing the name Gallé were not made by his hands, but were the fruit of his ideas, understanding of materials and techniques, collaboration with his design team (whose drafts he meticulously annotated), and close oversight of execution (fig. 5).

With a prescient instinct for public relations, Gallé was a regular presence at Paris's expositions, and won a prize representing his father's firm at the 1867 *Exposition Universelle*. His highly visible displays garnered international attention at the 1889 World's Fair (fig. 6). He showed

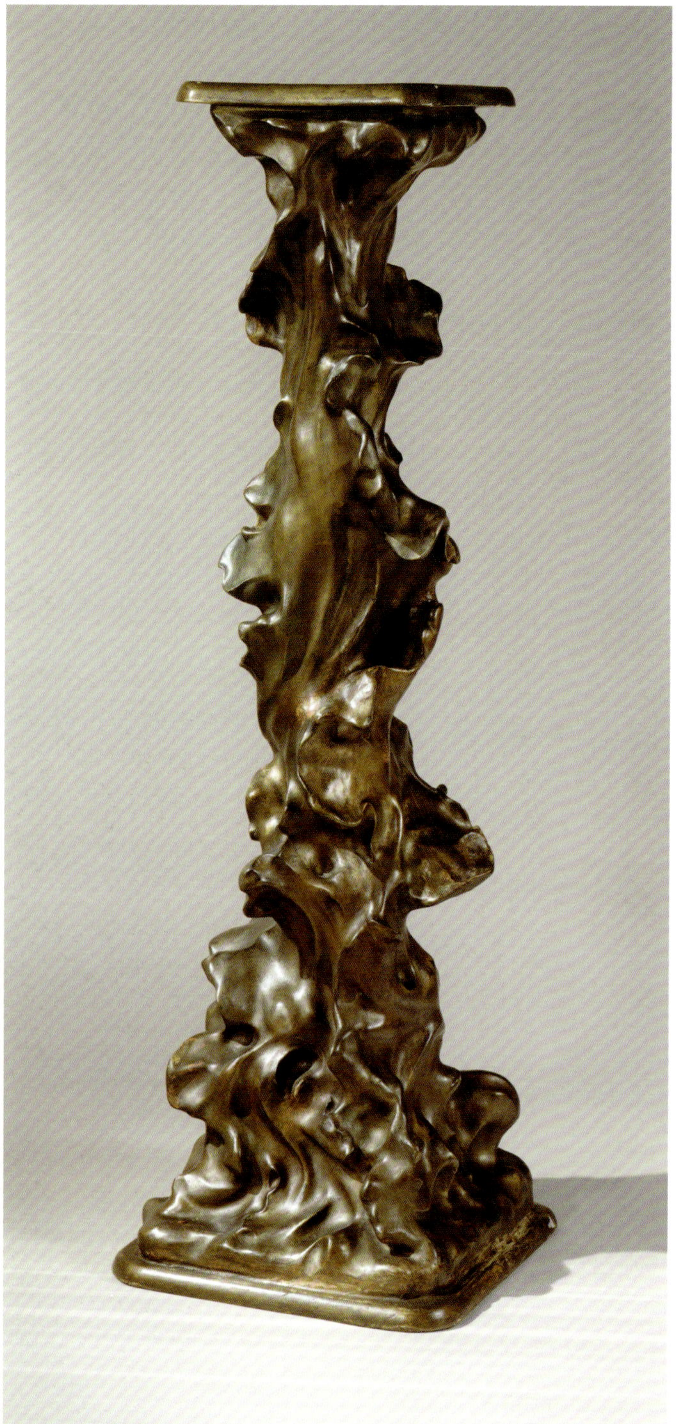

FIG. 3 Pedestal from Casa Milà. Antonio Gaudi (Spanish, 1852–1926). Spain, 1905–10. Gilded plaster over wood. Private collection

The eighteenth-century tradition of a tall gilded wood candlestand appears as a melted-down memory of Gaudí's design.

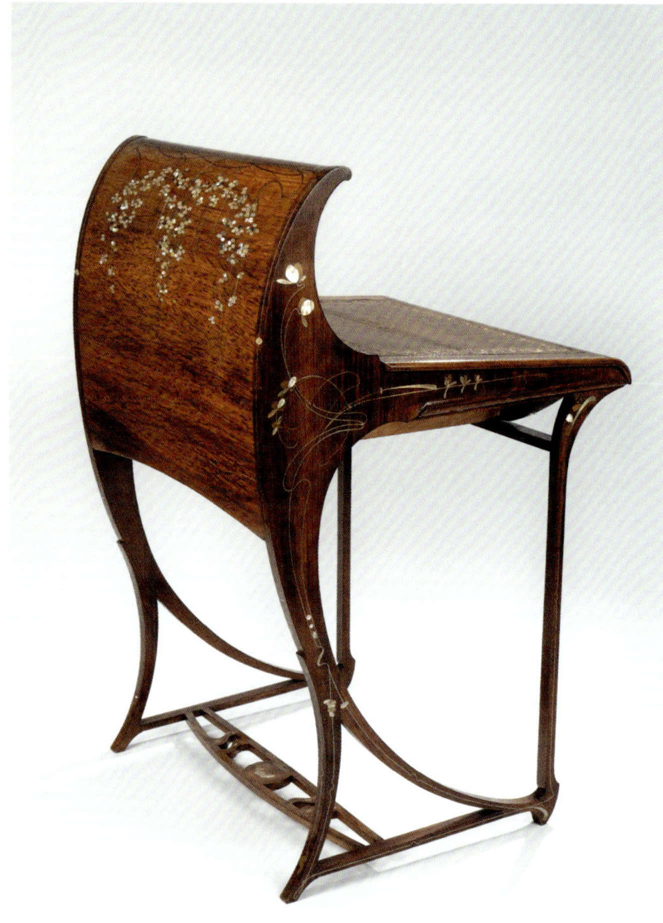

FIG. 4 Writing desk. Carlo Zen (Italian, 1851–1918). Milan, Italy, ca. 1902. Fruitwood, brass, white metal, mother-of-pearl, leather. Cooper-Hewitt, National Design Museum, Smithsonian Institution, Gift of John Goodwin, 1963-29-1

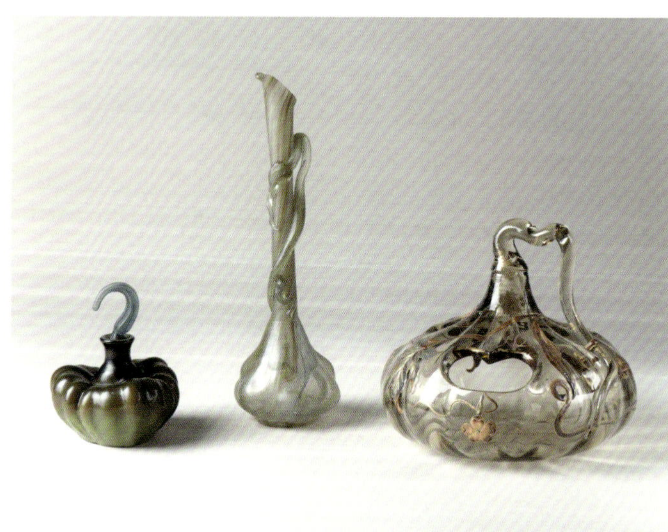

FIG. 5 "Pepper," "Garlic," and "Gourd" vases. Emile Gallé (French, 1846–1904). France, ca. 1900. Glass, enamel, gilding. The Collection of Eric Streiner

The "Garlic" vase was in the collection of the influential art critic Roger Marx.

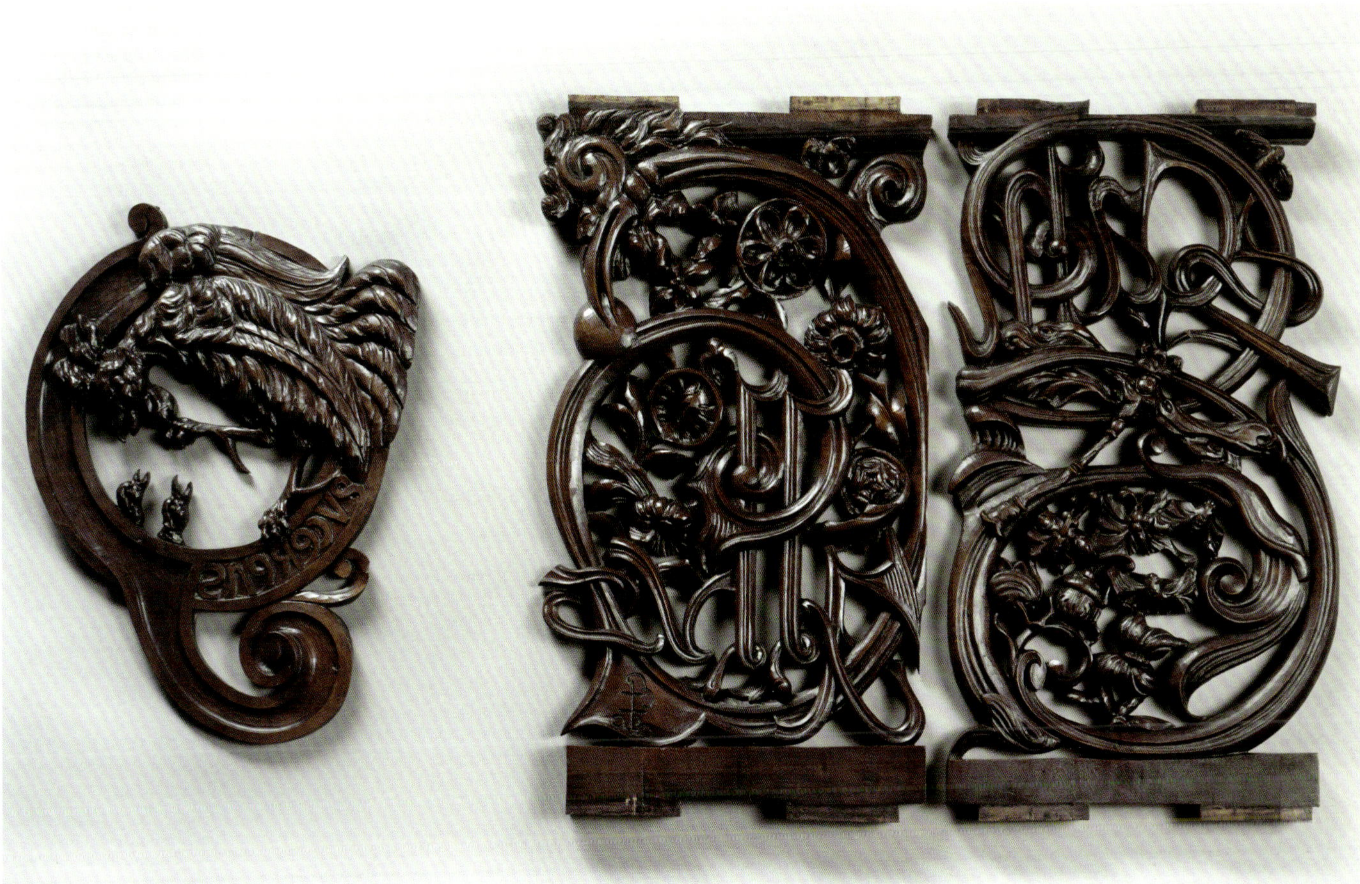

FIG. 6 Carved signs for Gallé's booth in the 1889 Paris World's Fair. Émile Gallé (French, 1846–1904) with Victor Prouvé (French, 1858–1943). Nancy, France, 1889. Carved fruitwood. Musée de l'Ecole de Nancy

with the Union centrale des arts décoratifs and the Société nationale des beaux-arts, organized exhibitions in Nancy, and forged relationships with the reigning arbiters of taste, Nancy-born critics Roger Marx and the Goncourt brothers, as well as Robert de Montesquieu. He mobilized his colleagues for triumphant presentations at the 1902 International Exhibition in Turin and the 1904 St. Louis World's Fair just months before his death.

As a teenager working in his father's establishment, Gallé moved production away from the popular pastiches of Louis XVI ornament toward a distillation of the Louis XV vocabulary.[4] One sheet in the collection of working drawings donated by Gallé's family to the Musée Ecole de Nancy, dated 1875, was inscribed "Garniture de toilette Polychrome/ Style LXV Rocailles" (figs. 7–9). Additional sheets from the design studio reveal that Gallé continued to explore the decorative vocabulary of eighteenth-century rococo even as he introduced themes from botany, Japanese art, and Symbolism. The fusion of these tendencies is most perfectly expressed in the jardinière he exhibited at the 1889 World's Fair and subsequently kept for his own collection.[5] (fig. 10) Its form evokes a Louis XV sleigh set on high cabriole legs. Two collaborators assisted Gallé in carrying out elements of the work *Flora marina, Flora exotica*. Victor Prouvé (1858–1943) designed a scene of females floating among plants that was executed in marquetry. Louis Hestaux (1858–1919), who headed Gallé's design atelier, created the vegetation and sea life carved on the base.

Glass emerged as a major medium in the Art Nouveau period, and, once Gallé established his own glass house in 1894, he took the medium to new heights. While the Nancy glass manufactory of Daum surpassed him in serial production, Gallé stood unchallenged in the creation of unique pieces charged with symbolic content. Engraved inscriptions enhanced the poetic intent of Gallé's so-called *vases parlantes*, or talking vases. Botanical and aquatic themes increasingly determined the form. As a result, the molten medium was coaxed into shapes imbued with the same sinuous sensuality as eighteenth-century rococo metalwork and ceramics. Gallé's achievement was recognized with a Grand Prix for glass at the 1900 World's Fair.

The addition of bronze mounts to selected glass pieces emphasized their preciousness by analogy to the oriental porcelains similarly mounted in the eighteenth century. The Paris sales firm Escalier de Cristal applied glittering gilt-bronze mounts in Louis XV style to glamorize select Gallé pieces. Gallé himself designed bronze or iron mounts that complemented the natural or symbolic themes of his vases. Around 1900, he added metalworkers to his atelier and ventured into electric lighting, with functional metal bases or brackets fashioned as leaves and branches (fig. 11). These final creations of his career at once brought him

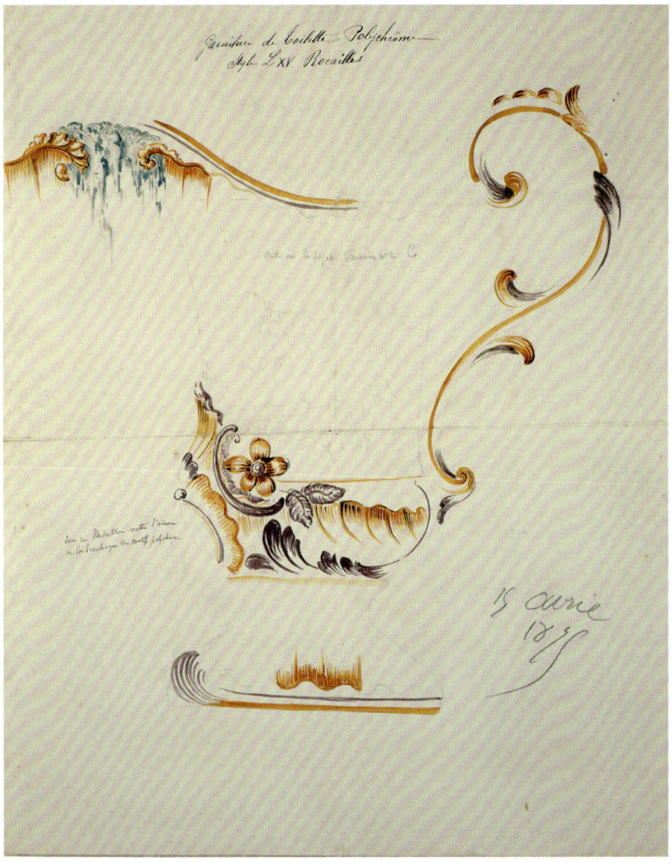

fig. 7 *Etude d'une garniture de toilette.* Atelier Gallé. France, 1875. Watercolor on paper. Musée de l'Ecole de Nancy, MOD15

This annotated study was produced in ceramic.

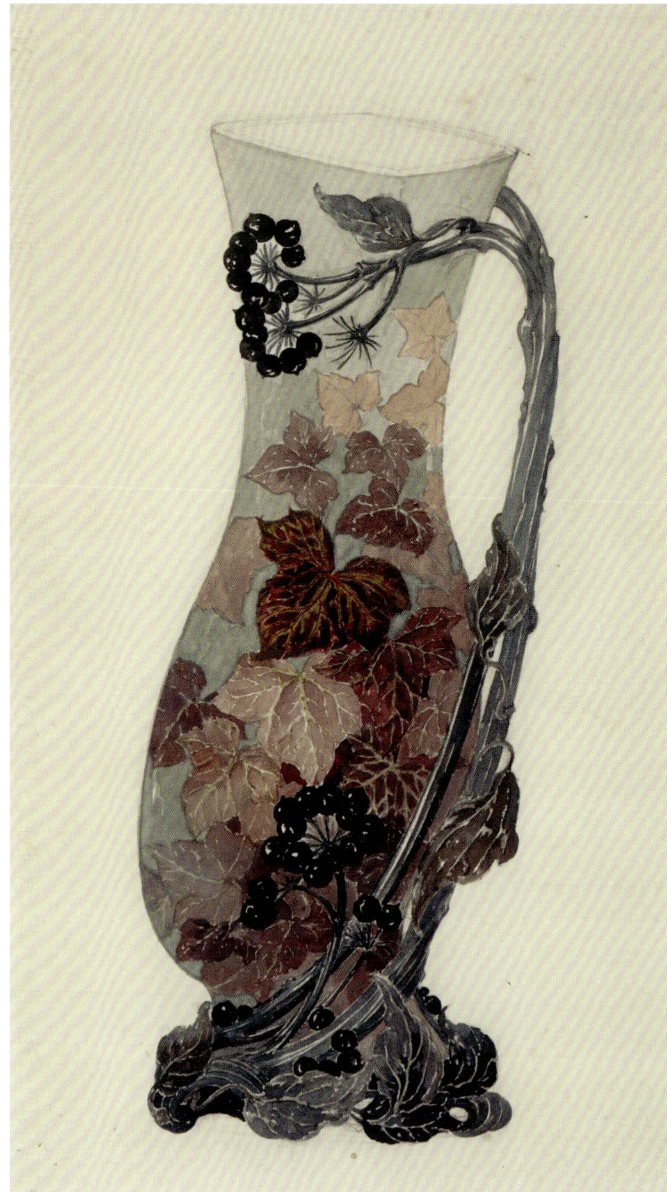

fig. 8 *Etude de cruche à décor de lierre.* Atelier Gallé. France, ca. 1885–1900. Watercolor and pencil on paper. Musée de l'Ecole de Nancy, MOD268

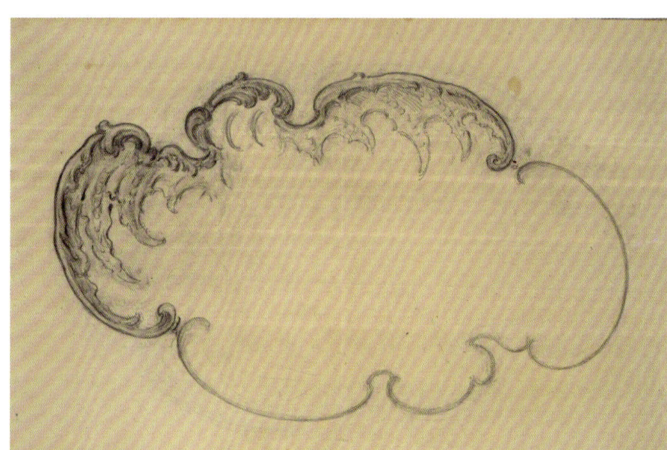

fig. 9 *Etude pour un plat en forme de coquillage.* Atelier Gallé. France, ca. 1875-85. Pencil on paper. Musée de l'Ecole de Nancy, MOD15

This design was produced in ceramic.

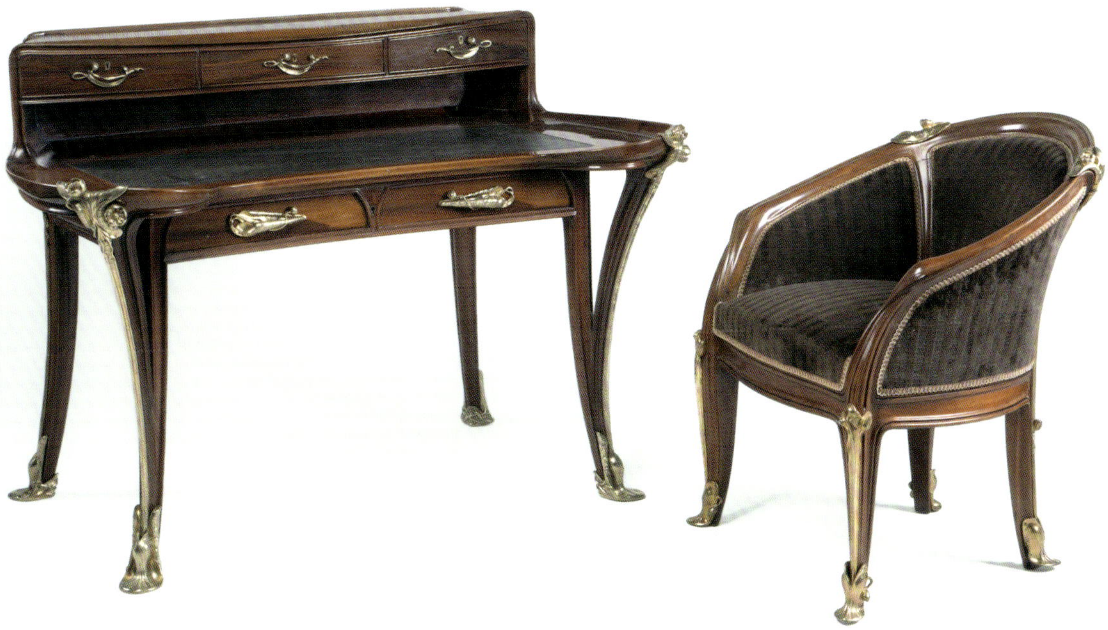

FIG. 12 "Nénuphar" desk and chair. Louis Majorelle (French, 1859–1926). France, ca. 1900. Mahogany, gilt bronze, leather. Virginia Museum of Fine Arts, Richmond. The Sydney and Frances Lewis Art Nouveau Fund, 72.31.1/2

closer to his ideal of originality within organic unity and bore kinship to his Louis XV candlesticks and wall lights.

LOUIS MAJORELLE

Louis Majorelle (1859–1926) was hailed by contemporaries as the Ecole de Nancy's master of furniture, and the rubric "majorellism" was coined to describe contemporary imitations of his pieces.[6] He took over the applied-arts firm of his father around 1882 and retooled it for factory production. He continued a historical line in the Louis XV style, even after 1894, when he became firmly aligned with the movement Gallé had initiated. He employed modern direct marketing techniques as well as advertising pamphlets and catalogs. In one pamphlet advertising the Majorelle Frères sideline of metalwork, an array of curvilinear silver-gilt objects, ranging stylistically from historicizing Louis XV to Art Nouveau, illustrates nature as the common source of inspiration.[7]

Majorelle translated the Ecole de Nancy's new nature-inspired ornament into traditional eighteenth-century carved seating furniture and bronze-mounted cabinetry. He adopted the eighteenth-century tradition of embellishing furniture with gilt-bronze *chutes* (corner mounts) and *sabots* (feet). Organic curves and discreet vegetal carvings graced even his simplest pieces, while gilt-bronze mounts complemented the sweeping arcs and swirling moldings of his high-end furniture. The massive forms clad in gilt-bronze leaves and flowers of the Nénuphar (water lily) and Orchidée (orchid) suites he introduced in 1898–99 and exhibited at the 1900 World's Fair in Paris took the boldest Louis XV models a step further (fig. 12).

Unable to find local metalworkers to realize his ambitious furniture ornaments, Majorelle opened his own foundry in Nancy around 1890. He soon executed commissions for balustrades, balconies, and architectural ornament that updated the local tradition of Jean Lamour. In 1902, Majorelle began a collaboration with Daum to exploit the potential of artistic lighting made possible by electricity. In a wide range of floral designs, bronze and iron structures by Majorelle supported Daum's cameo-glass lampshades in the form of glowing flowers.

VICTOR PROUVÉ

Victor Prouvé took over as president of a reorganized Ecole de Nancy in 1904, following the death of Gallé a year earlier. Starting out in the Gallé enterprise, Prouvé went on to a career as a painter, but remained a frequent participant in collaborative creations in every medium. He embodied the ideal of unity in the arts and encouraged the collaboration among artists, craftsmen, and industry that had been fundamental to the movement. Production of applied arts continued to flourish in Nancy, where more than 2,000 were employed in the field in 1905,[8] but the vigor of the organic design vocabulary gradually subsided.

SIEGFRIED BING

Though Nancy had taken the lead away from Paris in Art Nouveau, the French capital was still the stage on which innovation was presented and tested. The very term Art Nouveau came from the title of the Paris gallery opened in 1895 by Siegfried Bing (1838–1905).[9] A naturalized Frenchman, Bing was the scion of a merchant family in Hamburg, Germany, which

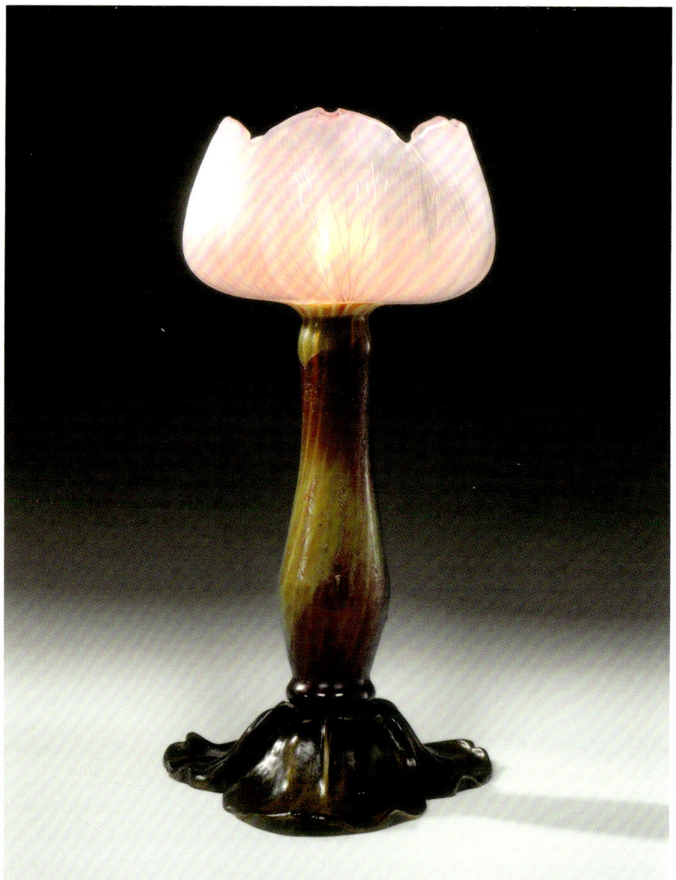

FIG. 11 "Corolla" lamp. Émile Gallé (French, 1846–1904). France, ca. 1900. Cameo glass and bronze. Minneapolis Institute of Arts, The Modernism Collection, gift of Wells Fargo, 98.276.239

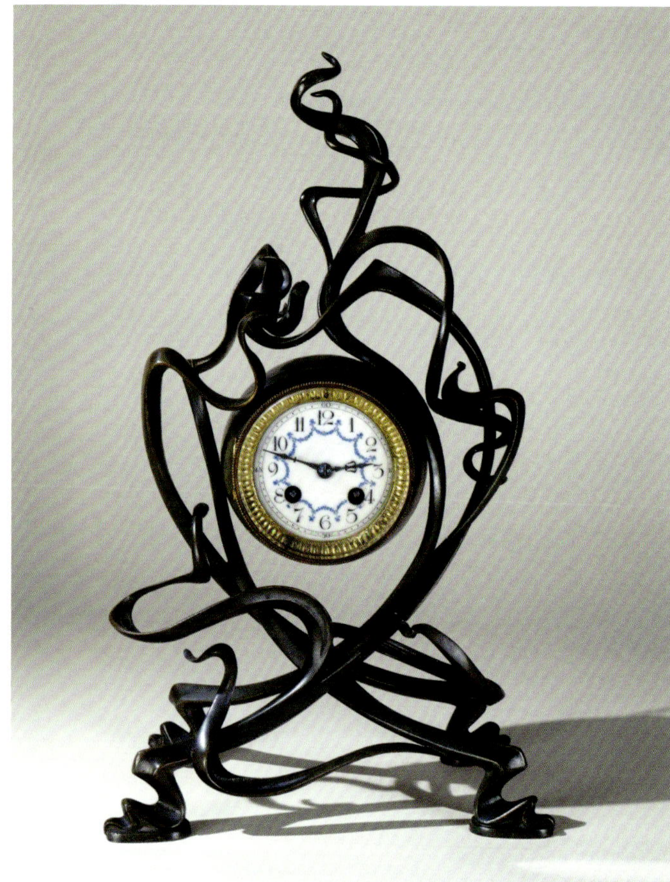

FIG. 13 Mantel clock. Victor Horta (Belgian, 1861–1947). France, ca. 1895. Bronze. Private collection

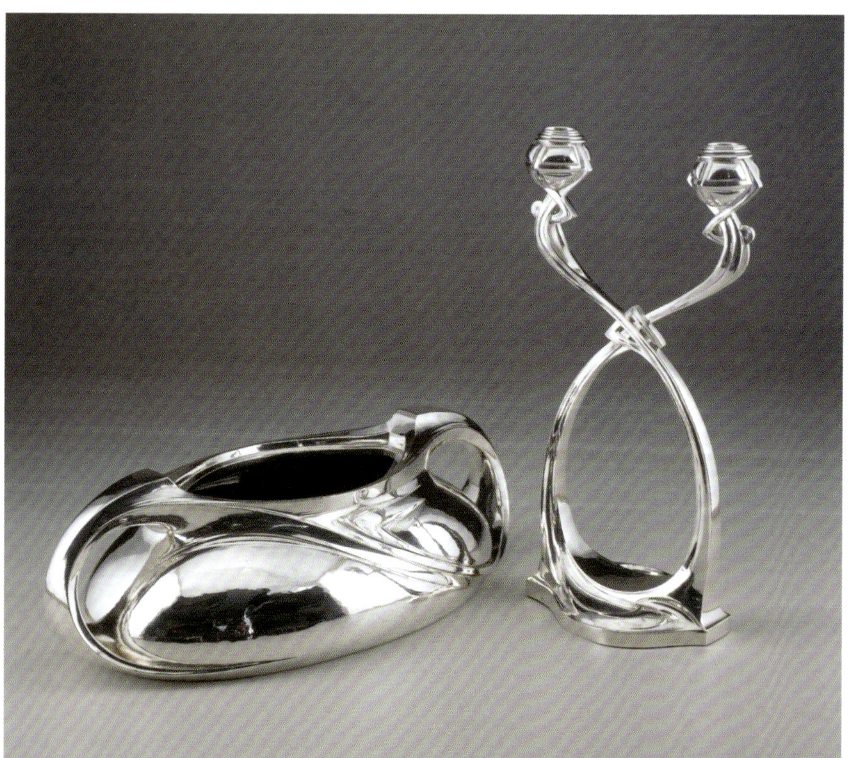

FIG. 14 Candlestick and jardinière. Henry van de Velde (Belgian, 1863–1957). Manufactured by Theodor-Müller. Germany, ca. 1900. Silver. Virginia Museum of Fine Arts, Richmond. The Sydney and Frances Lewis Art Nouveau Fund, 72.14.1-2

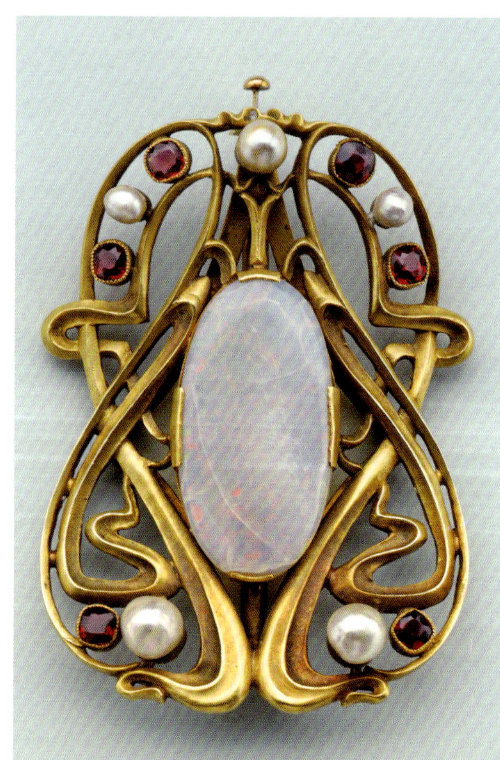

FIG. 15 Buckle. Attributed to Edward Colonna (French, 1862–1948). Paris, France, ca. 1900. Gold, opal, pearls, garnets. Cooper-Hewitt, National Design Museum, Smithsonian Institution, Gift of Mr. and Mrs. Maxime Hermanos, 1967-88-3

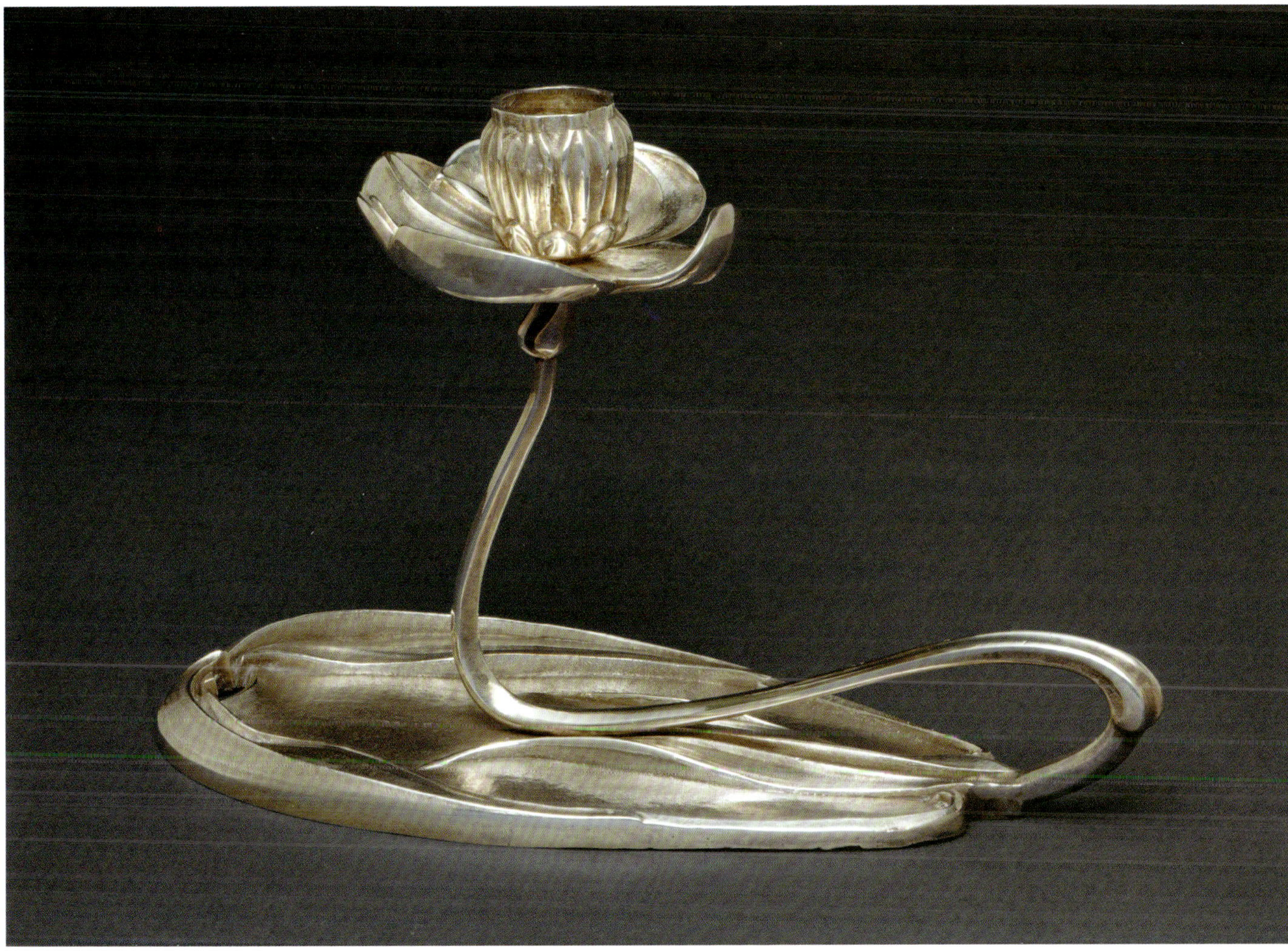

FIG. 16 Candlestick. Georges de Feure (French, 1868–1943). France, ca. 1901. Silverplate. Private collection

opened a porcelain manufactory in Paris producing and marketing subdued rococo-revival wares in the 1860s. After the Franco-Prussian War, Bing focused on dealing in Japanese art, which was fast becoming a mania in France. He perceived innovative talent in the applied arts across the world and determined to bring it together to create model environments for a new century.

Bing showcased work as disparate as the industrial English metal of W. A. S. Benson and the nature-inspired glass of Emile Gallé. Impressed by his visit to Tiffany's glass studio in New York, he induced Nabis painters to provide designs for Tiffany to execute in stained glass. Bing liked the whiplash ornament unleashed by the young Belgian architect Victor Horta (1861–1947) and was profoundly impressed by the more restrained organic sensibility of the Belgian painter Henri van de Velde (1863–1957), who turned to the applied arts in 1892 (figs. 13, 14). Bing enlisted both Belgians in the renovation of his townhouse on the rue de Provence, where he presented one-man shows as well as rooms of furniture ensembles.

Bing found he could not achieve the harmonics of a unified style as an agent for artists and craftsmen of different nationalities, so he set up studios on his own premises. There craftsmen executed the exclusive models of a trio of French designers: Edward Colonna (1862–1948), who specialized in whiplash curves; Eugène Gaillard (1862–1933), who designed simple furniture forms with swirls of carving and bronze mounts; and Georges de Feure, who created more subdued floral and female imagery.[10] (figs. 15, 16)

Bing fulfilled a role similar to that of the *marchands merciers* in eighteenth-century Paris, filtering the sinuous, sensuous impulse of his designers through his own sense of refinement, then showcasing and marketing the products. While he did not enjoy the same success as his predecessors in furnishing the homes of the Paris elite, museum directors from Germany and Scandinavia acquired individual works as models for local production. In 1904, the aging Bing gave up, selling his premises on the rue de Provence to Majorelle, who turned the emporium into a Parisian outpost of the Ecole de Nancy.[11]

PARISIAN ART NOUVEAU

For the visitors of the 1900 Paris World's Fair, the high temple of Art Nouveau was not Bing's pavilion, but rather the theater where the American dancer Loie Fuller (1862–1928) performed. Artists vied to

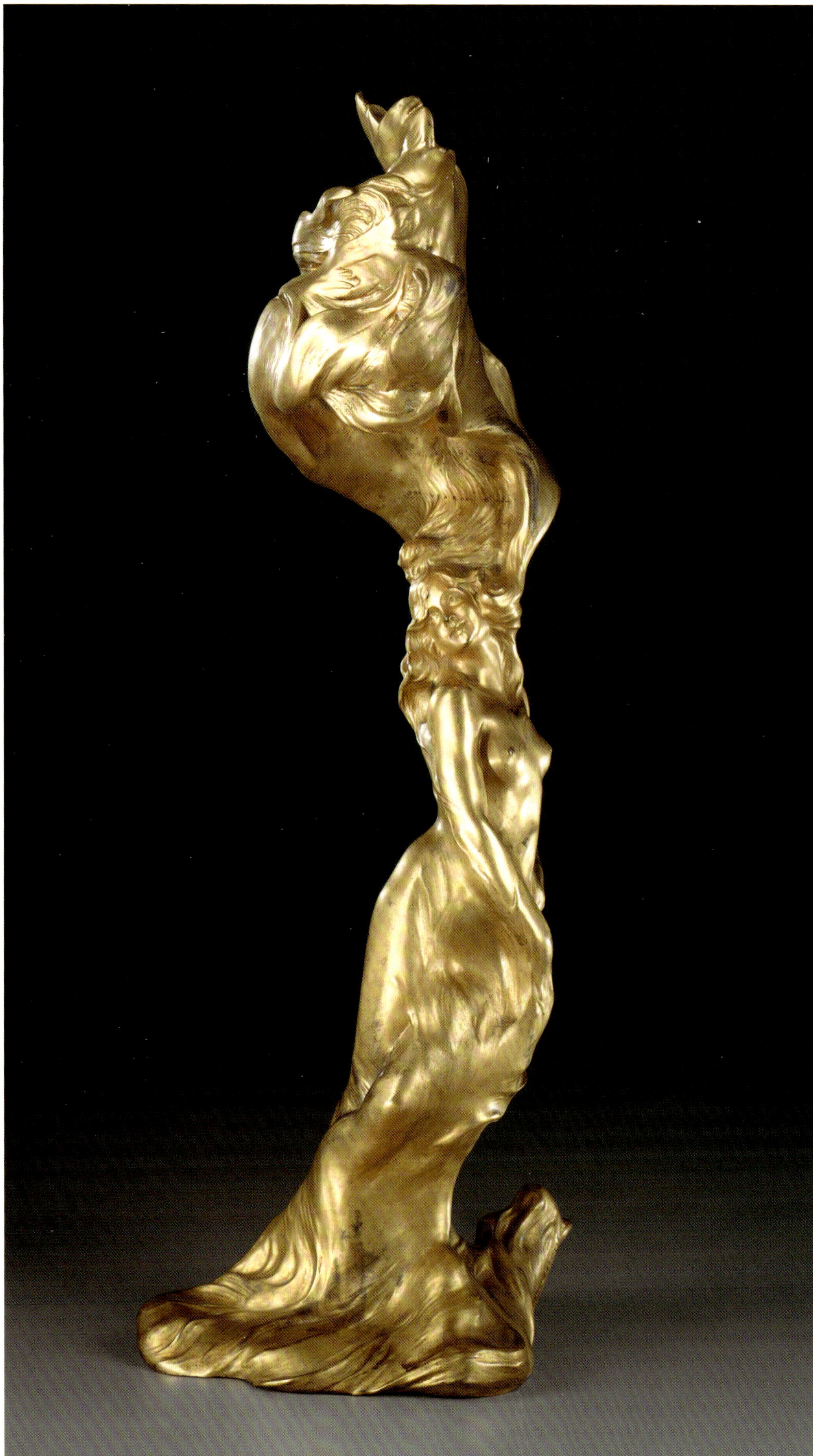

FIG. 17 "Loïe Fuller" lamp. Raoul-François Larche (French, 1860–1912). France, ca. 1896. Gilt bronze. Virginia Museum of Fine Arts, Richmond. The Sydney and Frances Lewis Art Nouveau Fund, 79.72

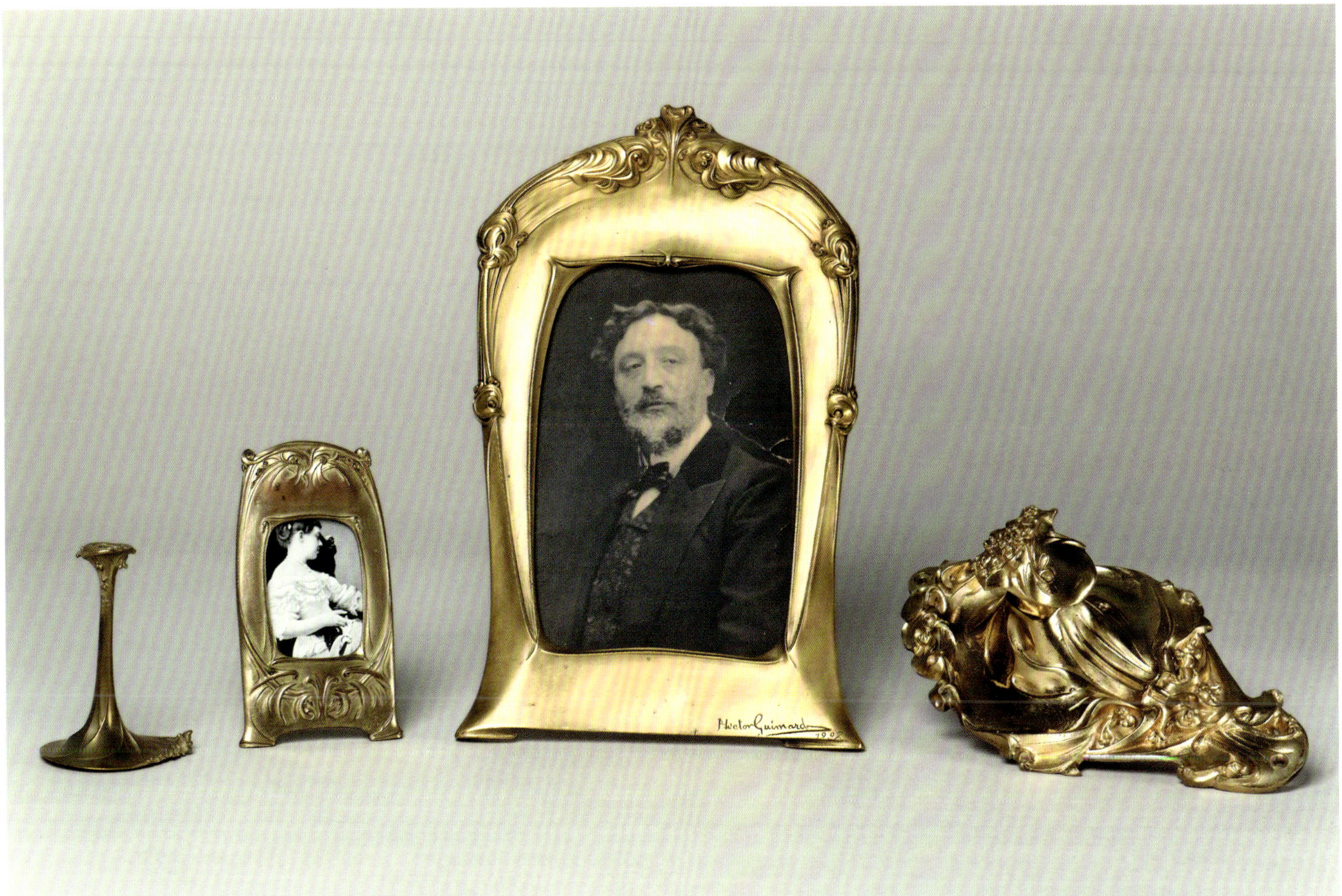

FIG. 19 Group of objects including frames, door pull, and seal. Hector Guimard (French 1867–1942). France, ca. 1900–10. Wood, bronze, glass. Cooper-Hewitt, National Design Museum, Smithsonian Institution, Gift of Mme. Hector Guimard, 1948-114-5, 1948-114-4a,b, 1956-76-4,5,6

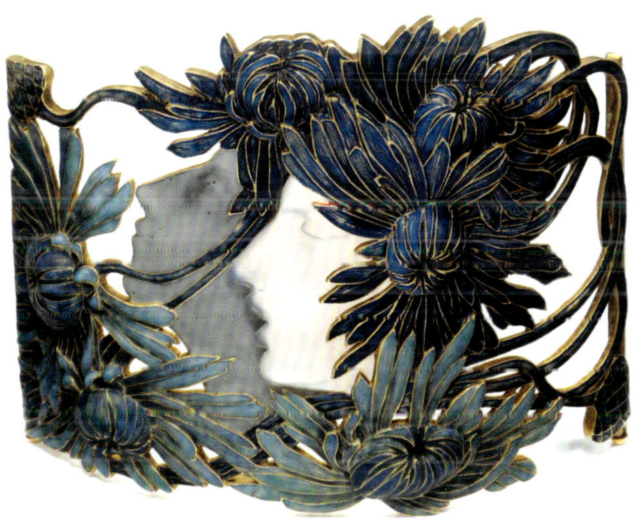

FIG. 18 "Narcisse" dog collar plaque. René Lalique (French, 1860–1945). Paris, France, ca. 1899–1900. Chased gold, opaque enamel on gold, glass. Private collection, New York

capture the essence of her image as she manipulated billowing veils under colored electric lights to personify a sensuous ideal (fig. 17).

At no other time and place in history did jewelry have greater artistic importance than turn-of-the-twentieth-century Paris. The brilliant René Lalique (1860–1945) brought together organic and Symbolist themes in designs that were soon emulated by established Parisian jewelry houses (fig. 18). Vever called on the talents of the Swiss designer Eugène Grasset (1845–1917) while Fouquet collaborated with the Czech graphic artist Alphonse Mucha (1860–1939; see Davidson, pp. 175, 176, figs. 12, 14). All three jewelers exhibited masterpieces featuring dreamy maidens with swirling hair to great acclaim at the 1900 World's Fair.

The Paris architect Hector Guimard (1867–1942) incorporated the whiplash of Horta in a fantastical, organic language (fig. 19). From his first major commission, the Castel Béranger of 1898, he detailed every aspect of his buildings, from doorknobs to lace curtains, with this original inspiration. Surging upward from Paris's sidewalks, Guimard's cast-iron Métro entrances, designed for the underground transit system built between 1899 and 1905, are lasting landmarks that have come to symbolize Art Nouveau style.

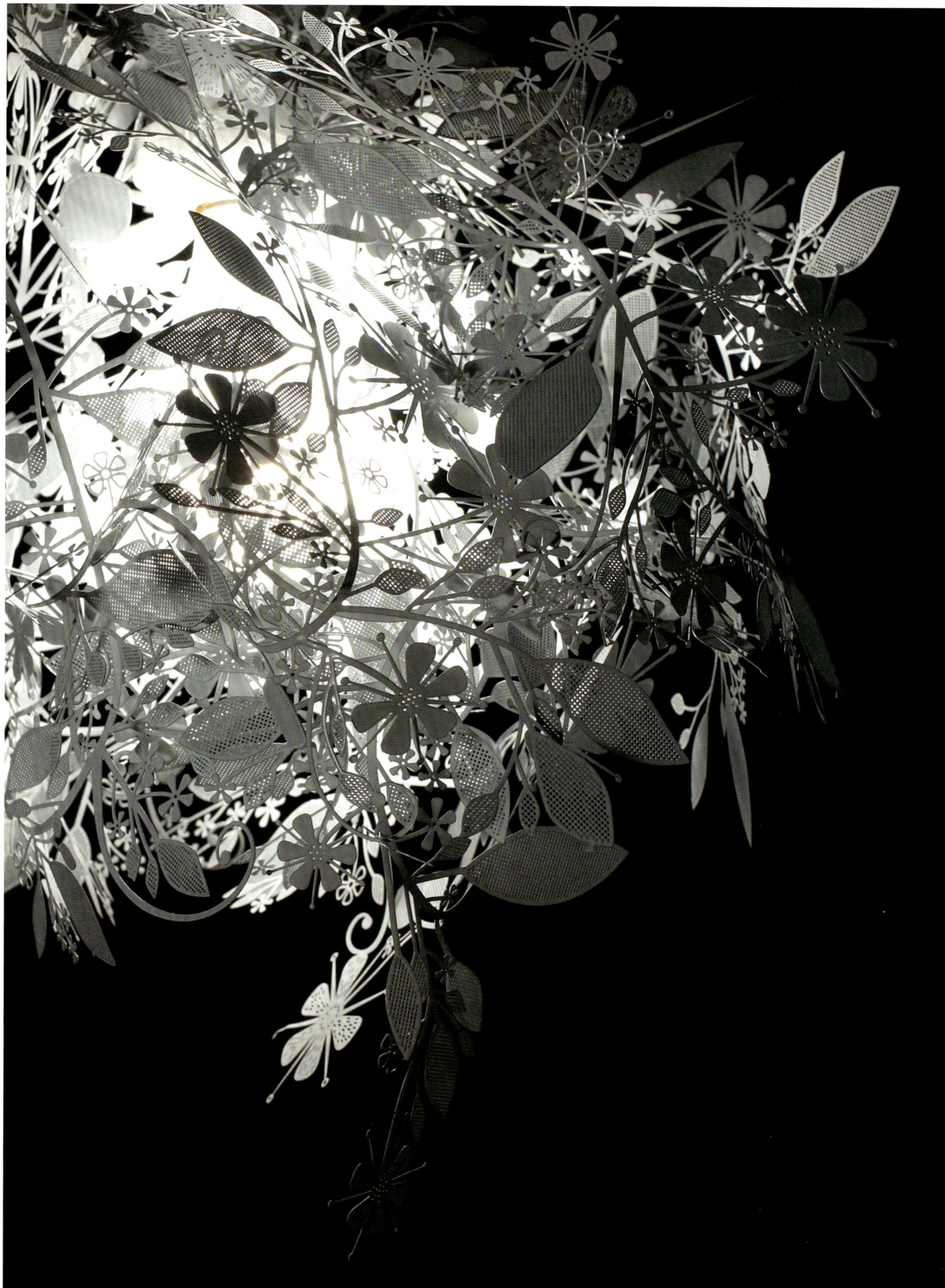

FIG. 1 Garland light. Tord Boontje (Dutch, b. 1968). Manufactured by Artecnica. Los Angeles, CA, 2004. Silver-plated, photographically etched stainless steel. Courtesy of Artecnica

The Modern Curve

FORM, STRUCTURE, AND IMAGE IN THE TWENTIETH CENTURY AND BEYOND

Ellen Lupton

Although the phrase "modern design" conjures orderly regiments of grids and cubes, the curve has always been at play within its discourse. Modern designers have repeatedly challenged classical stasis in favor of an open, inquisitive organicism. The contemporary American ceramicist Adrian Saxe, whose work combines historical and popular references, has said, "Modernism would not have happened without the Rococo."[1] The Dutch-born designer Tord Boontje designs delicate lampshades cut from Tyvek or paper-thin sheets of stainless steel that cascade around a simple fixture. Aiming to infuse daily life with sensuality and pleasure via intelligent, affordable products, Boontje says, "In a funny way, what I'm doing is very modern."[2] A respect for human comfort and delight underlies the continuing evolution of modern design. That sense of life-sustaining pleasure also characterizes rococo as a visual style and an outlook on the world (fig. 1).

This essay follows the path of the rococo impulse across twentieth- and twenty-first-century design, touching down to explore selected artifacts and ideas, from its role in early and mid-twentieth-century objects to its place in Pop, the international counter-movement that erupted in the 1950s and 1960s. Today, both the modernist view of technology and materials and the pop celebration of signs and surfaces continue to shape a diversity of design practices. Progressive designers are creating works that are abstract, referential, or both, informed by fascinations with structure, craft, and technology as well as with the history of ornament.

To speak of the "modern" is to speak of a particular time and philosophy. In the 1920s, thinkers such as Le Corbusier promoted the direct, transparent use of materials and manufacturing, as well as a democratic orientation toward markets[3]. The "modern" is not only a historic period, however; it is also an ongoing dialogue that designers and artists have sustained in relation to their own time and place. Modernism is at once a set of values grounded in a historical era and the framework for countless revolts launched against it.

Like modernism, the idea of rococo lives on multiple planes. Rococo is a period style, invented in early eighteenth-century France, that has been explicitly referenced and revived by designers, decorators, and manufacturers again and again since the birth and decline of the original movement. Rococo is also an outlook on life and form that resurfaces more abstractly in the work of many designers who might deny its direct inspiration, or who might see it as just one among many overlapping—even contradictory—currents of influence.

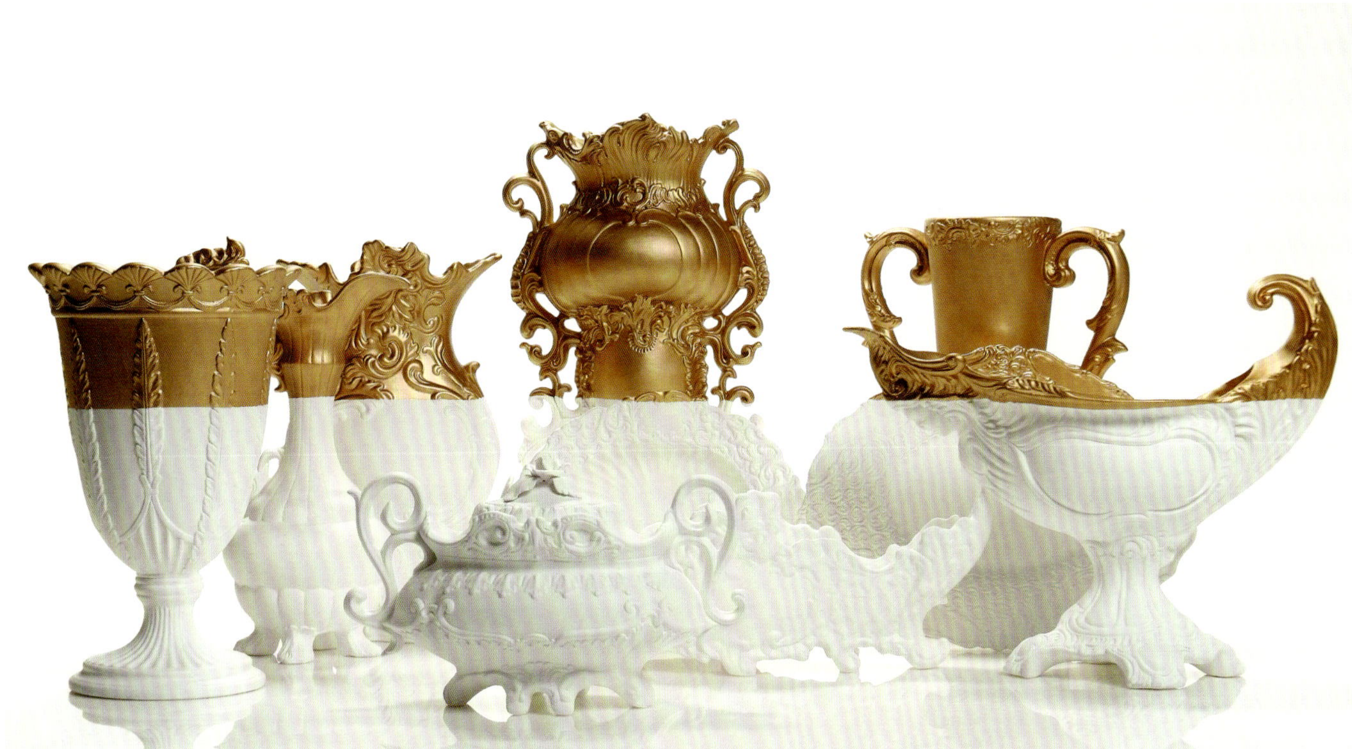

FIG. 2 We Are Typical vases and tableware. Fabrica (Sam Baron [French, b. 1976] and team). Manufactured by Stylnove. Bassano del Grappa, Italy, 2007. Varnished, gold-laquered earthenware. Courtesy of Fabrica

Styles such as baroque, rococo, and neoclassicism, once separated by time, place, and ideology, appear today side by side in the commercial catalogues of manufacturers and retailers worldwide. A recent project led by Sam Baron at the Fabrica workshop in Italy consisted of a suite of white objects taken from different points in history, each decorated with a band of gold across the top that hewed to a common horizon, as if the whole ensemble had been dipped simultaneously into a milky bath that coated its golden core. The taller the piece, the more gold peeked above the mass of white. The ensemble employed a graphic device to combine discordant histories into a simultaneous lexicon (fig. 2).

The definition of period styles dates to the nineteenth century, after the academic disciplines of art history and archaeology had established their places within the hierarchy of the arts and sciences. "Rococo" was officially canonized in 1843 in the *Dictionnaire de l'Académie Française* as a term "used colloquially for the kind of ornament, style, and design belonging to the school of the Louis XV and early Louis XVI reigns. This 'rococo' style both followed and preceded the style of Madame de Pompadour, which is just a nuance of rococo."[4] Art historians soon broadened this definition to encompass early eighteenth-century art more generally. Historicism, which looks for an era's distinctive styles, forms of organization, and Zeitgeist, is associated with the philosophy of Hegel, but also with the rise of history as an empirical discipline and with the rise of art history as the study of styles over time.[5]

Thus Rémy G. Saisselein has described rococo as a "dream of happiness," and a "style of living" that favored intimacy over grandeur and preferred wit and pleasure over pomp and ceremony. Rococo marked a shift away from the public showiness of the king's court in Versailles toward life played out in the private apartments of the aristocracy. The serpentine curves and repetitive flourishes emanating from French decorative arts in the first half of the eighteenth century have come to represent the spirit of an age—an attitude toward personal liberty expressed in painting, architecture, fashion, interiors, and more.

Architectural critic Deborah Fausch sees such a rococo worldview at play in works of late twentieth-century architecture that celebrate "the mobile, the ephemeral, the fragmented, and the fictitious." Those values are associated with Gilles Deleuze's theory of baroque style and the logic of the fold, which influenced many architects and designers at the turn of the twenty-first century. According to Fausch, those values are more tied to the restless, superficial wanderings of rococo than to muscular, masculine baroque. Tying contemporary design practices to the cleverness and convenience of rococo, Fausch concludes, "As the modernist style becomes ever more intelligent, beautiful, and bittersweet, it neither looks ahead to a millennial future nor back to a lost utopian past, but is content with the goal of making architecture more suitable to its present situation. Some of the best of our current architecture exhibits the economy, the elegance, and the assurance of this style."[6]

The story to be told in this essay concerns objects and decorative art rather than architecture, but it follows the idea of rococo as a broader vision of life and form. A look back over the last century and at what designers are doing today yields perspectives on design's ongoing dialogue about form, function, technology, materials, representation, and social life. Straight-up reproductions of gilt armoires or putti-infested wall coverings will not be found here; instead, there are works that tap the energy of the curve in order to form an original response to their makers' own situations in the world. These curves are complex rather than classical, lyrical and searching rather than strict and confined. In general,

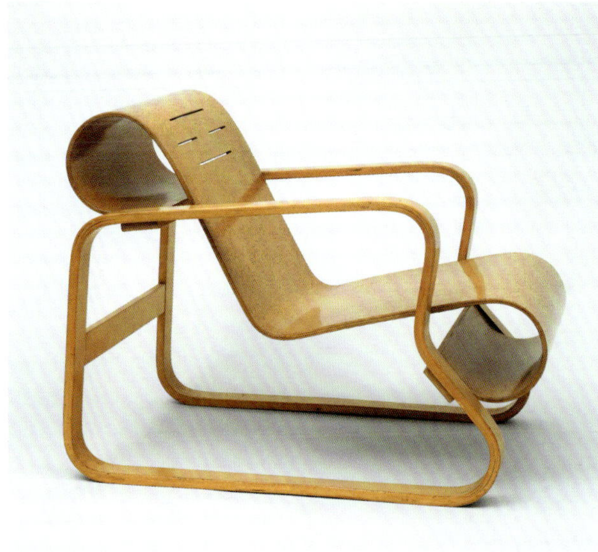

FIG. 3 Paimio chair. Alvar Aalto (Finish, 1898–1976). Manufactured by Oy Huonekalu-ja Rakennustyötehdas Ab. Turku, Finland, 1931–32. Bent plywood, bent laminated birch, solid birch. The Museum of Modern Art, New York, Gift of Edgar Kaufmann, Jr.

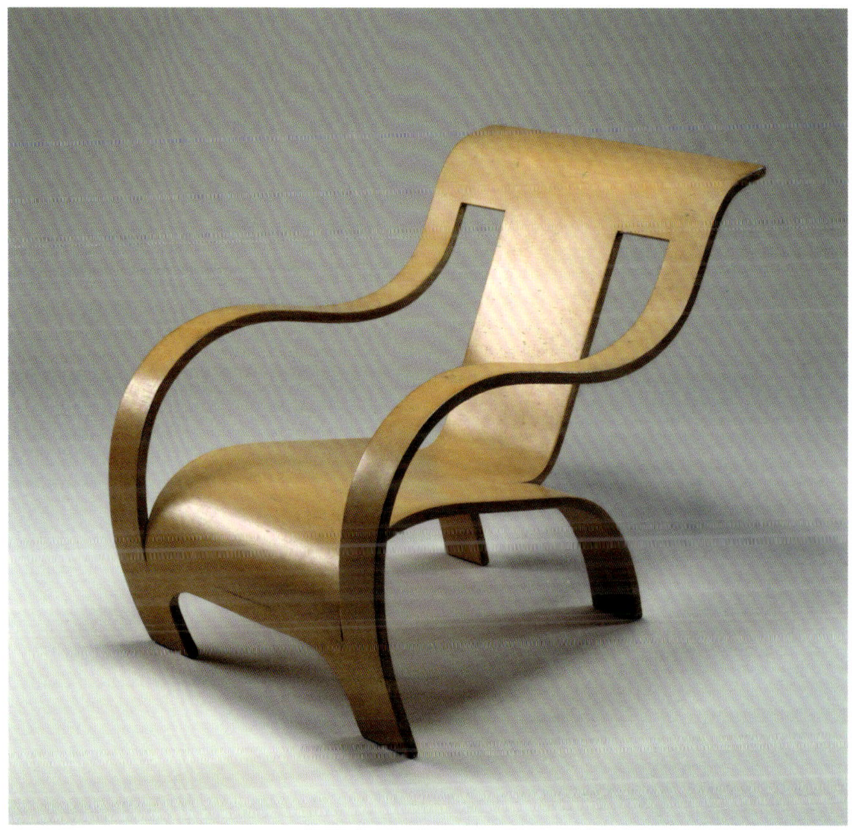

FIG. 4 Armchair. Gerald Summers (British, 1899–1967). Manufactured by Makers of Simple Furniture, Ltd. London, England, ca. 1934. Bent, laminated birch. Virginia Museum of Fine Arts, Richmond. The Sydney and Frances Lewis Endowment Fund, 88.128

rococo's modern vector beholds sweetness and light, seeking out beauty and comfort rather than Dionysian turmoil and rage.

Fascinated with the unique behavior of materials, designers have found ways to shape wood, glass, metal, and other substances into useful objects with organic contours. Bentwood furniture, initiated in the nineteenth century, is one such exploration on the behavior of materials.[7] A curved rod or plane, whether in wood, metal, or cardboard, has greater strength than a flat one. Furniture made from bent lengths of wood influenced the use of tubular steel by Marcel Breuer and others in the 1920s.[8] Alvar Aalto's Paimio chair of 1931–32 is considered one of the first chairs to use bent sheets of plywood. An unbroken loop of wood on either side of the chair combines arm and leg in a single unit. The back and seat are formed from a single plane that curves at the middle and ends in two scrolls. Additional slats hold the chair together.[9] (fig. 3)

More singular and concise, Gerald Summers's lounge chair of 1933–34 is made from just one piece of plywood, produced by cutting two parallel slots out of a sheet and then pulling the arm plane in a separate direction from the body and legs. Designed for use in tropical climates, the chair's lack of joinery and upholstery helps it endure extremes of temperature and humidity. The chair's lyrical confluence of opposing curves is motivated by functional considerations, celebrating an economy of means.[10] While the Paimio's curves are essentially classical, following the radius of a circle, the Summers chair follows rococo's emblematic S-curve (fig. 4).

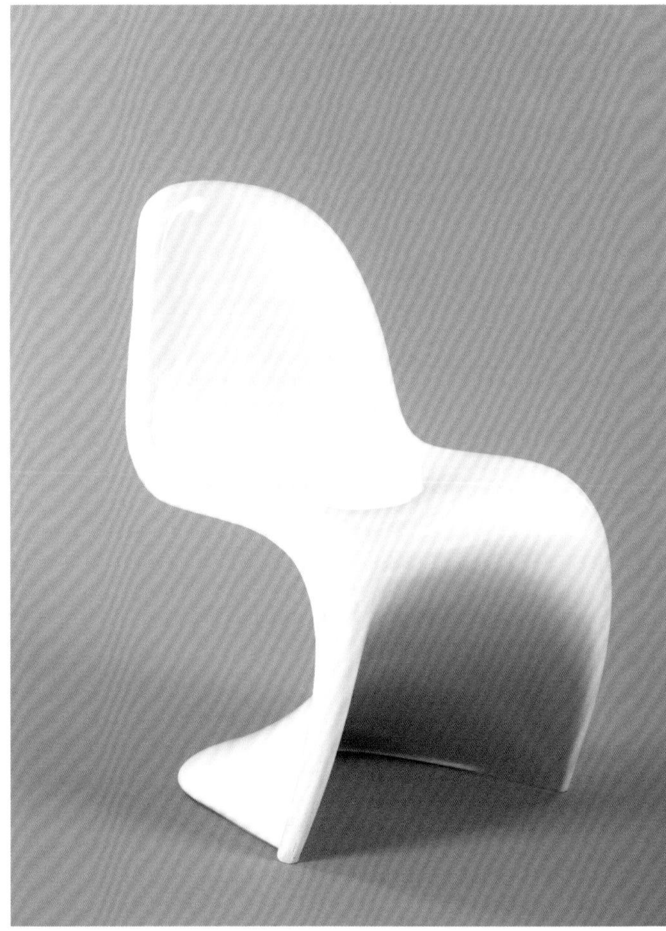

FIG. 5 Stacking Side Chair. Verner Panton (Danish, 1926–1998). Manufactured by Herman Miller. Zeeland, MI, 1960. Injection-molded thermoplastic. Cooper-Hewitt, National Design Museum, Smithsonian Institution, Gift of Robert Blaich, 1977-1-1

Eroticism, another rococo proclivity, was at play in the curved silhouettes shaped by Carlo Mollino, who often photographed his female acquaintances in provocative poses. The elegant contortions in Mollino's work also drew inspiration from Art Nouveau, surrealism, and futurism, as well as from aeronautics and the natural world. He belonged to a generation of Italian designers in the 1950s who turned against rectilinear modernism and Fascist neoclassicism in favor of an organic design vocabulary. Mollino's tea table of 1950 is made of a sinuous plane of bent plywood stabilized by two planes of glass (a tabletop and a lower shelf). Ocular shapes cut from the wood both diminish its weight and provide structural ribbing, functioning like the perforations in the longerons of an airplane wing.[11] (fig. 6)

Charles and Ray Eames furthered the complexity of the curve with their LCW (Lounge Chair Wood) of 1946, whose "potato chip" seat bends across both the x and y axes of a single plane. Such compound curves resulted from Ray Eames's abstract sculptural experiments with bent plywood.[12] Applied to the design of a chair, these double contours yield lyrical beauty, structural strength, and comfort. Compound curves underlay numerous other works by the Eameses, including the couple's hugely successful series of chairs made from molded fiberglass-reinforced plastic. La Chaise, a fiberglass-reinforced chair, was conceived for mass production in 1948 but proved too expensive to manufacture at the time. Named after Gaston La Chaise's 1927 sculpture *Reclining Nude*, a study in exaggerated femininity, La Chaise overflows with curves that step beyond frank utility into a dreamy and erotic realm, worthy of a rococo boudoir. The Eameses wrote, "The form can only suggest a freer adaptation of material to need and stimulate inquiry into what those needs may be."[13] Thus function did not dictate the form of La Chaise; rather, the form opened up avenues to functions not yet defined (fig. 7).

The Danish designer Verner Panton was among the first to produce a chair from a single piece of synthetic material. Like the Eameses, he sought to create affordable, practical seating. His goal was a single-piece chair whose production would require no hand-finishing or assembly, and used the curve to simplify a basic object of daily living. Designed in 1960, Panton's Stacking Side Chair combines seat, back, and legs into one continuous form. The American furniture company Herman Miller initially balked at the object's unprecedented form—design director George Nelson dismissed it as "at most a sculpture, but not a chair."[14] In Europe, Vitra began trying to manufacture the chair in 1963, releasing a viable model in 1968; the chair remains in production today in numerous colors. Animated by a swooping S-curve, the cantilevered chair built upon Panton's earlier work with bent plywood for Arne Jacobson. Panton also was inspired by cheap plastic buckets and fiberglass crash helmets (fig. 5).

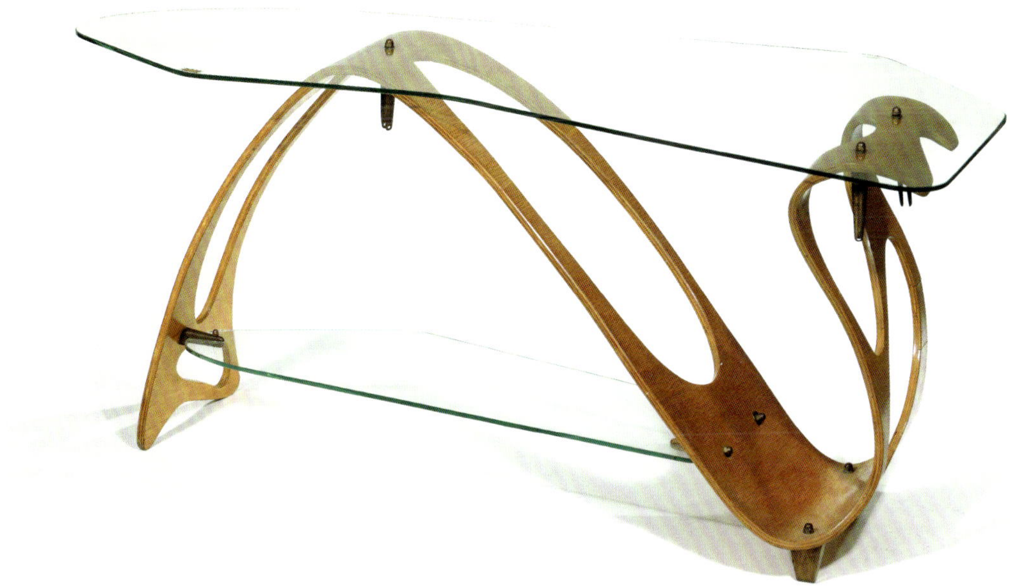

FIG. 6 Tea table with removable shelves. Carlo Mollino (Italian, 1905–1973). Manufactured by F. Apelli and L. Varesio. Turin, Italy, ca. 1950. Maple plywood, glass. Brooklyn Museum 54.64.231.a-c. Gift of the Italian Government

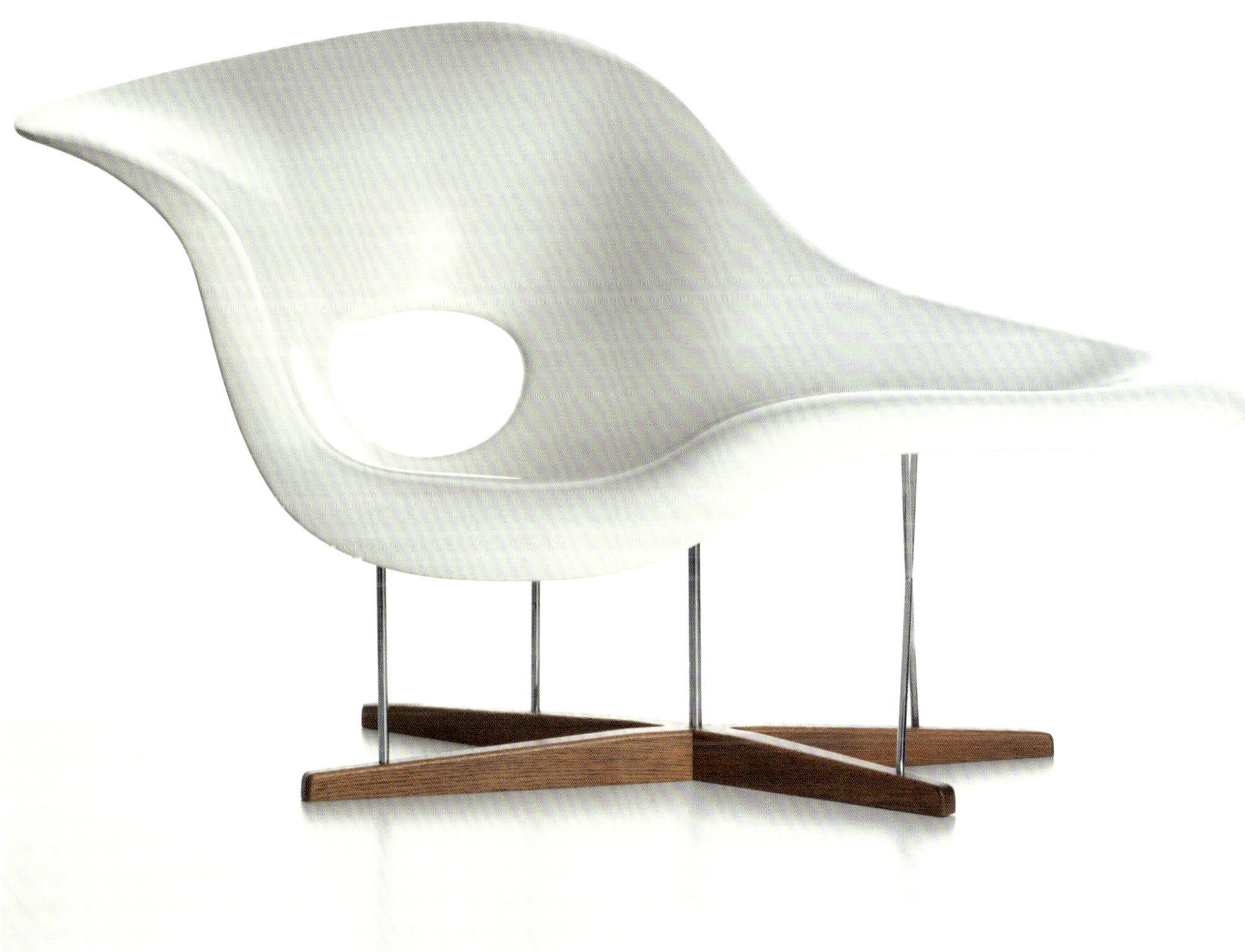

FIG. 7 La Chaise. Charles and Ray Eames (American, 1907–1978, 1912–1988). Manufactured by Vitra. Designed in United States, 1948, manufactured in Germany, 1990. Fiberglass, chrome-plated metal, oak. Courtesy of Vitra

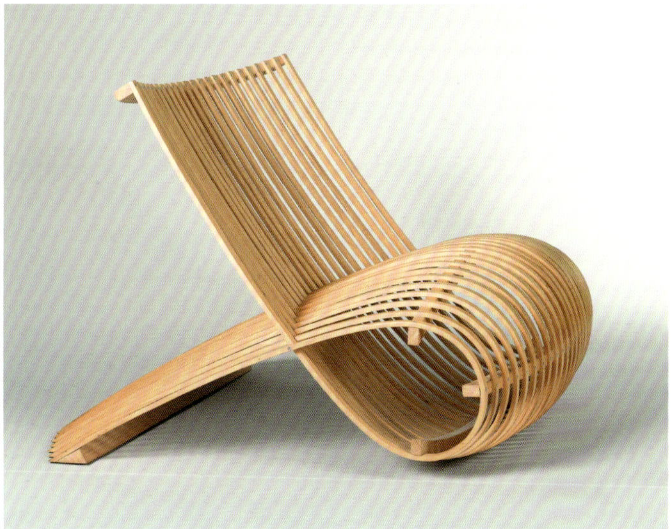

FIG. 8 Wood Chair. Marc Newson (Australian, b. 1962). Manufactured by Capellini. Italy, 1988. Bent beech wood. Cooper-Hewitt, National Design Museum, Smithsonian Institution, Museum purchase from General Acquisitions Endowment Fund, 2006-4-3

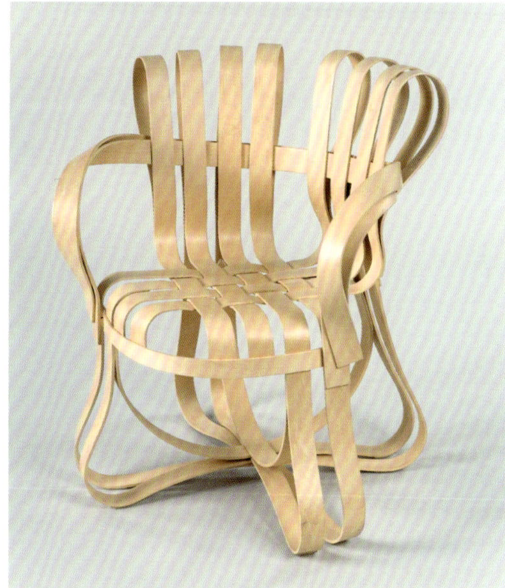

FIG. 9 Cross Check chair. Frank O. Gehry (American, born Canada, 1929). Manufactured by Knoll International. United States, 1994. Bent, laminated white maple. Cooper-Hewitt, National Design Museum, Smithsonian Institution, Gift of Joel and Anne Ehrenkranz, 2006-24-2

In Marc Newson's 1988 Wood Chair, two dozen strips of wood are fastened along a set of horizontal slats to create a curved plane. The surface bends over and passes through itself to create seat, back, and supporting legs. Each strip follows a simple path that changes from strip to strip, yielding a compound plane that bulges out towards the center of the seat. Frank Gehry's Cross Check chairs and table, created for Knoll in 1990, employ slender ribbons of wood as both structure and seat, giving shape, in Gehry's words, to a "single and continuous idea."[15] The Cross Check pieces implement the same technique used to make simple bushel baskets in an explosive and unexpected composition (figs. 8, 9).

The liquid substance of glass undulates across the history of modern design. René Lalique designed mass-produced luxury objects from glass in the first half of the twentieth century; the faceted surface of his power-pressed glass Tourbillon vase (1925) swirls with curves evoking whirlpools and the wind.[16] The continuous wall of Alvar Aalto's Savoy vase (ca. 1936–37) follows a serpentine path around the perimeter that descends at right angles towards a flat, horizontal bottom, creating a fluid form grounded against a stable base.[17] Aalto's vase was made by inflating a bubble of molten glass against the interior of a wooden mold.[18] Pipsan Saarinen Swanson explored a similar organicism in works such as her Flower floater/candleholder of 1947, conceived as part of a complete collection of modern home furnishings.[19] More effusive curves animate the Handkerchief vases designed by Fulvio Bianconi for Venini Glassworks. These pieces, emblems of the Venetian glass renaissance in the 1950s, capture the movement of a glass bowl as it is reheated and swung through the air, an action that generates exquisitely balanced folds and counterfolds.[20] (figs. 10–13)

The Seattle-based glass blower Dale Chihuly was the first American to study glassmaking at the Venini factory, going there on a Fulbright fellowship in the 1960s. The objects in Chihuly's Seaform series resemble bowls and vessels, but are not explicitly functional. The subtle grooves that run horizontally around the circumference of the pieces—made

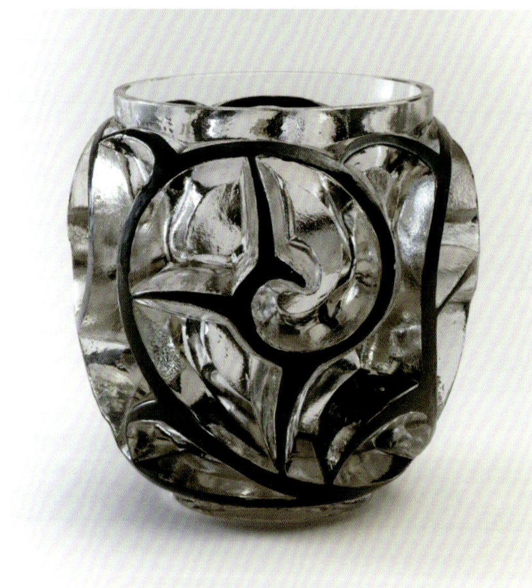

FIG. 10 Tourbillon (Whirlwind) vase. René Lalique (French, 1860–1945). Paris, France, ca. 1925. Glass, enamel. Cooper-Hewitt, National Design Museum, Smithsonian Institution, Museum purchase through gift of Anonymous Donor, 1969-20-1

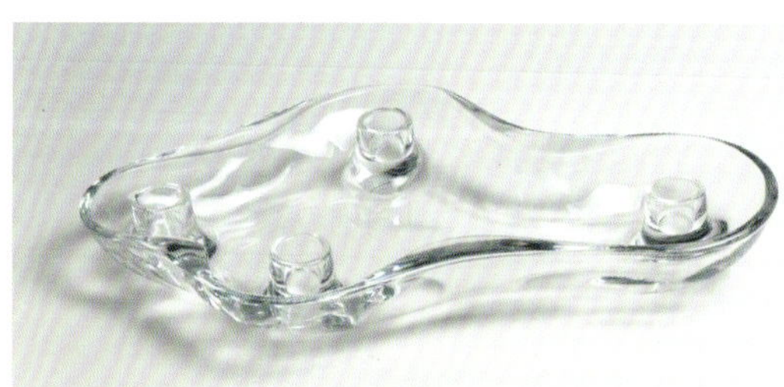

FIG. 11 Flower floater/ candle holder. Eva Lisa "Pipsan" Saarinen Swanson (American, born Finland, 1905–1979). Manufactured by U.S. Glass Company. Tiffin, OH, 1948–50. Glass. Cooper-Hewitt, National Design Museum, Smithsonian Institution, Gift of Ashley Dawn Brown, 2000-16-1 Photo: Matt Flynn

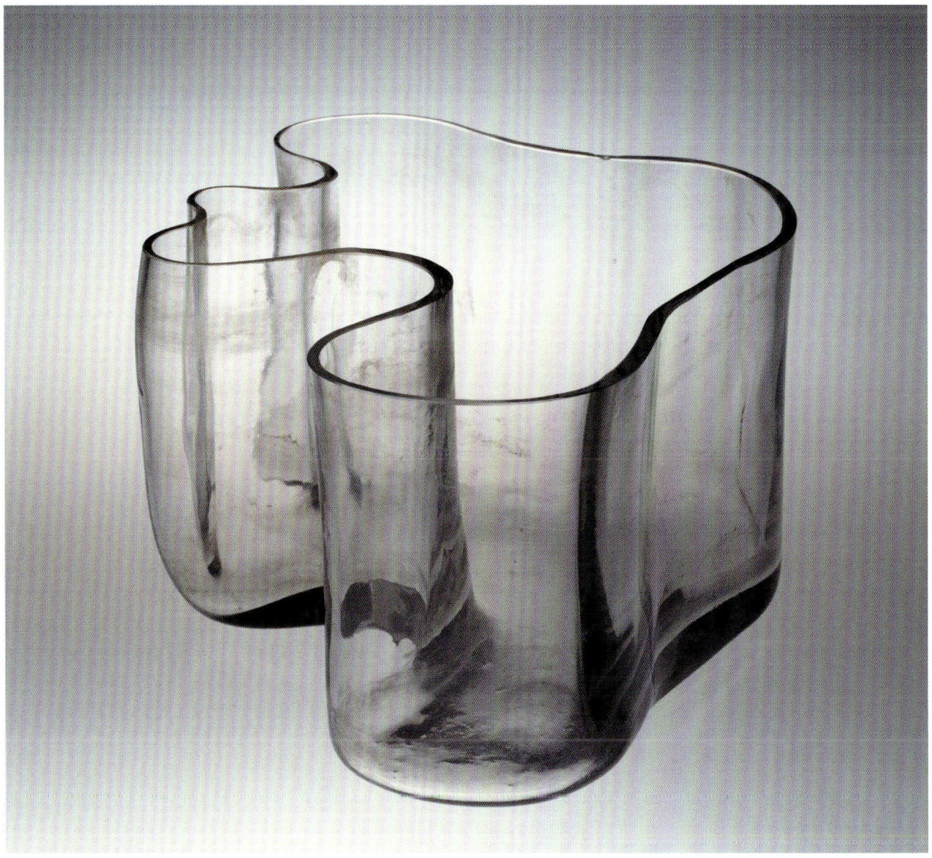

FIG. 12 Savoy vase. Alvar Aalto (Finnish, 1898–1976). Manufactured by Karhula Glassworks. Iittala, Finland, ca. 1936–37. Mold-blown glass. Cooper-Hewitt, National Design Museum, Smithsonian Institution, Gift of Harmon Goldstone, 1990-61-2

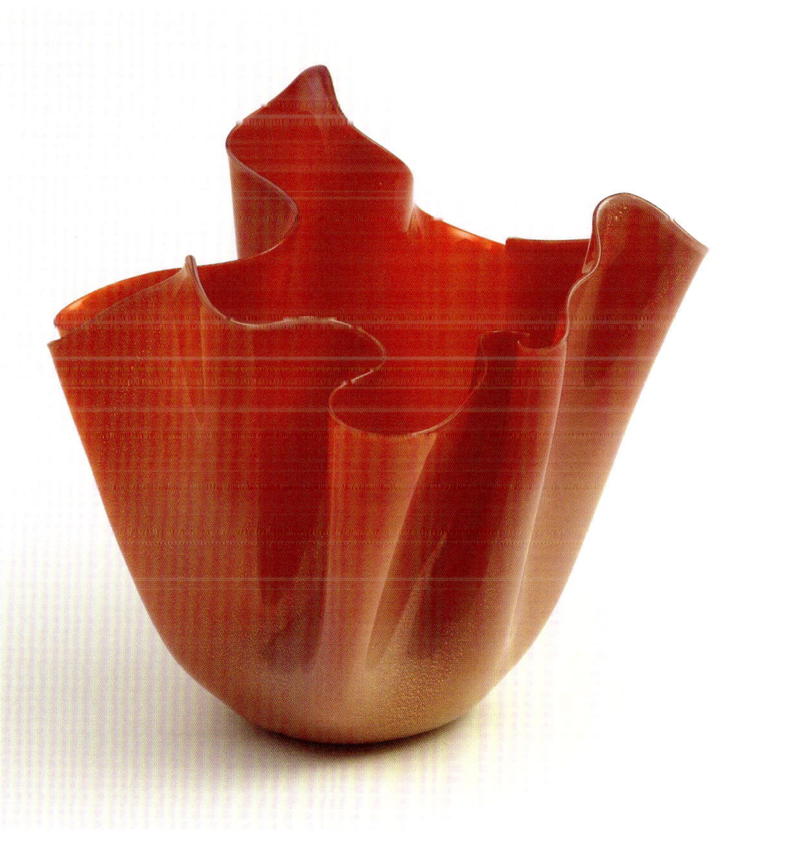

FIG. 13 Fazzoletto (Handkerchief) vase. Fulvio Bianconi (Italian, 1915–1996). Manufactured by Venini Glassworks. Murano, Italy, ca. 1955. Blown and cased glass. Cooper-Hewitt, National Design Museum, Smithsonian Institution, Gift of Christian Rohlfing, 1969-46-1

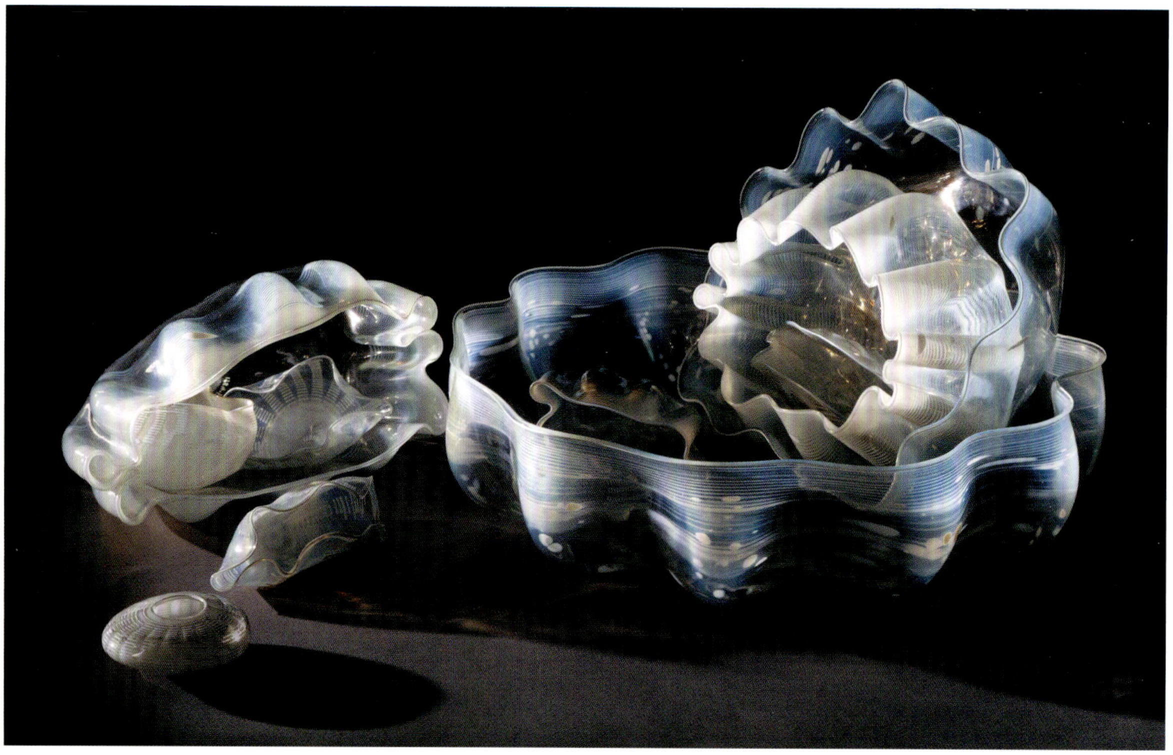

FIG. 14 White Seaform Group. Dale Chihuly (American, b. 1941). Seattle, WA, 1982. Blown glass. Cooper-Hewitt, National Design Museum, Smithsonian Institution, Gift of Dr. and Mrs. Joseph Chazen, 1984-137-1/11

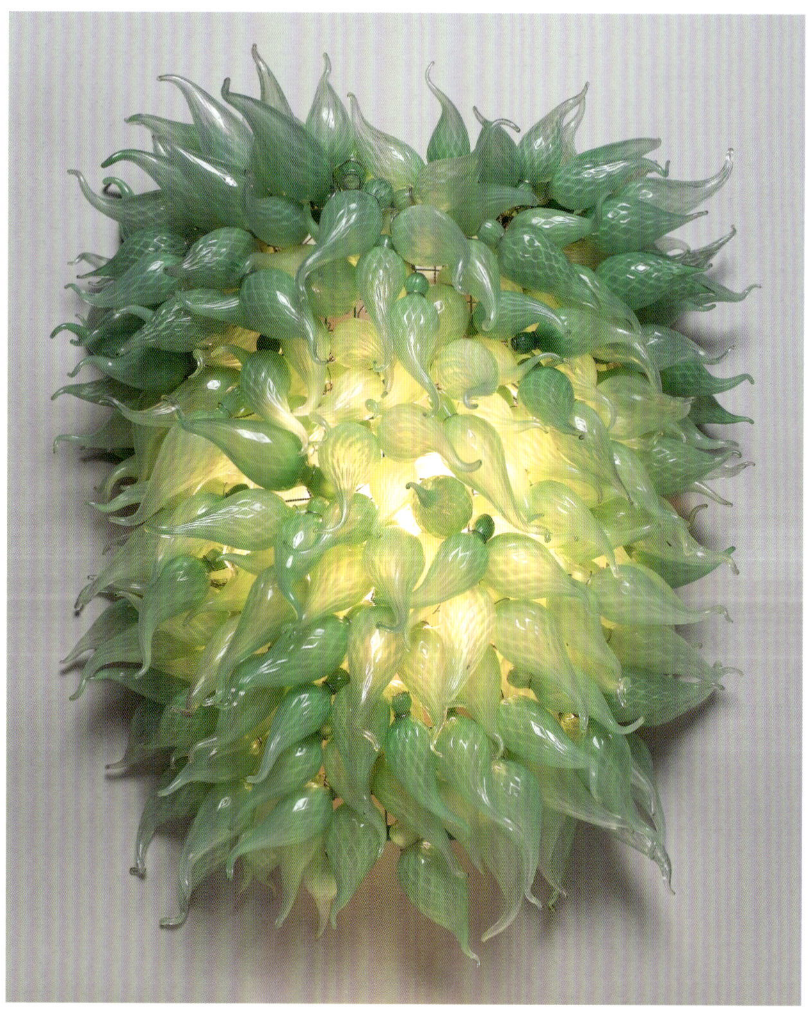

FIG. 15 Wall sconce (one of a pair). Dale Chihuly (American, b. 1941). Seattle, WA, 1996. Blown glass, metal. Cooper-Hewitt, National Design Museum, Smithsonian Institution, Gift of Barbaralee Diamonstein-Spielvogel, 2007-31-1

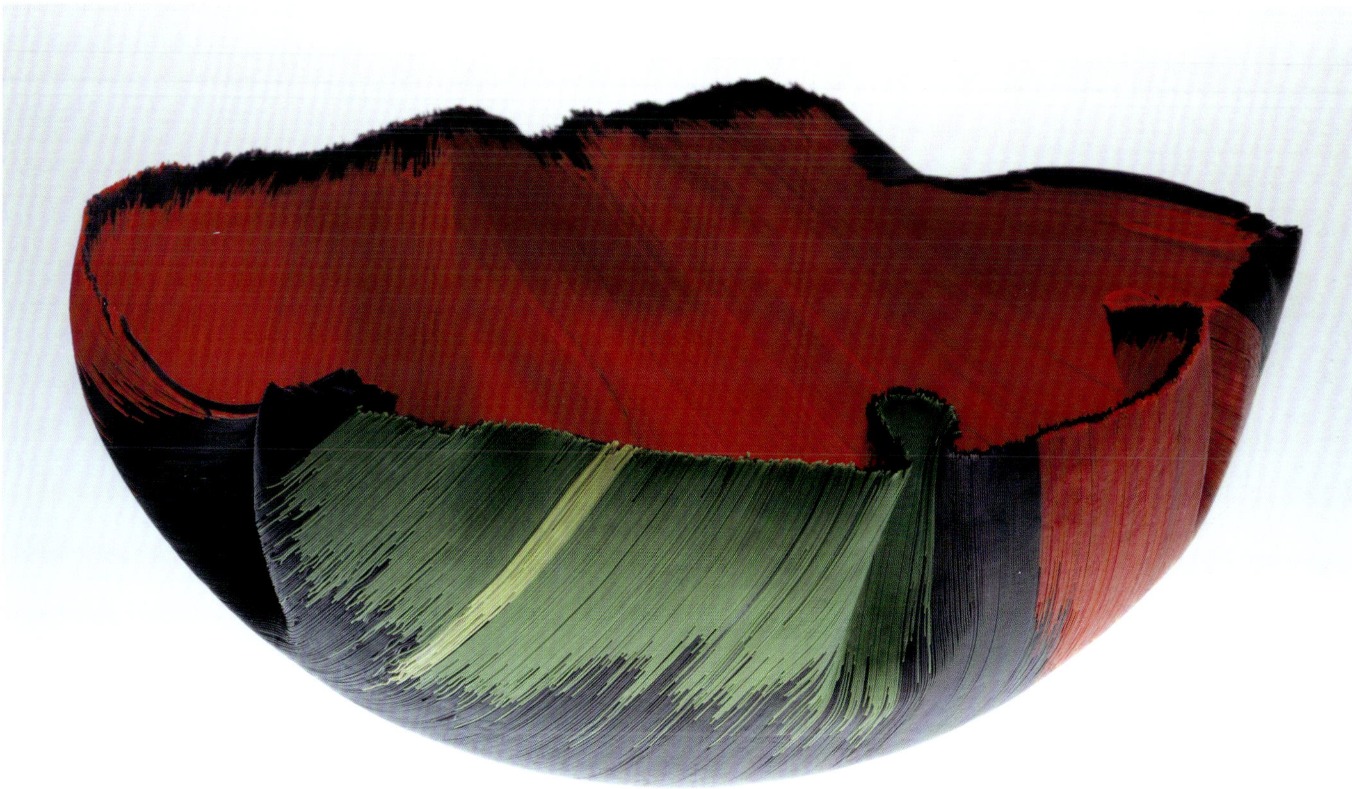

FIG. 16 Bowl. Mary Ann "Toots" Zynsky (American, b. 1951). Amsterdam, The Netherlands, 1985. Slumped, fused, and shaped glass threads. Cooper-Hewitt, National Design Museum, Smithsonian Institution, Museum Purchase through gift of Anonymous Donor, Carol B. Brener and Stephen W. Brener, Mr. and Mrs. Max B. Furman, Bequest of Mrs. John Innes Kane, James M. Osborn, and Thonet Industries, Inc., 1986-20-1

by pressing molten glass against a ribbed mold early in the process—strengthen the glass, just as corrugations strengthen a sheet of plywood. The vertical pleats and folds, made by swinging and crimping the heated volume, also produce both structural integrity and lyrical form.[21] More delicate folds and striations appear in the work of Mary Ann "Toots" Zynsky, whose filet de verre technique fuses together tiny threads of glass into an integral material.[22] (figs. 14–16) Although the curve may seem to deviate from modernism's baseline rationality, the projects discussed above share modernism's commitment to visual continuity and the direct, transparent manipulation of materials and techniques.

The international Pop movement took the curve in another direction, turning against wholeness and integrity toward a flamboyant exploration of signifying surfaces and unstructured forms and anti-forms. Pop artists and designers delighted in the "groovy" curves and soft edges of commercial culture, found everywhere from comic books and Cadillacs to the decorative tradition of Art Nouveau. They viewed technology not only in terms of new materials and mass-production techniques, but also as a driving feature in a consumer economy based on constant renewal and waste.[23] The rococo impulse was reborn in the 1960s as a language of ephemerality and revolt.

The curves of the Boalum lamp, designed by Livio Castiglioni and Gianfranco Frattini in 1969–70, behave in a wholly different manner from the meandering yet dignified path of Aalto's Savoy vase or the tautly engineered S of Panton's stacking chair. The lamp, whose serpentine, segmented body was inspired by the hose of an outdoor vacuum cleaner,

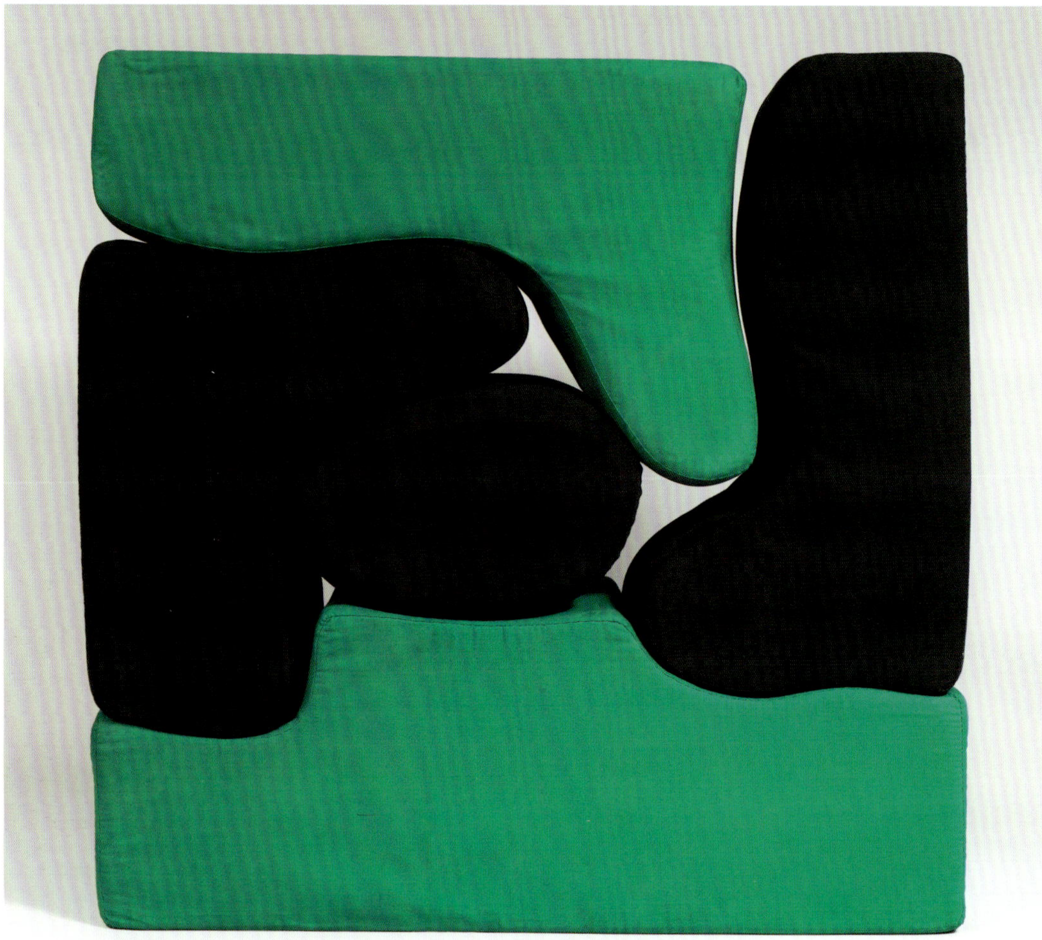

FIG. 17 Malitte seating system (lounge chairs and ottoman). Roberto Sebastian Matta (Chilean, 1911–2002). Manufactured by Gavina. Italy, ca. 1968. Polyurethane foam, cotton. Cooper-Hewitt, National Design Museum, Smithsonian Institution, Museum purchase from Decorative Arts Association Acquisition Fund, 1991-47-4a/e

consists of a double-spiral plastic tube lit from inside with incandescent bulbs. In place of precisely planned form and counter-form, weight and counter-weight, the shape of this worm-like tube changes depending on how the user drapes, coils, or piles it. Multiple units can be plugged together, creating more possibilities for shaping the fixture's body.[24] (fig. 18)

This casual anti-aesthetic takes shape in other ways as well. Several designers in the 1960s created furniture out of polyurethane foam to exploit the cheapness and lightness of this industrial material. One such system is Roberto Sebastian Antonio Matta Eschaurren's Malitte seating of 1966, whose elements fit together into a compact square when not in use (fig. 17). Some of the curved profiles of the individual pieces resemble, to varying degrees, the silhouettes of traditional chairs and lounges; others are wholly abstract, determined in relation to the graphic framework of the cube and the interlocking profiles of its parts. Speaking to a party lifestyle whose furnishings require no fixed position or function, these pieces can be picked up and pushed aside when not in use.

Working with wood, Wendell Castle created organically modeled furniture and sculptural objects in the 1960s, and translated that aesthetic into a series of plastic pieces created between 1968 and 1973. The Cloud shelf is a comic-book thought bubble materialized into a three-dimensional object. In several lamps, a single lighting element crowns a set of voluptuously curved, ecstatically splayed legs. Some pieces employ velvet flocking to create a soft, fleshy impression, while others use auto-body paint to display a hard and shiny surface.[25] (fig. 19)

Plastic lost some of its allure with the oil crisis of the 1970s and the growing awareness of the ecological impact of consumerism. Frank Gehry, known for mixing pop references with ordinary industrial materials, made his first cardboard furniture for a window display in 1972, an experiment that led to his Easy Edges line of inexpensive, mass-produced chairs and side tables. While the pieces are rectilinear, Gehry's later Experimental Edges series is loaded with curves. Made with the type of thick, fluted cardboard used inside hollow-core doors, pieces such as the 1979 Bubbles lounge take their curved arabesques from the behavior of the material itself, whose masses of folded matter soften with use. Gehry rejected design that was "ponderous, overpriced, and tyrannical" in favor of "structural and decorative shapes that were useful, clean, and liberating."[26] (fig. 20)

Pop design objects took cues from graphics and advertising. Many, such as the Matta seating system, were conceived (and photographed) as two-dimensional icons and driven by a graphic sensibility. Meanwhile, the graphic design of the period made its own contributions to the culture of the curve. The psychedelic posters of the 1960s were marketed as

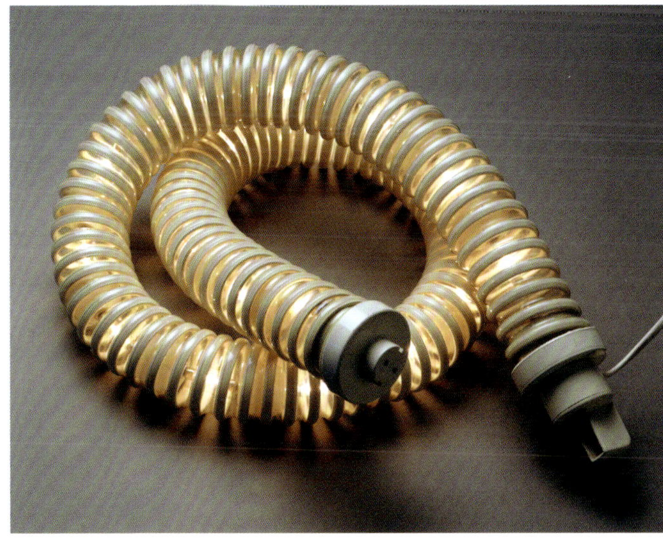

FIG. 18 Boalum lamp. Livio Castiglioni (Italian, 1911–1979) and Gianfranco Frattini (Italian, 1926–2004). Manufactured by Artemide. Milan, Italy, ca. 1969. PVC plastic, metal. Cooper-Hewitt, National Design Museum, Smithsonian Institution, Museum purchase from Decorative Arts Association Acquisition Fund, 1991-47-8

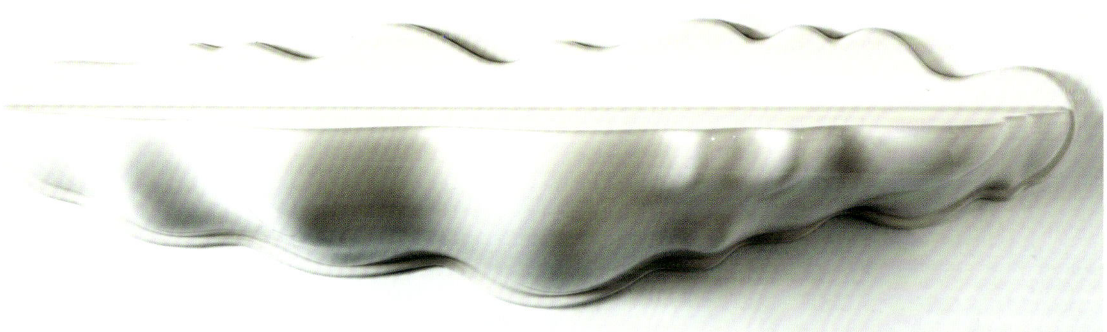

FIG. 19 Cloud shelf. Wendell Castle (American, b. 1932). United States, ca. 1969. Gel-coated, fiberglass reinforced plastic. Courtesy of R Gallery

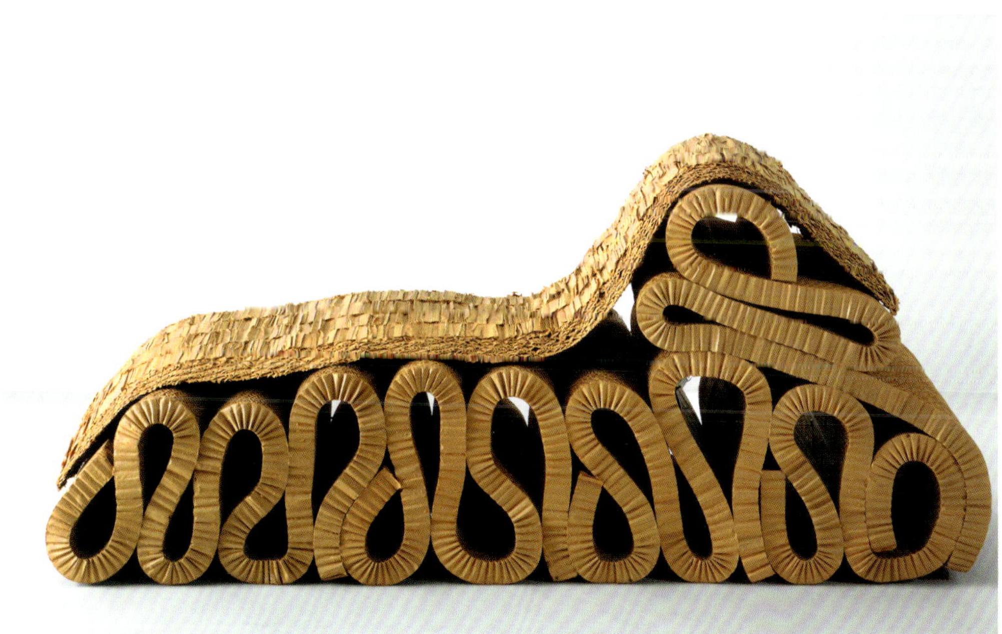

FIG. 20 Bubbles chaise longue. Frank O. Gehry (American, born Canada, 1929). Manufactured by New City Editions. Venice, CA, 1987. Corrugated cardboard with fire-retardant coating. The Museum of Modern Art, New York, Kenneth Walker Fund

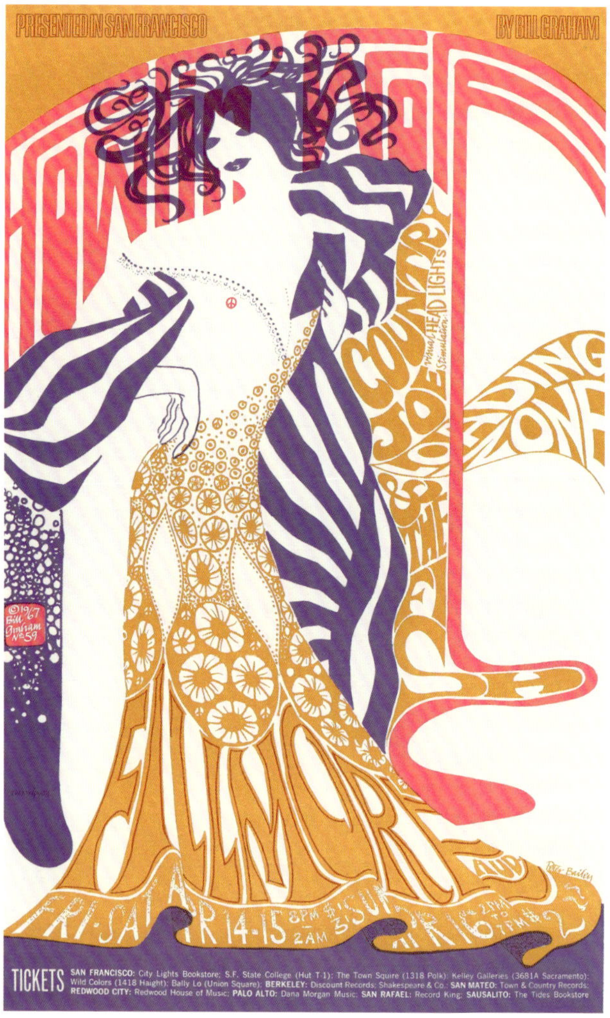

FIG. 21 *Howlin' Wolf.* Peter Bailey (American, active 1967–68). San Francisco, CA, 1967. Offset lithograph on white wove paper. Cooper-Hewitt, National Design Museum, Smithsonian Institution, Gift of Mr. and Mrs. Leslie J. Schreyer, 1979-34-1

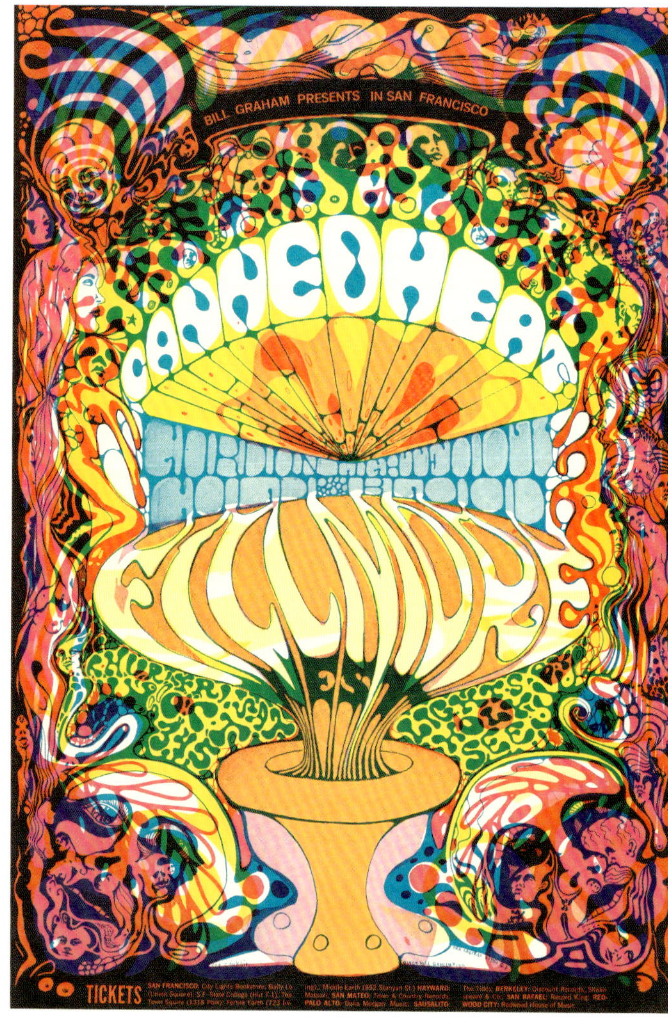

FIG. 22 *Canned Heat for Bill Graham.* Lee Conklin (American, b. 1941). Printed by Tea Lautrec. San Francisco, CA, 1968. Offset Lithograph on white wove paper. Cooper-Hewitt, National Design Museum, Smithsonian Institution, Gift of Mr. and Mrs. Leslie J. Schreyer, 1979-34-5

inexpensive art for a new generation that defined its own taste in music, art, sex, and drugs.[27] Designers such as Robert Wesley "Wes" Wilson and Peter Bailey appropriated ideas and imagery from Art Nouveau, merging word and image across surfaces that writhe with sinuous lines and intense colors. Posters featuring illustrations of pretty girls surrounded by dense fields of lettering directly referenced fin-de-siècle graphics, while others moved into more original territory. Wilson's poster for The Association, whose red, hand-lettered flames vibrate against an acid-green background, is an abstract optical assault. Larsen Design Studio explored similar ideas in textile designs printed on state-of-the-art synthetic fabrics. Reaching further back into history, a poster by Lee Conklin for the Grateful Dead recalls the densely packed framework of baroque and rococo title pages, revisioned as a drug-enhanced orgy set in a primeval forest (figs. 21–24).

The idea of appropriating historic styles and iconography became more nuanced in the postmodern discourse of the 1980s art world. Artist Jeff Koons exploited rococo style (and lifestyle) in objects whose defiant luxury tested the limits of taste. According to critic Robert Rosenblum, the rococo worldview permeates Koons's work, an oeuvre that forces us to "look head on at the weird, intricate fusion of the repellant and the

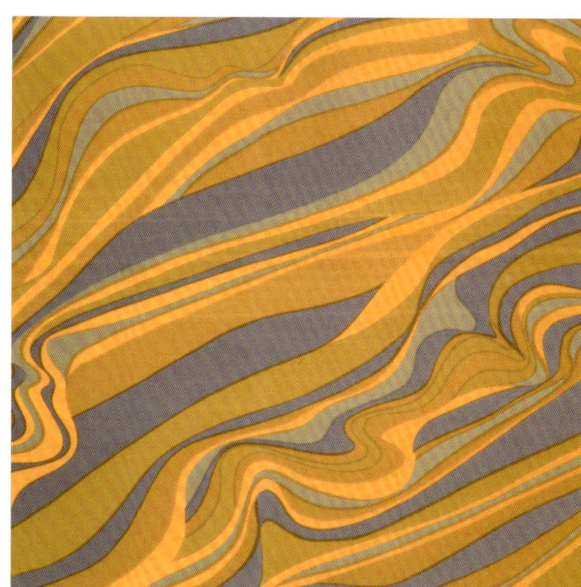

FIG. 23 *Bojangles,* from *The Butterflies,* a group of four designs. Larsen Design Studio. United States, 1967. Caprolan® nylon backed with polyester foam. Cooper-Hewitt, National Design Museum, Smithsonian Institution, Gift of Jack Lenor Larsen, 1968-47-1-c

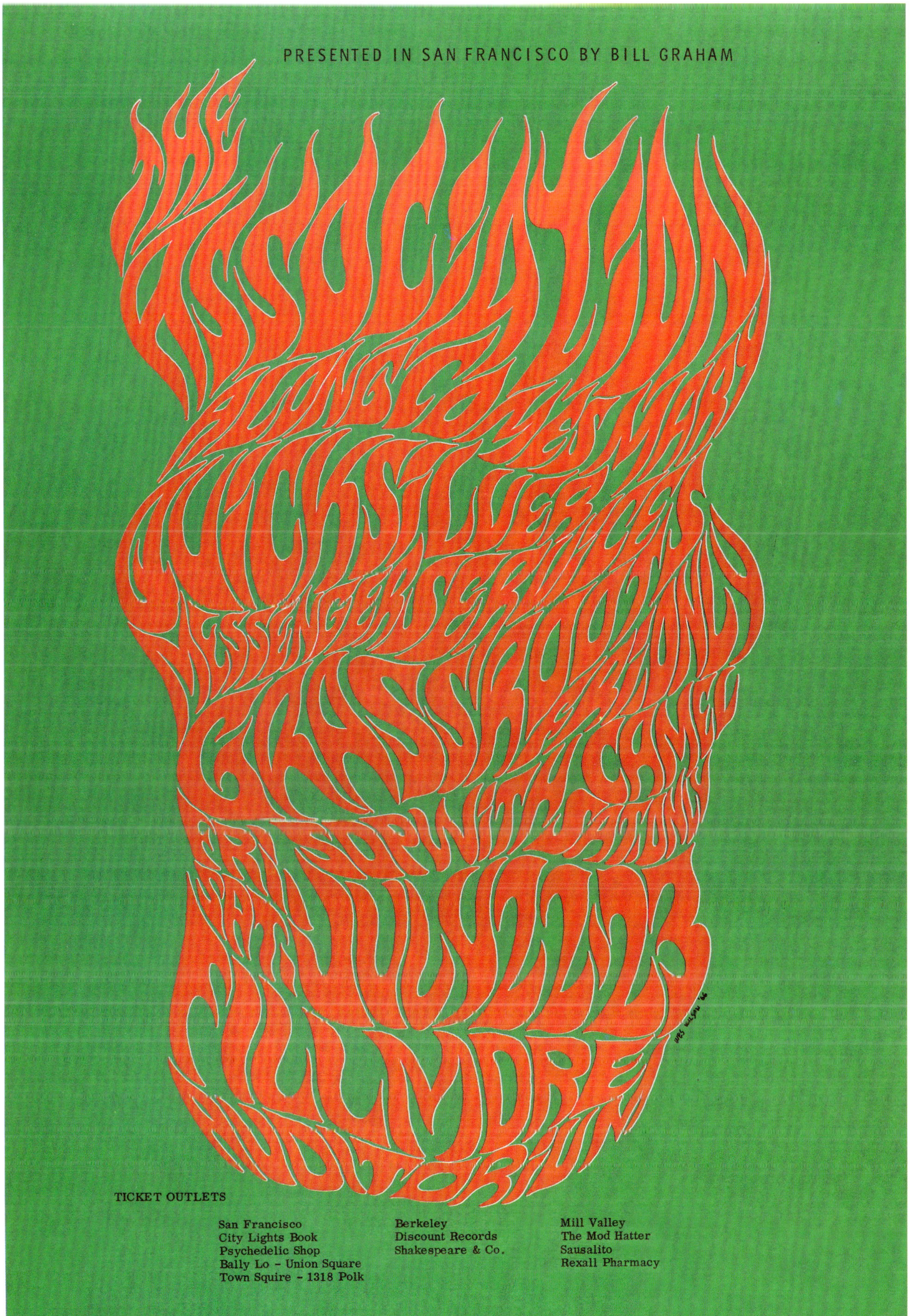

FIG. 24 *The Association.* Robert Wesley "Wes" Wilson (American, b. 1937). San Francisco, CA, 1966. Offset Lithograph on white wove paper. Cooper-Hewitt, National Design Museum, Smithsonian Institution, Gift of Mr. and Mrs. Leslie J. Schreyer, 1979-34-25

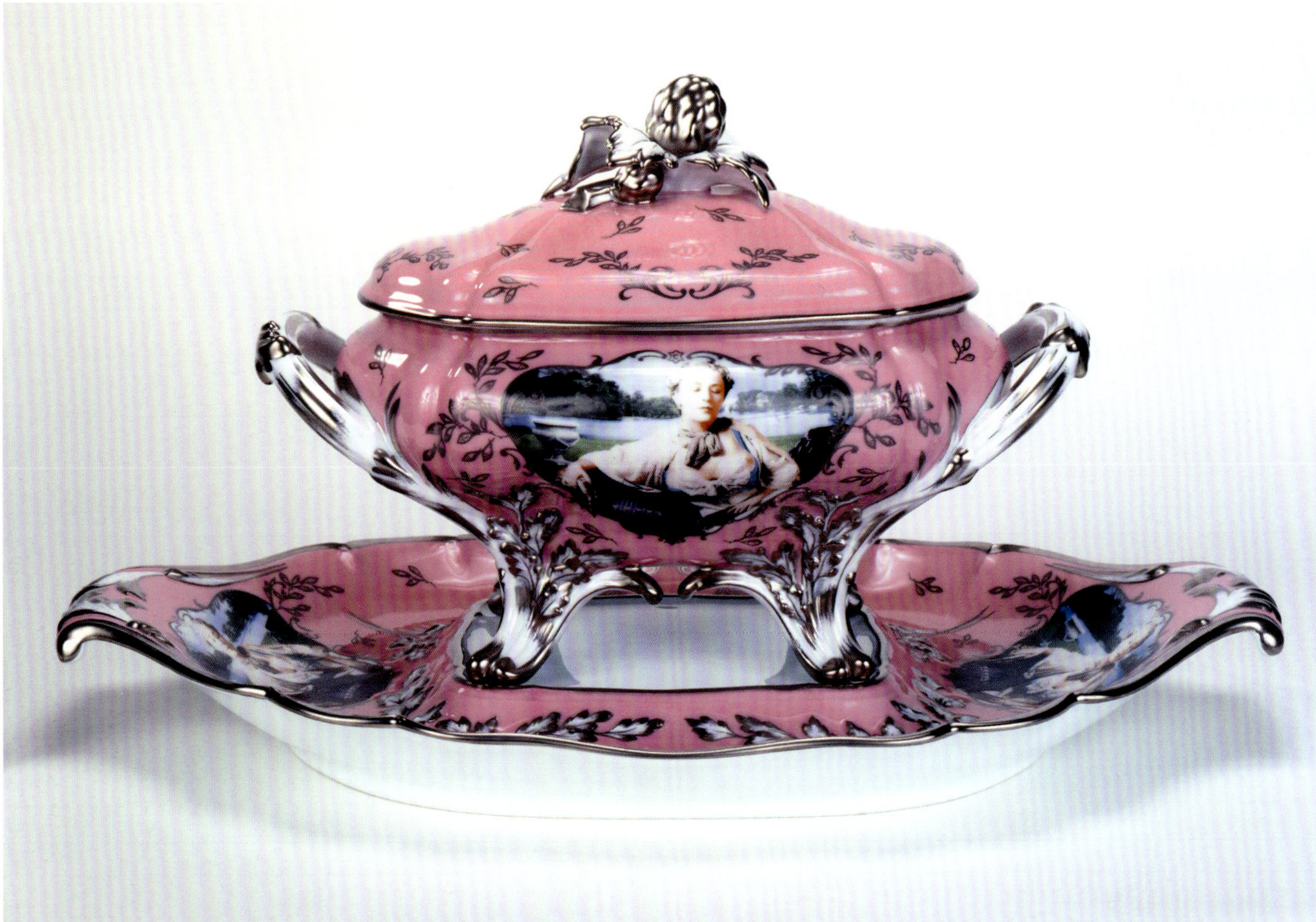

FIG. 25 Madame de Pompadour (née Poisson) covered tureen with tray. Cindy Sherman (American, b. 1954). Produced by Artes Magnus, NY. Manufactured by Ancienne Manufacture Royale de Limoges. France, 1990. Glazed porcelain, photo-transfer (silkscreen), painted-platinum decoration. Cooper-Hewitt, National Design Museum, Smithsonian Institution, Museum purchase from Charles E. Sampson Memorial Fund, 2003-4-1a/c

enticing that marks the world of kitsch."[28] The gilt frame of Koons's 1988 mirror Christ and the Lamb incorporates a tiny reference to Leonardo da Vinci's painting *Virgin, Child, and Saint Anne.* Explosive rivulets of decorative form engulf that dignified passage, overtaking the surface of the mirror (fig. 26). According to Koons, "When you go to church and you see the gold and the Rococo, it's there, they say, for the glory of God. But I believe it's there just to soothe the masses for the moment; to make them feel economically secure; to let something else—a spiritual experience, a manipulation—come into their lives."[29]

Artist Cindy Sherman is known for her photographic impersonations of archetypes from the history of film and art. In 1990, the New York firm Artes Magnus invited her to create a piece to be manufactured by the Ancienne Manufacture Royale de Limoges in France. Sherman photographed herself dressed as Madame de Pompadour—the supreme rococo—with wig, makeup, and prosthetic breasts (fig. 25). Her image, imprinted on eighteenth-century-style ceramic ware, is framed with seemingly traditional ornamentation. In place of acanthus leaves are little fishes that refer to Madame de Pompadour's maiden name, Poisson. The piece is less an embrace or revival of rococo style than a carefully constructed reference to a historical moment and to the preeminent consumer of an elite style.[30]

The ceramic objects of Adrian Saxe marry rococo with pop culture. Take-offs on the ormolu-mounted porcelains produced in Europe from the seventeenth through the nineteenth centuries, they are objects in which discordant histories and materials willfully embrace. Saxe's Untitled Ewer (Home Team Advantage) of 2004–05 is a precarious vessel pieced together from hybrid bits of cast ornament and hand-formed clay; topping the piece like a cherry is a commercial sports figurine. Diverse materials and surfaces likewise conjoin in Hella Jongerius's Layers vases: in one, a bronze bird integrated into an elaborately curved handle perches on the body of a classical ceramic urn (figs. 27, 28). Such objects reflect the craft revival that has invigorated art and design since the 1970s. Unruly ribbons of steel unfurl around the works of Albert Paley, a metalsmith inspired by the serpentine exercises of Art Nouveau, a period he avidly studies and collects. Subjecting steel to intense hammering and heat, Paley twists it into curls and tendrils to create candleholders, torchieres, and other objects.[31] (fig. 29)

Metalwork played a central role in the vigorous, anti-minimal design scene that played out in London in the 1980s. Tom Dixon was a leader in the "creative salvage" movement, whose designers harvested spare parts from London scrap yards and welded them into objects both brutal and decorative. The seat and back of Dixon's cantilevered steel

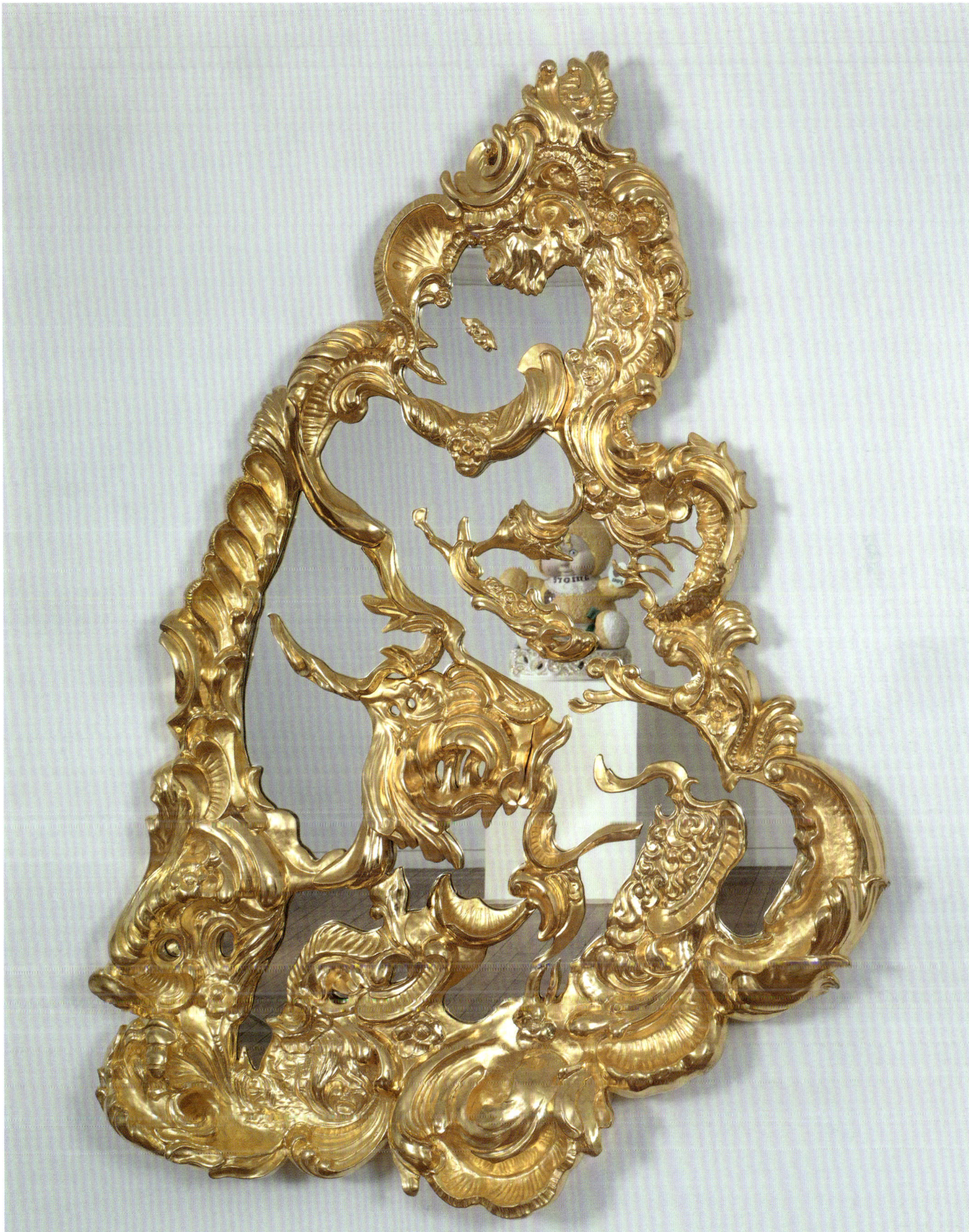

FIG. 26 Mirror: Christ and the Lamb. Jeff Koons (American, b. 1955). United States, 1988. Wood, gilding, mirror glass. Collection of Groninger Museum, Groningen

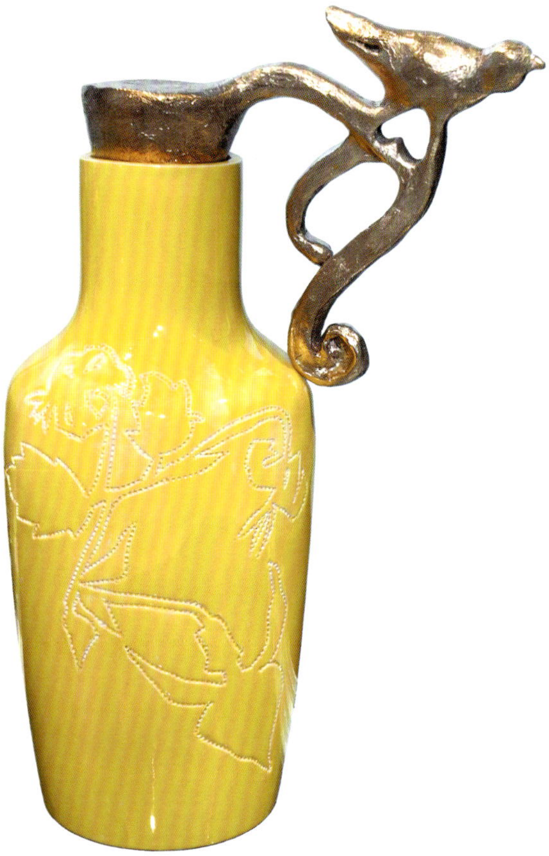

FIG. 27 Layers Bonanza jug. Hella Jongerius (Dutch, b. 1963). Manufactured by JongeriusLab. Rotterdam, the Netherlands, 2006. Glazed incised earthenware, bronze. Courtesy of Moss

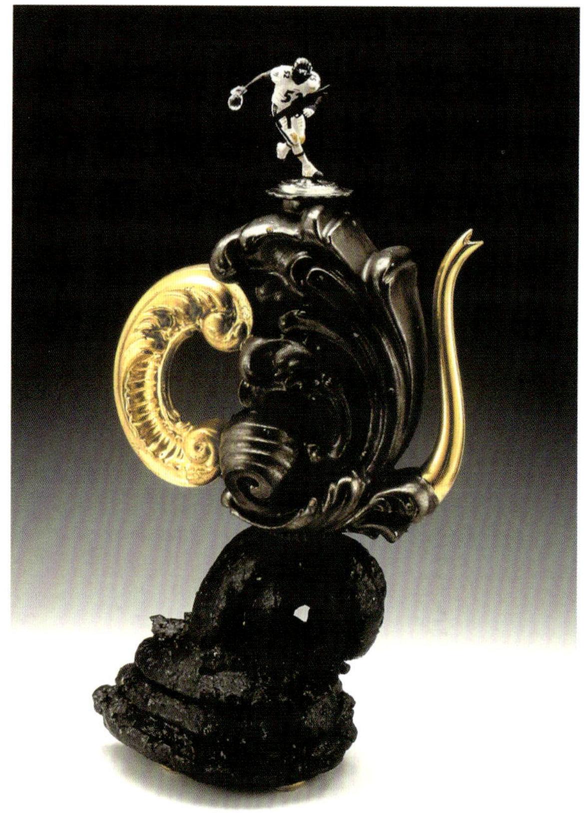

FIG. 28 Untitled ewer (Home Team Advantage). Adrian Saxe (American, b. 1943). Los Angeles, CA, 2004–05. Porcelain, stoneware, mixed media. Courtesy of Frank Lloyd Gallery

S chair (1988) (fig. 30) form a single continuous curve, flowing upward from a common point at the base. Early versions were wrapped in woven rush, and others were sheathed in stretch fabric, but the rubber-bound S speaks best of Dixon's punk origins.

Dixon, who began welding furniture after a motorcycle accident in 1983, invited the French-born artist and designer André Dubreuil to collaborate on an interior for a London chocolate shop called Rococo in 1985.[32] The shop, decorated with hand-painted pink and green arabesques and chandeliers assembled from industrial refuse, gave voice to an emerging spirit. As Dubreuil recalls, "It was a very opportune moment. There was plenty of money around, people were fed up with Minimalism and they wanted curves. They liked the slapped-together, scrap-yard, arts-and-crafts aspect of our pieces."

Dubreuil's Spine chair of 1986 is at once complex and coherent (fig. 31). Drawn in space with lines of metal, its primary plane is defined by the sweeping path of two lengths of steel emerging from a single point behind the back. These lyrical lines spread apart and scroll over to form a seat that appears to seamlessly merge with the supporting legs. Dubreuil made the first versions of the chair with concrete-reinforcing bar. This cheap, ordinary material, normally hidden inside slabs of poured concrete, can be easily shaped into curves. The chair's elegant, branch-like lines reflect Dubreuil's deep knowledge of furniture history—he had been a dealer of French antiques—and yet it is approachable and unpretentious, like a side chair in a café or ice-cream parlor.

The Israeli-born designer Ron Arad, who also took part in the London salvage scene, has been a presence in design and architecture since 1981. Arad's fascination with curvilinear forms is seen in his Looploop and other chairs of the early 1990s (fig. 32), in which ribbons of metal flow through space to create unexpected seating. Such works take inspiration from Hebrew lettering as well as from the fundamental behavior and abstract potential of bent planes of metal.[33]

The intersection of design, craft, and technology has been crucial to the design discourse of the early twenty-first century. The Nymphenburg Porcelain Manufactory, founded near Munich in the eighteenth century, began commissioning designers in 1997 to create objects and tableware from a contemporary point of view. The American designer Ted Muehling, working closely with Nymphenburg's master modelers, throwers, and formers, has designed numerous tabletop objects based on natural forms, including the Branch candlestick, whose upward-sweeping asymmetrical design and sculpturally grooved surface recalls rococo ornament.[34] (fig. 33) The American ceramicist Jennifer McCurdy throws porcelain vessels on the wheel and then alters them with whorls, swirls, and curves. With an Xacto knife, she cuts slits through the wall in various places; when the pieces are fired, the porcelain bends and deforms further in response to the grooves and openings in its skin.[35] (fig. 35) British silversmith Ndidi Ekubia makes fluid, asymmetrical vessels from planished sheets of metal, designed to show a different aspect from every direction (fig. 39). In the Netherlands, Marcel Wanders's Airborne Snotty vases employ digital pro-

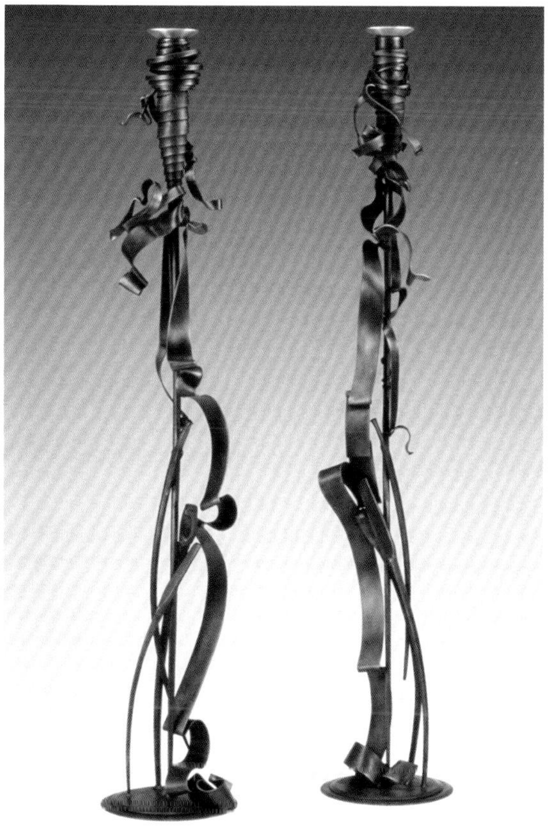

FIG. 29 Pair of candlestands. Albert Paley (American, b. 1944). United States, 1989. Forged and fabricated mild steel. Collection of Sydney and Frances Lewis

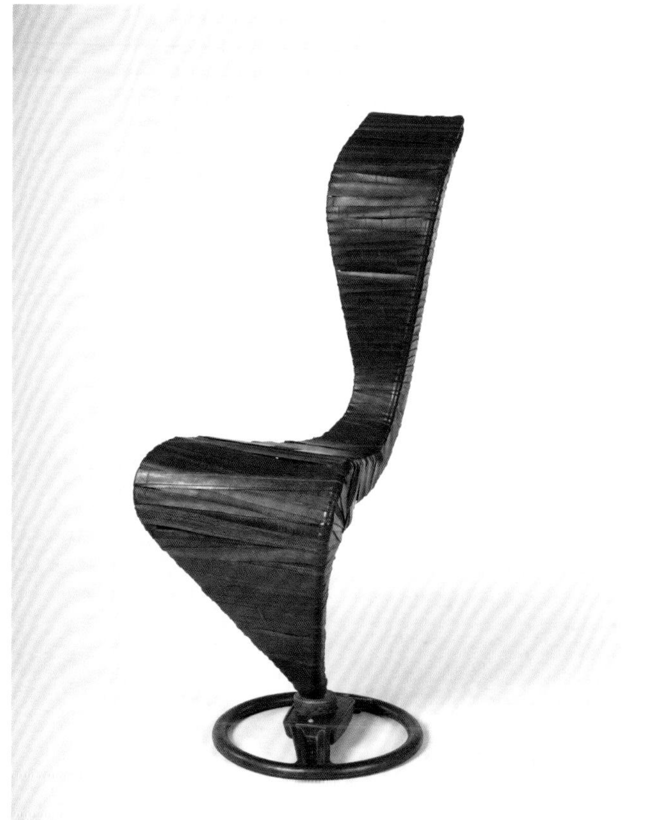

FIG. 30 S chair. Tom Dixon (British, b. 1959). England, 1988. Recycled rubber inner tube, steering wheel, steel. Cooper-Hewitt, National Design Museum, Smithsonian Institution, Museum purchase from General Acquisitions Endowment Fund, 2006-4-2

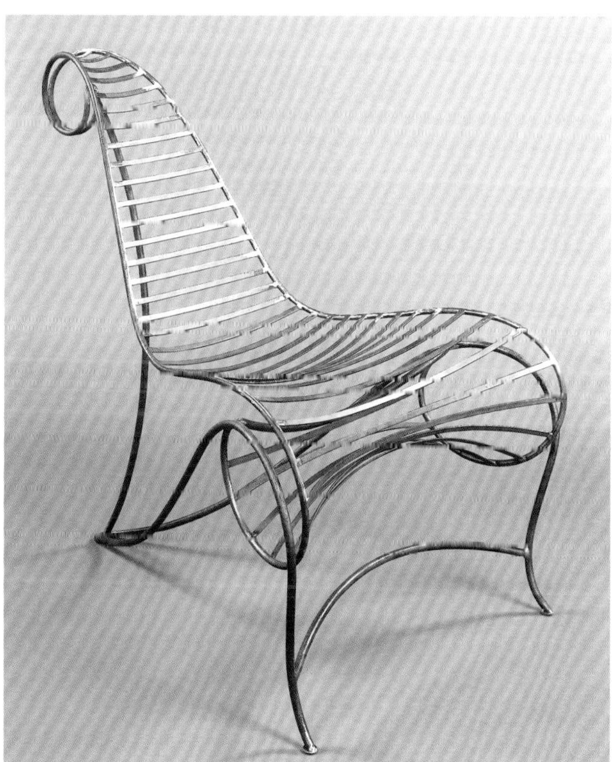

FIG. 31 Spine chair. André Dubreuil (French, active England, b. 1951). England, 1986. Steel. Cooper-Hewitt, National Design Museum, Smithsonian Institution, Museum purchase from Decorative Arts Association Acquisition Fund, 1992-36-1

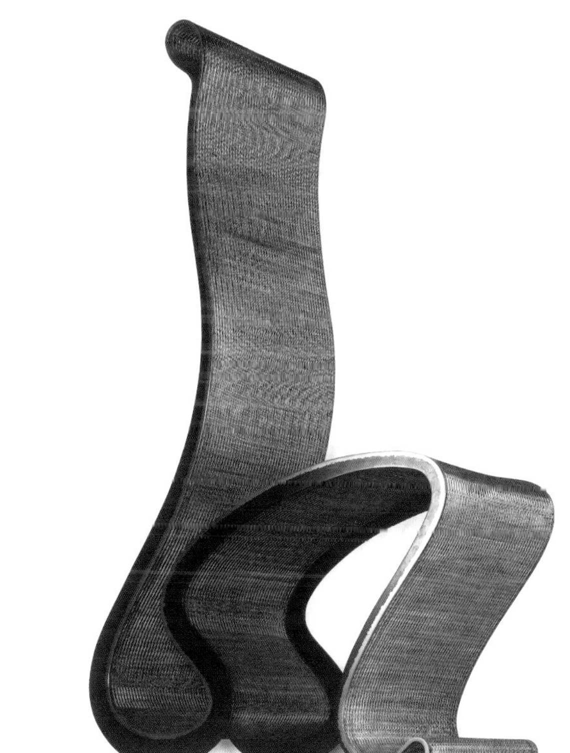

FIG. 32 Looploop chair. Designed by Ron Arad (Israeli, active England, b. 1951). London, England, 1992. Polished bronze mesh. Courtesy of Friedman Benda

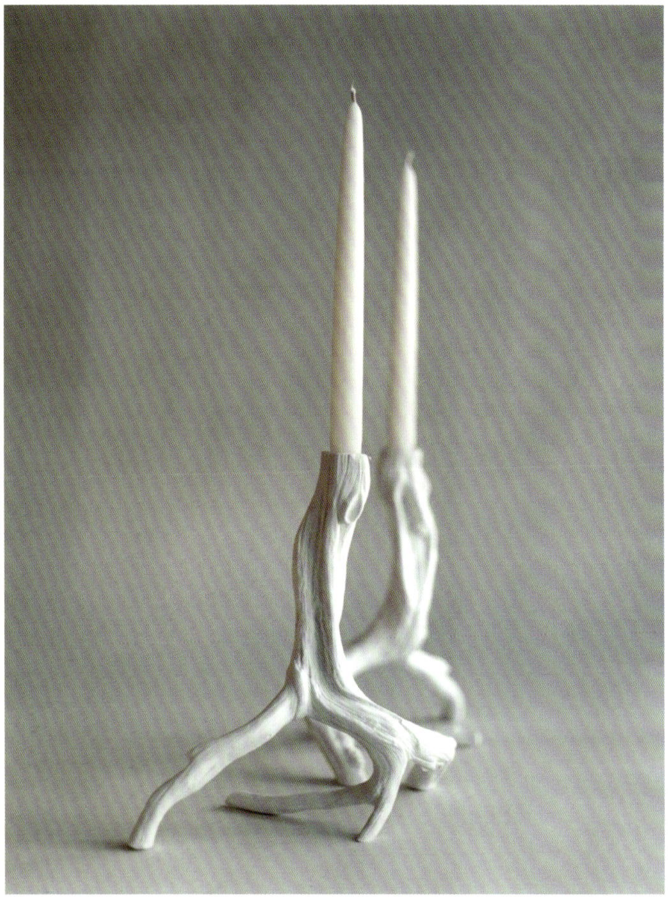

FIG. 33 Branch candlestick. Ted Muehling (American, b. 1953). Manufactured by Porzellan Manufaktur Nymphenburg. Munich, Germany, 2003. Porcelain bisque. Courtesy of Ted Muehling

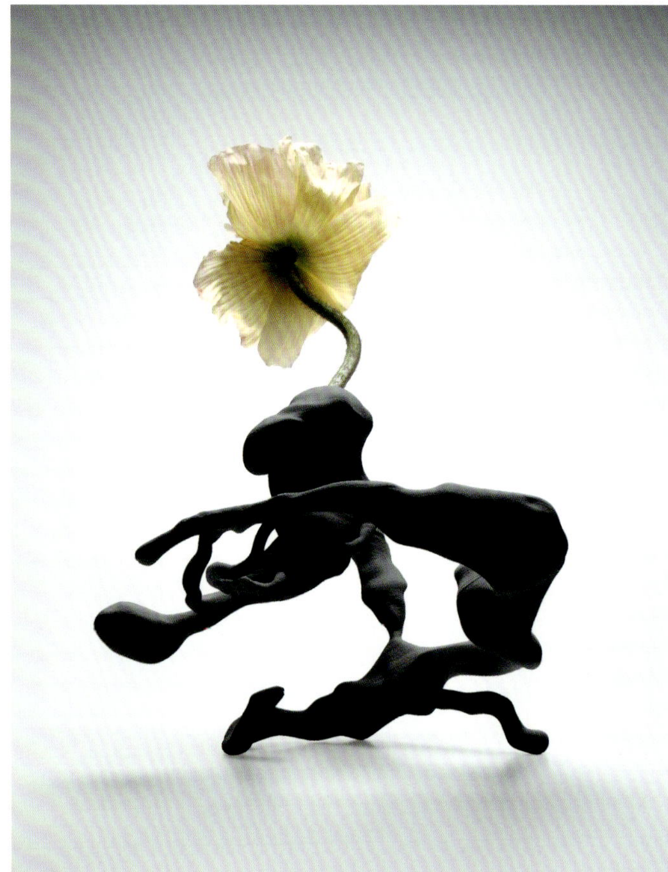

FIG. 34 Airborne Snotty vase: Coryza. Marcel Wanders (Dutch, b. 1963). Manufactured by Marcel Wanders Studio. The Netherlands, 2001. Polyamide. Courtesy of Marcel Wanders Studio

totyping technology to capture the shape of a human sneeze as particles of mucus fly through the air; the captured data are then transformed into a series of intricate and organic objects (fig. 34).

Like Wanders, the Swedish design collective Front employs digital technologies to generate unpredictable forms.[36] To create their Materialized Sketch pieces, the team used motion-capture technology to record the movement of drawings made in three-dimensional space, then converted the gestural lines into three-dimensional prints, built up with layers of thermoplastic powder. These hand-drawn yet computer-generated objects convey an unmistakable humanity at a peculiar, unsettling scale (fig. 37). Jeroen Verhoeven's Cinderella table, a masterpiece of computer-aided design and manufacturing, morphs the profiles of two seventeenth- and eighteenth-century tables into a single object, consisting of fifty-seven slices of laser-cut plywood bonded together and finished by hand.[37] (fig. 38)

Heralding from Antwerp, Studio Job's 2003 Rock furniture assembles graceful curves from aggregates of cubic elements. The designers build up the crystalline forms of these pieces by hand from blocks of foam, finish them with sculpture wax and paper, then cast them in bronze. The serene silhouette of a historic chair or table takes shape out of jagged elements. Designer Job Smeets explains, "We wanted objects that would look as if they were growing spontaneously, like a virus. We wanted it to be unclear whether the piece still needs to be finished or whether it is already crumbling, falling apart."[38] The project revisits a historic design vocabulary from a contemporary perspective, suggesting a narrative of growth and decay (fig. 36).

In the Netherlands, Joris Laarman has made a radiator out of modular units of ornament, cast from reinforced concrete. An industrial appliance grows across a wall, bringing beauty and glamour to an essential object of human comfort. Laarman explains, "I wanted to show that minimalist, industrial forms are not always more functional than decoration. A radiator needs a large surface to give its heat to the air, so in my project Baroque styling is more functional than a straight square. . . . The more decoration a radiator has, the better it works."[39] Laarman's Ivy Climbing Wall consists of polyester concrete ornaments that affix to a wall, serving as both decoration and as grips for indoor climbing. The product shifts the traditional idea of applied plaster ceiling ornament and shifts it to the wall, creating a form of decoration that is also functional. (The ivy climbs, but so too apartment dwellers can climb their own walls.) In the designer's words, "Climbing in a living room on enormous decorative grips is a lovely way of getting exercise, but also of seeing your interior from a different perspective."[40] (figs. 40, 41)

Laarman's objects revisit baroque and rococo forms in order to add functionality and depth to interior walls. Meanwhile, surface designers are infusing archetypal historic patterns with contemporary iconography. A curtain by Nicolette Brunklaus features an enormous photograph

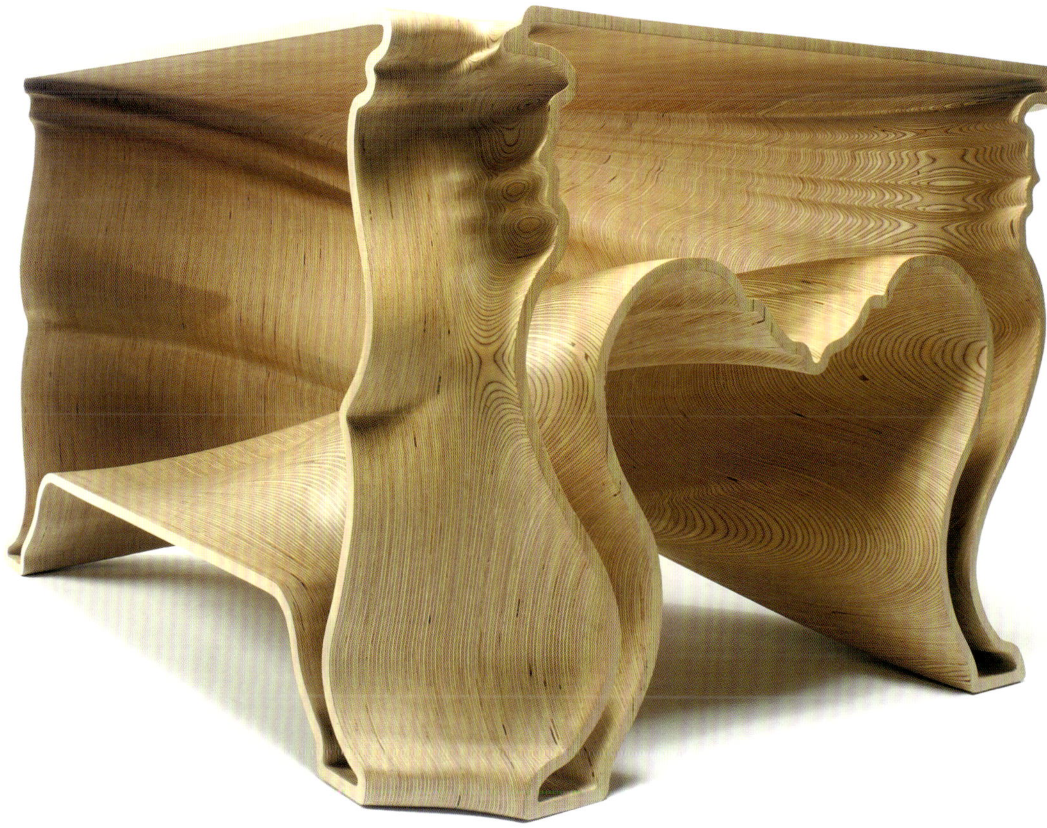

FIG. 35 Cinderella table. Jeroen Verhoeven (Dutch, b. 1976). Made by Demakersvan. The Netherlands, 2004. Birch plywood. Private collection

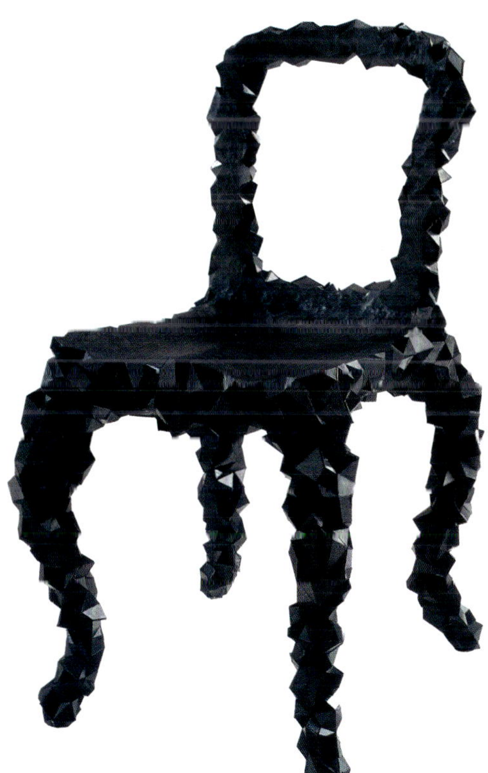

FIG. 36 Rock chair. Job Smeets (Belgian, b. 1970) and Nynke Tynagel (Dutch, b. 1977). Modeled by Studio Job, cast by Kemner & Zn. Belgium, 2003. Cast bronze. Courtesy of Boudwijn van Dishoeck

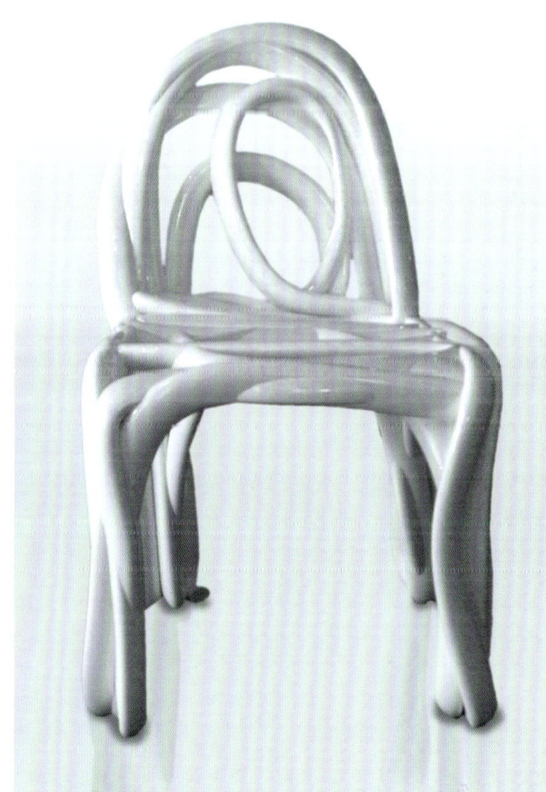

FIG. 37 Materialized Sketch chair. Front (Anna Lindgren, Katja Sävström, Sofia Lagerkvist, Charlotte van der Lancken). Sweden, 2006. Thermoplastic, rapid prototyping processes (stereolithography, selective laser sintering). Courtesy of Friedman Benda

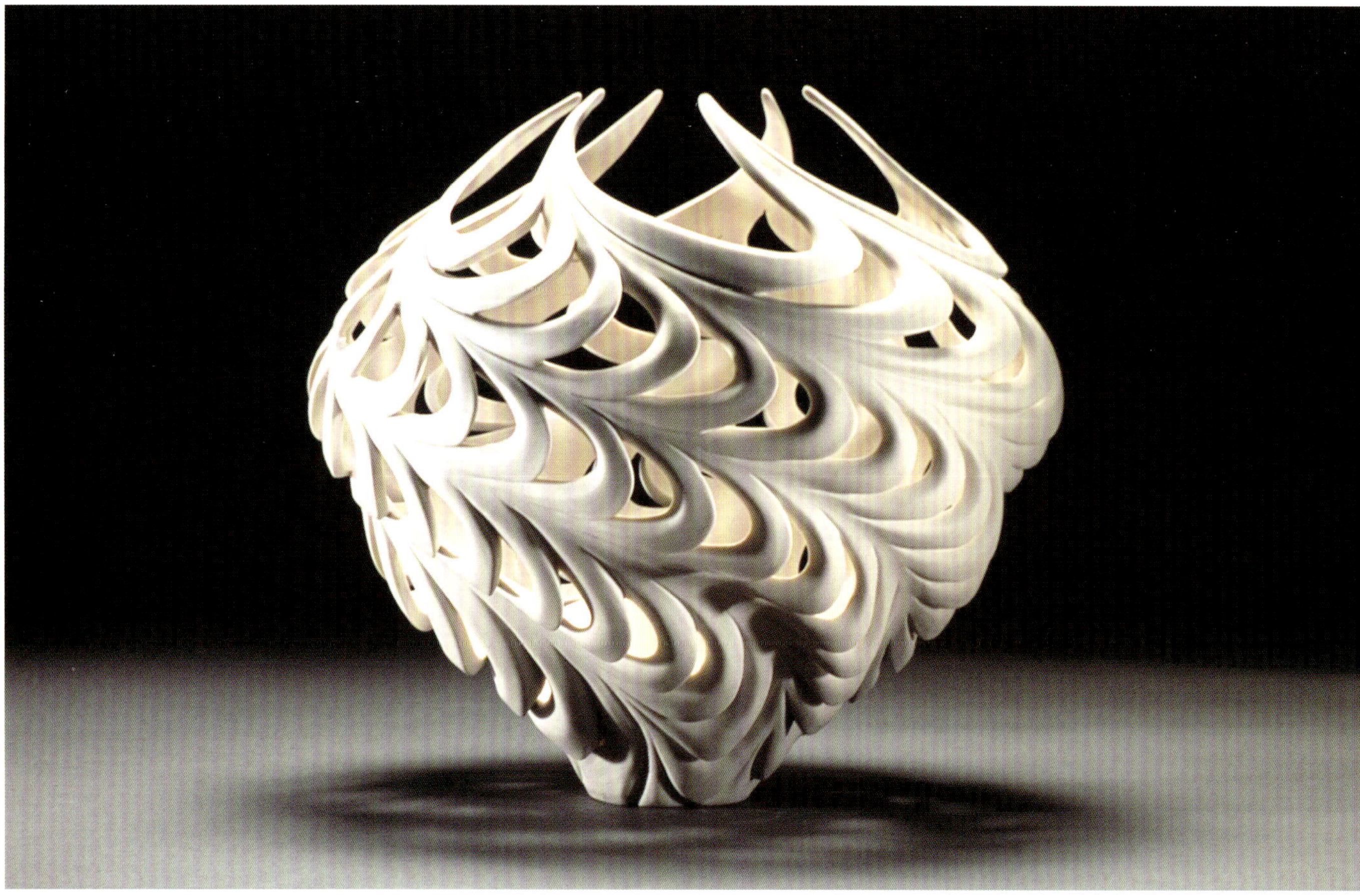

FIG. 38 Wave vessel. Jennifer C. McCurdy (American, b. 1955). Vineyard Haven, MA, 2007. Porcelain. Courtesy of Jennifer C. McCurdy

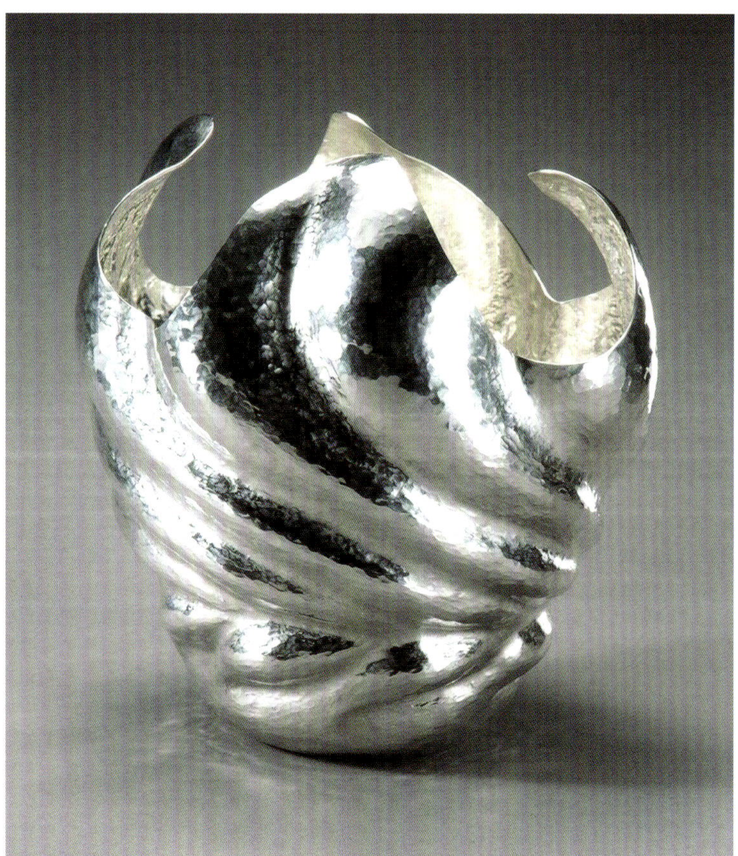

FIG. 39 Flame vase. Ndidi Ekubia (British, b. 1973). England, 2007. Sterling silver. Courtesy of Ndidi Ekubia

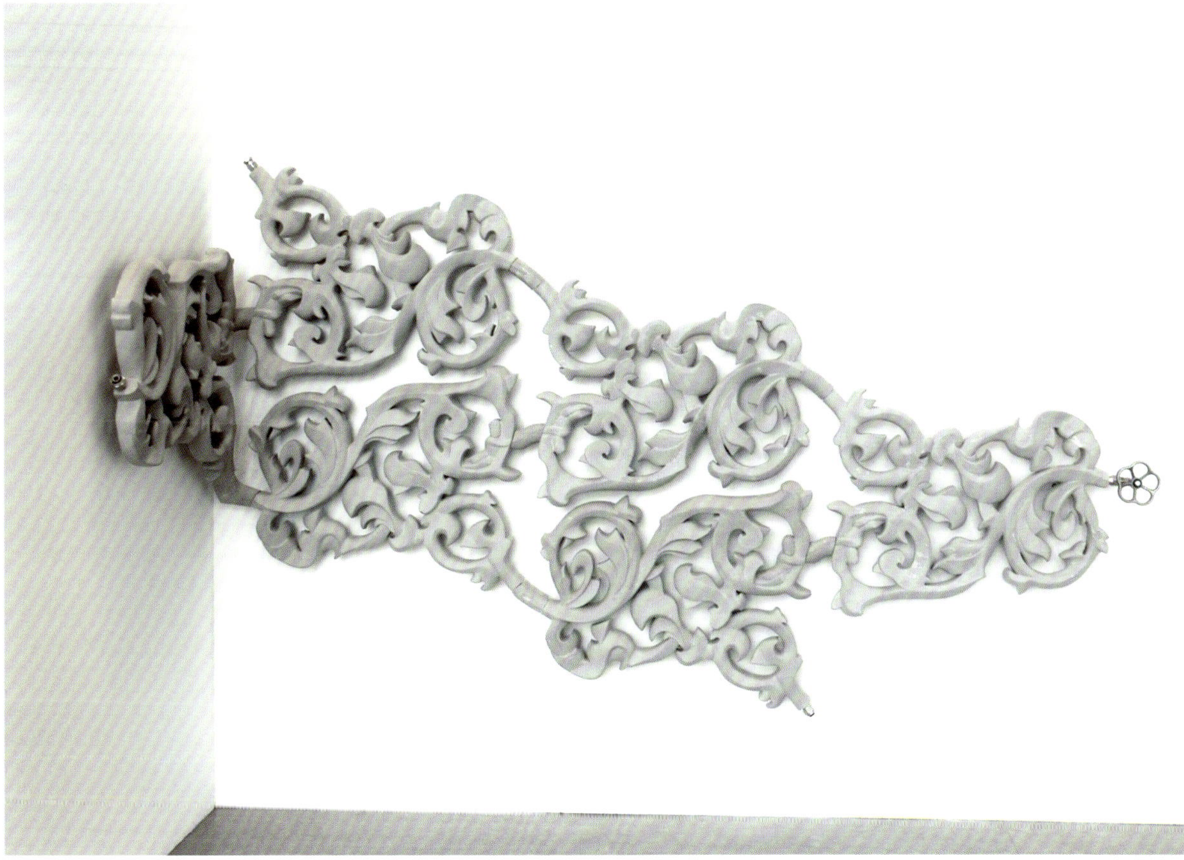

FIG. 40 Heatwave radiator. Joris Laarman (Dutch, b. 1979). Manufactured by Jaga, N.V. Belgium, 2003. Polyconcrete (polyester concrete). Courtesy of Jaga, N.V.

of blond hair—that undying icon of feminine allure—screenprinted on silk or velvet (fig. 42). Long lines of hair, flowing with the controlled abandon of an artificial waterfall, cascade downward into a swirling mass of curls. Creating textiles with physical depth, Claudy Jongstra uses various types of fleece (straight, long, curly) to produce felt panels that overflow with organic curves (fig. 43).

There has been a renaissance of the curve in graphic design at the turn of the twenty-first century as well. Designers are reviving the art and craft of hand-lettering, which marked American graphic bravado in the 1960s and 1970s. Among them is Marian Bantjes, a Vancouver-based designer who pulls strands of influence from the history of graphic art, from medieval and Celtic lettering and baroque and rococo ornament to Swiss typography and American psychedelia. From this dense tangle of influences, Bantjes has woven her own vocabulary of ravenous and excessive curves. Produced and printed digitally, her work originates with hand-drawn forms, which she sometimes translates into digital vectors but just as often scans from the original drawings.[41] (fig. 44)

One of our era's great craftsmen of the two-dimensional surface is the Swiss poster artist Ralph Schraivogel. This singular designer produces only a handful of posters each year, each one a piece of art that is worked and reworked before distilling to its final form. To produce several recent posters, Schraivogel combined digital tools and hand processes to build complex topographic surfaces that swarm with movement and mysterious depth. Schraivogel says, "I'm interested in conveying spaces on paper without using conventional tropes, like perspective, so that you can't imagine how the paper remains flat."[42] (fig. 45)

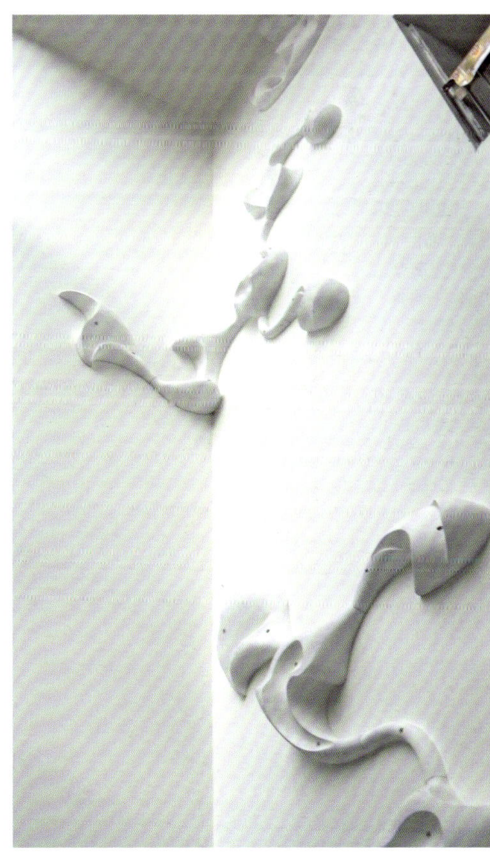

FIG. 41 Ivy climbing wall. Joris Laarman (Dutch, b. 1979). Manufactured by Joris Laarman Laboratory. The Netherlands, 2004. Polyconcrete (polyester concrete). Courtesy of Joris Laarman

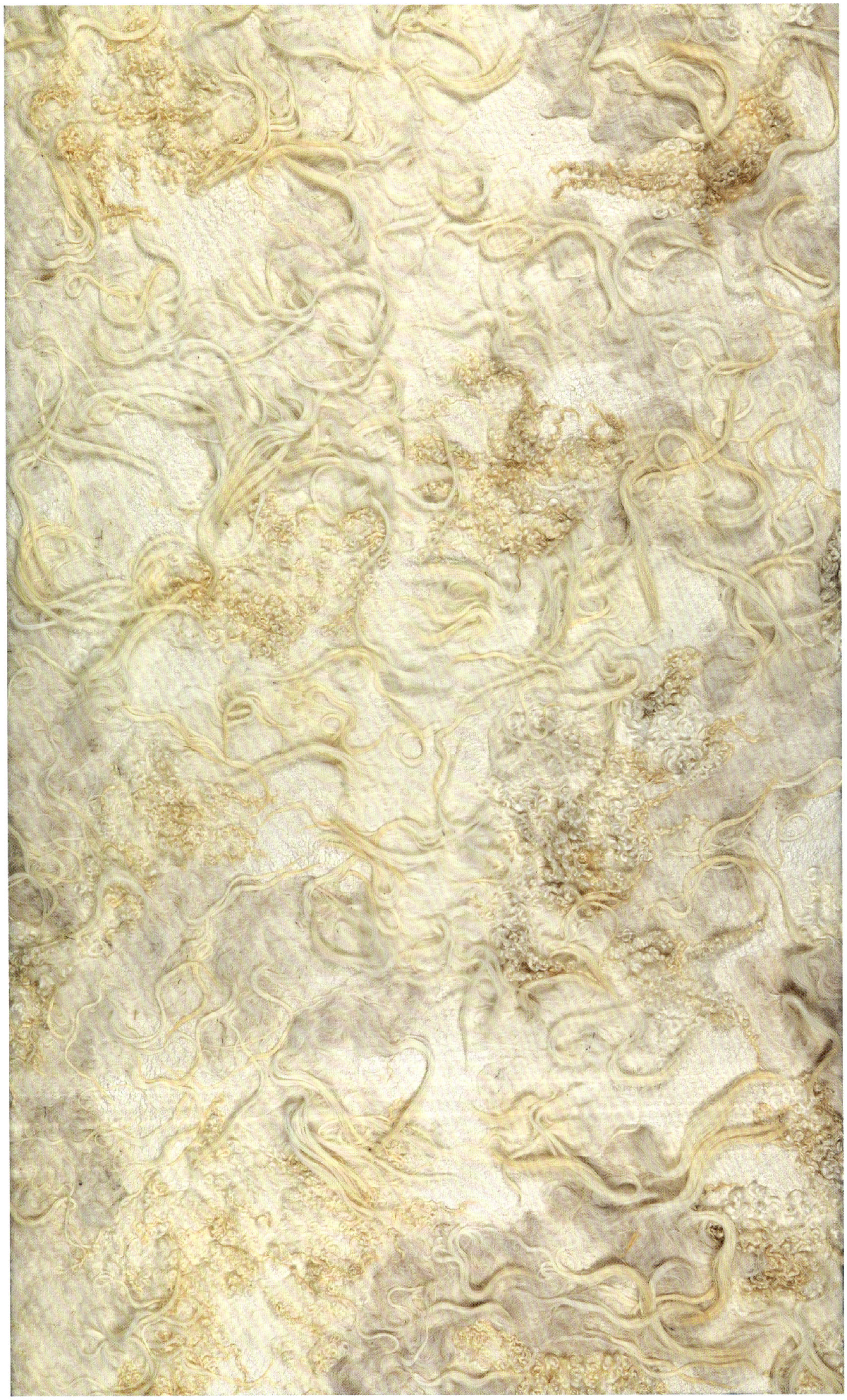

FIG. 43 Composition (DH/WD/SI 001). Claudy Jongstra (Dutch, b. 1963). The Netherlands, 2004. Merino, Drenthe Heath, Wensleydale wool, wild silk, cotton gauze. Cooper-Hewitt, National Design Museum, Smithsonian Institution, Museum purchase from General Acquisitions Endowment Fund, 2005-3-1

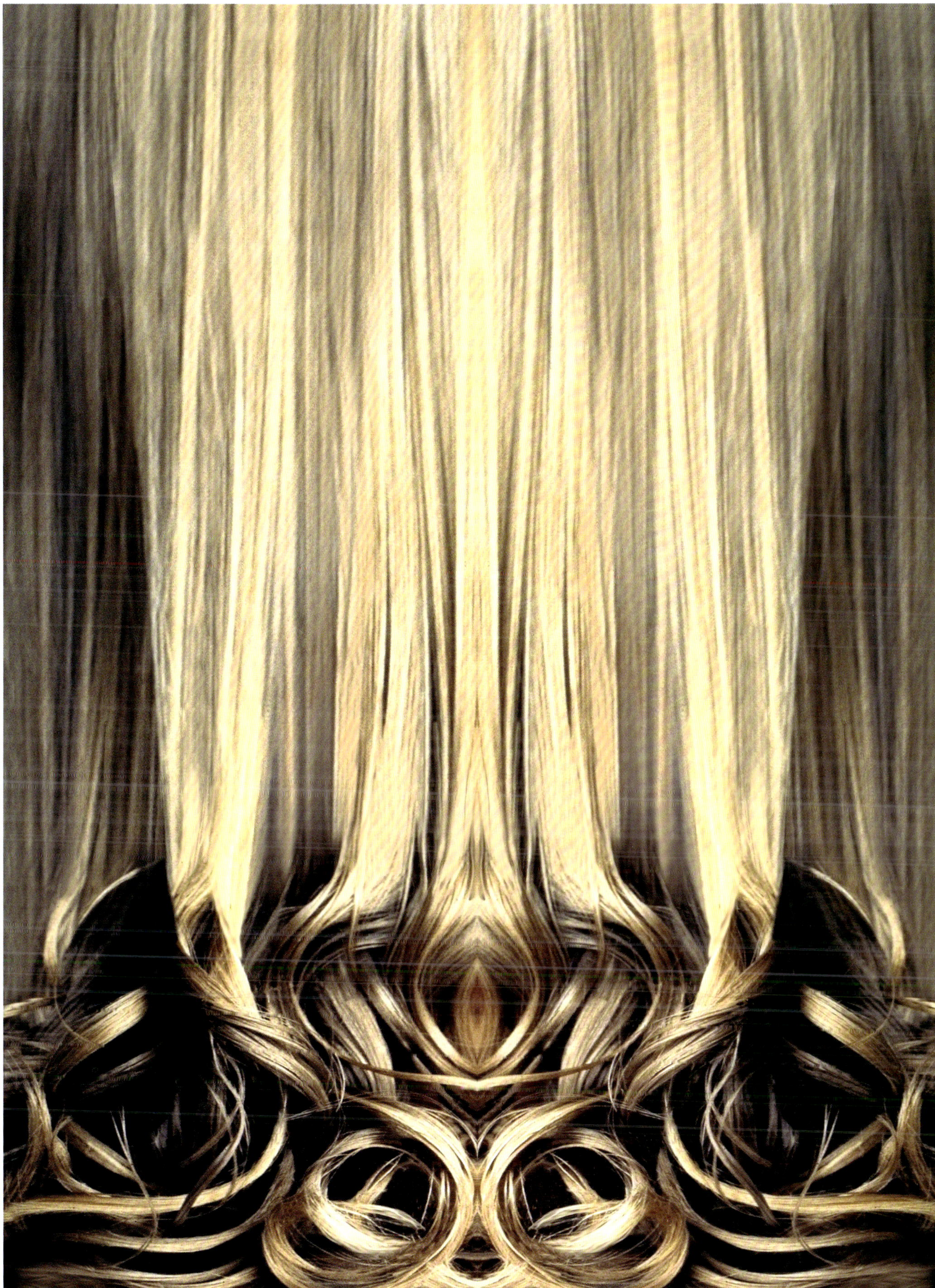

FIG. 42 Blond curtain. Nicolette Brunklaus (Dutch, b. 1959). Made by Brunklaus Amsterdam. The Netherlands, 2002. Screen print on velvet. Courtesy of Nicolette Brunklaus, Brunklaus Amsterdam

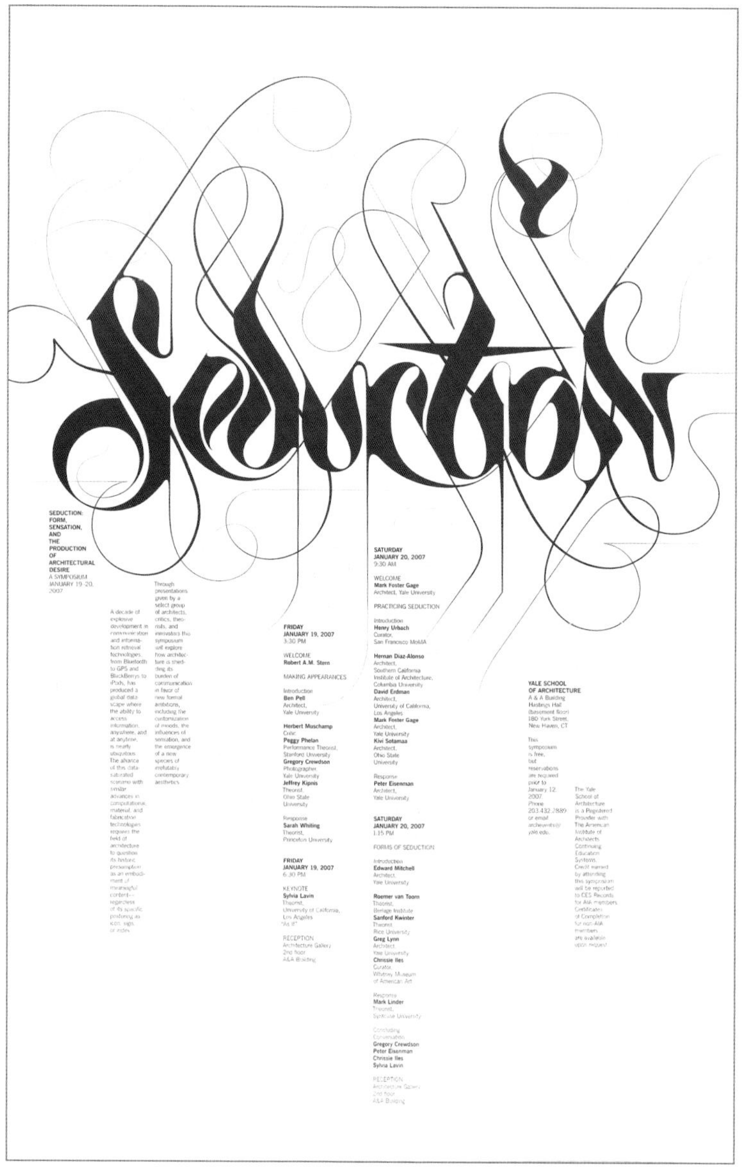

FIG. 44 Seduction, for the Yale School of Architecture Symposium, January 20–21, 2007. Marian Bantjes (Canadian, b. 1963) (lettering); Michael Bierut (American, b. 1958) and Michelle Leong (American, born Malaysia, 1978), Pentagram (poster). Canada and New York, NY, 2006. Offset lithography on white wove paper. Cooper-Hewitt, National Design Museum, Smithsonian Institution, Gift of Marian Bantjes, 2007-25-2

Many of the current period's fascinations converge in Bloom Field, a three-dimensional interpretation of a delicate and detailed line drawing by artist Leah Raintree. Created in collaboration with designer Ben Krone, this decorative wall panel is produced with a CNC (computer numerical control) router, which carves into a surface using data from a three-dimensional digital drawing. The computer controls the depth, position, and size of the tool as it moves across the surface. Drawings and engravings were essential to the spread of rococo style in the eighteenth and nineteenth centuries; today, new modes of drawing and making are giving rise to new practices (figs. 46–48).

In the twentieth and twenty-first centuries, the desire to create sensual, expressive curves has persisted alongside the rationality of the modern movement. The energy and attitude of rococo has continued to live and evolve, like a mutating germ passing through a gauntlet of host organisms. The irrepressible dynamic of the serpentine curve predates the historic rococo movement, and it will surely outlive the practices sketched out in this essay. Within the modern discourse, the curve has been function and simplicity as well as sensuality and delight. Wielding the curve, designers elaborate on form by spinning out complex and tangled tendrils of line and simplify form by subsuming an assembly of parts into continuous organic bodies. Rococo speaks of human life and happiness, of the openness of ideas and the beauty of natural phenomena. So, too, does modern design in its ongoing exploration of the nature of objects.

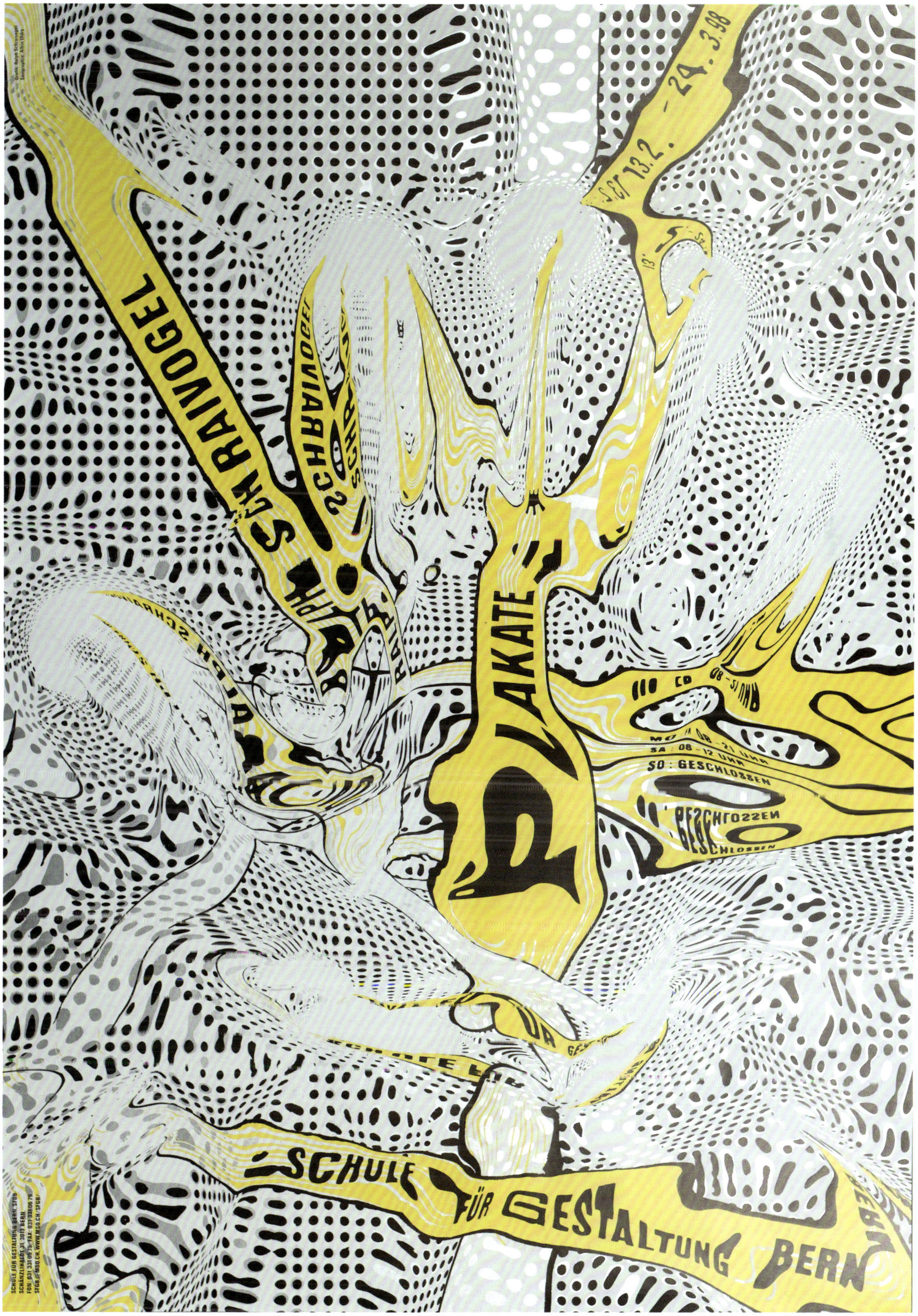

FIG. 45 Schule für Gestaltung Bern (Design School Bern). Ralph Schraivogel (Swiss, b. 1960). Printed by Albin Uldry. Switzerland, 1998. Screenprint on white wove paper. Cooper Hewitt, National Design Museum, Smithsonian Institution, Gift of Ralph Schraivogel, 2007-15-1

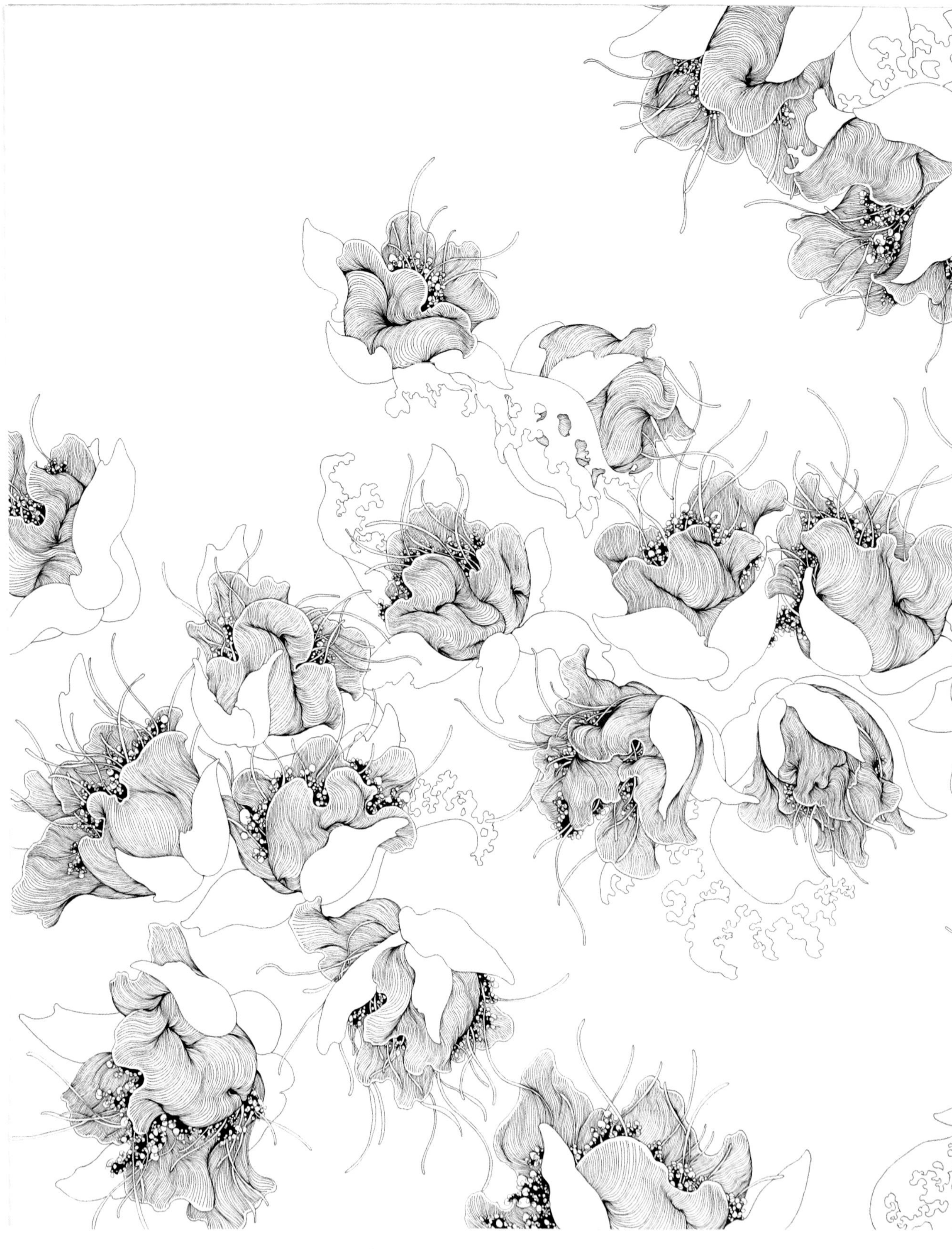

FIG. 46 Study for "Bloom Field." Leah Raintree (American, b. 1979). United States, 2007. Pen and black ink on white wove paper. Courtesy of Leah Raintree

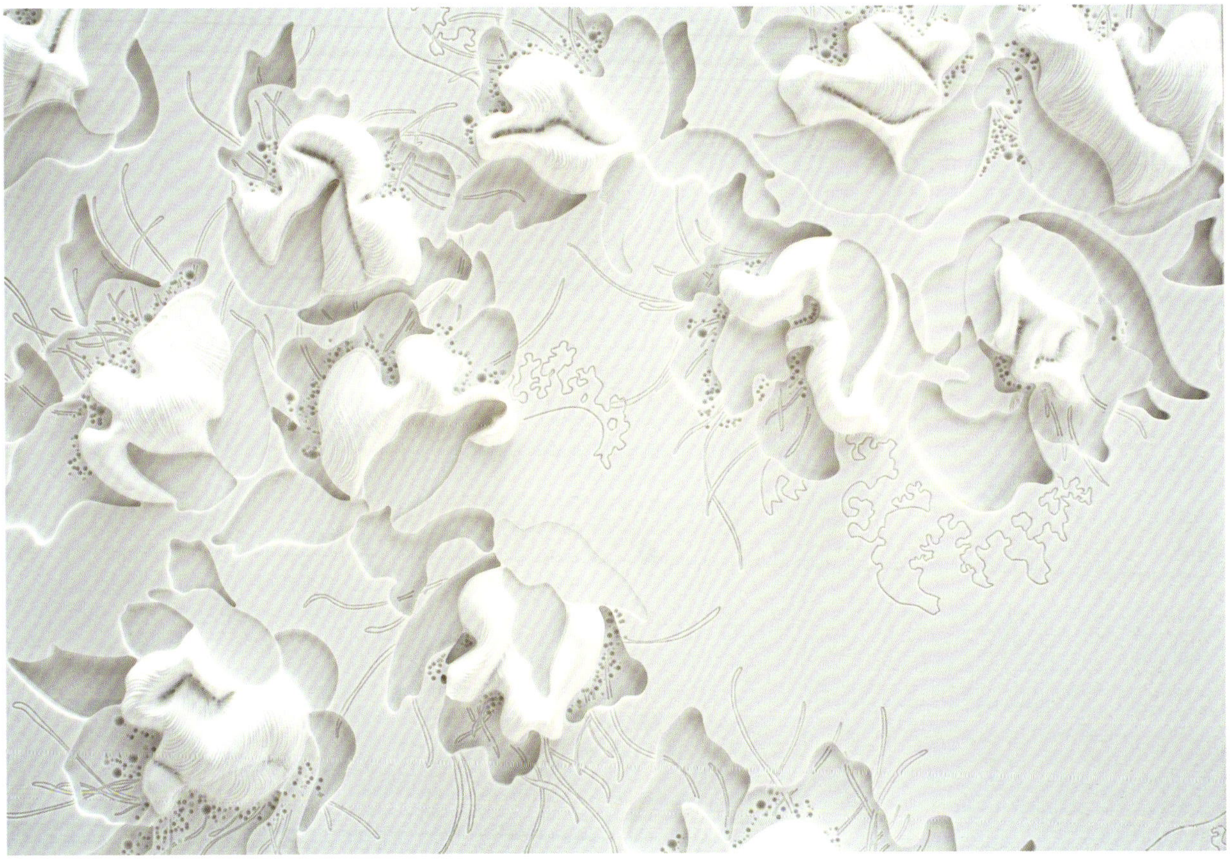

FIG. 47 Bloom Field project (detail)

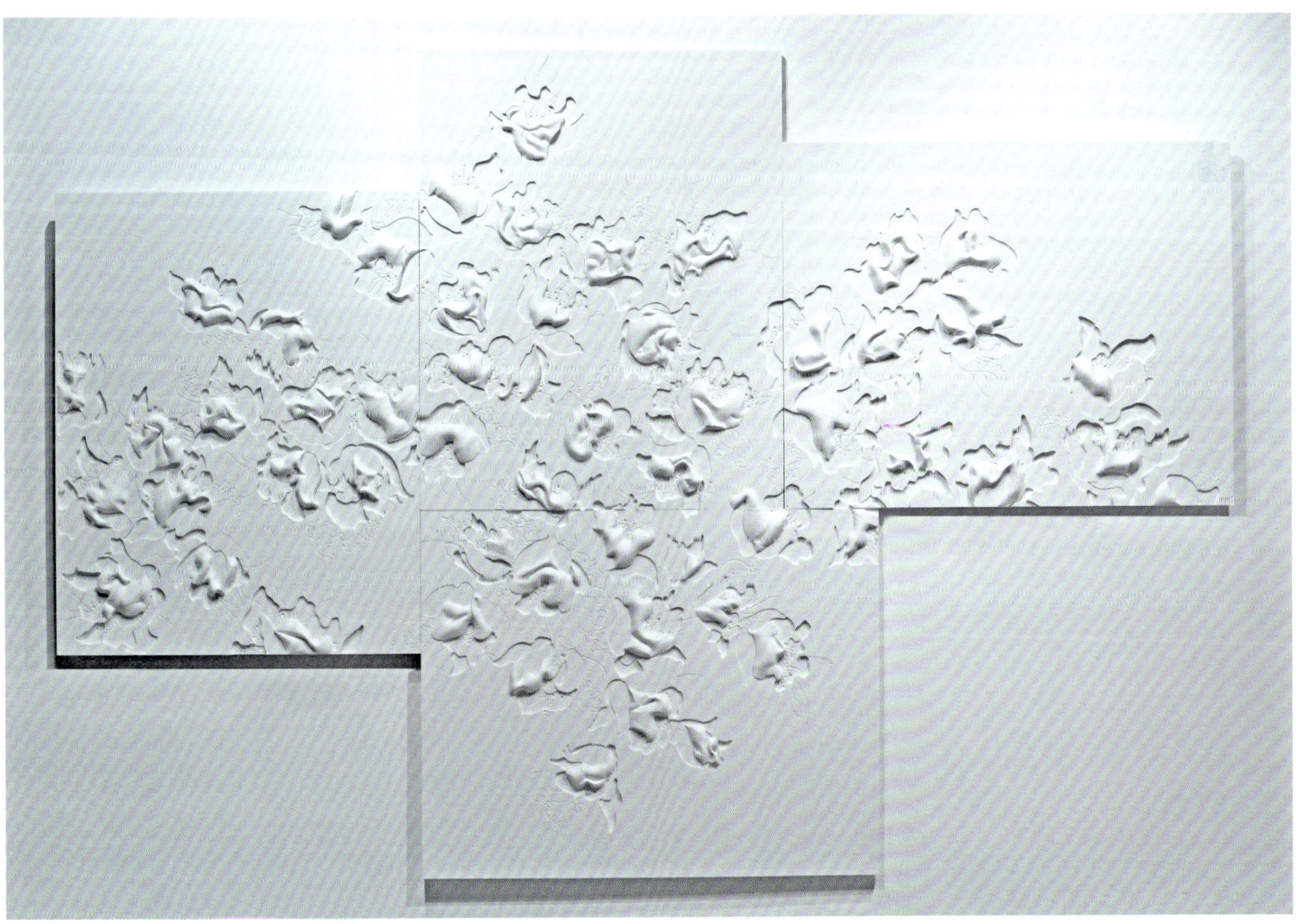

FIG. 48 Bloom Field project. Ben Krone (American, b. 1977), from a drawing by Leah Raintree (American, b. 1979). Manufactured by Associated Fabrication. New York, NY, 2007. CNC-routed Corian. Courtesy of William and Coren Sharples

Endnotes

Rococo Redux

MELISSA LEE HYDE

1. Already in 1850, the author of a notice in a British publication observed with puzzlement, "The history of this word appears to be involved in uncertainty." Martin de Albuquerque, ed., *Notes and Queries*, March 30, 1850 (Oxford, 1850): 356.

2. The 1771 edition of the Trévoux dictionary defined rocaille as "an assemblage of several kinds of shells and rough, unpolished stones that encrust certain rocks, which they are made to resemble. It is a rustic architectural composition imitating such natural rocks through the use of perforated stones, shells and coral of many colors, as seen in grottoes and fountain basins." Quoted in Bruno Pons, "The Rocaille," in Alain Gruber, ed., *The History of Decorative Arts. Classicism and the Baroque* (New York, 1992): 329.

3. See Mary Sheriff, "Rococo," in *Encyclopedia of the Enlightenment* (Oxford, 2002) 3: 466. The theory that *barocco* is etymologically linked to rococo may stem from the fact that the early nineteenth-century writer Stendhal declared Bernini to have been the "father" of French rococo; it was later shown by Fiske Kimball in *The Creation of the Rococo* (1943) to be an indigenous eighteenth-century French style, entirely distinct from baroque. Stendhal's references to Bernini and rococo are discussed in an important article by C. T. Carr, in which he argues against the etymological relationship between rococo and barocco, noting that the Italian form of the word did not appear in French sources, and was not used in the eighteenth century for a style of art. He points out that the French habit of forming colloquialisms by adding an o, as in aristo for "aristocrat," is suggestive of the colloquial origins of rococo. See C. T. Carr, "Two Words in Art History: II Rococo," in *Forum for Modern Language Studies* 1 (1965): 268–69.

4. Most French scholars tend to use these terms interchangeably to refer narrowly to a style of decoration and ornament. See Marianne Roland Michel, *Lajoüe et l'art rocaille* (Neuilly, 1984); and the recent ENSBA catalogue *Boucher, Watteau and the Origin of the Rococo* (Paris, 2003), especially the essay by Emmanuelle Brugerolles and David Guillet, p. 27. On the way in which elements of rococo style were absorbed into dress in France, see Aileen Ribeiro, *The Art of Dress. Fashion in England and France, 1750–1820* (New Haven, 1995): 53–54.

5. The frame was for an Oudry *Chasse du Roi* (destined for the Château de Marly), and is discussed in Peter Fuhring in "Boucher and Ornament Designers," in *Boucher, Watteau and the Origin of the Rococo*, p. 248.

6. "The expressions Pompadour and rococo, which are practically common parlance today for the taste that was in fashion during the reign of Louis XV, were used for the first time by Maurice Quai (a fellow student) in 1796–97. Back then, these locutions (one could say slang) were only used and understood in painting studios." See Etienne-Jean Delécluze, *Louis David, son école et son temps, souvenirs* (Paris, 1855): 82.

7. Stendhal used it to describe Bernini's art in his *Promenades dans Rome* (1829). This is usually credited as the first use of the word in a literary source. See Carr, p. 266. However, Etienne de Jouy used the term some six years earlier in "Les commis voyageurs" (June 1820), where he talked of seeing the church of St. Pierre in Besançon as "nouvellement construite" and "de ce style maniéré que les artistes appellent rococo." See *Oeuvres complètes, avec des éclaircissements et notes. Observations sur les Moeurs françaises au commencement du 19e siècle* (Paris: Didot ainé, 1823): XI: 119.

8. The 1842 supplement to the *Dictionnaire français* defined it thus: "Rococo se dit trivialement du genre d'ornement, de style et de dessin qui appartient à l'école du règne de Louis XV et du commencement de Louis XVI," adding "le genre rococo a suivi et précédé le 'Pompadour' qui n'est lui-même qu'une nuance du rococo."

9. "That part of the French population to whom the epithet of rococo is thus applied, may be understood to contain all varieties of old-fashionism, from the gentle advocate for laced coats and diamond sword-knots, up to the high-minded venerable loyalist, who only loves his rightful king the better because he has no means left to requite his love. Such is the interpretation of rococo in the mouth of a doctrinaire: but if a republican speaks it, he means that it should include also every gradation of orderly obedience, even to the powers that be; and in fact, whatever else may be considered as essentially connected with law or gospel." Frances Trollope, *Paris and the Parisians in 1835* (London, 1836): 15–16; discussed in Carr, p. 270.

10. Caroline Igra, "Reviving the Rococo: Enterprising Italian artists in Second Empire Paris," in *Art History* 28, no. 3 (2005): 340–56.

11. "Rococo Revival," in *Grove Dictionary of Art Online*. For the politically contestatory origins of rococo as a form a resistance to absolutist authority in the late seventeenth century, see Katie Scott, *The Rococo Interior* (New Haven, 1995).

12. Besides Le Pautre, Watteau, and Meissonnier, these artists included Pierre Lassurance, Jean Berain, Gilles-Marie Oppenord, Nicolas Pineau, and Jacques de Lajoüe.

13. Richard John, "Rococo," in *Grove Dictionary of Art*, p. 491.

14. Sheriff, p. 466.

15. Brugerolles and Guilliet, p. 27.

16. Ibid.

17. Ibid.

18. For a cogent discussion of other formal features of rococo painting, see Sheriff.

19. Edmond and Jules de Goncourt, *Madame de Pompadour* (1881, rpt, s.l.: Olivier Orban, 1982): 313.

20. Edmond and Jules de Goncourt, *La Revolution dans les moeurs: La Famille, le monde, la vielle femme, les jeunes gens, le mariage, les demoiselles à marier, les gens riches, les lettres et les arts, la pudeur sociale, le catholicisme* (Paris, 1854): 25.

21. For further discussion of critical responses to Boucher in gendered terms, see Melissa Lee Hyde, *Making Up the Rococo: François Boucher and His Critics* (Los Angeles, 2006).

22. Though, as Carol Duncan has argued, "there was both a survival of the Rococo tradition through the Neo-Classical era and a conscious revival of it beginning in the 1820s." See Carol Duncan, *The Persistence and Re-Emergence of the Rococo in French Romantic Painting* (UMI, 1970): 54.

23. At court, the Duchesse de Berry inspired a taste for the eighteenth century by organizing balls that "were consciously designed to recall the fêtes of Louis XV." See Duncan, 55–57.

24. For discussion of Romantic writers of this era inspired by rococo, see Duncan, 120ff, 169ff.

25. Ibid., p. 220.

26. Some of them discussed by Igra. See also Eric Zafran, *Cavaliers and Cardinals: Nineteenth-century French Anecdotal Paintings* (Cincinnati, 1992). On Meissonier, see Constance Cain Hungerford, *Ernest Meissonier: Master in His Genre* (Cambridge, 1999); and Marc Gottlieb, *The Plight of Emulation: Ernest Meissonier and French Salon Painting* (Princeton, 1996).

27. Igra, 347–48. See also Patricia Mainardi, *Art and Politics of the Second Empire* (New Haven, 1987).

28. Though her passion for the period, and especially for Marie-Antoinette, suggests more personal motivations as well. On this subject, see Christophe Pincemaille, *L'impératrice Eugénie du Suez à Sedan* (Paris, 2000).

29. For discussion of Eugénie's role in the rococo revival of the Second Empire, see Duncan, p. 222. On the "second Rococo," see Marianne Zweig, *Zweites Rokoko* (Vienna, 1926), and *The Second Empire, 1852–1870: Art in France under Napoleon III*, exh. cat (Philadelphia, 1978).

30. Christophe Pincemaille, "L'imperatrice Eugénie et Marie-Antoinette," in *Versalia* 6 (2003): 123–34.

31. The following year, Winterhalter portrayed her with her ladies-in-waiting in an imposing pseudo-rococo confection, in which the dainty aesthetic of the eighteenth century seems afflicted by a certain Second Empire gigantism. Discussed in Thérèse Dolan, "The Empress's New Clothes: Fashion and Politics in Second Empire France," in *Woman's Art Journal* 15 (1994).

32. On this artist, see Gabriel Weisberg, *Against the Modern: Dagnan-Bouveret and the Transformation of the Academic Tradition*, exh. cat. (New York: Dahesh Museum, 2002).

33. Debora Silverman, "The Brothers de Goncourts' Maison d'un Artiste: French Art Nouveau between History and the Psyche. 1869–1889," in *Arts Magazine*, LIX/9 (May 1985): 119–29.

34. On the Goncourts and their importance to Art Nouveau, see Debora Silverman, *Art Nouveau in Fin-de-siècle France* (1989): 28.

Juste-Aurèle Meissonnier and His Patrons

PETER FUHRING

1. Anthony Blunt, review of *The Creation of the Rococo* by Fiske Kimball, in *The Burlington Magazine* 88 (1946, 518): 128–29.

2. *Gazette des Beaux-Arts* XXIV (1943): 313–15.

3. Comte de Caylus, "Mémoire sur M. Messonnier," in *Mercure de France* (October 1750): 138–41. "Parce qu'il vouloit trouver du nouveau, paroître singulier, produire du piquant, en un mot devenir original, & sur tout ne ressembler à personne."

4. Le Blanc wrote a letter to Buffon, dated February 22, 1737. See London, British Library, Ms., Additional 22548, fol. 102–03: "Le plus habile Orfèvre de Londres n'est qu'un Ouvrier. Un Germain, un Messonier, sont tout autre chose, ce sont des Dessinateurs, ce sont des Sculpteurs, ce sont de grands Hommes en leur genre." See Peter Fuhring, *Un Génie du Rococo: Juste-Aurèle Meissonnier, 1695–1750* (Turin and London: Umberto Allemandi & C., 1999), vol. 2, chp. 4, documents no. 10, 422.

5. Paris, B.N., Estampes, Collection Deloynes, vol. IV, no. 45 [P.-J. Mariette], Obituary of Meissonnier: "Il vouloit être tout cela, pretendoit cy primer, tandis qu'il n'avoit de tous ces Arts qu'une connoissance telle que l'a peut donner le goût, mais qui n'est pas a beaucoup suffisante pour les exercer au lieu et avec s'il s'en fut tenu à la seule Orfevrerie qui étoit sa veritable profession & celle pour laquelle il étoit né. Il n'auroit eu pour émule que M. Germain & n'auroit redouté aucun concurrent."

6. Jacques-François Blondel, *Discours sur la nécessité de l'étude de l'architecture…* (Paris, 1754): 77–79: "Par ces connoissances, combien ne se sont pas illustrés les célébres MM. Germain & Meyssonier, qui joignant à la célébrité de leur Art la plus grande étude de l'Architecture, ont montré dans plus d'une occasion de quelle ressource cette étude leur avoit été?"

7. Not to be confused with the Royal goldsmiths employed by the court at a retainer, such as Thomas Germain, Nicolas Besnier, and Claude Ballin. See Fuhring, vol. 1, pp. 22–23, vol. 2, chp. 4, p. 407.

8. *Mercure de France* (December 1730): 2920–22: "Nous sommes trop attentifs à celebrer le progrès des beaux Arts en France, pour ne pas dire quelque chose d'un grand Ouvrage d'Orfévrerie, fait depuis peu par M. Meissonniere, & que quantité de Curieux ont été voir chez lui avec une très-grande satisfaction."

9. Sue Taylor and Richard A. Born, *The David and Alfred Smart Museum. A Guide of the Collection* (New York, 1990): 58, no. 19; G. Le Duc, *Porcelaine tendre de Chantilly au XVIIIe siècle* (Paris, 1996): 173, figs. pp. 174–75; Fuhring 1999, vol. 2, cat. works no. 41.

10. Fuhring 1999, vol. 2, cat. prints no. 66.

11. Ibid., cat. works no. 42, cat. prints nos. 72–73.

12. In the flattering introduction of Fraise to his *Livre de desseins chinois, tirés d'après les originaux de Perse, des Indes, de la Chine et du Japon, dessinés et gravés en taille-douce par le Sr Fraisse, peintre de S.A.S. Monseigneur le Duc, dédié à son altesse serenissime* (Paris, 1735), one reads about the porcelain and lackerwork: "Vous n'avez pas même dédaigné, MONSEIGNEUR, d'employer quelques momens à découvrir & à perfectionner ces Arts, qui sembloient jusqu'à présent reservés aux Peuples de l'autre Hémispere; & l'on voit avec admiration vos Ouvrages dans tous les genres, confondus avec ceux de la Chine & des Indes, sans que le plus habile connoisseur puisse les distinguer les uns des autres". Despite the confidential nature of Chantilly porcelain production, the factory had an outlet in Paris, where the public could inspect the latest creations. In *Les Affiches de Paris* (January, 1748), we learn that the shop had moved to a new location: "Le Magasin général des Porcelaines de la Manufacture Royale de Chantilly, se tient présentement rue de la vieille Draperie, au Magasin Anglois à Paris, chez le sieur de la Vigne, ci–devant Privilegié du Roi pour le similor."

13. Fuhring 1999, vol. 2, cat. works no. 4, and prints no. 101. The idea of the added "background," the corner of a room is likely a later idea and unrelated to the actual position of the cadran, drawn when the publisher Gabriel Huquier decided to opt for a folio-size publication of the artist's works. It is tempting to situate the cadran in the hôtel of the Duke of Mortemart, 14, rue Saint-Guillaume, in Paris, but the surviving documents, among which is the after-death inventory, do not identify such an object.

14. Fuhring 1999, vol. 2, cat. works no. 8, drawings no. 5 and prints no. 108.

15. The project was long dated to the 1740s in association with the town square competition of Louis XV of 1748, but the designs stem from twenty years earlier. See J. Garms, "Projects for the Pont Neuf and Place Dauphine in the First Half of the Eighteenth Century," in *Journal of the Society of Architectural Historians* XXVI (1967): 102–13; Dorothea Nyberg, "Meissonnier: An Eighteenth-century Maverick," in *Oeuvre de Juste-Aurèle Meissonnier* (New York: Benjamin Blom, 1969): 24, 31–32, and note 104, but the design stems from twenty years earlier. See Fuhring 1999, vol. 2, cat. works no. 15; Peter Fuhring, in A. Gady and J.-M. Pérouse de Montclos, eds., *De l'esprit des villes. Nancy et l'Europe urbaine au Siècle des Lumières 1720–1770*, exh. cat. (Nancy: Musée des Beaux-Arts, 2005): no. 111.

16. Fuhring 1999, vol. 2, cat. works no. 38, cat. prints no. 75.

17. Marie-Thérèse Mandroux-França, "Information artistique et 'mass-media' au XVIIIe siècle: la diffusion de l'ornement gravé rococo au Portugal," in *Bracara Augusta* XXVII (1973): 64 (76) (Braga, 1974): 1–36, especially 8, where the author rightly suggests in relationship to this series that Meissonnier was the first creator of true rococo ornament.

18. "Ce sont des Fontaines, des Cascades, des Ruines, des Rocailles, et Coquillages, des morceaux d'Architecture qui font des effets bizarres et pittoresques, par leurs formes piquantes et extraordinaires, dont souvent aucune partie ne répond à l'autre, sans que le sujet en paroisse moins riche et moins agréable. Il y a aussi des especes de plafonds avec figures et animaux, groupez avec intelligence, dont les bordures sont extrêmement ingénieuses et variées."

19. Marie-Thérèse Mandroux-França, "La Politique artistique européenne du roi Jean V de Portugal en direction de Paris. Sources raisonnées," in *Histoire du Portugal. Histoire Européenne, Actes du Colloque, Paris, May 22–23, 1986* (Paris: Fondation Calouste Gulbenkian, 1987): 111–45.

20. Peter Fuhring, *Designing the Décor: French Drawings of the Eighteenth Century*, exh. cat. (Lisbon: Calouste Gulbenkian Museum, 2005): nos. 23–24.

21. Marie-Thérèse Mandroux-França, 'Une collection 'Affaire d'Etat,' ", in P.-J. Mariette, *Catalogues de la collection d'estampes de Jean V, Roi du Portugal*, vol. 1, edited by Marie-Thérèse Mandroux-França and M. Préaud (Lisbon and Paris: Fundação Calouste Gulbenkian, 2003): 53–164, especially 90–91.

22. The house still stands, virtually unaltered, at the corner of the quai de la Nive and the rue du Pont-Mayou, subsequently called rue Chegaray; today, 1, rue Victor-Hugo.

23. G. Perrot, *Inventaire des arrêts du conseil du Roi* (janvier-février 1730; reprint Paris: Imprimeries "Les Presses modernes": 1937): 73, no. 171.

24. F. Kimball, "J.-A. Meissonnier and the Beginning of the 'Genre Pittoresque,' " in *Gazette des Beaux-Arts* 22 (1942): 33–34 (as 1733); F. Kimball, *The Creation of the Rococo* (Philadelphia, 1943): 158 (idem); L. Hautecœur, *Histoire de l'Architecture classique en France. Tome III. Première moitié du XVIIIe siècle. Le style Louis XV* (Paris, 1950): 194 and 263, note 8; and Nyberg, p. 28 (the years 1730). The two prints depicting the interior, etched by Gabriel Huquier, are not part of the original series depicting the house, but added to the *Oeuvre* in 1748. See Fuhring 1999, vol. 2, cat. prints nos. 12–13.

25. Fuhring 1999, vol. 2, cat. works no. 31, cat. prints no. 119.

26. Ibid., cat. works no. 61, cat. prints nos. 115–116; Peter Fuhring, "Libros de fiestas y exequias celebradas en la corte de Francia," in *La Real Biblioteca Pública 1711–1760 de Felipe V a Fernando VI*, exh. cat. (Madrid: Biblioteca Nacional, 2004): 285–99.

27. Fuhring 1999, vol. 2, cat. prints no. 94.

28. Ibid., cat. works no. 43.

29. Ibid., cat. works no. 47.

30. Ibid., cat. prints nos. 90–93. The four paintings made to be incorporated in the wainscoting seem to be the only surviving elements of the scheme.

31. *Gazette d'Utrecht* LXXVIII (September 29 [Paris, September 23], 1735): 3; see Fuhring 1999, vol. 2, chp. 4, p. 402.

32. *Mercure de France* (July 1736): 1691–94; see Fuhring 1999, vol. 2, chp. 4, Documents no. 7, p. 421 with previous bibliography.

33. Fuhring 1999, vol. 2, cat. works no. 55, cat. prints no. 97.

34. B.-G.-B. Pallot, *L'art du siège au XVIIIe siècle en France* (Paris: ACR-Gismondi Editeurs 1987): 122.

35. Peter Fuhring, "Juste-Aurèle Meissonnier: The Artist and His Work," introduction, sale catalogue, *The Thyssen Meissonnier Silver Tureen made for the 2nd Duke of Kingston* New York (Sotheby's, May 13, 1998): 10–49, especially 39–40, fig. 32.

36. Henry Hawley, "Meissonnier's Silver for the Duke of Kingston," in *The Bulletin of the Cleveland Museum of Art* LXV (1978): 10, p. 344, with a full transcription of the "Memoire de la Vaisselle que Monsieur le Duc de Kingston a acheté à Paris." See for a photograph of

the same document in Ph. and G. Glanville, " 'French Fancy' Silver from Paris and English patrons," in *Rococo Silver in England and Its Colonies*, papers from a symposium at Virginia Museum of Fine Arts, Richmond, 2004 (London: Silver Society, 2006): 20 and appendix 3.5, fig. 183.

37. For a first survey of such candlesticks, see Fuhring 1999, cat. works nos. 49a–h. Some of the gilt bronze versions are however of such an outstanding quality that one can not exclude that Meissonnier's original model should be considered as its starting point rather than the three prints in the *Oeuvre* of the artist. If one accepts this idea, one cannot exclude a second hypothesis, namely that Meissonnier may have participated in the organization of their production. As a member of the Parisian corporation of silversmiths he was certainly allowed to do so, but we have no information about Meissonnier's practical involvement given the dismantling of his goldsmith workshop before he died.

38. *Gazette d'Utrecht*, no. XXII, Monday 17 March, notice dated Paris 10 March: "Le Duc de Kingston a envoyé commission de Londres, de faire faire ici chez le Sieur Melier [sic], fameux Orfèvre, 2. Terrines d'argent, du poids de 80 marcs chacune, qui sont presque achévées, & qui surpassent tout ce qu'on a fait jusqu'à présent de beau dans ce genre."

39. Hawley 1978, pp. 322–23, 345, app. III.

40. Etienne de La Font de Saint-Yenne and Voltaire (François-Marie Arouet), *L'Ombre du grand Colbert. Le Louvre, et la ville de Paris, dialogue* (La Haye, 1749).

41. Alexandre Gady and Jean-Marie Pérouse de Montclos, eds., *De l'esprit des villes. Nancy et l'Europe urbaine au Siècle des Lumières 1720–1770*, exh. cat. dir. by A. Gady and J.-M. Pérouse de Montclos (Nancy: Musée des Beaux-Arts, 2005): fig. 37.

42. For a first discussion of this phenomenon in which a publisher collaborated with an artist, including Meissonnier and Oppenord, and possibly also Jacques de Lajoüe and François Boucher, see Peter Fuhring, "Two Title Page Designs by Gilles-Marie Oppenord for His Engraved Oeuvre," in *Drawing* XIV (1992): 3, 49–52.

43. Letter by Devalcourt to Prince Czartoryski, dated 11 February 1732, cited after I. Malinowska, "Kilka przyczunkow do historii stosunkow artystycznych miedzy Polska a Francja w l pol. XVIII w." In *Muzeum i Tworca* (Warsaw, 1969): 126, no. 8633: "Les desseins d'ornemens intérieurs sont des plus parfaits et du fameux Caffieri que Mr le Baron de Besenval a engagé à travailler dans le gout le plus nouveau; ils seront très difficiles pour l'Execution, Mr de Besenval même pensa que le seul Caffieri pourroit les faire Executer parfaitement icy, Soit en bois, soit en Carton pour les dorer en même tems et les envoyer Numerotés prêts à appliquer sur le muraille d'une chambre ou d'un cabinet après qu'on en auroit envoyé toutes les proportions; Votre Altesse en jugera et decidera."

44. The surviving elements are fully restored and part of the collection of the Przypkowski Museum in Poland. See Piotr Maciej Przypkowski, "Rokokowe boazerie w zbiorach Muzeum Im. Przypkowskich W Jedrzejowie," in *Rocznik Muzeum Swietokrzyskiego* IX (1975): 387–400 (with summary in Russian and English); Fuhring 1999, vol. 2, cat. works no. 64.

Ornament of Bizarre Imagination

GAIL S. DAVIDSON

* I would especially like to thank Dr. Peter Fuhring, Professor, Radboud University, Nijmegen, the Netherlands, whose publications and conversations on the subject of ornament prints have contributed much to my knowledge of this field, and who graciously reviewed my manuscript.

1. Jacques-François Blondel, *Cours d'Architecture ou traité de la decoration,...*, vol. 5 (Paris: Platte, 1777): 88; cited in Peter Fuhring, *Un Génie du Rococo: Juste-Aurèle Meissonier, 1695–1740*, 2 vols. (Turin and London: Umberto Allemandi & C., 1999): vol. 2, 435.

2. The ridicule lodged by Blondel against rococo style was preceded in public discourse by two articles in 1754 and 1755 by Charles-Nicolas Cochin fils in the *Mercure de France*. See Sidney Fiske Kimball, *The Creation of the Rococo* (Philadelphia: Philadelphia Museum of Art, 1943): 3–4; and Katie Scott, *The Rococo Interior, Decoration of Social Spaces in Early Eighteenth-century Paris* (New Haven and London: Yale University Press, 1995): 258–62.

3. See Peter Fuhring, "The Print Privilege in Eighteenth-century France I," in *Print Quarterly* 2, no. 3 (1985): 174–193; and "The Print Privilege in Eighteenth-century France II," in *Print Quarterly* 3, no. 1 (1986): 19–33.

4. Coined in the nineteenth century, ornament print refers to engravings, etchings, or other prints used in workshops as a resource or a model, to transfer a design into another medium, or as an educational tool to teach styles or drawing excellence.

5. Examples of these allegorical vignettes in the Decloux collection include: Claude Duflos after François Boucher, *Les Quatre Saisons* (1921-6-251-1/4); Jean Pillement, *Les Cinq Sens* (1921-6-381-1/5); Charles-Nicolas Cochin fils after Bellay, *Les Quatre Saisons* (1921-6-273-1/4); and others.

6. Susan Miller, "Jean-Antoine Fraisse, 'Gravé par Huquier,'" in *Metropolitan Museum Journal*, vol. 31 (1996): 127, quoting Peter Fuhring, "The Print Privilege in Eighteenth-century France II," p. 26; see also Fuhring, *Meissonnier*, vol. 1, p. 60, for other designers who applied for their own print privileges.

7. For a discussion of Meissonnier's application for print privilege and the plates published in the Widow Chéreau edition, see Peter Fuhring, *Meissonnier*, vol. 1: 53–56.

8. On the Chéreau family, see Maxime Préaud, Pierre Casselle, et al., *Dictionnaire des éditeurs d'estampes à Paris sous l'Ancien Régime* (Paris: Promodis, Editions du Cercle de la Libraire, 1986): 79–85.

9. On the work of Gabriel Huquier and his publication of oeuvre catalogues, see Yves Bruand, "Un grand collectionneur, marchand et graveur du XVIIIe siècle, Gabriel Huquier (1695–1772)," in *Gazette des Beaux-Arts*, vol. XXXVII (July–September 1950): 99–114; Yves Bruand, Michèle Hébert, and Yves Sjöberg, *Inventaire du fonds français, graveurs du XVIIIe siècle*, vol. XI (Paris: Bibliothèque Nationale, 1970): 446–538; Préaud, pp. 165–66; Peter Fuhring, "Two Title Page Designs by Gilles-Marie Oppenord for his Engraved Oeuvre," in *Drawing*, vol. XIV, no. 3 (September–October 1992): 49–52; Madeleine Barban, "Gabriel Huquier," in Jane Turner, ed., *Grove Dictionary of Art*, vol. 15 (London: Macmillan Publishers Ltd., 1996): 31; and Peter Fuhring, "Gabriel Huquier," in Emmanuelle Brugerolles, *François Boucher et l'art rocaille dans les collections de l' École des beaux-arts*, exh. cat. (Paris: Ecole Nationale Supérieure des Beaux-Arts, 2003): 276–79.

10. See Frits Lugt, *Les Marques de Collections de Dessins & d'Estampes...*, 2 vols. (Amsterdam: Vereenigde Drukkerijen, 1921): vol. 1, #75 (Bérard), #421 (Beurdely), #740 (Destailleur); vol. 2, supplement, #2078PaP (Piancastelli); and Peter Fuhring, *Design into Art, Drawings for Architecture and Ornament, the Lodewijk Houthakker Collection*, 2 vols. (London: Philip Wilson Publishers, 1989): vol. 1: 28–30.

11. On the Piancastelli purchases, see Marilyn Symmes, "Collecting for Inspiration and Instruction: Drawings at Cooper-Hewitt, National Design Museum," in *Drawing*, vol. XVII, nos. 4–6 (November 1995–March 1996): 73–79.

12. According to the records of the Archives de Sèvres (FR AC 92072; series F and G), in 1911, Decloux lived at 26, rue Croix-Bosset, in Sèvres. By 1919, he also gave a Paris address at 7, cité Malesherbes, and listed himself as a realtor of furnished apartments. By 1921, he was listed as without a profession.

13. Hôtel Drouot, Paris, April 27–28, 1891: Objets d'art et de haute curiosité, émaux peints de Limoges, faïences italiennes, hispano-mauresques et françaises, grès allemands, vitraux, bronzes d'art et d'ameublement, fers, bois, ivoires, miniatures, objets variés, meubles-broderies au point, composant la collection de M. Léon Decloux.

14. Hôtel Drouot, Paris, February 14–15, 1898: Dessins, Aquarelles, Gouaches et Tableaux du XVIIIe Siècle... composant la collection de M. Léon Decloux.

15. Eleanor Garnier Hewitt, *The Making of a Modern Museum*, 4th edition (Boston: The Merrymount Press, 1941): p. 12. I am grateful to Judith Bergoffen for her research on Marcellite Thorn Garner and her family.

16. To help cement the relationship, Decloux almost immediately donated to the museum fourteen fragments of eighteenth-century wood paneling (1907-6-1/14), and, the following year, the Museum Council purchased from him forty-nine pieces of wood paneling dating from ca. 1720–80, some coming from the Château d'Asnières (1908-24-1/49).

17. On the role of Charles W. Gould in acquiring the American landscape drawings for the Cooper Union Museum, see Gail S. Davidson, "Eliot Clark and the American Drawings Collection at Cooper–Hewitt, National Design Museum," in *Archives of the American Art Journal*, vol. 34, no. 4 (1994): 4–10.

18. Letters from Décloux to Eleanor Hewitt are in the Museum Advisory Council property file, Cooper-Hewitt, National Design Museum.

19. Hôtel Drouot, Paris, November 29–30, 1920: Catalogue des Tableaux, Dessins Miniatures & Objets d'Art du XIIIe siècle appartenant à M. L. Decloux.

20. From the start of his project for the Hewitt sisters, Decloux sought to purchase a copy of Meissonnier's *Oeuvre*. The example in the Museum's collection may well be the version "in a modern binding" that Decloux mentioned in his February 11, 1908, letter, which brought 4,200 francs at auction.

21. For a discussion of Meissonnier's critics, see Dorothea Nyberg, "Meissonnier, an Eighteenth-century Maverick," in *Oeuvre de Juste-Aurèle Meissonnier* (Bronx, New York: Benjamin Blom, Inc., 1969): 14–19; and Fuhring, *Meissonnier*, vol. 2, pp. 425–38.

22. See Fuhring, *Meissonnier*, vol. 2: 320, who pointed to the existence of Meissonnier prints of this model in the Meissen archives, which may have been acquired in 1735. On the Metropolitan Museum of Art's Meissen Candlestick, see Clare Le Corbeiller, "German Porcelain of the Eighteenth Century," in *Metropolitan Museum of Art Bulletin* (Spring 1990): 1, 29.

23. Regarding other Roëttiers designs for candlesticks and tureens in *Eléments d'orfèvrerie*, see additional plates 70–72, 81, 82, 86; see also Fuhring, *Designing the Décor, French Drawing from the Eighteenth Century*, exh. cat. (Lisbon: Calouste Gulbenkian foundation, 2000): 174–75, with other Roëttiers drawings.

24. On Lajoüe, see Marianne Roland Michel, *Lajoüe et L'Art Rocaille* (Neuilly-sur-Seine: Arthena, 1984); Peter Fuhring, *Boucher et l'art rocaille*: pp. 290–301, nos. 73–78 (illus.); and Peter Fuhring, *Designing the Décor*, p. 112, no. 31 (illus.).

25. Though the drawing was donated by the Hewitt sisters in 1914, there is good reason to believe that it came from the Decloux drawings purchase in 1911.

26. See Roland Michel, p. 316, G. 12 and fig. 205; this print was reproduced in reverse by Bickham, *The Universal Penman* (London, 1741): 119, to depict merchandise. Le Rouge and others used additional sea-themed cartouche designs for various maps; see Roland Michel, p. 153, G. 8; p. 316, G. 11; p. 317, G. 22.

27. See Roland Michel, p. 315; p. 16, G. 12; and p. 318, G.27–38; the publication *Sixty different sorts of Ornaments by Gaetano Brunetti* (1736), which reproduces three cartouches in reverse without the name of the designer, was discovered by Peter Fuhring.

28. Blondel, *L'homme du monde éclairé par les arts* (Paris: Chez M. Onory, 1774), notice 15, quoted in Roland Michel, p. 398.

29. See *Design for a Fire Screen*, in Roland Michel, p.271, D.175, fig. 259; and hand-fan prints, p. 346, G.138–43, figs. 432–34 and 439–41.

30. Patrick Mauriès, *Shell Shock, Conchological Curiosities* (London: Thames and Hudson Ltd., 1994): 44

31. Roland Michel, pp. 196–98; P. 57 A/F; figs. 88–99.

32. Musée des Arts Décoratifs, Inv. D. 11304. Roland Michel (p. 217, P. 167) called this painting a model for a larger decorative panel.

33. Roland Michel, p. 197.

34. On the identification of the Boucher drawing as a design for the panel of a coach, see Alastair Lang, "A Group of Boucher's Designs for Coach Panels," in Fuhring, *Design into Art*, vol. 1: 117–21.

35. Roland Michel, p. 180.

36. For recent literature on Peyrotte, see Fuhring, "Print Privilege I," p. 191; Jean-Nérée Ronfort, "1759, Bellevue et le Secrétaire du Dauphin," in *L'Estampille L'Objet d'Art*, no. 285/286 (November-December 1994): 118; Fuhring, "Boucher et les dessinateurs d'ornement," in *Boucher et L'Art Rocaille*, p. 257 and p. 318, no. 80; and Fuhring, *Designing the Décor*, pp. 150–53, no. 49; pp. 180–85; nos. 63–65; pp. 343–44.

37. Fuhring, "Boucher et les dessinateurs d'ornement," p. 257.

38. Examples of these etchings for fire screens are Cooper-Hewitt 1921-22-260 and -262, which came from the collection of Léon Decloux. Another example, *Repast of the Hunters*, etched by Gérard-Jean-Baptiste Scotin the Younger (1921-22-279), also from the Decloux collection, is one of the Peyrotte designs illegally re-published by Etienne Charpentier in Paris; on the suit by Pariset and Daudet against Charpentier, see Fuhring, "Print Privilege I," pp. 191–92.

39. On Peyrotte's découpure prints, see idem.; Simon Jervis, "Huquier's 'Second Livre,'" in *J. Paul Getty Museum Journal*, vol. 14 (1986): 113–20; Fuhring, "Boucher et les dessinateurs d'ornement," p. 257; and Fuhring, *Designing the Décor*, pp. 152–53. For a general discussion of the vogue for découpures, consult Scott, *The Rococo Interior*, p. 249.

40. See Peter Fuhring's identification and discussion of the album belonging to Fontanieu in the Bibliothèque Nationale (Hd64 Réserve), from which this sheet comes, containing sixty-two drawings by different designers for furniture and ornaments, in *Designing the Décor*, pp. 32–36.

41. Fuhring, *Design into Art*, vol. 1, pp. 20–21.

42. This textile dating from 1764 was produced by the Lyonnais silk manufacturer Jean-François Charton. See Svend Eriksen, *Early Neo-Classicism in France*, translated by Peter Thornton (London: Faber and Faber Ltd., 1974): 164–65.

43. See Mary L. Myers, *French Architectural and Ornament Drawings of the Eighteenth Century*, exh. cat. (New York: The Metropolitan Museum of Art, 1992): 167–68, no. 102 (illus.).

44. Fuhring, *Designing the Décor*, pp. 150–53, no. 49; pp. 180–85; nos. 63–65; pp. 343–44. In recognition of Fontanieu's support, the ornamentalist dedicated a series of prints after his designs to the intendant (*Nouveaux cartouches chinois*, 1738–49) and a second series to his wife Marie-Anne Pollart de Villequoy (*Nouveau livre de cartouches chinois*, before 1752), both published by Huquier.

45. This pattern of small floral sprigs embellished with pierced decorative bands replicates two other panels with honeysuckle sprays beneath bands of applied ornament in the same volume, which have been attributed to Peyrotte based on supporting documentation See Fuhring, *Designing the Décor*, pp. 150–51, no. 49 and fig. 48.

46. Prints after Peyrotte from the suite *Divers ornements* were used as educational tools in Britain to teach proper drawing of ornament. see Anne Puetz, "Design Instruction for Artisans in Eighteenth-century Britain," in *Journal of Design History*, vol. 12 no. 3 (1999): 225, fig. 3.

47. Blondel, p. 103, quoted in Roland Michel, p. 164.

48. For biographical information on Cuvilliés, see A. Bérard, *Catalogue de l'ouevre de Cuvilliés père et fils* (Paris: Veuve Jules Renouard, Libraire, 1859): 5–11; Jean Laran, *François de Cuvilliés Dessinateur et Architecte* (Paris: Henri Laurens, Éditeur, 1930): 1–4; Anthony Blunt et al., *Baroque and Rococo Architecture and Decoration* (New York, Hagerstown, San Francisco, London: Harper & Row, Publishers, 1978): 281–87; Wolfgang Braunfels, *François de Cuvilliés* (Munich: Süddeutscher Verlag, 1986); Gerhard Hojer, "(Jean) François (Vincent Joseph) de Cuvilliés I," in *Grove Dictionary of Art*, vol. 8: 288–91.

49. Roland Michel, p. 166 and p. 320, no. G 39–45. Plate 3 of Cuvilliés's series shows kettle drums similar to Lajoüe's plate 7; plate 4 of Cuvilliés's series uses a cannon running under the bottom of the cartouche, which appears in Lajoüe's plate 6, and so on.

50. Fuhring, *Meissonnier*, vol. 2, p. 358, no. 90a.

51. Adolf Feulner and Preston Remington, "Examples of South German Woodwork in the Metropolitan Museum," in *Metropolitan Museum Studies*, vol. 2, no. 2 (May 1930),: 152–66, figs. 4, 5.

52. On Nahl, see Friedrich Bleibaum, *Johann August Nahl, der künstler Friedrichs des Grossen und der landgrafen von Hessen-Kassel* (Baden bei Wein and Leipzig: R. M. Rohrer, ca. 1933); Thilo Eggeling, Studien zum friderizianischen Rokoko. George Wenceslaus von Knobelsdorff als Entwerfer von Innendekorationen (Berlin: Gebr. Mann Verlag, 1980); and Sabine Fett, Michaela Kalusok, and Ulrich Schmidt, *Die Künstlerfamilie Nahl: Rokoko under Klassizismus in Kassel*, exh. cat. (Kassel: Staatliche Museen Kassel, ca. 1994).

53. On the Hoppenhaupt brothers, see Wilhelm Kurth, *Die Raumkunst in Kupferstich des 17 und 18 Jahrhunderts* (Stuttgart: Julius Hoffmann Verlag, 1923): XLIV; *Sanssouci, Ein Beitrag zur Kunst des Deutschen Rokoko* (Berlin: Henschelverlag Kunst und Gesellschaft, 1962): 148–64 and 171–73; Thomas DaCosta Kaufmann, *Central European Drawings 1680–1800: A Selection from American Collections*, exh. cat. (Princeton: The Art Museum, Princeton University, 1989): 160, no. 57; and Thilo Eggling, "Johann Michael Hoppenhaupt II and Johann Christian Hoppenhaupt," in *Grove Dictionary of Art*, vol. 14: 750–51.

54. Kaufmann, pp. 158–59, no. 56 (illus.), on images of Nahl's designs for the Stadtschloss Bronzesaal and the Sanssouci Library, see Bleibaum, pls. 17, 27, and fig. 31.

55. For other drawings related to this series, see Fuhring, *Design into Art*, vol. 1, pp. 320 and 325, nos. 497–99; and Kaufmann, p. 162, no. 58 (illus.). See also Ebba Krull, *Franz Xaver Habermann, 1721–1796: Ein Augsburger Oramentist des Rokoko* (Abhandlungen zur Geschichte der stadt Augsburg, Band 23), Augsburg, 1977.

56. Sir Timothy Clifford, *Designs of Desire, Architectural and Ornament Prints and Drawings, 1500–1850* (Edinburgh: National Galleries of Scotland, 2000): 214, no. 101.

57. Similar ewer shaped ornaments resting on brackets were made for the Garden Room in the Franckenstein Pavilion, Schloss Seehof, Bamberg, Germany; see Daniëlle O. Kisluk-Grosheide, "The Garden Room from Schloss Seehof and Its Furnishings," in *Metropolitan Museum Journal*, vol. 25 (1990), p. 154, fig. 19, and p. 152, fig. 15.

58. Among the bibliographic references on Baumgartner, see Kaufmann, pp. 119–21, nos. 39–40 (illus.), pp. 174–75, no. 63 (illus.), and Gode Krämer, "Johann Wolfgang Baumgartner," in *Grove Dictionary of Art*, vol. 3, pp. 413–14.

Louis XV Style

PENELOPE HUNTER-STIEBEL

1. Penelope Hunter, "A Royal Taste: Louis XV–1738," in *Metropolitan Museum of Art Journal*, vol. 7 (1973): 89–113.

2. Pierre Verlet, *Le Mobilier Royal Français* (Paris: Editions d'Art et d'Histoire, 1945): nos. 19–22.

3. André-Jacob Roubo, *L'Art du menuisier*, vol. II (Paris, 1771): 653.

4. Whether or not they actually supplied design drawings, *marchands merciers* were editors, procuring and providing expensive materials, coordinating the efforts of specialists, and promoting the products. Madame de Pompadour was just one of the trendsetting clients of the marchand mercier Lazare Duvaux, whose transactions are known through his sales records; see Luis Courajod, ed., *Livre-Journal de Lazare Duvaux, Marchand-bijoutier ordinaire du roi, 1748–1758*, 2 vols. (Paris, 1873; republished by F. de Nobele, 1965).

5. Thibaut Wolvesperges, *Le Meuble Français en laque au XVIIIe Siècle* (Paris: L'Edition de l'Amateur , 2000): 182.

6. Calin Demetrescu, "D.F., un Ebéniste identifié," in *L'objet d'Art* (October 1992): 64–81.

7. Alexandre Pradère, *Les Ebénistes français de Louis XV à la Révolution* (Paris: Chene, 1989): 182–99.

8. Henry Hawley, "Jean-Pierre Latz, Cabinetmaker," in *The Bulletin of the Cleveland Museum of Art* (September/October 1970).

9. Marquetry of tortoiseshell and metal associated with the great Louis XIV ébéniste André-Charles Boulle (1642–1732).

10. Hawley, 204–05.

11. Gillian Wilson, *Selections from the Decorative Arts in the J. Paul Getty Museum* (Malibu: J. Paul Getty Museum, 1983): 50, no. 25.

12. Pierre Verlet, *Les Bronzes dorées français* (Paris: Picard, 1987): 193.

13. James Parker, *Decorative Art from the Samuel H. Kress Collection at the Metropolitan Museum of Art* (New York: Phaidon, 1964): 131.

14. Marie-Laure de Rochebrune, "La Passion de Madame de Pompadour pour la Porcelaine," in *Madame de Pompadour et les Arts* (Paris: Réunion des Musées Nationaux, 2002): 411, 439, 449.

Eighteenth-century Nancy

PENELOPE HUNTER-STIEBEL

1. Peter Fuhring, *Un Génie du Rococo: Juste-Aurèle Meissonnier*, vol. II (Turin: Umberto Allemandi, 1999): 270, no.14; 180, no. 14, preparatory drawing; 350, no.74, print.

2. Ibid., p. 435.

3. Quoted by Pierrre du Colombier, "Le Château de Lunéville," in *La Revue Française* (May 1958); author's translation.

4. *Stanislas, un roi de Pologne en Lorraine* (Nancy: Musée Lorrain, 2004): 1790.

5. See above for discussion of gilt bronzes.

6. Manuscript study by Frédéric Destreman in the archives of the Musée Lorrain, Nancy.

7. The archives of the Musée Lorrain show that 318 pieces were transferred to the museum in 1881; 232 are accounted for today, in varying states of conservation.

8. It was noted at the time that "he was the first example of a king who, in his own domain, erected a statue to his successor." Quoted from the *Comte general* (1761) by Mireille-Bénédicte Bouvet, "Places de Nancy au XVIIIe siècle," in *De l'Esprit des villes, Nancy et l'Europe urbaine au siècle des Lumières 1720–1770* (Nancy: Musée des Beaux-Arts, 2005): 74; author's translation. The figure of Louis XV was destroyed in the Revolution and replaced in 1831 by a monument to Stanislas, as the citizens of Nancy preferred to celebrate the golden years of his reign and their independence.

9. The only published study of Jean Lamour is the monograph by Albert France-Lanord, *Jean Lamour: Serrurier du Roi* (Nancy: Presses Universitaires, 1977). However, the archives of the Musée Lorrain contain a manuscript thesis by Aurore Baradol, *La Ferronerie de Jean Lamour* (2003–04).

10. The Musée Lorrain is undergoing a progressive renovation, to be completed in 2012.

11. Pierre-Yves Caillault, manuscript study preparatory to the restoration of the façade of the Pavillon Morey of the Palais Ducal, Nancy, p. 13014, in the archives of the Musée Lorrain.

12. Notre Dame de Bon Secours (1738), Château de Malgrange (1740), Château de Chanteheux (1741), Hôtel des Missions Royales (1741–43), Saint-Julien orphanage (1747).

Radiating Rococo

SARAH D. COFFIN

1. Serge Grandjean, *Les Tabatières du Musée du Louvre* (Paris: Réunion des Musées Nationaux, 1981): 109–10.

2. Peter Fuhring, "Juste-Aurèle Meissonnier: The Artist and His Work," in *The Thyssen Meissonnier Tureen Made for the Second Duke of Kingston* (Sotheby's, May 13, 1998): 14.

3. Grandjean, p. 110.

4. "Objects of Vertu" are small objects made to show off virtuosity of design and craftsmanship rather than serve a function.

5. Richard Edgcumbe, *The Art of the Gold Chaser* (New York: Oxford University Press, 2000): 52–53; Haidt had worked in Augsburg and Venice before coming to London, and may well be related to Johann Haidt, the Augsburg engraver who produced fine rococo cartouche ornamental engravings in the 1750s. Haidt left London for a Moravian community in Germany, then moved to another in Bethlehem, Pennsylvania, where he painted and drew.

6. Ibid., p. 86. Edgcumbe cites Vertue in 1745 as listing Haidt among the leading members of the St. Martin's Lane set, which also included Gravelot, Moser, Roubilliac, Wills, and Yeo. By 1746, Haidt is described after Hamon, Hogarth, Ellis, and Wills as one of the "principal Directors" of St. Martin's Lane Academy.

7. Burges(s) apprenticed to Laurence Ham(m)ond in 1731.

8. See Edgcumbe, who notes he may have been the son of goldsmith Michael Heckel.

9. George Vertue's notebooks cover much of the first half of the eighteenth century. Most of their contents were published by the Walpole Society in 1929–42 and 1948–50.

10. Vertue notebooks.

11. Michael Snodin, *Print Quarterly*, vol. XI, No.1 (March 1994): notes, p. 46.

12. P. von Stetten, *Kunst, Gewerk und Handwers Geschichte des Reichs-Stadt Augsburg* (Augsburg, 1779–88): i. 486, cited in Edgecombe, p. 66. The portrait was of George Ehret, the botanical artist whose works were the source for the Chelsea botanical plates from 1753–56. One is tempted to connect Heckel with the choice of Ehret's work as the source at Chelsea. His work was evidently still renowned many years later in Augsburg, as his sister and her husband received plaster casts of his work there.

13. Snodin, p. 46.

14. Gravelot's sinuous, curvilinear cartouche forms appear in John Pine's *The Tapestry Hangings of the House of Lords*, published in London in 1739, which depicted the defeat of the Spanish Armada. Gravelot designed the borders for two plates and the cartouche surround for the General Chart. His 1738 drawing for the latter, in Cooper-Hewitt's collection, was formerly in the collection of Horace Walpole.

15. This drawing (1948-40-185) is also similar to various German designs from both Dresden and Augsburg of this period. It is interesting to note that Crace's wife was the daughter of a German cabinetmaker working in London. A similar automaton, with an elephant instead of a horse, made probably for the Chinese market by Upjohn, is illustrated in a small booklet published by the Beijing Museum entitled *Clocks and Watches of the Qing Dynasty, from the Collection in the Forbidden City*, compiled by Liao Pin (Beijing: Foreign Languages Press, 2002). I am most grateful to Roger Smith for this information.

16. Quoted in A. Kenneth Snowman, *Eighteenth Century Gold Boxes of Europe* (Boston: Boston Book & Art Shop, 1966): 103.

17. Anna Somers Cocks and Charles Truman, *The Thyssen-Bornemisza Collection: Renaissance Jewels, Gold Boxes, Objets de Vertu* (New York and London: Vendome and Sotheby's, 1984): 278.

18. The latter became famous for his hardstone flowers in vases, and he almost replicated an English watch and nécessaire by Cox then in the imperial collection, probably to accommodate the English tastes of Empress Alexandra, wife of Nicholas II, now in the Walters Art Museum, Baltimore. The Fabergé version is now at Hillwood Museum and Gardens, Washington, D.C. Empress Alexandra was considered the favorite granddaughter of Queen Victoria, and spent much of her youth in England.

19. Tamara Rapp, "The History of the Furniture Collection in the Hermitage," in *Furniture History* (1993): 206.

20. Peter Fuhring, *Un Génie du Rococo: Juste-Aurèle Meissonnier, 1695–1750* (Turin: U. Allemandi, 1990). Pierre Germain, a probable relative of Thomas, was

from Marseille, from which there were other silversmiths of that name. It is interesting to consider the idea of the names of Meissonnier and Germain as references to an earlier origin such as from Meissen and "Germanium," as Provence had a large protestant influx in the sixteenth and seventeenth centuries.

21. A. Baudi de Vesme, *Schede Vesme: l'arte in Piemonte dal XVI al XVIII secolo* (Turin: Società piemontese di archeologica e belle arti, 1963): I:193, cited in Clare Le Corbeiller, "A Tale of Two Cities," in *Cleveland Studies in the History of Art*, vol. 8 (2003): 148–55.

22. See Charles Oman, "The Plate of the Sardinian Embassy," in *The Burlington Magazine*, vol. 108, No. 763 (October 1966): 500–03.

23. Recently parts of a silver centerpiece made for Fredrick, Prince of Wales, possibly as a collaboration between Paul Crespin, Paul de Lamerie, and Nicholas Sprimont, was found to have parts marked in Turin either being reused or newly incorporated.

24. Capodimonte was founded by Charles de Bourbon, crowned King of Naples and Sicily in 1734. He was married to the daughter of Augustus III, King of Saxony, partially as a result of the success of Meissen there.

25. Used for the ceremonial transport of a priest carrying the viaticum, or "bread of life," for the Eucharist from the church to the dwellings of the infirm. It is similar to others made for non-ecclesiastic use, not only in Spain but in Italy and elsewhere.

26. *Mercure de France* (May 1754): 156–58; cited in Maureen Cassidy-Geiger, " 'Quelque chose de beau et de bon goût': A Silver-gilt Toilet Service for the Dresden Doppelhochzeit of 1747," in *Rococo Silver in England and Its Colonies, Silver Studies*, no. 20 (2004): 113, appendix 1.5. For additional new insights into the spread of Meissonnier, Germain, and Ballin's designs through Count Brühl's acquisition and silver by Ballin and Germain's "Penthièvre" service, see Maureen Cassidy-Geiger, "Ein neues silbern Französisches Tafel Service: Linking the Penthièvre-Orléans Service to Dresden," in *Silver Studies: The Journal of the Silver Society*, no. 21 (2007): 123–52.

27. Hogarth was an apprentice to London goldsmith Ellis Gamble, with whom Lamerie had a business connection and who may have done some of Lamerie's engraving. See foreword by Tessa Murdoch in Ellenor Alcorn, *Beyond the Maker's Mark* (Cambridge: John Adamson, 2006): 16.

28. This salver, now in the Victoria and Albert Museum, has an engraved border possibly executed by Ellis Gamble, to whom Hogarth had been apprenticed and with whom Lamerie had a partnership, with Gamble possibly serving as a retailer as well. See Alcorn, pp. 16, 79. De Lamerie has been written on extensively, and he and other makers who worked in the early rococo idiom have been the subject of considerable recent scholarship, especially by Ellenor Alcorn, Tessa Murdoch, Timothy Schroder, Ubaldo Vitale, Peter Cameron, and Christopher Hartop. In addition to the above, see *Silver Studies: The Journal of the Silver Society*, no. 20 (2005); *Rococo Silver in England and Its Colonies*, based on a symposium held in Richmond, Virginia, in 2004; and Peter Cameron, "Henry Jernegan, the Kändlers and the Client Who Changed His Mind," in *Silver Studies: The Journal of the Silver Society*, no. 8 (1996): 487–501.

29. George Vertue, *Notebooks 1732 II*, p.63, cited in *The Walpole Society Journal XX* (1932), states "Mr Zincke often at Court drawing the pictures of the Royal Family."

30. For invaluable insight into the interconnections of the London arts scene through Old Slaughter's Coffee House, see Mark Girouard, "English Art and The Rococo: Coffee at Slaughter's," "Hogarth and his Friends," and "The Two Worlds of St. Martin's Lane," in *Country Life*, Jan 13, 1966: 58–61; Jan 27, 1966: 188–90; Feb 3, 1966: 224–27.

31. Ibid., p. 226.

32. Timothy Schroder, in "Evidence without Documents: Patterns of Ornament in Rococo and Régence Silver," in *Rococo Silver in England and Its Colonies, Silver Studies, The Journal of the Silver Society*, no. 20 (London, 2006): 58–71, notes this change.

33. This basin and an accompanying ewer have the arms without coronet of Stephen Fox and his second wife, and probably were commissioned shortly before he attained the peerage in 1741.

34. For further biographical information on Willaume, see Eileen Goodway, "David Willaume and His Apprentices, part II: further Research," in *Silver Studies: The Journal of the Silver Society*, no. 11 (1999): 140–42. Shruder is recorded in Mortimer's Universal Directory in 1763 as a "Modeller in Papier Maché Manufacturer." He witnessed Lamerie's will.

35. For a discussion of a coffeepot by Frederick Kandler of 1739–40 and a pair of beer jugs by Phillips Garden, which show a strong similarity to German porcelain, see Wolfram Koeppe, "Mit feiner Bildhauer Arbei & verfertigte Stücke," in *Kunst und Antiquitäte* (1989): 31–37.

36. Peter Cameron, "Henry Jernagen, the Kändlers and the Client Who Changes His Mind," in *Silver Studies: The Journal of the Silver Society* (1996): 487–501.

37. Maureen Cassidy-Geiger's discovery and recognition of these were first presented at the symposium Rococo Silver in England and its Colonies, Richmond 2004, and in *Silver Studies: The Journal of the Silver Society*, no. 20 (of the same name): 47–57.

38. Ellenor Alcorn, *Beyond the Maker's Mark: Paul de Lamerie Silver in the Cahn Collection* (Cambridge: John Adamson, 2006).

39. J.-V.-G. Mallet, "Rococo Designs in Porcelain," in *Apollo* (August 1969): 100–13

40. Hillary Young, *English Porcelain 1745–95* (London: V&A, 1999): 36.

41. Bernard Dragesco, *English Ceramics in French Archives. The Writings of Jean Hellot, the Adventures of Jacques Louis Brolliet and the Identification of 'The Girl in the Swing' Factory* (London: privately printed, 1993), cited in Young, p. 84.

42. Ibid.

43. See Jacob Simon, "A Chronology of Thomas Johnson's Life," based on Johnson's *The Life of the Author*, in *Furniture History Society Journal* (2003): 18–21. In 1755, Johnson published his own book of designs, *Twelve Gerandoles*, followed the next year by *A New Book of Ornaments*.

44. He also produced a number of other designs, the most important being one first issued with the engraver Henry Copland, in *A New Dictionary of Ornament* (1752).

45. *Cabinet and Chairmaker's Friend and Companion* (1765).

46. Francine Irwin, "Scottish Eighteenth-century Chintz and Its Design I," in *The Burlington Magazine*, vol. 107, no. 750 (September 1965): 455.

47. For a connection between Delacour and Newport, See Nancy Goyne Evans, "A Pair of Distinctive Chairs from Newport, Rhode Island," in *The Magazine Antiques*, vol. 145 (January 1994): 186–93.

48. For a full discussion of these carvers, see Luke Beckerdite, *The Magazine Antiques*, May 1984: 1120–33; 1985: 485–520; 1987: 1044–63.

49. Luke Beckerdite, "Immigrant Carvers and the Development of the Rococo Style in New York, 1750–1770," in *American Furniture* (1996): 233–65, pl. 247.

50. For a full discussion of Myers's work, see David Barquist, *Myer Myers, Jewish Silversmith in Colonial New York* (New Haven: Yale, 2001).

51. The difference in the quality of the chasing implies that Myers used different chasers and that the one for the buckles would have had to meet the sophisticated standards of the Irish-born patron.

52. Fueter advertised that he "informs the Public that Mr. John Anthony Beau, Chaiser, from Geneva works with him; where chaising in general viz. Snuff Boxes, Watch Cases &c &c. is done in the best and cheapest manner." Quoted in John Marshall Phillips, *American Silver* (New York: Chanticleer Press, 1949): 107

53. See the chronology from "Life of Thomas Johnson," in *Furniture History Society Journal* (2003): 19.

54. Benjamin Randolph receipt book 1763–77, and Cadwalader receipted bills, cited in Beckerdite II, p. 513.

55. Alexandria Alevizatos Kirtley, "Survival of the Fittest: The Lloyd Family's Furniture Legacy," in *American Furniture* (2002): 2–11.

56. Beckerdite I, p. 1121.

57. Advertisement in the *Pennsylvania Gazette* (November 25, 1762), cited in Beckerdite II, p. 498

58. (Charleston) *South Carolina Gazette* (October 12, 1765), cited in Beckerdite II, p. 510.

59. Michelle Erickson and Robert Hunter, "Making a Bonnin & Morris Pickle Stand," in Robert Hunter, ed., *Ceramics in America* (Milwaukee: Chipstone Foundation, 2004): 141–64. I am indebted to Rob Hunter for drawing my attention both to the presences of the fragments of an English sweetmeat/pickle stand in Williamsburg and for information on Bonnin & Morris's use of actuall shells in their production.

60. Presented by Thomas Savage at Winterthur Symposium, March 2007, after previous identification of Martin Pfenniger.

61. This mission ended in Ireland due to financial difficulties of the ship's captain. Roentgen returned from Ireland to Germany after two years in Holland. See Christine Cornet, "Roentgen Möebel in Münchner Museen," in *Weltkunst*, vol. 60, no. 3 (Feb. 1, 1990): 215

62. See David Dobson, *Scottish Emigration in Colonial America, 1607–1785* (Athens, GA: University of Georgia Press, 1009): 56; also see Elizabeth Packer, *Importation of English Furniture into Virginia, 1750–1800*, unpublished MA Thesis, Winterthur, University of Delaware.

63. Robert A. Leath, "Robert and William Walker and the 'Ne Plus Ultra': Scottish Design and Colonial Virginia Furniture 1730–75," in *American Furniture*, edited by Luke Beckerdite (2006): 54–95.

64. Tara Gleason Chicirda, "The Furniture of Fredericksburg, VA, 1740–1820," in *American Furniture*, edited by Luke Beckerdite (2006): 96–136.

65. For a discussion of Buckland's work, see Luke Beckerdite, "Architect-designed Furniture in Eighteenth-century Virginia: The Work of William Buckland and William Bernard Sears," in *American Furniture* (1998): 29–48.

German Rococo

ULRICH LEBEN

1. This essay tries to capture the input of those artists who mainly worked in Germany, and can only present a small choice of European artists who were at the same time working for the various German courts, but there were many, especially from France, who imported French pattern into Germany. See Ulrich Leben, *Les Arts decoratifs en France et en Allemagne au XVIIIe siècle: l'histoire d'un chassé-croisé…*, *Collection Rencontres de l'Ecole du Louvre, Actes du colloque Art français et art allemand au XVIIIe siècle* (Paris 2008); *Assimilation des modèles français dans les arts décoratifs en Allemagne au XVIIIe siècle*, Centre André Chastel (Bern: Editions Peter Lang AG, 2007).

2. The abolition of the Edict of Nantes in 1687 caused the emigration of French Protestants, many of whom were skilled in craft, industry, and commerce. European countries opened their borders happily to these able immigrants. The 1685 Tolerance Act of Potsdam made Prussia one of the most attractive destinations for the refugees.

3. Among other projects he had in Germany, the French architect Robert de Cotte got the commission to build the summer castle of Poppelsdorf, one mile outside of the residence of Bonn. The elector also commissioned furnishings in Paris, of which a great number survive in the treasures of the cathedral of Cologne and Aachen. See Dela von Boeselager, *Capella Clementina, Kurfürst Clemens August und die Krönung Kaiser Karls VII*, *Studien zum Kölner Dom* Band 8 (Cologne: Cologne Cathedral, 2001).

4. *Die Hugenotten-Zuwanderungsland Deutschland*, exh. cat., Deutsches Historisches Museum Berlin (Berlin: Edition Minerva, 2005); and Winfried Baer, *Prunk-Tabatièren Friedrichs des Grossen*, exh. cat. (Munich: Hirmer Verlag, 1993).

5. In comparison to French production, only a small number of commissions for gilt-bronze objects is documented in German residences, and the only court commissions were in Potsdam and Dresden. In other regions, patrons often imported bronze objects directly from Paris. The most elaborate examples for large-scale bronze objects in Berlin are the chandeliers conceived by Nahl (now at Charlottenburg) and one by the French immigrant bronze worker Geoffroy (d. 1765) and the gilders Jean Audibert and Nicolas Morel in the Chinese Teahouse in the garden at Sanssouci. There are some models of gilt-bronze commissions made by local craftsmen in Potsdam, such as wall brackets or the mounts of a writing table for Frederick made by the goldsmith C. G. Kelly (active 1734–70).

6. Another example is the Savonnerie-style Berlin pile carpet from the Charles Vigne carpet-weaving workshop, housed in one of the royal palaces. Framed by an elaborate rococo frame, the central motif is an asymmetrical cartouche, based on a typical French model for a cartouche but expanded to form the central motif of the carpet. It is a very particular interpretation, and this motif can only be found in works made by the Vigne workshop. See Josephine Gabler and Jürgen Julier, *Kaiserlicher Kunstbesitz aus dem holländischen Exil Haus Doorn*, exh. cat., (Berlin: Staatliche Schlösser und Gärten, 1991): illus. nos. 118, 119.

7. Höder was one of the few German artists to make engravings of his designs, some of which are now in the collection of the Kunstbibliothek Berlin: Friedrich Wilhelm Höder (active 1736–61), *Sammlung geätzter von F. W. Höder, im Verlage bey A. L. Krüger in Potsdam*, 1750; also see Catharina Berents, "Moderne Chinoiserien: Das Vorbild Jean Pillements," in *Art Déco in Deutschland: Das moderne Ornament*, Werkbund-Archiv 27 (Frankfurt: Anabas Verlag, 1998): 75.

8. The mirrors were imported from Paris. Their limited sizes facilitated their shipping and corresponded to the size of the window panes, thus enhancing the optical illusion. See Heinrich Kreisel, *Deutsche Spiegelkabinette*, Wohnkunst und Hausrat/ Einst uns Jetzt, Band 1 (Darmstadt: Franz Schneekluth Verlag, 1955).

9. Building was happening simultaneously in Charlottenburg, the Potsdam Stadtschloss (destroyed), and Sanssouci. For the interior architecture, Frederick applied decorative schemes he developed in intense collaboration with von Knobelsdorff on a more modest scale in the castle at Rheinsberg, where he lived before becoming king. The castle is currently underoing restoration, and these early interiors are being rediscovered as this is being written.

10. Eduard M. Fallet, *Der Bildhauer Johann August Nahl der Ältere, seine Berner Jahre* (Bern: Historischer Verein des Kantons, 1970); Friedrich Bleibaum, *Johann August Nahl der Künstler Friedrich des Grossen und der Landgrafen von Hessen-Kassel* (Wien-Leipzig, 1933); on furniture design by Knobelsdorff, see Tilo Eggeling, *Raum und Ornament G.W. Knobelsdorff und das friderizianische Rokoko* (Regensburg: Verlag Schnell & Steiner, 2003); Michael Hassels, *Potsdamer Schlösser und Gärten, Bau- und Gartenkunst vom 17. bis 20. Jahrhundert*, exh. cat. (Potsdam-Sanssouci, 1993): 72–103.

11. Filed as war-loss and only recently rediscovered. Since 2006, the Merseburg Spiegelkabinett has been reinstalled in the Berlin Kunstgewerbe Museum. See also Alexander Schreyer, *Die Möbelentwürfe Johann Michael Hoppenhaupts des älteren und ihre Beziehungen zu den Rokoko-Möbeln Friedrichs des Grossen*, Studien zur Deutschen Kunstgeschichte (Strasburg J.H.Ed. Heitz, 1932). A very elaborate state coach carved by Johann Michael Hoppenhaupt the Elder is today in the Armory at the Kremlin, in Moscow. *Von Sanssouci nach Europa, Geschenke Friedrichs des Grossen an europäische Höfe*, exh. cat. (Potsdam: Stiftung Schlösser und Gärten Potsdam-Sanssouci, 1994): 105–07.

12. This style was even exported to foreign countries, with buildings such as the Castle of Rundale in Kurland (Latvia). The interior decoration at Rundale used Berlin models and, in many cases, were made by craftsmen of German or Italian origin who had previously worked on the Berlin or Potsdam sites, such as the gilder Johann Michael Graff, who was in Kurland after 1750. The interpretation of the original schemes were enlarged in Rundale, but remained faithful to the Potsdam prototypes. Imants Lancmanis, *Le Château de Rundale* (Le Château de Rundale, 2005).

13. See Ulrich Leben works cited in note 1.

14. Maureen Cassidy-Geiger, "Graphic Sources for Meissen Porcelain: Origins of the Print Collection in the Meissen Archives," in *Metropolitan Museum Journal*, vol. 31 (1996): 99–126; *Meissen and France before and after the Seven Years' War: Artists, Espionage and Trade*, Collection Rencontres de l'Ecole du Louvre, Actes du colloque Art français et art allemand au XVIIIe siècle (Paris, 2007).

15. Thomas W. Gaehtgens, Dirk Syndram, and Béatrix Saule, *Splendeurs de la cour de Saxe, Dresde à Versailles*, exh. cat., Musée National des Châteaux de Versailles et de Trianon (Paris: RMN, 2006): 116; *Kaiserlicher Kunstbesitz aus dem holländischen Exil Haus Doorn*, exh. cat. (Berlin: Staatliche Schlösser und Gärten), 1991): 112.

16. There is only one engraving in a London edition, by the French engraver Pierre-Edmé Babel, which shows an armchair with sinuous armrests that might have influenced Nahl's work. This engraving was realized before Nahl's departure in 1743; see Geoffrey Beard, "Babel's 'A New Book of Ornaments,' 1752," in *Furniture History* 11 (1975): 31–32.

17. Peter O. Krückmann, *Paradies des Rokoko I & II, Das Bayreuth der Markgräfin Wilhelmine, Galli Bibiena und der Musenhof der Wilhelmine von Bayreuth* (Munich and New York: Prestel, 1998); concerning German furniture, the best reference for the period is Heinrich Kreisel and Georg Himmelheber, *Die Kunst des deutschen Möbels, Spätbarock und Rokoko* (Munich: C. H. Beck, 1970), and Heinrich Kreisel, *Fränkische Rokokomöbel*, Wohnkunst und Hausrat, einst und jetzt, Band 26 (Darmstadt: Franz Shneekluth Verlag, 1956).

18. Henry Hawley, "Jean-Pierre Latz, Cabinetmaker," in *The Bulletin of the Cleveland Museum of Art* (September–October 1970): 203–59.

19. Gisela Haase and Jürgen Karpinski, *Dresdener Möbel des 18. Jahrhunderts* (Leipzig: VEB E.A.Seemann, Buch- und Kunstverlag, 1986); Gisela Haase, *Der Kuppritzer Schreibschrank: das Meisterstück des Dresdener Hoftischlers Johann Christoph Hesse aus Schloss Kuppritz* (Munich: Röbbig, 2005); Christopher Wilk, *Western Furniture, 1350 to the Present Day* (London: Victoria & Albert Publications, 2001): 98.

20. A number of model books from the workshop of Wilhelm Kimbel in Mainz are today in the library at Cooper-Hewitt, National Design Museum, where they were deposited by a descendant of the firm of Anton Kimbel (1822–?) and Anton Bembé (1799–1861) in New York City. Some of the plates in these model books show neo-rococo designs from the second quarter of the nineteenth century and illustrate the interpretation of rococo by bourgeois society of that period. See also Heidrun Zinnkann, *Mainzer Möbelschreiner der ersten Hälfte des 19. Jahrhunderts*, Schriften des Historischen Museum Frankfurt am Main 17 (Frankfurt am Main: Kramer, 1985).

21. Afra Schick, *Furniture for the Dream King, Ludwig II and the Munich Court Cabinet-Maker Anton Pössenbacher* (Stuttgart: Arnoldsche, 2003): 38–69.

22. Julius Zwiener was trained in Paris as a cabinetmaker and bronze worker. From 1895 on he was listed in the Berlin address books, and received a lot of commissions from the crown. See Winfried Baer, *Eine Schlafzimmer-Ausstattung von Julius Zwiener. Ein Auftrag Kaiser Wilhelm II für das Berliner Schloss, 1895–1900* (Berlin: Kulturstiftung der Länder und der Verwaltung der Staatlichen Schlösser und Gärten, 1989): 12; and *Kaiserlicher Kunstbesitz aus dem holländischen Exil Haus Doorn*, exh. cat. (Berlin: Staatliche Schlösser und Gärten, 1991): 287–91.

23. The following books give good examples of interior schemes in rococo-revival style in early twentieth-century Germany: *Farbige Raumkunst*, Zweite Folge Band IX (Stuttgart: Verlag Julius Hofmann, 1914); *Farbige Raumkunst*, Dritte Folge, Band XVI (Stuttgart: Verlag Julius Hofmann, 1923); *Farbige Raumkunst*, Vierte Folge, Band XXII (Stuttgart: Verlag Julius Hofmann, 1927); also see illustrations in *Moderne Bauformen* (Stuttgart: Verlag, 1920).

24. Stephan Brakensiek, *Gelsenkirchener Barock*, Ausstellung Stadt Gelsenkirchen Städtisches Museum 1991 (Heidelberg: Ed. Braus, 1991).

Rococo in Holland

REINIER BAARSEN

1. This essay, the first general assessment in English of Dutch rococo, draws on much information presented in the catalogue of the first exhibition devoted to this style: Reinier Baarsen a.o., *Rococo in Holland*, exh. cat. (Amsterdam: Rijksmuseum, 2001–02).

2. See Reinier Baarsen, "The Court Style in Holland," in *Courts and Colonies, The Willam and Mary Style in Holland, England and America*, exh. cat. (New York and Pittsburgh: Cooper-Hewitt Museum and the Carnegie Museum of Art, 1988–89): 12–35.

3. See M. D. Ozinga, *Daniel Marot, De schepper van den Hollandschen Lodewijk XIV-stijl* (Amsterdam, 1938).

4. Rhijnvis Feith, *Dicht- en prozaïsche werken*, vol. II (Rotterdam, 1824): 87–88; quoted in Baarsen, *Rococo in Holland*, p. 179.

5. Katie Heyning, "Decoratief beeldhouwwerk in Den Haag tijdens het rococo," in Baarsen, *Rococo in Holland*, p. 26, figs. 15 and 16.

6. Baarsen, *Rococo in Holland*, pp. 179–80, fig. VII.1. On Xavery's decorative manner, see Reinier Baarsen, "Throne Chairs from the Workshop of Jan Baptist Xavery," in *Furniture History* 43 (2007): 101–13.

7. See Pieter Fischer, *Ignatius en Jan van Logteren, Beeldhouwers en stuckunstenaars in het Amsterdam van de 18de eeuw* (Alphen aan den Rijn, 2005).

8. R. Meischke, *Amsterdam Burgerweeshuis* (The Hague, 1975): 98, 232, fig. 142; and Baarsen, *Rococo in Holland*, cat. no. 99.

9. Meischke, pp. 231–32 and 246–47, figs. 297–301.

10. On these chairs and the career of Ermans, see Reinier Baarsen, "The First Amsterdam Rococo Chairs," in *Cleveland Studies in the History of Art* 8 (2003): 120–29.

11. Baarsen, *Rococo in Holland*, cat. no. 115. For more conventional versions of Dutch rococo clothes-presses, see C. H. de Jonge and W. Vogelsang, *Holländische Möbel und Raumkunst von 1650–1780* (The Hague, 1922): figs. 177–86.

12. Sale catalogue, Amsterdam, March 26, 1759 (F. Lugt, *Répertoire des catalogues de ventes publiques...*, vol. 1, The Hague, 1939, no. 1038), preface; Baarsen, *Rococo in Holland*, p. 180, fig. VII.5.

13. Advertisement in the *Amsterdamsche Courant* of October 3, 1765 (no. 119); Reinier Baarsen, *Dutch Furniture 1600–1800* (Amsterdam: Rijksmuseum, 1993): no. 43; Baarsen, *Rococo in Holland*, cat. no 105.

14. See Hans-Joachim Giersberg, *Friedrich als Bauherr, Studien zur Architektur des 18. Jahrhunderts in Berlin und Potsdam* (Berlin, 1986).

15. Freerk Schmidt, *Pieter de Swart, Architect van de achttiende eeuw* (Zwolle-Zeist, 1999): 81–105.

16. See Reinier Baarsen, "High Rococo in Holland: William IV and Agostino Carlini," in *The Burlington Magazine* 140 (1998): 173–76, figs. 16–18, 22.

17. See M. D. Ozinga, "Pieter de Swart architect der stadhouderlijke familie en zijn 'school'(Gunckel, Westenhout, Druck)," in *Oudheidkundig Jaarboek* 8 (1939): figs. 1, 3; Schmidt, pp. 184–87, figs. 179–80; Baarsen, *Rococo in Holland*, cat. no. 57.

18. Baarsen, *Rococo in Holland*, cat. no. 26; Baarsen, "High Rococo in Holland," pp. 175–80, figs. 19–21, 23–24, 28.

19. M. L. de Iongh, "Twee gouden bokalen door Louis en Philippe Metayer," in *Bulletin van het Rijksmuseum* 30 (1982): 115–32; Jan Rudolph de Lorm, *Amsterdams goud en zilver* (Amsterdam: Rijksmuseum, 1999): no. 262; Baarsen, *Rococo in Holland*, cat. nos. 28 and 29.

20. Jan Rudolph de Lorm, "Franse goudsmeden in Amsterdam," in Baarsen, *Rococo in Holland*, p. 103, fig. III.1.

21. De Lorm, nos. 255, 260; Baarsen, *Rococo in Holland*, cat. nos. 30, 35.

22. Marten Loonstra a.o., *Uit Koninklijk Bezit, Honderd jaar Koninklijk Huisarchief: de verzamelingen van de Oranjes* (Zwolle, 1996): 54–56, figs. 7, 51, cat. no. 68; Baarsen, *Rococo in Holland*, cat. no. 22.

23. Th. H. Lunsingh Scheurleer, "De stoel van de stadhouder," in *Oud Holland* 63 (1948): 199–200, fig. 7; Baarsen, *Rococo in Holland*, cat. no. 24; Baarsen, "Throne Chairs from the Workshop of Jan Baptist Xavery," pp. 106–08, figs. 6, 7.

24. Lunsingh Scheurleer, pp. 197–98, fig. 13; Heyning, p. 29; Baarsen, *Rococo in Holland*, cat. no. 23.

25. Sold at Christie's, Amsterdam, May 19–20, 1988, lot 752; Baarsen, *Rococo in Holland*, cat. no. 76.

26. Baarsen, *Rococo in Holland*, cat. no. 124; see Johannes Schiotling, *Een Amsterdamse zilversmid (1730–1799)*, exh. cat. (Amsterdam: Rijksmuseum, 1976–77); De Lorm, nos. 80, 92, 93, 104, 107, 115, 124, 129, 133, 295, p. 531; Baarsen, *Rococo in Holland*, nos. 65, 69 and 70; Hubert Vreeken, *Goud en zilver met Amsterdamse keuren, De verzameling van het Amsterdams Historisch Museum* (Zwolle, 2003): nos. 78, 84, 89, 92, 97, pp. 468–69.

27. Reinier Baarsen, *De Amsterdamse meubelloterijen en de geschiedenis van de meubelmakerij in de tweede helft van de achttiende eeuw* (Zwolle/Amsterdam, 1992): 56, fig. 4; De Lorm, no. 92; Baarsen, *Rococo in Holland*, cat. no. 64.

28. De Lorm, no. 62; Baarsen, *Rococo in Holland*, cat. no. 61.

29. *100 Jahre Lëtzebuerger Dynastie, Collections et Souvenirs de la Maison Grand-Ducale*, exh. cat. (Luxembourg: Musée National d'Histoire et d'Art, 1990–91): no. 131; Baarsen, *Rococo in Holland*, cat. no. 122.

30. "Keuze uit de aanwinsten," in *Bulletin van het Rijksmuseum* 31 (1983): 124, 130, fig. 3; see Baarsen, *Rococo in Holland*, cat. no. 81; and Jet Pijzel-Dommisse, *Haags goud en zilver* (The Hague and Zwolle: Gemeentemuseum, 2005): 218–19, cat. no. 35.

31. Reinier Baarsen, "'In the commode van Parijs tot Den Haag,' Matthijs Horrix (1735–1809), een meubelmaker in Den Haag in de tweede helft van de achttiende eeuw," in *Oud Holland* 107 (1993): 186–91, fig. 15; Reinier Baarsen, 'Matthijs Horrix, cabinetmaker from The Hague," in *The Magazine Antiques* 154 (1998): 521–25, fig. III.

Emulation and Subversion

GAIL S. DAVIDSON

1. Paul Greenhalgh, *Quotations and Sources on Design and the Decorative Arts, 1800–1900* (Manchester: Manchester University Press, 1993): 135.

2. Paul Greenhalgh, "Alternative Histories," in Paul Greenhalgh, ed., *Art Nouveau, 1890–1914* (London and Washington: Victoria and Albert Museum and National Gallery of Art, 2000): 41.

3. The Crace firm of coach painter and builders, headed by Edward Crace in the eighteenth century, undoubtedly had examples of cartouche ornament prints by various designers including their own to use as sources of inspiration.

4. Quoted in Mario Praz, *An Illustrated History of Interior Decoration from Pompeii to Art Nouveau* (London: Thames and Hudson, 2nd edition, 1982): 63.

5. It is worth noting that Guilmard was also a major contributor to the field of ornament and design history. His celebrated work *Les maîtres ornemanistes* (Paris: E. Plon et Cie, 1880–81), which catalogued French, German, and Netherlandish ornament prints from public and private European collections, was one of the earliest systematic catalogues of these objects.

6. *A Nineteenth century French Second Empire Interior, 1850–1870*, from Cooper-Hewitt's Eugene V. Thaw collection (2007-27-24), has a rococo-revival carpet very similar in color and design to this maquette; see also Charlotte Gere, *Nineteenth-century Decoration, the Art of the Interior* (New York: Harry N. Abrams, Inc., 1989): 259–60, fig. 301; and Sarah B. Sherrill, *Carpets and Rugs of Europe and America* (New York and London: Abbeville Press, 1996): 106, pl. 115.

7. Debora Silverman, *Art Nouveau in Fin-de-Siècle France, Politics, Psychology, and Style* (Berkeley, Los Angeles, and Oxford: University of California Press, 1992): 1–5.

8. Elie G. Haddad, "On Henry van de Velde's 'Manuscript on Ornament,'" in *Journal of Design History*, vol. 16, no. 2 (2003): 119–38.

9. "Ein Kapitel uber Entwurf und Bau moderner Mobel," in *Pan*, Jg 3 (1897–98): 260–64.

10. Writing his memoirs in hindsight, when he was most interested in separating himself from what he called the "brief interlude of art nouveau, that ephemeral will o' the wisp which knew no law other than its own caprice," and allying himself with the modernist movement, he said that he worked with Bing because he felt sorry him and did not want to see him fail. See P. Morton Shand, ed., "Henry van de Velde, Extracts from His Memoirs: 1891–1901," in *Architectural Review*, vol. 112 (September 1952): 154.

11. The following summarizes the discussion in Silverman, *Art Nouveau in Fin-de-Siècle France*.

12. Ibid., p. 143.

13. Ibid., p. 25.

14. Paul Greenhalgh, "Alternative Histories," p. 41.

15. Silverman, p. 35.

16. Ibid., pp. 109–18.

17. Ibid., pp. 126–33.

18. See M. F. Herne, *The Architectural Theory of Viollet-Le-Duc: Readings and Commentary* (Boston: Massachusetts Institute of Technology Press, 1990): 143.

19. Eugène Grasset, *La Plante et ses applications ornementales* (Paris: Librairie Centrale des Beaux-Arts, 1897 and 1900): iv.

20. Eugène Grasset, *Méthode de composition ornementale*, 2 vols. (Paris: Librairie Centrale des Beaux-Arts, 1905): vol. 1: vi. On the discussion early nineteenth-century naturalism and later nineteenth-century abstraction of nature, see Paul Greenhalgh, "The Cult of Nature," in *Art Nouveau*, 55–65.

21. For other publications on the abstraction of nature, see Greenhalgh, "The Cult of Nature," pp. 58–59.

22. See Davidson, pp. 13–16.

23. *Revue des Arts Décoratifs* (Paris, 1900): 24

24. Mucha agreed to have Champenois print all of his lithographs in return for a generous fixed salary. It was Champenois's idea to print Mucha's poster designs as panels on fabric without lettering to hang as wall decorations. See Julia King, *The Flowering of Art Nouveau Graphics* (London: Trefoil, 1990): 97.

25. Henri Vever, *La Bijouterie Française au XIXème siècle (1800–1900)*, 3 vols. (Paris: H. Floury, 1906–08): vol. 3: 624, fn. 1.

26. Ibid. pp. 624–26.

27. While the *Documents décoratifs* included realistic drawings after female models and the plant world, Mucha also used photography as a design tool, from which he created figurative posters and decorative panels.

28. This lush textile design corresponds to the observations of the French designer and critic M.-P. Verneuil, who wrote in "Adaptation du décor à la forme," in *Art de Décoration* (1903): 376, "Mucha's system of composition is often two-fold, in the sense that, in the same ornament, he combines purely conventional forms with natural elements scarcely interpreted. A floral decoration close to nature occupies the first plane and in the background a simple stylized form, sometimes very dry, completes the ensemble."

29. On this textile see, Linda Parry, "The New Textiles," in *Art Nouveau*, p. 186 and p. 438, note 13 (chapter 11).

30. See Yvonne Brunhammer, "The Lalique Epoch," in Yvonne Brunhammer, ed., *The Jewels of Lalique*, exh. cat. (Paris and New York: Flammarion, 1998): 8–30.

31. See Yvonne Brunhammer, *René Lalique, Bijoux d'exception, 1890–1912*, exh. cat. (Milan: Skira, 2007): 64, no. 10; 30 (illus.).

32. Theodore Duret, "On Combs," in *Le Japon Artistique* V (1890): 335–41.

33. Henri Vever, "Les Bijoux aux Salons de 1898," in *Art et Décoration* III (1898): 168–78.

34. Quoted in Vever, *La Bijouterie Française* III, p. 732.

35. Of particular note is a prototype molded and painted glass vase of two gurnards (flying fish), Friends of the Lalique Museum, Wingen-sur-Moder, France, whose bodies take the same form as the fish in Cooper-Hewitt's drawing. The vase has been dated before 1910 by Yvonne Brunhammer, *René Lalique*, p. 277, no. 309, p. 265 (illus).

36. This drawing was identified as the design for the "Night" jewel by Joan T. Rosasco, curator with Exhibitions International for the 1994 exhibition *Jewels of Lalique*.

37. Pol Neveux, "René Lalique," in *Art et Décoration* VIII (1900): 135.

38. Vever, *La Bijouterie Française* III, pp. 738–39.

The Rococo Revival in English and American Nineteenth-century Silver

SARAH D. COFFIN

1. This firm, comprised of Philip Rundell, John Bridge, and Edmund Rundell (Philip's nephew), took its name by 1803 after the latter Rundell joined the firm. The first two were appointed as goldsmith and jeweler to King George III in 1797. See Arthur G. Grimwade, *London Goldsmiths, 1697–1837* (London, 1976): 648–49.

2. For a more complete discussion of Kensington Lewis, see John Culme, "Kensington Lewis: A Nineteenth-century Businessman," in *Connoisseur* (September, 1975): 26–41. In his trade card, Lewis described himself as "Silversmith and Jeweller to his R.H. The Duke of York" and advertised "a Large Assortment of Antique and Second Hand Plate in General."

3. Paul Storr's first mark was recorded in 1792 in partnership with William Frisbee. He entered into a partnership with Rundell, Bridge, and Rundell, Royal Goldsmiths, from 1807 to 1817, throughout which time he maintained his own marks, as he did during a subsequent partnership with John Mortimer as Storr and Mortimer from 1823 to 1838.

4. Rachel Layton, "Uncovering the Past of a Caviar Pail," in *Carnegie Museum of Art Magazine* (September-October 1996).

"Equal to Any in the World"

JASON BUSCH

1. Benjamin Silliman, Jr., and Charles Rush Goodrich, eds., *The World of Science, Art, and Industry/ Illustrated from Examples in the New-York Exhibition, 1853–54* (New York: G. P. Putnam and Company, 1854): 185.

2. For explorations of the rococo-revival style in America, see Jason T. Busch, "The French Rococo Revival along the Mississippi River," in *The Magazine Antiques* (August 2004): 84–95; Jason T. Busch, " 'Handsomely Furnished in the Most Fashionable Style': Art and Decoration along the Mississippi River," in Jason T. Busch, Christopher Monkhouse, and Janet L. Whitmore, *Currents of Change/Art and Life Along the Mississippi River, 1850–1861* (Minneapolis: Minneapolis Institute of Arts, 2004): 62–139; and Catherine Hoover Voorsanger, " 'Gorgeous Articles of Furniture': Cabinetmaking in the Empire City," in John K. Howat and Catherine Hoover Voorsanger, eds., *Art and the Empire City: New York, 1825–1861* (New York: Metropolitan Museum of Art, 2000): 286–325.

3. Thomas Webster, *An Encyclopedia of Domestic Economy...* (New York: Harper & Brothers, 1845): 248.

4. For example, see Matthew Lock, *A Collection of Ornamental Designs, applicable to Furniture, Frames & the Decoration of Rooms, in the Style of Louis 14th – on 24 Plates, Chiefly after Thos. Chippendale* (England, 1838). The illustration of an English rococo-revival side chair, identified as "French Antique Chair" in George Smith's *Cabinet Maker's and Upholsterer's Guide...* (London: Jones & Co., 1826), plate CXLVI, p. 188, is remarkably similar to "A Mahogany Chair" illustrated in Joseph Meeks & Sons' famous broadside of 1833 (Metropolitan Museum of Art). The introduction of rococo-revival designs in England coincided with the 1820s invention of coiled springs for seating furniture, which were part and parcel of the stuffed, tufted, and heavily upholstered appearance of most chairs from the Western world in this style by the mid-nineteenth century.

5. Samuel Sloan, *Sloan's Homestead Architecture...* (Philadelphia: J. B. Lippincott & Co., 1861): 325–26.

6. "A Parlor View in a New York Dwelling House," in *Gleason's Pictorial Drawing-Room Companion* (November 11, 1854), illustrates a parlor decorated in rococo-revival style. At the time in America, the words "parlor" and "drawing room" were used interchangeably.

7. Andrew Jackson Downing, *The Architecture of Country Houses...* (New York: D. Appleton and Co., 1850): 410, 432.

8. Sloan, p. 326.

9. Parisian receipts are among the Shaw Papers, Missouri Botanical Garden, St. Louis.

10. For the Turnbulls, their European tour, and purchases, see Busch, " 'Handsomely Furnished in the Most Fashionable Style': Art and Decoration along the Mississippi River," pp. 79–80, 94–96.

11. David Bigelow, *History of Prominent Mercantile and Manufacturing Firms in the United States*, vol. 6 (Boston, 1857): 172. Similar to other manufacturers in the Northeast, Smallwood advertised for the western and southern market, and, between 1851 and 1856, he sent nearly a dozen orders of parlor furniture from Boston to furniture retailer Robert Stewart in Natchez, Mississippi. For Robert Stewart, Edwin Smallwood, and their trade, see Jason T. Busch, " 'Such a Paradise Can Be Made on Earth': Furniture Patronage and Consumption in Antebellum Natchez, Mississippi, 1828–1863," master's thesis, University of Delaware, Newark, 1998; for Edwin Smallwood, see Jan M. Seidler, "A Tradition in Transition: The Boston

Furniture Industry, 1840–1880," in Kenneth L. Ames, ed., *Victorian Furniture/Essays from a Victorian Society Autumn Symposium* (Philadelphia: Victorian Society of America, 1983): 69–71.

12. For Prudent Mallard, see Busch, "'Handsomely Furnished in the Most Fashionable Style': Art and Decoration along the Mississippi River," pp. 86–87; and Stephen G. Harrison, "The Nineteenth-century Furniture Trade in New Orleans," in *The Magazine Antiques* (May 1997): 748–59.

13. For Leon Marcotte and Ringuet Leprince, see Nina Gray, "Leon Marcotte: Cabinetmaker and Interior Decorator," in Luke Beckerdite, ed., *American Furniture* (Hanover, NH: University Press of New England for the Chipstone Foundation, 1994): 49–72.

14. The revival in "Boulle" work, characterized by ebony or ebonized furniture with marquetry, brass, and tortoise-shell inlay, was well described in George J. Henkels, *An Essay on Household Furniture...* (Philadelphia, PA, 1850) and Sloan's *Homestead Architecture* (p. 318), although few objects with a documented American provenance from the mid-nineteenth century have surfaced. Sloan commented, "The art of making boule [sic] work is not much known or practiced in this country, and it would not be of much benefit to the makers, as the demand for such expensive articles is so limited. It is mostly made in Paris, where they can duplicate designs or articles [which is the economy in its manufacture] to a great extent from having the whole world for customers." Several "Buhl" objects were listed in the 1857 auction of material from Alexander Roux of New York, but it is likely that the furnishings were imported through Roux's connections in France (see *Catalogue of Rich Cabinet Furniture, Comprising a large and rich assortment of Rosewood, Walnut, Oak, Buhl, and Marqueterie at Alex. Roux & Co., November 11, 1857*).

15. A handsomely carved ebony table by Doe, Hazleton & Co. of Boston was illustrated and described in *Art Journal Illustrated Catalogue/The Industry of All Nations 1851*, p. 232. Sloan's *Homestead Architecture*, which was written for an American audience, provided a detailed description of the process of making ebonized furniture with ormolu or gilt-bronze mounts, pp. 317–18.

16. A nearly complete collection of Désiré Guilmard's *Le garde-meuble, ancien et moderne* from 1841 to 1851 is in the collection of Cooper Hewitt, National Design Museum in New York, and is accessible on line through www.sil.si.edu/digitalcollections/art–design/garde-meuble.

17. George J. Henkels, *Catalogue of Furniture* (1850–57).

18. For German pattern books in mid-nineteenth-century America, see Charles Venable, "Germanic Craftsmen and Furniture Design in Philadelphia, 1820–1850," in Luke Beckerdite, ed., *American Furniture* (Hanover, NH: University Press of New England for the Chipstone Foundation, 1994): 41–80.

19. For Siebrecht and Stanton Hall, see Jason T. Busch, "Furniture Patronage in Antebellum Natchez," in *The Magazine Antiques* (May 2000): 804–13. Like other high-end furnishing retailers in America at the time, Siebrecht imported Italian, English, and German as well as French goods; see Stephen G. Harrison, *Furniture Trade in New Orleans, 1840–1880: The Largest Assortment Constantly on Hand*, master's thesis (University of Delaware, Newark, 1997): 44.

20. London 1851, New York City 1853, Paris 1855.

21. Charles H. White, *Chas H White/ Upholstery and Furniture Bazaar* (Philadelphia: Sickles & Reading, 1854), back of title page.

22. In a comparable situation, George Henkels of Philadelphia reproduced images from Désiré Guilmard's *Le Garde-meuble album de l'exposition de l'industrie, 1844* (Paris, 1844) in *An Essay on Essay Household Furniture...* (Philadelphia, PA, 1850). The correspondence of images is discussed in Kenneth L. Ames, "Designed in France/Notes on the Transmission of French Style to America," in *Winterthur Portfolio 12* (Charlottesville, VA: University Press of Virginia, 1977): 103–14.

23. White, p. 21.

24. A remarkably similar lady's armchair appears in an 1849 George Henkels advertisement in *Godey's Magazine and Lady's Book*.

25. White, p. 23.

26. While block-printed patterns on rococo-revival chairs are not commonly seen in examples with original upholstery, nor described in contemporaneous texts, the technique of using block prints in a similar manner was widely implemented in the scenic–wallpaper industry in France during the nineteenth century.

27. The suite was purchased by Willis Royal Peake (1836–1901), a banker and politician from Bristol, Vermont, who built an Italianate house there in 1863 (Registration Department files, Wadsworth Atheneum Museum of Art, Hartford, CT).

28. Another table with restored textile panels is in the collection of the Hunter Dawson House in New Madrid, Missouri, and is illustrated in Busch, "The French Rococo Revival along the Mississippi River," p. 95.

29. Charles Cist, *Sketches and Statistics of Cincinnati in 1851* (Cincinnati: William H. Moore & Co., 1851): 202.

30. The table descended in the family of Joseph Hibberson Wilby (1819–1903), a Boston tobacco agent who moved to Cincinnati and started Rawson, Wilby & Co. I am grateful to Amy [illegible] at the Cincinnati Art Museum for sharing information with me on the table as well as Squire James John and F. Weber.

31. Dissemination of furniture within America during the mid-nineteenth century was dependent on economic systems of transportation and agriculture. Ocean bound clipper ships from the East Coast, laden with manufactured domestic and imported goods such as furniture, porcelain, glass, and textiles, sailed into ports in the South, such as Mobile and New Orleans, and exchanged their goods primarily for cotton, destined for the mills of New England or Europe. The lower Mississippi Delta, from Natchez to New Orleans, is a unique time capsule in mid-nineteenth-century furnishings, especially those in the rococo-revival style, as many objects, if not nearly completely furnished homes, have remained intact since before the Civil War.

32. Sloan, p. 327.

33. "New Furniture" and "A Visit to Henkels' Wareroom," in *Godey's Magazine and Lady's Book* (February 1850): 123–24, 152–53. For the influence of Godey's, see Gail Caskey Winkler, "Influence of 'Godey's Lady's Book' on the American Woman and her Home: Contributions to a National Culture, 1830–1877," Ph.D. dissertation (University of Wisconsin, Madison, 1988).

34. John Henry Belter also exhibited a carved ivory and ebony table at the 1853 exhibition in New York, although it was not included in *The World of Science, Art, and Industry/Illustrated from Examples in the New-York Exhibition, 1853–54*.

35. Downing, p. 456.

36. As transcribed in Elizabeth A. Ingerman, "Personal Experiences of an old New York cabinetmaker," in *The Magazine Antiques* (November 1963): 579.

37. In *The Cabinet Maker's Assistant* (London, 1853), pp. 50, 51, Blackie & Son refer to rosewood as "likely to furnish a permanently fashionable material for drawing–room furniture. Besides being intrinsically beautiful, it contrasts admirably with the materials usually employed in drapery."

38. A parlor suite bought in 1855 for Green Hill Jordan of Milledgeville, Georgia, and documented in a receipt from Belter, is now in the Museum of Fine Arts, Houston; the suite was purchased for Jordan by Benjamin Smith Jordan, who also bought an identical suite for himself at the same time. A parlor set and other furniture were acquired by James B. Clay of Lexington, Kentucky, son of Henry Clay, in 1857. The two double parlor suites purchased by Eliza Wilson in 1858 for Rosalie, her villa in Natchez, Mississippi, remain there today.

39. Apparently, other furniture makers also realized Belter's innovative technique. Ernest Hagen described in detail how his employer, furniture maker Charles Baudouine, infringed on Belter's patent (Ingerman, p. 579).

40. There is an extensive bibliography of scholarship on John Henry Belter, including Marvin D. Schwartz, Edward J. Stanek, and Douglas K. True, eds., *The Furniture of John Henry Belter and the Rococo Revival* (New York: E. P. Dutton, 1981); and Ed Polk Douglas, "Rococo Revival: John Henry Belter," Art and Antiques, ed., *Nineteenth Century Furniture/Innovation, Revival, and Reform* (New York: Billboard, 1982).

41. For example, see J.O. & Co., *Designs of Cabinet Furniture* (England, ca. 1875).

42. Webster, p. 248.

Art Nouveau

PENELOPE HUNTER-STIEBEL

1. The 1901 statutes name Emile Gallé ceramist, furniture manufacturer, and master glass maker as president; with Antonin Daum, master glass maker, as vice-president and treasurer; Louis Majorelle, furniture manufacturer, as vice-president; and Eugène Vallin, cabinetwork manufacturer, as vice-president and secretary. See Christian Debize, *Emile Gallé and the Ecole de Nancy* (Metz: Editions Serpenoise, 1999): 112.

2. Ibid., p. 16.

3. François le Tacon and Flavien De Luca, *L'usine d'art Gallé à Nancy* (Nancy, 1999): 24.

4. Although 1867 is the date when Gallé became a principal in the family firm, the documents he filled out in 1900 at the time of his promotion to the grade of commander of the Légion d'honneur state that, from 1863, he was "coopérateur-artiste de Gallé-Reinemer, son père." See Philippe Thiébaut, "Gallé et l'art du

XVIIe siècle," in *Couleurs et formes: L'héritage du XVIIIe siècle dans l'Ecole de Nancy* (Musée de l'Ecole de Nancy, 2005): 29, 34, note 19.

5. The work remained in the Gallé family home until 1955, when it was offered at auction. See Jean-François Brabant, *Emile Gallé et Victor Prouvé: une alliance pour le mobilier* (Musée Ecole de Nancy, 2002): 24–25.

6. Debize, p. 22.

7. Roselyne Bouvier and Valérie Thomas, "Le XVIIIe siècle, de mille façons on le fait présent à notre esprit," in *Couleurs et formes: L'héritage du XVIIIe siècle dans l'Ecole de Nancy*, pp. 19–20, illus. 5.

8. Debize, pp. 40–41.

9. Gabriel Weisberg, *Art Nouveau Bing: Paris Style 1900* (Washington, D.C.: Smithsonian, 1986). Weisberg presents an in-depth study of Bing's career.

10. It was not initially known that de Feure was Dutch, not French.

11. Debize, p. 22.

The Modern Curve

ELLEN LUPTON

1. Quoted in Lisa Lyons, *Departures* (Los Angeles: J. Paul Getty Trust, 2000): 52.

2. Quoted in Josephine Minutillo, "Tord Boontje: A Modern Craftsman with a Human Touch," in *Architectural Record* (July 2004): 240.

3. Charlotte Benton, "Le Corbusier: Furniture and the Interior," in *Journal of Design History*, vol. 3, No. 2/3 (1990): 103–24.

4. Rémy G. Saisselein, "The Rococo as a Dream of Happiness," in *The Journal of Aesthetics and Art Criticism* 19, 2 (Winter, 1990): 145–52. Quotation translated from the French by Vivian Folkenflik.

5. On the history of art history, see Michael Ann Holly, *Panofsky and the Foundations of Art History* (Ithaca: Cornell University Press, 1984).

6. Deborah Fausch, "Rococo Modernism: The Elegance of Style," in *Perspecta* 32 (2001): 8–17.

7. William Rieder, "Bentwood Furniture," in *Architectural Digest*, vol. 53, Issue 8 (August 1996): 106.

8. "Tubular Steel Furniture: Antecedents and Early History," in *Journal of Design History*, vol. 3, No. 2/3 (1990): 166–70.

9. Paola Antonelli, *Objects of Design from the Museum of Modern Art* (New York: Museum of Modern Art, 2003): 130.

10. Kathryn B. Hiesinger and George H. Marcus, *Landmarks of Twentieth-Century Design: An Illustrated Handbook* (New York: Abbeville Press, 1993): 129.

11. Fulvio Ferrari and Napoleone Ferrari, *The Furniture of Carlo Mollino* (London: Phaidon Press, 2006).

12. Joseph Giovannini has analyzed in-depth the curved furniture of Charles and Ray Eames; he asserts the leadership of Ray Eames (née Kaiser) in developing the couple's legendary formal vocabulary. See Joseph Giovannini, "The Office of Charles and Ray Eames: The Material Trail," in Donald Albrecht et al., *The Work of Charles and Ray Eames: A Legacy of Invention* (New York: Harry N. Abrams, 1997): 45–71. The mid-century period was filled with designers who celebrated the curve as a form both abstract and humane, including Harry Bertoia, Eero Saarinen, Frederick Kiesler, and many others.

13. Antonelli, p. 134.

14. Ibid., p. 145. See also Hanne Horsfeld, Poul Hvidberg-Hansen, Barbel Birkelbach, Sabine Epple, and Mathias Remmele, *Verner Panton: The Collected Works* (Weil am Rhein, Germany: Vitra Design Stiftung, 2003); and Charlotte and Peter Fiell, *Design of the Twentieth Century* (New York: Taschen, 1999): 542.

15. Quoted in David A. Hanks and Anne Hoy, *Design for Living: Furniture and Lighting 1950–2000* (New York: Flammarion, 2000): 202.

16. Jacques Jugeat, *Lalique Glass from the Collection of Charles and Mary Magriel*, exh. cat. (Williamstown, MA: Sterling and Francine Clark Institute, 1986).

17. Brooke Kamin Rapaport and Kevin L. Stayton, *Vital Forms: American Art and Design in the Atomic Age, 1940–1960* (New York: Brooklyn Museum, 2001).

18. Today, the vase is made with a steel mold. This and other changes in production methods at the Iittala factory in Finland result in a more uniform product than was possible in Aalto's day. See Laurie Manfra, "Alvar's Icon," in *Metropolis* (May 2006): 121–26.

19. Pipsan Saarinen Swanson, *Backgrounds for Modern Living: Furniture, Textile, and Fashion Designs* (Bloomfield Hills, MI: Cranbrook Academy of Art, 1999). See also press release, "Presentation of The Saarinen-Swanson Design Group at the Johnson Furniture Co. Showroom, Grand Rapids, Michigan," June 5, 1947 (photocopy in Cooper-Hewitt, National Design Museum research files).

20. Peter Leyton, *Glass Art* (Seattle: University of Washington Press, 1996) and Franco Deboni, *The Venini Glass* (Umberto Allemandi and Co., 1996).

21. Joan Seeman Robinson, "Chihuly Seaforms," in *Portland Press* (1995); and Jack Cowart and Karen Chambers, *Chihuly: A Decade of Glass* (Bellevue, WA: Bellevue Art Museum).

22. Toots Zynsky: *Oeuvres* (Paris: Clara Scremini, 1987); and *Toots Zynsky: Tierra del Fuego Series*, exh. cat. (Amsterdam: Stejelijk Museum, 1989).

23. David A. Hanks and Nancy Hoy describe the 1960s as an era whose economic liquidity was reflected in its fluid design vocabulary: "Consumption mattered more than production; and markets were viewed not as monolithic but as multifaceted and fluid." *Design for Living*, p. 65.

24. Ibid., p. 117.

25. Donald Albrecht, curator, *Wendell Castle, 1968–1973*, exhibition at R 20th Century, New York.

26. Quoted in Peter Reed, "Mind Over Matter," in Antonelli, p. 151. See also Hanks, p. 150.

27. David Kunzle, *American Posters of Protest, 1966–70*, exh. cat. (New York: New School Art Center, 1971).

28. Robert Rosenblum, "Jeff Koons: Christ and the Lamb," in *Artforum International* (September 1993). See also Karen Wright, "Koons," in *Modern Painters* (June 2006): 64–66, 68–71.

29. Quoted in Rosenblum.

30. Linsdey Morton, "Louis XV Soup Tureen Serves as Inspiration, and Medium, for Modernist," in *Inside Smithsonian Research* 4 (Spring 2004); Susan Tallman, "Feet of Clay: Limoges Porcelain by Contemporary Artists," in *Arts Magazine*.

31. Marcia Westby, *Baroque Modernism: New Work by Albert Paley* (Peter Joseph Gallery, 1992).

32. Jean-Louis Gaillemin provides a rich portrait of the entire London "creative salvage" scene in his book *André Dubreuil: Poet of Iron* (Paris: Editions Norma, 2006).

33. Raymond Guidot and Oliver Boissere, *Ron Arad* (Paris: Editions Dis Voir, 1997).

34. Andrea DiNoto, "Once Upon a Gingko Leaf: Ted Muchling," in *American Craft* (February/March 2001): 70–75.

35. Gail S. Davidson, interview with the artist, May 2007.

36. Jamer Hunt, "A Manifesto for Postindustrial Design," in I.D. (December 2005): 120–21.

37. http://www.vam.ac.uk/collections/furniture/object_stories/cinderella_table/index.html (referenced April 9, 2007).

38. Interview with the author, April 2007.

39. Quoted in Loredana Mascheroni, "Joris vs. Vico," in *Domus*, no. 878 (February 2005): 86–93.

40. "Wall Lingerie," in *Domus*, no. 868 (March 2004): 64–71. Text by Joris Laarman, edited by Francesca Picchi.

41. Alice Twemlow, "Ornamentality," in *Eye*, no. 58 (Winter 2005): 232.

42. Quoted in Dan Nadel, "The Flat Earth," in *Print* (May/June 2004): 44–51. See also Felix Studinka, "Ralph Schraivogel: The Craftsman's Contract," in *Graphis* 351, 60 (May/June 2004).

Selected Bibliography

Alcorn, Ellenor M. Beyond the Maker's Mark: Paul de Lamerie Silver in the Cahn Collection. Cambridge: John Adamson, 2006.

_____. English Silver in the Museum of Fine Arts, Boston. Boston: Museum of Fine Arts/Northeastern University Press, 1993.

_____. Rococo Silver in England and Its Colonies: Papers from a Symposium at Virginia Museum of Fine Arts, Richmond. Silver Studies 20. London: The Silver Society, 2006.

Allen, Brian. "Carl Marcus Tuscher: A German Artist in London." In Apollo 122 (July 1985): 32–35.

Ames, Kenneth L. "Designed in France: Notes on the Transmission of French Style to America." In Winterthur Portfolio 12 (1977): 103–14.

Antonelli, Paola. Objects of Design from The Museum of Modern Art. New York: The Museum of Modern Art, 2003.

Baarsen, Reinier. "The Court Style in Holland." In Courts and Colonies, the William and Mary Style in Holland, England and America, exh. cat. New York: Cooper-Hewitt Museum, 1988: 12–35.

_____. De Amsterdamse meubelloterijen en de geschiedenis van de meubelmakerij in de tweede helft van de achttiende eeuw. Publikaties van het Gemeentearchief Amsterdam 20. Zwolle: Waanders; Amsterdam: Gemeentearchief, 1992.

_____. Nederlandse meubelen, 1600–1800. Amsterdam: Rijksmuseum; Zwolle: Waanders, 1993.

_____. "The First Amsterdam Rococo chairs." In Cleveland Studies in the History of Art 8 (2003): 120–29.

_____. "High Rococo in Holland: William IV and Agostino Carlini." In The Burlington Magazine 140 (March 1998): 172–83.

_____. " 'In the commode van Parijs tot Den Haag,' Matthijs Horrix (1735–1809), een meubelmaker in Den Haag in de tweede helft van de achttiende eeuw." In Oud Holland 107, no. 2 (1993): 161–255.

_____ "Matthijs Horrix, Cabinetmaker from The Hague." In The Magazine Antiques 154 (1998): 521–25.

Baarsen, Reinier, ed., et al. Rococo in Nederland, exh. cat. Amsterdam: Rijksmuseum; Zwolle: Waanders, 2001.

_____. "Throne chairs from the workshop of Jan Baptist Xavery." In Furniture History 43 (2007).

Backgrounds for Modern Living: Furniture, Textile, and Fashion Designs by Pipsan Saarinen Swanson, with text by Ashley Brown. Bloomfield Hills, MI: Cranbrook Academy of Art, 1999.

Baer, Winfried. Eine Schlafzimmer-Ausstattung von Julius Zweiner. Ein Auftrag Kaiser Wilhelm II für das Berliner Schloss, 1895–1900. Kulturstiftung der Länder 3. Berlin: Kulturstiftung der Länder und der Verwaltung der Staatlichen Schlösser und Gärten, 1989.

_____, ed. Prunk-Tabatièren Friedrichs des Grossen, exh. cat. Munich: Hirmer Verlag, 1993.

Barquist, David, ed. Myer Myers: Jewish Silversmith in Colonial New York, exh. cat. New Haven and London: Yale University Press, 2001.

Baumstark, Reinhold, et al. Silber und Gold: Augsburger Goldschmiedekunst für die Höfe Europas, exh. cat. Munich: Bayerisches Nationalmuseum, 1994.

Beard, Geoffrey W. " 'Babel's A New Book of Ornaments,' 1752." In The Furniture History Society Journal 11 (1975): 31–32.

_____. Craftsmen and Interior Decoration in England, 1660–1820. New York: Holmes & Meier, 1981.

_____. Italian Stuccoists in Yorkshire. York, England: York Civic Trust and Maxiprint Colour Printers, 1896.

_____. "Philadelphia Carving Shops. Part I: James Reynolds." In The Magazine Antiques (May 1984): 1120–33.

_____. "Philadelphia Carving Shops. Part II: Bernard and Jugiez." In The Magazine Antiques (Sept. 1985): 498–513.

_____. "Philadelphia Carving Shops. Part III: Hercules Courtenay and His School." In The Magazine Antiques (May 1987): 1044–63.

Becker, Vivienne, ed. The Jewellery of René Lalique, exh. cat. London: Goldsmith's Company, 1987.

Beckerdite, Luke. "The Origins of Rococo Style in New York Furniture and Interior Architecture." In Luke Beckerdite, ed. American Furniture (Hanover, NH: University Press of New England for the Chipstone Foundation, 1994): 15–37.

_____. "William Buckland and William Bernard Sears: the Designer and the Carver." In Journal of Early Southern Decorative Arts 8 (1982): 7–41.

_____. ed., American Furniture. Hanover, NH: University Press of New England for the Chipstone Foundation, 1994.

Beet, Brian. "Foreign Snuffbox makers in Eighteenth century London." In The Silver Society Journal (2002): 49–78.

Beneke, Sabine, and Hans Ottomeyer, eds. Zuwanderungsland Deutschland: die Hugenotten, exh. cat. Berlin: Deutsches Historisches Museum; Wolfratshausen: Edition Minerva, 2005.

Benton, Charlotte. "Le Corbusier: Furniture and the Interior." In Journal of Design History 3, no. 2/3 (1990): 103–24.

Bérard, M. Catalogue de l'Oeuvre de Cuvilliés Père et Fils. Paris: Veuve Jules Renouard, Libraire, 1859.

Berents, Catharina. "Moderne Chinoiserien: Das Vorbild Jean Pillements." In Art Déco in Deutschland, Das moderne Ornament, Werkbund-Archiv 27. Frankfurt-am-Mein: Anabas Verlag, 1998.

Bigelow, David. History of Prominent Mercantile and Manufacturing Firms in the United States, vol. 6. Boston: D. Bigelow, 1857.

Bivins, John, Jr. "Charleston Rococo Interiors, 1765–1775: The 'Sommers' Carver.' " In Journal of Early Southern Decorative Arts 12 (1986): 1–129.

Bjurström, Per. The Art of Drawing in France, 1400–1900: Drawings from the Nationalmuseum, Stockholm. London and New York: Sotheby's Publications, 1987.

Blackie & Sons. The Cabinet Maker's Assistant. London, 1853. Reprinted as The Victorian Cabinet-Maker's Assistant. New York: Dover, 1970.

Bleibaum, Friedrich. Johann August Nahl, der Künstler Friedrich des Grossen und der Landgrafen von Hessen-Kassel. Baden-bei-Wien and Leipzig: R. M. Rohrer, 1933.

Blunt, Anthony, et al. Baroque and Rococo Architecture and Decoration. New York and London: Harper & Row Publishers, 1978.

_____. Review of The Creation of Rococo by Fiske Kimball. In The Burlington Magazine 88, no. 518 (1946): 128–29.

_____. "Cooper-Hewitt Union Drawings." In The Burlington Magazine 115, no. 845 (August 1973): 562–63.

Bott, Gerhard. Sitz-Gelegenheiten: Bugholz und Stahlrohrmöbel von Thonet, exh. cat. Nürnberg: Germanisches Nationalmuseum, 1989.

Bouvet, Mireille-Bénédicte. "Places de Nancy au XVIIIe siècle." In Alexandre Gady and Jean-Marie Pérouse de Montclose, eds., De l'Esprit des villes, Nancy et l'Europe urbaine au siècle des Lumières 1720–1770. Nancy: Musée des Beaux-Arts, 2005.

Bouvier, Roselyne, and Valérie Thomas. "Le XVIIIe siècle, de mille façons on le fait présent à notre esprit." In Couleurs et Formes: L'héritage du XVIIIe siècle dans l'Ecole de Nancy, exh. cat. Nancy: Musée de l'Ecole de Nancy, 2005.

Brabant, Jean-François. Emile Gallé et Victor Prouvé: un alliance pour le mobilier, exh. cat. Nancy: Musée Ecole de Nancy, 2002.

Brakensiek, Stephan, ed. Gelsenkirchener Barock, exh. cat. Gelsenkirchen, Germany: Edition Braus, 1991.

Braunfels, Wolfgang. François de Cuvilliés: Der Baumeister Der Galanten Architektur Des Rokoko. Munich: Süddeutscher Verlag, 1986.

Bremer-David, Charissa. French Tapestries and Textiles in the J. Paul Getty Museum. Los Angeles: J. Paul Getty Museum, 1997.

Bremer-David, Charissa, et al. Decorative Arts: An Illustrated Summary Catalogue of the Collections of the J. Paul Getty Museum. Malibu: J. Paul Getty Museum, 1993.

Brown, Peter, "Derby Porcelain." In The Magazine Antiques (2003): 103–11.

Bruand, Yves. "Un grand collectionneur, marchand et graveur du XVIIe siècle, Gabriel Huquier (1695–1772)." In *Gazette des Beaux-Arts* 37 (July–September 1950): 99–114.

Brunhammer, Yvonne, et al. *Art Nouveau, Belgium, France*. Houston: Institute for the Arts, Rice University, 1976.

_____. *René Lalique: Bijoux d'exception, 1890–1912*, exh. cat. Milan: Skira, 2007.

Brunhammer, Yvonne, ed. "The Lalique Epoch." In *The Jewels of Lalique*, exh. cat. Paris and New York: Flammarion, 1998.

Brugerolles, Emmanuelle, ed. *Boucher, Watteau and the Origin of the Rococo*, exh. cat. Paris: Ecole Nationale Supérieure des Beaux-Arts, 2004.

Buhler, Kathryn C., and Graham Hood. *American Silver: Garvan and Other Collections in the Yale University Art Gallery*. New Haven and London: Yale University Press, 1970.

Busch, Jason T. "The French Rococo Revival along the Mississippi River." In *The Magazine Antiques* 66, no. 2 (August 2004): 84–95.

_____. "Furniture Patronage in Antebellum Natchez." In *The Magazine Antiques* 157, no. 5 (May 2000): 804–13.

_____. " 'Such a Paradise Can Be Made on Earth': Furniture Patronage and Consumption in Antebellum Natchez, Mississippi, 1828–1863." Master's thesis, University of Delaware, Newark, DE, 1998.

Busch, Jason T., Christopher P. Monkhouse, and Janet L. Whitmore, eds. *Currents of Change: The Art and Life along the Mississippi River, 1850–1861*, exh. cat. Minneapolis: Minneapolis Institute of Arts, 2004.

Cameron, Peter. "Henry Jernegan, the Kandlers and the Client Who Changed His Mind." In *Silver Society Journal* 8 (1996): 487–501.

Carlson, Victor I., John W. Ittmann, and David B. Becker, eds. *Regency to Empire: French Printmaking, 1715–1814*, exh. cat. Baltimore: Baltimore Museum of Art, 1984.

Carr, C. T. "Two Words in Art History II: Rococo." In *Forum for Modern Language Studies* 1 (1965): 266–81.

Cassidy-Geiger, Maureen. "Graphic Sources for Meissen Porcelain: Origins of the Print Collection in the Meissen Archives." In *Metropolitan Museum Journal* 31 (1996): 99–126.

_____. "Ein neues silbern Französisches Tafel Service: Linking the Penthièvre-Orléans Service to Dresden." In *Silver Studies: The Journal of the Silver Society* 21 (November 2007): 123–54.

_____. " 'Quelque chose de beau et de bon goût': A Silver-gilt Toilet Service for the Dresden Doppelhochzeit of 1747." In *Rococo Silver in England and Its Colonies*. In *Silver Studies: The Journal of the Silver Society* 20 (2004).

_____. "Meissen and France before and after the Seven Years' War: Artists, Espionage and Trade." In *Collection Rencontres de l'Ecole du Louvre, Actes du colloque Art français et art allemande au XVIII siècle*. Paris, 2007.

Chapman, Martin. "A Diplomatic Gift from Turin." In *Apollo* 147 (January 1998): 3–9.

Chicirda, Tara Gleason. "The Furniture of Fredericksburg, VA, 1740–1820." In Luke Beckerdite, ed., *American Furniture*. Hanover, NH: University Press of New England for the Chipstone Foundation, 1994.

Clark, Alvin L., et al. *Mastery & Elegance: Two Centuries of French Drawings from the Collection of Jeffrey E. Horvitz*. Cambridge: Harvard University Art Museums, 1998.

Clifford, Sir Timothy. *Designs of Desire: Architectural and Ornament Prints and Drawings, 1500–1850*. Edinburgh: National Galleries of Scotland, 1999.

du Colombier, Pierre. "Le Chateau de Lunéville." In *La Revue Française* (May 1958).

Corrin, Lisa G., and Joaneath Spicer. *Going for Baroque: 18 Contemporary Artists Fascinated with the Baroque and Rococo*. Baltimore: The Contemporary/The Walters Art Gallery, 1995.

Courajod, Luis. ed. *Livre-Journal de Lazare Duvaux, Marchand-bijoutier ordinaire du roi, 1748–1758*, 2 vols. Paris, 1873. Reprinted Paris: F. de Nobele, 1965.

Cowart, Jack, and Karen Chambers. *Chihuly: A Decade of Glass*. Bellevue, WA: Bellevue Art Museum, 1984.

Culme, John. *The Directory of Gold & Silversmiths: Jewellers & Allied Traders, 1833–1914, from the London Assay Office Registers*, vol. 1. Woodbridge, Suffolk: Antique Collectors' Club, 1987.

_____. *Nineteenth-century Silver*. London: Hamlyn for Country Life Books, 1977.

Culme, John, and John G. Strang. *Antique Silver and Silver Collecting*. London: Hamlyn, 1973.

Davidson, Gail S. "Eliot Clark and the American Drawings Collection at Cooper-Hewitt, National Design Museum." In *Archives of American Art Journal* 34, no. 4 (1994): 4–10.

Debize, Christian. *Emile Gallé and the "Ecole de Nancy."* Metz, Germany: Editions Serpenoise, 1999.

Deboni, Franco. *Venini Glasswares*. Woodbridge, Suffolk: Umberto Allemandi and Co., 1996.

Demetrescu, Calin. "D.F. un Ebéniste identifié." In *L'objet d'Art* 262 (October 1992): 64–81.

DiNoto, Andrea. "Once Upon a Gingko Leaf: Ted Muehling." In *American Craft* 61, no. 1 (February/March 2001): 70–75.

Donnell, Edna. "Juste-Aurèle Meissonnier and the Rococo Style." In *Bulletin of the Metropolitan Museum of Art* 12 (1941): 254–60.

Douglas, Ed Polk. "Rococo Revival: John Henry Belter." In *Nineteenth Century Furniture: Innovation, Revival and Reform*. New York: Art and Antiques, 1982, 26–35.

Dragesco, Bernard. *English Ceramics in French Archives: The Writings of Jean Hellot, the Adventures of Jacques Louis Brolliet and the Identification of 'Girl in the Swing' Factory*. London: B. Dragesco, 1993.

Duret, Theodore. "On Combs." In *Le Japon Artistique* 5 (1890): 335–41.

Edgcumbe, Richard. *The Art of the Gold Chaser in Eighteenth-century London*. Oxford: Oxford University Press, 2000.

Elling, Christian. *Amalienborg Interiører: Christian VII's Palæ, 1750–1800*. Copenhagen: Glyndendal, 1945.

Eriksen, Svend. *Early Neo-classicism in France*. Translated by Peter Thornton. London: Faber and Faber, 1974.

Fausch, Deborah. "Rococo Modernism: The Elegance of Style." In *Perspecta* 32 (2001): 8–17.

Fennimore, Donald L., and Patricia A. Halfpenny with Kate Duffy and Janice Carlson. *Campbell Collection of Soup Tureens at Winterthur*. Hanover, NH: Henry Francis du Pont Winterthur Museum, 2000.

Ferrari, Fulvio, and Napoleone Ferrari. *The Furniture of Carlo Mollino*. London: Phaidon Press, 2006.

Ferraris, Giancarlo. *Pietro Piffetti e gli ebanisti a Torino, 1670–1838*. Turin: U. Allemandi, 1992.

Fett, Sabine, Michaela Kalusok, and Ulrich Schmidt, eds. *Die Künstlerfamilie Nahl: Rokoko under Klassizismus in Kassel*, exh. cat. Kassel: Staatliche Museen Kassel, 1994.

Feulner, Adolf, and Preston Remington. "Examples of South German Woodwork in the Metropolitan Museum." In *Metropolitan Museum Studies* 2, no. 2 (May 1930): 152–70.

Fiell, Charlotte, and Peter Fiell. *Design of the Twentieth Century*. New York: Taschen, 1999.

Fischer, Peter M. *Ignatius en Jan van Logteren, Beeldhouwers en stuckunstenaars in het Amsterdam van de 18de eeuw*. Alphen aan den Rijn: Canaletto, 2005.

FitzGerald, Desmond. "Gravelot and His Influence on English Furniture." In *Apollo* 90 (1969): 140–47.

FitzGerald, Desmond: Knight of Glin, and James Peill. *Irish Furniture: Woodwork and Carving in Ireland from the Earliest Times to the Act of Union*. New Haven: Yale University Press, 2007.

France-Lanord, Albert. *Jean Lamour: Serrurier du Roi, 1698–1771*. Nancy: Université de Nancy II, Service des Publications, 1977.

Fuhring, Peter. *Design into Art: Drawings for Architecture and Ornament: The Lodewijk Houthakker Collection*, 2 vols. The Hague: G. Schwartz; London: Philip Wilson Publishers, 1989.

_____. *Designing the Décor: French Drawings from the Eighteenth Century*. Lisbon: Calouste Gulbenkian Foundation, 2005.

_____. *Un Génie du Rococo: Juste-Aurèle Meissonnier, 1695–1750*, 2 vols. Turin and London: Umberto Allemandi & Co., 1999.

_____. "The Print Privilege in Eighteenth-century France, I." *Print Quarterly* 2, no. 3 (September 1985): 174–93.

_____. "The Print Privilege in Eighteenth-century France, II." *Print Quarterly* 3, no. 1 (March 1986): 19–33.

_____. "Two Title Page Designs by Gilles-Marie Oppenord for His Engraved Oeuvre." In *Drawing* 14, no. 3 (September-October 1992): 49–52.

Fuhring, Peter, et al. "Juste-Aurèle Meissonnier: The Artist and His Work." In *The Thyssen Meissonnier Silver Tureen Made for the 2nd Duke of Kingston*. New York: Sotheby's, 1998.

Gabler, Josephine, and Jürgen Julier. *Kaiserlicher Kunstbesitz aus dem holländischen Exil Haus Doorn*. Berlin: Staatliche Schlösser und Gärten, 1991.

Gady, Alexandre, and Jean-Marie Pérouse de Montclos, eds. *De l'Esprit des villes: Nancy et l'Europe urbaine au siècle des lumières, 1720–1770*, exh. cat. Nancy: Musée des Beaux-Arts, 2005.

Gaehtgens, Thomas E., Dirk Syndram, and Béatrix Saule, eds. *Splendeurs de la cour de Saxe, Dresde à Versailles*, exh. cat. Paris: Réunion des Musées Nationaux, 2006.

Gaillemin, Jean-Louis. *André Dubreuil: Poet of Iron*. Paris: Editions Norma, 2006.

Gere, Charlotte, John Culme, and William Summers. *Garrard: The Crown Jewelers for 150 years, 1843–1993*. London: Quartet Books, 1993.

Giersberg, Hans-Joachim. *Friedrich als Bauherr: Studien zur Architektur des 18. Jahrhunderts in Berlin und Potsdam*. Berlin: Siedler, 1986.

Girouard, Mark. "English Art and the Rococo," in *Country Life* I: "Coffee at Slaughter's," Jan 13, 1966, 58–61; II: "Hogarth and his Friends," Jan 27, 1966, 188–90; III: "The Two Worlds of St. Martin's Lane," February 3, 1966, 224–27.

Glanville, Philippa, ed. *Silver: History & Design*. New York: Harry N. Abrams, 1997.

_____. *Silver in England*. New York: Holmes & Meier, 1987.

Glanville, Philippa, and Hilary Young, eds. *Elegant Eating: Four Hundred Years of Dining in Style*. London: V & A Publications, 2002.

Goodman-Soellner, Elise. "Boucher's Madame de Pompadour at her Toilette." In *Simiolus* 17 (May 1987): 41–58.

de Goncourt, Edmond and Jules. *Madame de Pompadour*. Paris: G. Charpentier, 1881. Reprint Paris: O. Orban, 1982.

González-Palacios, Alvar. *The Age of Louis XV*. London: Cassell, 1988 (originally published 1969).

Greenhalgh, Paul. *Quotations and Sources on Design and the Decorative Arts 1800–1900*. Manchester: Manchester University Press, 1993.

_____, ed. *Art Nouveau, 1890–1914*, exh. cat. London: Victoria & Albert Museum; Washington, DC: National Gallery of Art, 2000.

Gray, Nina. "Leon Marcotte: Cabinetmaker and Interior Decorator." In Luke Beckerdite, ed., *American Furniture* (Hanover, NH: University Press of New England for the Chipstone Foundation, 1994): 49–72.

Grier, Katherine C. *Culture & Comfort: Parlor Making and Middle-class Identity, 1850–1930*. Washington, DC: Smithsonian Institution Press, 1997.

Guidot, Raymond, and Olivier Boissière. *Ron Arad*. Paris: Editions Dis Voir, 1997.

Haaff, Rainer. *Louis-Philippe Furniture, Early Historicism (1850–1870)*. Stuttgart: Arnoldsche, 2004.

Haase, Gisela, and Jürgen Karpinski. *Dresdener Möbel des 18. Jahrhunderts*. Leipzig: VEB E.A. Seemann, Buch-und-Kunstverlag, 1986.

_____. *Der Kuppritzer Schreibschrank: das Meisterstück des Dresdener Hoftischlers Johann Christoph Hesse aus Shloss Luppritz*. Munich: Röbbig, 2005.

Hackenbroch, Yvonne, and James Parker. *The Lesley and Emma Sheafer Collection: A Selective Presentation Opening, July 16, 1975*. New York: The Metropolitan Museum of Art, 1975.

Haddad, Elie G. "On Henry van de Velde's 'Manuscript on Ornament.'" In *Journal of Design History* 16, no. 2 (2003): 119–38.

Hanks, David A., and Anne Hoy. *Design for Living: Furniture and Lighting 1950–2000*. New York and Paris: Flammarion, 2000.

_____. "The Nineteenth-century Furniture Trade in New Orleans." In *Antiques* 151, no. 5 (May 1998): 748–59.

Hartop, Christopher. *Royal Goldsmiths: The Art of Rundell & Bridge, 1797–1843*. Cambridge: John Adamson, 2005.

Hassels, Michael. *Potsdamer Schlösser und Gärten, Bau - und Gartenkunst vom 17. bis 20. Jarhundert*, exh. cat. Potsdam: Stiftung Schlösser und Gärten Potsdam-Sanssouci, 1993.

Hautecœur, L. *Histoire de l'Architecture Classique en France*, vol. 3, *Première Moitié du XVIII siècle, Le Style Louis XV*, new ed. Paris: A. et J. Picard, 1950.

Hawes, Vivian, and Christina S. Corsiglia. *The Rita and Frits Markus Collection of European Ceramics and Enamels*. Boston: Museum of Fine Arts, 1984.

Hawley, Henry. "Jean-Pierre Latz, Cabinetmaker." In *The Bulletin of the Cleveland Museum of Art* 57 (September–October 1970): 203–59.

_____. "Meissonnier's Silver for the Duke of Kingston." In *The Bulletin of the Cleveland Museum of Art* 65, no. 10 (1978): 312–52.

Heckscher, Morrison H. "English Furniture Pattern Books in Eighteenth-century America." In Luke Beckerdite, ed., *American Furniture* (Hanover, NH: University Press of New England for the Chipstone Foundation, 1994): 173–205.

Heckscher, Morrison H. "Gideon Saint; an Eighteenth-Century Carver and His Scrapbook." In *Metropolitan Museum of Art Bulletin* 27 (1969): 299–311.

Heckscher, Morrison H., and Leslie Greene Bowman. *American Rococo 1750–1775: Elegance in Ornament*. New York: Harry N. Abrams, 1992.

Hearn, M. F., ed. *The Architectural Theory of Viollet-Le-Duc. Readings and Commentary*. Cambridge, MA: MIT Press, 1990.

Hewitt, Eleanor Garnier. *The Making of a Modern Museum*, 4th ed. Boston: The Merrymount Press, 1941.

Hiesinger, Kathryn B. *The Second Empire, 1852–1870: Art in France under Napoleon III*, exh. cat. Philadelphia: Philadelphia Museum of Art, 1978.

Hiesinger, Kathryn B., and George H. Marcus. *Landmarks of Twentieth-century Design: An Illustrated Handbook*. New York: Abbeville Press, 1993.

High Museum of Art. *Selected Works: Outstanding Painting, Sculpture, and Decorative Art from the Permanent Collection*. Atlanta: High Museum of Art, 1987.

Hind, Charles, ed. *The Rococo in England: A Symposium*. London: Victoria and Albert Museum, 1986.

Holloway, Owen E. *French Rococo Book Illustration*. New York: Transatlantic Arts, 1969.

Howat, John K., and Catherine Hoover Voorsanger. *Art and the Empire City, New York 1825–1861*, exh. cat. New York: Metropolitan Museum of Art, 2000.

Horsfeld, Hanne, Poul Hvidberg-Hansen, Barbel Birkelbach, Sabine Epple, and Mathias Remmele. *Verner Panton: The Collected Works*. Weil am Rhein: Vitra Design Stiftung, 2003.

Hungerford, Constance Cain. *Ernest Meissonier: Master in His Genre*. Cambridge and New York: Cambridge University Press, 1999.

Hunt, Jamer. "A Manifesto for Postindustrial Design." In *I.D.* 52, no. 8 (December 2005): 120–21.

Hunter, Penelope. "A Royal Taste: Louis XV–1738." In *Metropolitan Museum of Art Journal* 7 (1973): 89–113.

Hunter-Stiebel, Penelope. *Louis XV and Madame de Pompadour: A Love Affair with Style*. New York: Rosenberg and Stiebel, 1990.

Hurst, Ronald. "Irish Influences on Cabinetmaking in Virginia's Rappahannock River Basin." In Luke Beckerdite, ed., *American Furniture* (Hanover and London: Chipstone Foundation, 1997): 170–95.

Hyde, Melissa Lee. *Making Up the Rococo: François Boucher and His Critics*. Los Angeles: Getty Research Institute, 2006.

Igra, Caroline. "Reviving the Rococo: Enterprising Italian Artists in Second Empire Paris." In *Art History* 28, no. 3 (2005): 340–56.

Irwin, Francine. "Scottish Eighteenth-century Chintz and Its Design - I." In *The Burlington Magazine*, vol. 107, no. 750, September 1965.

Jervis, Simon. "Huquier's 'Second Livre.'" In *The J. Paul Getty Museum Journal* 14 (1986): 113–20.

Jessen, Peter. *Rococo Engravings: Two Hundred Plates of the Eighteenth Century*. London: Benn Brothers, 1922.

Jones, Colin. *Madame de Pompadour: Images of a Mistress*. London: National Gallery Company, 2002.

de Jonge, C. H., and W. Vogelsang. *Holländische Möbel und Raumkunst von 1650–1780*. The Hague, 1922.

Kaufmann, Thomas DaCosta, ed. *Central European Drawings, 1680–1800: A Selection from American Collections*. Princeton: Art Museum, Princeton University/Princeton University Press, 1989.

Keefe, John Webster. *Paris Porcelains in the New Orleans Museum of Art*, exh. cat. New Orleans: New Orleans Museum of Art, 1998.

Kimball, Fiske. *The Creation of the Rococo*. Philadelphia: Philadelphia Museum of Art, 1943. Reprint New York: W. W. Norton & Co., 1964.

_____. "Juste-Aurèle Meissonnier and the Beginning of the 'Genre Pittoresque.'" In *Gazette des Beaux Arts* 22, no. 6 (1942): 33–34.

King, Julia. *The Flowering of Art Nouveau Graphics*. London: Trefoil; Salt Lake City: Peregrine Smith Books, 1990.

Kirtley, Alexandra Alevizatos. "Survival of the Fittest: the Lloyd Family's Furniture Legacy." In Luke Beckerdite, ed., *American Furniture* (London: Chipstone Foundation, 2002). 3–21.

Kisluk-Grosheide, Daniëlle O. "The Garden Room from Schloss Seehof and Its Furnishings." In Metropolitan Museum of Art Journal 25 (1990): 143–72.

Klien, Laurence Eliot. Shaftesbury and the Culture of Politeness: Moral Discourse and Cultural Politics in Early 18th Century England. Cambridge: Cambridge University Press, 1994.

von Koeppe, Wolfram. "Tafelleuchter und Girandolen." In Kunst & Antiquitäten (1993): 48–50.

Kreisel, Henrich. Fränkische Rokokomöbel. Wohnkunst und Hausrat 26. Darmstadt: Franz Schneekluth Verlag, 1956.

Kreisel, Heinrich, and Georg Himmelheber. Die Kunst des Deutschen Möbels: Möbels und Vertäfelungen des deutschen Sprachraums von den Anfänge bis zum Jugendstil. Vol. 2 Spätbarock und Rokoko. Munich: C. H. Beck, 1970.

Krückmann, Peter Olaf. Paradies des Rokoko, exh. cat., 2 vols. Munich and New York: Prestel, 1998.

Kurth, Wilhelm. Die Raumkunst in Kupferstich des 17 und 18 Jahrhunderts. Stuttgart: Julius Hoffman Verlag, 1923.

———. Sanssouci, Ein Beitrag zur Kunst des Deutschen Rokoko. Berlin: Henschelverlag Kunst und Gesellschaft, 1962.

Laarman, Joris, and Francesca Picchi, ed. "Wall Lingerie." In Domus, no. 868 (March 2004): 64–71.

Lacmanis, Imants. Le Château de Rundale. Bauska: Le Château de Rundale, 2005.

Lang, Alastair. "A Group of Boucher's Designs for Coach Panels." In Peter Fuhring, ed., Design into Art: Drawings for Architecture and Ornament: the Lodewijk Houthakker Collection, 2 vols. (The Hague: G. Schwartz; London: Philip Wilson Publishers, 1989): vol. 1.

Laran, Jean. François de Cuvilliés: Dessinateur et Architecte. Paris: Henri Laurens, 1925.

Layton, Peter. Glass Art. Seattle: University of Washington Press, 1996.

Leath, Robert A. "Robert and William Walker and the 'Ne Plus Ultra': Scottish Design and Colonial Virginia Furniture 1730–75." In Luke Beckerdite, ed., American Furniture, 2006.

Le Corbeiller, Clare. European and American Snuff Boxes, 1730–1830. New York: Viking, 1966.

———. "German Porcelain of the Eighteenth Century." In Metropolitan Museum of Art Bulletin 49, no. 4 (Spring 1990): 1–58.

———. "A Tale of Two Cities." In Cleveland Studies in the History of Art 8 (Cleveland, 2003): 148–55.

Leben, Ulrich. "La France et l'Allemagne et le domaine des arts décoratifs au 18e siècle: Histoire d'une assimilation d'idées en chassé-croisé." In Collection Rencontres de l'Ecole du Louvre, Actes du Colloque Art Français et Art Allemande au XVIIIe siècle (Paris, 2007).

———. "Assimilation des Modèles Français dans les arts décoratifs en Allemagne au XXIIIe Siècle." In Marie-Claude Chaudonneret, ed., Les Artistes étrangers à Paris : de la fin du Moyen Age aux années 1920: actes de journées d'études organisées par le Centre André Chastel (Bern: Center André Chastel, Editions Peter Lang AG, 2007).

Le Duc, Geneviève. Porcelain tendre de Chantilly au XVIIIe siècle. Paris: Hazan, 1996.

Le Tacon, François, and Flavien de Luca. L'usine d'art Gallé à Nancy. Nancy, 1999.

Levey, Michael, and Wend Von Kalnein. Art and Architecture of the Eighteenth Century in France. Harmondsworth: Penguin Books, 1972.

Lindsey, Jack L. "The Cadwalader Town House and Its Furnishings." In Philadelphia Museum of Art Bulletin 91 (1996): 10–23.

Llongueras, Lourdes de Sanjosé, ed. The Collection of Alcora Ceramics. New York: Hispanic Society of America, 2005.

Lock, Matthew. A Collection of Ornamental Designs, Applicable to Furniture, Frames & the Decoration of Rooms, in the Style of Louis 14th – on 24 Plates, Chiefly after Thos. Chippendale. England, 1838.

de Lorm, Jan Rudolph, and Dirk Jan Biemond. Amsterdams goud en zilver. Amsterdam: Waander Uitgevers; Rijksmuseum, 1999.

Lyons, Lisa. Departures: 11 Artists at the Getty. Los Angeles: J. Paul Getty Museum, 2000.

Mainardi, Patricia. Art and Politics of the Second Empire: The Universal Expositions of 1855 and 1867. New Haven: Yale University Press, 1987.

Mallett, J. V. G. The Spirit of the Rococo: Reflections of Summer. London: Mallett, 2004.

———. "Rococo Designs in Porcelain." In Apollo (August 1969): 100–13.

Mandroux-França, Marie-Thérèse. "Information Artistique et 'Mass-Media' au XVIIIe siècle: La Diffusion de l'Ornement Gravé Rococo au Portugal." In Bracara Augusta 27, no. 64 (1973): 1–36.

Manfra, Laurie. "Alvar's Icon." In Metropolis 25, no. 9 (May 2006): 121–26.

Mascheroni, Loredana. "Joris vs. Vico." In Domus, no. 878 (February 2005): 86–93.

Mathias, Martine, ed. Stanislas, un roi de Pologne en Lorraine., Nancy: Musée Lorrain, 2004.

Mauriès, Patrick. Shell Shock: Conchological Curiosities. London: Thames and Hudson, 1994.

Mayhew, Edgar de Noailles, and Minor Myers, Jr. "The Rococo Style, 1850–1870." In A Documentary History of American Interiors from the Colonial Era to 1915. New York: Scribner and Sons, 1980.

Meckel, Claudia, Susanne Evers, and Ute-G. Weickardt, eds. Von Sanssouci nach Europa: Geschenke Friedrichs des Grossen an Europäische Höfe, exh. cat. Potsdam: Stiftung Schlösser und Gärten Potsdam-Sanssouci, 1994.

McCarthy, Michael. "The Building of Hagley Hall, Worcestershire." In The Burlington Magazine 118 (1976): 214–25.

Michel, Marianne Roland. Le Dessin Français au XVIII Siècle. Fribourg: Office du Livre, 1987.

———. Lajoüe et L'Art Rocaille. Neuilly-sur-Seine: Arthena, 1984.

Minutillo, Josephine. "Tord Boontje: A Modern Craftsman with a Human Touch." In Architectural Record 192, no. 7 (July 2004): 240.

Morton, Lindsey. "Louis XV Soup Tureen Serves as Inspiration, and Medium, for Modernist." In Inside Smithsonian Research 4 (Spring 2004).

Murdoch, Tessa V. Boughton House: The English Versailles. London: Faber and Faber, 1992.

Musée National de Versailles. Marie-Antoinette: Archiduchesse, Dauphine, et Reine, exh. cat. Paris: Editions des Musées Nationaux, 1955.

Myers, Mary L., ed. French Architectural and Ornament Drawings of the Eighteenth Century, exh. cat. New York: The Metropolitan Museum of Art, 1992.

Nicolle, Jean. Madame de Pompadour et la société de son temps. Paris: Albatros, 1980.

Noco, Henry, and Carle Dreyfus. Tabatières: Boîtes et Étuis. Paris: Les Editions G. Van Oest, 1969.

Nyberg, Dorothea. "Meissonnier, an Eighteenth-century Maverick," introduction to Oeuvre de Juste-Aurèle Meissonnier by Juste-Aurèle Meissonnier. New York: Benjamin Blom, Inc. 1969.

Pallot, Bill G. B. L'art du Siège au XVIIIe Siècle en France. Courbevoie and Paris: ACR-Gismondi Editeurs, 1987.

Parker, James. Decorative Art from the Samuel H. Kress Collection at the Metropolitan Museum of Art. New York: Phaidon, 1964.

Perrin, Christiane. François Thomas Germain: Orfèvre des rois. Saint-Rémy-en-l'Eau: Editions d'Art Monelle Hayot, 1993.

Perrot, Georges. Inventaire des Arrêts du Conseil du Roi (Janvier–Février 1730). Reprint, Paris: Les Presses modernes, 1937.

von Pfeil, Christoph Graf. Die Möbel der Residenz Ansbach. 2 vols. Munich: Prestel, 1999.

Picchi, Francesca. "Ron Arad MT3." In Domus (December 2005): 77–80.

Pietsch, Ulrich, ed. Schwanenservice: Meissener Porzellan für Heinrich Graf von Brühl, exh. cat. Berlin: Staatliche Kunstsammlungen Dresden, 2000.

Pinot de Villechenon, Marie-Noëlle. Sèvres: Porcelain from the Sèvres Museum, 1740 to the Present Day, translated by John Gilbert. London: Lund Humphries Publishers, 1993.

Pons, Bruno. "The Rocaille." In Alain Gruber, ed., The History of Decorative Arts. Classicism and the Baroque. New York and Oxford: Abbeville Press, 1996.

Pradère, Alexandre. Les Ebénistes français de Louis XV à la Révolution. Paris: Chêne, 1989.

Préaud, Maxime, Pierre Casselle, et al., Dictionnaire des éditeurs d'estampes à Paris sous l'Ancien Régime. Paris: Promodis, Editions du Cercle de la Librairie, 1986.

"Presentation of The Saarinen Swanson Design Group at the Johnson Furniture Co. Showroom, Grand Rapids, Michigan," June 5, 1947 (photocopy in Cooper-Hewitt, National Design Museum research files). Press release.

Puetz, Anne. "Design Instruction for Artisans in Eighteenth-century Britain." In Journal of Design History 12, no. 3 (1999): 217–39.

Rapaport, Brooke Kamin, and Kevin L. Stayton. *Vital Forms: American Art and Design in the Atomic Age, 1940–1960*. New York: Brooklyn Museum, 2001.

Reed, Peter. "Mind over Matter." In Paola Antonelli, *Objects of Design from the Museum of Modern Art*. New York: The Museum of Modern Art, 2003.

Richards, Sarah. *Eighteenth-century Ceramics: Products for a Civilized Society*. Manchester: Manchester University Press, 1999.

Rieder, William. "Bentwood Furniture." In *Architectural Digest* 53, no. 8 (August 1996): 106–11.

Robinson, Joan Seeman. *Chihuly Seaforms*. Seattle: Portland Press, 1995.

von Roda, Brukard. "The Design for the 'Berceau' Room at Seehof." In *Metropolitan Museum Journal* 25 (1990): 161–68.

Ronfort, Jean-Nérée. "1759, Bellevue et le Secrétaire du Dauphin." In L'Estampille L'Objet D'Art, no. 285/286 (November–December 1994): 104–23.

Rosenblum, Robert. "Jeff Koons: Christ and the Lamb." In *Artforum International* 32, no. 1 (September 1993): 148.

Saisselin, Rémy G. "The Rococo as a Dream of Happiness." In *Journal of Aesthetics and Art Criticism* 19, no. 2 (Winter 1960): 145–52.

Salmon, Xavier, ed. *Madame de Pompadour et les arts*, exh. cat. Paris: Réunion des Musées Nationaux, 2002.

Sassoon, Adrian. *Vincennes and Sèvres Porcelain: Catalogue of the Collections*. Malibu: J. Paul Getty Museum, 1991.

Sassoon, Adrian, and Gillian Wilson. *Decorative Arts: A Handbook of the J. Paul Getty Museum*. Malibu: J. Paul Getty Museum, 1986.

Saule, Béatrix, and Dirk Syndram, ed. *Splendeurs de la cour de Saxe, Dresde à Versailles*, exh. cat. Paris: Réunion des Musées Nationaux, 2006.

Savil, Rosalind. *The Wallace Collection Catalogue of Sèvres Porcelain*. 3 vols. London: The Trustees of the Wallace Collection, 1988.

Schick, Afra. *Furniture for the Dream King: Ludwig II and the Munich Court Cabinet–Maker Anton Pössenbacher*. Stuttgart: Arnoldsche, 2003.

Schmidt, Freek. *Pieter de Swart, Architect van de achttiende eeuw*. Zwolle-Zeist, 1999.

Schreyer, Alexander. *Die Möbelentwürfe Johann Michael Hoppenhaupts des älteren und ihre Beziehungen zu den Rokoko-Möbeln Friedrichs des Grossen*. Studien zur Deutschen Kunstgeschichte 288. Strasbourg: J. H. E. Heitz, 1932.

Schwartz, Marvin D., Edward J. Stanek, and Douglas K. True, eds. *The Furniture of John Henry Belter and the Rococo Revival*. New York: E. P. Dutton, 1981.

Scott, Katie. *The Rococo Interior: Decoration and Social Spaces in Early Eighteenth-century Paris*. New Haven and London: Yale University Press, 1995.

Sergène, André, et al. *Les porcelainiers du XVIIIe siècle français*. Paris: Hachette, 1964.

Shand, P. Morton, ed. "Henry van de Velde: Extracts from His Memoirs, 1891–1901." In *Architectural Review* 112 (September 1952): 148–155.

Sheriff, Mary. "Rococo." In Alan Charles Kors, ed., *Encyclopedia of the Enlightenment*, vol. 3, Mably-Ruysch. Oxford and New York: Oxford University Press, 2003.

Silverman, Debora. *Art Nouveau in Fin-de-Siècle France: Politics, Psychology, and Style*. Berkeley and Los Angeles: University of California Press, Ltd., 1989.

_____. "The Brothers de Goncourt; Maison d'un artiste: French Art Nouveau between History and the Psyche: 1869–1889." In *Arts Magazine*, 59 (May 1985): 119–29.

Simon, Jacob. "A Chronology of Thomas Johnson's Life." In *Furniture History Society Journal* (2003): 18–21.

Snodin, Michael. Print Quarterly, vol. XI, No.1, March 1994.

_____, ed. *Rococo Art and Design in Hogarth's England*, exh. cat. London: Trefoil Books and Victoria and Albert Museum, 1984.

Snowman, Kenneth. *Eighteenth Century Gold Boxes of Europe*. Boston: Boston Book & Art Shop, 1966.

Studinka, Felix. "Schraivogel: The Craftsman's Contract." In *Graphis* 351, 60 (May/June 2004): 39–52.

Sutton, Denys. "Rococo Furniture from Schloss Seehof." In *Apollo* 116 (1982): 263–66.

Symmes, Marilyn. "Collecting for Inspiration and Instruction: Drawings at Cooper-Hewitt, National Design Museum." In *Drawing* 17, nos. 4–6 (November 1995–March 1996): 73–79.

Tallman, Susan. "Feet of Clay: Limoges Porcelain by Contemporary Artists." In *Arts Magazine*.

Taylor, Sue, and Richard A. Born, eds. *The David and Alfred Smart Museum. A Guide of the Collection*. New York: Hudson Hills Press in Association with the Smart Museum, 1990.

Thiébaut, Philippe. "Gallé et l'art du XVIIe siècle." In *Couleurs et Formes: L'héritage du XVIIIe siècle dans l'Ecole de Nancy*. Nancy: Musée de l'Ecole de Nancy, 2005.

Towne-Markus, Elana, ed. *Masterpieces of the J. Paul Getty Museum: Decorative Arts*. Los Angeles: J. Paul Getty Museum, 1997.

Twemlow, Alice. "Ornamentality." In *Eye* 58 (Winter 2005): 232.

Toots Zynsky: Oeuvres. Paris: Clara Scremini, 1987.

Toots Zynsky: Tierra del Fuego Series, exh. cat. Amsterdam: Stedelijk Museum, 1989.

Venable, Charles. "Germanic Craftsmen and Furniture Design in Philadelphia, 1820–1850." In Luke Beckerdite, ed., *American Furniture*. Hanover, NH: University Press of New England for the Chipstone Foundation, 1994, pp. 41–80.

Verlet, Pierre. *Les Bronzes dorés français*. Paris: Picard, 1987.

_____. *The Eighteenth Century in France: Society, Decoration, and Furniture*. Rutland, VT: Charles E. Tuttle Company, 1967.

_____. *Le Mobilier Royal Français*. Paris: Editions d'Art et d'Histoire, 1945.

Verlet, Pierre, and Marcel Brunet. *Sèvres*, 2 vols. Paris: Gérard le Prat, 1953.

Vertue, George. "Notebooks." In *The Volume of the Walpole Society*, XVIII (1929–30), XX (1931–32), XXII (1933–34), XXIV (1935–36), XXVI (1937–38), XXIV (1947; index), XXX (1951–52; index).

Victoria and Albert Museum. *Rococo Silks*. Exeter, UK: Webb and Bower, 1985.

Vreeken, Hubert. *Goud en zilver met Amsterdamse keuren, De verzameling van het Amsterdams Historisch Museum*. Zwolle: Waanders, 2003.

Ward-Jackson, Peter. *Rococo Ornament: A History in Pictures*. Edited by Michael Snodin. London: Victoria and Albert Museum, 1984.

Watson, F. J. B., Gillian Wilson, and Anthony Derham. *Mounted Oriental Porcelains in the J. Paul Getty Museum*. Malibu: J. Paul Getty Museum, 1982.

Weisberg, Gabriel. *Against the Modern: Dagnan-Bouveret and the Transformation of the Academic Tradition*, exh. cat. New York: Dahesh Museum of Art; New Brunswick, NJ: Rutgers University Press, 2002.

_____. *Art Nouveau Bing: Paris Style 1900*. Washington, DC: Smithsonian Institution, 1986.

Westby, Marcia. *Baroque Modernism: New Work by Albert Paley*. New York: Peter Joseph Gallery, 1992.

Wilk, Christopher. *Western Furniture, 1350 to the Present Day*. London: Victoria & Albert Publications, 2001.

Wilson, Gillian. *Selections for the Decorative Arts Collection in the J. Paul Getty Museum*. Malibu: J. Paul Getty Museum, 1983.

_____. *Clocks: French Eighteenth-century Clocks in the J. Paul Getty Museum*. Malibu: J. Paul Getty Museum, 1976.

Wolvesperges, Thibaut. *Le Meuble Français en laque au XVIIIe Siècle*. Paris: L'Edition de l'Amateur, 2000.

Wrightsman, Charles B., et al. *The Wrightsman Collection*, 5 vols. New York: Metropolitan Museum of Art, 1966.

Young, Hillary. *English Porcelain 1745–95*. London: V&A, 1999.

Zweig, Marianne. *Zweites rokoko: innenräume und hausrat in Wien um 1830–1860*. Vienna: A. Schroll & Co., 1924.

Acknowledgments

The curators and Cooper-Hewitt, National Design Museum are grateful for the extraordinary level of help from the following individuals and organizations, especially Reinier Baarsen, Jason Busch, Stephen Harrison, Patricia Kane, Wolfram Koeppe, Juan Pablo Molyneux, and Maxime Préaud. The curators acknowledge in particular the enthusiastic support of Tracey Albainy, Russell B. and Andree Beauchamp Stearns Senior Curator of Decorative Arts and Sculpture Art of Europe, Museum of Fine Arts, Boston, whose untimely death is a great loss.

EXHIBITION LENDERS

Bibliothèque Nationale de France: Jean-Noël Jeanneney, Sylvie Aubenas, Barbara Brejon de Lavergnée, Maxime Préaud

Brooklyn Museum: Arnold Lehman, Charles Desmarais, Elisa Flynn, Barry Harwood

Carnegie Museum of Art: Richard Armstrong, Jason Busch, Rachel Delphia

Cincinnati Art Museum: Aaron Betsky, Amy Dehan, Anita Ellis, Rebecca Posage

Cleveland Museum of Art: Timothy Rub, Carol Ciulla, Stephen Harrison, Catherine Walworth, Gretchen Shie Miller, Charles Venable

Dallas Museum of Art: John R. Lane, Marci Driggers Caslin, Kevin Tucker, Erin Murphy

Fine Arts Museums of San Francisco: John E. Buchanan, Martin Chapman, Maria Reilly

Groninger Museum: Kees van Twist, Caspar Martens

Hillwood Estate, Museum & Gardens: Frederick J. Fisher, David T. Johnson, Karen Kettering, Liana Paredes, Ruthann Uithol

Hispanic Society of America: Mitchell Codding, Marcus Burke, Margaret Connors McQuade

J. Paul Getty Museum: Michael Brand, David Bomford, Antonia Böstrom, Charissa Bremer-David, Marc Harnley, Lee Hendrix, Sally Hibbard, Stephanie Schrader, Jeffrey Weaver

Metropolitan Museum of Art: Philippe de Montebello, Jane Adlin, Kit Basquin, Elaine Bradson, Julia Colchie, George R. Goldner, Roger Haapala, Morrison Heckscher, Catherine Jenkins, Laurence Kanter, Peter M. Kenny, Daniëlle O. Kisluk-Grosheide, Wolfram Koeppe, Ricky Luna, Jessie McNab, Jeffrey H. Munger, Michelle Povilaitis, Melissa Smith, Perrin Stein, Saskia Verlaan, Clare Vincent, Ian Wardropper, Beth Carver Wees, Mary Zuber

Minneapolis Institute of Arts: William Griswold, Jennifer Carlquist, Christopher Monkhouse, Tanya Morrison

Musée de l'Ecole de Nancy: Valérie Thomas

Musée Lorrain: Eric Moinet, Muriel Barbier, Bénédicte Pasques, Claire Tiné

Museum of Art, Rhode Island School of Design: Hope Alswang, Linda Catano, Jan Howard, Gloria Martinez, Emily Peters

Museum of Early Southern Decorative Arts: Johanna M. Brown, Robert Leath

Museum of Fine Arts, Boston: Malcolm Rogers, Edward Saywell, Barbara Shapiro, Rebecca Tilles

Museum of International Folk Art: Joyce Lee, Barbara Mauldin

Museum of Modern Art: Glenn D. Lowry, Candace Banks, Barry Bergdoll, Christian Larsen, Pamela Popeson, Emily Talbot, Deborah Wye

Museum of the City of New York: Susan Henshaw Jones, Deborah Waters

Ville de Nancy: André Rossinot, Laurent Hénart

National Gallery of Art: Earl A. Powell III, Margaret Morgan Grasselli, Gregory Jecman, Ginger Hammer, Nicholas Penny

Philadelphia Museum of Art: Anne d'Harnoncourt, David Barquist, Donna Corbin, Kathryn B. Hiesinger, Alexandra Kirtley

Rijksmuseum: Ronald de Leeuw, Reinier Baarsen, Wendela Brouwer, Jan Rudolph de Lorme, J. P. Sigmond

Saint Louis Art Museum: Brent Benjamin

Smart Museum, University of Chicago: Anthony Hirschel, Richard Born, Natasha Derrickson

Smithsonian American Art Museum: Elizabeth Broun, Alison H. Fenn, Helen Ingalls, Jane Milosch

Smithsonian Institution Libraries: Nancy E. Gwinn, Eliza Gilligan, Vanessa Haight

Sterling and Francine Clark Art Institute: Michael Conforti, Kathleen Morris

Virginia Museum of Fine Arts, Richmond: Alexander Nyerges, Frederick Brandt, Barry Schifman, Mary Sullivan

Winterthur Museum, Gardens & Library: Thomas Savage, Leslie Bowman, Wendy Cooper, Pat Halfpenny, Ann Verplank, Anne Wagner

Yale University Art Gallery: Jock Reynolds, Vicki Caine, Patricia Kane

A la Vieille Russie: Peter and Paul Schaffer

L'Antiquaire & The Connoisseur, Inc.: Helen Fioratti, Catherine Turer

The Arnhold Collection: Henry Arnhold, Maureen Cassidy Geiger

Artecnica: Jackie Fan, Tamineh Javanbakht

Horace Wood Brock

Brunklaus, Amsterdam: Nicolette Brunklaus, Han van Dien

Collection of Sydney & Frances Lewis: Frances Lewis, Jay Barrows

Dalva Brothers: Leon Dalva

Ndidi Ekubia

Ralph Esmerian

Fabrica: Sam Barron, Valentina Carretta

Friedman Benda Gallery: Rachel Compton

Mr. and Mrs. Jon Gerstenfeld

Joanne and Roberto de Guardiola

Carlton Hobbs

The Horvitz Collection, Boston: Jeffrey Horvitz, Dr. Alvin L. Clark, Jr.

Jason Jacques

Jaga, N.V.: Tony Michiels

Boudewijn Jansen & Yvette van Dishoeck

Linda Kaufman

Robert P. and Arlene R. Kogod

Ben Krone

Diana Kunkel

Joris Laarman Studio: Joris Laarman, Anita Star, William Strafford

Frank Lloyd

Marcel Wanders Studio: Marcel Wanders, Fabiana Vidal Leao de Aquino

Jennifer C. McCurdy

Miu Miu: Miuccia Prada, Erika Albies

Moss: Murray Moss, Bret Pittman

National Park Service, Melrose Plantation: Kathleen McClain Jenkins

Colección Patricia Phelps de Cisneros: Patricia Phelps de Cisneros, Guilermo Ovalle

R 20th Century: Evan Snyderman

Leah Raintree

William & Coren Sharples

Roger Smith

Elizabeth Stafford

Eric Streiner

Laurence Strenger

Vitra AG: Fernanda Chandoha

OTHER SUPPORT

Art Institute of Chicago: Ghenete Zelleke

Library of Congress: Katherine L. Blood

Municipal Archives, Sèvres, France: Franz Joyot

Musée des Arts Décoratifs: Chantal Bouchon, Constance Rubinie

Musée du Petit Palais: Patrick Lemasson, Marie-Christine Boucher, Charles de Santi,

Smithsonian National Museum of American History: Brent Glass, Bill Yeingst

Victoria and Albert Museum: Frances Collard, Tessa Murdoch, Michael Snodin

Ellenor Alcorn

Luke Beckerdite

H. Blairman and Sons Ltd.: Martin Levy

Christie's: Edward Clive, Jeanne Sloane, William Strafford

Dr. James and Mrs. Ruth Coy

Princesse Minnie de Beauvau Craon

Daniel Denise

Bruno and Jeannie Eberli

Philippa Glanville

Mr. and Mrs. Robert Hermanos

Joern Lohmann

Mallett's: Henry Neville

Manufacture Nationale de Sèvres: Tamara Préaud

Marks Gallery, London: John Culme

Sotheby's: Peter Lang, Kevin Tierney, John Ward, James Zemaitis

Stanton Hall: Ethel Banta, Mimi Miller

Eugene V. and Clare E. Thaw

Tsang Seymour Design: Catarina Tsang, Patrick Seymour, Laura Howell, Susan Brzozowski, Thomas Ryun, Loren Flaherty

John Wilton-Ely

Rococo: The Continuing Curve
HONORARY ADVISORY COMMITTEE:

Michèle Gerber Klein
Albert Bouilhet
Horace Wood Brock
Janna Bullock
Georgette Farkas
Philips Hathaway
Susan Hermanos
Olivier Kraemer
Juan Pablo Molyneux
Judith Price
Eli Wilner

AT COOPER-HEWITT:

Communications and Marketing: William Berry, Jennifer Northrop, Laurie Olivieri, Mara Sorkin; Conservation: Perry C. Choe, Lucy Commoner, Sarah Scaturro; Curatorial: Susan Brown, Gregory Herringshaw, Floramae McCarron-Cates, Matilda McQuaid; Development and External Affairs: Caroline Baumann, Deborah Fitzgerald, Anne Shisler-Hughes; Education: Caroline Payson and team; Exhibitions: Matthew O'Connor, Mathew Weaver; Finance: Christopher Jeannopoulos; Registrar: Steven Langehough, Melanie Fox, Bethany Romanowski, Wendy Rogers, Larry Silver; Library: Stephen Van Dyk, Elizabeth Broman, Jennifer Cohlman

Cooper-Hewitt volunteers, interns, and fellows: Sarah Alexander, Talia Avisar, Judith Bergoffen, Emma Bowen, Caroline Cole, Carla Deluise, Lauren DiGiulio, Helen Esberg, Alexandra Gilbert, Elizabeth Griswold, Mary Hermes, Susie Hermanos, Alexis Jarossy, Allison Krier, Erin Leary, Caroline Lefevre, Michelle Mandville, Aidan O'Connor, Christine Ritok, Quillan Rosen, Emily Segal, Kristen Windmuller, Sung Won, Alessandra Wood

Photographic Credits

Cooper-Hewitt, National Design Museum is grateful to the following organizations and individuals for their permission to reproduce images in this book. Every effort has been made to trace and contact the copyright holders of the images reproduced; any errors or omissions shall be corrected in subsequent editions.

All photos © Cooper-Hewitt, National Design Museum, Smithsonian Institution, photo by Matt Flynn, except the images listed below. Numerals indicate figure numbers in each essay.

TITLE PAGE:
Courtesy of Horace Wood Brock, photo by Matt Flynn.

FOREWORD:
© Carlton Hobbs LLC, photo by Matt Flynn.

HUNTER-STIEBEL, The Continuing Curve:
© The Metropolitan Museum of Art: 1, 3, 5; © The Cleveland Museum of Art: 2; © Colecciòn Patricia Phelps de Cisneros, Caracas, photo by Mark Morosse Photography: 4; © Musée Lorrain, Nancy: 6; private collection, photo by Matt Flynn: 7; © The Sterling and Francine Clark Art Institute: 8; © Yale University Art Gallery: 9; © Musée de l'Ecole de Nancy, photo by C. Philippot: 11; © Virginia Museum of Fine Arts, photo by Katherine Wetzel: 12; © Fred Leighton: 14; © Smithsonian American Art Museum: 15.

HYDE, Rococo Redux:
© Réunion des Musées Nationaux/Art Resource, NY: 1, photo by Hervé Lewandowski: 6, 9, photo by Daniel Arnaudet: 10; © Museum of Fine Arts, Boston: 3; © Bridgeman-Giradon/Art Resource, NY, photo by Bulloz: 5; © Trustees of the Wallace Collection: 7; © The J. Paul Getty Museum, Los Angeles: 8; © The State Hermitage Museum, Saint Petersburg: 11.

FUHRING, Juste-Aurèle Meissonnier and His Patrons:
© The David and Alfred Smart Museum of Art: 2; © Bibliothèque Nationale de France: 9; © Musée des Arts Décoratifs, photo by Jean Tholance: 13; © The Cleveland Museum of Art: 15; private collection, photo courtesy of Sotheby's: 16; © Bibliothèque de l'Institut National d'Histoire de l'Art, Collections Jacques Doucet: 17; © The Przypkowskis Museum of Jedrzejow, photo by Mgr. Piotr Maciej Przypkowski: 20.

DAVIDSON, *Ornament of Bizarre Imagination*:
© Smithsonian Institution, photo by Andrew Garn: 43; © The Metropolitan Museum of Art: 8, 16, 18, 23, 37; © Bibliothèque Nationale de France: 11, 24, 27, 29; © Musée du Petit Palais, Patrick Pierrain/Petit Palais/Roger-Viollet: 19; © Musée des Arts Décoratifs, photo by Laurent Sully Jaulmes: 20; © The Horvitz Collection: 21; © L'Antiquaire and the Connoisseur, Inc., photo by Matt Flynn: 22, photo by Andrew Garn: 43; © The J. Paul Getty Museum: 35; © The Bayerische Verwaltung der staatlichen Schlösser, Gärten und Seen: 38; © Museum of Art, Rhode Island School of Design, photo by Erik Gould: 41; © Horace Wood Brock, photography courtesy of The J. Paul Getty Museum: 44–48.

HUNTER-STIEBEL, Louis XV Style:
© Horace Wood Brock, photo by Matt Flynn: 1; © Réunion des Musées Nationaux/Art Resource, NY, photo by Gérard Blot: 2–6; private collection, photo by Andrew Garn: 7; © Hillwood Estate, Museum & Gardens, photo by E. Owen: 8; © National Gallery of Art, photo by Phillip A. Charles: 10; © Fine Arts Museums of San Francisco: 11, 12, 19, 20; © Cincinnati Art Museum: 13; © Dalva Brothers: 14; © The J. Paul Getty Museum: 15, 16, 18; © The Cleveland Museum of Art: 17; © The Metropolitan Museum of Art: 21; © The Philadelphia Museum of Art: 22; rivate collection, photo by Matt Flynn: 23, 24.

HUNTER-STIEBEL, Eighteenth-century Nancy:
All photos © Musée Lorrain, Nancy; except: Musée Lorrain, Nancy, photo by C. Philippot: 1, 9; photo by Martine-Beck Coppola: 3, 5, photo by G. Mangin: 10, 14, 15; photo by Daniel Denise: 6, 7, 11; © Cooper-Hewitt, National Design Museum, Smithsonian Institution, photo by Matt Flynn: 12, 13.

COFFIN, Radiating Rococo:
private collection, photo by Matt Flynn: 1, 11; private collection: 2; © The Metropolitan Museum of Art: 3, 5, 7, 8, 15, 38, 53, 57; © The Cleveland Museum of Art: 4, 34; © Réunion des Musées Nationaux/Art Resource, NY, photo by Daniel Arnaudet: 6; © Yale University Art Gallery: 9, 50, 51, 58, 59; © A la Vieille Russie, photo by Andrew Garn: 10, 12, 19; © Horace Wood Brock, photo by Matt Flynn: 13, photo by Andrew Garn: 14; private collection, photo by Andrew Garn: 16; © V&A Images/Victoria and Albert Museum: 17, 48; © Hillwood Estate, Museum & Gardens, photo by E. Owen: 18; © The Art Institute of Chicago: 20, 23; private collection, photo courtesy of Museum of Fine Arts, Boston: 21; © Minneapolis Institute of Arts: 22; private collection, photo © Christie's Images: 25; © The Museum of Fine Arts, Boston: 26, 31, 35, 40; © The Hispanic Society of America, New York: 27, 28; © Samuel S. Fleischer Art Memorial, photo © The Philadelphia Museum of Art: 29; © Tate, London 2006: 30; © Cincinnati Art Museum: 32; private collection, photo © V&A Images/Victoria and Albert Museum: 33; © Collection of Laurence N. Strenger, photo by Andrew Garn: 36, 41; © Virginia Museum of Fine Arts, photo by Katherine Wetzel: 37; © Dallas Museum of Art: 42; © Minneapolis Institute of Arts: 43; © Carlton Hobbs LLC: 44; © The Gerstenfeld Collection, photo by Reid Baker, courtesy of Christie's: 45, 46; © Smithsonian Institution, photo by Andrew Garn: 49; © Winterthur Museum: 54, 61; © The Philadelphia Museum of Art: 55; private collection, photo by Gavin Ashworth: 56; © Museum of Early Southern Decorative Arts, Old Salem Museums & Gardens: 60, 62.

LEBEN, German Rococo:
© The Metropolitan Museum of Art: 3, 10, 11; © Waddesdon, the Rothschild Collection (The National Trust), photo by Jèrôme Letellier: 4, photo by Francis Carver: 6, photo by Eost & MacDonald: 8, photo by Mike Fear: 12; © The National Trust: 5; © Horace Wood Brock, photo courtesy of Mallett Antiques, New York: 7; © Smithsonian Institution Libraries: 14, 15.

BAARSEN, Rococo in Holland:
All photos © Rijksmuseum, Amsterdam; except: © The Hague Town Hall, photo courtesy of the Rijksmuseum, Amsterdam: 1; © Waddesdon, The Rothschild Collection (The National Trust), photo by Mike Fear: 2; © Amsterdams Historisch Museum: 3; © Rijksdienst voor de Monumentenzorg, Zeist: 4; private collection, photo courtesy of the Rijksmuseum: 8, 19; © Royal Picture Gallery Mauritshuis, the Hague: 9; © Historisch Centrum, Leeuwarden: 10; © Royal Collection, The Netherlands, photo courtesy of the Rijksmuseum, Amsterdam: 11; © House of Orange-Nassau Historic Collections Trust: 16; © Collection of His Royal Highness the Grand-Duke of Luxemburg: 23; private collection, photo courtesy of Christie's: 25.

DAVIDSON, Emulation and Subversion:
© Smithsonian Institution Libraries: 3, photo by Matt Flynn: 9, 10; © Brooklyn Museum: 4; The Museum of Modern Art, © 2008 Mucha Trust/ADAGP, Paris/ARS, NY, digital image licensed by SCALA/Art Resource, NY: 13; © Virginia Museum of Fine Arts, photo by Katherine Wetzel: 14; The New York Public Library, Astor, Lenox, and Tilden Foundations, © 2008 Mucha Trust/ADAGP, Paris/ARS, NY: 15; Smithsonian Institution, © 2008 Mucha Trust/ADAGP, Paris/ARS, NY, photo by Matt Flynn: 16, 17; The New York Public Library, Astor, Lenox, and Tilden Foundations, © 2008 Artist Rights Society (ARS), New York/ADAGP, Paris: 18; Smithsonian Institution, © 2008 Artist Rights Society (ARS), New York/ADAGP, Paris, photo by Matt Flynn: 19, 20.

COFFIN, The Rococo Revival in English and American Nineteenth-century Silver:
© A. M. Marks Ltd., London, England: 1, 13; © Sotheby's: 2; © Hillwood Estate, Museum & Gardens, photo by E. Owen: 3; © The Metropolitan Museum of Art: 4, 8, 18; © The Philadelphia Museum of Art: 7; © Smithsonian Institution, photo by Andrew Garn: 9, 16; © Carnegie Museum of Art, Pittsburgh: 10; © Smithsonian Institution Libraries, photo by Matt Flynn: 12; © J. H. Bourdon-Smith Ltd.: 14; © Collection of Eric Streiner, photo by Andrew Garn: 17.

BUSCH, "Equal to Any in the World":
© The Maryland Historical Society, Baltimore: 2; © Louisiana State Museum, New Orleans: 3; © Carnegie Museum of Art, Pittsburgh: 4, 9; © Minneapolis Institute of Arts: 5, 14; © National Park Service, photo by William Beane: 6; © Smithsonian Institution Libraries: 7; © The Athenæum of Philadelphia: 8; © Wadsworth Atheneum Museum of Art: 10; © Cincinnati Art Museum: 11; © The Winterthur Library, Printed Book and Periodical Collection: 12; © Museum of the City of New York, photo by Matt Flynn: 15.

HUNTER-STIEBEL, Art Nouveau:
© Virginia Museum of Fine Arts, Richmond, photo by Katherine Wetzel: 1, 12, 14, 17; © Dallas Museum of Art: 2; private collection, photo by Robert Lorenzson: 3, 13, 16; © Collection of Laurence N. Strenger, photo by Andrew Garn: 5; © Musée de l' Ecole de Nancy, photo by Studio Image: 10, photo by C. Philippot: 6, 7, 8, 9; © Minneapolis Institute of Arts: 11; © Smithsonian Institution, photo by Dennis Cowley: 15; private collection, photo by David Behl: 18; © Smithsonian Institution, photo by Andrew Garn: 19.

LUPTON, The Modern Curve:
© Artecnica, photo by Nemat Sharifpour: 1; © Fabrica: 2; The Museum of Modern Art, digital image © 2007 Licensed by SCALA / Art Resource, NY: 3, 20; © Virginia Museum of Fine Arts, photo by Katherine Wetzel: 4; © Brooklyn Museum: 6; © Vitra, photo by Hans Hansen: 7; © Smithsonian Institution, photo by John White: 12, 16; © Smithsonian Institution, photo by Andrew Garn: 17; © R Gallery: 19; © Collection Groninger Museum, Groningen: 26; © Moss: 27; © The Frank Lloyd Gallery, photo by Anthony Cuñha: 28; © Collection of Sydney and Frances Lewis, photo by Dennis McWaters: 29; © Smithsonian Institution, photo by Steve Tague: 31; © Ron Arad Associates, photo by Tom Vack: 32; © Ted Muehling, photo by Don Freeman: 33; © Marcel Wanders Studio, photo by Maarten van Houten: 34; © Sotheby's: 35; © Studio Job: 36; © Front: 37 ; © Jennifer C. McCurdy, photo by Katherine Ross: 38; © Ndidi Ekubia, photo by Stephen Brayne: 39; © Joris Laarman, photo by Bas Helbers: 40, photo by Anita Star: 41; © Nicolette Brunklaus: 43; © Leah Raintree, photo by Hermann Feldhaus: 46; © Collection of William and Coren Sharples, photo by Natalie Gruppuso and Jared Holstein: 47.

FRONT COVER:
© Cooper-Hewitt, National Design Museum, Smithsonian Institution, photo by Matt Flynn.

BACK COVER:
© Ron Arad Associates, photo by Tom Vack.

Selected Index of Names

ROCOCO: THE CONTINUING CURVE, 1730–2008

Published by
Cooper-Hewitt, National Design Museum
Smithsonian Institution
2 East 91st Street
New York, NY 10128, USA
www.cooperhewitt.org

Published on the occasion of the exhibition
Rococo: The Continuing Curve, 1730–2008
at Cooper-Hewitt, National Design Museum,
Smithsonian Institution,
March 7–July 6, 2008.

Rococo: The Continuing Curve, 1730–2008 is made possible in part by The Grand Marnier Foundation, Kay Allaire, the Consulate-General of The Netherlands, Furthermore: a program of the J. M. Kaplan Fund, and an anonymous donor.

This publication is made possible in part by The Andrew W. Mellon Foundation.

Distributed to the trade worldwide by
Assouline Publishing
601 West 26th Street, 18th floor
New York, NY 10001, USA
www.assouline.com

First edition: March 2008

ISBN: 978-0-910503-92-1 (hardcover)
978-0-910503-91-4 (paperback)
Library of Congress CIP data available from the publisher.

Museum Editor: Chul R. Kim, Head of Publications
Image Editors: Jill Bloomer, Annie Chambers
Design: Ellen Lupton with Tsang Seymour Design, Inc.
Printed in China by Oceanic Graphic Printing.

FRONT COVER: *Winged Griffon on a Rocaille Bracket*, plate 6 in *Première Partie divers Ornements*. Alexis Peyrotte (French, 1699–1769). Etched by Gabriel Huquier (French, 1695–1772). Paris, France, ca. 1745. Etching on white laid paper. Cooper-Hewitt, National Design Museum, Smithsonian Institution, Purchased for the Museum by the Advisory Council, 1921-6-213-6

BACK COVER: Looploop chair. Ron Arad (Israeli, active England, b. 1951). London, England, 1992. Polished bronze mesh. Courtesy of Friedman Benda

TITLE PAGE: Petrified wood in mount (one of a pair). France, ca. 1740. Petrified wood, gilt bronze. Courtesy of Horace Wood Brock